CCENT/CCNA ICND1
Official Exam Certification Guide, Second Edition

Wendell Odom,
CCIE No. 1624

Cisco Press

800 East 96th Street
Indianapolis, Indiana 46240 USA

CCENT/CCNA ICND1 Official Exam Certification Guide, Second Edition

Wendell Odom

Copyright© 2008 Cisco Systems, Inc.

Published by:
Cisco Press
800 East 96th Street
Indianapolis, IN 46240 USA

Printed in the United States of America

Sixth Printing, February 2009

Library of Congress Cataloging-in-Publication Data.

Odom, Wendell.

  CCENT/CCNA ICND1 official exam certification guide / Wendell Odom.

    p. cm.

  ISBN 978-1-58720-182-0 (hardback w/cd) 1. Electronic data processing personnel--Certification. 2. Computer networks--Examinations--Study guides. I. Title.

  QA76.3.O358 2007

  004.6--dc22

                         2007029241

ISBN-13: 978-1-58720-182-0

ISBN-10: 1-58720-182-8

Warning and Disclaimer

Trademark Acknowledgments

All terms mentioned in this book that are known to be trademarks or service marks have been appropriately capitalized. Cisco Press or Cisco Systems, Inc. cannot attest to the accuracy of this information. Use of a term in this book should not be regarded as affecting the validity of any trademark or service mark.

Corporate and Government Sales

The publisher offers excellent discounts on this book when ordered in quantity for bulk purchases or special sales, which may include electronic versions and/or custom covers and content particular to your business, training goals, marketing focus, and branding interests. For more information, please contact: **U.S. Corporate and Government Sales** 1-800-382-3419 **corpsales@pearsontechgroup.com**

For sales outside the United States please contact: **International Sales** international@pearsoned.com

Feedback Information

At Cisco Press, our goal is to create in-depth technical books of the highest quality and value. Each book is crafted with care and precision, undergoing rigorous development that involves the unique expertise of members of the professional technical community.

Reader feedback is a natural continuation of this process. If you have any comments about how we could improve the quality of this book, or otherwise alter it to better suit your needs, you can contact us through e-mail at feedback@ciscopress.com. Please be sure to include the book title and ISBN in your message.

We greatly appreciate your assistance.

Publisher: Paul Boger

Associate Publisher: Dave Dusthimer

Cisco Representative: Anthony Wolfenden

Cisco Press Program Manager: Jeff Brady

Executive Editor: Brett Bartow

Managing Editor: Patrick Kanouse

Senior Development Editor: Christopher Cleveland

Senior Project Editor: San Dee Phillips and Meg Shaw

Copy Editor: Gayle Johnson and Bill McManus

Technical Editors: Teri Cook, Brian D'Andrea, and Steve Kalman

Editorial Assistant: Vanessa Evans

Book and Cover Designer: Louisa Adair

Composition: ICC Macmillan Inc.

Indexer: Tim Wright

Proofreader: Suzanne Thomas

ıｌｉｌｉｌｉｌｉ
CISCO.

Americas Headquarters
Cisco Systems, Inc.
170 West Tasman Drive
San Jose, CA 95134-1706
USA
www.cisco.com
Tel: 408 526-4000
800 553-NETS (6387)
Fax: 408 527-0883

Asia Pacific Headquarters
Cisco Systems, Inc.
168 Robinson Road
#28-01 Capital Tower
Singapore 068912
www.cisco.com
Tel: +65 6317 7777
Fax: +65 6317 7799

Europe Headquarters
Cisco Systems International BV
Haarlerbergpark
Haarlerbergweg 13-19
1101 CH Amsterdam
The Netherlands
www-europe.cisco.com
Tel: +31 0 800 020 0791
Fax: +31 0 20 357 1100

Cisco has more than 200 offices worldwide. Addresses, phone numbers, and fax numbers are listed on the Cisco Website at **www.cisco.com/go/offices.**

©2007 Cisco Systems, Inc. All rights reserved. CCVP, the Cisco logo, and the Cisco Square Bridge logo are trademarks of Cisco Systems, Inc.; Changing the Way We Work, Live, Play, and Learn is a service mark of Cisco Systems, Inc.; and Access Registrar, Aironet, BPX, Catalyst, CCDA, CCDP, CCIE, CCIP, CCNA, CCNP, CCSP, Cisco, the Cisco Certified Internetwork Expert logo, Cisco IOS, Cisco Press, Cisco Systems, Cisco Systems Capital, the Cisco Systems logo, Cisco Unity, Enterprise/Solver, EtherChannel, EtherFast, EtherSwitch, Fast Step, Follow Me Browsing, FormShare, GigaDrive, GigaStack, HomeLink, Internet Quotient, IOS, IP/TV, iQ Expertise, the iQ logo, iQ Net Readiness Scorecard, iQuick Study, LightStream, Linksys, MeetingPlace, MGX, Networking Academy, Network Registrar, Packet, PIX, ProConnect, RateMUX, ScriptShare, SlideCast, SMARTnet, StackWise, The Fastest Way to Increase Your Internet Quotient, and TransPath are registered trademarks of Cisco Systems, Inc. and/or its affiliates in the United States and certain other countries.

All other trademarks mentioned in this document or Website are the property of their respective owners. The use of the word partner does not imply a partnership relationship between Cisco and any other company. (0609R)

About the Author

Wendell Odom, CCIE No. 1624, has been in the networking industry since 1981. He currently teaches QoS, MPLS, and CCNA courses for Skyline Advanced Technology Services (http://www.skyline-ats.com). He has also worked as a network engineer, consultant, systems engineer, instructor, and course developer. He is the author of all previous editions of the *CCNA Exam Certification Guide*, as well as the *Cisco QOS Exam Certification Guide*, Second Edition, *Computer Networking First-Step*, *CCIE Routing and Switching Official Exam Certification Guide*, Second Edition, and *CCNA Video Mentor*—all from Cisco Press.

About the Technical Reviewers

Teri Cook (CCSI, CCDP, CCNP, CCDA, CCNA, MCT, and MCSE 2000/2003: Security) has more than ten years of experience in the IT industry. She has worked with different types of organizations in the private business and DoD sectors, providing senior-level network and security technical skills in the design and implementation of complex computing environments. Since obtaining her certifications, Teri has been committed to bringing quality IT training to IT professionals as an instructor. She is an outstanding instructor who uses real-world experience to present complex networking technologies. As an IT instructor, Teri has been teaching Cisco classes for more than five years.

Brian D'Andrea (CCNA, CCDA, MCSE, A+, and Net+) has 11 years of IT experience in both medical and financial environments, where planning and supporting critical networking technologies were his primary responsibilities. For the last five years he has dedicated himself to technical training. Brian spends most of his time with The Training Camp, an IT boot camp provider. Using his real-world experience and his ability to break difficult concepts into a language that students can understand, Brian has successfully trained hundreds of students for both work and certification endeavors.

Stephen Kalman is a data security trainer. He is the author or tech editor of more than 20 books, courses, and CBT titles. His most recent book is *Web Security Field Guide*, published by Cisco Press. In addition to those responsibilities he runs a consulting company, Esquire Micro Consultants, which specializes in network security assessments and forensics.

Mr. Kalman holds SSCP, CISSP, ISSMP, CEH, CHFI, CCNA, CCSA (Checkpoint), A+, Network+ and Security+ certifications and is a member of the New York State Bar.

Dedication

For Brett Bartow. Thanks for being such a steady, insightful, and incredibly trustworthy guide through the publishing maze.

Acknowledgments

The team who helped produce this book has been simply awesome. Everyone who touched this book has made it better, and they've been particularly great at helping catch the errors that always creep into the manuscript.

Brian, Teri, and Steve all did a great job TEing the book. Besides helping a lot with technical accuracy, Brian made a lot of good suggestions about traps that he sees when teaching CCNA classes, helping the book avoid those same pitfalls. Teri's ability to see each phrase in the context of an entire chapter, or the whole book, was awesome, helping catch things that no one would otherwise catch. Steve spent most of his TE time on the ICND2 book, but he did lend great help with this one, particularly with his reviews of the security-oriented topics, an area in which he's an expert. And more so than any other book I've written, the TEs really sunk their teeth into the specifics of every example, helping catch errors. Thanks so much!

Another (ho-hum) all-star performance from Chris Cleveland, who developed the book. Now I empathize with sports writers who have to write about the local team's star who bats .300, hits 40 homers, and drives in 100 runs, every year, for his whole career. How many ways can you say he does a great job? I'll keep it simple: Thanks, Chris.

The wonderful and mostly hidden production folks did their usual great job. When every time I see how they reworded something, and think, "Wow; why didn't I write that?", it makes me appreciate the kind of team we have at Cisco Press. The final copy edit, figure review, and pages review process required a fair amount of juggling and effort as well – thanks to Patrick's team, especially San Dee, Meg, Tonya, for working so well with all the extra quality initiatives we've implemented. Thanks to you all!

Additionally, several folks who didn't have any direct stake in the book also helped it along. Thanks to Frank Knox for the discussions on the exams, why they're so difficult, and about troubleshooting. Thanks to Rus Healy for the help with wireless. Thanks to the Mikes at Skyline for making my schedule work to get this book (and the ICND2 book) out the door. And thanks to the course and exam teams at Cisco for the great early communications and interactions about the changes to the courses and exams.

Finally, thanks to my wife Kris for all her support with my writing efforts, her prayers, and her understanding when the deadline didn't quite match with our vacation plans this summer. And thanks to Jesus Christ—all this effort is just striving after the wind without Him.

This Book Is Safari Enabled

The Safari® Enabled icon on the cover of your favorite technology book means that the book is available through Safari Bookshelf. When you buy this book, you get free access to the online edition for 45 days.

Safari Bookshelf is an electronic reference library that lets you easily search thousands of technical books, find code samples, download chapters, and access technical information whenever and wherever you need it.

To gain 45-day Safari Enabled access to this book:

- Go to http://www.ciscopress.com/safarienabled.

- Complete the brief registration form.

- Enter the coupon code 6EM9-WNXL-7Z1E-9UL2-KAEC.

If you have difficulty registering on Safari Bookshelf or accessing the online edition, please e-mail customer-service@safari-booksonline.com.

Contents at a Glance

Contents

Part VII CD-only

Icons Used in This Book

 Web Server

 Web Browser

 PC

 Laptop

Server

 Printer

 Phone

 IP Phone

 Cable Modem

 CSU/DSU

 Router

 Multiservice Switch

 Switch

 ATM Switch

 Frame Relay Switch

PBX

Access Point

ASA

DSLAM

WAN Switch

Hub

PIX Firewall

Bridge

 Wireless Connection

Network Cloud

 Ethernet Connection

 Serial Line Connection

Virtual Circuit

Command Syntax Conventions

The conventions used to present command syntax in this book are the same conventions used in the IOS Command Reference. The Command Reference describes these conventions as follows:

- **Bold** indicates commands and keywords that are entered literally as shown. In actual configuration examples and output (not general command syntax), bold indicates commands that the user enters (such as a **show** command).

- *Italic* indicates arguments for which you supply actual values.

- Vertical bars (|) separate alternative, mutually exclusive elements.

- Square brackets ([ ]) indicate an optional element.

- Braces ({ }) indicate a required choice.

- Braces within brackets ([{ }]) indicate a required choice within an optional element.

Foreword

CCENT/CCNA ICND1 Official Exam Certification Guide, Second Edition, is an excellent self-study resource for the CCENT and CCNA ICND1 exam. Passing the ICND1 exam validates the knowledge and skills required to successfully install, operate, and troubleshoot a small branch office network. It is the sole required exam for CCENT certification and the first of two exams required for CCNA certification.

Gaining certification in Cisco technology is key to the continuing educational development of today's networking professional. Through certification programs, Cisco validates the skills and expertise required to effectively manage the modern Enterprise network.

Cisco Press exam certification guides and preparation materials offer exceptional—and flexible—access to the knowledge and information required to stay current in your field of expertise, or to gain new skills. Whether used as a supplement to more traditional training or as a primary source of learning, these materials offer users the information and knowledge validation required to gain new understanding and proficiencies.

Developed in conjunction with the Cisco certifications and training team, Cisco Press books are the only self-study books authorized by Cisco. They offer students a series of exam practice tools and resource materials to help ensure that learners fully grasp the concepts and information presented.

Additional authorized Cisco instructor-led courses, e-learning, labs, and simulations are available exclusively from Cisco Learning Solutions Partners worldwide. To learn more, visit http://www.cisco.com/go/training.

I hope that you find these materials to be an enriching and useful part of your exam preparation.

Erik Ullanderson
Manager, Global Certifications
Learning@Cisco
August 2007

Introduction

Congratulations! If you're reading this Introduction, you've probably already decided to go for your Cisco certification. If you want to succeed as a technical person in the networking industry, you need to know Cisco. Cisco has a ridiculously high market share in the router and switch marketplace—more than 80 percent in some markets. In many geographies and markets around the world, networking equals Cisco. If you want to be taken seriously as a network engineer, Cisco certification makes sense.

Historically speaking, the first entry-level Cisco certification has been the Cisco Certified Network Associate (CCNA) certification, first offered in 1998. The first three versions of the CCNA certification (1998, 2000, and 2002) required that you pass a single exam to become certified. However, over time, the exam kept growing, both in the amount of material covered and the difficulty level of the questions. So, for the fourth major revision of the exams, announced in 2003, Cisco continued with a single certification (CCNA) but offered two certification options: a single exam option and a two-exam option. The two-exam option allowed people to study roughly half the material and then take and pass one exam before moving on to the next.

Cisco announced changes to the CCNA certification and exams in June 2007. This announcement includes many changes; here are the most notable:

- The exams collectively cover a broader range of topics.

- The exams increase the focus on proving the test taker's skills (as compared with just testing knowledge).

- Cisco created a new entry-level certification: Cisco Certified Entry Networking Technician (CCENT).

For the current certifications, announced in June 2007, Cisco created the ICND1 (640-822) and ICND2 (640-816) exams, along with the CCNA (640-802) exam. To become CCNA certified, you can pass both the ICND1 and ICND2 exams, or just the CCNA exam. The CCNA exam simply covers all the topics on the ICND1 and ICND2 exams, giving you two options for gaining your CCNA certification. The two-exam path gives people with less experience a chance to study for a smaller set of topics at one time. The one-exam option provides a more cost-effective certification path for those who want to prepare for all the topics at once.

Although the two-exam option is useful for some certification candidates, Cisco designed the ICND1 exam with a much more important goal in mind. The CCNA certification grew to the point that it tested knowledge and skills beyond what an entry-level network technician would need. Cisco needed a certification that better reflected the skills required for entry-level networking jobs. So Cisco designed its Interconnecting Cisco Networking Devices 1 (ICND1) course, and the corresponding ICND1 640-822 exam, to include the knowledge and skills most needed by an entry-level technician in a small Enterprise network. And so that you can prove that you have the skills required for those entry-level jobs, Cisco created a new certification, CCENT.

Figure I-1 shows the basic organization of the certifications and the exams used to get your CCENT and CCNA certifications. (Note that there is no separate certification for passing the ICND2 exam.)

Figure I-1   *Cisco Entry-Level Certifications and Exams*

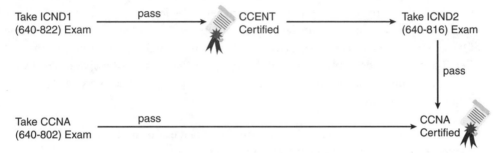

As you can see, although you can obtain the CCENT certification by taking the ICND1 exam, you do not have to be CCENT certified before getting your CCNA certification. You can choose to take just the CCNA exam and bypass the CCENT certification.

The ICND1 and ICND2 exams cover different sets of topics, with a minor amount of overlap. For example, ICND1 covers IP addressing and subnetting, and ICND2 covers a more complicated use of subnetting called variable-length subnet masking (VLSM). Therefore, ICND2 must then cover subnetting to some degree. The CCNA exam covers all the topics covered on both the ICND1 and ICND2 exams.

Although the popularity of the CCENT certification cannot be measured until a few years have passed, certainly the Cisco CCNA is the most popular entry-level networking certification program. A CCNA certification proves that you have a firm foundation in the most important components of the Cisco product line—routers and switches. It also proves that you have broad knowledge of protocols and networking technologies.

Format of the CCNA Exams

The ICND1, ICND2, and CCNA exams all follow the same general format. When you get to the testing center and check in, the proctor gives you some general instructions and then takes you into a quiet room containing a PC. When you're at the PC, you have a few things to do before the timer starts on your exam. For instance, you can take a sample quiz to get accustomed to the PC and the testing engine. Anyone who has user-level skills in getting around a PC should have no problems with the testing environment. Additionally, Chapter 18, "Final Preparation," points to a Cisco website where you can see a demo of Cisco's actual test engine.

When you start the exam, you are asked a series of questions. You answer them and then move on to the next question. *The exam engine does not let you go back and change your answer.* Yes, it's true. When you move on to the next question, that's it for the preceding question.

The exam questions can be in one of the following formats:

- Multiple choice (MC)

- Testlet

- Drag-and-drop (DND)

- Simulated lab (sim)

- Simlet

The first three types of questions are relatively common in many testing environments. The multiple-choice format simply requires that you point and click a circle beside the correct answer(s). Cisco traditionally tells you how many answers you need to choose, and the testing software prevents you from choosing too many. Testlets are questions with one general scenario and several multiple-choice questions about the overall scenario. Drag-and-drop questions require you to click and hold, move a button or icon to another area, and release the mouse button to place the object somewhere else—typically in a list. For some questions, to get the question correct, you might need to put a list of five things in the proper order.

The last two types of questions use a network simulator to ask questions. Interestingly, the two types actually allow Cisco to assess two very different skills. First, sim questions generally describe a problem, and your task is to configure one or more routers and switches to fix it. The exam then grades the question based on the configuration you changed or added. Interestingly, sim questions are the only questions (to date) for which Cisco has openly confirmed it gives partial credit for.

The simlet questions may well be the most difficult style of question. Simlet questions also use a network simulator, but instead of having you answer by changing the configuration, the question includes one or more multiple-choice questions. The questions require that you use the simulator to examine a network's current behavior, interpreting the output of any

show commands you can remember to answer the question. Whereas sim questions require you to troubleshoot problems related to a configuration, simlets require you to analyze both working networks and networks with problems, correlating **show** command output with your knowledge of networking theory and configuration commands.

What's on the CCNA Exam(s)?

Ever since I was in grade school, whenever the teacher announced that we were having a test soon, someone would always ask, "What's on the test?" Even in college, people would try to get more information about what would be on the exams. The goal is to know what to study a lot, what to study a little, and what to not study at all.

Cisco wants the public to know the variety of topics and have an idea of the kinds of knowledge and skills required for each topic, for every Cisco certification exam. To that end, Cisco publishes a set of objectives for each exam. The objectives list the specific topics such as IP addressing, RIP, and VLANs. The objectives also imply the kinds of skills required for that topic. For example, one objective might start with "Describe...", and another might begin with "Describe, configure, and troubleshoot...". The second objective clearly states that you need a thorough understanding of that topic. By listing the topics and skill level, Cisco helps you prepare for the exams.

Although the exam objectives are helpful, keep in mind that Cisco adds a disclaimer that the posted exam topics for all its certification exams are *guidelines*. Cisco makes an effort to keep the exam questions within the confines of the stated exam objectives. I know from talking to those involved that every question is analyzed to ensure that it fits within the stated exam topics.

ICND1 Exam Topics

Table I-1 lists the exam topics for the ICND1 exam. The ICND2 exam topics follow in Table I-2. Although the posted exam topics are not numbered at Cisco.com, Cisco Press numbers them for easier reference. The tables also note the book parts in which each exam topic is covered. Because the exam topics may change over time, it may be worth it to double-check the exam topics listed on Cisco.com (go to http://www.cisco.com/go/ccna). If Cisco does happen to add exam topics at a later date, note that Appendix C, "ICND1 Exam Updates," describes how to go to http://www.ciscopress.com and download additional information about those newly added topics.

> **NOTE** The table includes gray highlights that are explained in the upcoming section "CCNA Exam Topics."

Table I-1 *ICND1 Exam Topics*

Reference Number	Book Part(s) Where Topic Is Covered	Exam Topic
		Describe the operation of data networks
1	I	Describe the purpose and functions of various network devices
2	I	Select the components required to meet a given network specification
3	I, II, III	Use the OSI and TCP/IP models and their associated protocols to explain how data flows in a network
4	I	Describe common networking applications including web applications
5	I	Describe the purpose and basic operation of the protocols in the OSI and TCP models
6	I	Describe the impact of applications (Voice Over IP and Video Over IP) on a network
7	I–IV	Interpret network diagrams
8	I–IV	Determine the path between two hosts across a network
9	I, III, IV	Describe the components required for network and Internet communications
10	I–IV	Identify and correct common network problems at Layers 1, 2, 3, and 7 using a layered model approach
11	II, III	Differentiate between LAN/WAN operation and features
		Implement a small switched network
12	II	Select the appropriate media, cables, ports, and connectors to connect switches to other network devices and hosts
13	II	Explain the technology and media access control method for Ethernet technologies
14	II	Explain network segmentation and basic traffic management concepts
15	II	Explain the operation of Cisco switches and basic switching concepts
16	II	Perform, save, and verify initial switch configuration tasks including remote access management

continues

Table I-1 *ICND1 Exam Topics (Continued)*

Reference Number	Book Part(s) Where Topic Is Covered	Exam Topic
17	II	Verify network status and switch operation using basic utilities (including: ping, traceroute, Telnet, SSH, ARP, ipconfig), show and debug commands
18	II	Implement and verify basic security for a switch (port security, deactivate ports)
19	II	Identify, prescribe, and resolve common switched network media issues, configuration issues, autonegotiation, and switch hardware failures
		Implement an IP addressing scheme and IP services to meet network requirements for a small branch office
20	I, III	Describe the need for and role of addressing in a network
21	I, III	Create and apply an addressing scheme to a network
22	III	Assign and verify valid IP addresses to hosts, servers, and networking devices in a LAN environment
23	IV	Explain the basic uses and operation of NAT in a small network connecting to one ISP
24	I, III	Describe and verify DNS operation
25	III, IV	Describe the operation and benefits of using private and public IP addressing
26	III, IV	Enable NAT for a small network with a single ISP and connection using SDM and verify operation using CLI and ping
27	III	Configure, verify, and troubleshoot DHCP and DNS operation on a router (including: CLI/SDM)
28	III	Implement static and dynamic addressing services for hosts in a LAN environment
29	III	Identify and correct IP addressing issues
		Implement a small routed network
30	I, III	Describe basic routing concepts (including: packet forwarding, router lookup process)
31	III	Describe the operation of Cisco routers (including: router bootup process, POST, router components)

Table I-1 *ICND1 Exam Topics (Continued)*

Reference Number	Book Part(s) Where Topic Is Covered	Exam Topic
32	I, III	Select the appropriate media, cables, ports, and connectors to connect routers to other network devices and hosts
33	III	Configure, verify, and troubleshoot RIPv2
34	III	Access and utilize the router CLI to set basic parameters
35	III	Connect, configure, and verify operation status of a device interface
36	III	Verify device configuration and network connectivity using ping, traceroute, Telnet, SSH, or other utilities
37	III	Perform and verify routing configuration tasks for a static or default route given specific routing requirements
38	III	Manage IOS configuration files (including: save, edit, upgrade, restore)
39	III	Manage Cisco IOS
40	III	Implement password and physical security
41	III	Verify network status and router operation using basic utilities (including: ping, traceroute, Telnet, SSH, ARP, ipconfig), show and debug commands
		Explain and select the appropriate administrative tasks required for a WLAN
42	II	Describe standards associated with wireless media (including: IEEE, Wi-Fi Alliance, ITU/FCC)
43	II	Identify and describe the purpose of the components in a small wireless network (including: SSID, BSS, ESS)
44	II	Identify the basic parameters to configure on a wireless network to ensure that devices connect to the correct access point
45	II	Compare and contrast wireless security features and capabilities of WPA security (including: open, WEP, WPA-1/2)
46	II	Identify common issues with implementing wireless networks

continues

Table I-1 *ICND1 Exam Topics (Continued)*

Reference Number	Book Part(s) Where Topic Is Covered	Exam Topic
		Identify security threats to a network and describe general methods to mitigate those threats
47	I	Explain today's increasing network security threats and the need to implement a comprehensive security policy to mitigate the threats
48	I	Explain general methods to mitigate common security threats to network devices, hosts, and applications
49	I	Describe the functions of common security appliances and applications
50	I, II, III	Describe security recommended practices including initial steps to secure network devices
		Implement and verify WAN links
51	IV	Describe different methods for connecting to a WAN
52	IV	Configure and verify a basic WAN serial connection

ICND2 Exam Topics

Table I-2 lists the exam topics for the ICND2 (640-816) exam, along with the book parts in the *CCNA ICND2 Official Exam Certification Guide* in which each topic is covered.

Table I-2 *ICND2 Exam Topics*

Reference Number	Book Part(s) Where Topic Is Covered (in ICND2)	Exam Topic
		Configure, verify, and troubleshoot a switch with VLANs and interswitch communications
101	I	Describe enhanced switching technologies (including: VTP, RSTP, VLAN, PVSTP, 802.1q)
102	I	Describe how VLANs create logically separate networks and the need for routing between them
103	I	Configure, verify, and troubleshoot VLANs
104	I	Configure, verify, and troubleshoot trunking on Cisco switches

Table I-2 *ICND2 Exam Topics (Continued)*

Reference Number	Book Part(s) Where Topic Is Covered (in ICND2)	Exam Topic
105	II	Configure, verify, and troubleshoot interVLAN routing
106	I	Configure, verify, and troubleshoot VTP
107	I	Configure, verify, and troubleshoot RSTP operation
108	I	Interpret the output of various show and debug commands to verify the operational status of a Cisco switched network
109	I	Implement basic switch security (including: port security, unassigned ports, trunk access, etc.)
		Implement an IP addressing scheme and IP Services to meet network requirements in a medium-size Enterprise branch office network
110	II	Calculate and apply a VLSM IP addressing design to a network
111	II	Determine the appropriate classless addressing scheme using VLSM and summarization to satisfy addressing requirements in a LAN/WAN environment
112	V	Describe the technological requirements for running IPv6 (including: protocols, dual stack, tunneling, etc.)
113	V	Describe IPv6 addresses
114	II, III	Identify and correct common problems associated with IP addressing and host configurations
		Configure and troubleshoot basic operation and routing on Cisco devices
115	III	Compare and contrast methods of routing and routing protocols
116	III	Configure, verify, and troubleshoot OSPF
117	III	Configure, verify, and troubleshoot EIGRP
118	II, III	Verify configuration and connectivity using ping, traceroute, and Telnet or SSH
119	II, III	Troubleshoot routing implementation issues

continues

Table I-2 *ICND2 Exam Topics (Continued)*

Reference Number	Book Part(s) Where Topic Is Covered (in ICND2)	Exam Topic
120	II, III, IV	Verify router hardware and software operation using show and debug commands
121	II	Implement basic router security
		Implement, verify, and troubleshoot NAT and ACLs in a medium-size Enterprise branch office network
122	II	Describe the purpose and types of access control lists
123	II	Configure and apply access control lists based on network filtering requirements
124	II	Configure and apply an access control list to limit Telnet and SSH access to the router
125	II	Verify and monitor ACLs in a network environment
126	II	Troubleshoot ACL implementation issues
127	V	Explain the basic operation of NAT
128	V	Configure Network Address Translation for given network requirements using CLI
129	V	Troubleshoot NAT implementation issues
		Implement and verify WAN links
130	IV	Configure and verify Frame Relay on Cisco routers
131	IV	Troubleshoot WAN implementation issues
132	IV	Describe VPN technology (including: importance, benefits, role, impact, components)
133	IV	Configure and verify PPP connection between Cisco routers

CCNA Exam Topics

In the previous version of the exams, the CCNA exam covered a lot of what was in the ICND (640-811) exam, plus some coverage of topics in the INTRO (640-821) exam. The new CCNA exam (640-802) covers all the topics on both the ICND1 (640-822) and ICND2 (640-816) exams. One of the reasons for more-balanced coverage in the exams is that some of the topics that used to be in the second exam have been moved to the first exam.

The CCNA (640-802) exam covers all the topics in both the ICND1 and ICND2 exams. The official CCNA 640-802 exam topics, posted at http://www.cisco.com, include all the topics listed in Table I-2 for the ICND2 exam, plus most of the exam topics for the ICND1 exam listed in Table I-1. The only exam topics from these two tables that are not listed as CCNA exam topics are the topics highlighted in gray in Table I-1. However, note that the gray topics are still covered on the CCNA 640-802 exam. Those topics are just not listed in the CCNA exam topics because one of the ICND2 exam topics refers to the same concepts.

ICND1 and ICND2 Course Outlines

Another way to get some direction about the topics on the exams is to look at the course outlines for the related courses. Cisco offers two authorized CCNA-related courses: Interconnecting Cisco Network Devices 1 (ICND1) and Interconnecting Cisco Network Devices 2 (ICND2). Cisco authorizes Certified Learning Solutions Providers (CLSP) and Certified Learning Partners (CLP) to deliver these classes. These authorized companies can also create unique custom course books using this material—in some cases to teach classes geared toward passing the CCNA exam.

About the *CCENT/CCNA ICND1 Official Exam Certification Guide* and *CCNA ICND2 Official Exam Certification Guide*

As mentioned earlier, Cisco has separated the content covered by the CCNA exam into two parts: topics typically used by engineers who work in small Enterprise networks (ICND1), and topics commonly used by engineers in medium-sized Enterprises (ICND2). Likewise, the Cisco Press *CCNA Exam Certification Guide* series includes two books for CCNA—*CCENT/CCNA ICND1 Official Exam Certification Guide* and *CCNA ICND2 Official Exam Certification Guide*. These two books cover the breadth of topics on each exam, typically to a little more depth than is required for the exams, to ensure that the books prepare you for the more difficult exam questions.

This section lists the variety of book features in both this book and the *CCNA ICND2 Official Exam Certification Guide*. Both books have the same basic features, so if you are reading both this book and the ICND2 book, there is no need to read the Introduction to the second book. Also, if you're using both books to prepare for the CCNA 640-802 exam (rather than taking the two-exam option), the end of this Introduction lists a suggested reading plan.

Objectives and Methods

The most important and somewhat obvious objective of this book is to help you pass the ICND1 exam or the CCNA exam. In fact, if the primary objective of this book were different, the book's title would be misleading! However, the methods used in this book to help you pass the exams are also designed to make you much more knowledgeable about how to do your job.

This book uses several key methodologies to help you discover the exam topics on which you need more review, to help you fully understand and remember those details, and to help you prove to yourself that you have retained your knowledge of those topics. So, this book does not try to help you pass the exams only by memorization, but by truly learning and understanding the topics. The CCNA certification is the foundation for many of the Cisco professional certifications, and it would be a disservice to you if this book did not help you truly learn the material. Therefore, this book helps you pass the CCNA exam by using the following methods:

- Helping you discover which exam topics you have not mastered

- Providing explanations and information to fill in your knowledge gaps

- Supplying exercises that enhance your ability to recall and deduce the answers to test questions

- Providing practice exercises on the topics and the testing process via test questions on the CD

Book Features

To help you customize your study time using these books, the core chapters have several features that help you make the best use of your time:

- **"Do I Know This Already?" Quizzes:** Each chapter begins with a quiz that helps you determine how much time you need to spend studying that chapter.

- **Foundation Topics:** These are the core sections of each chapter. They explain the protocols, concepts, and configuration for the topics in that chapter.

- **Exam Preparation Tasks:** After the Foundation Topics section, the "Exam Preparation Tasks" section lists a series of study activities you should perform. Each chapter includes the activities that make the most sense for studying the topics in that chapter. The activities include the following:

  — **Review All the Key Topics:** The key topics icon appears next to the most important items in the Foundation Topics section. The "Review All the Key Topics" activity lists the key topics from the chapter and the page on which they appear. Although the contents of the entire chapter could be on the exam, you should definitely know the information listed in each key topic.

— **Complete the Tables and Lists from Memory:** To help you memorize some lists of facts, many of the more important lists and tables from the chapter are included in Appendix H on the CD. This document lists only some of the information, allowing you to complete the table or list. Appendix I lists the same tables and lists, completed, for easy comparison.

— **Definitions of Key Terms:** Although the exams may be unlikely to ask a question such as "Define this term," the CCNA exams do require that you learn and know a lot of networking terminology. This section lists the most important terms from the chapter, asking you to write a short definition and compare your answer to the glossary at the end of the book.

— **Command Reference tables:** Some book chapters cover a large number of configuration and EXEC commands. These tables list and describe the commands introduced in the chapter. For exam preparation, use this section for reference, but also read through the table when performing the Exam Preparation Tasks to make sure you remember what all the commands do.

■ **CD-based practice exam:** The companion CD contains an exam engine (from Boson software, http://www.boson.com) that includes a large number of exam-realistic practice questions. You can take simulated ICND1 exams, as well as simulated CCNA exams, using this book's CD. (You can take simulated ICND2 and CCNA exams using the CD in the *CCNA ICND2 Official Exam Certification Guide*.)

■ **Subnetting videos:** The companion DVD contains a series of videos that show you how to figure out various facts about IP addressing and subnetting—in particular, using the shortcuts described in this book.

■ **Subnetting practice:** CD Appendix D contains a large set of subnetting practice problems, including the answers and explanations of how they were arrived at. This is a great resource to help you get ready to do subnetting well and fast.

■ **CD-based practice scenarios:** CD Appendix F contains several networking scenarios for additional study. These scenarios describe various networks and requirements, taking you through conceptual design, configuration, and verification. These scenarios are useful for building your hands-on skills, even if you do not have lab gear.

■ **Companion website:** The website http://www.ciscopress.com/title/1587201828 posts up-to-the-minute materials that further clarify complex exam topics. Check this site regularly for new and updated postings written by the author that provide further insight into the more troublesome topics on the exam.

How This Book Is Organized

This book contains 18 core chapters. The final one includes summary materials and suggestions on how to approach the exams. Each chapter covers a subset of the topics on the ICND1 exam. The chapters are organized into parts and cover the following topics:

■ **Part I: Networking Fundamentals**

— **Chapter 1, "Introduction to Computer Networking Concepts,"** provides a basic introduction in case you're new to networking.

— **Chapter 2, "The TCP/IP and OSI Networking Models,"** introduces the terminology used with two different networking architectures— Transmission Control Protocol/Internet Protocol (TCP/IP) and Open Systems Interconnection (OSI).

— **Chapter 3, "Fundamental of LANs,"** covers the concepts and terms used with the most popular option for the data link layer for local-area networks (LANs)—namely, Ethernet.

— **Chapter 4, "Fundamentals of WANs,"** covers the concepts and terms used with the most popular options for the data link layer for wide-area networks (WANs), including High-Level Data Link Control (HDLC), Point-to-Point Protocol (PPP), and Frame Relay.

— **Chapter 5, "Fundamentals of IP Addressing and Routing,"** covers the main network layer protocol for TCP/IP—Internet Protocol (IP). This chapter introduces the basics of IP, including IP addressing and routing.

— **Chapter 6, "Fundamentals of TCP/IP Transport, Applications, and Security,"** covers the main transport layer protocols for TCP/IP— Transmission Control Protocol (TCP) and User Datagram Protocol (UDP). This chapter introduces the basics of TCP and UDP.

■ **Part II: LAN Switching**

— **Chapter 7, "Ethernet LAN Switching Concepts,"** deepens and expands the introduction to LANs from Chapter 3, completing most of the conceptual materials for Ethernet in this book.

— **Chapter 8, "Operating Cisco LAN Switches,"** explains how to access, examine, and configure Cisco Catalyst LAN switches.

— **Chapter 9, "Ethernet Switch Configuration,"** shows you how to configure a variety of switch features, including duplex and speed, port security, securing the CLI, and the switch IP address.

— **Chapter 10, "Ethernet Switch Troubleshooting,"** focuses on how to tell if the switch is doing what it is supposed to, mainly through the use of **show** commands.

— **Chapter 11, "Wireless LANs,"** explains the basic operation concepts of wireless LANs, along with addressing some of the most common security concerns.

■ **Part III: IP Routing**

— **Chapter 12, "IP Addressing and Subnetting,"** completes the explanation of subnetting that was introduced in Chapter 5. More importantly, it describes in detail how to perform the math and processes to find the answers to many varieties of subnetting questions.

— **Chapter 13, "Operating Cisco Routers,"** is like Chapter 8, but with a focus on routers instead of switches.

— **Chapter 14, "Routing Protocol Concepts and Configuration,"** explains how routers forward (route) IP packets and how IP routing protocols work to find all the best routes to each subnet. This chapter includes the details of how to configure static routes and RIP version 2.

— **Chapter 15, "Troubleshooting IP Routing,"** suggests hints and tips about how to troubleshoot problems related to layer 3 routing, including a description of several troubleshooting tools.

■ **Part IV: Wide-Area Networks**

— **Chapter 16, "WAN Concepts,"** completes the conceptual materials for WANs, continuing the coverage from Chapter 4 by touching on Internet access technologies such as DSL and cable. It also covers the concepts of Network Address Translation (NAT).

— **Chapter 17, "WAN Configuration,"** completes the main technical topics, focusing on a few small WAN configuration tasks. It also covers the WAN configuration tasks and NAT configuration using Cisco Security Device Manager (SDM).

■ **Part V: Final Preparation**

— **Chapter 18, "Final Preparation,"** suggests a plan for final preparation after you have finished the core parts of the book. It also explains the many study options available in the book.

■ **Part VI: Appendixes (in the Book)**

— **Appendix A, "Answers to the "Do I Know This Already?" Quizzes,"** includes the answers to all the questions from Chapters 1 through 17.

- — **Appendix B, "Decimal to Binary Conversion Table,"** lists decimal values 0 through 255, along with their binary equivalents.

- — **Appendix C, "ICND1 Exam Updates,"** covers a variety of short topics that either clarify or expand on topics covered earlier in the book. This appendix is updated from time to time and is posted at http://www.ciscopress.com/ccna. The most recent version available at the time this book was published is included in this book as Appendix C. (The first page of the appendix includes instructions on how to check to see if a later version of Appendix C is available online.)

- — The **glossary** defines all the terms listed in the "Definitions of Key Terms" section at the conclusion of Chapters 1 through 17.

■ **Part VII: Appendixes (on the CD)**

The following appendixes are available in PDF format on the CD that accompanies this book:

- — **Appendix D, "Subnetting Practice,"** includes a large number of subnetting practice problems. It gives the answers as well as explanations of how to use the processes described in Chapter 12 to find the answers.

- — **Appendix E, "Subnetting Reference Pages."** Chapter 12 explains in detail how to calculate the answers to many subnetting questions. This appendix summarizes the process of finding the answers to several key questions, with the details on a single page. The goal is to give you a handy reference page to refer to when you're practicing subnetting.

- — **Appendix F, "Additional Scenarios."** One method to improve your troubleshooting and network analysis skills is to examine as many unique network scenarios as possible, think about them, and then get some feedback on whether you came to the right conclusions. This appendix provides several such scenarios.

- — **Appendix G, "Subnetting Video Reference."** The DVD includes several subnetting videos that show you how to use the processes covered in Chapter 12. This appendix contains copies of the key elements from those videos, which may be useful when you're watching the videos (so that you do not have to keep moving back and forth in the video).

- — **Appendix H, "Memory Tables,"** contains the key tables and lists from each chapter, with some of the content removed. You can print this appendix and, as a memory exercise, complete the tables and lists. The goal is to help you memorize facts that can be useful on the exams.

- — **Appendix I, "Memory Tables Answer Key,"** contains the answer key for the exercises in Appendix H.

— **Appendix J, "ICND1 Open-Ended Questions,"** is a holdover from the previous edition of this book. The first edition had some open-ended questions to help you study for the exam, but the newer features make these questions unnecessary. For convenience, the old questions are included here, unedited since the last edition.

How to Use This Book to Prepare for the ICND1 (640–822) Exam and CCENT Certification

This book was designed with two primary goals in mind: to help you study for the ICND1 exam (and get your CCENT certification), and to help you study for the CCNA exam by using both this book and the *CCNA ICND2 Official Exam Certification Guide*. Using this book to prepare for the ICND1 exam is pretty straightforward. You read each chapter in succession and follow the study suggestions in Chapter 18.

For Chapters 1 through 17, you have some choices as to how much of the chapter you read. In some cases, you may already know most or all of the information covered in a given chapter. To help you decide how much time to spend on each chapter, the chapters begin with a "Do I Know This Already?" quiz. If you get all the quiz questions correct, or if you miss just one, you may want to skip to the "Exam Preparation Tasks" section at the end of the chapter and perform those activities. Figure I-2 shows the overall plan.

Figure I-2 *How to Approach Each Chapter of This Book*

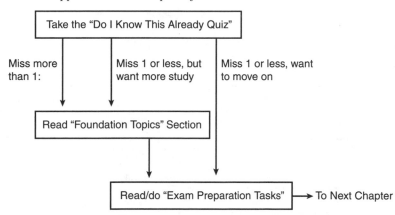

When you have completed Chapters 1 through 17, you can use the guidance listed in Chapter 18 to perform the rest of the exam preparation tasks. That chapter includes the following suggestions:

■ Check http://www.ciscopress.com for the latest copy of Appendix C, which may include additional topics for study.

- Practice subnetting using the tools available in the CD appendixes.

- Repeat the tasks in all the chapters' "Exam Preparation Tasks" chapter-ending sections.

- Review the scenarios in CD Appendix F.

- Review all the "Do I Know This Already?" questions.

- Practice the exam using the exam engine.

How to Use These Books to Prepare for the CCNA 640–802 Exam

If you plan to get your CCNA certification using the one-exam option of taking the CCNA 640-802 exam, you can use this book with the *CCNA ICND2 Official Exam Certification Guide*. If you haven't yet bought either book, you generally can get the pair cheaper by buying both books as a two-book set called the *CCNA Certification Library*.

These two books were designed to be used together when you study for the CCNA exam. You have two good options for the order in which to read the two books. The first and most obvious option is to read this book and then move on to the ICND2 book. The other option is to read all of ICND1's coverage of one topic area, and then read ICND2's coverage of the same topics, and then return to ICND1. Figure I-3 outlines my suggested plan for reading the two books.

Figure I-3 *Reading Plan When You're Studying for the CCNA Exam*

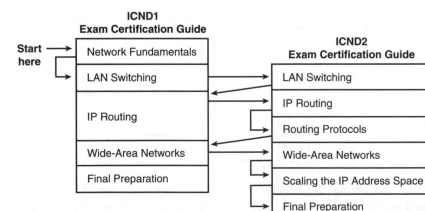

Both reading plan options have some benefits. Moving back and forth between books helps you focus on one general topic at a time. However, note that there is some overlap between the two exams, so there is some overlap between the two books as well. From reader comments about the previous edition of these books, readers who were new to networking tended to do better by completing all of the first book and then moving on to the second. Readers who had more experience and knowledge before starting the books tended to prefer following a reading plan like the one shown in Figure I-3.

Note that for final preparation, you can use the final chapter (Chapter 18) of the ICND2 book rather than the "Final Preparation" chapter (Chapter 18) of this book. Chapter 18 of ICND2 covers the same basic activities as does this book's Chapter 18, with reminders of any exam preparation materials from this book that should be useful.

In addition to the flow shown in Figure I-3, when you study for the CCNA exam (rather than the ICND1 and ICND2 exams), it is important to master IP subnetting before moving on to the IP routing and routing protocol parts of the ICND2 book. The ICND2 book does not review subnetting or the underlying math, assuming that you know how to find the answers. Those ICND2 chapters, particularly Chapter 5 ("VLSM and Route Summarization"), are much easier to understand if you can do the related subnetting math pretty easily.

For More Information

If you have any comments about this book, you can submit them via http://www.ciscopress.com. Just go to the website, select Contact Us, and enter your message.

Cisco might occasionally make changes that affect the CCNA certification. You should always check http://www.cisco.com/go/ccna and http://www.cisco.com/go/ccent for the latest details.

The CCNA certification is arguably the most important Cisco certification, although the new CCENT certification might surpass CCNA in the future. CCNA certainly is the most popular Cisco certification to date. It's required for several other certifications, and it's the first step in distinguishing yourself as someone who has proven knowledge of Cisco.

The *CCENT/CCNA ICND1 Official Exam Certification Guide* is designed to help you attain both CCENT and CCNA certification. This is the CCENT/CCNA ICND1 certification book from the only Cisco-authorized publisher. We at Cisco Press believe that this book can help you achieve CCNA certification, but the real work is up to you! I trust that your time will be well spent.

Cisco Published ICND1 Exam Topics* Covered in This Part:

Describe the operation of data networks

- Describe the purpose and functions of various network devices
- Select the components required to meet a given network specification
- Use the OSI and TCP/IP models and their associated protocols to explain how data flows in a network
- Describe common networking applications including web applications
- Describe the purpose and basic operation of the protocols in the OSI and TCP models
- Describe the impact of applications (Voice Over IP and Video Over IP) on a network
- Describe the components required for network and Internet communications
- Identify and correct common network problems at Layers 1, 2, 3, and 7 using a layered model approach

Implement an IP addressing scheme and IP services to meet network requirements for a small branch office

- Describe the need for and role of addressing in a network
- Create and apply an addressing scheme to a network
- Describe and verify DNS operation

Implement a small routed network

- Describe basic routing concepts (including: packet forwarding, router lookup process)
- Select the appropriate media, cables, ports, and connectors to connect routers to other network devices and hosts

Identify security threats to a network and describe general methods to mitigate those threats

- Explain today's increasing network security threats and the need to implement a comprehensive security policy to mitigate the threats
- Explain general methods to mitigate common security threats to network devices, hosts, and applications
- Describe the functions of common security appliances and applications
- Describe security recommended practices including initial steps to secure network devices

*Always check http://www.cisco.com for the latest posted exam topics.

Part I: Networking Fundamentals

CHAPTER 1

Introduction to Computer Networking Concepts

This chapter gives you a light-hearted perspective about networks, how they were originally created, and why networks work the way they do. Although no specific fact from this chapter happens to be on any of the CCNA exams, this chapter helps you prepare for the depth of topics you will start to read about in Chapter 2, "The TCP/IP and OSI Networking Models." If you are brand new to networking, this short introductory chapter will help you get ready for the details to follow. If you already understand some of the basics of TCP/IP, Ethernet, switches, routers, IP addressing, and the like, go ahead and skip on to Chapter 2. The rest of you will probably want to read through this short introductory chapter before diving into the details.

Perspectives on Networking

So, you are new to networking. You might have seen or heard about different topics relating to networking, but you are only just now getting serious about learning the details. Like many people, your perspective about networks might be that of a user of the network, as opposed to the network engineer who builds networks. For some, your view of networking might be based on how you use the Internet, from home, using a high-speed Internet connection. Others of you might use a computer at a job or at school, again connecting to the Internet; that computer is typically connected to a network via some cable. Figure 1-1 shows both perspectives of networking.

Figure 1-1 *End-User Perspective on Networks*

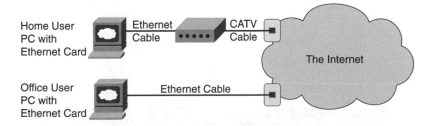

The top part of the figure shows a typical high-speed cable Internet user. The PC connects to a cable modem using an Ethernet cable. The cable modem then connects to a cable TV (CATV) outlet on the wall using a round coaxial cable—the same kind of cable used to connect your TV to the CATV wall outlet. Because cable Internet services provide service continuously, the user can just sit down at the PC and start sending e-mail, browsing websites, making Internet phone calls, and using other tools and applications as well.

Similarly, an employee of a company or a student at a university views the world as a connection through a wall plug. Typically, this connection uses a type of local-area network (LAN) called Ethernet. Instead of needing a cable modem, the PC connects directly to an Ethernet-style socket in a wall plate (the socket is much like the typical socket used for telephone cabling today, but the connector is a little larger). As with high-speed cable Internet connections, the Ethernet connection does not require the PC user to do anything first to connect to the network—it is always there waiting to be used, similar to the power outlet.

From the end-user perspective, whether at home, at work, or at school, what happens behind the wall plug is magic. Just as most people do not really understand how cars work, how TVs work, and so on, most people who use networks do not understand how they work. Nor do they want to! But if you have read this much into Chapter 1, you obviously have a little more interest in networking than a typical end user. By the end of this book, you will have a pretty thorough understanding of what is behind that wall plug in both cases shown in Figure 1-1.

The CCNA exams, and particularly the ICND1 (640-822) exam, focus on two major branches of networking concepts, protocols, and devices. One of these two major branches is called enterprise networking. An enterprise network is a network created by one corporation, or enterprise, for the purpose of allowing its employees to communicate. For example, Figure 1-2 shows the same type of PC end-user shown in Figure 1-1, who is now communicating with a web server through the enterprise network (represented by a cloud) created by Enterprise #2. The end-user PC can communicate with the web server to do something useful for the company—for instance, the user might be on the phone with a customer, with the user typing in the customer's new order in the ordering system that resides in the web server.

Figure 1-2 *An Example Representation of an Enterprise Network*

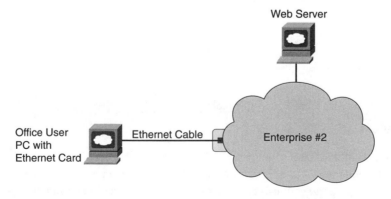

> **NOTE**   In networking diagrams, a cloud represents a part of a network whose details
> are not important to the purpose of the diagram. In this case, Figure 1-2 ignores the
> details of how to create an enterprise network.

The second major branch of networking covered on the ICND1 exam is called small office/
home office, or SOHO. This branch of networking uses the same concepts, protocols, and
devices used to create enterprise networks, plus some additional features that are not
needed for enterprises. SOHO networking allows a user to connect to the Internet using
a PC and any Internet connection, such as the high-speed cable Internet connection shown
in Figure 1-1. Because most enterprise networks also connect to the Internet, the SOHO
user can sit at home, or in a small office, and communicate with servers at the enterprise
network, as well as with other hosts in the Internet. Figure 1-3 shows the concept.

Figure 1-3   *SOHO User Connecting to the Internet and Other Enterprise Networks*

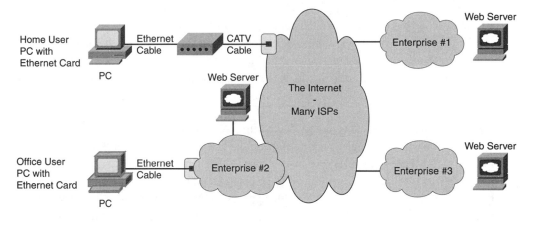

The Internet itself consists of most every enterprise network in the world, plus billions of
devices connecting to the Internet directly through Internet service providers (ISPs). In fact,
the term itself—Internet—is formed by shortening the phrase "interconnected networks."
To create the Internet, ISPs offer Internet access, typically using either a cable TV line, a
phone line using digital subscriber line (DSL) technology, or a telephone line with a modem.
Each enterprise typically connects to at least one ISP, using permanent connections
generally called wide-area network (WAN) links. Finally, the ISPs of the world also
connect to each other. These interconnected networks—from the smallest single-PC home
network, to cell phones and MP3 players, to enterprise networks with thousands of
devices—all connect to the global Internet.

Most of the details about standards for enterprise networks were created in the last quarter of the 20th century. You might have become interested in networking after most of the conventions and rules used for basic networking were created. However, you might understand the networking rules and conventions more easily if you take the time to pause and think about what you would do if you were creating these standards. The next section takes you through a somewhat silly example of thinking through some imaginary early networking standards, but this example has real value in terms of exploring some of the basic concepts behind enterprise networking and some of the design trade-offs.

The Flintstones Network: The First Computer Network?

The Flintstones are a cartoon family that, according to the cartoon, lived in prehistoric times. Because I want to discuss the thought process behind some imaginary initial networking standards, the Flintstones seem to be the right group of people to put in the example.

Fred is the president of FredsCo, where his wife (Wilma), buddy (Barney), and buddy's wife (Betty) all work. They all have phones and computers, but they have no network because no one has ever made up the idea of a network before. Fred sees all his employees exchanging data by running around giving each other disks with files on them, and it seems inefficient. So, Fred, being a visionary, imagines a world in which people can connect their computers somehow and exchange files, without having to leave their desks. The (imaginary) first network is about to be born.

Fred's daughter, Pebbles, has just graduated from Rockville University and wants to join the family business. Fred gives her a job, with the title First-Ever Network Engineer. Fred says to Pebbles, "Pebbles, I want everyone to be able to exchange files without having to get up from their desks. I want them to be able to simply type in the name of a file and the name of the person, and poof! The file appears on the other person's computer. And because everyone changes departments so often around here, I want the workers to be able to take their PCs with them and just have to plug the computer into a wall socket so that they can send and receive files from the new office to which they moved. I want this network thing to be like the electrical power thing your boyfriend, Bamm-Bamm, created for us last year—a plug in the wall near every desk, and if you plug in, you are on the network!"

Pebbles first decides to do some research and development. If she can get two PCs to transfer files in a lab, then she ought to be able to get all the PCs to transfer files, right? She writes a program called Fred's Transfer Program, or FTP, in honor of her father.

The program uses a new networking card that Pebbles built in the lab. This networking card uses a cable with two wires in it—one wire to send bits and one wire to receive bits. Pebbles puts one card in each of the two computers and cables the computers together with a cable with two wires in it. The FTP software on each computer sends the bits that comprise the files by using the networking cards. If Pebbles types a command such as **ftp send filename**, the software transfers the file called filename to the computer at the other end of the cable. Figure 1-4 depicts the first network test at FredsCo.

Figure 1-4   *Two PCs Transfer Files in the Lab*

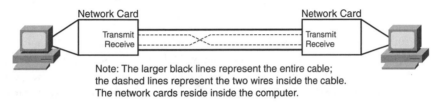

Pebbles' new networking cards use wire 1 to send bits and wire 2 to receive bits, so the cable used by Pebbles connects wire 1 on PC1 to wire 2 on PC2, and vice versa. That way, both cards can send bits using wire 1, and those bits will enter the other PC on the other PC's wire 2.

Bamm-Bamm stops by to give Pebbles some help after hearing about the successful test. "I am ready to start deploying the network!" she exclaims. Bamm-Bamm, the wizened one-year veteran of FredsCo who graduated from Rockville University a year before Pebbles, starts asking some questions. "What happens when you want to connect three computers together?" he asks. Pebbles explains that she can put two networking cards in each computer and cable each computer to each other. "So what happens when you connect 100 computers to the network, in each building?" Pebbles then realizes that she has a little more work to do. She needs a scheme that allows her network to scale to more than two users. Bamm-Bamm then offers a suggestion, "We ran all the electrical power cables from the wall plug at each cube back to the broom closet. We just send electricity from the closet out to the wall plug near every desk. Maybe if you did something similar, you could find a way to somehow make it all work."

With that bit of input, Pebbles has all the inspiration she needs. Emboldened by the fact that she has already created the world's first PC networking card, she decides to create a device that will allow cabling similar to Bamm-Bamm's electrical cabling plan. Pebble's solution to this first major hurdle is shown in Figure 1-5.

Figure 1-5   *Star Cabling to a Repeater*

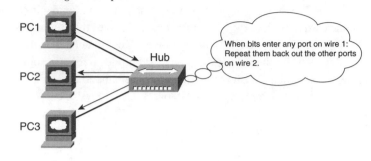

Pebbles follows Bamm-Bamm's advice about the cabling. However, she needs a device into which she can plug the cables—something that will take the bits sent by a PC, and reflect, or repeat, the bits back to all the other devices connected to this new device. Because the networking cards send bits using wire 1, Pebbles builds this new device in such a way that when it receives bits coming in wire 1 on one of its ports, it repeats the same bits, but repeats them out wire 2 on all the other ports, so that the other PCs get those bits on the receive wire. (Therefore, the cabling does not have to swap wires 1 and 2—this new device takes care of that.) And because she is making this up for the very first time in history, she needs to decide on a name for this new device: She names the device a hub.

Before deploying the first hub and running a bunch of cables, Pebbles does the right thing: She tests it in a lab, with three PCs connected to the world's first hub. She starts FTP on PC1, transfers the file called recipe.doc, and sees a window pop up on PC2 saying that the file was received, just like normal. "Fantastic!" she thinks, until she realizes that PC3 also has the same pop-up window on it. She has transferred the file to both PC2 and PC3! "Of course!" she thinks. "If the hub repeats everything out every cable connected to it, then when my FTP program sends a file, everyone will get it. I need a way for FTP to send a file to a specific PC!"

At this point, Pebbles thinks of a few different options. First, she thinks that she will give each computer the same name as the first name of the person using the computer. She will then change FTP to put the name of the PC that the file was being sent to in front of the file contents. In other words, to send her mom a recipe, she will use the **ftp Wilma recipe.doc** command. So, even though each PC will receive the bits because the hub repeats the signal to everyone connected to it, only the PC whose name is the one in front of the file should actually create the file. Then her dad walks in: "Pebbles, I want you to meet Barney Fife, our new head of security. He needs a network connection as well—you are going to be finished soon, right?"

So much for using first names for the computers, now that there are two people named Barney at FredsCo. Pebbles, being mathematically inclined and in charge of creating all the hardware, decides on a different approach. "I will put a unique numeric address on each networking card—a four-digit decimal number," she exclaims. Because Pebbles created all the cards, she will make sure that the number used on each card is unique. Also, with a four-digit number, she will never run out of unique numbers—she has 10,000 (10^4) to choose from and only 200 employees at FredsCo.

By the way, because she is making all this up for the very first time, Pebbles calls these built-in numbers on the cards *addresses*. When anyone wants to send a file, they can just use the **ftp** command, but with a number instead of a name. For instance, **ftp 0002 recipe.doc** will send the recipe.doc file to the PC whose network card has the address 0002. Figure 1-6 depicts the new environment in the lab.

Figure 1-6 *The First Network Addressing Convention*

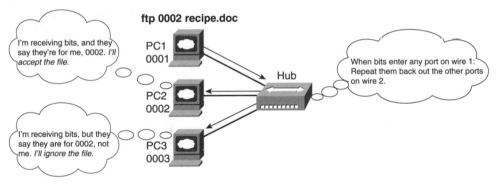

Now, with some minor updates to the Fred Transfer Program, the user can type **ftp 0002 recipe.doc** to send the file recipe.doc to the PC with address 0002. Pebbles tests the software and hardware in the lab again, and although the hub forwards the frames from PC1 to both PC2 and PC3, only PC2 processes the frames and creates a copy of the file. Similarly, when Pebbles sends the file to address 0003, only PC3 processes the received frames and creates a file. She is now ready to deploy the first computer network.

Pebbles now needs to build all the hardware required for the network. She first creates 200 network cards, each with a unique address. She installs the FTP program on all 200 PCs and installs the cards in each PC. Then she goes back to the lab and starts planning how many cables she will need and how long each cable should be. At this point, Pebbles realizes that she will need to run some cables a long way. If she puts the hub in the bottom floor of building A, the PCs on the fifth floor of building B will need a really long cable to connect to the hub. Cables cost money, and the longer the cable is, the more expensive the cable is. Besides, she has not yet tested the network with longer cables; she has been using cables that are only a couple of meters long.

Bamm-Bamm walks by and sees that Pebbles is stressed. Pebbles vents a little: "Daddy wants this project finished, and you know how demanding he is. And I didn't think about how long the cables will be—I will be way over budget. And I will be installing cables for weeks!" Bamm-Bamm, being a little less stressed, having just come from a lunchtime workout at the club, knows that Pebbles already has the solution—she is too stressed to see it. Of course, the solution is not terribly different from how Bamm-Bamm solved a similar problem with the electrical cabling last year. "Those hubs repeat everything they hear, right? So, why not make a bunch of hubs. Put one hub on each floor, and run cables from all the PCs. Then run one cable from the hub on each floor to a hub on the first floor. Then, run one cable between the two main hubs in the two buildings. Because they repeat everything, every PC should receive the signal when just one PC sends, whether they are attached to the same hub or are four hubs away." Figure 1-7 depicts Bamm-Bamm's suggested design.

Figure 1-7 *Per-Floor Hubs, Connected Together*

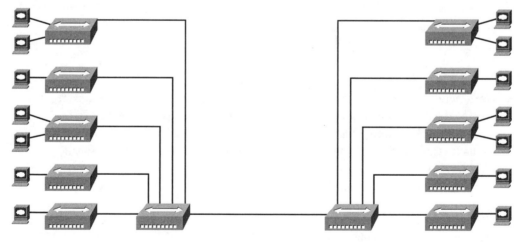

Pebbles loves the idea. She builds and connects the new hubs in the lab, just to prove the concept. It works! She makes the (now shorter) cables, installs the hubs and cables, and is ready to test. She goes to a few representative PCs and tests, and it all works! The first network has now been deployed.

Wanting to surprise Poppa Fred, Pebbles writes a memo to everyone in the company, telling them how to use the soon-to-be-famous Fred Transfer Program to transfer files. Along with the memo, she puts a list of names of people and the four-digit network address to be used to send files to each PC. She puts the memos in everyone's mail slot and waits for the excitement to start.

Amazingly, it all works. The users are happy. Fred treats Pebbles and Bamm-Bamm to a nice dinner—at home, cooked by Wilma, but a good meal nonetheless.

Pebbles thinks she did it—created the world's first computer network, with no problems—until a few weeks pass. "I can't send files to Fred anymore!" exclaims Barney Rubble. "Ever since Fred got that new computer, he is too busy to go bowling, and now I can't even send files to him to tell him how much we need him back on the bowling team!" Then it hits Pebbles—Fred had just received a new PC and a new networking card. Fred's network address has changed. If the card fails and it has to be replaced, the address changes.

About that time, Wilma comes in to say hi. "I love that new network thing you built. Betty and I can type notes to each other, put them in a file, and send them anytime. It is almost like working on the same floor!" she says. "But I really don't remember the numbers so well. Couldn't you make that FTP thing work with names instead of addresses?"

In a fit of inspiration, Pebbles sees the answer to the first problem in the solution to her mom's problem. "I will change FTP to use names instead of addresses. I will make everyone tell me what name they want to use—maybe Barney Rubble will use BarneyR, and Barney Fife will use BarneyF, for instance. I will change FTP to accept names as well as numbers. Then I will tell FTP to look in a table that I will put on each PC that correlates the names to the numeric addresses. That way, if I ever need to replace a LAN card, all I have to do is update the list of names and addresses and put a copy on everyone's PC, and no one will know that anything has changed!" Table 1-1 lists Pebbles' first name table.

Table 1-1   *Pebbles' First Name/Address Table*

Person's Name	Computer Name	Network Address
Fred Flintstone	Fred	0001
Wilma Flintstone	Wilma	0002
Barney Rubble	BarneyR	0011
Betty Rubble	Betty	0012
Barney Fife	BarneyF	0022
Pebbles Flintstone	Netguru	0030
Bamm-Bamm Rubble	Electrical-guy	0040

Pebbles tries out the new FTP program and name/address table in the lab, and it works. She deploys the new FTP software, puts the name table on everyone's PC, and sends another memo. Now she can accommodate changes easily by separating the physical details, such as addresses on the networking cards, from what the end users need to know.

Like all good network engineers, Pebbles thought through the design and tested it in a lab before deploying the network. For the problems she did not anticipate, she found a reasonable solution to get around the problem.

So ends the story of the obviously contrived imaginary first computer network. What purpose did this silly example really serve? First, you have now been forced to think about some basic design issues that confronted the people who created the networking tools that you will be learning about for the CCNA exams. Although the example with Pebbles might have been fun, the problems that she faced are the same problems faced—and solved—by the people who created the original networking protocols and products.

The other big benefit to this story, particularly for those of you brand new to networking, is that you already know some of the more important concepts in networking:

Ethernet networks use cards inside each computer.

The cards have unique numeric addresses, similar to Pebbles' networking cards.

Ethernet cables connect PCs to Ethernet hubs—hubs that repeat each received signal out all other ports.

The cabling is typically run in a star configuration—in other words, all cables run from a cubicle to a wiring (not broom!) closet.

Applications such as the contrived Fred Transfer Program or the real-life File Transfer Protocol (FTP) ask the underlying hardware to transfer the contents of files. Users can use names—for instance, you might surf a website called www.fredsco.com—but the name gets translated into the correct address.

Now on to the real chapters, with real protocols and devices, with topics that you could see on the ICND1 exam.

This chapter covers the following subjects:

The TCP/IP Protocol Architecture: This section explains the terminology and concepts behind the world's most popular networking model, TCP/IP.

The OSI Reference Model: This section explains the terminology behind the OSI networking model in comparison to TCP/IP.

CHAPTER 2

The TCP/IP and OSI Networking Models

The term *networking model*, or *networking architecture*, refers to an organized set of documents. Individually, these documents describe one small function required for a network. These documents may define a protocol, which is a set of logical rules that devices must follow to communicate. Other documents may define some physical requirements for networking, for example, it may define the voltage and current levels used on a particular cable. Collectively, the documents referenced in a networking model define all the details of how to create a complete working network.

To create a working network, the devices in that network need to follow the details referenced by a particular networking model. When multiple computers and other networking devices implement these protocols, physical specifications, and rules, and the devices are then connected correctly, the computers can successfully communicate.

You can think of a networking model as you think of a set of architectural plans for building a house. Sure, you can build a house without the architectural plans, but it will work better if you follow the plans. And because you probably have a lot of different people working on building your house, such as framers, electricians, bricklayers, painters, and so on, it helps if they can all reference the same plan. Similarly, you could build your own network, write your own software, build your own networking cards, and create a network without using any existing networking model. However, it is much easier to simply buy and use products that already conform to some well-known networking model. And because the networking product vendors use the same networking model, their products should work well together.

The CCNA exams include detailed coverage of one networking model—the Transmission Control Protocol/Internet Protocol, or TCP/IP. TCP/IP is the most pervasively used networking model in the history of networking. You can find support for TCP/IP on practically every computer operating system in existence today, from mobile phones to mainframe computers. Almost every network built using Cisco products today supports TCP/IP. Not surprisingly, the CCNA exams focus heavily on TCP/IP.

The ICND1 exam, and the ICND2 exam to a small extent, also covers a second networking model, called the Open System Interconnection (OSI) reference model. Historically, OSI was the first large effort to create a vendor-neutral networking model, a model that was intended to be used by any and every computer in the world. Because OSI was the first major effort to create a vendor-neutral networking architectural model, many of the terms used in networking today come from the OSI model.

"Do I Know This Already?" Quiz

The "Do I Know This Already?" quiz allows you to assess if you should read the entire chapter. If you miss no more than one of these 10 self-assessment questions, you might want to move ahead to the "Exam Preparation Tasks" section. Table 2-1 lists the major headings in this chapter and the "Do I Know This Already?" quiz questions covering the material in those headings so you can assess your knowledge of these specific areas. The answers to the "Do I Know This Already?" quiz appear in Appendix A.

Table 2-1   *"Do I Know This Already?" Foundation Topics Section-to-Question Mapping*

Foundation Topics Section	Questions
The TCP/IP Protocol Architecture	1–6
The OSI Reference Model	7–10

1. Which of the following protocols are examples of TCP/IP transport layer protocols?

    a.   Ethernet

    b.   HTTP

    c.   IP

    d.   UDP

    e.   SMTP

    f.   TCP

2. Which of the following protocols are examples of TCP/IP network access layer protocols?

    a.   Ethernet

    b.   HTTP

    c.   IP

    d.   UDP

    e.   SMTP

f. TCP

g. PPP

3. The process of HTTP asking TCP to send some data and make sure that it is received correctly is an example of what?

   a. Same-layer intcraction

   b. Adjacent-layer interaction

   c. The OSI model

   d. All the other answers are correct.

4. The process of TCP on one computer marking a segment as segment 1, and the receiving computer then acknowledging the receipt of segment 1, is an example of what?

   a. Data encapsulation

   b. Same-layer interaction

   c. Adjacent-layer interaction

   d. The OSI model

   e. None of these answers are correct.

5. The process of a web server adding a TCP header to a web page, followed by adding an IP header, and then a data link header and trailer is an example of what?

   a. Data encapsulation

   b. Same-layer interaction

   c. The OSI model

   d. All of these answers are correct.

6. Which of the following terms is used specifically to identify the entity that is created when encapsulating data inside data link layer headers and trailers?

   a. Data

   b. Chunk

   c. Segment

   d. Frame

   e. Packet

   f. None of these—there is no encapsulation by the data link layer.

7. Which OSI layer defines the functions of logical network-wide addressing and routing?

   a. Layer 1

   b. Layer 2

   c. Layer 3

   d. Layer 4

   e. Layer 5

   f. Layer 6

   g. Layer 7

8. Which OSI layer defines the standards for cabling and connectors?

   a. Layer 1

   b. Layer 2

   c. Layer 3

   d. Layer 4

   e. Layer 5

   f. Layer 6

   g. Layer 7

9. Which OSI layer defines the standards for data formats and encryption?

   a. Layer 1

   b. Layer 2

   c. Layer 3

   d. Layer 4

   e. Layer 5

   f. Layer 6

   g. Layer 7

10. Which of the following terms are not valid terms for the names of the seven OSI layers?

   a. Application

   b. Data link

   c. Transmission

   d. Presentation

   e. Internet

   f. Session

Foundation Topics

It is practically impossible to find a computer today that does not support the set of networking protocols called TCP/IP. Every Microsoft, Linux, and UNIX operating system includes support for TCP/IP. Hand-held digital assistants and cell phones support TCP/IP. And because Cisco sells products that create the infrastructure that allows all of these computers to talk with each other using TCP/IP, Cisco products also include extensive support for TCP/IP.

The world has not always been so simple. Once upon a time, there were no networking protocols, including TCP/IP. Vendors created the first networking protocols; these protocols supported only that vendor's computers, and the details were not even published to the public. As time went on, vendors formalized and published their networking protocols, enabling other vendors to create products that could communicate with their computers. For instance, IBM published its Systems Network Architecture (SNA) networking model in 1974. After SNA was published, other computer vendors created products that allowed their computers to communicate with IBM computers using SNA. This solution worked, but it had some negatives, including the fact that it meant that the larger computer vendors tended to rule the networking market.

A better solution was to create an open standardized networking model that all vendors would support. The International Organization for Standardization (ISO) took on this task starting as early as the late 1970s, beginning work on what would become known as the Open System Interconnection (OSI) networking model. ISO had a noble goal for the OSI model: to standardize data networking protocols to allow communication between all computers across the entire planet. ISO worked toward this ambitious and noble goal, with participants from most of the technologically developed nations on Earth participating in the process.

A second, less formal effort to create a standardized, public networking model sprouted forth from a U.S. Defense Department contract. Researchers at various universities volunteered to help further develop the protocols surrounding the original department's work. These efforts resulted in a competing networking model called TCP/IP.

By the late 1980s, the world had many competing vendor-proprietary networking models plus two competing standardized networking models. So what happened? TCP/IP won in the end. Proprietary protocols are still in use today in many networks, but much less so than in the 1980s and 1990s. The OSI model, whose development suffered in part because of a slower formal standardization process as compared with TCP/IP, never succeeded in the marketplace. And TCP/IP, the networking model created almost entirely by a bunch of volunteers, has become the most prolific set of data networking protocols ever.

In this chapter, you will read about some of the basics of TCP/IP. Although you will learn some interesting facts about TCP/IP, the true goal of this chapter is to help you understand what a networking model or networking architecture really is and how one works.

Also in this chapter, you will learn about some of the jargon used with OSI. Will any of you ever work on a computer that is using the full OSI protocols instead of TCP/IP? Probably not. However, you will often use terms relating to OSI. Also, the ICND1 exam covers the basics of OSI, so this chapter also covers OSI to prepare you for questions about it on the exam.

The TCP/IP Protocol Architecture

TCP/IP defines a large collection of protocols that allow computers to communicate. TCP/IP defines the details of each of these protocols inside documents called Requests for Comments (RFC). By implementing the required protocols defined in TCP/IP RFCs, a computer can be relatively confident that it can communicate with other computers that also implement TCP/IP.

An easy comparison can be made between telephones and computers that use TCP/IP. You go to the store and buy a phone from one of a dozen different vendors. When you get home and plug in the phone to the same cable in which your old phone was connected, the new phone works. The phone vendors know the standards for phones in their country and build their phones to match those standards. Similarly, a computer that implements the standard networking protocols defined by TCP/IP can communicate with other computers that also use the TCP/IP standards.

Like other networking architectures, TCP/IP classifies the various protocols into different categories or layers. Table 2-2 outlines the main categories in the TCP/IP architectural model.

Table 2-2 *TCP/IP Architectural Model and Example Protocols*

TCP/IP Architecture Layer	Example Protocols
Application	HTTP, POP3, SMTP
Transport	TCP, UDP
Internet	IP
Network access	Ethernet, Frame Relay

The TCP/IP model represented in column 1 of the table lists the four layers of TCP/IP, and column 2 of the table lists several of the most popular TCP/IP protocols. If someone makes up a new application, the protocols used directly by the application would be considered to be application layer protocols. For example, when the World Wide Web (WWW) was first created, a new application layer protocol was created for the purpose of asking for web pages and receiving the contents of the web pages. Similarly, the network access layer includes protocols and standards such as Ethernet. If someone makes up a new type of LAN, those protocols would be considered to be a part of the network access layer. In the next several sections, you will learn the basics about each of these four layers in the TCP/IP architecture and how they work together.

The TCP/IP Application Layer

TCP/IP application layer protocols provide services to the application software running on a computer. The application layer does not define the application itself, but rather it defines services that applications need—such as the capability to transfer a file in the case of HTTP. In short, the application layer provides an interface between software running on a computer and the network itself.

Arguably, the most popular TCP/IP application today is the web browser. Many major software vendors either have already changed or are changing their software to support access from a web browser. And thankfully, using a web browser is easy—you start a web browser on your computer and select a website by typing in the name of the website, and the web page appears.

What really happens to allow that web page to appear on your web browser?

Imagine that Bob opens his browser. His browser has been configured to automatically ask for web server Larry's default web page, or *home page*. The general logic looks like that in Figure 2-1.

Figure 2-1 *Basic Application Logic to Get a Web Page*

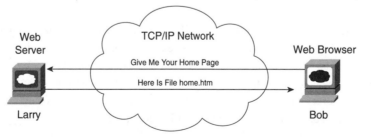

So what really happened? Bob's initial request actually asks Larry to send his home page back to Bob. Larry's web server software has been configured to know that the default web page is contained in a file called home.htm. Bob receives the file from Larry and displays the contents of the file in the web browser window.

Taking a closer look, this example uses two TCP/IP application layer protocols. First, the request for the file and the actual transfer of the file are performed according to the Hypertext Transfer Protocol (HTTP). Many of you have probably noticed that most websites' URLs—universal resource locators (often called web addresses), the text that identifies web pages—begin with the letters "http," to imply that HTTP will be used to transfer the web pages.

The other protocol used is the Hypertext Markup Language (HTML). HTML is one of many specifications that define how Bob's web browser should interpret the text inside the file he just received. For instance, the file might contain directions about making certain text be a certain size, color, and so on. In most cases, the file also includes directions about other files that Bob's web browser should get—files that contain such things as pictures and animation. HTTP would then be used to get those additional files from Larry, the web server.

A closer look at how Bob and Larry cooperate in this example reveals some details about how networking protocols work. Consider Figure 2-2, which simply revises Figure 2-1, showing the locations of HTTP headers and data.

Figure 2-2   *HTTP Get Request and HTTP Reply*

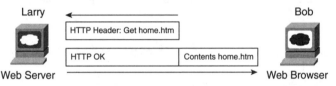

To get the web page from Larry, Bob sends something called an HTTP header to Larry. This header includes the command to "get" a file. The request typically contains the name of the file (home.htm in this case), or, if no filename is mentioned, the web server assumes that Bob wants the default web page.

The response from Larry includes an HTTP header as well, with something as simple as "OK" returned in the header. In reality, the header includes an HTTP return code, which indicates whether the request can be serviced. For instance, if you have ever looked for a web page that was not found, then you received an HTTP 404 "not found" error, which means that you received an HTTP return code of 404. When the requested file is found, the return code is 200, meaning that the request is being processed.

This simple example between Bob and Larry introduces one of the most important general concepts behind networking models: when a particular layer on one computer wants to communicate with the same layer on another computer, the two computers use headers to hold the information that they want to communicate. The headers are part of what is transmitted between the two computers. This process is called *same-layer interaction*.

The application layer protocol (HTTP, in this case) on Bob is communicating with Larry's application layer. They each do so by creating and sending application layer headers to each other—sometimes with application data following the header and sometimes not, as seen in Figure 2-2. Regardless of what the application layer protocol happens to be, they all use the same general concept of communicating with the application layer on the other computer using application layer headers.

TCP/IP application layer protocols provide services to the application software running on a computer. The application layer does not define the application itself, but rather it defines services that applications need, such as the ability to transfer a file in the case of HTTP. In short, the application layer provides an interface between software running on a computer and the network itself.

The TCP/IP Transport Layer

The TCP/IP application layer includes a relatively large number of protocols, with HTTP being only one of those. The TCP/IP transport layer consists of two main protocol options: the *Transmission Control Protocol* (TCP) and the *User Datagram Protocol* (UDP). To get a true appreciation for what TCP/IP transport layer protocols do, read Chapter 6, "Fundamentals of TCP/IP Transport, Applications, and Security." However, in this section, you will learn about one of the key features of TCP, which enables us to cover some more general concepts about how networking models behave.

To appreciate what the transport layer protocols do, you must think about the layer above the transport layer, the application layer. Why? Well, each layer provides a service to the layer above it. For example, in Figure 2-2, Bob and Larry used HTTP to transfer the home page from Larry to Bob. But what would have happened if Bob's HTTP get request had been lost in transit through the TCP/IP network? Or, what would have happened if Larry's response, which included the contents of the home page, had been lost? Well, as you might expect, in either case the page would not have shown up in Bob's browser.

So, TCP/IP needs a mechanism to guarantee delivery of data across a network. Because many application layer protocols probably want a way to guarantee delivery of data across a network, TCP provides an error-recovery feature to the application protocols by using acknowledgments. Figure 2-3 outlines the basic acknowledgment logic.

NOTE   The data shown in the rectangles in Figure 2-3, which includes the transport layer header and its encapsulated data, is called a *segment*.

Figure 2-3 *TCP Services Provided to HTTP*

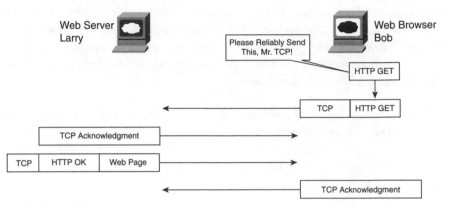

As Figure 2-3 shows, the HTTP software asks for TCP to reliably deliver the HTTP get request. TCP sends the HTTP data from Bob to Larry, and the data arrives successfully. Larry's TCP software acknowledges receipt of the data and also gives the HTTP get request to the web server software. The reverse happens with Larry's response, which also arrives at Bob successfully.

Of course, the benefits of TCP error recovery cannot be seen unless the data is lost. (Chapter 6 shows an example of how TCP recovers lost data.) For now, assume that if either transmission in Figure 2-3 were lost, HTTP would not take any direct action, but TCP would resend the data and ensure that it was received successfully. This example demonstrates a function called *adjacent-layer interaction*, which defines the concepts of how adjacent layers in a networking model, on the same computer, work together. The higher-layer protocol (HTTP) needs to do something it cannot do (error recovery). So, the higher layer asks for the next lower-layer protocol (TCP) to perform the service, and the next lower layer performs the service. The lower layer provides a service to the layer above it. Table 2-3 summarizes the key points about how adjacent layers work together on a single computer and how one layer on one computer works with the same networking layer on another computer.

Table 2-3 *Summary: Same-Layer and Adjacent-Layer Interactions*

Key Topic

Concept	Description
Same-layer interaction on different computers	The two computers use a protocol to communicate with the same layer on another computer. The protocol defined by each layer uses a header that is transmitted between the computers, to communicate what each computer wants to do.
Adjacent-layer interaction on the same computer	On a single computer, one layer provides a service to a higher layer. The software or hardware that implements the higher layer requests that the next lower layer perform the needed function.

All the examples describing the application and transport layers ignored many details relating to the physical network. The application and transport layers work the same way regardless of whether the endpoint host computers are on the same LAN or are separated by the entire Internet. The lower two layers of TCP/IP, the internet layer and the network access layer, must understand the underlying physical network because they define the protocols used to deliver the data from one host to another.

The TCP/IP Internet Layer

Imagine that you just wrote a letter to your favorite person on the other side of the country and that you also wrote a letter to someone on the other side of town. It is time to send the letters. Is there much difference in how you treat each letter? Not really. You put a different address on the envelope for each letter because the letters need to go to two different places. You put stamps on both letters and put them in the same mailbox. The postal service takes care of all the details of figuring out how to get each letter to the right place, whether it is across town or across the country.

When the postal service processes the cross-country letter, it sends the letter to another post office, then another, and so on, until the letter gets delivered across the country. The local letter might go to the post office in your town and then simply be delivered to your friend across town, without going to another post office.

So what does this all matter to networking? Well, the internet layer of the TCP/IP networking model, primarily defined by the *Internet Protocol* (IP), works much like the postal service. IP defines addresses so that each host computer can have a different IP address, just as the postal service defines addressing that allows unique addresses for each house, apartment, and business. Similarly, IP defines the process of routing so that devices called routers can choose where to send packets of data so that they are delivered to the correct destination. Just as the postal service created the necessary infrastructure to be able to deliver letters—post offices, sorting machines, trucks, planes, and personnel—the internet layer defines the details of how a network infrastructure should be created so that the network can deliver data to all computers in the network.

Chapter 5, "Fundamentals of IP Addressing and Routing," describes the TCP/IP internet layer further, with other details scattered throughout this book and the *CCNA ICND2 Official Exam Certification Guide*. But to help you understand the basics of the internet layer, take a look at Bob's request for Larry's home page, now with some information about IP, in Figure 2-4. The LAN cabling details are not important for this figure, so both LANs simply are represented by the lines shown near Bob and Larry, respectively. When Bob sends the data, he is sending an IP packet, which includes the IP header, the transport layer header (TCP, in this example), the application header (HTTP, in this case), and any application data (none, in this case). The IP header includes both a source and a destination

IP address field, with Larry's IP address (1.1.1.1) as the destination address and Bob's IP address (2.2.2.2) as the source.

Figure 2-4 *IP Services Provided to TCP*

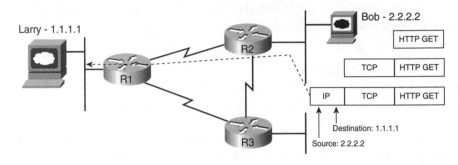

> **NOTE**   The data shown in the bottom rectangle in Figure 2-4, which includes the internet layer header and its encapsulated data, is called a *packet*.

Bob sends the packet to R2. R2 then examines the destination IP address (1.1.1.1) and makes a routing decision to send the packet to R1, because R2 knows enough about the network topology to know that 1.1.1.1 (Larry) is on the other side of R1. Similarly, when R1 gets the packet, it forwards the packet over the Ethernet to Larry. And if the link between R2 and R1 fails, IP allows R2 to learn of the alternate route through R3 to reach 1.1.1.1.

IP defines logical addresses, called *IP addresses*, which allow each TCP/IP-speaking device (called IP hosts) to have an address with which to communicate. IP also defines routing, the process of how a router should forward, or route, packets of data.

All the CCNA exams cover IP fairly deeply. For the ICND1 exam, this book's Chapter 5 covers more of the basics, with Chapters 11 through 15 covering IP in much more detail.

The TCP/IP Network Access Layer

The network access layer defines the protocols and hardware required to deliver data across some physical network. The term *network access* refers to the fact that this layer defines how to physically connect a host computer to the physical media over which data can be transmitted. For instance, Ethernet is one example protocol at the TCP/IP network access layer. Ethernet defines the required cabling, addressing, and protocols used to create an Ethernet LAN. Likewise, the connectors, cables, voltage levels, and protocols used to deliver data across WAN links are defined in a variety of other protocols that also fall into the network access layer. Chapters 3 and 4 cover the fundamentals of LANs and WANs, respectively.

Just like every layer in any networking model, the TCP/IP network access layer provides services to the layer above it in the model. The best way to understand the basics of the TCP/IP network access layer is to examine the services that it provides to IP. IP relies on the network access layer to deliver IP packets across a physical network. IP understands the overall network topology, things such as which routers are connected to each other, which host computers are connected to which physical networks, and what the IP addressing scheme looks like. However, the IP protocol purposefully does not include the details about each of the underlying physical networks. Therefore, the Internet layer, as implemented by IP, uses the services of the network access layer to deliver the packets over each physical network, respectively.

The network access layer includes a large number of protocols. For instance, the network access layer includes all the variations of Ethernet protocols and other LAN standards. This layer also includes the popular WAN standards, such as the Point-to-Point Protocol (PPP) and Frame Relay. The same familiar network is shown in Figure 2-5, with Ethernet and PPP used as the two network access layer protocols.

Figure 2-5 *Ethernet and PPP Services Provided to IP*

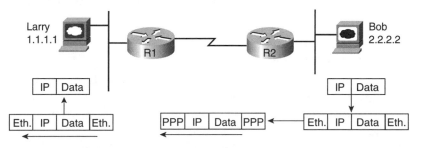

> **NOTE** The data shown in several of the rectangles in Figure 2-5—those including the Ethernet header/trailer and PPP header/trailer—are called *frames*.

To fully appreciate Figure 2-5, first think a little more deeply about how IP accomplishes its goal of delivering the packet from Bob to Larry. To send a packet to Larry, Bob sends the IP packet to router R2. To do so, Bob uses Ethernet to get the packet to R2—a process that requires Bob to follow Ethernet protocol rules, placing the IP packet (IP header and data) between an Ethernet header and Ethernet trailer.

Because the goal of the IP routing process is to deliver the IP packet—the IP header and data—to the destination host, R2 no longer needs the Ethernet header and trailer received from Bob. So, R2 strips the Ethernet header and trailer, leaving the original IP packet. To send the IP packet from R2 to R1, R2 places a PPP header in front of the IP packet and a PPP trailer at the end, and sends this data frame over the WAN link to R1.

Similarly, after the packet is received by R1, R1 removes the PPP header and trailer because PPP's job is to deliver the IP packet across the serial link. R1 then decides that it should forward the packet over the Ethernet to Larry. To do so, R1 adds a brand-new Ethernet header and trailer to the packet and forwards it to Larry.

In effect, IP uses the network access layer protocols to deliver an IP packet to the next router or host, with each router repeating the process until the packet arrives at the destination. Each network access protocol uses headers to encode the information needed to successfully deliver the data across the physical network, in much the same way as other layers use headers to achieve their goals.

> **CAUTION**   Many people describe the network access layer of the TCP/IP model as two layers, the data link layer and the physical layer. The reasons for the popularity of these alternate terms are explained in the section covering OSI, because the terms originated with the OSI model.

In short, the TCP/IP network access layer includes the protocols, cabling standards, headers, and trailers that define how to send data across a wide variety of types of physical networks.

Data Encapsulation Terminology

As you can see from the explanations of how HTTP, TCP, IP, and the network access layer protocols Ethernet and PPP do their jobs, each layer adds its own header (and sometimes trailer) to the data supplied by the higher layer. The term *encapsulation* refers to the process of putting headers and trailers around some data. For example, the web server encapsulated the home page inside an HTTP header in Figure 2-2. The TCP layer encapsulated the HTTP headers and data inside a TCP header in Figure 2-3. IP encapsulated the TCP headers and the data inside an IP header in Figure 2-4. Finally, the network access layer encapsulated the IP packets inside both a header and a trailer in Figure 2-5.

The process by which a TCP/IP host sends data can be viewed as a five-step process. The first four steps relate to the encapsulation performed by the four TCP/IP layers, and the last step is the actual physical transmission of the data by the host. The steps are summarized in the following list:

Step 1   **Create and encapsulate the application data with any required application layer headers.** For example, the HTTP OK message can be returned in an HTTP header, followed by part of the contents of a web page.

Step 2   **Encapsulate the data supplied by the application layer inside a transport layer header.** For end-user applications, a TCP or UDP header is typically used.

Step 3   **Encapsulate the data supplied by the transport layer inside an internet layer (IP) header.** IP is the only protocol available in the TCP/IP network model.

Step 4   **Encapsulate the data supplied by the internet layer inside a network access layer header and trailer.** This is the only layer that uses both a header and a trailer.

Step 5   **Transmit the bits**. The physical layer encodes a signal onto the medium to transmit the frame.

The numbers in Figure 2-6 correspond to the five steps in the list, graphically showing the same concepts. Note that because the application layer often does not need to add a header, the figure does not show a specific application layer header.

Figure 2-6   *Five Steps of Data Encapsulation—TCP/IP*

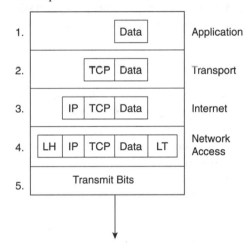

*The letters LH and LT stand for link header and link trailer, respectively, and refer to the data link layer header and trailer.

Finally, take particular care to remember the terms *segment*, *packet*, and *frame*, and the meaning of each. Each term refers to the headers and possibly trailers defined by a particular layer, and the data encapsulated following that header. Each term, however, refers to a different layer—segment for the transport layer, packet for the internet layer, and frame for the network access layer. Figure 2-7 shows each layer along with the associated term.

Figure 2-7   *Perspectives on Encapsulation and "Data"*

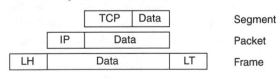

Note that Figure 2-7 also shows the encapsulated data as simply "data." When focusing on the work done by a particular layer, the encapsulated data typically is unimportant. For example, an IP packet may indeed have a TCP header after the IP header, an HTTP header after the TCP header, and data for a web page after the HTTP header—but when discussing IP, you probably just care about the IP header, so everything after the IP header is just called "data." So, when drawing IP packets, everything after the IP header is typically shown simply as "data."

The OSI Reference Model

To pass the ICND1 exam, you must be conversant in a protocol specification with which you are very unlikely to ever have any hands-on experience—the OSI reference model. The difficulty these days when discussing the OSI protocol specifications is that you have no point of reference, because most people cannot simply walk down the hall and use a computer whose main, or even optional, networking protocols conform to the entire OSI model.

OSI is the Open System Interconnection reference model for communications. OSI as a whole never succeeded in the marketplace, although some of the original protocols that comprised the OSI model are still used. So, why do you even need to think about OSI for the CCNA exams? Well, the OSI model now is mainly used as a point of reference for discussing other protocol specifications. And because being either a CCENT or CCNA requires you to understand some of the concepts and terms behind networking architecture and models, and because other protocols (including TCP/IP) are almost always compared to OSI, using OSI terminology, you need to know some things about OSI.

Comparing OSI and TCP/IP

The OSI reference model consists of seven layers. Each layer defines a set of typical networking functions. When OSI was in active development in the 1980s and 1990s, the OSI committees created new protocols and specifications to implement the functions specified by each layer. In other cases, just as for TCP/IP, the OSI committees did not create new protocols or standards, but instead referenced other protocols that were already defined. For instance, the IEEE defines Ethernet standards, so the OSI committees did not waste time specifying a new type of Ethernet; it simply referred to the IEEE Ethernet standards.

Today the OSI model can be used as a standard of comparison to other networking models. Figure 2-8 compares the seven-layer OSI model with the four-layer TCP/IP model. Also, for perspective, the figure also shows some example protocols and the related layers.

Figure 2-8 *Using OSI Layers for Referencing Other Protocols*

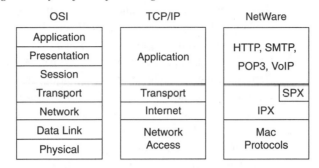

Because OSI does have a very well-defined set of functions associated with each of its seven layers, you can examine any networking protocol or specification and make some determination of whether it most closely matches OSI Layer 1, 2, or 3, and so on. For instance, TCP/IP's internet layer, as implemented mainly by IP, equates most directly to the OSI network layer. So, most people say that IP is a network layer protocol, or a Layer 3 protocol, using OSI terminology and numbers for the layer. Of course, if you numbered the TCP/IP model, starting at the bottom, IP would be in Layer 2—but, by convention, everyone uses the OSI standard when describing other protocols. So, using this convention, IP is a network layer protocol.

While Figure 2-8 seems to imply that the OSI network layer and the TCP/IP internet layer are at least similar, the figure does not point out why they are similar. To appreciate why the TCP/IP layers correspond to a particular OSI layer, you need to have a better understanding of OSI. For example, the OSI network layer defines logical addressing and routing, as does the TCP/IP internet layer. While the details differ significantly, because the OSI network layer and TCP/IP internet layer define similar goals and features, the TCP/IP internet layer matches the OSI network layer. Similarly, the TCP/IP transport layer defines many functions, including error recovery, as does the OSI transport layer—so TCP is called a *transport layer*, or *Layer 4*, protocol.

Not all TCP/IP layers correspond to a single OSI layer. In particular, the TCP/IP network access layer defines both the physical network specifications and the protocols used to control the physical network. OSI separates the physical network specifications into the physical layer and the control functions into the data link layer. In fact, many people think of TCP/IP as a five-layer model, replacing the TCP/IP's network access layer with two layers, namely a physical layer and a data link layer, to match OSI.

NOTE For the exams, be aware of both views about whether TCP/IP has a single network access layer or two lower layers (data link and physical).

OSI Layers and Their Functions

Cisco requires that CCNAs demonstrate a basic understanding of the functions defined by each OSI layer, as well as remembering the names of the layers. It is also important that, for each device or protocol referenced throughout the book, you understand which layers of the OSI model most closely match the functions defined by that device or protocol. The upper layers of the OSI reference model (application, presentation, and session—Layers 7, 6, and 5) define functions focused on the application. The lower four layers (transport, network, data link, and physical—Layers 4, 3, 2, and 1) define functions focused on end-to-end delivery of the data. The CCNA exams focus on issues in the lower layers—in particular, with Layer 2, upon which LAN switching is based, and Layer 3, upon which routing is based. Table 2-4 defines the functions of the seven layers.

Table 2-4 *OSI Reference Model Layer Definitions*

Layer	Functional Description
7	Layer 7 provides an interface between the communications software and any applications that need to communicate outside the computer on which the application resides. It also defines processes for user authentication.
6	This layer's main purpose is to define and negotiate data formats, such as ASCII text, EBCDIC text, binary, BCD, and JPEG. Encryption also is defined by OSI as a presentation layer service.
5	The session layer defines how to start, control, and end conversations (called sessions). This includes the control and management of multiple bidirectional messages so that the application can be notified if only some of a series of messages are completed. This allows the presentation layer to have a seamless view of an incoming stream of data.
4	Layer 4 protocols provide a large number of services, as described in Chapter 6 of this book. Although OSI Layers 5 through 7 focus on issues related to the application, Layer 4 focuses on issues related to data delivery to another computer—for instance, error recovery and flow control.
3	The network layer defines three main features: logical addressing, routing (forwarding), and path determination. The routing concepts define how devices (typically routers) forward packets to their final destination. Logical addressing defines how each device can have an address that can be used by the routing process. Path determination refers to the work done by routing protocols by which all possible routes are learned, but the best route is chosen for use.
2	The data link layer defines the rules (protocols) that determine when a device can send data over a particular medium. Data link protocols also define the format of a header and trailer that allows devices attached to the medium to send and receive data successfully. The data link trailer, which follows the encapsulated data, typically defines a Frame Check Sequence (FCS) field, which allows the receiving device to detect transmission errors.
1	This layer typically refers to standards from other organizations. These standards deal with the physical characteristics of the transmission medium, including connectors, pins, use of pins, electrical currents, encoding, light modulation, and the rules for how to activate and deactivate the use of the physical medium.

Table 2-5 lists most of the devices and protocols covered in the CCNA exams, and their comparable OSI layers. Note that many of the devices must actually understand the protocols at multiple OSI layers, so the layer listed in the table actually refers to the highest layer that the device normally thinks about when performing its core work. For example, routers need to think about Layer 3 concepts, but they must also support features at both Layers 1 and 2.

Table 2-5   *OSI Reference Model—Example Devices and Protocols*

Layer Name	Protocols and Specifications	Devices
Application, presentation, session (Layers 5–7)	Telnet, HTTP, FTP, SMTP, POP3, VoIP, SNMP	Firewall, intrusion detection system
Transport (Layer 4)	TCP, UDP	
Network (Layer 3)	IP	Router
Data link (Layer 2)	Ethernet (IEEE 802.3), HDLC, Frame Relay, PPP	LAN switch, wireless access point, cable modem, DSL modem
Physical (Layer 1)	RJ-45, EIA/TIA-232, V.35, Ethernet (IEEE 802.3)	LAN hub, repeater

Besides remembering the basics of the features of each OSI layer (as in Table 2-4), and some example protocols and devices at each layer (as in Table 2-5), you should also memorize the names of the layers. You can simply memorize them, but some people like to use a mnemonic phrase to make memorization easier. In the following three phrases, the first letter of each word is the same as the first letter of an OSI layer name, in the order specified in parentheses:

■   All People Seem To Need Data Processing (Layers 7 to 1)

■   Please Do Not Take Sausage Pizzas Away (Layers 1 to 7)

■   Pew! Dead Ninja Turtles Smell Particularly Awful (Layers 1 to 7)

OSI Layering Concepts and Benefits

Many benefits can be gained from the process of breaking up the functions or tasks of networking into smaller chunks, called *layers*, and defining standard interfaces between these layers. The layers break a large, complex set of concepts and protocols into smaller pieces, making it easier to talk about, easier to implement with hardware and software, and easier to troubleshoot. The following list summarizes the benefits of layered protocol specifications:

■   **Less Complex**—Compared to not using a model, network models break the concepts into smaller parts.

- **Standard Interfaces**—The standard interface definitions between each layer allow for multiple vendors to create products that compete to be used for a given function, along with all the benefits of open competition.

- **Easier to learn**—Humans can more easily discuss and learn about the many details of a protocol specification.

- **Easier to develop**—Reduced complexity allows easier program changes and faster product development.

- **Multivendor interoperability**—Creating products to meet the same networking standards means that computers and networking gear from multiple vendors can work in the same network.

- **Modular engineering**—One vendor can write software that implements higher layers—for example, a web browser—and another vendor can write software that implements the lower layers—for example, Microsoft's built-in TCP/IP software in its operating systems.

The benefits of layering can be seen in the familiar postal service analogy. A person writing a letter does not have to think about how the postal service will deliver a letter across the country. The postal worker in the middle of the country does not have to worry about the contents of the letter. Likewise, layering enables one software package or hardware device to implement functions from one layer and assume that other software/hardware will perform the functions defined by the other layers. For instance, a web browser does not need to think about what the network topology looks like, the Ethernet card in the PC does not need to think about the contents of the web page, and a router in the middle of the network does not need to worry about the contents of the web page or whether the computer that sent the packet was using an Ethernet card or some other networking card.

OSI Encapsulation Terminology

Like TCP/IP, OSI defines processes by which a higher layer asks for services from the next lower layer. To provide the services, the lower layer encapsulates the higher layer's data behind a header. The final topic of this chapter explains some of the terminology and concepts related to OSI encapsulation.

The TCP/IP model uses terms such as segment, packet, and frame to refer to various layers and their respective encapsulated data (see Figure 2-7). OSI uses a more generic term: *protocol data unit*, or *PDU*. A PDU represents the bits that include the headers and trailers for that layer, as well as the encapsulated data. For instance, an IP packet, as shown in Figure 2-7, is a PDU. In fact, an IP packet is a *Layer 3 PDU* because IP is a Layer 3 protocol. The term *L3PDU* is a shorter version of the phrase *Layer 3 PDU*. So, rather than use the terms segment, packet, or frame, OSI simply refers to the "Layer x PDU," with "x" referring to the number of the layer being discussed.

OSI defines encapsulation similarly to how TCP/IP defines it. All layers except the lowest layer define a header, with the data from the next higher layer being encapsulated behind the header. The data link layer defines both a header and a trailer and places the Layer 3 PDU between the header and trailer. Figure 2-9 represents the typical encapsulation process, with the top of the figure showing the application data and application layer header, and the bottom of the figure showing the L2PDU that is transmitted onto the physical link.

Figure 2-9 *OSI Encapsulation and Protocol Data Units*

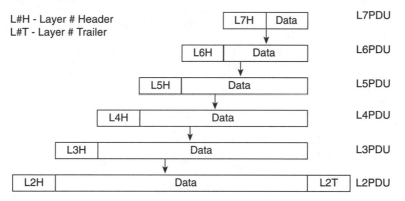

Exam Preparation Tasks

Review all the Key Topics

Key
Topic

Review the most important topics from inside the chapter, noted with the key topics icon in the outer margin of the page. Table 2-6 lists a reference of these key topics and the page number on which each is found.

Table 2-6 *Key Topics for Chapter 2*

	Description	Page Number
Table 2-3	Provides definitions of same-layer and adjacent-layer interaction	26
Figure 2-5	Depicts the data-link services provided to IP for the purpose of delivering IP packets from host to host	29
Figure 2-7	Shows the meaning of the terms segment, packet, and frame	31
Figure 2-8	Compares the OSI and TCP/IP network models	33
List	Lists the benefits of using a layered networking model	35-36

Complete the Tables and Lists from Memory

Print a copy of Appendix H (found on the CD), or at least the section for this chapter, and complete the tables and lists from memory. Appendix I includes completed tables and lists to check your work.

Definitions of Key Terms

Define the following key terms from this chapter, and check your answers in the glossary.

adjacent-layer interaction, decapsulation, encapsulation, frame, networking model, packet, protocol data unit (PDU), same-layer interaction, segment

OSI Reference

You should memorize the names of the layers of the OSI model. Table 2-7 lists a summary of OSI functions at each layer, along with some sample protocols at each layer.

Table 2-7 *OSI Functional Summary*

Layer	Functional Description
Application (7)	Interfaces between network and application software. Also includes authentication services.
Presentation (6)	Defines the format and organization of data. Includes encryption.
Session (5)	Establishes and maintains end-to-end bidirectional flows between endpoints. Includes managing transaction flows.
Transport (4)	Provides a variety of services between two host computers, including connection establishment and termination, flow control, error recovery, and segmentation of large data blocks into smaller parts for transmission.
Network (3)	Logical addressing, routing, and path determination.
Data link (2)	Formats data into frames appropriate for transmission onto some physical medium. Defines rules for when the medium can be used. Defines means by which to recognize transmission errors.
Physical (1)	Defines the electrical, optical, cabling, connectors, and procedural details required for transmitting bits, represented as some form of energy passing over a physical medium.

This chapter covers the following subjects:

An Overview of Modern Ethernet LANs:
Provides some perspectives for those who have
used Ethernet at the office or school but have not
examined the details.

A Brief History of Ethernet: Examines several
old options for Ethernet cabling and devices as a
point of comparison for today's cabling, devices,
and terminology.

Ethernet UTP Cabling: Explains the options for
cabling and cable pinouts.

**Improving Performance by Using Switches
Instead of Hubs:** A more detailed examination
of the performance improvements made by using
switches instead of older Ethernet hubs.

Ethernet Data-Link Protocols: Explains the
meaning and purpose of the fields in the Ethernet
header and trailer.

CHAPTER 3

Fundamentals of LANs

Physical and data link layer standards work together to allow computers to send bits to each other over a particular type of physical networking medium. The Open Systems Interconnection (OSI) physical layer (Layer 1) defines how to physically send bits over a particular physical networking medium. The data link layer (Layer 2) defines some rules about the data that is physically transmitted, including addresses that identify the sending device and the intended recipient, and rules about when a device can send (and when it should be silent), to name a few.

This chapter explains some of the basics of local-area networks (LAN). The term LAN refers to a set of Layer 1 and 2 standards designed to work together for the purpose of implementing geographically small networks. This chapter introduces the concepts of LANs—in particular, Ethernet LANs. More-detailed coverage of LANs appears in Part II (Chapters 7 through 11).

"Do I Know This Already?" Quiz

The "Do I Know This Already?" quiz allows you to assess whether you should read the entire chapter. If you miss no more than one of these 11 self-assessment questions, you might want to move ahead to the "Exam Preparation Tasks" section. Table 3-1 lists the major headings in this chapter and the "Do I Know This Already?" quiz questions covering the material in those sections. This helps you assess your knowledge of these specific areas. The answers to the "Do I Know This Already?" quiz appear in Appendix A.

Table 3-1 *"Do I Know This Already?" Foundation Topics Section-to-Question Mapping*

Foundation Topics Section	Questions
An Overview of Modern Ethernet LANs	1
A Brief History of Ethernet	2
Ethernet UTP Cabling	3, 4
Improving Performance by Using Switches Instead of Hubs	5–7
Ethernet Data-Link Protocols	8–11

1. Which of the following is true about the cabling of a typical modern Ethernet LAN?

   a. Connect each device in series using coaxial cabling

   b. Connect each device in series using UTP cabling

   c. Connect each device to a centralized LAN hub using UTP cabling

   d. Connect each device to a centralized LAN switch using UTP cabling

2. Which of the following is true about the cabling of a 10BASE2 Ethernet LAN?

   a. Connect each device in series using coaxial cabling

   b. Connect each device in series using UTP cabling

   c. Connect each device to a centralized LAN hub using UTP cabling

   d. Connect each device to a centralized LAN switch using UTP cabling

3. Which of the following is true about Ethernet crossover cables?

   a. Pins 1 and 2 are reversed on the other end of the cable.

   b. Pins 1 and 2 on one end of the cable connect to pins 3 and 6 on the other end of the cable.

   c. Pins 1 and 2 on one end of the cable connect to pins 3 and 4 on the other end of the cable.

   d. The cable can be up to 1000 meters long to cross over between buildings.

   e. None of the other answers is correct.

4. Each answer lists two types of devices used in a 100BASE-TX network. If these devices were connected with UTP Ethernet cables, which pairs of devices would require a straight-through cable?

   a. PC and router

   b. PC and switch

   c. Hub and switch

   d. Router and hub

   e. Wireless access point (Ethernet port) and switch

5. Which of the following is true about the CSMA/CD algorithm?

   a. The algorithm never allows collisions to occur.

   b. Collisions can happen, but the algorithm defines how the computers should notice a collision and how to recover.

   c. The algorithm works with only two devices on the same Ethernet.

   d. None of the other answers is correct.

6. Which of the following is a collision domain?

   a. All devices connected to an Ethernet hub

   b. All devices connected to an Ethernet switch

   c. Two PCs, with one cabled to a router Ethernet port with a crossover cable and the other PC cabled to another router Ethernet port with a crossover cable

   d. None of the other answers is correct.

7. Which of the following describe a shortcoming of using hubs that is improved by instead using switches?

   a. Hubs create a single electrical bus to which all devices connect, causing the devices to share the bandwidth.

   b. Hubs limit the maximum cable length of individual cables (relative to switches)

   c. Hubs allow collisions to occur when two attached devices send data at the same time.

   d. Hubs restrict the number of physical ports to at most eight.

8. Which of the following terms describe Ethernet addresses that can be used to communicate with more than one device at a time?

   a. Burned-in address

   b. Unicast address

   c. Broadcast address

   d. Multicast address

9. Which of the following is one of the functions of OSI Layer 2 protocols?

    a. Framing

    b. Delivery of bits from one device to another

    c. Error recovery

    d. Defining the size and shape of Ethernet cards

10. Which of the following are true about the format of Ethernet addresses?

    a. Each manufacturer puts a unique code into the first 2 bytes of the address.

    b. Each manufacturer puts a unique code into the first 3 bytes of the address.

    c. Each manufacturer puts a unique code into the first half of the address.

    d. The part of the address that holds this manufacturer's code is called the MAC.

    e. The part of the address that holds this manufacturer's code is called the OUI.

    f. The part of the address that holds this manufacturer's code has no specific name.

11. Which of the following is true about the Ethernet FCS field?

    a. It is used for error recovery.

    b. It is 2 bytes long.

    c. It resides in the Ethernet trailer, not the Ethernet header.

    d. It is used for encryption.

    e. None of the other answers is correct.

Foundation Topics

A typical Enterprise network consists of several sites. The end-user devices connect to a LAN, which allows the local computers to communicate with each other. Additionally, each site has a router that connects to both the LAN and a wide-area network (WAN), with the WAN providing connectivity between the various sites. With routers and a WAN, the computers at different sites can also communicate.

This chapter describes the basics of how to create LANs today, with Chapter 4, "Fundamentals of WANs," describing the basics of creating WANs. Ethernet is the undisputed king of LAN standards today. Historically speaking, several competing LAN standards existed, including Token Ring, Fiber Distributed Data Interface (FDDI), and Asynchronous Transfer Mode (ATM). Eventually, Ethernet won out over all the competing LAN standards, so that today when you think of LANs, no one even questions what type— it's Ethernet.

An Overview of Modern Ethernet LANs

The term *Ethernet* refers to a family of standards that together define the physical and data link layers of the world's most popular type of LAN. The different standards vary as to the speed supported, with speeds of 10 megabits per second (Mbps), 100 Mbps, and 1000 Mbps (1 gigabit per second, or Gbps) being common today. The standards also differ as far as the types of cabling and the allowed length of the cabling. For example, the most commonly used Ethernet standards allow the use of inexpensive *unshielded twisted-pair* (UTP) cabling, whereas other standards call for more expensive fiber-optic cabling. Fiber-optic cabling might be worth the cost in some cases, because the cabling is more secure and allows for much longer distances between devices. To support the widely varying needs for building a LAN—needs for different speeds, different cabling types (trading off distance requirements versus cost), and other factors—many variations of Ethernet standards have been created.

The Institute of Electrical and Electronics Engineers (IEEE) has defined many Ethernet standards since it took over the LAN standardization process in the early 1980s. Most of the standards define a different variation of Ethernet at the physical layer, with differences in speed and types of cabling. Additionally, for the data link layer, the IEEE separates the functions into two sublayers:

- The 802.3 Media Access Control (MAC) sublayer

- The 802.2 Logical Link Control (LLC) sublayer

In fact, MAC addresses get their name from the IEEE name for this lower portion of the data link layer Ethernet standards.

Each new physical layer standard from the IEEE requires many differences at the physical layer. However, each of these physical layer standards uses the exact same 802.3 header, and each uses the upper LLC sublayer as well. Table 3-2 lists the most commonly used IEEE Ethernet physical layer standards.

Table 3-2 *Today's Most Common Types of Ethernet*

Key
Topic

Common Name	Speed	Alternative Name	Name of IEEE Standard	Cable Type, Maximum Length
Ethernet	10 Mbps	10BASE-T	IEEE 802.3	Copper, 100 m
Fast Ethernet	100 Mbps	100BASE-TX	IEEE 802.3u	Copper, 100 m
Gigabit Ethernet	1000 Mbps	1000BASE-LX, 1000BASE-SX	IEEE 802.3z	Fiber, 550 m (SX) 5 km (LX)
Gigabit Ethernet	1000 Mbps	1000BASE-T	IEEE 802.3ab	100 m

The table is convenient for study, but the terms in the table bear a little explanation. First, beware that the term *Ethernet* is often used to mean "all types of Ethernet," but in some cases it is used to mean "10BASE-T Ethernet." (Because the term Ethernet sometimes can be ambiguous, this book refers to 10-Mbps Ethernet as 10BASE-T when the specific type of Ethernet matters to the discussion.) Second, note that the alternative name for each type of Ethernet lists the speed in Mbps—namely, 10 Mbps, 100 Mbps, and 1000 Mbps. The *T* and *TX* in the alternative names refer to the fact that each of these standards defines the use of UTP cabling, with the *T* referring to the T in *twisted pair*.

To build and create a modern LAN using any of the UTP-based types of Ethernet LANs listed in Table 3-2, you need the following components:

■ Computers that have an Ethernet network interface card (NIC) installed

■ Either an Ethernet hub or Ethernet switch

■ UTP cables to connect each PC to the hub or switch

Figure 3-1 shows a typical LAN. The NICs cannot be seen, because they reside in the PCs. However, the lines represent the UTP cabling, and the icon in the center of the figure represents a LAN switch.

Figure 3-1 *Typical Small Modern LAN*

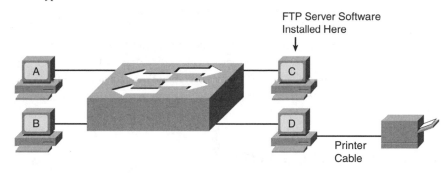

> **NOTE** Figure 3-1 applies to all the common types of Ethernet. The same basic design and topology are used regardless of speed or cabling type.

Most people can build a LAN like the one shown in Figure 3-1 with practically no real knowledge of how LANs work. Most PCs contain an Ethernet NIC that was installed at the factory. Switches do not need to be configured for them to forward traffic between the computers. All you have to do is connect the switch to a power cable and plug in the UTP cables from each PC to the switch. Then the PCs should be able to send Ethernet frames to each other.

You can use such a small LAN for many purposes, even without a WAN connection. Consider the following functions for which a LAN is the perfect, small-scale solution:

File sharing: Each computer can be configured to share all or parts of its file system so that the other computers can read, or possibly read and write, the files on another computer. This function typically is simply part of the PC operating system.

Printer sharing: Computers can share their printers as well. For example, PCs A, B, and C in Figure 3-1 could print documents on PC D's printer. This function is also typically part of the PC's operating system.

File transfers: A computer could install a file transfer server, thereby allowing other computers to send and receive files to and from that computer. For example, PC C could install File Transfer Protocol (FTP) server software, allowing the other PCs to use FTP client software to connect to PC C and transfer files.

Gaming: The PCs could install gaming software that allows multiple players to play in the same game. The gaming software would then communicate using the Ethernet.

The goal of the first half of this chapter is to help you understand much of the theory and practical knowledge behind simple LAN designs such as the one illustrated in Figure 3-1. To fully understand modern LANs, it is helpful to understand a bit about the history of Ethernet, which is covered in the next section. Following that, this chapter examines the physical aspects (Layer 1) of a simple Ethernet LAN, focusing on UTP cabling. Then this chapter compares the older (and slower) Ethernet hub with the newer (and faster) Ethernet switch. Finally, the LAN coverage in this chapter ends with the data-link (Layer 2) functions on Ethernet.

A Brief History of Ethernet

Like many early networking protocols, Ethernet began life inside a corporation that was looking to solve a specific problem. Xerox needed an effective way to allow a new invention, called the personal computer, to be connected in its offices. From that, Ethernet was born. (Go to http://inventors.about.com/library/weekly/aa111598.htm for an interesting story on the history of Ethernet.) Eventually, Xerox teamed with Intel and Digital Equipment Corp. (DEC) to further develop Ethernet, so the original Ethernet became known as *DIX Ethernet*, referring to DEC, Intel, and Xerox.

These companies willingly transitioned the job of Ethernet standards development to the IEEE in the early 1980s. The IEEE formed two committees that worked directly on Ethernet—the IEEE 802.3 committee and the IEEE 802.2 committee. The 802.3 committee worked on physical layer standards as well as a subpart of the data link layer called *Media Access Control (MAC)*. The IEEE assigned the other functions of the data link layer to the 802.2 committee, calling this part of the data link layer the *Logical Link Control (LLC)* sublayer. (The 802.2 standard applied to Ethernet as well as to other IEEE standard LANs such as Token Ring.)

The Original Ethernet Standards: 10BASE2 and 10BASE5

Ethernet is best understood by first considering the two early Ethernet specifications, 10BASE5 and 10BASE2. These two Ethernet specifications defined the details of the physical and data link layers of early Ethernet networks. (10BASE2 and 10BASE5 differ in their cabling details, but for the discussion in this chapter, you can consider them as behaving identically.) With these two specifications, the network engineer installs a series of coaxial cables connecting each device on the Ethernet network. There is no hub, switch, or wiring panel. The Ethernet consists solely of the collective Ethernet NICs in the computers and the coaxial cabling. The series of cables creates an electrical circuit, called a bus, which is shared among all devices on the Ethernet. When a computer wants to send some bits to another computer on the bus, it sends an electrical signal, and the electricity propagates to all devices on the Ethernet.

Figure 3-2 shows the basic logic of an old Ethernet 10BASE2 network, which uses a single electrical bus, created with coaxial cable and Ethernet cards.

Figure 3-2 *Small Ethernet 10BASE2 Network*

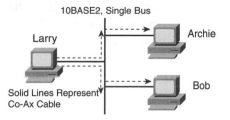

The solid lines in the figure represent the physical network cabling. The dashed lines with arrows represent the path that Larry's transmitted frame takes. Larry sends an electrical signal across his Ethernet NIC onto the cable, and both Bob and Archie receive the signal. The cabling creates a physical electrical bus, meaning that the transmitted signal is received by all stations on the LAN. Just like a school bus stops at every student's house along a route, the electrical signal on a 10BASE2 or 10BASE5 network is propagated to each station on the LAN.

Because the network uses a single bus, if two or more electrical signals were sent at the same time, they would overlap and collide, making both signals unintelligible. So, unsurprisingly, Ethernet also defined a specification for how to ensure that only one device sends traffic on the Ethernet at one time. Otherwise, the Ethernet would have been unusable. This algorithm, known as the *carrier sense multiple access with collision detection (CSMA/CD)* algorithm, defines how the bus is accessed.

In human terms, CSMA/CD is similar to what happens in a meeting room with many attendees. It's hard to understand what two people are saying at the same time, so generally, one person talks and the rest listen. Imagine that Bob and Larry both want to reply to the current speaker's comments. As soon as the speaker takes a breath, Bob and Larry both try to speak. If Larry hears Bob's voice before Larry makes a noise, Larry might stop and let Bob speak. Or, maybe they both start at almost the same time, so they talk over each other and no one can hear what is said. Then there's the proverbial "Pardon me; go ahead with what you were saying," and eventually Larry or Bob talks. Or perhaps another person jumps in and talks while Larry and Bob are both backing off. These "rules" are based on your culture; CSMA/CD is based on Ethernet protocol specifications and achieves the same type of goal.

Basically, the CSMA/CD algorithm can be summarized as follows:

Key Topic

■   A device that wants to send a frame waits until the LAN is silent—in other words, no frames are currently being sent—before attempting to send an electrical signal.

■   If a collision still occurs, the devices that caused the collision wait a random amount of time and then try again.

In 10BASE5 and 10BASE2 Ethernet LANs, a collision occurs because the transmitted electrical signal travels along the entire length of the bus. When two stations send at the same time, their electrical signals overlap, causing a collision. So, all devices on a 10BASE5 or 10BASE2 Ethernet need to use CSMA/CD to avoid collisions and to recover when inadvertent collisions occur.

Repeaters

Like any type of LAN, 10BASE5 and 10BASE2 had limitations on the total length of a cable. With 10BASE5, the limit was 500 m; with 10BASE2, it was 185 m. Interestingly, the 5 and 2 in the names 10BASE5 and 10BASE2 represent the maximum cable length—with the 2 referring to 200 meters, which is pretty close to the actual maximum of 185 meters. (Both of these types of Ethernet ran at 10 Mbps.)

In some cases, the maximum cable length was not enough, so a device called a *repeater* was developed. One of the problems that limited the length of a cable was that the signal sent by one device could attenuate too much if the cable was longer than 500 m or 185 m. *Attenuation* means that when electrical signals pass over a wire, the signal strength gets weaker the farther along the cable it travels. It's the same concept behind why you can hear someone talking right next to you, but if that person speaks at the same volume and you are on the other side of a crowded room, you might not hear her because the sound waves have attenuated.

Repeaters connect to multiple cable segments, receive the electrical signal on one cable, interpret the bits as 1s and 0s, and generate a brand-new, clean, strong signal out the other cable. A repeater does not simply amplify the signal, because amplifying the signal might also amplify any noise picked up along the way.

NOTE   Because the repeater does not interpret what the bits mean, but it does examine and generate electrical signals, a repeater is considered to operate at Layer 1.

You should not expect to need to implement 10BASE5 or 10BASE2 Ethernet LANs today. However, for learning purposes, keep in mind several key points from this section as you move on to concepts that relate to today's LANs:

■   The original Ethernet LANs created an electrical bus to which all devices connected.

■   Because collisions could occur on this bus, Ethernet defined the CSMA/CD algorithm, which defined a way to both avoid collisions and take action when collisions occurred.

■   Repeaters extended the length of LANs by cleaning up the electrical signal and repeating it—a Layer 1 function—but without interpreting the meaning of the electrical signal.

Building 10BASE-T Networks with Hubs

The IEEE later defined new Ethernet standards besides 10BASE5 and 10BASE2. Chronologically, the 10BASE-T standard came next (1990), followed by 100BASE-TX (1995), and then 1000BASE-T (1999). To support these new standards, networking devices called hubs and switches were also created. This section defines the basics of how these three popular types of Ethernet work, including the basic operation of hubs and switches.

10BASE-T solved several problems with the early 10BASE5 and 10BASE2 Ethernet specifications. 10BASE-T allowed the use of UTP telephone cabling that was already installed. Even if new cabling needed to be installed, the inexpensive and easy-to-install UTP cabling replaced the old expensive and difficult-to-install coaxial cabling.

Another major improvement introduced with 10BASE-T, and that remains a key design point today, is the concept of cabling each device to a centralized connection point. Originally, 10BASE-T called for the use of Ethernet *hubs*, as shown in Figure 3-3.

Figure 3-3 *Small Ethernet 10BASE-T Network Using a Hub*

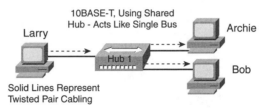

When building a LAN today, you could choose to use either a hub or a switch as the centralized Ethernet device to which all the computers connect. Even though modern Ethernet LANs typically use switches instead of hubs, understanding the operation of hubs helps you understand some of the terminology used with switches, as well as some of their benefits.

Hubs are essentially repeaters with multiple physical ports. That means that the hub simply regenerates the electrical signal that comes in one port and sends the same signal out every other port. By doing so, any LAN that uses a hub, as in Figure 3-3, creates an electrical bus, just like 10BASE2 and 10BASE5. Therefore, collisions can still occur, so CSMA/CD access rules continue to be used.

10BASE-T networks using hubs solved some big problems with 10BASE5 and 10BASE2. First, the LAN had much higher availability, because a single cable problem could, and probably did, take down 10BASE5 and 10BASE2 LANs. With 10BASE-T, a cable connects each device to the hub, so a single cable problem affects only one device. As mentioned earlier, the use of UTP cabling, in a star topology (all cables running to a centralized connection device), lowered the cost of purchasing and installing the cabling.

Today, you might occasionally use LAN hubs, but you will more likely use switches instead of hubs. Switches perform much better than hubs, support more functions than hubs, and typically are priced almost as low as hubs. However, for learning purposes, keep in mind several key points from this section about the history of Ethernet as you move on to concepts that relate to today's LANs:

■ The original Ethernet LANs created an electrical bus to which all devices connected.

■ 10BASE2 and 10BASE5 repeaters extended the length of LANs by cleaning up the electrical signal and repeating it—a Layer 1 function—but without interpreting the meaning of the electrical signal.

■ Hubs are repeaters that provide a centralized connection point for UTP cabling—but they still create a single electrical bus, shared by the various devices, just like 10BASE5 and 10BASE2.

■ Because collisions could occur in any of these cases, Ethernet defines the CSMA/CD algorithm, which tells devices how to both avoid collisions and take action when collisions do occur.

The next section explains the details of the UTP cabling used by today's most commonly used types of Ethernet.

Ethernet UTP Cabling

The three most common Ethernet standards used today—10BASE-T (Ethernet), 100BASE-TX (Fast Ethernet, or FE), and 1000BASE-T (Gigabit Ethernet, or GE)—use UTP cabling. Some key differences exist, particularly with the number of wire pairs needed in each case, and in the type (category) of cabling. This section examines some of the details of UTP cabling, pointing out differences among these three standards along the way. In particular, this section describes the cables and the connectors on the ends of the cables, how they use the wires in the cables to send data, and the pinouts required for proper operation.

UTP Cables and RJ-45 Connectors

The UTP cabling used by popular Ethernet standards include either two or four pairs of wires. Because the wires inside the cable are thin and brittle, the cable itself has an outer jacket of flexible plastic to support the wires. Each individual copper wire also has a thin plastic coating to help prevent the wire from breaking. The plastic coating on each wire has a different color, making it easy to look at both ends of the cable and identify the ends of an individual wire.

The cable ends typically have some form of connector attached (typically RJ-45 connectors), with the ends of the wires inserted into the connectors. The RJ-45 connector has eight specific physical locations into which the eight wires in the cable can be inserted, called *pin positions*, or simply *pins*. When the connectors are added to the end of the cable, the ends of the wires must be correctly inserted into the correct pin positions.

> **NOTE**   If you have an Ethernet UTP cable nearby, it would be useful to closely examine the RJ-45 connectors and wires as you read through this section.

As soon as the cable has RJ-45 connectors on each end, the RJ-45 connector needs to be inserted into an RJ-45 receptacle, often called an *RJ-45 port*. Figure 3-4 shows photos of the cables, connectors, and ports.

Figure 3-4   *RJ-45 Connectors and Ports*

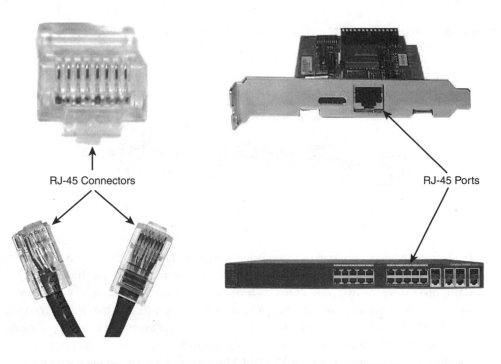

RJ-45 Connectors

RJ-45 Ports

> **NOTE**   The RJ-45 connector is slightly wider, but otherwise similar, to the RJ-11 connectors commonly used for telephone cables in homes in North America.

The figure shows three separate views of an RJ-45 connector on the left. The head-on view in the upper-left part of the figure shows the ends of the eight wires in their pin positions inside the UTP cable. The upper-right part of the figure shows an Ethernet NIC that is not yet installed in a computer. The RJ-45 port on the NIC would be exposed on the side of the computer, making it easily accessible as soon as the NIC has been installed into a computer. The lower-right part of the figure shows the side of a Cisco 2960 switch, with multiple RJ-45 ports, allowing multiple devices to easily connect to the Ethernet network.

Although RJ-45 connectors and ports are popular, engineers might want to purchase Cisco LAN switches that have a few physical ports that can be changed without having to purchase a whole new switch. Many Cisco switches have a few interfaces that use either Gigabit Interface Converters (GBIC) or Small-Form Pluggables (SFP). Both are small removable devices that fit into a port or slot in the switch. Because Cisco manufactures a wide range of GBICs and SFPs, for every Ethernet standard, the switch can use a variety of cable connectors and types of cabling and support different cable lengths—all by just switching to a different kind of GBIC or SFP. Figure 3-5 shows a 1000BASE-T GBIC, ready to be inserted into a LAN switch.

Figure 3-5   *1000BASE-T GBIC with an RJ-45 Connector*

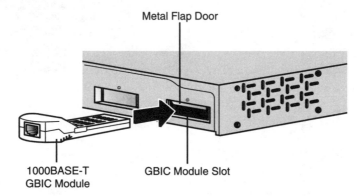

If a network engineer needs to use an existing switch in a new role in a campus network, the engineer could simply buy a new 1000BASE-LX GBIC to replace the old 1000BASE-T GBIC and reduce the extra cost of buying a whole new switch. For example, when using a switch so that it connects only to other switches in the same building, the switch could use 1000BASE-T GBICs and copper cabling. Later, if the company moved to another location, the switch could be repurposed by using a different GBIC that supported fiber-optic cabling, and different connectors, using 1000BASE-LX to support a longer cabling distance.

Transmitting Data Using Twisted Pairs

UTP cabling consists of matched pairs of wires that are indeed twisted together—hence the name *twisted pair*. The devices on each end of the cable can create an electrical circuit using a pair of wires by sending current on the two wires, in opposite directions. When current passes over any wire, that current induces a magnetic field outside the wire; the magnetic field can in turn cause electrical noise on other wires in the cable. By twisting together the wires in the same pair, with the current running in opposite directions on each wire, the magnetic field created by one wire mostly cancels out the magnetic field created by the other wire. Because of this feature, most networking cables that use copper wires and electricity use twisted pairs of wires to send data.

To send data over the electrical circuit created over a wire pair, the devices use an *encoding scheme* that defines how the electrical signal should vary, over time, to mean either a binary 0 or 1. For example, 10BASE-T uses an encoding scheme that encodes a binary 0 as a transition from higher voltage to lower voltage during the middle of a 1/10,000,000th-of-a-second interval. The electrical details of encoding are unimportant for the purposes of this book. But it is important to realize that networking devices create an electrical circuit using each wire pair, and vary the signal as defined by the encoding scheme, to send bits over the wire pair.

UTP Cabling Pinouts for 10BASE-T and 100BASE-TX

The wires in the UTP cable must be connected to the correct pin positions in the RJ-45 connectors in order for communication to work correctly. As mentioned earlier, the RJ-45 connector has eight *pin positions*, or simply *pins*, into which the copper wires inside the cable protrude. The wiring *pinouts*—the choice of which color wire goes into which pin position—must conform to the Ethernet standards described in this section.

Interestingly, the IEEE does not actually define the official standards for cable manufacturing, as well as part of the details of the conventions used for the cabling pinouts. Two cooperating industry groups, the Telecommunications Industry Association (TIA) and the Electronics Industry Alliance (EIA), define standards for UTP cabling, color coding for wires, and standard pinouts on the cables. (See http://www.tiaonline.org and http://www.eia.org.) Figure 3-6 shows two pinout standards from the EIA/TIA, with the color coding and pair numbers listed.

Figure 3-6 *EIA/TIA Standard Ethernet Cabling Pinouts*

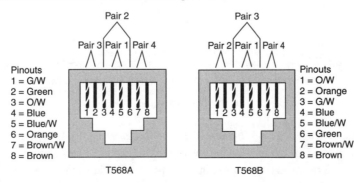

To understand the acronyms listed in the figure, note that the eight wires in a UTP cable have either a solid color (green, orange, blue, or brown) or a striped color scheme using white and one of the other four colors. Also, a single-wire pair uses the same base color. For example, the blue wire and the blue/white striped wire are paired and twisted. In Figure 3-6, the notations with a / refer to the striped wires. For example, "G/W" refers to the green-and-white striped wire.

> **NOTE** A UTP cable needs two pairs of wires for 10BASE-T and 100BASE-TX and four pairs of wires for 1000BASE-T. This section focuses on the pinouts for two-pair wiring, with four-pair wiring covered next.

To build a working Ethernet LAN, you must choose or build cables that use the correct wiring pinout on each end of the cable. 10BASE-T and 100BASE-TX Ethernet define that one pair should be used to send data in one direction, with the other pair used to send data in the other direction. In particular, Ethernet NICs should send data using the pair connected to pins 1 and 2—in other words, pair 3 according to the T568A pinout standard shown in Figure 3-6. Similarly, Ethernet NICs should expect to receive data using the pair at pins 3 and 6—pair 2 according to the T568A standard. Knowing what the Ethernet NICs do, hubs and switches do the opposite—they receive on the pair at pins 1,2 (pair 3 per T568A), and they send on the pair at pins 3,6 (pair 2 per T568A).

Figure 3-7 shows this concept, with PC Larry connected to a hub. Note that the figure shows the two twisted pairs inside the cable, and the NIC outside the PC, to emphasize that the cable connects to the NIC and hub and that only two pairs are being used.

Figure 3-7   *Ethernet Straight-Through Cable Concept*

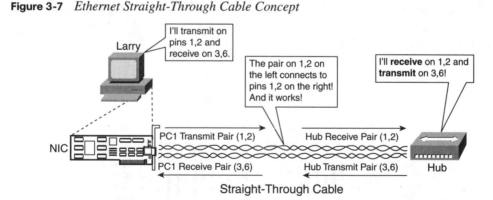

The network shown in Figure 3-7 uses a *straight-through* cable. An Ethernet straight-through cable connects the wire at pin 1 on one end of the cable to pin 1 at the other end of the cable; the wire at pin 2 needs to connect to pin 2 on the other end of the cable; pin 3 on one end connects to pin 3 on the other; and so on. (To create a straight-through cable, both ends of the cable use the same EIA/TIA pinout standard on each end of the cable.)

A straight-through cable is used when the devices on the ends of the cable use opposite pins when they transmit data. However, when connecting two devices that both use the same pins to transmit, the pinouts of the cable must be set up to swap the wire pair. A cable that swaps the wire pairs inside the cable is called a *crossover cable*. For example, many LANs inside an Enterprise network use multiple switches, with a UTP cable connecting the switches. Because both switches send on the pair at pins 3,6, and receive on the pair at pins 1,2, the cable must swap or cross the pairs. Figure 3-8 shows several conceptual views of a crossover cable.

Figure 3-8 *Crossover Ethernet Cable*

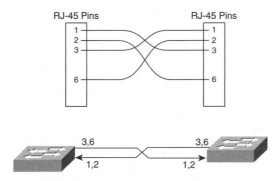

Key
Topic

The top part of the figure shows the pins to which each wire is connected. Pin 1 on the left end connects to pin 3 on the right end, pin 2 on the left to pin 6 on the right, pin 3 on the left to pin 1 on the right, and pin 6 on the left to pin 2 on the right. The bottom of the figure shows that the wires at pins 3,6 on each end—the pins each switch uses to transmit—connect to pins 1,2 on the other end, thereby allowing the devices to receive on pins 1,2.

For the exam, you should be well prepared to choose which type of cable (straight-through or crossover) is needed in each part of the network. In short, devices on opposite ends of a cable that use the same pair of pins to transmit need a crossover cable. Devices that use an opposite pair of pins to transmit need a straight-through cable. Table 3-3 lists the devices mentioned in this book and the pin pairs they use, assuming that they use 10BASE-T and 100BASE-TX.

Table 3-3 *10BASE-T and 100BASE-TX Pin Pairs Used*

Key
Topic

Devices That Transmit on 1,2 and Receive on 3,6	Devices That Transmit on 3,6 and Receive on 1,2
PC NICs	Hubs
Routers	Switches
Wireless Access Point (Ethernet interface)	—
Networked printers (printers that connect directly to the LAN)	—

For example, Figure 3-9 shows a campus LAN in a single building. In this case, several straight-through cables are used to connect PCs to switches. Additionally, the cables connecting the switches—referred to as *trunks*—require crossover cables.

Figure 3-9 *Typical Uses for Straight-Through and Crossover Ethernet Cables*

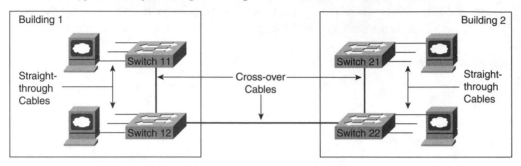

1000BASE-T Cabling

As noted earlier, 1000BASE-T differs from 10BASE-T and 100BASE-TX as far as the cabling and pinouts. First, 1000BASE-T requires four wire pairs. Also, Gigabit Ethernet transmits and receives on each of the four wire pairs simultaneously.

However, Gigabit Ethernet does have a concept of straight-through and crossover cables, with a minor difference in the crossover cables. The pinouts for a straight-through cable are the same—pin 1 to pin 1, pin 2 to pin 2, and so on. The crossover cable crosses the same two-wire pair as the crossover cable for the other types of Ethernet—the pair at pins 1,2 and 3,6—as well as crossing the two other pairs (the pair at pins 4,5 with the pair at pins 7,8).

> **NOTE**   If you have some experience with installing LANs, you might be thinking that you have used the wrong cable before (straight-through or crossover), but the cable worked. Cisco switches have a feature called auto-mdix that notices when the wrong cabling pinouts are used. This feature readjusts the switch's logic and makes the cable work. For the exams, be ready to identify whether the correct cable is shown in figures.

Next, this chapter takes a closer look at LAN hubs and the need for LAN switches.

Improving Performance by Using Switches Instead of Hubs

This section examines some of the performance problems created when using hubs, followed by explanations of how LAN switches solve the two largest performance problems encountered with hubs. To better appreciate the problem, consider Figure 3-10, which shows what happens when a single device sends data through a hub.

NOTE   The figure and the logic describing it apply to any hub, whether 10BASE-T, 100BASE-TX, or even 1000BASE-T.

Figure 3-10 *Hub Creates One Shared Electrical Bus*

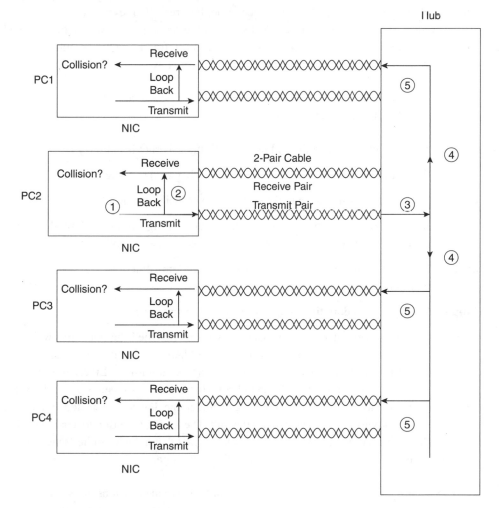

The figure outlines how a hub creates an electrical bus. The steps illustrated in Figure 3-10 are as follows:

Step 1   The network interface card (NIC) sends a frame.

Step 2   The NIC loops the sent frame onto its receive pair internally on the card.

Step 3   The hub receives the electrical signal, interpreting the signal as bits so that it can clean up and repeat the signal.

Step 4   The hub's internal wiring repeats the signal out all other ports, but not back to the port from which the signal was received.

Step 5   The hub repeats the signal to each receive pair on all other devices.

In particular, note that a hub always repeats the electrical signal out all ports, except the port from which the electrical signal was received. Also, Figure 3-10 does not show a collision. However, if PC1 and PC2 sent an electrical signal at the same time, at Step 4 the electrical signals would overlap, the frames would collide, and both frames would be either completely unintelligible or full of errors.

CSMA/CD logic helps prevent collisions and also defines how to act when a collision does occur. The CSMA/CD algorithm works like this:

Step 1   A device with a frame to send listens until the Ethernet is not busy.

Step 2   When the Ethernet is not busy, the sender(s) begin(s) sending the frame.

Step 3   The sender(s) listen(s) to make sure that no collision occurred.

Step 4   If a collision occurs, the devices that had been sending a frame each send a jamming signal to ensure that all stations recognize the collision.

Step 5   After the jamming is complete, each sender randomizes a timer and waits that long before trying to resend the collided frame.

Step 6   When each random timer expires, the process starts over with Step 1.

CSMA/CD does not prevent collisions, but it does ensure that the Ethernet works well even though collisions may and do occur. However, the CSMA/CD algorithm does create some performance issues. First, CSMA/CD causes devices to wait until the Ethernet is silent before sending data. This process helps avoid collisions, but it also means that only one device can send at any one instant in time. As a result, all the devices connected to the same hub share the bandwidth available through the hub. The logic of waiting to send until the LAN is silent is called *half duplex*. This refers to the fact that a device either sends or receives at any point in time, but never both at the same time.

The other main feature of CSMA/CD defines what to do when collisions do occur. When a collision occurs, CSMA/CD logic causes the devices that sent the colliding data frames to wait a random amount of time, and then try again. This again helps the LAN to function, but again it impacts performance. During the collision, no useful data makes it across the LAN. Also, the offending devices have to wait longer before trying to use the LAN. Additionally, as the load on an Ethernet increases, the statistical chance for collisions increases as well. In fact, during the years before LAN switches became more affordable and solved some of these performance problems, the rule of thumb was that an Ethernet's performance began to degrade when the load began to exceed 30 percent utilization, mainly as a result of increasing collisions.

Increasing Available Bandwidth Using Switches

The term *collision domain* defines the set of devices whose frames could collide. All devices on a 10BASE2, 10BASE5, or any network using a hub risk collisions between the frames that they send, so all devices on one of these types of Ethernet networks are in the same collision domain. For example, all four devices connected to the hub in Figure 3-10 are in the same collision domain. To avoid collisions, and to recover when they occur, devices in the same collision domain use CSMA/CD.

LAN switches significantly reduce, or even eliminate, the number of collisions on a LAN. Unlike hubs, switches do not create a single shared bus, forwarding received electrical signals out all other ports. Instead, switches do the following:

■ Switches interpret the bits in the received frame so that they can typically send the frame out the one required port, rather than all other ports

■ If a switch needs to forward multiple frames out the same port, the switch buffers the frames in memory, sending one at a time, thereby avoiding collisions

For example, Figure 3-11 illustrates how a switch can forward two frames at the same time while avoiding a collision. In Figure 3-11, both PC1 and PC3 send at the same time. In this case, PC1 sends a data frame with a destination address of PC2, and PC3 sends a data frame with a destination address of PC4. (More on Ethernet addressing is coming up later in this chapter.) The switch looks at the destination Ethernet address and sends the frame from PC1 to PC2 at the same instant as the frame is sent by PC3 to PC4. Had a hub been used, a collision would have occurred; however, because the switch did not send the frames out all other ports, the switch prevented a collision.

> **NOTE**   The switch's logic requires that the switch look at the Ethernet header, which is considered a Layer 2 feature. As a result, switches are considered to operate as a Layer 2 device, whereas hubs are Layer 1 devices.

Buffering also helps prevent collisions. Imagine that PC1 and PC3 both send a frame to PC4 at the same time. The switch, knowing that forwarding both frames to PC4 at the same time would cause a collision, buffers one frame (in other words, temporarily holds it in memory) until the first frame has been completely sent to PC4.

These seemingly simple switch features provide significant performance improvements as compared with using hubs. In particular:

■ If only one device is cabled to each port of a switch, no collisions can occur.

■ Devices connected to one switch port do not share their bandwidth with devices connected to another switch port. Each has its own separate bandwidth, meaning that a switch with 100-Mbps ports has 100 Mbps of bandwidth *per port*.

Figure 3-11 *Basic Switch Operation*

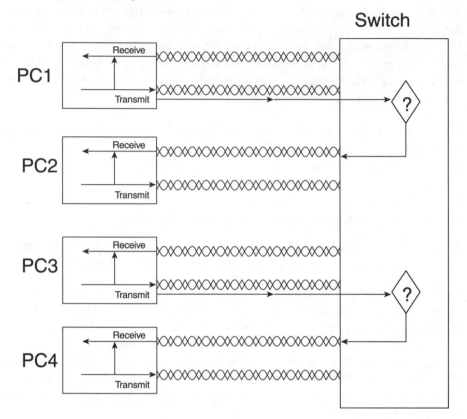

The second point refers to the concepts behind the terms *shared Ethernet* and *switched Ethernet*. As mentioned earlier in this chapter, shared Ethernet means that the LAN bandwidth is shared among the devices on the LAN because they must take turns using the LAN because of the CSMA/CD algorithm. The term switched Ethernet refers to the fact that with switches, bandwidth does not have to be shared, allowing for far greater performance. For example, a hub with 24 100-Mbps Ethernet devices connected to it allows for a theoretical maximum of 100 Mbps of bandwidth. However, a switch with 24 100-Mbps Ethernet devices connected to it supports 100 Mbps for each port, or 2400 Mbps (2.4 Gbps) theoretical maximum bandwidth.

Doubling Performance by Using Full-Duplex Ethernet

Any Ethernet network using hubs requires CSMA/CD logic to work properly. However, CSMA/CD imposes half-duplex logic on each device, meaning that only one device can send at a time. Because switches can buffer frames in memory, switches can completely eliminate collisions on switch ports that connect to a single device. As a result, LAN switches with only one device cabled to each port of the switch allow the use of *full-duplex* operation. Full duplex means that an Ethernet card can send and receive concurrently.

To appreciate why collisions cannot occur, consider Figure 3-12, which shows the full-duplex circuitry used with a single PC's connection to a LAN switch.

Figure 3-12 *Full-Duplex Operation Using a Switch*

With only the switch and one device connected to each other, collisions cannot occur. When you implement full duplex, you disable CSMA/CD logic on the devices on both ends of the cable. By doing so, neither device even thinks about CSMA/CD, and they can go ahead and send data whenever they want. As a result, the performance of the Ethernet on that cable has been doubled by allowed simultaneous transmission in both directions.

Ethernet Layer 1 Summary

So far in this chapter, you have read about the basics of how to build the Layer 1 portions of Ethernet using both hubs and switches. This section explained how to use UTP cables, with RJ-45 connectors, to connect devices to either a hub or a switch. It also explained the general theory of how devices can send data by encoding different electrical signals over an electrical circuit, with the circuit being created using a pair of wires inside the UTP cable. More importantly, this section explained which wire pairs are used to transmit and receive data. Finally, the basic operations of switches were explained, including the potential elimination of collisions, which results in significantly better performance than hubs.

Next, this chapter examines the data link layer protocols defined by Ethernet.

Ethernet Data-Link Protocols

One of the most significant strengths of the Ethernet family of protocols is that these protocols use the same small set of data-link standards. For instance, Ethernet addressing works the same on all the variations of Ethernet, even back to 10BASE5, up through 10-Gbps Ethernet—including Ethernet standards that use other types of cabling besides UTP. Also, the CSMA/CD algorithm is technically a part of the data link layer, again applying to most types of Ethernet, unless it has been disabled.

This section covers most of the details of the Ethernet data-link protocols—in particular, Ethernet addressing, framing, error detection, and identifying the type of data inside the Ethernet frame.

Ethernet Addressing

Ethernet LAN addressing identifies either individual devices or groups of devices on a LAN. Each address is 6 bytes long, is usually written in hexadecimal, and, in Cisco devices, typically is written with periods separating each set of four hex digits. For example, 0000.0C12.3456 is a valid Ethernet address.

Unicast Ethernet addresses identify a single LAN card. (The term *unicast* was chosen mainly for contrast with the terms *broadcast*, *multicast*, and *group addresses*.) Computers use unicast addresses to identify the sender and receiver of an Ethernet frame. For instance, imagine that Fred and Barney are on the same Ethernet, and Fred sends Barney a frame. Fred puts his own Ethernet MAC address in the Ethernet header as the source address and uses Barney's Ethernet MAC address as the destination. When Barney receives the frame, he notices that the destination address is his own address, so he processes the frame. If Barney receives a frame with some other device's unicast address in the destination address field, he simply does not process the frame.

The IEEE defines the format and assignment of LAN addresses. The IEEE requires globally unique unicast MAC addresses on all LAN interface cards. (IEEE calls them MAC addresses because the MAC protocols such as IEEE 802.3 define the addressing details.) To ensure a unique MAC address, the Ethernet card manufacturers encode the MAC address onto the card, usually in a ROM chip. The first half of the address identifies the manufacturer of the card. This code, which is assigned to each manufacturer by the IEEE, is called the *organizationally unique identifier (OUI)*. Each manufacturer assigns a MAC address with its own OUI as the first half of the address, with the second half of the address being assigned a number that this manufacturer has never used on another card. Figure 3-13 shows the structure.

Figure 3-13 *Structure of Unicast Ethernet Addresses*

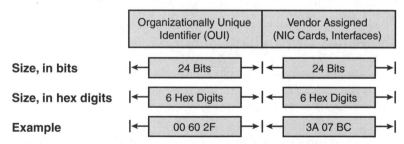

Organizationally Unique Identifier (OUI)	Vendor Assigned (NIC Cards, Interfaces)

Size, in bits	24 Bits	24 Bits
Size, in hex digits	6 Hex Digits	6 Hex Digits
Example	00 60 2F	3A 07 BC

Many terms can be used to describe unicast LAN addresses. Each LAN card comes with a *burned-in address (BIA)* that is burned into the ROM chip on the card. BIAs sometimes are called *universally administered addresses (UAA)* because the IEEE universally (well, at least worldwide) administers address assignment. Regardless of whether the BIA is used or another address is configured, many people refer to unicast addresses as either LAN addresses, Ethernet addresses, hardware addresses, physical addresses, or MAC addresses.

Group addresses identify more than one LAN interface card. The IEEE defines two general categories of group addresses for Ethernet:

■ **Broadcast addresses:** The most often used of the IEEE group MAC addresses, the broadcast address, has a value of FFFF.FFFF.FFFF (hexadecimal notation). The broadcast address implies that all devices on the LAN should process the frame.

■ **Multicast addresses:** Multicast addresses are used to allow a subset of devices on a LAN to communicate. When IP multicasts over an Ethernet, the multicast MAC addresses used by IP follow this format: 0100.5e*xx.xxxx*, where any value can be used in the last half of the address.

Table 3-4 summarizes most of the details about MAC addresses.

Table 3-4   *LAN MAC Address Terminology and Features*

Key
Topic

LAN Addressing Term or Feature	Description
MAC	Media Access Control. 802.3 (Ethernet) defines the MAC sublayer of IEEE Ethernet.
Ethernet address, NIC address, LAN address	Other names often used instead of MAC address. These terms describe the 6-byte address of the LAN interface card.
Burned-in address	The 6-byte address assigned by the vendor making the card.
Unicast address	A term for a MAC that represents a single LAN interface.
Broadcast address	An address that means "all devices that reside on this LAN right now."
Multicast address	On Ethernet, a multicast address implies some subset of all devices currently on the Ethernet LAN.

Ethernet Framing

Framing defines how a string of binary numbers is interpreted. In other words, framing defines the meaning behind the bits that are transmitted across a network. The physical layer helps you get a string of bits from one device to another. When the receiving device gets the bits, how should they be interpreted? The term *framing* refers to the definition of the fields assumed to be in the data that is received. In other words, framing defines the meaning of the bits transmitted and received over a network.

For instance, you just read an example of Fred sending data to Barney over an Ethernet. Fred put Barney's Ethernet address in the Ethernet header so that Barney would know that the Ethernet frame was meant for him. The IEEE 802.3 standard defines the location of the destination address field inside the string of bits sent across the Ethernet.

The framing used for Ethernet has changed a couple of times over the years. Xerox defined one version of the framing, which the IEEE then changed when it took over Ethernet standards in the early 1980s. The IEEE finalized a compromise standard for framing in 1997 that includes some of the features of the original Xerox Ethernet framing, along with the framing defined by the IEEE. The end result is the bottom frame format shown in Figure 3-14.

Figure 3-14 *LAN Header Formats*

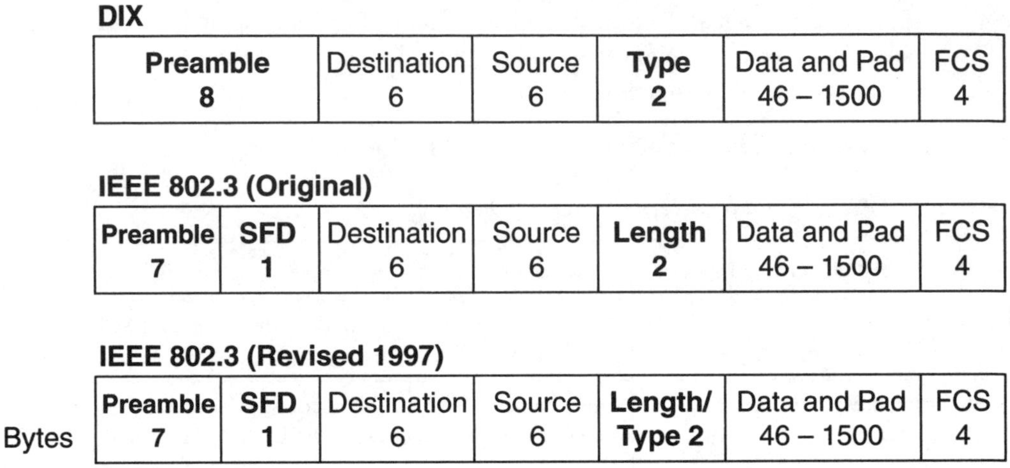

DIX

Preamble 8	Destination 6	Source 6	Type 2	Data and Pad 46 – 1500	FCS 4

IEEE 802.3 (Original)

Preamble 7	SFD 1	Destination 6	Source 6	Length 2	Data and Pad 46 – 1500	FCS 4

IEEE 802.3 (Revised 1997)

	Preamble 7	SFD 1	Destination 6	Source 6	Length/ Type 2	Data and Pad 46 – 1500	FCS 4
Bytes							

Most of the fields in the Ethernet frame are important enough to be covered at some point in this chapter. For reference, Table 3-5 lists the fields in the header and trailer, and a brief description, for reference.

Table 3-5 *IEEE 802.3 Ethernet Header and Trailer Fields*

Field	Field Length in Bytes	Description
Preamble	7	Synchronization
Start Frame Delimiter (SFD)	1	Signifies that the next byte begins the Destination MAC field
Destination MAC address	6	Identifies the intended recipient of this frame
Source MAC address	6	Identifies the sender of this frame
Length	2	Defines the length of the data field of the frame (either length or type is present, but not both)
Type	2	Defines the type of protocol listed inside the frame (either length or type is present, but not both)

Table 3-5 *IEEE 802.3 Ethernet Header and Trailer Fields (Continued)*

Field	Field Length in Bytes	Description
Data and Pad[*]	46–1500	Holds data from a higher layer, typically an L3 PDU (generic), and often an IP packet
Frame Check Sequence (FCS)	4	Provides a method for the receiving NIC to determine if the frame experienced transmission errors

[*]The IEEE 802.3 specification limits the data portion of the 802.3 frame to a maximum of 1500 bytes. The Data field was designed to hold Layer 3 packets; the term maximum transmission unit (MTU) defines the maximum Layer 3 packet that can be sent over a medium. Because the Layer 3 packet rests inside the data portion of an Ethernet frame, 1500 bytes is the largest IP MTU allowed over an Ethernet.

Identifying the Data Inside an Ethernet Frame

Over the years, many different network layer (Layer 3) protocols have been designed. Most of these protocols were part of larger network protocol models created by vendors to support their products, such as IBM Systems Network Architecture (SNA), Novell NetWare, Digital Equipment Corporation's DECnet, and Apple Computer's AppleTalk. Additionally, the OSI and TCP/IP models also defined network layer protocols.

All these Layer 3 protocols, plus several others, could use Ethernet. To use Ethernet, the network layer protocol would place its packet (generically speaking, its L3 PDU) into the data portion of the Ethernet frame shown in Figure 3-14. However, when a device receives such an Ethernet frame, that receiving device needs to know what type of L3 PDU is in the Ethernet frame. Is it an IP packet? an OSI packet? SNA? and so on.

To answer that question, most data-link protocol headers, including Ethernet, have a field with a code that defines the type of protocol header that follows. Generically speaking, these fields in data-link headers are called *Type fields*. For example, to imply that an IP packet is inside an Ethernet frame, the Type field (as shown in Figure 3-14) would have a value of hexadecimal 0800 (decimal 2048). Other types of L3 PDUs would be implied by using a different value in the Type field.

Interestingly, because of the changes to Ethernet framing over the years, another popular option exists for the protocol Type field, particularly when sending IP packets. If the 802.3 Type/Length field (in Figure 3-14) has a value less than hex 0600 (decimal 1536), the Type/Length field is used as a Length field for that frame, identifying the length of the entire Ethernet frame. In that case, another field is needed to identify the type of L3 PDU inside the frame.

To create a Type field for frames that use the Type/Length field as a Length field, either one or two additional headers are added after the Ethernet 802.3 header but before the

Layer 3 header. For example, when sending IP packets, the Ethernet frame has two additional headers:

■ An IEEE 802.2 Logical Link Control (LLC) header

■ An IEEE Subnetwork Access Protocol (SNAP) header

Figure 3-15 shows an Ethernet frame with these additional headers. Note that the SNAP header Type field has the same purpose, with the same reserved values, as the Ethernet Type/Length field.

Figure 3-15 *802.2 SNAP Headers*

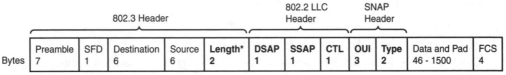

* To be a Length field, this value must be less than decimal 1536.

Error Detection

The final Ethernet data link layer function explained here is error detection. Error detection is the process of discovering if a frame's bits changed as a result of being sent over the network. The bits might change for many small reasons, but generally such errors occur as a result of some kind of electrical interference. Like every data-link protocol covered on the CCNA exams, Ethernet defines both a header and trailer, with the trailer containing a field used for the purpose of error detection.

The Ethernet Frame Check Sequence (FCS) field in the Ethernet trailer—the only field in the Ethernet trailer—allows a device receiving an Ethernet frame to detect whether the bits have changed during transmission. To detect an error, the sending device calculates a complex mathematical function, with the frame contents as input, putting the result into the frame's 4-byte FCS field. The receiving device does the same math on the frame; if its calculation matches the FCS field in the frame, no errors occurred. If the result doesn't match the FCS field, an error occurred, and the frame is discarded.

Note that error detection does not also mean error recovery. Ethernet defines that the errored frame should be discarded, but Ethernet takes no action to cause the frame to be retransmitted. Other protocols, notably TCP (as covered in Chapter 6, "Fundamentals of TCP/IP Transport, Applications, and Security"), can notice the lost data and cause error recovery to occur.

Exam Preparation Tasks

Review All the Key Topics

Review the most important topics from this chapter, noted with the key topics icon. Table 3-6 lists these key topics and where each is discussed.

Key Topic

Table 3-6 *Key Topics for Chapter 3*

Key Topic Element	Description	Page Number
Table 3-2	The four most popular types of Ethernet LANs and some details about each	46
List	Summary of CSMA/CD logic	49
Figure 3-6	EIA/TIA standard Ethernet Cabling Pinouts	55
Figure 3-7	Straight-through cable concept	56
Figure 3-8	Crossover cable concept	57
Table 3-3	List of devices that transmit on wire pair 1,2 and pair 3,6	57
List	Detailed CSMA/CD logic	60
Figure 3-13	Structure of a unicast Ethernet address	64
Table 3-4	Key Ethernet addressing terms	65

Complete the Tables and Lists from Memory

Print a copy of Appendix H, "Memory Tables" (found on the CD), or at least the section for this chapter, and complete the tables and lists from memory. Appendix I, "Memory Tables Answer Key," also on the CD, includes completed tables and lists for you to check your work.

Definitions of Key Terms

Define the following key terms from this chapter and check your answers in the glossary.

1000BASE-T, 100BASE-TX, 10BASE-T, crossover cable, CSMA/CD, full duplex, half duplex, hub, pinout, protocol type, shared Ethernet, straight-through cable, switch, switched Ethernet, twisted pair

This chapter covers the following subjects:

OSI Layer 1 for Point-to-Point WANs: This section explains the physical cabling and devices used to create the customer portions of a leased circuit.

OSI Layer 2 for Point-to-Point WANs: This section introduces the data link layer protocols used on point-to-point leased lines, namely HDLC and PPP.

Frame Relay and Packet-Switching Services: This section explains the concept of a WAN packet-switching service, with particular attention given to Frame Relay.

CHAPTER 4

Fundamentals of WANs

In the previous chapter, you learned more details about how Ethernet LANs perform the functions defined by the two lowest OSI layers. In this chapter, you will learn about how wide-area network (WAN) standards and protocols also implement OSI Layer 1 (physical layer) and Layer 2 (data link layer). The OSI physical layer details are covered, along with three popular WAN data link layer protocols: High-Level Data Link Control (HDLC), Point-to-Point Protocol (PPP), and Frame Relay.

"Do I Know This Already?" Quiz

The "Do I Know This Already?" quiz allows you to assess if you should read the entire chapter. If you miss no more than one of these eight self-assessment questions, you might want to move ahead to the "Exam Preparation Tasks" section. Table 4-1 lists the major headings in this chapter and the "Do I Know This Already?" quiz questions covering the material in those headings so you can assess your knowledge of these specific areas. The answers to the "Do I Know This Already?" quiz appear in Appendix A.

Table 4-1   *"Do I Know This Already?" Foundation Topics Section-to-Question Mapping*

Foundation Topics Section	Questions
OSI Layer 1 for Point-to-Point WANs	1–4
OSI Layer 2 for Point-to-Point WANs	5, 6
Frame Relay and Packet-Switching Services	7, 8

1.   Which of the following best describes the main function of OSI Layer 1 protocols?

   a.   Framing

   b.   Delivery of bits from one device to another

   c.   Addressing

   d.   Local Management Interface (LMI)

   e.   DLCI

2. Which of the following typically connects to a four-wire line provided by a telco?

    a. Router serial interface

    b. CSU/DSU

    c. Transceiver

    d. Switch serial interface

3. Which of the following typically connects to a V.35 or RS-232 end of a cable when cabling a leased line?

    a. Router serial interface

    b. CSU/DSU

    c. Transceiver

    d. Switch serial interface

4. On a point-to-point WAN link using a leased line between two routers located hundreds of miles apart, what devices are considered to be the DTE devices?

    a. Routers

    b. CSU/DSU

    c. The central office equipment

    d. A chip on the processor of each router

    e. None of these answers are correct.

5. Which of the following functions of OSI Layer 2 is specified by the protocol standard for PPP, but is implemented with a Cisco proprietary header field for HDLC?

    a. Framing

    b. Arbitration

    c. Addressing

    d. Error detection

    e. Identifying the type of protocol that is inside the frame

6. Imagine that Router1 has three point-to-point serial links, one link each to three remote routers. Which of the following is true about the required HDLC addressing at Router1?

    a. Router1 must use HDLC addresses 1, 2, and 3.

    b. Router1 must use any three unique addresses between 1 and 1023.

    c. Router1 must use any three unique addresses between 16 and 1000.

    d. Router1 must use three sequential unique addresses between 1 and 1023.

    e. None of these answers are correct.

7. What is the name of the Frame Relay field used to identify Frame Relay virtual circuits?

    a. Data-link connection identifier

    b. Data-link circuit identifier

    c. Data-link connection indicator

    d. Data-link circuit indicator

    e. None of these answers are correct.

8. Which of the following is true about Frame Relay virtual circuits (VCs)?

    a. Each VC requires a separate access link.

    b. Multiple VCs can share the same access link.

    c. All VCs sharing the same access link must connect to the same router on the other side of the VC.

    d. All VCs on the same access link must use the same DLCI.

Foundation Topics

As you read in the previous chapter, the OSI physical and data link layers work together to deliver data across a wide variety of types of physical networks. LAN standards and protocols define how to network between devices that are relatively close together, hence the term *local-area* in the acronym LAN. WAN standards and protocols define how to network between devices that are relatively far apart—in some cases, even thousands of miles apart—hence the term *wide-area* in the acronym WAN.

LANs and WANs both implement the same OSI Layer 1 and Layer 2 functions, but with different mechanisms and details. This chapter points out the similarities between the two, and provides details about the differences.

The WAN topics in this chapter describe mainly how enterprise networks use WANs to connect remote sites. Part IV of this book covers a broader range of WAN topics, including popular Internet access technologies such as digital subscriber line (DSL) and cable, along with a variety of configuration topics. The *CCNA ICND2 Official Exam Certification Guide* covers Frame Relay in much more detail than this book, as well as the concepts behind Internet virtual private networks (VPN), which is a way to use the Internet instead of traditional WAN links.

OSI Layer 1 for Point-to-Point WANs

The OSI physical layer, or Layer 1, defines the details of how to move data from one device to another. In fact, many people think of OSI Layer 1 as "sending bits." Higher layers encapsulate the data, as described in Chapter 2, "The TCP/IP and OSI Networking Models." No matter what the other OSI layers do, eventually the sender of the data needs to actually transmit the bits to another device. The OSI physical layer defines the standards and protocols used to create the physical network and to send the bits across that network.

A point-to-point WAN link acts like an Ethernet trunk between two Ethernet switches in many ways. For perspective, look at Figure 4-1, which shows a LAN with two buildings and two switches in each building. As a brief review, remember that several types of Ethernet use one twisted pair of wires to transmit and another twisted pair to receive, in order to reduce electromagnetic interference. You typically use straight-through Ethernet cables between end-user devices and the switches. For the trunk links between the switches, you use crossover cables because each switch transmits on the same pair of pins on the connector, so the crossover cable connects one device's transmit pair to the other device's receive pair. The lower part of Figure 4-1 reminds you of the basic idea behind a crossover cable.

Figure 4-1 *Example LAN, Two Buildings*

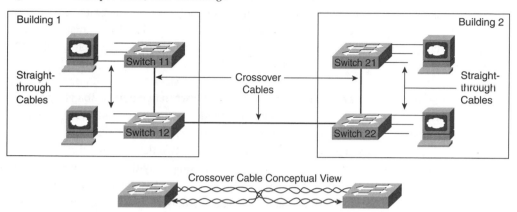

Now imagine that the buildings are 1000 miles apart instead of right next to each other. You are immediately faced with two problems:

■   Ethernet does not support any type of cabling that allows an individual trunk to run for 1000 miles.

■   Even if Ethernet supported a 1000-mile trunk, you do not have the rights-of-way needed to bury a cable over the 1000 miles of real estate between buildings.

The big distinction between LANs and WANs relates to how far apart the devices can be and still be capable of sending and receiving data. LANs tend to reside in a single building or possibly among buildings in a campus using optical cabling approved for Ethernet. WAN connections typically run longer distances than Ethernet—across town or between cities. Often, only one or a few companies even have the rights to run cables under the ground between the sites. So, the people who created WAN standards needed to use different physical specifications than Ethernet to send data 1000 miles or more (WAN).

> **NOTE** Besides LANs and WANs, the term metropolitan-area network (MAN) is sometimes used for networks that extend between buildings and through rights-of-ways. The term MAN typically implies a network that does not reach as far as a WAN, generally in a single metropolitan area. The distinctions between LANs, MANs, and WANs are blurry—there is no set distance that means a link is a LAN, MAN, or WAN link.

To create such long links, or circuits, the actual physical cabling is owned, installed, and managed by a company that has the right of way to run cables under streets. Because a company that needs to send data over the WAN circuit does not actually own the cable or line, it is called a *leased line*. Companies that can provide leased WAN lines typically started life as the local telephone company, or telco. In many countries, the telco is still a government-regulated or government-controlled monopoly; these companies are sometimes called public telephone and telegraph (PTT) companies. Today, many people use the generic term *service provider* to refer to a company that provides any form of WAN connectivity, including Internet services.

Point-to-point WAN links provide basic connectivity between two points. To get a point-to-point WAN link, you would work with a service provider to install a circuit. What the phone company or service provider gives you is similar to what you would have if you made a phone call between two sites, but you never hung up. The two devices on either end of the WAN circuit could send and receive bits between each other any time they want, without needing to dial a phone number. Because the connection is always available, a point-to-point WAN connection is sometimes called a *leased circuit* or *leased line* because you have the exclusive right to use that circuit, as long as you keep paying for it.

Now back to the comparison of the LAN between two nearby buildings versus the WAN between two buildings that are 1000 miles apart. The physical details are different, but the same general functions need to be accomplished, as shown in Figure 4-2.

Figure 4-2   *Conceptual View of Point-to-Point Leased Line*

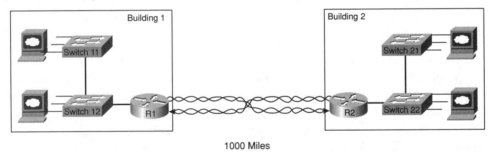

1000 Miles

Keep in mind that Figure 4-2 provides a conceptual view of a point-to-point WAN link. In concept, the telco installs a physical cable, with a transmit and a receive twisted pair, between the buildings. The cable has been connected to each router, and each router, in turn, has been connected to the LAN switches. As a result of this new physical WAN link and the logic used by the routers connected to it, data now can be transferred between the two sites. In the next section, you will learn more about the physical details of the WAN link.

NOTE   Ethernet switches have many different types of interfaces, but all the interfaces are some form of Ethernet. Routers provide the capability to connect many different types of OSI Layer 1 and Layer 2 technologies. So, when you see a LAN connected to some other site using a WAN connection, you will see a router connected to each, as in Figure 4-2.

WAN Connections from the Customer Viewpoint

The concepts behind a point-to-point connection are simple. However, to fully understand what the service provider does to build its network to support your point-to-point line, you would need to spend lots of time studying and learning technologies outside the scope of the ICND1 exam. However, most of what you need to know about WANs for the ICND1 exam relates to how WAN connections are implemented between the telephone company and a customer site. Along the way, you will need to learn a little about the terminology used by the provider.

In Figure 4-2, you saw that a WAN leased line acts as if the telco gave you two twisted pairs of wires between the two sites on each end of the line. Well, it is not that simple. Of course, a lot more underlying technology must be used to create the circuit, and telcos use a lot of terminology that is different from LAN terminology. The telco seldom actually runs a 1000-mile cable for you between the two sites. Instead, it has built a large network already and even runs extra cables from the local central office (CO) to your building (a CO is just a building where the telco locates the devices used to create its own network). Regardless of what the telco does inside its own network, what you receive is the equivalent of a four-wire leased circuit between two buildings.

Figure 4-3 introduces some of the key concepts and terms relating to WAN circuits.

Figure 4-3 *Point-to-Point Leased Line: Components and Terminology*

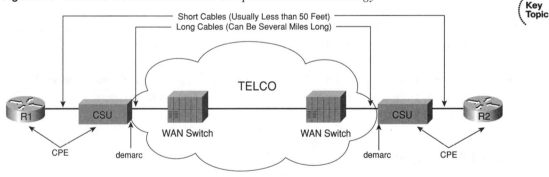

Typically, routers connect to a device called an external channel service unit/data service unit (CSU/DSU). The router connects to the CSU/DSU with a relatively short cable, typically less than 50 feet long, because the CSU/DSUs typically get placed in a rack near the router. The much longer four-wire cable from the telco plugs into the CSU/DSU. That cable leaves the building, running through the hidden (typically buried) cables that you sometimes see phone company workers fixing by the side of the road. The other end of that cable ends up in the CO, with the cable connecting to a CO device generically called a WAN switch.

The same general physical connectivity exists on each side of the point-to-point WAN link. In between the two COs, the service provider can build its network with several competing different types of technology, all of which is beyond the scope of any of the CCNA exams. However, the perspective in Figure 4-2 remains true—the two routers can send and receive data simultaneously across the point-to-point WAN link.

From a legal perspective, two different companies own the various components of the equipment and lines in Figure 4-3. For instance, the router cable and typically the CSU/ DSU are owned by the telco's customer, and the wiring to the CO and the gear inside the CO are owned by the telco. So, the telco uses the term *demarc*, which is short for demarcation point, to refer to the point at which the telco's responsibility is on one side and the customer's responsibility is on the other. The demarc is not a separate device or cable, but rather a concept of where the responsibilities of the telco and customer end.

In the United States, the demarc is typically where the telco physically terminates the set of two twisted pairs inside the customer building. Typically, the customer asks the telco to terminate the cable in a particular room, and most, if not all, the lines from the telco into that building terminate in the same room.

The term customer premises equipment (CPE) refers to devices that are at the customer site, from the telco's perspective. For instance, both the CSU/DSU and the router are CPE devices in this case.

The demarc does not always reside where it is shown in Figure 4-3. In some cases, the telco actually could own the CSU/DSU, and the demarc would be on the router side of the CSU/ DSU. In some cases today, the telco even owns and manages the router at the customer site, again moving the point that would be considered the demarc. Regardless of where the demarc sits from a legal perspective, the term CPE still refers to the equipment at the telco customer's location.

WAN Cabling Standards

Cisco offers a large variety of different WAN interface cards for its routers, including synchronous and asynchronous serial interfaces. For any of the point-to-point serial links or Frame Relay links in this chapter, the router uses an interface that supports synchronous communication.

Synchronous serial interfaces in Cisco routers use a variety of proprietary physical connector types, such as the 60-pin D-shell connector shown at the top of the cable drawings in Figure 4-4. The cable connecting the router to the CSU/DSU uses a connector that fits the router serial interface on the router side, and a standardized WAN connector type that matches the CSU/DSU interface on the CSU/DSU end of the cable. Figure 4-4 shows a typical connection, with some of the serial cabling options listed.

Figure 4-4 *Serial Cabling Options*

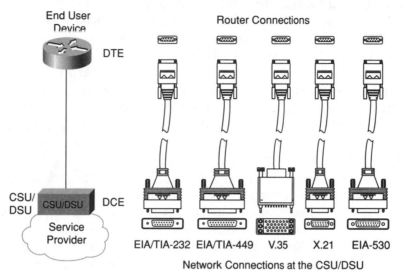

The engineer who deploys a network chooses the cable based on the connectors on the router and the CSU/DSU. Beyond that choice, engineers do not really need to think about how the cabling and pins work—they just work! Many of the pins are used for control functions, and a few are used for the transmission of data. Some pins are used for clocking, as described in the next section.

> **NOTE** The Telecommunications Industry Association (TIA) is accredited by the American National Standards Institute (ANSI) to represent the United States in work with international standards bodies. The TIA defines some of the WAN cabling standards, in addition to LAN cabling standards. For more information on these standards bodies, and to purchase copies of the standards, refer to the websites http://www.tiaonline.org and http://www.ansi.org.

The cable between the CSU/DSU and the telco CO typically uses an RJ-48 connector to connect to the CSU/DSU; the RJ-48 connector has the same size and shape as the RJ-45 connector used for Ethernet cables.

Many Cisco routers support serial interfaces that have an integrated internal CSU/DSU. With an internal CSU/DSU, the router does not need a cable connecting it to an external CSU/DSU because the CSU/DSU is internal to the router. In these cases, the serial cables shown in Figure 4-4 are not needed, and the physical line from the telco is connected to a port on the router, typically an RJ-48 port in the router serial interface card.

Clock Rates, Synchronization, DCE, and DTE

An enterprise network engineer who wants to install a new point-to-point leased line between two routers has several tasks to perform. First, the network engineer contacts a service provider and orders the circuit. As part of that process, the network engineer specifies how fast the circuit should run, in kilobits per second (kbps). While the telco installs the circuit, the engineer purchases two CSU/DSUs, installs one at each site, and configures each CSU/DSU. The network engineer also purchases and installs routers, and connects serial cables from each router to the respective CSU/DSU using the cables shown in Figure 4-4. Eventually, the telco installs the new line into the customer premises, and the line can be connected to the CSU/DSUs, as shown in Figure 4-3.

Every WAN circuit ordered from a service provider runs at one of many possible predefined speeds. This speed is often referred to as the clock rate, bandwidth, or link speed. The enterprise network engineer (the customer) must specify the speed when ordering a circuit, and the telco installs a circuit that runs at that speed. Additionally, the enterprise network engineer must configure the CSU/DSU on each end of the link to match the defined speed.

To make the link work, the various devices need to synchronize their clocks so that they run at exactly the same speed—a process called synchronization. *Synchronous circuits* impose time ordering at the link's sending and receiving ends. Essentially, all devices agree to try to run at the exact same speed, but it is expensive to build devices that truly can operate at exactly the same speed. So, the devices operate at close to the same speed and listen to the speed of the other device on the other side of the link. One side makes small adjustments in its rate to match the other side.

Synchronization occurs between the two CSU/DSUs on a leased line by having one CSU/DSU (the slave) adjust its clock to match the clock rate of the other CSU/DSU (the master). The process works almost like the scenes in spy novels in which the spies synchronize their watches; in this case, the networking devices synchronize their clocks several times per second.

In practice, the clocking concept includes a hierarchy of different clock sources. The telco provides clocking information to the CSU/DSUs based on the transitions in the electrical signal on the circuit. The two CSU/DSUs then adjust their speeds to match the clocking signals from the telco. The CSU/DSUs each supply clocking signals to the routers so that the routers simply react, sending and receiving data at the correct rate. So, from the routers' perspectives, the CSU/DSU is considered to be *clocking* the link.

A couple of other key WAN terms relate to the process of clocking. The device that provides clocking, typically the CSU/DSU, is considered to be the data communications equipment (DCE). The device receiving clocking, typically the router, is referred to as data terminal equipment (DTE).

Building a WAN Link in a Lab

On a practical note, when purchasing serial cables from Cisco, you can pick either a DTE or a DCE cable. You pick the type of cable based on whether the router is acting like DTE or DCE. In most cases with a real WAN link, the router acts as DTE, so the router must use a DTE cable to connect to the CSU/DSU.

You can build a serial link in a lab without using any CSU/DSUs, but to do so, one router must supply clocking. When building a lab to study for any of the Cisco exams, you do not need to buy CSU/DSUs or order a WAN circuit. You can buy two routers, a DTE serial cable for one router, and a DCE serial cable for the other, and connect the two cables together. The router with the DCE cable in it can be configured to provide clocking, meaning that you do not need a CSU/DSU. So, you can build a WAN in your home lab, saving hundreds of dollars by not buying CSU/DSUs. The DTE and DCE cables can be connected to each other (the DCE cable has a female connector and the DTE cable has a male connector) and to the two routers. With one additional configuration command on one of the routers (the **clock rate** command), you have a point-to-point serial link. This type of connection between two routers sometimes is called a back-to-back serial connection.

Figure 4-5 shows the cabling for a back-to-back serial connection and also shows that the combined DCE/DTE cables reverse the transmit and receive pins, much like a crossover Ethernet cable allows two directly connected devices to communicate.

Figure 4-5 *Serial Cabling Uses a DTE Cable and a DCE Cable*

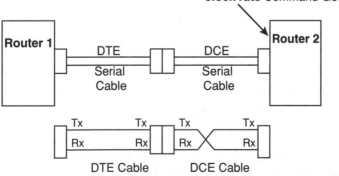

As you see in Figure 4-5, the DTE cable, the same cable that you typically use to connect to a CSU/DSU, does not swap the Tx and Rx pins. The DCE cable swaps transmit and receive, so the wiring with one router's Tx pin connected to the other router's Rx, and vice versa, remains intact. The router with the DCE cable installed needs to supply clocking, so the **clock rate** command will be added to that router to define the speed.

Link Speeds Offered by Telcos

No matter what you call them—telcos, PTTs, service providers—these companies do not simply let you pick the exact speed of a WAN link. Instead, standards define how fast a point-to-point link can run.

For a long time, the telcos of the world made more money selling voice services than selling data services. As technology progressed during the mid-twentieth century, the telcos of the world developed a standard for sending voice using digital transmissions. Digital signaling inside their networks allowed for the growth of more profitable data services, such as leased lines. It also allowed better efficiencies, making the build-out of the expanding voice networks much less expensive.

The original mechanism used for converting analog voice to a digital signal is called pulse code modulation (PCM). PCM defines that an incoming analog voice signal should be sampled 8000 times per second, and each sample should be represented by an 8-bit code. So, 64,000 bits were needed to represent 1 second of voice. When the telcos of the world built their first digital networks, they chose a baseline transmission speed of 64 kbps because that was the necessary bandwidth for a single voice call. The term digital signal level 0 (DS0) refers to the standard for a single 64-kbps line.

Today, most telcos offer leased lines in multiples of 64 kbps. In the United States, the digital signal level 1 (DS1) standard defines a single line that supports 24 DS0s, plus an 8-kbps overhead channel, for a speed of 1.544 Mbps. (A DS1 is also called a T1 line.) Another option is a digital signal level 3 (DS3) service, also called a T3 line, which holds 28 DS1s. Other parts of the world use different standards, with Europe and Japan using standards that hold 32 DS0s, called an E1 line, with an E3 line holding 16 E1s.

> **NOTE**   The combination of multiple slower-speed lines and channels into one faster-speed line or channel—for instance, combining 24 DS0s into a single T1 line—is generally called time-division multiplexing (TDM).

Table 4-2 lists some of the standards for WAN speeds. Included in the table are the type of line, plus the type of signaling (for example, DS1). The signaling specifications define the electrical signals that encode a binary 1 or 0 on the line. You should be aware of the general idea, and remember the key terms for T1 and E1 lines in particular, for the ICND1 exam.

Table 4-2 *WAN Speed Summary*

Key
Topic

Name(s) of Line	Bit Rate
DS0	64 kbps
DS1 (T1)	1.544 Mbps (24 DS0s, plus 8 kbps overhead)
DS3 (T3)	44.736 Mbps (28 DS1s, plus management overhead)
E1	2.048 Mbps (32 DS0s)
E3	34.064 Mbps (16 E1s, plus management overhead)
J1 (Y1)	2.048 Mbps (32 DS0s; Japanese standard)

The leased circuits described so far in this chapter form the basis for the WAN services used by many enterprises today. Next, this chapter explains the data link layer protocols used when a leased circuit connects two routers.

OSI Layer 2 for Point-to-Point WANs

WAN protocols used on point-to-point serial links provide the basic function of data delivery across that one link. The two most popular data link layer protocols used on point-to-point links are High-Level Data Link Control (HDLC) and Point-to-Point Protocol (PPP).

HDLC

Because point-to-point links are relatively simple, HDLC has only a small amount of work to do. In particular, HDLC needs to determine if the data passed the link without any errors; HDLC discards the frame if errors occurred. Additionally, HDLC needs to identify the type of packet inside the HDLC frame so the receiving device knows the packet type.

To achieve the main goal of delivering data across the link and to check for errors and identify the packet type, HDLC defines framing. The HDLC header includes an Address field and a Protocol Type field, with the trailer containing a frame check sequence (FCS) field. Figure 4-6 outlines the standard HDLC frame and the HDLC frame that is Cisco proprietary.

HDLC defines a 1-byte Address field, although on point-to-point links, it is not really needed. Having an Address field in HDLC is sort of like when I have lunch with my friend Gary, and only Gary. I do not need to start every sentence with "Hey Gary"—he knows I am talking to him. On point-to-point WAN links, the router on one end of the link knows that there is only one possible recipient of the data—the router on the other end of the link—so the address does not really matter today.

Figure 4-6 *HDLC Framing*

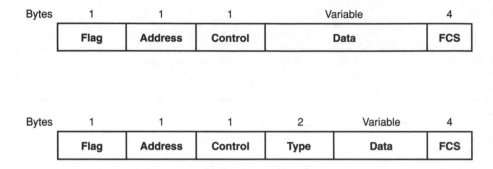

> **NOTE**   The Address field was useful in years past, when the telco would sell multidrop circuits. These circuits had more than two devices on the circuit, so an Address field was needed.

HDLC performs error detection just like Ethernet—it uses an FCS field in the HDLC trailer. And just like Ethernet, if a received frame has errors in it, the device receiving the frame discards the frame, with no error recovery performed by HDLC.

HDLC also performs the function of identifying the encapsulated data, just like Ethernet. When a router receives an HDLC frame, it wants to know what type of packet is held inside the frame. The Cisco implementation of HDLC includes a *Protocol Type* field that identifies the type of packet inside the frame. Cisco uses the same values in its 2-byte HDLC Protocol Type field as it does in the Ethernet Protocol Type field.

The original HDLC standards did not include a Protocol Type field, so Cisco added one to support the first serial links on Cisco routers, back in the early days of Cisco in the latter 1980s. By adding something to the HDLC header, Cisco made its version of HDLC proprietary. So, the Cisco implementation of HDLC will not work when connecting a Cisco router to another vendor's router.

HDLC is very simple. There simply is not a lot of work for the point-to-point data link layer protocols to perform.

Point-to-Point Protocol

The International Telecommunications Union (ITU), previously known as the Consultative Committee for International Telecommunications Technologies (CCITT), first defined HDLC. Later, the Internet Engineering Task Force (IETF) saw the need for another data link layer protocol for use between routers over a point-to-point link. In RFC 1661 (1994), the IETF created the Point to Point Protocol (PPP).

Comparing the basics, PPP behaves much like HDLC. The framing looks identical to the Cisco proprietary HDLC framing. There is an Address field, but the addressing does not matter. PPP does discard errored frames that do not pass the FCS check. Additionally, PPP uses a 2-byte Protocol Type field. However, because the Protocol Type field is part of the standard for PPP, any vendor that conforms to the PPP standard can communicate with other vendor products. So, when connecting a Cisco router to another vendor's router over a point-to-point serial link, PPP is the data link layer protocol of choice.

PPP was defined much later than the original HDLC specifications. As a result, the creators of PPP included many additional features that had not been seen in WAN data link layer protocols up to that time, so PPP has become the most popular and feature-rich of WAN data link layer protocols.

Point-to-Point WAN Summary

Point-to-point WAN leased lines and their associated data link layer protocols use another set of terms and concepts beyond those covered for LANs, as outlined in Table 4-3.

Table 4-3 *WAN Terminology*

Term	Definition
Synchronous	The imposition of time ordering on a bit stream. Practically, a device tries to use the same speed as another device on the other end of a serial link. However, by examining transitions between voltage states on the link, the device can notice slight variations in the speed on each end and can adjust its speed accordingly.
Clock source	The device to which the other devices on the link adjust their speed when using synchronous links.
CSU/DSU	Channel service unit/data service unit. Used on digital links as an interface to the telephone company in the United States. Routers typically use a short cable from a serial interface to a CSU/DSU, which is attached to the line from the telco with a similar configuration at the other router on the other end of the link.
Telco	Telephone company.

continues

Table 4-3   *WAN Terminology (Continued)*

Term	Definition
Four-wire circuit	A line from the telco with four wires, composed of two twisted-pair wires. Each pair is used to send in one direction, so a four-wire circuit allows full-duplex communication.
T1	A line from the telco that allows transmission of data at 1.544 Mbps.
E1	Similar to a T1, but used in Europe. It uses a rate of 2.048 Mbps and 32 64-kbps channels.

Also, just for survival when talking about WANs, keep in mind that all the following terms may be used to refer to a point-to-point leased line as covered so far in this chapter:

leased line, leased circuit, link, serial link, serial line, point-to-point link, circuit

Frame Relay and Packet-Switching Services

Service providers offer a class of WAN services, different from leased lines, that can be categorized as *packet-switching services*. In a packet-switching service, physical WAN connectivity exists, similar to a leased line. However, a company can connect a large number of routers to the packet-switching service, using a single serial link from each router into the packet-switching service. Once connected, each router can send packets to all the other routers—much like all the devices connected to an Ethernet hub or switch can send data directly to each other.

Two types of packet-switching service are very popular today, Frame Relay and Asynchronous Transfer Mode (ATM), with Frame Relay being much more common. This section introduces the main concepts behind packet-switching services, and explains the basics of Frame Relay.

The Scaling Benefits of Packet Switching

Point-to-point WANs can be used to connect a pair of routers at multiple remote sites. However, an alternative WAN service, Frame Relay, has many advantages over point-to-point links, particularly when you connect many sites via a WAN. To introduce you to Frame Relay, this section focuses on a few of the key benefits compared to leased lines, one of which you can easily see when considering the illustration in Figure 4-7.

Figure 4-7   *Two Leased Lines to Two Branch Offices*

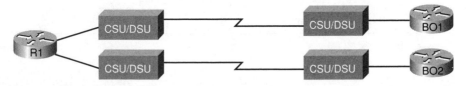

In Figure 4-7, a main site is connected to two branch offices, labeled BO1 and BO2. The main site router, R1, requires two serial interfaces and two separate CSU/DSUs. But what happens when the company grows to 10 sites? Or 100 sites? Or 500 sites? For each point-to-point line, R1 needs a separate physical serial interface and a separate CSU/DSU. As you can imagine, growth to hundreds of sites will take many routers, with many interfaces each, and lots of rack space for the routers and CSU/DSUs.

Now imagine that the phone company salesperson says the following to you when you have two leased lines, or circuits, installed (as shown in Figure 4-7):

> You know, we can install Frame Relay instead. You will need only one serial interface on R1 and one CSU/DSU. To scale to 100 sites, you might need two or three more serial interfaces on R1 for more bandwidth, but that is it. And by the way, because your leased lines run at 128 kbps today, we will guarantee that you can send and receive that much data to and from each site. We will upgrade the line at R1 to T1 speed (1.544 Mbps). When you have more traffic than 128 kbps to a site, go ahead and send it! If we have capacity, we will forward it, with no extra charge. And by the way, did I tell you that it is cheaper than leased lines anyway?

You consider the facts for a moment: Frame Relay is cheaper, it is at least as fast as (probably faster than) what you have now, and it allows you to save money when you grow. So, you quickly sign the contract with the Frame Relay provider, before the salesperson can change their mind, and migrate to Frame Relay. Does this story seem a bit ridiculous? Sure. The cost and scaling benefits of Frame Relay, as compared to leased lines, however, are very significant. As a result, many networks moved from using leased lines to Frame Relay, particularly in the 1990s, with a significantly large installed base of Frame Relay networks today. In the next few pages, you will see how Frame Relay works and realize how Frame Relay can provide functions claimed by the fictitious salesperson.

Frame Relay Basics

Frame Relay networks provide more features and benefits than simple point-to-point WAN links, but to do that, Frame Relay protocols are more detailed. Frame Relay networks are multiaccess networks, which means that more than two devices can attach to the network, similar to LANs. To support more than two devices, the protocols must be a little more detailed. Figure 4-8 introduces some basic connectivity concepts for Frame Relay.
Figure 4-8 reflects the fact that Frame Relay uses the same Layer 1 features as a point-to-point leased line. For a Frame Relay service, a leased line is installed between each router and a nearby Frame Relay switch; these links are called *access links*. The access links run at the same speed and use the same signaling standards as do point-to-point leased lines. However, instead of extending from one router to the other, each leased line runs from one router to a Frame Relay switch.

Figure 4-8 *Frame Relay Components*

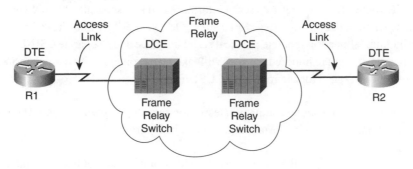

The difference between Frame Relay and point-to-point links is that the equipment in the telco actually examines the data frames sent by the router. Frame Relay defines its own data-link header and trailer. Each Frame Relay header holds an address field called a data-link connection identifier (DLCI). The WAN switch forwards the frame based on the DLCI, sending the frame through the provider's network until it gets to the remote-site router on the other side of the Frame Relay cloud.

> **NOTE** The Frame Relay header and trailer are defined by a protocol called Link Access Procedure – Frame (LAPF).

Because the equipment in the telco can forward one frame to one remote site and another frame to another remote site, Frame Relay is considered to be a form of *packet switching*. This term means that the service provider actually chooses where to send each data packet sent into the provider's network, switching one packet to one device, and the next packet to another. However, Frame Relay protocols most closely resemble OSI Layer 2 protocols; the term usually used for the bits sent by a Layer 2 device is *frame*. So, Frame Relay is also called a *frame-switching service*, while the term packet switching is a more general term.

The terms DCE and DTE actually have a second set of meanings in the context of any packet-switching or frame-switching service. With Frame Relay, the Frame Relay switches are called DCE, and the customer equipment—routers, in this case—are called DTE. In this case, DCE refers to the device providing the service, and the term DTE refers to the device needing the frame-switching service. At the same time, the CSU/DSU provides clocking to the router, so from a Layer 1 perspective, the CSU/DSU is still the DCE and the router is still the DTE. It is just two different uses of the same terms.

Figure 4-8 depicted the physical and logical connectivity at each connection to the Frame Relay network. In contrast, Figure 4-9 shows the end-to-end connectivity associated with a virtual circuit (VC).

Figure 4-9   *Frame Relay VC Concepts*

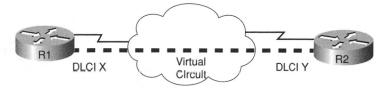

The logical path that a frame travels between each pair of routers is called a Frame Relay VC. In Figure 4-9, a single VC is represented by the dashed line between the routers. Typically, the service provider preconfigures all the required details of a VC; these VCs are called permanent virtual circuits (PVC). When R1 needs to forward a packet to R2, it encapsulates the Layer 3 packet into a Frame Relay header and trailer and then sends the frame. R1 uses a Frame Relay address called a DLCI in the Frame Relay header, with the DLCI identifying the correct VC to the provider. This allows the switches to deliver the frame to R2, ignoring the details of the Layer 3 packet and looking at only the Frame Relay header and trailer. Recall that on a point-to-point serial link, the service provider forwards the frame over a physical circuit between R1 and R2. This transaction is similar in Frame Relay, where the provider forwards the frame over a logical VC from R1 to R2.

Frame Relay provides significant advantages over simply using point-to-point leased lines. The primary advantage has to do with VCs. Consider Figure 4-10 with Frame Relay instead of three point-to-point leased lines. Frame Relay creates a logical path (a VC) between two Frame Relay DTE devices. A VC acts like a point-to-point circuit, but physically it is not—it is virtual. For example, R1 terminates two VCs—one whose other endpoint is R2 and one whose other endpoint is R3. R1 can send traffic directly to either of the other two routers by sending it over the appropriate VC, although R1 has only one physical access link to the Frame Relay network.

VCs share the access link and the Frame Relay network. For example, both VCs terminating at R1 use the same access link. So, with large networks with many WAN sites that need to connect to a central location, only one physical access link is required from the main site router to the Frame Relay network. By contrast, using point-to-point links would require a physical circuit, a separate CSU/DSU, and a separate physical interface on the router for each point-to-point link. So, Frame Relay enables you to expand the WAN but add less hardware to do so.

Figure 4-10 *Typical Frame Relay Network with Three Sites*

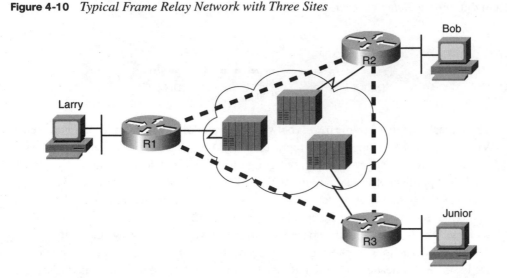

Many customers of a single Frame Relay service provider share that provider's Frame Relay network. Originally, people with leased-line networks were reluctant to migrate to Frame Relay because they would be competing with other customers for the provider's capacity inside the service provider's network. To address these fears, Frame Relay is designed with the concept of a committed information rate (CIR). Each VC has a CIR, which is a guarantee by the provider that a particular VC gets at least that much bandwidth. You can think of the CIR of a VC like the bandwidth or clock rate of a point-to-point circuit, except that it is the minimum value—you can actually send more, in most cases.

Even in this three-site network, it is probably less expensive to use Frame Relay than to use point-to-point links. Now imagine a much larger network, with a 100 sites, that needs any-to-any connectivity. A point-to-point link design would require 4950 leased lines! In addition, you would need 99 serial interfaces per router. By contrast, with a Frame Relay design, you could have 100 access links to local Frame Relay switches (1 per router) with 4950 VCs running over the access links. Also, you would need only one serial interface on each router. As a result, the Frame Relay topology is easier for the service provider to implement, costs the provider less, and makes better use of the core of the provider's network. As you would expect, that makes it less expensive to the Frame Relay customer as well. For connecting many WAN sites, Frame Relay is simply more cost-effective than leased lines.

Exam Preparation Tasks

Review All the Key Topics

Review the most important topics from inside the chapter, noted with the key topics icon in the outer margin of the page. Table 4-4 lists a reference of these key topics and the page numbers on which each is found.

Table 4-4 *Key Topics for Chapter 4*

Key Topic Element	Description	Page Number
Figure 4-3	Shows typical cabling diagram of CPE for a leased line	77
Table 4-2	Typical speeds for WAN leased lines	83
Figure 4-6	HDLC framing	84
Table 4-3	List of key WAN terminology	85-86
Paragraph	List of synonyms for "point-to-point leased line"	86
Figure 4-10	Diagram of Frame Relay virtual circuits	90

Key
Topic

Complete the Tables and Lists from Memory

Print a copy of Appendix H, "Memory Tables" (found on the CD-ROM), or at least the section for this chapter, and complete the tables and lists from memory. Appendix I, "Memory Tables Answer Key," also on the CD-ROM, includes completed tables and lists to check your work.

Definitions of Key Terms

Define the following key terms from this chapter, and check your answers in the glossary.

access link, back-to-back link, clocking, DTE (Layer 1), CSU/DSU, DCE (Layer 1), DS0, DS1, Frame Relay, HDLC, leased line, packet switching, PPP, serial cable, synchronous, T1, virtual circuit

This chapter covers the following subjects:

Overview of Network Layer Functions: The first section introduces the concepts of routing, logical addressing, and routing protocols.

IP Addressing: Next, the basics of 32-bit IP addresses are explained, with emphasis on how the organization aids the routing process.

IP Routing: This section explains how hosts and routers decide how to forward a packet.

IP Routing Protocols: This brief section explains the basics of how routing protocols populate each router's routing tables.

Network Layer Utilities: This section introduces several other functions useful to the overall process of packet delivery.

CHAPTER 5

Fundamentals of IP Addressing and Routing

The OSI physical layer (Layer 1) defines how to transmit bits over a particular type of physical network. The OSI data link layer (Layer 2) defines the framing, addressing, error detection, and rules for when to use the physical medium. Although they are important, these two layers do not define how to deliver data between devices that exist far from each other, with many different physical networks sitting between the two computers.

This chapter explains the function and purpose of the OSI network layer (Layer 3): the end-to-end delivery of data between two computers. Regardless of the type of physical network to which each endpoint computer is attached, and regardless of the types of physical networks used between the two computers, the network layer defines how to forward, or route, data between the two computers.

This chapter covers the basics of how the network layer routes data packets from one computer to another. After reviewing the full story at a basic level, this chapter examines in more detail the network layer of TCP/IP, including IP addressing (which enables efficient routing), IP routing (the forwarding process itself), IP routing protocols (the process by which routers learn routes), and several other small but important features of the network layer.

"Do I Know This Already?" Quiz

The "Do I Know This Already?" quiz allows you to assess whether you should read the entire chapter. If you miss no more than one of these 13 self-assessment questions, you might want to move ahead to the "Exam Preparation Tasks" section. Table 5-1 lists the major headings in this chapter and the "Do I Know This Already?" quiz questions covering the material in those sections. This helps you assess your knowledge of these specific areas. The answers to the "Do I Know This Already?" quiz appear in Appendix A.

Table 5-1   *"Do I Know This Already?" Foundation Topics Section-to-Question Mapping*

Foundation Topics Section	Questions
Overview of Network Layer Functions	1 – 3
IP Addressing	4 – 8
IP Routing	9, 10
IP Routing Protocols	11
Network Layer Utilities	12, 13

1. Which of the following are functions of OSI Layer 3 protocols?

   a. Logical addressing

   b. Physical addressing

   c. Path selection

   d. Arbitration

   e. Error recovery

2. Imagine that PC1 needs to send some data to PC2, and PC1 and PC2 are separated by several routers. What are the largest entities that make it from PC1 to PC2?

   a. Frame

   b. Segment

   c. Packet

   d. L5 PDU

   e. L3 PDU

   f. L1 PDU

3. Imagine a network with two routers that are connected with a point-to-point HDLC serial link. Each router has an Ethernet, with PC1 sharing the Ethernet with Router1, and PC2 sharing the Ethernet with Router2. When PC1 sends data to PC2, which of the following is true?

   a. Router1 strips the Ethernet header and trailer off the frame received from PC1, never to be used again.

   b. Router1 encapsulates the Ethernet frame inside an HDLC header and sends the frame to Router2, which extracts the Ethernet frame for forwarding to PC2.

    c.   Router1 strips the Ethernet header and trailer off the frame received from PC1, which is exactly re-created by R2 before forwarding data to PC2.

    d.   Router1 removes the Ethernet, IP, and TCP headers and rebuilds the appropriate headers before forwarding the packet to Router2.

4.   Which of the following are valid Class C IP addresses that can be assigned to hosts?

    a.   1.1.1.1

    b.   200.1.1.1

    c.   128.128.128.128

    d.   224.1.1.1

    e.   223.223.223.255

5.   What is the range of values for the first octet for Class A IP networks?

    a.   0 to 127

    b.   0 to 126

    c.   1 to 127

    d.   1 to 126

    e.   128 to 191

    f.   128 to 192

6.   PC1 and PC2 are on two different Ethernets that are separated by an IP router. PC1's IP address is 10.1.1.1, and no subnetting is used. Which of the following addresses could be used for PC2?

    a.   10.1.1.2

    b.   10.2.2.2

    c.   10.200.200.1

    d.   9.1.1.1

    e.   225.1.1.1

    f.   1.1.1.1

7. Each Class B network contains how many IP addresses that can be assigned to hosts?

  a. 16,777,214

  b. 16,777,216

  c. 65,536

  d. 65,534

  e. 65,532

  f. 32,768

  g. 32,766

8. Each Class C network contains how many IP addresses that can be assigned to hosts?

  a. 65,534

  b. 65,532

  c. 32,768

  d. 32,766

  e. 256

  f. 254

9. Which of the following does a router normally use when making a decision about routing TCP/IP packets?

  a. Destination MAC address

  b. Source MAC address

  c. Destination IP address

  d. Source IP address

  e. Destination MAC and IP address

10. Which of the following are true about a LAN-connected TCP/IP host and its IP routing (forwarding) choices?

  a. The host always sends packets to its default gateway.

  b. The host sends packets to its default gateway if the destination IP address is in a different class of IP network than the host.

  c. The host sends packets to its default gateway if the destination IP address is in a different subnet than the host.

  d. The host sends packets to its default gateway if the destination IP address is in the same subnet as the host.

11. Which of the following are functions of a routing protocol?

    a. Advertising known routes to neighboring routers.

    b. Learning routes for subnets directly connected to the router.

    c. Learning routes, and putting those routes into the routing table, for routes advertised to the router by its neighboring routers.

    d. To forward IP packets based on a packet's destination IP address.

12. Which of the following protocols allows a client PC to discover the IP address of another computer based on that other computer's name?

    a. ARP

    b. RARP

    c. DNS

    d. DHCP

13. Which of the following protocols allows a client PC to request assignment of an IP address as well as learn its default gateway?

    a. ARP

    b. RARP

    c. DNS

    d. DHCP

Foundation Topics

OSI Layer 3-equivalent protocols define how packets can be delivered from the computer that creates the packet all the way to the computer that needs to receive the packet. To reach that goal, an OSI network layer protocol defines the following features:

Routing: The process of forwarding packets (Layer 3 PDUs).

Logical addressing: Addresses that can be used regardless of the type of physical networks used, providing each device (at least) one address. Logical addressing enables the routing process to identify a packet's source and destination.

Routing protocol: A protocol that aids routers by dynamically learning about the groups of addresses in the network, which in turn allows the routing (forwarding) process to work well.

Other utilities: The network layer also relies on other utilities. For TCP/IP, these utilities include Domain Name System (DNS), Dynamic Host Configuration Protocol (DHCP), Address Resolution Protocol (ARP), and ping.

NOTE The term *path selection* sometimes is used to mean the same thing as routing protocol, sometimes is used to refer to the routing (forwarding) of packets, and sometimes is used for both functions.

This chapter begins with an overview of routing, logical addressing, and routing protocols. Following that, the text moves on to more details about the specifics of the TCP/IP network layer (called the internetwork layer in the TCP/IP model). In particular, the topics of IP addressing, routing, routing protocols, and network layer utilities are covered.

Overview of Network Layer Functions

A protocol that defines routing and logical addressing is considered to be a network layer, or Layer 3, protocol. OSI does define a unique Layer 3 protocol called Connectionless Network Services (CLNS), but, as usual with OSI protocols, you rarely see it in networks today. In the recent past, you might have seen many other network layer protocols, such as Internet Protocol (IP), Novell Internetwork Packet Exchange (IPX), or AppleTalk Datagram Delivery Protocol (DDP). Today, the only Layer 3 protocol that is used widely is the TCP/IP network layer protocol—specifically, IP.

The main job of IP is to route data (packets) from the source host to the destination host. Because a network might need to forward large numbers of packets, the IP routing process is very simple. IP does not require any overhead agreements or messages before sending a packet, making IP a connectionless protocol. IP tries to deliver each packet, but if a router or host's IP process cannot deliver the packet, it is discarded—with no error recovery. The goal with IP is to deliver packets with as little per-packet work as possible, which allows for large packet volumes. Other protocols perform some of the other useful networking functions. For example, Transmission Control Protocol (TCP), which is described in detail in Chapter 6, "Fundamentals of TCP/IP Transport, Applications, and Security," provides error recovery, resending lost data, but IP does not.

IP routing relies on the structure and meaning of IP addresses, and IP addressing was designed with IP routing in mind. This first major section of this chapter begins by introducing IP routing, with some IP addressing concepts introduced along the way. Then, the text examines IP addressing fundamentals.

Routing (Forwarding)

Routing focuses on the end-to-end logic of forwarding data. Figure 5-1 shows a simple example of how routing works. The logic illustrated by the figure is relatively simple. For PC1 to send data to PC2, it must send something to router R1, which sends it to router R2, and then to router R3, and finally to PC2. However, the logic used by each device along the path varies slightly.

Figure 5-1 *Routing Logic: PC1 Sending to PC2*

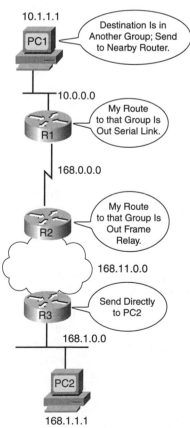

PC1's Logic: Sending Data to a Nearby Router

In this example, illustrated in Figure 5-1, PC1 has some data to send to PC2. Because PC2 is not on the same Ethernet as PC1, PC1 needs to send the packet to a router that is attached to the same Ethernet as PC1. The sender sends a data-link frame across the medium to the nearby router; this frame includes the packet in the data portion of the frame. That frame uses data link layer (Layer 2) addressing in the data-link header to ensure that the nearby router receives the frame.

The main point here is that the computer that created the data does not know much about the network—just how to get the data to some nearby router. Using a post office analogy, it's like knowing how to get to the local post office, but nothing more. Likewise, PC1 needs to know only how to get the packet to R1, not the rest of the path used to send the packet to PC2.

R1 and R2's Logic: Routing Data Across the Network

R1 and R2 both use the same general process to route the packet. The *routing table* for any particular network layer protocol contains a list of network layer address *groupings*. Instead of a single entry in the routing table per individual destination network layer address, there is one routing table entry per group. The router compares the destination network layer address in the packet to the entries in the routing table and makes a match. This matching entry in the routing table tells this router where to forward the packet next. The words in the bubbles in Figure 5-1 point out this basic logic.

The concept of network layer address grouping is similar to the U.S. zip code system. Everyone living in the same vicinity is in the same zip code, and the postal sorters just look for the zip codes, ignoring the rest of the address. Likewise, in Figure 5-1, everyone in this network whose IP address starts with 168.1 is on the Ethernet on which PC2 resides, so the routers can have just one routing table entry that means "all addresses that start with 168.1."

Any intervening routers repeat the same process: the router compares the packet's destination network layer (Layer 3) address to the groups listed in its routing table, and the matched routing table entry tells this router where to forward the packet next. Eventually, the packet is delivered to the router connected to the network or subnet of the destination host (R3), as shown in Figure 5-1.

R3's Logic: Delivering Data to the End Destination

The final router in the path, R3, uses almost the exact same logic as R1 and R2, but with one minor difference. R3 needs to forward the packet directly to PC2, not to some other router. On the surface, that difference seems insignificant. In the next section, when you read about how the network layer uses the data link layer, the significance of the difference will become obvious.

Network Layer Interaction with the Data Link Layer

When the network layer protocol is processing the packet, it decides to send the packet out the appropriate network interface. Before the actual bits can be placed onto that physical interface, the network layer must hand off the packet to the data link layer protocols, which, in turn, ask the physical layer to actually send the data. And as was described in Chapter 3, "Fundamentals of LANs," the data link layer adds the appropriate header and trailer to the packet, creating a frame, before sending the frames over each physical network. The routing process forwards the packet, and only the packet, end-to-end through the network, *discarding data-link headers and trailers along the way.* The network layer processes deliver the packet end-to-end, using successive data-link headers and trailers just to get the packet to the next router or host in the path. Each successive data link layer just gets the packet from one device to the next. Figure 5-2 points out the key encapsulation logic on each device, using the same examples as in Figure 5-1.

Figure 5-2   *Network Layer and Data Link Layer Encapsulation*

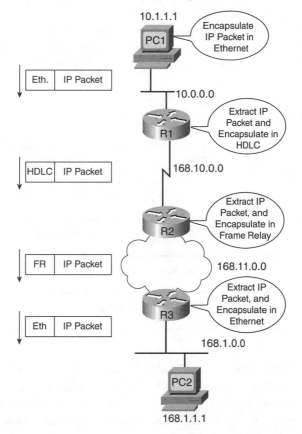

Because the routers build new data-link headers and trailers (trailers not shown in the figure), and because the new headers contain data-link addresses, the PCs and routers must have some way to decide what data-link addresses to use. An example of how the router determines which data-link address to use is the IP Address Resolution Protocol (ARP). *ARP is used to dynamically learn the data-link address of an IP host connected to a LAN.* You will read more about ARP later in this chapter.

Routing as covered so far has two main concepts:

■ The process of routing forwards Layer 3 packets, also called *Layer 3 protocol data units* (*L3 PDU*), based on the destination Layer 3 address in the packet.

■ The routing process uses the data link layer to encapsulate the Layer 3 packets into Layer 2 frames for transmission across each successive data link.

IP Packets and the IP Header

The IP packets encapsulated in the data-link frames shown in Figure 5-2 have an IP header, followed by additional headers and data. For reference, Figure 5-3 shows the fields inside the standard 20-byte IPv4 header, with no optional IP header fields, as is typically seen in most networks today.

Figure 5-3 *IPv4 Header*

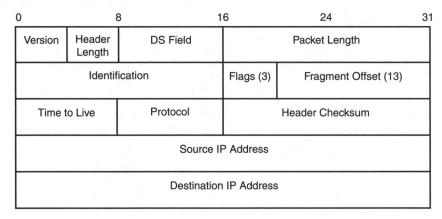

Of the different fields inside the IPv4 header, this book, and the companion *ICND2 Official Exam Certification Guide*, ignore all the fields except the Time-To-Live (TTL) (covered in Chapter 15 in this book), protocol (Chapter 6 of the ICND2 book), and the source and destination IP address fields (scattered throughout most chapters). However, for reference, Table 5-2 briefly describes each field.

Table 5-2 *IPv4 Header Fields*

Field	Meaning
Version	Version of the IP protocol. Most networks use version 4 today.
IHL	IP Header Length. Defines the length of the IP header, including optional fields.
DS Field	Differentiated Services Field. It is used for marking packets for the purpose of applying different quality-of-service (QoS) levels to different packets.
Packet length	Identifies the entire length of the IP packet, including the data.
Identification	Used by the IP packet fragmentation process; all fragments of the original packet contain the same identifier.
Flags	3 bits used by the IP packet fragmentation process.
Fragment offset	A number used to help hosts reassemble fragmented packets into the original larger packet.
TTL	Time to live. A value used to prevent routing loops.
Protocol	A field that identifies the contents of the data portion of the IP packet. For example, protocol 6 implies that a TCP header is the first thing in the IP packet data field.
Header Checksum	A value used to store an FCS value, whose purpose is to determine if any bit errors occurred in the IP header.
Source IP address	The 32-bit IP address of the sender of the packet.
Destination IP address	The 32-bit IP address of the intended recipient of the packet.

This section next examines the concept of network layer addressing and how it aids the routing process.

Network Layer (Layer 3) Addressing

Network layer protocols define the format and meaning of logical addresses. (The term *logical address* does not really refer to whether the addresses make sense, but rather to contrast these addresses with physical addresses.) Each computer that needs to communicate will have (at least) one network layer address so that other computers can send data packets to that address, expecting the network to deliver the data packet to the correct computer.

One key feature of network layer addresses is that they were designed to allow logical grouping of addresses. In other words, something about the numeric value of an address implies a group or set of addresses, all of which are considered to be in the same grouping. With IP addresses, this group is called a *network* or a *subnet*. These groupings work just like USPS zip (postal) codes, allowing the routers (mail sorters) to speedily route (sort) lots of packets (letters).

Just like postal street addresses, network layer addresses are grouped based on physical location in a network. The rules differ for some network layer protocols, but with IP addressing, the first part of the IP address is the same for all the addresses in one grouping. For example, in Figures 5-1 and 5-2, the following IP addressing conventions define the groups of IP addresses (IP networks) for all hosts on that internetwork:

■ Hosts on the top Ethernet: Addresses start with 10

■ Hosts on the R1-R2 serial link: Addresses start with 168.10

■ Hosts on the R2-R3 Frame Relay network: Addresses start with 168.11

■ Hosts on the bottom Ethernet: Addresses start with 168.1

NOTE   To avoid confusion when writing about IP networks, many resources (including this one) use the term *internetwork* to refer more generally to a network made up of routers, switches, cables, and other equipment, and the word *network* to refer to the more specific concept of an IP network.

Routing relies on the fact that Layer 3 addresses are grouped. The routing tables for each network layer protocol can have one entry for the group, not one entry for each individual address. Imagine an Ethernet with 100 TCP/IP hosts. A router that needs to forward packets to any of those hosts needs only one entry in its IP routing table, with that one routing table entry representing the entire group of hosts on the Ethernet. This basic fact is one of the key reasons that routers can scale to allow hundreds of thousands of devices. It's very similar to the USPS zip code system. It would be ridiculous to have people in the same zip code live far from each other, or to have next-door neighbors be in different zip codes. The poor postman would spend all his time driving and flying around the country! Similarly, to make routing more efficient, network layer protocols group addresses.

Routing Protocols

Conveniently, the routers in Figures 5-1 and 5-2 somehow know the correct steps to take to forward the packet from PC1 to PC2. To make the correct choices, each router needs a routing table, with a route that matches the packet sent to PC2. The routes tell the router where to send the packet next.

In most cases, routers build their routing table entries dynamically using a routing protocol. Routing protocols learn about all the locations of the network layer "groups" in a network and advertise the groups' locations. As a result, each router can build a good routing table dynamically. Routing protocols define message formats and procedures, just like any other protocol. The end goal of each routing protocol is to fill the routing table with all known destination groups and with the best route to reach each group.

The terminology relating to routing protocols sometimes can get in the way. A *routing protocol* learns routes and puts those routes in a routing table. A *routed protocol* defines the type of packet forwarded, or routed, through a network. In Figures 5-1 and 5-2, the figures represent how IP packets are routed, so IP would be the *routed protocol*. If the routers used Routing Information Protocol (RIP) to learn the routes, RIP would be the *routing protocol*. Later in this chapter, the section "IP Routing Protocols" shows a detailed example of how routing protocols learn routes.

Now that you have seen the basic function of the OSI network layer at work, the rest of this chapter examines the key components of the end-to-end routing process for TCP/IP.

IP Addressing

IP addressing is absolutely the most important topic for the CCNA exams. By the time you have completed your study, you should be comfortable and confident in your understanding of IP addresses, their formats, the grouping concepts, how to subdivide groups into subnets, how to interpret the documentation for existing networks' IP addressing, and so on. Simply put, you had better know addressing and subnetting!

This section introduces IP addressing and subnetting and also covers the concepts behind the structure of an IP address, including how it relates to IP routing. In Chapter 12, "IP Addressing and Subnetting," you will read about the math behind IP addressing and subnetting.

IP Addressing Definitions

If a device wants to communicate using TCP/IP, it needs an IP address. When the device has an IP address and the appropriate software and hardware, it can send and receive IP packets. Any device that can send and receive IP packets is called an *IP host*.

> **NOTE** IP Version 4 (IPv4) is the most widely used version of IP. The *ICND2 Official Exam Certification Guide* covers the newer version of IP, IPv6. This book only briefly mentions IPv6 in Chapter 12 and otherwise ignores it. So, all references to IP addresses in this book should be taken to mean "IP version 4" addresses.

IP addresses consist of a 32-bit number, usually written in *dotted-decimal notation*. The "decimal" part of the term comes from the fact that each byte (8 bits) of the 32-bit IP address is shown as its decimal equivalent. The four resulting decimal numbers are written in sequence, with "dots," or decimal points, separating the numbers—hence the name *dotted decimal*. For instance, 168.1.1.1 is an IP address written in dotted-decimal form; the actual binary version is 10101000 00000001 00000001 00000001. (You almost never need to write down the binary version, but you will see how to convert between the two formats in Chapter 12.)

Each decimal number in an IP address is called an *octet*. The term *octet* is just a vendor-neutral term for *byte*. So, for an IP address of 168.1.1.1, the first octet is 168, the second octet is 1, and so on. The range of decimal numbers in each octet is between 0 and 255, inclusive.

Finally, note that each network interface uses a unique IP address. Most people tend to think that their computer has an IP address, but actually their computer's network card has an IP address. If you put two Ethernet cards in a PC to forward IP packets through both cards, they both would need unique IP addresses. Also, if your laptop has both an Ethernet NIC and a wireless NIC working at the same time, your laptop will have an IP address for each NIC. Similarly, routers, which typically have many network interfaces that forward IP packets, have an IP address for each interface.

Now that you have some idea of the basic terminology, the next section relates IP addressing to the routing concepts of OSI Layer 3.

How IP Addresses Are Grouped

The original specifications for TCP/IP grouped IP addresses into sets of consecutive addresses called *IP networks*. The addresses in a single network have the same numeric value in the first part of all addresses in the network. Figure 5-4 shows a simple internetwork that has three separate IP networks.

Figure 5-4   *Sample Network Using Class A, B, and C Network Numbers*

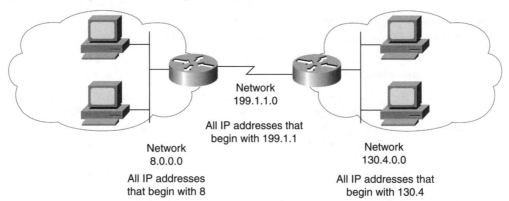

Network
199.1.1.0

All IP addresses that
begin with 199.1.1

Network
8.0.0.0

All IP addresses
that begin with 8

Network
130.4.0.0

All IP addresses that
begin with 130.4

The conventions of IP addressing and IP address grouping make routing easy. For example, all IP addresses that begin with 8 are in the IP network that contains all the hosts on the Ethernet on the left. Likewise, all IP addresses that begin with 130.4 are in another IP network that consists of all the hosts on the Ethernet on the right. Along the same lines, 199.1.1 is the prefix for all IP addresses on the network that includes the addresses on the serial link. (The only two IP addresses in this last grouping will be the IP addresses on each of the two routers.) By following this convention, the routers build a routing table with three entries—one for each prefix, or network number. For example, the router on the left can have one route that refers to all addresses that begin with 130.4, with that route directing the router to forward packets to the router on the right.

The example indirectly points out a couple of key points about how IP addresses are organized. To be a little more explicit, the following two rules summarize the facts about which IP addresses need to be in the same grouping:

- All IP addresses in the same group must not be separated by a router.

- IP addresses separated by a router must be in different groups.

Key Topic

As mentioned earlier in this chapter, IP addressing behaves similarly to zip codes. Everyone in my zip code lives in a little town in Ohio. If some members of my zip code were in California, some of my mail might be sent to California by mistake. Likewise, IP routing relies on the fact that all IP addresses in the same group (called either a network or a subnet) are in the same general location. If some of the IP addresses in my network or subnet were allowed to be on the other side of the internetwork compared to my computer, the routers in the network might incorrectly send some of the packets sent to my computer to the other side of the network.

Classes of Networks

Figure 5-4 and the surrounding text claim that the IP addresses of devices attached to the Ethernet on the left all start with 8 and that the IP addresses of devices attached to the Ethernet on the right all start with 130.4. Why only one number (8) for the "prefix" on the Ethernet on the left and two numbers (130 and 4) on the Ethernet on the right? Well, it all has to do with IP address classes.

RFC 791 defines the IP protocol, including several different classes of networks. IP defines three different network classes for addresses used by individual hosts—addresses called unicast IP addresses. These three network classes are called A, B, and C. TCP/IP defines Class D (multicast) addresses and Class E (experimental) addresses as well.

By definition, all addresses in the same Class A, B, or C network have the same numeric value *network* portion of the addresses. The rest of the address is called the *host* portion of the address.

Using the post office example, the network part of an IP address acts like the zip (postal) code, and the host part acts like the street address. Just as a letter-sorting machine three states away from you cares only about the zip code on a letter addressed to you, a router three hops away from you cares only about the network number that your address resides in.

Class A, B, and C networks each have a different length for the part that identifies the network:

■ Class A networks have a 1-byte-long network part. That leaves 3 bytes for the rest of the address, called the host part.

■ Class B networks have a 2-byte-long network part, leaving 2 bytes for the host portion of the address.

■ Class C networks have a 3-byte-long network part, leaving only 1 byte for the host part.

For example, Figure 5-4 lists network 8.0.0.0 next to the Ethernet on the left. Network 8.0.0.0 is a Class A network, which means that only 1 octet (byte) is used for the network part of the address. So, all hosts in network 8.0.0.0 begin with 8. Similarly, Class B network 130.4.0.0 is listed next to the Ethernet on the right. Because it is a Class B network, 2 octets define the network part, and all addresses begin with 130.4 as the first 2 octets.

When listing network numbers, the convention is to write down the network part of the number, with all decimal 0s in the host part of the number. So, Class A network "8," which consists of all IP addresses that begin with 8, is written as 8.0.0.0. Similarly, Class B network "130.4," which consists of all IP addresses that begin with 130.4, is written as 130.4.0.0, and so on.

Now consider the size of each class of network. Class A networks need 1 byte for the network part, leaving 3 bytes, or 24 bits, for the host part. There are 2^{24} different possible values in the host part of a Class A IP address. So, each Class A network can have 2^{24} IP addresses—except for two reserved host addresses in each network, as shown in the last column of Table 5-3. The table summarizes the characteristics of Class A, B, and C networks.

Key Topic

Table 5-3 *Sizes of Network and Host Parts of IP Addresses with No Subnetting*

Any Network of This Class	Number of Network Bytes (Bits)	Number of Host Bytes (Bits)	Number of Addresses Per Network[*]
A	1 (8)	3 (24)	$2^{24} - 2$
B	2 (16)	2 (16)	$2^{16} - 2$
C	3 (24)	1 (8)	$2^{8} - 2$

[*]There are two reserved host addresses per network.

Based on the three examples from Figure 5-4, Table 5-4 provides a closer look at the numeric version of the three network numbers: 8.0.0.0, 130.4.0.0, and 199.1.1.0.

Table 5-4 *Sample Network Numbers, Decimal and Binary*

Network Number	Binary Representation, with the Host Part in Bold
8.0.0.0	00001000 **00000000 00000000 00000000**
130.4.0.0	10000010 00000100 **00000000 00000000**
199.1.1.0	11000111 00000001 00000001 **00000000**

Even though the network numbers look like addresses because of their dotted-decimal format, network numbers cannot be assigned to an interface to be used as an IP address. Conceptually, network numbers represent the group of all IP addresses in the network, much like a zip code represents the group of all addresses in a community. It would be confusing to have a single number represent a whole group of addresses and then also use that same number as an IP address for a single device. So, the network numbers themselves are reserved and cannot be used as an IP address for a device.

Besides the network number, a second dotted-decimal value in each network is reserved. Note that the first reserved value, the network number, has all binary 0s in the host part of the number (see Table 5-4). The other reserved value is the one with all binary 1s in the host part of the number. This number is called the *network broadcast* or *directed broadcast* address. This reserved number cannot be assigned to a host for use as an IP address. However, packets sent to a network broadcast address are forwarded to all devices in the network.

Also, because the network number is the lowest numeric value inside that network and the broadcast address is the highest numeric value, all the numbers between the network number and the broadcast address are the valid, useful IP addresses that can be used to address interfaces in the network.

The Actual Class A, B, and C Network Numbers

The Internet is a collection of almost every IP-based network and almost every TCP/IP host computer in the world. The original design of the Internet required several cooperating features that made it technically possible as well as administratively manageable:

- Each computer connected to the Internet needs a unique, nonduplicated IP address.

- Administratively, a central authority assigned Class A, B, or C networks to companies, governments, school systems, and ISPs based on the size of their IP network (Class A for large networks, Class B for medium networks, and Class C for small networks).

- The central authority assigned each network number to only one organization, helping ensure unique address assignment worldwide.

- Each organization with an assigned Class A, B, or C network then assigned individual IP addresses inside its own network.

By following these guidelines, as long as each organization assigns each IP address to only one computer, every computer in the Internet has a globally unique IP address.

> **NOTE**   The details of address assignment have changed over time, but the general idea described here is enough detail to help you understand the concept of different Class A, B, and C networks.

The organization in charge of universal IP address assignment is the Internet Corporation for Assigned Network Numbers (ICANN, www.icann.org). (The Internet Assigned Numbers Authority (IANA) formerly owned the IP address assignment process.) ICANN, in turn, assigns regional authority to other cooperating organizations. For example, the American Registry for Internet Numbers (ARIN, www.arin.org) owns the address assignment process for North America.

Table 5-5 summarizes the possible network numbers that ICANN and other agencies could have assigned over time. Note the total number for each network class and the number of hosts in each Class A, B, and C network.

Key Topic

Table 5-5   *All Possible Valid Network Numbers**

Class	First Octet Range	Valid Network Numbers*	Total Number for This Class of Network	Number of Hosts Per Network
A	1 to 126	1.0.0.0 to 126.0.0.0	$2^7 - 2$ (126)	$2^{24} - 2$ (16,777,214)
B	128 to 191	128.0.0.0 to 191.255.0.0	2^{14} (16,384)	$2^{16} - 2$ (65,534)
C	192 to 223	192.0.0.0 to 223.255.255.0	2^{21} (2,097,152)	$2^8 - 2$ (254)

*The Valid Network Numbers column shows actual network numbers. Networks 0.0.0.0 (originally defined for use as a broadcast address) and 127.0.0.0 (still available for use as the loopback address) are reserved.

Memorizing the contents of Table 5-5 should be one of the first things you do in preparation for the CCNA exam(s). Engineers should be able to categorize a network as Class A, B, or C with ease. Also, memorize the number of octets in the network part of Class A, B, and C addresses, as shown in Table 5-4.

IP Subnetting

Subnetting is one of the most important topics on the ICND1, ICND2, and CCNA exams. You need to know how it works and how to "do the math" to figure out issues when subnetting is in use, both in real life and on the exam. Chapter 12 covers the details of subnetting concepts, motivation, and math, but you should have a basic understanding of the concepts before covering the topics between here and Chapter 12. IP subnetting takes a single Class A, B, or C network and subdivides it into a number of smaller groups of IP addresses. The Class A, B, and C rules still exist, but now, a single Class A, B, or C network can be subdivided into many smaller groups. Subnetting treats a subdivision of a single Class A, B, or C network as if it were a network itself. In fact, the name "subnet" is just shorthand for "subdivided network."

You can easily discern the concepts behind subnetting by comparing one network topology that does not use subnetting with the same topology but with subnetting implemented. Figure 5-5 shows such a network, without subnetting.

Figure 5-5 *Backdrop for Discussing Numbers of Different Networks/Subnetworks*

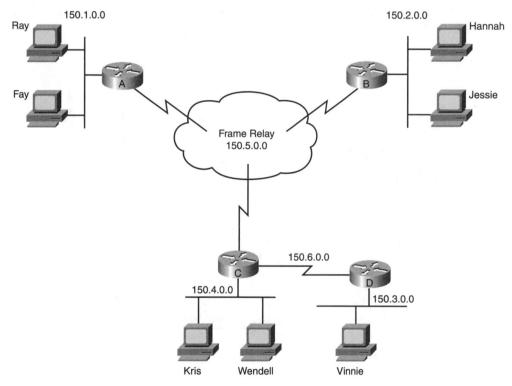

The design in Figure 5-5 requires six groups of IP addresses, each of which is a Class B network in this example. The four LANs each use a single Class B network. In other words, each of the LANs attached to routers A, B, C, and D is in a separate IP network. Additionally, the two serial interfaces composing the point-to-point serial link between routers C and D use one IP network because these two interfaces are not separated by a router. Finally, the three router interfaces composing the Frame Relay network with routers A, B, and C are not separated by an IP router and would use a sixth IP network.

Each Class B network has $2^{16} - 2$ host addresses—far more than you will ever need for each LAN and WAN link. For example, the upper-left Ethernet should contain all addresses that begin with 150.1. Therefore, addresses that begin with 150.1 cannot be assigned anywhere else in the network, except on the upper-left Ethernet. So, if you ran out of IP addresses somewhere else, you could not use the large number of unused addresses that begin with 150.1. As a result, the addressing design shown in Figure 5-5 wastes a lot of addresses.

In fact, this design would not be allowed if it were connected to the Internet. The ICANN member organization would not assign six separate registered Class B network numbers. In fact, you probably would not get even one Class B network, because most of the Class B addresses are already assigned. You more likely would get a couple of Class C networks with the expectation that you would use subnetting. Figure 5-6 illustrates a more realistic example that uses basic subnetting.

Figure 5-6 *Using Subnets*

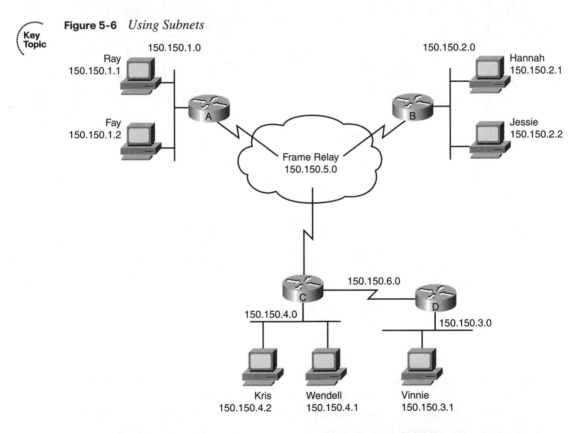

As in Figure 5-5, the design in Figure 5-6 requires six groups. Unlike Figure 5-5, this figure uses six subnets, each of which is a subnet of a single Class B network. This design subdivides the Class B network 150.150.0.0 into six subnets. To perform subnetting, the third octet (in this example) is used to identify unique subnets of network 150.150.0.0.

Notice that each subnet number in the figure shows a different value in the third octet, representing each different subnet number. In other words, this design numbers or identifies each different subnet using the third octet.

When subnetting, a third part of an IP address appears between the network and host parts of the address—namely, the *subnet part* of the address. This field is created by "stealing" or "borrowing" bits from the host part of the address. The size of the network part of the address never shrinks. In other words, Class A, B, and C rules still apply when defining the size of the network part of an address. The host part of the address shrinks to make room for the subnet part of the address. Figure 5-7 shows the format of addresses when subnetting, representing the number of bits in each of the three parts of an IP address.

Figure 5-7 *Address Formats When Subnetting Is Used (Classful)*

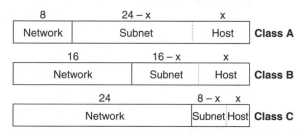

Now, instead of routing based on the network part of an address, routers can route based on the combined network and subnet parts. For example, when Kris (150.150.4.2) sends a packet to Hannah (150.150.2.1), router C has an IP route that lists information that means "all addresses that begin with 150.150.2." That same route tells router C to forward the packet to router B next. Note that the information in the routing table includes both the network and subnet part of the address, because both parts together identify the group.

Note that the concepts shown in Figure 5-7, with three parts of an IP address (network, subnet, and host), are called *classful addressing*. The term *classful addressing* refers to how you can think about IP addresses—specifically, that they have three parts. In particular, classful addressing means that you view the address as having a network part that is determined based on the rules about Class A, B, and C addressing—hence the word "classful" in the term.

Because the routing process considers the network and subnet parts of the address together, you can take an alternative view of IP addresses called *classless addressing*. Instead of three parts, each address has two parts:

■ The part on which routing is based

■ The host part

This first part—the part on which routing is based—is the combination of the network and subnet parts from the classful addressing view. This first part is often simply called the subnet part, or sometimes the *prefix*. Figure 5-8 shows the concepts and terms behind classless IP addressing.

Figure 5-8 *Address Formats When Subnetting Is Used (Classless)*

Finally, IP addressing with subnetting uses a concept called a *subnet mask*. A subnet mask helps define the structure of an IP address, as shown in Figures 5-7 and 5-8. Chapter 12 explains the details of subnet masks.

IP Routing

In the first section of this chapter, you read about the basics of routing using a network with three routers and two PCs. Armed with more knowledge of IP addressing, you now can take a closer look at the process of routing IP. This section focuses on how the originating host chooses where to send the packet, as well as how routers choose where to route or forward packets to the final destination.

Host Routing

Hosts actually use some simple routing logic when choosing where to send a packet. This two-step logic is as follows:

Step 1 If the destination IP address is in the same subnet as I am, send the packet directly to that destination host.

Step 2 If the destination IP address is not in the same subnet as I am, send the packet to my *default gateway* (a router's Ethernet interface on the subnet).

For example, consider Figure 5-9, and focus on the Ethernet LAN at the top of the figure. The top Ethernet has two PCs, labeled PC1 and PC11, plus router R1. When PC1 sends a packet to 150.150.1.11 (PC11's IP address), PC1 sends the packet over the Ethernet to PC11—there's no need to bother the router.

Figure 5-9 *Host Routing Alternatives*

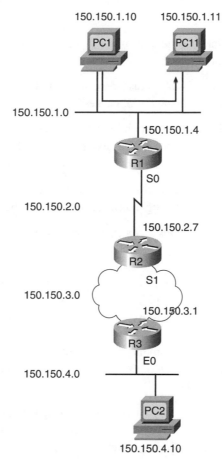

Alternatively, when PC1 sends a packet to PC2 (150.150.4.10), PC1 forwards the packet to its default gateway of 150.150.1.4, which is R1's Ethernet interface IP address according to Step 2 in the host routing logic. The next section describes an example in which PC1 uses its default gateway.

Router Forwarding Decisions and the IP Routing Table

Earlier in this chapter, Figures 5-1 and 5-2 (and the associated text) described generally how routers forward packets, making use of each successive physical network to forward packets to the next device. To better appreciate a router's forwarding decision, this section uses an example that includes three different routers forwarding a packet.

A router uses the following logic when receiving a data-link frame—a frame that has an IP packet encapsulated in it:

Key Topic

Step 1   Use the data-link FCS field to ensure that the frame had no errors; if errors occurred, discard the frame.

Step 2   Assuming the frame was not discarded at step 1, discard the old data-link header and trailer, leaving the IP packet.

Step 3   Compare the IP packet's destination IP address to the routing table, and find the route that matches the destination address. This route identifies the outgoing interface of the router, and possibly the next-hop router.

Step 4   Encapsulate the IP packet inside a new data-link header and trailer, appropriate for the outgoing interface, and forward the frame.

With these steps, each router sends the packet to the next location until the packet reaches its final destination.

Next, focus on the routing table and the matching process that occurs at Step 3. The packet has a destination IP address in the header, whereas the routing table typically has a list of networks and subnets. To match a routing table entry, the router thinks like this:

> Network numbers and subnet numbers represent a group of addresses that begin with the same prefix. In which of the groups in my routing table does this packet's destination address reside?

As you might guess, routers actually turn that logic into a math problem, but the text indeed shows what occurs. For example, Figure 5-10 shows the same network topology as Figure 5-9, but now with PC1 sending a packet to PC2.

> **NOTE**   Note that the routers all know in this case that "subnet 150.150.4.0" means "all addresses that begin with 150.150.4."

The following list explains the forwarding logic at each step in the figure. (Note that all references to Steps 1, 2, 3, and 4 refer to the list of routing logic at the top of this page.)

Step A   **PC1 sends the packet to its default gateway.** PC1 first builds the IP packet, with a destination address of PC2's IP address (150.150.4.10). PC1 needs to send the packet to R1 (PC1's default gateway) because the destination address is on a different subnet. PC1 places the IP packet into an Ethernet frame, with a destination Ethernet address of R1's Ethernet address. PC1 sends the frame onto the Ethernet.

Figure 5-10 *Simple Routing Example, with IP Subnets*

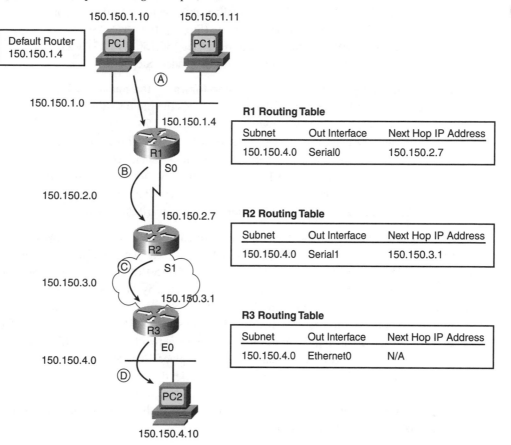

Step B **R1 processes the incoming frame and forwards the packet to R2.**
Because the incoming Ethernet frame has a destination MAC of R1's
Ethernet MAC, R1 copies the frame off the Ethernet for processing. R1
checks the frame's FCS, and no errors have occurred (Step 1). R1 then
discards the Ethernet header and trailer (Step 2). Next, R1 compares the
packet's destination address (150.150.4.10) to the routing table and finds the
entry for subnet 150.150.4.0—which includes addresses 150.150.4.0 through
150.150.4.255 (Step 3). Because the destination address is in this group,
R1 forwards the packet out interface Serial0 to next-hop router R2
(150.150.2.7) after encapsulating the packet in an HDLC frame (step 4).

Step C **R2 processes the incoming frame and forwards the packet to R3.**
R2 repeats the same general process as R1 when R2 receives the HDLC
frame. R2 checks the FCS field and finds that no errors occurred (Step 1).
R2 then discards the HDLC header and trailer (Step 2). Next, R2 finds its

route for subnet 150.150.4.0—which includes the address range
150.150.4.0–150.150.4.255—and realizes that the packet's destination
address 150.150.4.10 matches that route (Step 3). Finally, R2 sends the
packet out interface serial1 to next-hop router 150.150.3.1 (R3) after
encapsulating the packet in a Frame Relay header (Step 4).

Step D   R3 processes the incoming frame and forwards the packet to PC2.
Like R1 and R2, R3 checks the FCS, discards the old data-link header
and trailer, and matches its own route for subnet 150.150.4.0. R3's
routing table entry for 150.150.4.0 shows that the outgoing interface is
R3's Ethernet interface, but there is no next-hop router, because R3 is
connected directly to subnet 150.150.4.0. All R3 has to do is encapsulate
the packet inside an Ethernet header and trailer, with a destination
Ethernet address of PC2's MAC address, and forward the frame.

The routing process relies on the rules relating to IP addressing. For instance, why does
150.150.1.10 (PC1) assume that 150.150.4.10 (PC2) is not on the same Ethernet? Well,
because 150.150.4.0, PC2's subnet, is different from 150.150.1.0, which is PC1's subnet.
Because IP addresses in different subnets must be separated by a router, PC1 needs to send
the packet to a router—and it does. Similarly, all three routers list a route to subnet
150.150.4.0, which, in this example, includes IP addresses 150.150.4.1 to 150.150.4.254.
What if someone tried to put PC2 somewhere else in the network, still using 150.150.4.10?
The routers then would forward packets to the wrong place. So, Layer 3 routing relies on
the structure of Layer 3 addressing to route more efficiently.

Chapter 12 covers IP addressing in much more detail. Next, this chapter briefly introduces
the concepts behind IP routing protocols.

IP Routing Protocols

The routing (forwarding) process depends heavily on having an accurate and up-to-date
IP routing table on each router. IP routing protocols fill the routers' IP routing tables with
valid, loop-free routes. Each route includes a subnet number, the interface out which to
forward packets so that they are delivered to that subnet, and the IP address of the next
router that should receive packets destined for that subnet (if needed) (as shown in the
example surrounding Figure 5-10).

Before examining the underlying logic used by routing protocols, you need to consider the
goals of a routing protocol. The goals described in the following list are common for any
IP routing protocol, regardless of its underlying logic type:

■   To dynamically learn and fill the routing table with a route to all subnets in the
network.

- If more than one route to a subnet is available, to place the best route in the routing table.

- To notice when routes in the table are no longer valid, and to remove them from the routing table.

- If a route is removed from the routing table and another route through another neighboring router is available, to add the route to the routing table. (Many people view this goal and the preceding one as a single goal.)

- To add new routes, or to replace lost routes, with the best currently available route as quickly as possible. The time between losing the route and finding a working replacement route is called *convergence* time.

- To prevent routing loops.

Routing protocols can become rather complicated, but the basic logic that they use is relatively simple. Routers follow these general steps for advertising routes in a network:

Step 1 Each router adds a route to its routing table for each subnet directly connected to the router.

Step 2 Each router's routing protocol tells its neighbors about all the routes in its routing table, including the directly connected routes and routes learned from other routers.

Step 3 After learning a new route from a neighbor, the router's routing protocol adds a route to its routing table, with the next-hop router typically being the neighbor from which the route was learned.

For example, Figure 5-11 shows the same sample network as in Figures 5-9 and 5-10, but now with focus on how the three routers each learned about subnet 150.150.4.0. Note that routing protocols do more work than is implied in the figure; this figure just focuses on how the routers learn about subnet 150.150.4.0.

Again, follow the items A, B, C, and D shown in the figure to see how each router learns its route to 150.150.4.0. All references to Steps 1, 2, and 3 refer to the list just before Figure 5-11.

Step A R3 learns a route that refers to its own E0 interface because subnet 150.150.4.0 is directly connected (Step 1).

Step B R3 sends a routing protocol message, called a *routing update*, to R2, causing R2 to learn about subnet 150.150.4.0 (Step 2).

Figure 5-11 *Router R1 Learning About Subnet 150.150.4.0*

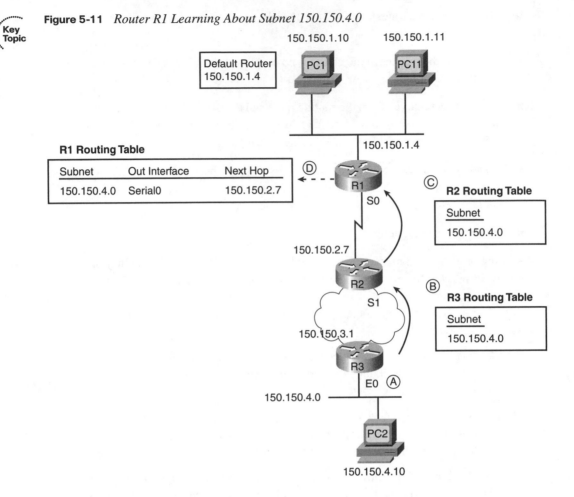

Step C R2 sends a similar routing update to R1, causing R1 to learn about subnet
150.150.4.0 (Step 2).

Step D R1's route to 150.150.4.0 lists 150.150.2.7 (R2's IP address) as the next-
hop address because R1 learned about the route from R2. The route also
lists R1's outgoing interface as Serial0, because R1 learned about the
route from the update that came in serial0 (at Step C in the figure).

> **NOTE** Routes do not always refer to the neighboring router's IP address as the next-hop
> IP address, but for protocols and processes covered for the ICND1 and CCNA exams,
> the routes typically refer to a neighboring router as the next hop.

Chapter 14, "Routing Protocol Concepts and Configuration," covers routing protocols in
more detail. Next, the final major section of this chapter introduces several additional

functions related to how the network layer forwards packets from source to destination through an internetwork.

Network Layer Utilities

So far this chapter has described the main features of the OSI network layer—in particular, the TCP/IP internetwork layer, which defines the same general features as OSI Layer 3. To close the chapter, this section covers four tools used almost every day in almost every TCP/IP network in the world to help the network layer with its task of routing packets from end to end through an internetwork:

- Address Resolution Protocol (ARP)

- Domain Name System (DNS)

- Dynamic Host Configuration Protocol (DHCP)

- Ping

Address Resolution Protocol and the Domain Name System

Network designers should try to make using the network as simple as possible. At most, users might want to remember the name of another computer with which they want to communicate, such as remembering the name of a website. They certainly do not want to remember the IP address, nor do they want to try to remember any MAC addresses! So, TCP/IP needs protocols that dynamically discover all the necessary information to allow communications, without the user knowing more than a name.

You might not even think that you need to know the name of another computer. For instance, when you open your browser, you probably have a default home page configured that the browser immediately downloads. You might not think of that universal resource locator (URL) string as a name, but the URL for the home page has a name embedded in it. For example, in a URL such as http://www.cisco.com/go/prepcenter, the www.cisco.com part is the name of the Cisco web server. So, whether you enter the name of another networked computer or it is implied by what you see on the screen, the user typically identifies a remote computer by using a name.

So, TCP/IP needs a way to let a computer find the IP address of another computer based on its name. TCP/IP also needs a way to find MAC addresses associated with other computers on the same LAN subnet. Figure 5-12 outlines the problem.

In this example, Hannah needs to communicate with a server on PC Jessie. Hannah knows her own name, IP address, and MAC address. *What Hannah does not know are Jessie's IP and MAC addresses.* To find the two missing facts, Hannah uses DNS to find Jessie's IP address and ARP to find Jessie's MAC address.

Figure 5-12 *Hannah Knows Jessie's Name, Needs IP Address and MAC Address*

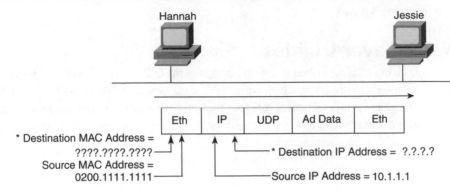

* Destination MAC Address =
         ????.????.????
  Source MAC Address =
         0200.1111.1111

* Destination IP Address = ?.?.?.?

Source IP Address = 10.1.1.1

* Information that Hannah Needs to Learn

DNS Name Resolution

Hannah knows the IP address of a DNS server because the address was either preconfigured on Hannah's machine or was learned with DHCP, as covered later in this chapter. As soon as Hannah somehow identifies the name of the other computer (for example, jessie.example.com), she sends a *DNS request* to the DNS, asking for Jessie's IP address. The DNS replies with the address, 10.1.1.2. Figure 5-13 shows the simple process.

Key Topic

Figure 5-13 *DNS Request and Reply*

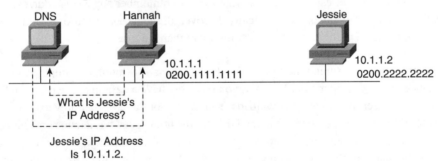

Hannah simply sends a DNS request to the server, supplying the name jessie, or jessie.example.com, and the DNS replies with the IP address (10.1.1.2 in this case). Effectively, the same thing happens when you surf the Internet and connect to any website. Your PC sends a request, just like Hannah's request for Jessie, asking the DNS to resolve the name into an IP address. After that happens, your PC can start requesting that the web page be sent.

The ARP Process

As soon as a host knows the IP address of the other host, the sending host may need to know the MAC address used by the other computer. For example, Hannah still needs to know the Ethernet MAC address used by 10.1.1.2, so Hannah issues something called an *ARP broadcast*. An ARP broadcast is sent to a broadcast Ethernet address, so everyone on the LAN receives it. Because Jessie is on the same LAN, she receives the ARP broadcast. Because Jessie's IP address is 10.1.1.2 and the ARP broadcast is looking for the MAC address associated with 10.1.1.2, Jessie replies with her own MAC address. Figure 5-14 outlines the process.

Figure 5-14 *Sample ARP Process*

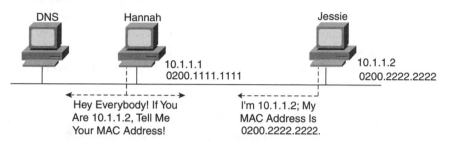

Now Hannah knows the destination IP and Ethernet addresses that she should use when sending frames to Jessie, and the packet shown in Figure 5-12 can be sent successfully.

Hosts may or may not need to ARP to find the destination host's MAC address based on the two-step routing logic used by a host. If the destination host is on the same subnet, the sending host sends an ARP looking for the destination host's MAC address, as shown in Figure 5-14. However, if the sending host is on a different subnet than the destination host, the sending host's routing logic results in the sending host needing to forward the packet to its default gateway. For example, if Hannah and Jessie had been in different subnets in Figures 5-12 through 5-14, Hannah's routing logic would have caused Hannah to want to send the packet to Hannah's default gateway (router). In that case, Hannah would have used ARP to find the router's MAC address instead of Jessie's MAC address.

Additionally, hosts need to use ARP to find MAC addresses only once in a while. Any device that uses IP should retain, or cache, the information learned with ARP, placing the information in its *ARP cache*. Each time a host needs to send a packet encapsulated in an Ethernet frame, it first checks its ARP cache and uses the MAC address found there. If the correct information is not listed in the ARP cache, the host then can use ARP to discover the MAC address used by a particular IP address. Also, a host learns ARP information when receiving an ARP as well. For example, the ARP process shown in Figure 5-14 results in both Hannah and Jessie learning the other host's MAC address.

NOTE You can see the contents of the ARP cache on most PC Operating Systems by using the **arp -a** command from a command prompt.

Address Assignment and DHCP

Every device that uses TCP/IP—in fact, every interface on every device that uses TCP/IP—needs a valid IP address. For some devices, the address can and should be statically assigned by configuring the device. For example, all commonly used computer operating systems that support TCP/IP allow the user to statically configure the IP address on each interface. Routers and switches typically use statically configured IP addresses as well.

Servers also typically use statically configured IP addresses. Using a statically configured and seldom-changed IP address helps because all references to that server can stay the same over time. This is the same concept that it's good that the location of your favorite grocery store never changes. You know where to go to buy food, and you can get there from home, on the way home from work, or from somewhere else. Likewise, if servers have a static, unchanging IP address, the users of that server know how to reach the server, from anywhere, consistently.

However, the average end-user host computer does not need to use the same IP address every day. Again thinking about your favorite grocery store, you could move to a new apartment every week, but you'd still know where the grocery store is. The workers at the grocery store don't need to know where you live. Likewise, servers typically don't care that your PC has a different IP address today as compared to yesterday. End-user hosts can have their IP addresses dynamically assigned, and even change their IP addresses over time, because it does not matter if the IP address changes.

DHCP defines the protocols used to allow computers to request a lease of an IP address. DHCP uses a server, with the server keeping a list of pools of IP addresses available in each subnet. DHCP clients can send the DHCP server a message, asking to borrow or lease an IP address. The server then suggests an IP address. If accepted, the server notes that the address is no longer available for assignment to any other hosts, and the client has an IP address to use.

DHCP supplies IP addresses to clients, and it also supplies other information. For example, hosts need to know their IP address, plus the subnet mask to use, plus what default gateway to use, as well as the IP address(es) of any DNS servers. In most networks today, DHCP supplies all these facts to a typical end-user host.

Figure 5-15 shows a typical set of four messages used between a DHCP server to assign an IP address, as well as other information. Note that the first two messages are both IP broadcast messages.

Figure 5-15 shows the DHCP server as a PC, which is typical in an Enterprise network. However, as covered in Chapter 17, "WAN Configuration," routers can and do provide DHCP services as well. In fact, routers can provide a DHCP server function, dynamically assigning IP addresses to the computers in a small or home office, using DHCP client functions to dynamically lease IP addresses from an Internet service provider (ISP). However, the need for these functions is closely related to features most often used with connections to the Internet, so more details about a router's implementation of DHCP server and DHCP client functions are saved for Chapter 17.

Figure 5-15   *DHCP Messages to Acquire an IP Address*

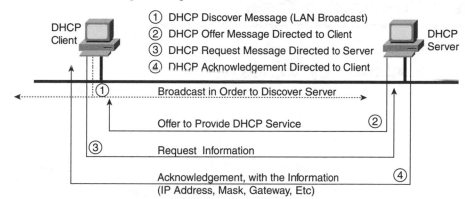

DHCP has become a prolific protocol. Most end-user hosts on LANs in corporate networks get their IP addresses and other basic configuration via DHCP.

ICMP Echo and the ping Command

After you have implemented a network, you need a way to test basic IP connectivity without relying on any applications to be working. The primary tool for testing basic network connectivity is the **ping** command. **ping** (Packet Internet Groper) uses the *Internet Control Message Protocol (ICMP)*, sending a message called an *ICMP echo request* to another IP address. The computer with that IP address should reply with an *ICMP echo reply.* If that works, you successfully have tested the IP network. In other words, you know that the network can deliver a packet from one host to the other, and back. ICMP does not rely on any application, so it really just tests basic IP connectivity—Layers 1, 2, and 3 of the OSI model. Figure 5-16 outlines the basic process.

Figure 5-16   *Sample Network,* **ping** *Command*

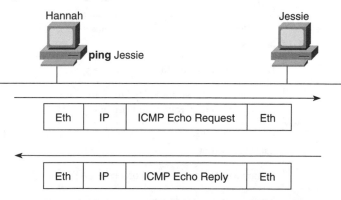

Chapter 15, "Troubleshooting IP Routing," gives you more information about and examples of ping and ICMP.

Exam Preparation Tasks

Review All the Key Topics

Review the most important topics from this chapter, noted with the key topics icon. Table 5-6 lists these key topics and where each is discussed.

Table 5-6 *Key Topics for Chapter 5*

Key Topic Element	Description	Page Number
List	Two statements about how IP expects IP addresses to be grouped into networks or subnets	107
Table 5-3	List of the three types of unicast IP networks and the size of the network and host parts of each type of network	108
Paragraph	Explanation of the concept of a network broadcast or directed broadcast address	109
Table 5-5	Details about the actual Class A, B, and C networks	110
Figure 5-6	Conceptual view of how subnetting works	112
Figure 5-7	Structure of subnetted Class A, B, and C IP addresses, classful view	113
Figure 5-8	Structure of a subnetted unicast IP address, classless view	114
List	Two-step process of how hosts route (forward) packets	114
List	Four-step process of how routers route (forward) packets	116
Figure 5-10	Example of the IP routing process	117
Figure 5-11	Example that shows generally how a routing protocol can cause routers to learn new routes	120
Figure 5-13	Example that shows the purpose and process of DNS name resolution	122
Figure 5-14	Example of the purpose and process of ARP	123
Paragraph	The most important information learned by a host acting as a DHCP client	124

Complete the Tables and Lists from Memory

Print a copy of Appendix H, "Memory Tables" (found on the CD), or at least the section for this chapter, and complete the tables and lists from memory. Appendix I, "Memory Tables Answer Key," also on the CD, includes completed tables and lists for you to check your work.

Definitions of Key Terms

Define the following key terms from this chapter, and check your answers in the glossary.

ARP, default gateway/default router, DHCP, DNS, host part, IP address, logical address, network broadcast address, network number/network address, network part, routing table, subnet broadcast address, subnet number/subnet address, subnet part

This chapter covers the following subjects:

TCP/IP Layer 4 Protocols: TCP and UDP:
This section explains the functions and
mechanisms used by TCP and UDP, including
error recovery and port numbers.

TCP/IP Applications: This section explains the
purpose of TCP/IP application layer protocols,
focusing on HTTP as an example.

Network Security: This section provides some
perspectives on the security threats faced by
networks today, introducing some of the key tools
used to help prevent and reduce the impact of
those threats.

CHAPTER 6

Fundamentals of TCP/IP Transport, Applications, and Security

The CCNA exams focus mostly on a deeper and broader examination of the topics covered in Chapter 3 (LANs), Chapter 4 (WANs), and Chapter 5 (routing). This chapter explains the basics of a few topics that receive less attention on the exams: the TCP/IP transport layer, the TCP/IP application layer, and TCP/IP network security. Although all three topics are covered on the various CCNA exams, the extent of that coverage is much less compared to LANs, WANs, and routing.

"Do I Know This Already?" Quiz

The "Do I Know This Already?" quiz allows you to assess whether you should read the entire chapter. If you miss no more than one of these ten self-assessment questions, you might want to move ahead to the "Exam Preparation Tasks" section. Table 6-1 lists the major headings in this chapter and the "Do I Know This Already?" quiz questions covering the material in those sections. This helps you assess your knowledge of these specific areas. The answers to the "Do I Know This Already?" quiz appear in Appendix A.

Table 6-1 *"Do I Know This Already?" Foundation Topics Section-to-Question Mapping*

Foundation Topics Section	Questions
TCP/IP Layer 4 Protocols: TCP and UDP	1–6
TCP/IP Applications	7, 8
Network Security	9, 10

1. PC1 is using TCP and has a window size of 4000. PC1 sends four segments to PC2 with 1000 bytes of data each, with sequence numbers 2000, 3000, 4000, and 5000. PC1 does not recieve an acknowledgment within its current timeout value for this connection. What should PC1 do next?

   a. Increase its window to 5000 or more segments

   b. Send the next segment, with sequence number 6000

   c. Resend the segment whose sequence number was 5000

   d. Resend all four previously sent segments

2. Which of the following are not features of a protocol that is considered to match OSI Layer 4?

    a. Error recovery

    b. Flow control

    c. Segmenting of application data

    d. Conversion from binary to ASCII

3. Which of the following header fields identify which TCP/IP application gets data received by the computer?

    a. Ethernet Type

    b. SNAP Protocol Type

    c. IP Protocol Field

    d. TCP Port Number

    e. UDP Port Number

    f. Application ID

4. Which of the following are not typical functions of TCP?

    a. Windowing

    b. Error recovery

    c. Multiplexing using port numbers

    d. Routing

    e. Encryption

    f. Ordered data transfer

5. Which of the following functions is performed by both TCP and UDP?

    a. Windowing

    b. Error recovery

    c. Multiplexing using port numbers

    d. Routing

    e. Encryption

    f. Ordered data transfer

6. What do you call data that includes the Layer 4 protocol header, and data given to Layer 4 by the upper layers, not including any headers and trailers from Layers 1 to 3?

   a. Bits

   b. Chunk

   c. Segment

   d. Packet

   e. Frame

   f. L4PDU

   g. L3PDU

7. In the URL http://www.fredsco.com/name.html, which part identifies the web server?

   a. http

   b. www.fredsco.com

   c. fredsco.com

   d. http://www.fredsco.com

   e. The file name.html includes the hostname.

8. When comparing VoIP with an HTTP-based mission-critical business application, which of the following statements are accurate about the quality of service needed from the network?

   a. VoIP needs better (lower) packet loss.

   b. HTTP needs less bandwidth.

   c. HTTP needs better (lower) jitter.

   d. VoIP needs better (lower) delay.

9. Which of the following is a device or function whose most notable feature is to examine trends over time to recognize different known attacks as compared to a list of common attack signatures?

   a. VPN

   b. Firewall

   c. IDS

   d. NAC

10. Which of the following is a device or function whose most notable feature is to encrypt packets before they pass through the Internet?

    a. VPN

    b. Firewall

    c. IDS

    d. NAC

Foundation Topics

This chapter begins by examining the functions of Transmission Control Protocol (TCP), which are many, as compared to the functions of User Datagram Protocol (UDP), of which there are few. The second major section of the chapter examines the TCP/IP application layer, including some discussion of how DNS name resolution works. Finally, the third major section examines the importance and concepts of network security, introducing some of the core concepts, terminology, and functions important for security today.

TCP/IP Layer 4 Protocols: TCP and UDP

The OSI transport layer (Layer 4) defines several functions, the most important of which are error recovery and flow control. Likewise, the TCP/IP transport layer protocols also implement these same types of features. Note that both the OSI model and TCP/IP model call this layer the transport layer. But as usual, when referring to the TCP/IP model, the layer name and number are based on OSI, so any TCP/IP transport layer protocols are considered Layer 4 protocols.

The key difference between TCP and UDP is that TCP provides a wide variety of services to applications, whereas UDP does not. For example, routers discard packets for many reasons, including bit errors, congestion, and instances in which no correct routes are known. As you have read already, most data-link protocols notice errors (a process called *error detection*) but then discard frames that have errors. TCP provides for retransmission (error recovery) and help to avoid congestion (flow control), whereas UDP does not. As a result, many application protocols choose to use TCP.

However, do not let UDP's lack of services make you think that UDP is worse than TCP. By providing few services, UDP needs fewer bytes in its header compared to TCP, resulting in fewer bytes of overhead in the network. UDP software does not slow down data transfer in cases where TCP may purposefully slow down. Also, some applications, notably today voice over IP (VoIP) and video over IP, do not need error recovery, so they use UDP. So, UDP also has an important place in TCP/IP networks today.

Table 6-2 lists the main features supported by TCP and/or UDP. Note that only the first item listed in the table is supported by UDP, whereas all items in the table are supported by TCP.

Table 6-2 *TCP/IP Transport Layer Features*

Function	Description
Multiplexing using ports	Function that allows receiving hosts to choose the correct application for which the data is destined, based on the port number.
Error recovery (reliability)	Process of numbering and acknowledging data with Sequence and Acknowledgment header fields.
Flow control using windowing	Process that uses window sizes to protect buffer space and routing devices.
Connection establishment and termination	Process used to initialize port numbers and Sequence and Acknowledgment fields.
Ordered data transfer and data segmentation	Continuous stream of bytes from an upper-layer process that is "segmented" for transmission and delivered to upper-layer processes at the receiving device, with the bytes in the same order.

Next, this section describes the features of TCP, followed by a brief comparison to UDP.

Transmission Control Protocol

Each TCP/IP application typically chooses to use either TCP or UDP based on the application's requirements. For instance, TCP provides error recovery, but to do so, it consumes more bandwidth and uses more processing cycles. UDP does not perform error recovery, but it takes less bandwidth and uses fewer processing cycles. Regardless of which of the two TCP/IP transport layer protocols the application chooses to use, you should understand the basics of how each of these transport layer protocols works.

TCP, as defined in RFC 793, accomplishes the functions listed in Table 6-2 through mechanisms at the endpoint computers. TCP relies on IP for end-to-end delivery of the data, including routing issues. In other words, TCP performs only part of the functions necessary to deliver the data between applications. Also, the role that it plays is directed toward providing services for the applications that sit at the endpoint computers. Regardless of whether two computers are on the same Ethernet or are separated by the entire Internet, TCP performs its functions the same way.

Figure 6-1 shows the fields in the TCP header. Although you don't need to memorize the names of the fields or their locations, the rest of this section refers to several of the fields, so the entire header is included here for reference.

Figure 6-1 *TCP Header Fields*

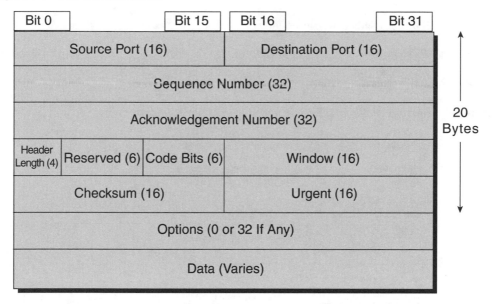

Multiplexing Using TCP Port Numbers

TCP provides a lot of features to applications, at the expense of requiring slightly more processing and overhead, as compared to UDP. However, TCP and UDP both use a concept called *multiplexing*. Therefore, this section begins with an explanation of multiplexing with TCP and UDP. Afterward, the unique features of TCP are explored.

Multiplexing by TCP and UDP involves the process of how a computer thinks when receiving data. The computer might be running many applications, such as a web browser, an e-mail package, or an Internet VoIP application (for example, Skype). TCP and UDP multiplexing enables the receiving computer to know which application to give the data to.

Some examples will help make the need for multiplexing obvious. The sample network consists of two PCs, labeled Hannah and Jessie. Hannah uses an application that she wrote to send advertisements that appear on Jessie's screen. The application sends a new ad to Jessie every 10 seconds. Hannah uses a second application, a wire-transfer application, to send Jessie some money. Finally, Hannah uses a web browser to access the web server that runs on Jessie's PC. The ad application and wire-transfer application are imaginary, just for this example. The web application works just like it would in real life.

Figure 6-2 shows the sample network, with Jessie running three applications:

■   A UDP-based ad application

■   A TCP-based wire-transfer application

■   A TCP web server application

Figure 6-2   *Hannah Sending Packets to Jessie, with Three Applications*

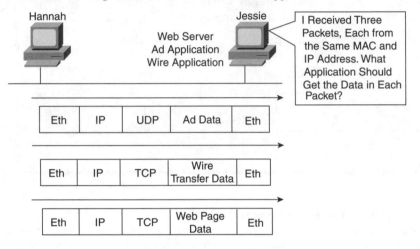

Jessie needs to know which application to give the data to, but *all three packets are from the same Ethernet and IP address.* You might think that Jessie could look at whether the packet contains a UDP or TCP header, but, as you see in the figure, two applications (wire transfer and web) are using TCP.

TCP and UDP solve this problem by using a port number field in the TCP or UDP header, respectively. Each of Hannah's TCP and UDP segments uses a different *destination port number* so that Jessie knows which application to give the data to. Figure 6-3 shows an example.

Multiplexing relies on a concept called a *socket*. A socket consists of three things:

■   An IP address

■   A transport protocol

■   A port number

Figure 6-3 *Hannah Sending Packets to Jessie, with Three Applications Using Port Numbers to Multiplex*

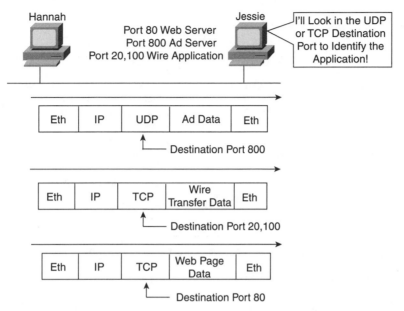

So, for a web server application on Jessie, the socket would be (10.1.1.2, TCP, port 80) because, by default, web servers use the well-known port 80. When Hannah's web browser connects to the web server, Hannah uses a socket as well—possibly one like this: (10.1.1.1, TCP, 1030). Why 1030? Well, Hannah just needs a port number that is unique on Hannah, so Hannah sees that port 1030 is available and uses it. In fact, hosts typically allocate *dynamic port numbers* starting at 1024 because the ports below 1024 are reserved for well-known applications, such as web services.

In Figure 6-3, Hannah and Jessie use three applications at the same time—hence, three socket connections are open. Because a socket on a single computer should be unique, a connection between two sockets should identify a unique connection between two computers. This uniqueness means that you can use multiple applications at the same time, talking to applications running on the same or different computers. Multiplexing, based on sockets, ensures that the data is delivered to the correct applications. Figure 6-4 shows the three socket connections between Hannah and Jessie.

Port numbers are a vital part of the socket concept. Well-known port numbers are used by servers; other port numbers are used by clients. Applications that provide a service, such as FTP, Telnet, and web servers, open a socket using a well-known port and listen for connection requests. Because these connection requests from clients are required to include both the source and destination port numbers, the port numbers used by the servers must be well-known. Therefore, each server has a hard-coded, well-known port number. The well-known ports are listed at http://www.iana.org/assignments/port-numbers.

Figure 6-4   *Connections Between Sockets*

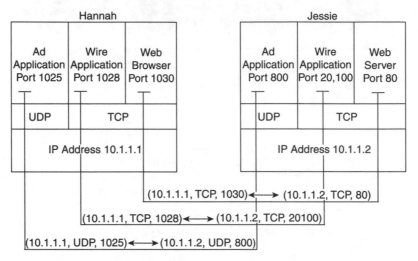

On client machines, where the requests originate, any unused port number can be allocated. The result is that each client on the same host uses a different port number, but a server uses the same port number for all connections. For example, 100 web browsers on the same host computer could each connect to a web server, but the web server with 100 clients connected to it would have only one socket and, therefore, only one port number (port 80 in this case). The server can tell which packets are sent from which of the 100 clients by looking at the source port of received TCP segments. The server can send data to the correct web client (browser) by sending data to that same port number listed as a destination port. The combination of source and destination sockets allows all participating hosts to distinguish between the data's source and destination. Although the example explains the concept using 100 TCP connections, the same port numbering concept applies to UDP sessions in the same way.

NOTE   You can find all RFCs online at http://www.isi.edu/in-notes/rfc*xxxx*.txt, where *xxxx* is the number of the RFC. If you do not know the number of the RFC, you can try searching by topic at http://www.rfc-editor.org/rfcsearch.html.

Popular TCP/IP Applications

Throughout your preparation for the CCNA exams, you will come across a variety of TCP/IP applications. You should at least be aware of some of the applications that can be used to help manage and control a network.

The World Wide Web (WWW) application exists through web browsers accessing the content available on web servers. Although it is often thought of as an end-user application, you can actually use WWW to manage a router or switch. You enable a web server function in the router or switch and use a browser to access the router or switch.

The Domain Name System (DNS) allows users to use names to refer to computers, with DNS being used to find the corresponding IP addresses. DNS also uses a client/server model, with DNS servers being controlled by networking personnel, and DNS client functions being part of most any device that uses TCP/IP today. The client simply asks the DNS server to supply the IP address that corresponds to a given name.

Simple Network Management Protocol (SNMP) is an application layer protocol used specifically for network device management. For instance, Cisco supplies a large variety of network management products, many of them in the CiscoWorks network management software product family. They can be used to query, compile, store, and display information about a network's operation. To query the network devices, CiscoWorks software mainly uses SNMP protocols.

Traditionally, to move files to and from a router or switch, Cisco used Trivial File Transfer Protocol (TFTP). TFTP defines a protocol for basic file transfer—hence the word "trivial." Alternatively, routers and switches can use File Transfer Protocol (FTP), which is a much more functional protocol, to transfer files. Both work well for moving files into and out of Cisco devices. FTP allows many more features, making it a good choice for the general end-user population. TFTP client and server applications are very simple, making them good tools as embedded parts of networking devices.

Some of these applications use TCP, and some use UDP. As you will read later, TCP performs error recovery, whereas UDP does not. For instance, Simple Mail Transport Protocol (SMTP) and Post Office Protocol version 3 (POP3), both used for transferring mail, require guaranteed delivery, so they use TCP. Regardless of which transport layer protocol is used, applications use a well-known port number so that clients know which port to attempt to connect to. Table 6-3 lists several popular applications and their well-known port numbers.

Table 6-3 *Popular Applications and Their Well-Known Port Numbers*

> Key
> Topic

Port Number	Protocol	Application
20	TCP	FTP data
21	TCP	FTP control
22	TCP	SSH

continues

Table 6-3 *Popular Applications and Their Well-Known Port Numbers (Continued)*

Port Number	Protocol	Application
23	TCP	Telnet
25	TCP	SMTP
53	UDP, TCP	DNS
67, 68	UDP	DHCP
69	UDP	TFTP
80	TCP	HTTP (WWW)
110	TCP	POP3
161	UDP	SNMP
443	TCP	SSL
16,384–32,767	UDP	RTP-based Voice (VoIP) and Video

Error Recovery (Reliability)

TCP provides for reliable data transfer, which is also called *reliability* or *error recovery*, depending on what document you read. To accomplish reliability, TCP numbers data bytes using the Sequence and Acknowledgment fields in the TCP header. TCP achieves reliability in both directions, using the Sequence Number field of one direction combined with the Acknowledgment field in the opposite direction. Figure 6-5 shows the basic operation.

Figure 6-5 *TCP Acknowledgment Without Errors*

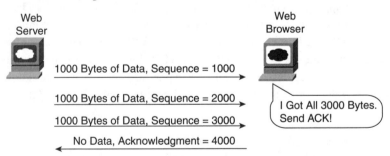

In Figure 6-5, the Acknowledgment field in the TCP header sent by the web client (4000) implies the next byte to be received; this is called *forward acknowledgment*. The sequence number reflects the number of the first byte in the segment. In this case, each TCP segment is 1000 bytes long; the Sequence and Acknowledgment fields count the number of bytes.

Figure 6-6 depicts the same scenario, but the second TCP segment was lost or is in error. The web client's reply has an ACK field equal to 2000, implying that the web client is expecting byte number 2000 next. The TCP function at the web server then could recover lost data by resending the second TCP segment. The TCP protocol allows for resending just that segment and then waiting, hoping that the web client will reply with an acknowledgment that equals 4000.

Figure 6-6 *TCP Acknowledgment with Errors*

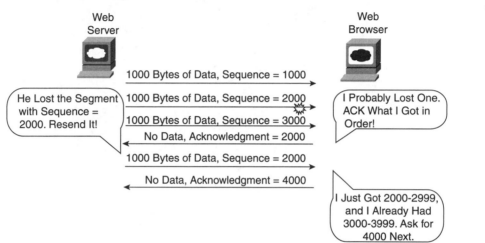

Although not shown, the sender also sets a retransmission timer, awaiting acknowledgment, just in case the acknowledgment is lost or all transmitted segments are lost. If that timer expires, the TCP sender sends all segments again.

Flow Control Using Windowing

TCP implements flow control by taking advantage of the Sequence and Acknowledgment fields in the TCP header, along with another field called the Window field. This Window field implies the maximum number of unacknowledged bytes that are allowed to be outstanding at any instant in time. The window starts small and then grows until errors occur. The size of the window changes over time, so it is sometimes called a *dynamic window*. Additionally, because the actual sequence and acknowledgment numbers grow over time, the window is sometimes called a *sliding window*, with the numbers sliding (moving) upward. When the window is full, the sender does not send, which controls the flow of data. Figure 6-7 shows windowing with a current window size of 3000. Each TCP segment has 1000 bytes of data.

Notice that the web server must wait after sending the third segment because the window is exhausted. When the acknowledgment has been received, another window can be sent. Because no errors have occurred, the web client grants a larger window to the server, so now 4000 bytes can be sent before the server receives an acknowledgment. In other words, the receiver uses the Window field to tell the sender how much data it can send before it must stop and wait for the next acknowledgment. As with other TCP features, windowing is symmetrical. Both sides send and receive, and, in each case, the receiver grants a window to the sender using the Window field.

Figure 6-7   *TCP Windowing*

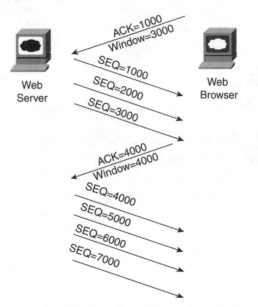

Windowing does not require that the sender stop sending in all cases. If an acknowledgment is received before the window is exhausted, a new window begins, and the sender continues sending data until the current window is exhausted. (The term *Positive Acknowledgment and Retransmission [PAR]* is sometimes used to describe the error recovery and windowing processes that TCP uses.)

Connection Establishment and Termination

TCP connection establishment occurs before any of the other TCP features can begin their work. Connection establishment refers to the process of initializing sequence and acknowledgment fields and agreeing on the port numbers used. Figure 6-8 shows an example of connection establishment flow.

This three-way connection establishment flow must end before data transfer can begin. The connection exists between the two sockets, although the TCP header has no single socket field. Of the three parts of a socket, the IP addresses are implied based on the source and destination IP addresses in the IP header. TCP is implied because a TCP header is in use, as specified by the protocol field value in the IP header. Therefore, the only parts of the socket that need to be encoded in the TCP header are the port numbers.

Figure 6-8 *TCP Connection Establishment*

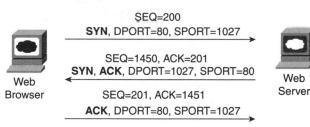

TCP signals connection establishment using 2 bits inside the flag fields of the TCP header. Called the SYN and ACK flags, these bits have a particularly interesting meaning. SYN means "Synchronize the sequence numbers," which is one necessary component in initialization for TCP. The ACK field means "The Acknowledgment field is valid in this header." Until the sequence numbers are initialized, the Acknowledgment field cannot be very useful. Also notice that in the initial TCP segment in Figure 6-8, no acknowledgment number is shown; this is because that number is not valid yet. Because the ACK field must be present in all the ensuing segments, the ACK bit continues to be set until the connection is terminated.

TCP initializes the Sequence Number and Acknowledgment Number fields to any number that fits into the 4-byte fields; the actual values shown in Figure 6-8 are simply sample values. The initialization flows are each considered to have a single byte of data, as reflected in the Acknowledgment Number fields in the example.

Figure 6-9 shows TCP connection termination. This four-way termination sequence is straightforward and uses an additional flag, called the *FIN bit*. (FIN is short for "finished," as you might guess.) One interesting note: Before the device on the right sends the third TCP segment in the sequence, it notifies the application that the connection is coming down. It then waits on an acknowledgment from the application before sending the third segment in the figure. Just in case the application takes some time to reply, the PC on the right sends the second flow in the figure, acknowledging that the other PC wants to take down the connection. Otherwise, the PC on the left might resend the first segment repeatedly.

Figure 6-9 *TCP Connection Termination*

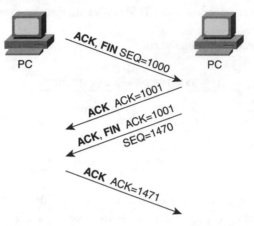

TCP establishes and terminates connections between the endpoints, whereas UDP does not. Many protocols operate under these same concepts, so the terms *connection-oriented* and *connectionless* are used to refer to the general idea of each. More formally, these terms can be defined as follows:

- **Connection-oriented protocol:** A protocol that requires an exchange of messages before data transfer begins or that has a required preestablished correlation between two endpoints

- **Connectionless protocol:** A protocol that does not require an exchange of messages and that does not require a preestablished correlation between two endpoints

Data Segmentation and Ordered Data Transfer

Applications need to send data. Sometimes the data is small—in some cases, a single byte. In other cases, such as with a file transfer, the data might be millions of bytes.

Each different type of data-link protocol typically has a limit on the *maximum transmission unit (MTU)* that can be sent inside a data link layer frame. In other words, the MTU is the size of the largest Layer 3 packet that can sit inside a frame's data field. For many data-link protocols, Ethernet included, the MTU is 1500 bytes.

TCP handles the fact that an application might give it millions of bytes to send by *segmenting* the data into smaller pieces, called *segments*. Because an IP packet can often be no more than 1500 bytes because of the MTU restrictions, and because IP and TCP headers are 20 bytes each, TCP typically segments large data into 1460-byte chunks.

The TCP receiver performs reassembly when it receives the segments. To reassemble the data, TCP must recover lost segments, as discussed previously. However, the TCP receiver must also reorder segments that arrive out of sequence. Because IP routing can choose to balance traffic across multiple links, the actual segments may be delivered out of order. So, the TCP receiver also must perform *ordered data transfer* by reassembling the data into the original order. The process is not hard to imagine: If segments arrive with the sequence numbers 1000, 3000, and 2000, each with 1000 bytes of data, the receiver can reorder them, and no retransmissions are required.

You should also be aware of some terminology related to TCP segmentation. The TCP header and the data field together are called a *TCP segment*. This term is similar to a data-link frame and an IP packet in that the terms refer to the headers and trailers for the respective layers, plus the encapsulated data. The term *L4PDU* also can be used instead of the term *TCP segment* because TCP is a Layer 4 protocol.

User Datagram Protocol

UDP provides a service for applications to exchange messages. Unlike TCP, UDP is connectionless and provides no reliability, no windowing, no reordering of the received data, and no segmentation of large chunks of data into the right size for transmission. However, UDP provides some functions of TCP, such as data transfer and multiplexing using port numbers, and it does so with fewer bytes of overhead and less processing required than TCP.

UDP data transfer differs from TCP data transfer in that no reordering or recovery is accomplished. Applications that use UDP are tolerant of the lost data, or they have some application mechanism to recover lost data. For example, VoIP uses UDP because if a voice packet is lost, by the time the loss could be noticed and the packet retransmitted, too much delay would have occurred, and the voice would be unintelligible. Also, DNS requests use UDP because the user will retry an operation if the DNS resolution fails. As another example, the Network File System (NFS), a remote file system application, performs recovery with application layer code, so UDP features are acceptable to NFS.

Figure 6-10 shows TCP and UDP header formats. Note the existence of both Source Port and Destination Port fields in the TCP and UDP headers, but the absence of Sequence Number and Acknowledgment Number fields in the UDP header. UDP does not need these fields because it makes no attempt to number the data for acknowledgments or resequencing.

UDP gains some advantages over TCP by not using the Sequence and Acknowledgment fields. The most obvious advantage of UDP over TCP is that there are fewer bytes of overhead. Not as obvious is the fact that UDP does not require waiting on acknowledgments or holding the data in memory until it is acknowledged. This means that UDP applications are not artificially slowed by the acknowledgment process, and memory is freed more quickly.

Figure 6-10 *TCP and UDP Headers*

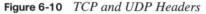

2	2	4	4	4 bits	6 bits	6 bits	2	2	2	3	1
Source Port	Dest. Port	Sequence Number	Ack. Number	Offset	Reserved	Flags	Window Size	Checksum	Urgent	Options	PAD

TCP Header

2	2	2	2
Source Port	Dest. Port	Length	Checksum

UDP Header

* Unless Specified, Lengths Shown
  Are the Numbers of Bytes

TCP/IP Applications

The whole goal of building an Enterprise network, or connecting a small home or office network to the Internet, is to use applications—applications such as web browsing, text messaging, e-mail, file downloads, voice, and video. This section examines a few issues related to network design in light of the applications expected in an internetwork. This is followed by a much deeper look at one particular application—web browsing using Hypertext Transfer Protocol (HTTP).

QoS Needs and the Impact of TCP/IP Applications

The needs of networked applications have changed and grown significantly over the years. When networks first became popular in Enterprises in the 1970s, the network typically supported only data applications, mainly text-only terminals and text-only printers. A single user might generate a few hundred bytes of data for the network every time he or she pressed the Enter key, maybe every 10 seconds or so.

The term quality of service (QoS) refers to the entire topic of what an application needs from the network service. Each type of application can be analyzed in terms of its QoS requirements on the network, so if the network meets those requirements, the application will work well. For example, the older text-based interactive applications required only a small amount of bandwidth, but they did like low delay. If those early networks supported a round-trip delay of less than 1 second, users were generally happy, because they had to wait less than 1 second for a response.

The QoS needs of data applications have changed over the years. Generally speaking, applications have tended to need more bandwidth, with lower delay as well. From those early days of networking to the present, here are some of the types of data applications that entered the marketplace, and their impact on the network:

■ Graphics-capable terminals and printers, which increased the required bytes for the same interaction as the old text-based terminals and printers

■ File transfers, which introduced much larger volumes of data, but with no significant response time requirements

■ File servers, which allow users to store files on a server—which might require a large volume of data transfer, but with a much smaller end-user response time requirement

■ The maturation of database technology, making vast amounts of data available to casual users, vastly increasing the number of users wanting access to data

■ The migration of common applications to web browsers, which encourages more users to access data

■ The general acceptance of e-mail as both a personal and business communications service, both inside companies and with other companies

■ The rapid commercialization of the Internet, enabling companies to offer data directly to their customers via the data network rather than via phone calls

Besides these and many other trends in the progression of data applications over the years, voice and video are in the middle of a migration onto the data network. Before the mid-to-late 1990s, voice and video typically used totally separate networking facilities. The migration of voice and video to the data network puts even more pressure on the data network to deliver the required quality of network service. Most companies today have either begun or plan on a migration to use IP phones, which pass voice traffic over the data network inside IP packets using application protocols generally referred to as voice over IP (VoIP). Additionally, several companies sell Internet phone service, which sends voice traffic over the Internet, again using VoIP packets. Figure 6-11 shows a few of the details of how VoIP works from a home high-speed Internet connection, with a generic voice adapter (VA) converting the analog voice signal from the normal telephone to an IP packet.

Figure 6-11 *Converting from Sound to Packets with a VA*

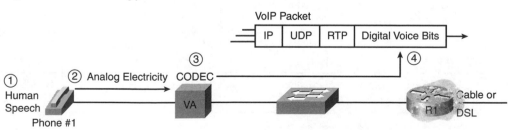

A single VoIP call that passes over a WAN typically takes less than 30 kbps of bandwidth, which is not a lot compared with many data applications today. In fact, most data applications consume as much bandwidth as they can grab. However, VoIP traffic has several other QoS demands on the network before the VoIP traffic will sound good:

■ **Low delay:** VoIP requires a very low delay between the sending phone and the receiving phone—typically less than 200 milliseconds (.2 seconds). This is a much lower delay than what is required by typical data applications.

■ **Low jitter:** Jitter is the variation in delay. VoIP requires very low jitter as well, whereas data applications can tolerate much higher jitter. For example, the jitter for consecutive VoIP packets should not exceed 30 milliseconds (.03 seconds), or the quality degrades.

■ **Loss:** If a VoIP packet is lost in transit because of errors or because a router doesn't have room to store the packet while waiting to send it, the VoIP packet is not delivered across the network. Because of the delay and jitter issues, there is no need to try to recover the lost packet. It would be useless by the time it was recovered. Lost packets can sound like a break in the sound of the VoIP call.

Video over IP has the same performance issues, except that video requires either more bandwidth (often time 300 to 400 kbps) or a lot more bandwidth (3 to 10 Mbps per video). The world of video over IP is also going through a bit of transformation with the advent of high-definition video over IP, again increasing demands on the bandwidth in the network.

For perspective, Table 6-4 summarizes some thoughts about the needs of various types of applications for the four main QoS requirements—bandwidth, delay, jitter, and packet loss. Memorizing the table is not important, but it is important to note that although VoIP requires relatively little bandwidth, it also requires low delay/jitter/loss for high quality. It is also important to note that video over IP has the same requirements, except for medium to large amounts of bandwidth.

Table 6-4   *Comparing Applications' Minimum Needs*

Type of Application	Bandwidth	Delay	Jitter	Loss
VoIP	Low	Low	Low	Low
Two-way video over IP (such as videoconferencing)	Medium/high	Low	Low	Low
One-way video over IP (such as security cameras)	Medium	Medium	Medium	Low
Interactive mission-critical data (such as web-based payroll)	Medium	Medium	High	High

Table 6-4 *Comparing Applications' Minimum Needs (Continued)*

Type of Application	Bandwidth	Delay	Jitter	Loss
Interactive business data (such as online chat with a coworker)	Low/medium	Medium	High	High
File transfer (such as backing up disk drives)	High	High	High	High
Nonbusiness (such as checking the latest sports scores)	Medium	High	High	High

To support the QoS requirements of the various applications, routers and switches can be configured with a wide variety of QoS tools. They are beyond the scope of the CCNA exams (but are covered on several of the Cisco professional-level certifications). However, the QoS tools must be used for a modern network to be able to support high-quality VoIP and video over IP.

Next we examine the most popular application layer protocol for interactive data applications today—HTTP and the World Wide Web (WWW). The goal is to show one example of how application layer protocols work.

The World Wide Web, HTTP, and SSL

The *World Wide Web* (WWW) consists of all the Internet-connected web servers in the world, plus all Internet-connected hosts with web browsers. *Web servers*, which consist of web server software running on a computer, store information (in the form of *web pages*) that might be useful to different people. *Web browsers*, which is software installed on an end user's computer, provide the means to connect to a web server and display the web pages stored on the web server.

> **NOTE** Although most people use the term web browser, or simply browser, web browsers are also called *web clients*, because they obtain a service from a web server.

For this process to work, several specific application-layer functions must occur. The user must somehow identify the server, the specific web page, and the protocol used to get the data from the server. The client must find the server's IP address, based on the server's name, typically using DNS. The client must request the web page, which actually consists of multiple separate files, and the server must send the files to the web browser. Finally, for electronic commerce (e-commerce) applications, the transfer of data, particularly sensitive financial data, needs to be secure, again using application layer features. The following sections address each of these functions.

Universal Resource Locators

For a browser to display a web page, the browser must identify the server that has the web page, plus other information that identifies the particular web page. Most web servers have many web pages. For example, if you use a web browser to browse http://www.cisco.com, and you click around that web page, you'll see another web page. Click again, and you'll see another web page. In each case, the clicking action identifies the server's IP address and the specific web page, with the details mostly hidden from you. (These clickable items on a web page, which in turn bring you to another web page, are called *links*.)

The browser user can identify a web page when you click something on a web page or when you enter a *Universal Resource Locator* (URL) (often called a *web address*) in the browser's address area. Both options—clicking a link and entering a URL—refer to a URL, because when you click a link on a web page, that link actually refers to a URL.

> **NOTE**   To see the hidden URL referenced by a link, open a browser to a web page, hover the mouse pointer over a link, right-click, and select **Properties**. The pop-up window should display the URL to which the browser would be directed if you clicked that link.

Each URL defines the protocol used to transfer data, the name of the server, and the particular web page on that server. The URL can be broken into three parts:

- The protocol is listed before the //.

- The hostname is listed between the // and the /.

- The name of the web page is listed after the /.

For example:

    http://www.cisco.com/go/prepcenter

In this case, the protocol is *Hypertext Transfer Protocol* (HTTP), the hostname is www.cisco.com, and the name of the web page is go/prepcenter. This URL is particularly useful, because it is the base web page for the Cisco CCNA Prep Center.

Finding the Web Server Using DNS

As mentioned in Chapter 5, "Fundamentals of IP Addressing and Routing," a host can use DNS to discover the IP address that corresponds to a particular hostname. Although URLs may include the IP address of the web server instead of the name of the web server, URLs typically list the hostname. So, before the browser can send a packet to the web server, the browser typically needs to resolve the name in the URL to that name's corresponding IP address.

To pull together several concepts, Figure 6-12 shows the DNS process as initiated by a web browser, as well as some other related information. From a basic perspective, the user enters the URL (http://www.cisco.com/go/prepcenter), resolves the www.cisco.com name into the correct IP address, and starts sending packets to the web server.

Figure 6-12 *DNS Resolution and Requesting a Web Page*

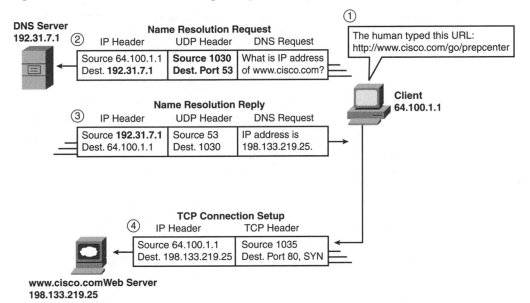

The steps shown in the figure are as follows:

1. The user enters the URL, http://www.cisco.com/go/prepcenter, into the browser's address area.

2. The client sends a DNS request to the DNS server. Typically, the client learns the DNS server's IP address via DHCP. Note that the DNS request uses a UDP header, with a destination port of the DNS well-known port of 53. (See Table 6-3, earlier in this chapter, for a list of popular well-known ports.)

3. The DNS server sends a reply, listing IP address 198.133.219.25 as www.cisco.com's IP address. Note also that the reply shows a destination IP address of 64.100.1.1, the client's IP address. It also shows a UDP header, with source port 53; the source port is 53 because the data is sourced, or sent by, the DNS server.

4. The client begins the process of establishing a new TCP connection to the web server. Note that the destination IP address is the just-learned IP address of the web server. The packet includes a TCP header, because HTTP uses TCP. Also note the destination TCP port is 80, the well-known port for HTTP. Finally, the SYN bit is shown, as a reminder that the TCP connection establishment process begins with a TCP segment with the SYN bit turned on (binary 1).

At this point in the process, the web browser is almost finished setting up a TCP connection to the web server. The next section picks up the story at that point, examining how the web browser then gets the files that comprise the desired web page.

Transferring Files with HTTP

After a web client (browser) has created a TCP connection to a web server, the client can begin requesting the web page from the server. Most often, the protocol used to transfer the web page is HTTP. The HTTP application-layer protocol, defined in RFC 2616, defines how files can be transferred between two computers. HTTP was specifically created for the purpose of transferring files between web servers and web clients.

HTTP defines several commands and responses, with the most frequently used being the HTTP GET request. To get a file from a web server, the client sends an HTTP GET request to the server, listing the filename. If the server decides to send the file, the server sends an HTTP GET response, with a return code of 200 (meaning "OK"), along with the file's contents.

> **NOTE**   Many return codes exist for HTTP requests. For instance, when the server does not have the requested file, it issues a return code of 404, which means "file not found." Most web browsers do not show the specific numeric HTTP return codes, instead displaying a response such as "page not found" in reaction to receiving a return code of 404.

Web pages typically consist of multiple files, called *objects*. Most web pages contain text as well as several graphical images, animated advertisements, and possibly voice or video. Each of these components is stored as a different object (file) on the web server. To get them all, the web browser gets the first file. This file may (and typically does) include references to other URLs, so the browser then also requests the other objects. Figure 6-13 shows the general idea, with the browser getting the first file and then two others.

In this case, after the web browser gets the first file—the one called "/go/ccna" in the URL—the browser reads and interprets that file. Besides containing parts of the web page, the file refers to two other files, so the browser issues two additional HTTP get requests.

Note that, even though it isn't shown in the figure, all these commands flow over one (or possibly more) TCP connections between the client and the server. This means that TCP would provide error recovery, ensuring that the data was delivered.

Figure 6-13 *Multiple HTTP Get Requests/Responses*

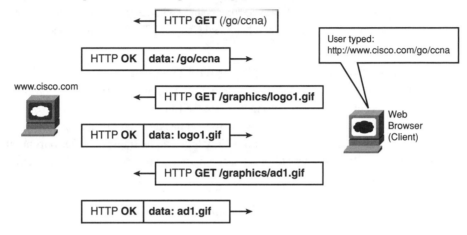

This chapter ends with an introduction to network security.

Network Security

In years past, security threats came from geniuses or nerdy students with lots of time. The numbers of these people were relatively small. Their main motivation was to prove that they could break into another network. Since then, the number of potential attackers and the sophistication of the attacks have increased exponentially. Attacks that once required attackers to have an advanced degree in computing now can be done with easily downloaded and freely available tools that the average junior-high student can figure out how to use. Every company and almost every person connects to the Internet, making essentially the whole world vulnerable to attack.

The biggest danger today may be the changes in attackers' motivation. Instead of looking for a challenge, or to steal millions, today's attackers can be much more organized and motivated. Organized crime tries to steal billions by extorting companies by threatening a denial of service (DoS) attack on the companies' public web servers. Or they steal identity and credit card information for sometimes hundreds of thousands of people with one sophisticated attack. Attacks might come from nation-states or terrorists. Not only might they attack military and government networks, but they might try to disrupt infrastructure services for utilities and transportation and cripple economies.

Security is clearly a big issue, and one that requires serious attention. For the purposes of this book, and for the ICND1 exam, the goal is to know some of the basic terminology, types of security issues, and some of the common tools used to mitigate security risks. To that end, this final section of the chapter gives you some perspectives on attacks, and then it introduces four classes of security tools. Beyond this introduction, this book also examines device security—the securing of access to routers and switches in this case—as part of Chapter 8, "Operating Cisco LAN Switches," and Chapter 13, "Operating Cisco Routers."

Perspectives on the Sources and Types of Threats

Figure 6-14 shows a common network topology with a firewall. Firewalls are probably the best-known security appliance, sitting between the Enterprise network and the dark, cold, unsecure Internet. The firewall's role is to stop packets that the network or security engineer has deemed unsafe. The firewall mainly looks at the transport layer port numbers and the application layer headers to prevent certain ports and applications from getting packets into the Enterprise.

Figure 6-14 *Typical Enterprise Internet Connection with a Firewall*

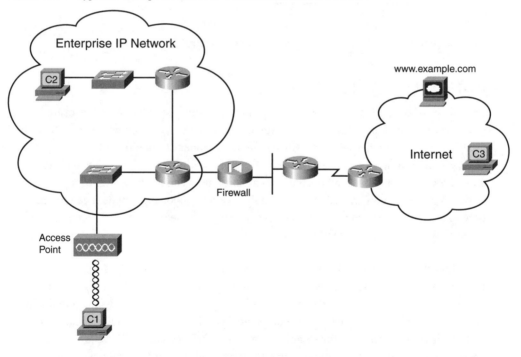

Figure 6-14 might give an average employee of the Enterprise a false sense of security. He or she might think the firewall provides protection from all the dangers of connecting to the Internet. However, a perimeter firewall (a firewall on the edge, or perimeter, of the network) does not protect the Enterprise from all the dangers possible through the Internet connection. Not only that, a higher percentage of security attacks actually come from inside the Enterprise network, and the firewall does not even see those packets.

To appreciate a bit more about the dangers inside the Enterprise network, it helps to understand a bit more about the kinds of attacks that might occur:

- **Denial of service (DoS) attacks:** An attack whose purpose is to break things. DoS attacks called *destroyers* try to harm the hosts, erasing data and software. DoS attacks called *crashers* cause harm by causing hosts to fail or causing the machine to no longer be able to connect to the network. Also, DoS attacks called *flooders* flood the network with packets to make the network unusable, preventing any useful communications with the servers.

- **Reconnaissance attacks:** This kind of attack may be disruptive as a side effect, but its goal is gathering information to perform an access attack. An example is learning IP addresses and then trying to discover servers that do not appear to require encryption to connect to the server.

- **Access attacks:** An attempt to steal data, typically data for some financial advantage, for a competitive advantage with another company, or even for international espionage.

Computer viruses are just one tool that can be used to carry out any of these attacks. A virus is a program that is somehow transferred onto an unsuspecting computer, possibly through an e-mail attachment or website download. A virus could just cause problems on the computer, or it could steal information and send it back to the attacker.

Today, most computers use some type of anti-virus software to watch for known viruses and prevent them from infecting the computer. Among other activities, the anti-virus software loads a list of known characteristics of all viruses, with these characteristics being known as virus *signatures*. By periodically downloading the latest virus signatures, the anti-virus software knows about all the latest viruses. By watching all packets entering the computer, the anti-virus software can recognize known viruses and prevent the computer from being infected. These programs also typically run an automatic periodic scan of the entire contents of the computer disk drives, looking for any known viruses.

To appreciate some of the security risks inherent in an Enterprise network that already has a quality perimeter firewall, consider Figure 6-15. The list following the figure explains three ways in which the Enterprise network is exposed to the possibility of an attack from within.

Figure 6-15 *Common Security Issues in an Enterprise*

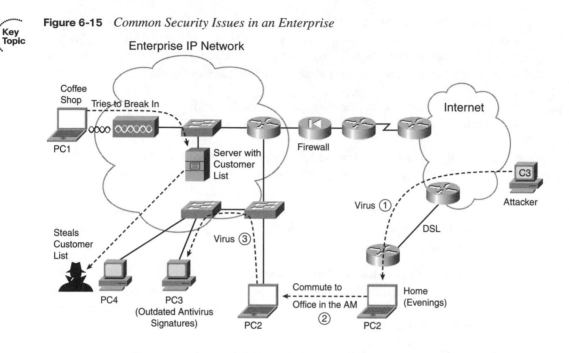

The following types of problems could commonly occur in this Enterprise:

■ **Access from the wireless LAN:** Wireless LANs allow users to access the rest of the devices in the Enterprise. The wireless radio signals might leave the building, so an unsecured wireless LAN allows the user across the street in a coffee shop to access the Enterprise network, letting the attacker (PC1) begin the next phase of trying to gain access to the computers in the Enterprise.

■ **Infected mobile laptops:** When an employee brings his or her laptop (PC2) home, with no firewall or other security, the laptop may become infected with a virus. When the user returns to the office in the morning, the laptop connects to the Enterprise network, with the virus spreading to other PCs, such as PC3. PC3 may be vulnerable in part because the users may have avoided running the daily anti-virus software scans that, although useful, can annoy the user.

■ **Disgruntled employees:** The user at PC4 is planning to move to a new company. He steals information from the network and loads it onto an MP3 player or USB flash drive. This allows him to carry the entire customer database in a device that can be easily concealed and removed from the building.

These attacks are just a few examples; a large number of variations and methods exist. To prevent such problems, Cisco suggests a security model that uses tools that automatically work to defend the network, with security features located throughout the network. Cisco uses the term *security in depth* to refer to a security design that includes security tools throughout the network, including features in routers and switches. Cisco also uses the term "self-defending network" to refer to automation in which the network devices automatically react to network problems.

For example, Network Admission Control (NAC) is one security tool to help prevent two of the attacks just described. Among other things, NAC can monitor when devices first connect to a LAN, be they wireless or wired. The NAC feature, partly implemented by features in the LAN switches, would prevent a computer from connecting to the LAN until its virus definitions were updated, with a requirement for a recent full virus scan. NAC also includes a requirement that the user supply a username and password before being able to send other data into the LAN, helping prevent the guy at the coffee shop from gaining access. However, NAC does not prevent a disgruntled employee from causing harm, because the employee typically has a working username/password to be authenticated with NAC.

Besides viruses, many other tools can be used to form an attack. The following list summarizes some of the more common terms for the tools in an attacker's toolkit:

- **Scanner:** A tool that sends connection requests to different TCP and UDP ports, for different applications, in an attempt to discover which hosts run which IP services, and possibly the operating system used on each host.

- **Spyware:** A virus that looks for private or sensitive information, tracking what the user does with the computer, and passing the information back to the attacker in the Internet.

- **Worm:** A self-propagating program that can quickly replicate itself around Enterprise networks and the Internet, often performing DoS attacks, particularly on servers.

- **Keystroke logger:** A virus that logs all keystrokes, or possibly just keystrokes from when secure sites are accessed, reporting the information to the attacker. Loggers can actually capture your username and password to secure sites before the information leaves the computer, which could give the attacker access to your favorite financial websites.

■ **Phishing:** The attacker sets up a website that outwardly looks like a legitimate website, often for a bank or credit card company. The phisher sends e-mails listing the illegitimate website's URL but making it look like the real company (for example, "Click here to update the records for your credit card to make it more secure."). The phisher hopes that a few people will take the bait, connect to the illegitimate website, and enter information such as their name, address, credit card number, social security number (in the U.S.), or other national government ID number. The best defense for phishing attacks may well be better user training and more awareness about the exposure.

■ **Malware:** This refers to a broad class of malicious viruses, including spyware.

The solution to these and the many other security issues not mentioned here is to provide security in depth throughout the network. The rest of this section introduces a few of the tools that can be used to provide that in-depth security.

Firewalls and the Cisco Adaptive Security Appliance (ASA)

Firewalls examine all packets entering and exiting a network for the purpose of filtering unwanted traffic. Firewalls determine the allowed traffic versus the disallowed traffic based on many characteristics of the packets, including their destination and source IP addresses and the TCP and UDP port numbers (which imply the application protocol). Firewalls also examine the application layer headers.

The term firewall is taken from the world of building and architecture. A firewall in a building has two basic requirements. It must be made of fire-resistant materials, and the architect limits the number of openings in the wall (doors, conduits for wires and plumbing), limiting the paths through which the fire can spread. Similarly, a network firewall must itself be hardened against security attacks. It must disallow all packets unless the engineer has configured a firewall rule that allows the traffic—a process often called "opening a hole," again with analogies to a firewall in a building.

Firewalls sit in the packet-forwarding path between two networks, often with one LAN interface connecting to the secure local network, and one to the other, less-secure network (often the Internet). Additionally, because some hosts in the Enterprise need to be accessible from the Internet—an inherently less secure practice—the firewall typically also has an interface connected to another small part of the Enterprise network, called the demilitarized zone (DMZ). The DMZ LAN is a place to put devices that need to be accessible, but that access puts them at higher risk. Figure 6-16 shows a sample design, with a firewall that has three interfaces.

Figure 6-16 *Common Internet Design Using a Firewall*

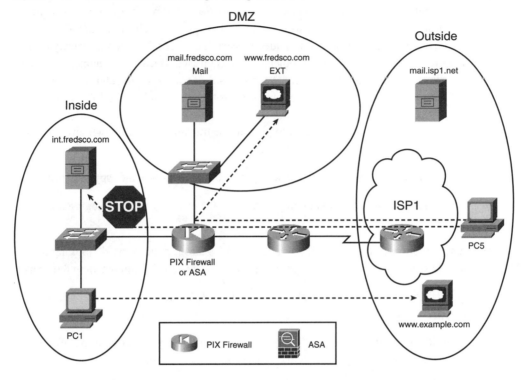

To do its job, the firewall needs to be configured to know which interfaces are connected to the inside, outside, and DMZ parts of the network. Then, a series of rules can be configured that tell the firewall which traffic patterns are allowed and which are not. The figure shows two typically allowed flows and one typical disallowed flow, shown with dashed lines:

- Allow web clients on the inside network (such as PC1) to send packets to web servers (such as the www.example.com web server)

- Prevent web clients in the outside network (such as PC5) from sending packets to web servers in the inside network (such as the internal web server int.fredsco.com)

- Allow web clients in the outside network (such as PC5) to connect to DMZ web servers (such as the www.fredsco.com web server)

In years past, Cisco sold firewalls with the trade name PIX firewall. A few years ago, Cisco introduced a whole new generation of network security hardware using the trade name Adaptive Security Appliance (ASA). ASA hardware can act as a firewall, in other security roles, and in a combination of roles. So, when speaking about security, the term firewall still refers to the functions, but today the Cisco product may be an older still-installed PIX firewall or a newer ASA. (Figure 6-16 shows the ASA icon at the bottom.)

Anti-x

A comprehensive security plan requires several functions that prevent different known types of problems. For example, host-based anti-virus software helps prevent the spread of viruses. Cisco ASA appliances can provide or assist in the overall in-depth security design with a variety of tools that prevent problems such as viruses. Because the names of several of the individual tools start with "anti-," Cisco uses the term *anti-x* to refer to the whole class of security tools that prevent these various problems, including the following:

- **Anti-virus:** Scans network traffic to prevent the transmission of known viruses based on virus signatures.

- **Anti-spyware:** Scans network traffic to prevent the transmission of spyware programs.

- **Anti-spam:** Examines e-mail before it reaches the users, deleting or segregating junk e-mail.

- **Anti-phishing:** Monitors URLs sent in messages through the network, looking for the fake URLs inherent in phishing attacks, preventing the attack from reaching the users.

- **URL filtering:** Filters web traffic based on URL to prevent users from connecting to inappropriate sites.

- **E-mail filtering:** Provides anti-spam tools. Also filters e-mails containing offensive materials, potentially protecting the Enterprise from lawsuits.

The Cisco ASA appliance can be used to perform the network-based role for all these anti-x functions.

Intrusion Detection and Prevention

Some types of attacks cannot be easily found with anti-x tools. For example, if a known virus infects a computer solely through an e-mail attachment of a file called this-is-a-virus.exe, the anti-virus software on the ASA or the end-user computer can easily identify and delete the virus. However, some forms of attacks can be more sophisticated. The attacks may not even include the transfer of a file, instead using a myriad of other, more-challenging methods, often taking advantage of new bugs in the operating system.

The world of network security includes a couple of types of tools that can be used to help prevent the more sophisticated kinds of attacks: Intrusion Detection Systems (IDS) and Intrusion Prevention Systems (IPS). IDS and IPS tools detect these threats by watching for trends, looking for attacks that use particular patterns of messages, and other factors. For instance, an IDS or IPS can track sequences of packets between hosts to look for a file being sent to more and more hosts, as might be done by a worm trying to spread inside a network.

IDS and IPS systems differ mainly in how they monitor the traffic and how they can respond to a perceived threat. IDS tools typically receive a copy of packets via a monitoring port, rather than being part of the packets' forwarding path. The IDS can then rate and report on each potential threat, and potentially ask other devices, such as firewalls and routers, to help prevent the attack (if they can). IPS tools often sit in the packets' forwarding path, giving the IPS the capability to perform the same functions as the IDS, but also to react and filter the traffic. The ability to react is important with some threats, such as the Slammer worm in 2003, which doubled the number of infected hosts every 9 seconds or so, infecting 75,000 hosts in the first 10 minutes of the attack. This kind of speed requires the use of reactive tools, rather than waiting on an engineer to see a report and take action.

Virtual Private Networks (VPN)

The last class of security tool introduced in this chapter is the virtual private network (VPN), which might be better termed a virtual private WAN. A leased line is inherently secure, effectively acting like an electrical circuit between the two routers. VPNs send packets through the Internet, which is a public network. However, VPNs make the communication secure, like a private leased line.

Without VPN technology, the packets sent between two devices over the Internet are inherently unsecure. The packets flowing through the Internet could be intercepted by attackers in the Internet. In fact, along with the growth of the Internet, attackers found ways to redirect packets and examine the contents, both to see the data and to find additional information (such as usernames and passwords) as part of a reconnaissance attack. Additionally, users and servers might not be able to tell the difference between a legitimate packet from an authentic user and a packet from an attacker who is trying to gain even more information and access.

VPNs provide a solution to allow the use of the Internet without the risks of unknowingly accepting data from attacking hosts and without the risk of others reading the data in transit. VPNs authenticate the VPN's endpoints, meaning that both endpoints can be sure that the other endpoint of the VPN connection is legitimate. Additionally, VPNs encrypt the original IP packets so that even if an attacker managed to get a copy of the packets as they pass through the Internet, he or she cannot read the data. Figure 16-17 shows the general idea, with an intranet VPN and an access VPN.

The figure shows an example of two types of VPNs: an *access VPN* and a *site-to-site intranet VPN*. An access VPN supports a home or small-office user, with the remote office's PC typically encrypting the packets. A site-to-site intranet VPN typically connects two sites of the same Enterprise, effectively creating a secure connection between two different parts inside (intra) the same Enterprise network. For intranet VPNs, the encryption could be done for all devices using different kinds of hardware, including routers, firewalls, purpose-built VPN concentrator hardware, or ASAs, as shown in the main site of the Enterprise.

Figure 6-17 *Sample VPNs*

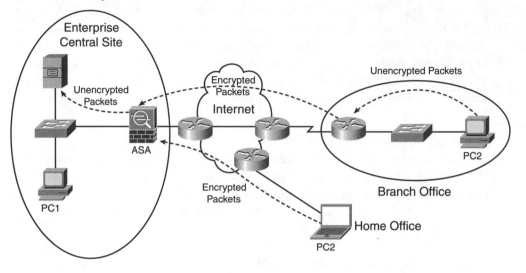

Figure 6-17 shows how VPNs can use end-to-end encryption, in which the data remains encrypted while being forwarded through one or more routers. Additionally, link encryption can be used to encrypt data at the data link layer, so the data is encrypted only as it passes over one data link. Chapter 11, "Wireless LANs," shows an example of link encryption.

Exam Preparation Tasks

Review All the Key Topics

Review the most important topics from this chapter, noted with the key topics icon. Table 6-5 lists these key topics and where each is discussed.

Key Topic

Table 6-5 *Key Topics for Chapter 6*

Key Topic Element	Description	Page Number
Table 6-2	Functions of TCP and UDP	134
Table 6-3	Well-known TCP and UDP port numbers	139-140
Figure 6-6	Example of TCP error recovery using forward acknowledgments	141
Figure 6-7	Example of TCP sliding windows	142
Figure 6-8	Example of TCP connection establishment	143
List	Definitions of connection-oriented and connectionless	144
List	QoS requirements for VoIP	148
List	Three types of attacks	155
Figure 6-15	Examples of common security exposures in an Enterprise	156

Complete the Tables and Lists from Memory

Print a copy of Appendix H, "Memory Tables" (found on the CD), or at least the section for this chapter, and complete the tables and lists from memory. Appendix I, "Memory Tables Answer Key," also on the CD, includes completed tables and lists for you to check your work.

Definitions of Key Terms

Define the following key terms from this chapter and check your answers in the glossary:

Anti-x, connection establishment, DoS, error detection, error recovery, firewall, flow control, forward acknowledgment, HTTP, Intrusion Detection System, Intrusion Prevention System, ordered data transfer, port, Positive Acknowledgment and Retransmission (PAR), segment, sliding windows, URL, virtual private network, VoIP, web server

Cisco Published ICND1 Exam Topics* Covered in This Part:

Describe the operation of data networks.

- Use the OSI and TCP/IP models and their associated protocols to explain how data flows in a network
- Interpret network diagrams
- Determine the path between two hosts across a network
- Identify and correct common network problems at Layers 1, 2, 3, and 7 using a layered model approach
- Differentiate between LAN/WAN operation and features

Implement a small switched network

- Select the appropriate media, cables, ports, and connectors to connect switches to other network devices and hosts
- Explain the technology and media access control method for Ethernet technologies
- Explain network segmentation and basic traffic management concepts
- Explain the operation of Cisco switches and basic switching concepts
- Perform, save, and verify initial switch configuration tasks including remote access management
- Verify network status and switch operation using basic utilities (including: ping, traceroute, Telnet, SSH, ARP, ipconfig), show and debug commands
- Implement and verify basic security for a switch (port security, deactivate ports)
- Identify, prescribe, and resolve common switched network media issues, configuration issues, autonegotiation, and switch hardware failures

Explain and select the appropriate administrative tasks required for a WLAN

- Describe standards associated with wireless media (including: IEEE Wi-Fi Alliance, ITU/FCC)
- Identify and describe the purpose of the components in a small wireless network (including: SSID, BSS, ESS)
- Identify the basic parameters to configure on a wireless network to ensure that devices connect to the correct access point
- Compare and contrast wireless security features and capabilities of WPA security (including: open, WEP, WPA-1/2)
- Identify common issues with implementing wireless networks

Identify security threats to a network and describe general methods to mitigate those threats

- Describe security recommended practices including initial steps to secure network devices

*Always recheck http://www.cisco.com for the latest posted exam topics.

Part II: LAN Switching

This chapter covers the following subjects:

LAN Switching Concepts: Explains the basic processes used by LAN switches to forward frames.

LAN Design Considerations: Describes the reasoning and terminology for how to design a switched LAN that operates well.

CHAPTER 7

Ethernet LAN Switching Concepts

Chapter 3, "Fundamentals of LANs," covered the conceptual and physical attributes of Ethernet LANs in a fair amount of detail. That chapter explains a wide variety of Ethernet concepts, including the basics of UTP cabling, the basic operation of and concepts behind hubs and switches, comparisons of different kinds of Ethernet standards, and Ethernet data link layer concepts such as addressing and framing.

The chapters in Part II, "LAN Switching," complete this book's coverage of Ethernet LANs, with one additional chapter (Chapter 11) on wireless LANs. This chapter explains most of the remaining Ethernet concepts that were not covered in Chapter 3. In particular, it contains a more detailed examination of how switches work, as well as the LAN design implications of using hubs, bridges, switches, and routers. Chapters 8 through 10 focus on how to access and use Cisco switches. Chapter 8, "Operating Cisco LAN Switches," focuses on the switch user interface. Chapter 9, "Ethernet Switch Configuration," shows you how to configure a Cisco switch. Chapter 10, "Ethernet Switch Troubleshooting," shows you how to troubleshoot problems with Cisco switches. Chapter 11, "Wireless LANs," concludes Part II with a look at the concepts behind wireless LANs.

"Do I Know This Already?" Quiz

The "Do I Know This Already?" quiz allows you to assess whether you should read the entire chapter. If you miss no more than one of these eight self-assessment questions, you might want to move ahead to the "Exam Preparation Tasks" section. Table 7-1 lists the major headings in this chapter and the "Do I Know This Already?" quiz questions covering the material in those sections. This helps you assess your knowledge of these specific areas. The answers to the "Do I Know This Already?" quiz appear in Appendix A.

Table 7-1 *"Do I Know This Already?" Foundation Topics Section-to-Question Mapping*

Foundation Topics Section	Questions
LAN Switching Concepts	1–5
LAN Design Considerations	6–8

1. Which of the following statements describes part of the process of how a switch decides to forward a frame destined for a known unicast MAC address?

    a. It compares the unicast destination address to the bridging, or MAC address, table.

    b. It compares the unicast source address to the bridging, or MAC address, table.

    c. It forwards the frame out all interfaces in the same VLAN except for the incoming interface.

    d. It compares the destination IP address to the destination MAC address.

    e. It compares the frame's incoming interface to the source MAC entry in the MAC address table.

2. Which of the following statements describes part of the process of how a LAN switch decides to forward a frame destined for a broadcast MAC address?

    a. It compares the unicast destination address to the bridging, or MAC address, table.

    b. It compares the unicast source address to the bridging, or MAC address, table.

    c. It forwards the frame out all interfaces in the same VLAN except for the incoming interface.

    d. It compares the destination IP address to the destination MAC address.

    e. It compares the frame's incoming interface to the source MAC entry in the MAC address table.

3. Which of the following statements best describes what a switch does with a frame destined for an unknown unicast address?

    a. It forwards out all interfaces in the same VLAN except for the incoming interface.

    b. It forwards the frame out the one interface identified by the matching entry in the MAC address table.

    c. It compares the destination IP address to the destination MAC address.

    d. It compares the frame's incoming interface to the source MAC entry in the MAC address table.

4. Which of the following comparisons does a switch make when deciding whether a new MAC address should be added to its bridging table?

    a. It compares the unicast destination address to the bridging, or MAC address, table.

    b. It compares the unicast source address to the bridging, or MAC address, table.

    c. It compares the VLAN ID to the bridging, or MAC address, table.

    d. It compares the destination IP address's ARP cache entry to the bridging, or MAC address, table.

5. PC1, with MAC address 1111.1111.1111, is connected to Switch SW1's Fa0/1 interface. PC2, with MAC address 2222.2222.2222, is connected to SW1's Fa0/2 interface. PC3, with MAC address 3333.3333.3333, connects to SW1's Fa0/3 interface. The switch begins with no dynamically learned MAC addresses, followed by PC1 sending a frame with a destination address of 2222.2222.2222. If the next frame to reach the switch is a frame sent by PC3, destined for PC2's MAC address of 2222.2222.2222, which of the following are true?

    a. The switch forwards the frame out interface Fa0/1.

    b. The switch forwards the frame out interface Fa0/2.

    c. The switch forwards the frame out interface Fa0/3.

    d. The switch discards (filters) the frame.

6. Which of the following devices would be in the same collision domain as PC1?

    a. PC2, which is separated from PC1 by an Ethernet hub

    b. PC3, which is separated from PC1 by a transparent bridge

    c. PC4, which is separated from PC1 by an Ethernet switch

    d. PC5, which is separated from PC1 by a router

7. Which of the following devices would be in the same broadcast domain as PC1?

    a. PC2, which is separated from PC1 by an Ethernet hub

    b. PC3, which is separated from PC1 by a transparent bridge

    c. PC4, which is separated from PC1 by an Ethernet switch

    d. PC5, which is separated from PC1 by a router

8. Which of the following Ethernet standards support a maximum cable length of longer than 100 meters?

   a. 100BASE-TX

   b. 1000BASE-LX

   c. 1000BASE-T

   d. 100BASE-FX

Foundation Topics

This chapter begins by covering LAN concepts—in particular, the mechanics of how LAN switches forward Ethernet frames. Following that, the next major section focuses on campus LAN design concepts and terminology. It includes a review of some of the Ethernet types that use optical cabling and therefore support longer cabling distances than do the UTP-based Ethernet standards.

LAN Switching Concepts

Chapter 3 introduced Ethernet, including the concept of LAN hubs and switches. When thinking about how LAN switches work, it can be helpful to think about how earlier products (hubs and bridges) work. The first part of this section briefly looks at why switches were created. Following that, this section explains the three main functions of a switch, plus a few other details.

Historical Progression: Hubs, Bridges, and Switches

As mentioned in Chapter 3, Ethernet started out with standards that used a physical electrical bus created with coaxial cabling. 10BASE-T Ethernet came next. It offered improved LAN availability, because a problem on a single cable did not affect the rest of the LAN—a common problem with 10BASE2 and 10BASE5 networks. 10BASE-T allowed the use of unshielded twisted-pair (UTP) cabling, which is much cheaper than coaxial cable. Also, many buildings already had UTP cabling installed for phone service, so 10BASE-T quickly became a popular alternative to 10BASE2 and 10BASE5 Ethernet networks. For perspective and review, Figure 7-1 depicts the typical topology for 10BASE2 and for 10BASE-T with a hub.

Figure 7-1   *10BASE2 and 10BASE-T (with a Hub) Physical Topologies*

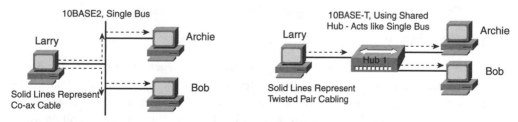

Although using 10BASE-T with a hub improved Ethernet as compared to the older standards, several drawbacks continued to exist, even with 10BASE-T using hubs:

- Any device sending a frame could have the frame collide with a frame sent by any other device attached to that LAN segment.

- Only one device could send a frame at a time, so the devices shared the (10-Mbps) bandwidth.

- Broadcasts sent by one device were heard by, and processed by, all other devices on the LAN.

When these three types of Ethernet were introduced, a shared 10 Mbps of bandwidth was a huge amount! Before the introduction of LANs, people often used dumb terminals, with a 56-kbps WAN link being a really fast connection to the rest of the network—and that 56 kbps was shared among everyone in a remote building. So, in the days when 10BASE-T was first used, getting a connection to a 10BASE-T Ethernet LAN was like getting a Gigabit Ethernet connection for your work PC today. It was more bandwidth than you thought you would ever need.

Over time, the performance of many Ethernet networks started to degrade. People developed applications to take advantage of the LAN bandwidth. More devices were added to each Ethernet. Eventually, an entire network became congested. The devices on the same Ethernet could not send (collectively) more than 10 Mbps of traffic because they all shared the 10 Mbps of bandwidth. In addition, the increase in traffic volumes increased the number of collisions. Long before the overall utilization of an Ethernet approached 10 Mbps, Ethernet began to suffer because of increasing collisions.

Ethernet bridges were created to solve some of the performance issues. Bridges solved the growing Ethernet congestion problem in two ways:

- They reduced the number of collisions that occurred in the network.

- They added bandwidth to the network.

Figure 7-2 shows the basic premise behind an Ethernet transparent bridge. The top part of the figure shows a 10BASE-T network before adding a bridge, and the lower part shows the network after it has been *segmented* using a bridge. The bridge creates two separate *collision domains*. Fred's frames can collide with Barney's, but they cannot collide with Wilma's or Betty's. If one LAN segment is busy, and the bridge needs to forward a frame onto the busy segment, the bridge simply buffers the frame (holds the frame in memory) until the segment is no longer busy. Reducing collisions, and assuming no significant change in the number of devices or the load on the network, greatly improves network performance.

Figure 7-2   *Bridge Creates Two Collision Domains and Two Shared Ethernets*

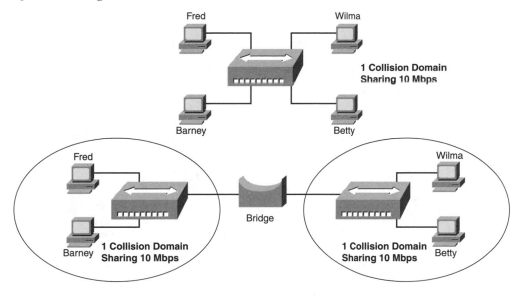

Adding a bridge between two hubs really creates two separate 10BASE-T networks—one on the left and one on the right. The 10BASE-T network on the left has its own 10 Mbps to share, as does the network on the right. So, in this example, the total network bandwidth is doubled to 20 Mbps, as compared with the 10BASE-T network at the top of the figure.

LAN switches perform the same basic core functions as bridges, but with many enhanced features. Like bridges, switches segment a LAN into separate parts, each part being a separate collision domain. Switches have potentially large numbers of interfaces, with highly optimized hardware, allowing even small Enterprise switches to forward millions of Ethernet frames per second. By creating a separate collision domain for each interface, switches multiply the amount of available bandwidth in the network. And, as mentioned in Chapter 3, if a switch port connects to a single device, that Ethernet segment can use full-duplex logic, essentially doubling the speed on that segment.

NOTE   A switch's effect of segmenting an Ethernet LAN into one collision domain per interface is sometimes called *microsegmentation*.

Figure 7-3 summarizes some of these key concepts, showing the same hosts as in Figure 7-2, but now connected to a switch. In this case, all switch interfaces are running at 100 Mbps, with four collision domains. Note that each interface also uses full duplex. This is possible because only one device is connected to each port, essentially eliminating collisions for the network shown.

Figure 7-3 *Switch Creates Four Collision Domains and Four Ethernet Segments*

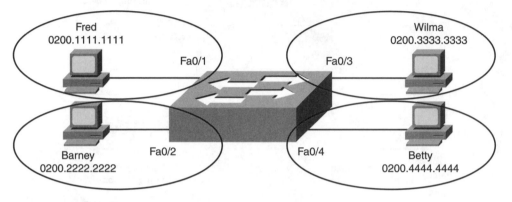

The next section examines how switches forward Ethernet frames.

Switching Logic

Ultimately, the role of a LAN switch is to forward Ethernet frames. To achieve that goal, switches use logic—logic based on the source and destination MAC address in each frame's Ethernet header. To help you appreciate how switches work, first a review of Ethernet addresses is in order.

The IEEE defines three general categories of Ethernet MAC addresses:

■ **Unicast addresses:** MAC addresses that identify a single LAN interface card.

■ **Broadcast addresses:** A frame sent with a destination address of the broadcast address (FFFF.FFFF.FFFF) implies that all devices on the LAN should receive and process the frame.

■ **Multicast addresses:** Multicast MAC addresses are used to allow a dynamic subset of devices on a LAN to communicate.

> **NOTE**   The IP protocol supports the multicasting of IP packets. When IP multicast packets are sent over an Ethernet, the multicast MAC addresses used in the Ethernet frame follow this format: 0100.5e*xx.xxxx*, where a value between 00.0000 and 7f.ffff can be used in the last half of the address. Ethernet multicast MAC addresses are not covered in this book.

The primary job of a LAN switch is to receive Ethernet frames and then make a decision: either forward the frame out some other port(s), or ignore the frame. To accomplish this primary mission, transparent bridges perform three actions:

1. Deciding when to forward a frame or when to filter (not forward) a frame, based on the destination MAC address

2. Learning MAC addresses by examining the source MAC address of each frame received by the bridge

3. Creating a (Layer 2) loop-free environment with other bridges by using Spanning Tree Protocol (STP)

The first action is the switch's primary job, whereas the other two items are overhead functions. The next sections examine each of these steps in order.

The Forward Versus Filter Decision

To decide whether to forward a frame, a switch uses a dynamically built table that lists MAC addresses and outgoing interfaces. Switches compare the frame's destination MAC address to this table to decide whether the switch should forward a frame or simply ignore it. For example, consider the simple network shown in Figure 7-4, with Fred sending a frame to Barney.

Figure 7-4 shows an example of both the forwarding decision and the filtering decision. Fred sends a frame with destination address 0200.2222.2222 (Barney's MAC address). The switch compares the destination MAC address (0200.2222.2222) to the MAC address table, finding the matching entry. This is the interface out which a frame should be sent to deliver it to that listed MAC address (0200.2222.2222). Because the interface in which the frame arrived (Fa0/1) is different than the listed outgoing interface (Fa0/2), the switch decides to forward the frame out interface Fa0/2, as shown in the figure's table.

> **NOTE** A switch's MAC address table is also called the switching table, or bridging table, or even the Content Addressable Memory (CAM), in reference to the type of physical memory used to store the table.

The key to anticipating where a switch should forward a frame is to examine and understand the address table. The table lists MAC addresses and the interface the switch should use when forwarding packets sent to that MAC address. For example, the table lists 0200.3333.3333 off Fa0/3, which is the interface out which the switch should forward frames sent to Wilma's MAC address (0200.3333.3333).

Key Topic

Figure 7-4 *Sample Switch Forwarding and Filtering Decision*

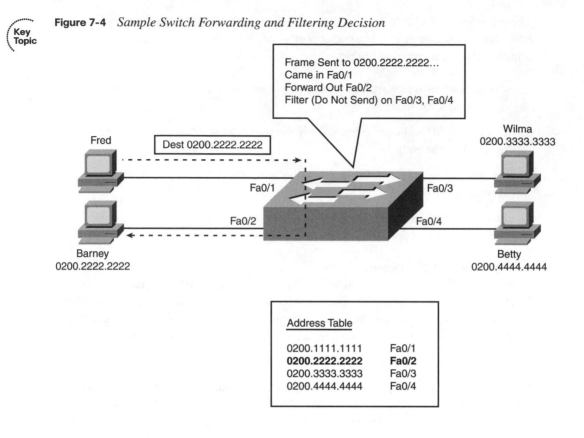

Frame Sent to 0200.2222.2222...
Came in Fa0/1
Forward Out Fa0/2
Filter (Do Not Send) on Fa0/3, Fa0/4

Fred

Dest 0200.2222.2222

Wilma
0200.3333.3333

Fa0/1

Fa0/3

Fa0/2

Fa0/4

Barney
0200.2222.2222

Betty
0200.4444.4444

Address Table

0200.1111.1111	Fa0/1
0200.2222.2222	**Fa0/2**
0200.3333.3333	Fa0/3
0200.4444.4444	Fa0/4

- - - - - - - - - - - - - - - ➤
Path of Frame Transmission

Figure 7-5 shows a different perspective, with the switch making a filtering decision. In this case, Fred and Barney connect to a hub, which is then connected to the switch. The switch's MAC address table lists both Fred's and Barney's MAC addresses off that single switch interface (Fa0/1), because the switch would forward frames to both Fred and Barney out its FA0/1 interface. So, when the switch receives a frame sent by Fred (source MAC address 0200.1111.1111) to Barney (destination MAC address 0200.2222.2222), the switch thinks like this: "Because the frame entered my Fa0/1 interface, and I would send it out that same Fa0/1 interface, do not send it (filter it), because sending it would be pointless."

Figure 7-5 *Sample Switch Filtering Decision*

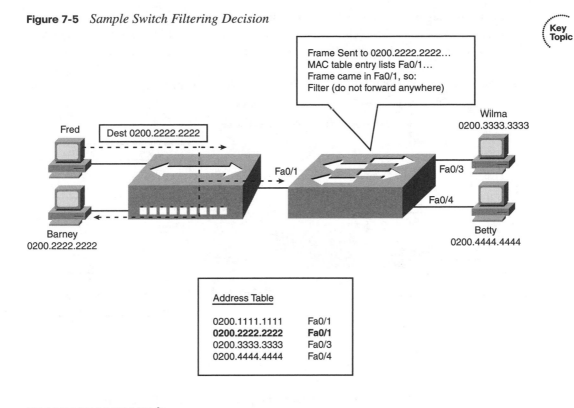

Frame Sent to 0200.2222.2222…
MAC table entry lists Fa0/1…
Frame came in Fa0/1, so:
Filter (do not forward anywhere)

Address Table

0200.1111.1111   Fa0/1
0200.2222.2222   Fa0/1
0200.3333.3333   Fa0/3
0200.4444.4444   Fa0/4

- - - - - - - - - - - - - - ►
Path of Frame Transmission

Note that the hub simply regenerates the electrical signal out each interface, so the hub forwards the electrical signal sent by Fred to both Barney and the switch. The switch decides to filter (not forward) the frame, noting that the MAC address table's interface for 0200.2222.2222 (Fa0/1) is the same as the incoming interface.

How Switches Learn MAC Addresses

The second main function of a switch is to learn the MAC addresses and interfaces to put into its address table. With a full and accurate MAC address table, the switch can make accurate forwarding and filtering decisions.

Switches build the address table by listening to incoming frames and examining the *source MAC address* in the frame. If a frame enters the switch and the source MAC address is not in the MAC address table, the switch creates an entry in the table. The MAC address is placed in the table, along with the interface from which the frame arrived. Switch learning logic is that simple.

Figure 7-6 depicts the same network as Figure 7-4, but before the switch has built any address table entries. The figure shows the first two frames sent in this network—first a frame from Fred, addressed to Barney, and then Barney's response, addressed to Fred.

Figure 7-6 *Switch Learning: Empty Table and Adding Two Entries*

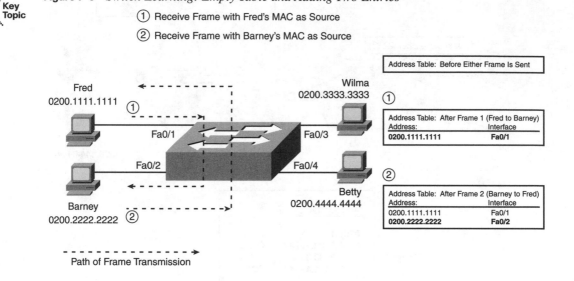

As shown in the figure, after Fred sends his first frame (labeled "1") to Barney, the switch adds an entry for 0200.1111.1111, Fred's MAC address, associated with interface Fa0/1. When Barney replies in Step 2, the switch adds a second entry, this one for 0200.2222.2222, Barney's MAC address, along with interface Fa0/2, which is the interface in which the switch received the frame. Learning always occurs by looking at the source MAC address in the frame.

Flooding Frames

Now again turn your attention to the forwarding process, using Figure 7-6. What do you suppose the switch does with Fred's first frame in Figure 7-6, the one that occurred when there were no entries in the MAC address table? As it turns out, when there is no matching entry in the table, switches forward the frame out all interfaces (except the incoming interface). Switches forward these *unknown unicast frames* (frames whose destination MAC addresses are not yet in the bridging table) out all other interfaces, with the hope that the unknown device will be on some other Ethernet segment and will reply, allowing the switch to build a correct entry in the address table.

For example, in Figure 7-6, the switch forwards the first frame out Fa0/2, Fa0/3, and Fa0/4, even though 0200.2222.2222 (Barney) is only off Fa0/2. The switch does not forward the frame back out Fa0/1, because a switch never forwards a frame out the same interface on which it arrived. (As a side note, Figure 7-6 does not show the frame being forwarded out interfaces Fa0/3 and Fa0/4, because this figure is focused on the learning process.) When Barney replies to Fred, the switch correctly adds an entry for 0200.2222.2222 (Fa0/2) to its address table. Any later frames sent to destination address 0200.2222.2222 will no longer need to be sent out Fa0/3 and Fa0/4, only being forwarded out Fa0/2.

The process of sending frames out all other interfaces, except the interface on which the frame arrived, is called *flooding*. Switches flood unknown unicast frames as well as broadcast frames. Switches also flood LAN multicast frames out all ports, unless the switch has been configured to use some multicast optimization tools that are not covered in this book.

Switches keep a timer for each entry in the MAC address table, called an *inactivity timer*. The switch sets the timer to 0 for new entries. Each time the switch receives another frame with that same source MAC address, the timer is reset to 0. The timer counts upward, so the switch can tell which entries have gone the longest time since receiving a frame from that device. If the switch ever runs out of space for entries in the MAC address table, the switch can then remove table entries with the oldest (largest) inactivity timers.

Avoiding Loops Using Spanning Tree Protocol

The third primary feature of LAN switches is loop prevention, as implemented by Spanning Tree Protocol (STP). Without STP, frames would loop for an indefinite period of time in Ethernet networks with physically redundant links. To prevent looping frames, STP blocks some ports from forwarding frames so that only one active path exists between any pair of LAN segments (collision domains). The result of STP is good: frames do not loop infinitely, which makes the LAN usable. However, although the network can use some redundant links in case of a failure, the LAN does not load-balance the traffic.

To avoid Layer 2 loops, all switches need to use STP. STP causes each interface on a switch to settle into either a blocking state or a forwarding state. *Blocking* means that the interface cannot forward or receive data frames. *Forwarding* means that the interface can send and receive data frames. If a correct subset of the interfaces is blocked, a single currently active logical path exists between each pair of LANs.

> **NOTE** STP behaves identically for a transparent bridge and a switch. Therefore, the terms *bridge*, *switch*, and *bridging device* all are used interchangeably when discussing STP.

A simple example makes the need for STP more obvious. Remember, switches flood frames sent to both unknown unicast MAC addresses and broadcast addresses.

Figure 7-7 shows that a single frame, sent by Larry to Bob, loops forever because the network has redundancy but no STP.

Figure 7-7 *Network with Redundant Links But Without STP: The Frame Loops Forever*

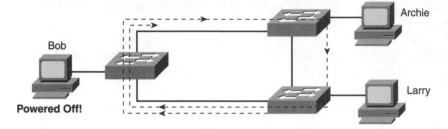

Larry sends a single unicast frame to Bob's MAC address, but Bob is powered off, so none of the switches has learned Bob's MAC address yet. Bob's MAC address would be an unknown unicast address at this point in time. Therefore, frames destined for Bob's MAC address are forwarded by each switch out every port. These frames loop indefinitely. Because the switches never learn Bob's MAC address (remember, he's powered off and can send no frames), they keep forwarding the frame out all ports, and copies of the frame go around and around.

Similarly, switches flood broadcasts as well, so if any of the PCs sent a broadcast, the broadcast would also loop indefinitely.

One way to solve this problem is to design the LAN with no redundant links. However, most network engineers purposefully design LANs to use physical redundancy between the switches. Eventually, a switch or a link will fail, and you want the network to still be available by having some redundancy in the LAN design. The right solution includes switched LANs with physical redundancy, while using STP to dynamically block some interface(s) so that only one active path exists between two endpoints at any instant in time.

Chapter 2, "Spanning Tree Protocol," in the *CCNA ICND2 Official Exam Certification Guide* covers the details of how STP prevents loops.

Internal Processing on Cisco Switches

This chapter has already explained how switches decide whether to forward or filter a frame. As soon as a Cisco switch decides to forward a frame, the switch can use a couple of different types of internal processing variations. Almost all of the more recently released switches use store-and-forward processing, but all three types of these internal processing methods are supported in at least one type of currently available Cisco switch.

Some switches, and transparent bridges in general, use *store-and-forward processing*. With store-and-forward, the switch must receive the entire frame before forwarding the first bit of the frame. However, Cisco also offers two other internal processing methods for switches: *cut-through* and *fragment-free*. Because the destination MAC address occurs very early in the Ethernet header, a switch can make a forwarding decision long before the switch has received all the bits in the frame. The cut-through and fragment-free processing methods allow the switch to start forwarding the frame before the entire frame has been received, reducing time required to send the frame (the latency, or delay).

With *cut-through* processing, the switch starts sending the frame out the output port as soon as possible. Although this might reduce latency, it also propagates errors. Because the frame check sequence (FCS) is in the Ethernet trailer, the switch cannot determine if the frame had any errors before starting to forward the frame. So, the switch reduces the frame's latency, but with the price of having forwarded some frames that contain errors.

Fragment-free processing works similarly to cut-through, but it tries to reduce the number of errored frames that it forwards. One interesting fact about Ethernet carrier sense multiple access with collision detection (CSMA/CD) logic is that collisions should be detected within the first 64 bytes of a frame. Fragment-free processing works like cut-through logic, but it waits to receive the first 64 bytes before forwarding a frame. The frames experience less latency than with store-and-forward logic and slightly more latency than with cut-through, but frames that have errors as a result of collisions are not forwarded.

With many links to the desktop running at 100 Mbps, uplinks at 1 Gbps, and faster application-specific integrated circuits (ASIC), today's switches typically use store-and-forward processing, because the improved latency of the other two switching methods is negligible at these speeds.

The internal processing algorithms used by switches vary among models and vendors; regardless, the internal processing can be categorized as one of the methods listed in Table 7-2.

Table 7-2 *Switch Internal Processing*

Switching Method	Description
Store-and-forward	The switch fully receives all bits in the frame (store) before forwarding the frame (forward). This allows the switch to check the FCS before forwarding the frame.
Cut-through	The switch forwards the frame as soon as it can. This reduces latency but does not allow the switch to discard frames that fail the FCS check.
Fragment-free	The switch forwards the frame after receiving the first 64 bytes of the frame, thereby avoiding forwarding frames that were errored due to a collision.

LAN Switching Summary

Switches provide many additional features not offered by older LAN devices such as hubs and bridges. In particular, LAN switches provide the following benefits:

Key Topic

■ Switch ports connected to a single device microsegment the LAN, providing dedicated bandwidth to that single device.

■ Switches allow multiple simultaneous conversations between devices on different ports.

■ Switch ports connected to a single device support full duplex, in effect doubling the amount of bandwidth available to the device.

■ Switches support rate adaptation, which means that devices that use different Ethernet speeds can communicate through the switch (hubs cannot).

Switches use Layer 2 logic, examining the Ethernet data-link header to choose how to process frames. In particular, switches make decisions to forward and filter frames, learn MAC addresses, and use STP to avoid loops, as follows:

Key Topic

Step 1   Switches forward frames based on the destination address:

a. If the destination address is a broadcast, multicast, or unknown destination unicast (a unicast not listed in the MAC table), the switch floods the frame.

b. If the destination address is a known unicast address (a unicast address found in the MAC table):

i. If the outgoing interface listed in the MAC address table is different from the interface in which the frame was received, the switch forwards the frame out the outgoing interface.

ii. If the outgoing interface is the same as the interface in which the frame was received, the switch filters the frame, meaning that the switch simply ignores the frame and does not forward it.

Step 2   Switches use the following logic to learn MAC address table entries:

a. For each received frame, examine the source MAC address and note the interface from which the frame was received.

b. If they are not already in the table, add the address and interface, setting the inactivity timer to 0.

c. If it is already in the table, reset the inactivity timer for the entry to 0.

Step 3   Switches use STP to prevent loops by causing some interfaces to block, meaning that they do not send or receive frames.

LAN Design Considerations

So far, the LAN coverage in this book has mostly focused on individual functions of LANs. For example, you have read about how switches forward frames, the details of UTP cables and cable pinouts, the CSMA/CD algorithm that deals with the issue of collisions, and some of the differences between how hubs and switches operate to create either a single collision domain (hubs) or many collision domains (switches).

This section now takes a broader look at LANs—particularly, how to design medium to larger LANs. When building a small LAN, you might simply buy one switch, plug in cables to connect a few devices, and you're finished. However, when building a medium to large LAN, you have more product choices to make, such as when to use hubs, switches, and routers. Additionally, you must weigh the choice of which LAN switch to choose (switches vary in size, number of ports, performance, features, and price). The types of LAN media differ as well. Engineers must weigh the benefits of UTP cabling, like lower cost and ease of installation, versus fiber optic cabling options, which support longer distances and better physical security.

This section examines a variety of topics that all relate to LAN design in some way. In particular, this section begins by looking at the impact of the choice of using a hub, switch, or router to connect parts of LANs. Following that, some Cisco design terminology is covered. Finishing this section is a short summary of some of the more popular types of Ethernet and cabling types, and cable length guidelines for each.

Collision Domains and Broadcast Domains

When creating any Ethernet LAN, you use some form of networking devices—typically switches today—a few routers, and possibly a few hubs. The different parts of an Ethernet LAN may behave differently, in terms of function and performance, depending on which types of devices are used. These differences then affect a network engineer's decision when choosing how to design a LAN.

The terms *collision domain* and *broadcast domain* define two important effects of the process of segmenting LANs using various devices. This section examines the concepts behind Ethernet LAN design. The goal is to define these terms and to explain how hubs, switches, and routers impact collision domains and broadcast domains.

Collision Domains

As mentioned earlier, a *collision domain* is the set of LAN interfaces whose frames could collide with each other, but not with frames sent by any other devices in the network. To review the core concept, Figure 7-8 illustrates collision domains.

Figure 7-8 *Collision Domains*

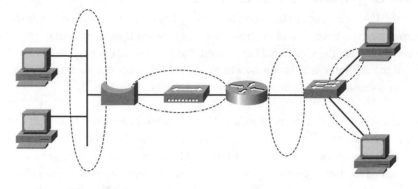

> **NOTE**   The LAN design in Figure 7-8 is not a typical design today. Instead, it simply provides enough information to help you compare hubs, switches, and routers.

Each separate segment, or collision domain, is shown with a dashed-line circle in the figure. The switch on the right separates the LAN into different collision domains for each port. Likewise, both bridges and routers also separate LANs into different collision domains (although this effect with routers was not covered earlier in this book). Of all the devices in the figure, only the hub near the center of the network does not create multiple collision domains for each interface. It repeats all frames out all ports without any regard for buffering and waiting to send a frame onto a busy segment.

Broadcast Domains

The term *broadcast domain* relates to where broadcasts can be forwarded. A *broadcast domain* encompasses a set of devices for which, when one of the devices sends a broadcast, all the other devices receive a copy of the broadcast. For example, switches flood broadcasts and multicasts on all ports. Because broadcast frames are sent out all ports, a switch creates a single broadcast domain.

Conversely, only routers stop the flow of broadcasts. For perspective, Figure 7-9 provides the broadcast domains for the same network depicted in Figure 7-8.

Broadcasts sent by a device in one broadcast domain are not forwarded to devices in another broadcast domain. In this example, there are two broadcast domains. For instance, the router does not forward a LAN broadcast sent by a PC on the left to the network segment on the right. In the old days, the term *broadcast firewall* described the fact that routers did not forward LAN broadcasts.

Figure 7-9   *Broadcast Domains*

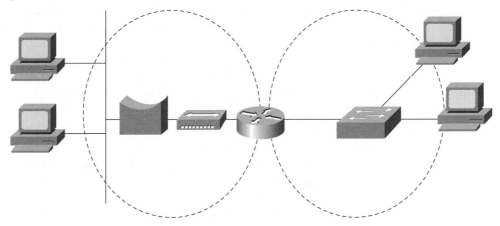

General definitions for a collision domain and a broadcast domain are as follows:

- A *collision domain* is a set of network interface cards (NIC) for which a frame sent by one NIC could result in a collision with a frame sent by any other NIC in the same collision domain.

- A *broadcast domain* is a set of NICs for which a broadcast frame sent by one NIC is received by all other NICs in the same broadcast domain.

The Impact of Collision and Broadcast Domains on LAN Design

When designing a LAN, you need to keep in mind the trade-offs when choosing the number of devices in each collision domain and broadcast domain. First, consider the devices in a single collision domain for a moment. For a single collision domain:

- The devices share the available bandwidth.

- The devices may inefficiently use that bandwidth due to the effects of collisions, particularly under higher utilization.

For example, you might have ten PCs with 10/100 Ethernet NICs. If you connect all ten PCs to ten different ports on a single 100-Mbps hub, you have one collision domain, and the PCs in that collision domain share the 100 Mbps of bandwidth. That may work well and meet the needs of those users. However, with heavier traffic loads, the hub's performance would be worse than it would be if you had used a switch. Using a switch instead of a hub, with the same topology, would create ten different collision domains, each with 100 Mbps of bandwidth. Additionally, with only one device on each switch interface, no collisions would occur. This means that you could enable full duplex on each interface, effectively giving each interface 200 Mbps, and a theoretical maximum of 2 Gbps of bandwidth—a considerable improvement!

Using switches instead of hubs seems like an obvious choice given the overwhelming performance benefits. Frankly, most new installations today use switches exclusively. However, vendors still offer hubs, mainly because hubs are still slightly less expensive than switches, so you may still see hubs in networks today.

Now consider the issue of broadcasts. When a host receives a broadcast, the host must process the received frame. This means that the NIC must interrupt the computer's CPU, and the CPU must spend time thinking about the received broadcast frame. All hosts need to send some broadcasts to function properly. (For example, IP ARP messages are LAN broadcasts, as mentioned in Chapter 5, "Fundamentals of IP Addressing and Routing.") So, broadcasts happen, which is good, but broadcasts do require all the hosts to spend time processing each broadcast frame.

Next, consider a large LAN, with multiple switches, with 500 PCs total. The switches create a single broadcast domain, so a broadcast sent by any of the 500 hosts should be sent to, and then processed by, all 499 other hosts. Depending on the number of broadcasts, the broadcasts could start to impact performance of the end-user PCs. However, a design that separated the 500 PCs into five groups of 100, separated from each other by a router, would create five broadcast domains. Now, a broadcast by one host would interrupt only 99 other hosts, and not the other 400 hosts, resulting in generally better performance on the PCs.

> **NOTE**   Using smaller broadcast domains can also improve security, due to limiting broadcasts, and due to robust security features in routers.

The choice about when to use a hub versus a switch was straightforward, but the choice of when to use a router to break up a large broadcast domain is more difficult. A meaningful discussion of the trade-offs and options is beyond the scope of this book. However, you should understand the concepts behind broadcast domains—specifically, that a router breaks LANs into multiple broadcast domains, but switches and hubs do not.

More importantly for the CCNA exams, you should be ready to react to questions in terms of the benefits of LAN segmentation instead of just asking for the facts related to collision domains and broadcast domains. Table 7-3 lists some of the key benefits. The features in the table should be interpreted within the following context: "Which of the following benefits are gained by using a hub/switch/router between Ethernet devices?"

Table 7-3 *Benefits of Segmenting Ethernet Devices Using Hubs, Switches, and Routers*

Feature	Hub	Switch	Router
Greater cabling distances are allowed	Yes	Yes	Yes
Creates multiple collision domains	No	Yes	Yes
Increases bandwidth	No	Yes	Yes
Creates multiple broadcast domains	No	No	Yes

Virtual LANs (VLAN)

Most every Enterprise network today uses the concept of virtual LANs (VLAN). Before understanding VLANs, you must have a very specific understanding of the definition of a LAN. Although you can think about and define the term "LAN" from many perspectives, one perspective in particular will help you understand VLANs:

> A LAN consists of all devices in the same broadcast domain.

Without VLANs, a switch considers all interfaces on the switch to be in the same broadcast domain. In other words, all connected devices are in the same LAN. (Cisco switches accomplish this by putting all interfaces in VLAN 1 by default.) With VLANs, a switch can put some interfaces into one broadcast domain and some into another based on some simple configuration. Essentially, the switch creates multiple broadcast domains by putting some interfaces into one VLAN and other interfaces into other VLANs. These individual broadcast domains created by the switch are called virtual LANs.

So, instead of all ports on a switch forming a single broadcast domain, the switch separates them into many, based on configuration. It's really that simple.

The next two figures compare two LANs for the purpose of explaining a little more about VLANs. First, before VLANs existed, if a design specified two separate broadcast domains, two switches would be used—one for each broadcast domain, as shown in Figure 7-10.

Figure 7-10 *Sample Network with Two Broadcast Domains and No VLANs*

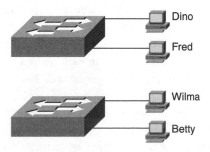

Alternately, you can create multiple broadcast domains using a single switch. Figure 7-11 shows the same two broadcast domains as in Figure 7-10, now implemented as two different VLANs on a single switch.

Key
Topic

Figure 7-11   *Sample Network with Two VLANs Using One Switch*

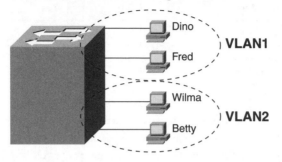

In a network as small as the one shown in Figure 7-11, you might not really need to use VLANs. However, there are many motivations for using VLANs, including the following:

■ To create more flexible designs that group users by department, or by groups that work together, instead of by physical location

■ To segment devices into smaller LANs (broadcast domains) to reduce overhead caused to each host in the VLAN

■ To reduce the workload for STP by limiting a VLAN to a single access switch

■ To enforce better security by keeping hosts that work with sensitive data on a separate VLAN

■ To separate traffic sent by an IP phone from traffic sent by PCs connected to the phones

The *CCNA ICND2 Official Exam Certification Guide* explains VLAN configuration and troubleshooting.

Campus LAN Design Terminology

The term *campus LAN* refers to the LAN created to support larger buildings, or multiple buildings in somewhat close proximity to one another. For instance, a company might lease office space in several buildings in the same office park. The network engineers can then build a campus LAN that includes switches in each building, plus Ethernet links between the switches in the buildings, to create a larger campus LAN.

When planning and designing a campus LAN, the engineers must consider the types of Ethernet available and the cabling lengths supported by each type. The engineers also need to choose the speeds required for each Ethernet segment. Additionally, some thought needs to be given to the idea that some switches should be used to connect directly to end-user devices, whereas other switches might need to simply connect to a large number of these end-user switches. Finally, most projects require that the engineer consider the type of equipment that is already installed and whether an increase in speed on some segments is worth the cost of buying new equipment.

For example, the vast majority of PCs that are already installed in networks today have 10/100 NICs, with many new PCs today having 10/100/1000 NICs built into the PC. Assuming that the appropriate cabling has been installed, a 10/100/1000 NIC can use autonegotiation to use either 10BASE-T (10 Mbps), 100BASE-TX (100 Mbps), or 1000BASE-T (1000 Mbps, or 1 Gbps) Ethernet, each using the same UTP cable. However, one trade-off the engineer must make is whether to buy switches that support only 10/100 interfaces or that support 10/100/1000 interfaces. At the time this book was published (summer 2007), the price difference between switches that support only 10/100 interfaces, versus 10/100/1000 interfaces, was still large enough to get management's attention. However, spending the money on switches that include 10/100/1000 interfaces allows you to connect pretty much any end-user device. You'll also be ready to migrate from 100 Mbps to the desktop device to 1000 Mbps (gigabit) as new PCs are bought.

To sift through all the requirements for a campus LAN, and then have a reasonable conversation about it with peers, most Cisco-oriented LAN designs use some common terminology to refer to the design. For this book's purposes, you should be aware of some of the key campus LAN design terminology. Figure 7-12 shows a typical design of a large campus LAN, with the terminology included in the figure. Explanations of the terminology follow the figure.

Cisco uses three terms to describe the role of each switch in a campus design: *access*, *distribution*, and *core*. The roles differ mainly in two main concepts:

■   Whether the switch should connect to end-user devices

■   Whether the switch should forward frames between other switches by connecting to multiple different switches

Access switches connect directly to end users, providing access to the LAN. Under normal circumstances, access switches normally send traffic to and from the end-user devices to which they are connected. However, access switches should not, at least by design, be expected to forward traffic between two other switches. For example, in Figure 7-12, switch Access1 normally would not forward traffic going from PCs connected to switch Access3 to a PC off switch Access4. Because access layer switches support only the traffic for the locally attached PCs, access switches tend to be smaller and less expensive, often supporting just enough ports to support a particular floor of a building.

Figure 7-12   *Campus LAN with Design Terminology Listed*

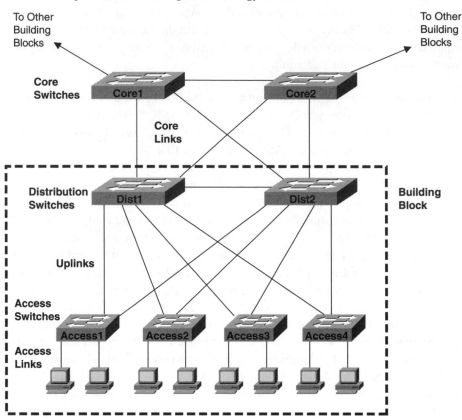

In larger campus LANs, distribution switches provide a path through which the access switches can forward traffic to each other. By design, each of the access switches connects to at least one distribution switch. However, designs use at least two uplinks to two different distribution switches (as shown in Figure 7-12) for redundancy.

Using distribution switches provides some cabling advantages and potential performance advantages. For example, if a network had 30 access layer switches, and the network engineer decided that each access layer switch should be cabled directly to every other access layer switch, the LAN would need 435 cables between switches! Furthermore, that design includes only one segment between each pair of switches. A possibly worse side effect is that if a link fails, the access layer switches may forward traffic to and from other switches, stressing the performance of the access switch, which typically is a less expensive but less powerful switch. Instead, by connecting each of the 30 access switches to two different distribution switches, only 60 cables are required. Well-chosen distribution switches, with faster forwarding rates, can handle the larger amount of traffic between switches. Additionally, the design with two distribution switches, with two uplinks from each access switch to the distribution switches, actually has more redundancy and therefore better availability.

Core switches provide even more aggregation benefits than do the distribution switches. Core switches provide extremely high forwarding rates—these days into the hundreds of millions of frames per second. The reasons for core switches are generally the same as for distribution switches. However, medium to smaller campus LANs often forego the concept of core switches.

The following list summarizes the terms that describe the roles of campus switches:

- **Access:** Provides a connection point (access) for end-user devices. Does not forward frames between two other access switches under normal circumstances.

- **Distribution:** Provides an aggregation point for access switches, forwarding frames between switches, but not connecting directly to end-user devices.

- **Core:** Aggregates distribution switches in very large campus LANs, providing very high forwarding rates.

Ethernet LAN Media and Cable Lengths

When designing a campus LAN, an engineer must consider the length of each cable run and then find the best type of Ethernet and cabling type that supports that length of cable. For example, if a company leases space in five buildings in the same office park, the engineer needs to figure out how long the cables between the buildings need to be and then pick the right type of Ethernet.

The three most common types of Ethernet today (10BASE-T, 100BASE-TX, and 1000BASE-T) have the same 100-meter cable restriction, but they use slightly different cables. The EIA/TIA defines Ethernet cabling standards, including the cable's quality. Each Ethernet standard that uses UTP cabling lists a cabling quality category as the minimum category that the standard supports. For example, 10BASE-T allows for Category 3 (CAT3) cabling or better, whereas 100BASE-TX calls for higher-quality CAT5 cabling, and 1000BASE-TX requires even higher-quality CAT5e or CAT6 cabling. If an engineer plans on using existing cabling, he or she must be aware of the types of UTP cables and the speed restrictions implied by the type of Ethernet the cabling supports.

Several types of Ethernet define the use of fiber-optic cables. UTP cables include copper wires over which electrical currents can flow, whereas optical cables include ultra-thin strands of glass through which light can pass. To send bits, the switches can alternate between sending brighter and dimmer light to encode 0s and 1s on the cable.

Optical cables support a variety of much longer distances than the 100 meters supported by Ethernet on UTP cables. Optical cables experience much less interference from outside sources as compared to copper cables. Additionally, switches can use lasers to generate the light, as well as light-emitting diodes (LED). Lasers allow for even longer cabling distances, up to 100 km today, at higher cost, whereas less-expensive LEDs may well support plenty of distance for campus LANs in most office parks.

Finally, the type of optical cabling can also impact the maximum distances per cable. Of the two types, multimode fiber supports shorter distances, but it is generally cheaper cabling, and it works fine with less-expensive LEDs. The other optical cabling type, single-mode fiber, supports the longest distances but is more expensive. Also note that the switch hardware to use LEDs (often with multimode fiber) is much less expensive than the switch hardware to support lasers (often with single-mode fiber).

Table 7-4 lists the more common types of Ethernet and their cable types and length limitations.

Table 7-4 *Ethernet Types, Media, and Segment Lengths (Per IEEE)*

Ethernet Type	Media	Maximum Segment Length
10BASE-T	TIA/EIA CAT3 or better, two pair	100 m (328 feet)
100BASE-TX	TIA/EIA CAT5 UTP or better, two pair	100 m (328 feet)
100BASE-FX	62.5/125-micron multimode fiber	400 m (1312.3 feet)
1000BASE-CX	STP	25 m (82 feet)
1000BASE-T	TIA/EIA CAT5e UTP or better, four pair	100 m (328 feet)
1000BASE-SX	Multimode fiber	275 m (853 feet) for 62.5-micron fiber 550 m (1804.5 feet) for 50-micron fiber
1000BASE-LX	Multimode fiber	550 m (1804.5 feet) for 50- and 62.5-micron fiber
1000BASE-LX	9-micron single-mode fiber	10 km (6.2 miles)

Most engineers simply remember the general distance limitations and then use a reference chart (such as Table 7-4) to remember each specific detail. An engineer must also consider the physical paths that the cables will use to run through a campus or building and the impact on the required cable length. For example, a cable might have to run from one end of the building to the other, and then through a conduit that connects the floors of the building, and then horizontally to a wiring closet on another floor. Often those paths are not the shortest way to get from one place to the other. So the chart's details are important to the LAN planning process and the resulting choice of LAN media.

Exam Preparation Tasks

Review All the Key Topics

Key Topic

Review the most important topics from this chapter, noted with the key topics icon. Table 7-5 lists these key topics and where each is discussed.

Table 7-5 *Key Topics for Chapter 7*

Key Topic Element	Description	Page Number
List	LAN switch actions	175
Figure 7-4	Example of switch forwarding logic	176
Figure 7-5	Example of switch filtering logic	177
Figure 7-6	Example of how a switch learns MAC addresses	178
Table 7-2	Summary of three switch internal forwarding options	181
List	Some of the benefits of switching	182
List	Summary of logic used to forward and filter frames and to learn MAC addresses	182
List	Definitions of collision domain and broadcast domain	185
Table 7-3	Four LAN design feature comparisons with hubs, switches, and routers	187
Figure 7-11	Illustration of the concept of a VLAN	188

Complete the Tables and Lists from Memory

Print a copy of Appendix H, "Memory Tables" (found on the CD), or at least the section for this chapter, and complete the tables and lists from memory. Appendix I, "Memory Tables Answer Key," also on the CD, includes completed tables and lists for you to check your work.

Definitions of Key Terms

Define the following key terms from this chapter, and check your answers in the glossary:

broadcast domain, broadcast frame, collision domain, cut-through switching, flooding, fragment-free switching, microsegmentation, segmentation, Spanning Tree Protocol (STP), store-and-forward switching, unknown unicast frame, virtual LAN

This chapter covers the following subjects:

Accessing the Cisco Catalyst 2960 Switch CLI: This section examines Cisco 2960 switches and shows you how to gain access to the command-line interface (CLI) from which you can issue commands to the switch.

Configuring Cisco IOS Software: This section shows you how to tell the switch different operational parameters using the CLI.

CHAPTER 8

Operating Cisco LAN Switches

LAN switches may be the most common networking device found in the Enterprise today. Most new end-user computers sold today include a built-in Ethernet NIC of some kind. Switches provide a connection point for the Ethernet devices so that the devices on the LAN can communicate with each other and with the rest of an Enterprise network or with the Internet.

Cisco routers also happen to use the exact same user interface as the Cisco Catalyst switches described in this chapter. So, even though this chapter is called "Operating Cisco LAN Switches," keep in mind that the user interface of Cisco routers works the same way. Chapter 13, "Operating Cisco Routers," begins by summarizing the features covered in this chapter that also apply to routers.

"Do I Know This Already?" Quiz

The "Do I Know This Already?" quiz allows you to assess whether you should read the entire chapter. If you miss no more than one of these seven self-assessment questions, you might want to move ahead to the "Exam Preparation Tasks" section. Table 8-1 lists the major headings in this chapter and the "Do I Know This Already?" quiz questions covering the material in those sections. This helps you assess your knowledge of these specific areas. The answers to the "Do I Know This Already?" quiz appear in Appendix A.

Table 8-1   *"Do I Know This Already?" Foundation Topics Section-to-Question Mapping*

Foundation Topics Section	Questions
Accessing the Cisco Catalyst 2960 Switch CLI	1–3
Configuring Cisco IOS Software	4–7

1. In what modes can you execute the command **show mac-address-table**?

    a. User mode

    b. Enable mode

    c. Global configuration mode

    d. Setup mode

    e. Interface configuration mode

2. In which of the following modes of the CLI could you issue a command to reboot the switch?

    a. User mode

    b. Enable mode

    c. Global configuration mode

    d. Interface configuration mode

3. Which of the following is a difference between Telnet and SSH as supported by a Cisco switch?

    a. SSH encrypts the passwords used at login, but not other traffic; Telnet encrypts nothing.

    b. SSH encrypts all data exchange, including login passwords; Telnet encrypts nothing.

    c. Telnet is used from Microsoft operating systems, and SSH is used from UNIX and Linux operating systems.

    d. Telnet encrypts only password exchanges; SSH encrypts all data exchanges.

4. What type of switch memory is used to store the configuration used by the switch when it is up and working?

    a. RAM

    b. ROM

    c. Flash

    d. NVRAM

    e. Bubble

5. What command copies the configuration from RAM into NVRAM?

    a. **copy running-config tftp**

    b. **copy tftp running-config**

    c. **copy running-config start-up-config**

    d. **copy start-up-config running-config**

    e. **copy startup-config running-config**

    f. **copy running-config startup-config**

6. Which mode prompts the user for basic configuration information?

    a. User mode

    b. Enable mode

    c. Global configuration mode

    d. Setup mode

    e. Interface configuration mode

7. A switch user is currently in console line configuration mode. Which of the following would place the user in enable mode?

    a. Using the **exit** command once

    b. Using the **exit** command twice in a row

    c. Pressing the **Ctrl-z** key sequence

    d. Using the **quit** command

Foundation Topics

When you buy a Cisco Catalyst switch, you can take it out of the box, power on the switch by connecting the power cable to the switch and a power outlet, and connect hosts to the switch using the correct UTP cables, and the switch works. You do not have to do anything else, and you certainly do not have to tell the switch to start forwarding Ethernet frames. The switch uses default settings so that all interfaces will work, assuming that the right cables and devices connect to the switch, and the switch forwards frames in and out of each interface.

However, most Enterprises will want to be able to check on the switch's status, look at information about what the switch is doing, and possibly configure specific features of the switch. Engineers will also want to enable security features that allow them to securely access the switches without being vulnerable to malicious people breaking into the switches. To perform these tasks, a network engineer needs to connect to the switch's user interface.

This chapter explains the details of how to access a Cisco switch's user interface, how to use commands to find out how the switch is currently working, and how to configure the switch to tell it what to do. This chapter focuses on the processes, as opposed to examining a particular set of commands. Chapter 9, "Ethernet Switch Configuration," then takes a closer look at the variety of commands that can be used from the switch user interface.

Cisco has two major brands of LAN switching products. The Cisco Catalyst switch brand includes a large collection of switches, all of which have been designed with Enterprises (companies, governments, and so on) in mind. The Catalyst switches have a wide range of sizes, functions, and forwarding rates. The Cisco Linksys switch brand includes a variety of switches designed for use in the home. The CCNA exams focus on how to implement LANs using Cisco Catalyst switches, so this chapter explains how to gain access to a Cisco Catalyst switch to monitor, configure, and troubleshoot problems. However, both the Catalyst and Linksys brands of Cisco switches provide the same base features, as covered earlier in Chapters 3 and 7.

Note that for the rest of this chapter, all references to a "Cisco switch" refer to Cisco Catalyst switches, not Cisco Linksys switches.

Accessing the Cisco Catalyst 2960 Switch CLI

Cisco uses the same concept of a *command-line interface* (CLI) with its router products and most of its Catalyst LAN switch products. The CLI is a text-based interface in which the user, typically a network engineer, enters a text command and presses Enter. Pressing Enter sends the command to the switch, which tells the device to do something. The switch does what the command says, and in some cases, the switch replies with some messages stating the results of the command.

Before getting into the details of the CLI, this section examines the models of Cisco LAN switches typically referenced for CCNA exams. Then this section explains how a network engineer can get access to the CLI to issue commands.

Cisco Catalyst Switches and the 2960 Switch

Within the Cisco Catalyst brand of LAN switches, Cisco produces a wide variety of switch series or families. Each switch series includes several specific models of switches that have similar features, similar price-versus-performance trade-offs, and similar internal components.

Cisco positions the 2960 series (family) of switches as full-featured, low-cost wiring closet switches for Enterprises. That means that you would expect to use 2960 switches as access switches, as shown in Figure 7-12 in Chapter 7, "Ethernet LAN Switching Concepts." Access switches provide the connection point for end-user devices, with cabling running from desks to the switch in a nearby wiring closet. 2960 access switches would also connect to the rest of the Enterprise network using a couple of uplinks, often connecting to distribution layer switches. The distribution layer switches are often from a different Cisco switch family, typically a more powerful and more expensive product family.

Figure 8-1 shows a photo of the 2960 switch series from Cisco. Each switch is a different specific model of switch inside the 2960 series. For example, the top switch in Figure 8-1 (model WS-2960-24TT-L) has 24 RJ-45 UTP 10/100 ports, meaning that these ports can negotiate the use of 10BASE-T or 100BASE-TX Ethernet. The WS-2960-24TT-L switch has two additional RJ-45 ports on the right that are 10/100/1000 interfaces, intended to connect to the core of an Enterprise campus LAN.

Cisco refers to a switch's physical connectors as either *interfaces* or *ports*. Each interface has a number in the style *x/y*, where *x* and *y* are two different numbers. On a 2960, the number before the / is always 0. The first 10/100 interface on a 2960 is numbered starting at 0/1, the second is 0/2, and so on. The interfaces also have names; for example, "interface FastEthernet 0/1" is the first of the 10/100 interfaces. Any Gigabit-capable interfaces would be called "GigabitEthernet" interfaces. For example, the first 10/100/1000 interface on a 2960 would be "interface gigabitethernet 0/1."

Figure 8-1   *Cisco 2960 Catalyst Switch Series*

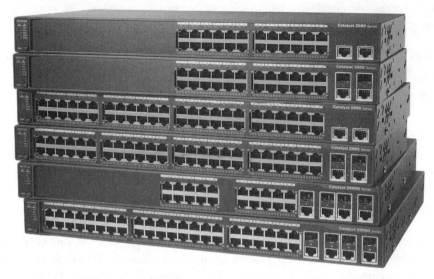

Cisco supports two major types of switch operating systems: *Internetwork Operating System* (IOS) and *Catalyst Operating System* (Cat OS). Most Cisco Catalyst switch series today run only Cisco IOS, but for some historical reasons, some of the high-end Cisco LAN switches support both Cisco IOS and Cat OS. For the purposes of the CCNA exams, you can ignore Cat OS, focusing on Cisco IOS. However, keep in mind that you might see terminology and phrasing such as "IOS-based switch," referring to the fact that the switch runs Cisco IOS, not Cat OS.

> **NOTE**   For the real world, note that Cisco's most popular core switch product, the 6500 series, can run either Cisco IOS or Cat OS. Cisco also uses the term *hybrid* to refer to 6500 switches that use Cat OS and the term *native* to refer to 6500 switches that use Cisco IOS.

Switch Status from LEDs

When an engineer needs to examine how a switch is working to verify its current status and to troubleshoot any problems, the vast majority of the time is spent using commands from the Cisco IOS CLI. However, the switch hardware does include several LEDs that provide some status and troubleshooting information, both during the time right after the switch has been powered on and during ongoing operations. Before moving on to discuss the CLI, this brief section examines the switch LEDs and their meanings.

Most Cisco Catalyst switches have some LEDs, including an LED for each physical Ethernet interface. For example, Figure 8-2 shows the front of a 2960 series switch, with five LEDs on the left, one LED over each port, and a mode button.

Figure 8-2 *2960 LEDs and a Mode Button*

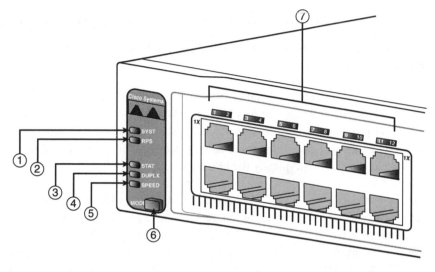

The figure points out the various LEDs, with various meanings. Table 8-2 summarizes the LEDs, and additional explanations follow the table.

Table 8-2 *LEDs in Figure 8-2*

Number in Figure 8-2	Name	Description
1	SYST (system)	Implies the overall system status
2	RPS (Redundant Power Supply)	Suggests the status of the extra (redundant) power supply
3	STAT (Status)	If on (green), implies that each port LED implies that port's status
4	DUPLX (duplex)	If on (green), each port LED implies that port's duplex (on/green is full; off means half)
5	SPEED	If on (green), each port LED implies the speed of that port, as follows: off means 10 Mbps, solid green means 100 Mbps, and flashing green means 1 Gbps.
7	Port	Has different meanings, depending on the port mode as toggled using the mode button

A few specific examples can help make sense of the LEDs. For example, consider the SYST LED for a moment. This LED provides a quick overall status of the switch, with three simple states on most 2960 switch models:

- **Off:** The switch is not powered on

- **On (green):** The switch is powered on and operational (Cisco IOS has been loaded)

- **On (amber):** The switch's Power-On Self Test (POST) process failed, and the Cisco IOS did not load.

So, a quick look at the SYST LED on the switch tells you whether the switch is working and, if it isn't, whether this is due to a loss of power (the SYST LED is off) or some kind of POST problem (LED amber). In this last case, the typical response is to power the switch off and back on again. If the same failure occurs, a call to the Cisco Technical Assistance Center (TAC) is typically the next step.

Besides the straightforward SYST LED, the port LEDs—the LEDs sitting above or below each Ethernet port—means something different depending on which of three port LED modes is currently used on the switch. The switches have a mode button (labelled with number 6 in Figure 8-2) that, when pressed, cycles the port LEDs through three modes: STAT, DUPLX, and SPEED. The current port LED mode is signified by a solid green STAT, DUPLX, or SPEED LED (the lower three LEDs on the left part of Figure 8-2, labeled 3, 4, and 5). To move to another port LED mode, the engineer simply presses the mode button another time or two.

Each of the three port LED modes changes the meaning of the port LEDs associated with each port. For example, in STAT (status) mode, each port LED implies status information about that one associated port. For example:

- **Off:** The link is not working.

- **Solid green:** The link is working, but there's no current traffic.

- **Flashing green:** The link is working, and traffic is currently passing over the interface.

- **Flashing amber:** The interface is administratively disabled or has been dynamically disabled for a variety of reasons.

In contrast, in SPEED port LED mode, the port LEDs imply the operating speed of the interface, with a dark LED meaning 10 Mbps, a solid green light meaning 100 Mbps, and flashing green meaning 1000 Mbps (1 Gbps).

The particular details of how each LED works differ between different Cisco switch families and with different models inside the same switch family. So, memorizing the specific meaning of particular LED combinations is probably not required, and this chapter does not attempt to cover all combinations for even a single switch. However, it is important to remember the general ideas, the concept of a mode button that changes the meaning of the port LEDs, and the three meanings of the SYST LED mentioned earlier in this section.

The vast majority of the time, switches power up just fine and load Cisco IOS, and then the engineer simply accesses the CLI to operate and examine the switch. Next, the chapter focuses on the details of how to access the CLI.

Accessing the Cisco IOS CLI

Cisco IOS Software for Catalyst switches implements and controls logic and functions performed by a Cisco switch. Besides controlling the switch's performance and behavior, Cisco IOS also defines an interface for humans called the CLI. The Cisco IOS CLI allows the user to use a terminal emulation program, which accepts text entered by the user. When the user presses Enter, the terminal emulator sends that text to the switch. The switch processes the text as if it is a command, does what the command says, and sends text back to the terminal emulator.

The switch CLI can be accessed through three popular methods—the console, Telnet, and Secure Shell (SSH). Two of these methods (Telnet and SSH) use the IP network in which the switch resides to reach the switch. The console is a physical port built specifically to allow access to the CLI. Figure 8-3 depicts the options.

Figure 8-3   *CLI Access*

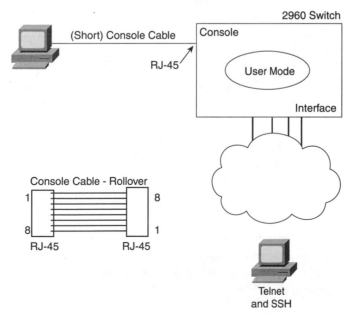

NOTE   You can also use a web browser to configure a switch, but the interface is not the CLI interface. This interface uses a tool called either the Cisco Device Manager (CDM) or Cisco Security Device Manager (SDM). Some SDM coverage is included in Chapter 17, "WAN Configuration," in relation to configuring a router.

Next, this section examines each of these three access methods in more detail.

CLI Access from the Console

The console port provides a way to connect to a switch CLI even if the switch has not been connected to a network yet. Every Cisco switch has a console port, which is physically an RJ-45 port. A PC connects to the console port using a UTP rollover cable, which is also connected to the PC's serial port. The UTP rollover cable has RJ-45 connectors on each end, with pin 1 on one end connected to pin 8 on the other, pin 2 to pin 7, pin 3 to pin 6, and pin 4 to pin 5. In some cases, a PC's serial interface does not use an RJ-45 connector, an adapter must be used to convert from the PC's physical interface—typically either a nine-pin connector or a USB connector—to an RJ-45. Figure 8-4 shows the RJ-45 end of the console cable connected to a switch and the DB-9 end connected to a laptop PC.

Figure 8-4   *Console Connection to a Switch*

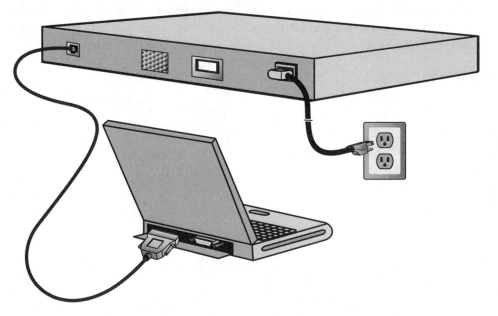

As soon as the PC is physically connected to the console port, a terminal emulator software package must be installed and configured on the PC. Today, terminal emulator software includes support for Telnet and Secure Shell (SSH), which can be used to access the switch CLI via the network, but not through the console.

Figure 8-5 shows the window created by the Tera Term Pro software package (available free from http://www.ayera.com). The emulator must be configured to use the PC's serial port, matching the switch's console port settings. The default console port settings on a switch are as follows:

- 9600 bits/second

- No hardware flow control

- 8-bit ASCII

- No parity bits

- 1 stop bit

Note that the last three parameters are referred to collectively as "8N1."

Figure 8-5 *Terminal Settings for Console Access*

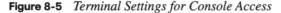

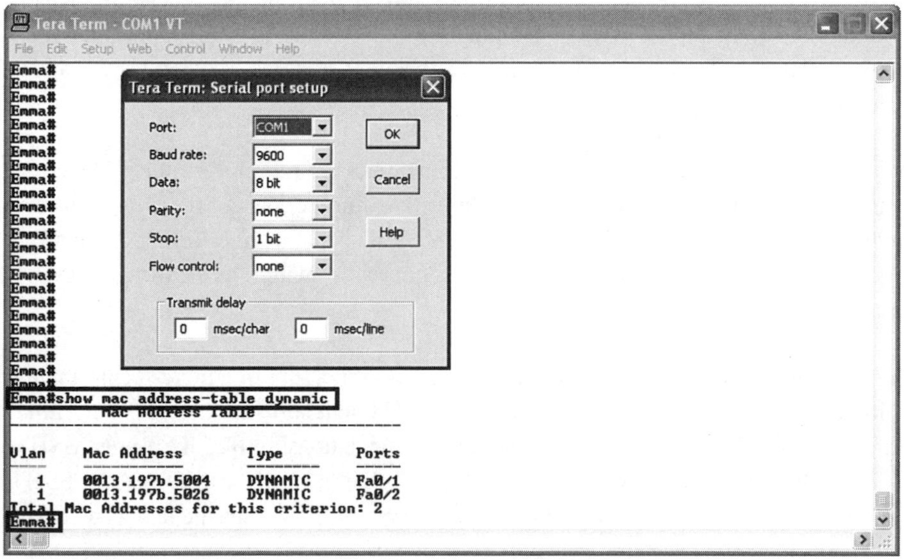

Figure 8-5 shows a terminal emulator window with some command output. It also shows the configuration window for the settings just listed.

The figure shows the window created by the emulator software. Note that the first highlighted portion shows the text **Emma#show mac address-table dynamic**. The **Emma#** part is the command prompt, which typically shows the hostname of the switch (Emma in this case). The prompt is text created by the switch and sent to the emulator. The **show mac address-table dynamic** part is the command that the user entered. The text shown beneath the command is the output generated by the switch and sent to the emulator. Finally, the lower highlighted text **Emma#** shows the command prompt again, as sent to the emulator by the switch. The window would remain in this state until the user entered something else at the command line.

Accessing the CLI with Telnet and SSH

The TCP/IP Telnet application allows a terminal emulator to communicate with a device, much like what happens with an emulator on a PC connected to the console. However, Telnet uses an IP network to send and receive the data, rather than a specialized cable and physical port on the device. The Telnet application protocols call the terminal emulator a *Telnet client* and the device that listens for commands and replies to them a *Telnet server*. Telnet is a TCP-based application layer protocol that uses well-known port 23.

To use Telnet, the user must install a Telnet client software package on his or her PC. (As mentioned earlier, most terminal emulator software packages today include both Telnet and SSH client functions.) The switch runs Telnet server software by default, but the switch does need to have an IP address configured so that it can send and receive IP packets. (Chapter 9 covers switch IP address configuration in greater detail.) Additionally, the network between the PC and switch needs to be up and working so that the PC and switch can exchange IP packets.

Many network engineers habitually use a Telnet client to monitor switches. The engineer can sit at his or her desk without having to walk to another part of the building—or go to another state or country—and still get into the CLI of that device. Telnet sends all data (including any username and password for login to the switch) as clear-text data, which presents a potential security risk.

Secure Shell (SSH) does the same basic things as Telnet, but in a more secure manner by using encryption. Like the Telnet model, the SSH client software includes a terminal emulator and the capability to send and receive the data using IP. Like Telnet, SSH uses TCP, while using well-known port 22 instead of Telnet's 23. As with Telnet, the SSH server (on the switch) receives the text from each SSH client, processes the text as a command, and sends messages back to the client. The key difference between Telnet and SSH lies in the fact that all the communications are encrypted and therefore are private and less prone to security risk.

Password Security for CLI Access

By default, a Cisco switch is very secure as long as the switch is locked inside a room. By default, a switch allows only console access, but no Telnet or SSH access. From the console, you can gain full access to all switch commands, and if so inclined, you can stop all functions of the switch. However, console access requires physical access to the switch, so allowing console access for switches just removed from the shipping boxes is reasonable.

Regardless of the defaults, it makes sense to password-protect console access, as well as Telnet and SSH access. To add basic password checking for the console and for Telnet, the engineer needs to configure a couple of basic commands. The configuration process is covered a little later in this chapter, but you can get a general idea of the commands by looking in the last column of Table 8-3. The table lists the two commands that configure the console and vty passwords. After it is configured, the switch supplies a simple password prompt (as a result of the **login** command), and the switch expects the user to enter the password listed in the **password** command.

Table 8-3 *CLI Password Configuration: Console and Telnet*

Access From	Password Type	Sample Configuration
Console	Console password	**line console 0** **login** **password faith**
Telnet	vty password	**line vty 0 15** **login** **password love**

Cisco switches refer to the console as a console line—specifically, console line 0. Similarly, switches support 16 concurrent Telnet sessions, referenced as virtual terminal (vty) lines 0 through 15. (The term vty refers to an old name for terminal emulators.) The **line vty 0 15** configuration command tells the switch that the commands that follow apply to all 16 possible concurrent virtual terminal connections to the switch, which includes Telnet as well as SSH access.

NOTE   Some older versions of switch software supported only five vty lines, 0 through 4.

After adding the configuration shown in Table 8-3, a user connecting to the console would be prompted for a password, and he or she would have to supply the word **faith** in this case. New Telnet users would also be prompted for a password, with **love** being the required password. Also, with this configuration, no username is required—just a simple password.

Configuring SSH requires a little more effort than the console and Telnet password configuration examples shown in Table 8-3. SSH uses public key cryptography to exchange a shared session key, which in turn is used for encryption. Additionally, SSH requires slightly better login security, requiring at least a password and a username. The section "Configuring Usernames and Secure Shell (SSH)" in Chapter 9 shows the configuration steps and a sample configuration to support SSH.

User and Enable (Privileged) Modes

All three CLI access methods covered so far (console, Telnet, and SSH) place the user in an area of the CLI called *user EXEC mode*. User EXEC mode, sometimes also called *user mode*, allows the user to look around but not break anything. The "EXEC mode" part of the name refers to the fact that in this mode, when you enter a command, the switch executes the command and then displays messages that describe the command's results.

Cisco IOS supports a more powerful EXEC mode called *enable* mode (also known as *privileged* mode or *privileged EXEC* mode). Enable mode is so named because the **enable** command is used to reach this mode, as shown in Figure 8-6. Privileged mode earns its name because powerful, or privileged, commands can be executed there. For example, you can use the **reload** command, which tells the switch to reinitialize or reboot Cisco IOS, only from enable mode.

Figure 8-6 *User and Privileged Modes*

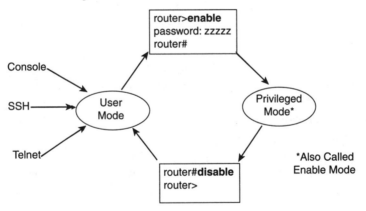

> **NOTE**   If the command prompt lists the hostname followed by a >, the user is in user mode; if it is the hostname followed by the #, the user is in enable mode.

The preferred configuration command for configuring the password for reaching enable mode is the **enable secret** *password* command, where *password* is the text of the password. Note that if the enable password is not configured (the default), Cisco IOS prevents Telnet and SSH users from getting into enable mode, but Cisco IOS does allow a console user to reach enable mode. This default action is consistent with the idea that, by default, users outside the locked room where the switch sits cannot get access without additional configuration by the engineer.

> **NOTE**   The commands that can be used in either user (EXEC) mode or enable (EXEC) mode are called EXEC commands.

So far, this chapter has pointed out some of the first things you should know when unpacking and installing a switch. The switch will work without any configuration—just plug in the power and Ethernet cables, and it works. However, you should at least connect to the switch console port and configure passwords for the console, Telnet, SSH, and the enable secret password.

Next, this chapter examines some of the CLI features that exist regardless of how you access the CLI.

CLI Help Features

If you printed the Cisco IOS Command Reference documents, you would end up with a stack of paper several feet tall. No one should expect to memorize all the commands—and no one does. You can use several very easy, convenient tools to help remember commands and save time typing. As you progress through your Cisco certifications, the exams will cover progressively more commands. However, you should know the methods of getting command help.

Table 8-4 summarizes command-recall help options available at the CLI. Note that, in the first column, *command* represents any command. Likewise, *parm* represents a command's parameter. For instance, the third row lists *command* **?**, which means that commands such as **show ?** and **copy ?** would list help for the **show** and **copy** commands, respectively.

Table 8-4   *Cisco IOS Software Command Help*

What You Enter	What Help You Get
?	Help for all commands available in this mode.
help	Text describing how to get help. No actual command help is given.
command **?**	Text help describing all the first parameter options for the command.
com?	A list of commands that start with **com**.
*command parm***?**	This style of help lists all parameters beginning with **parm**. (Notice that there is no space between *parm* and the **?**.)
command parm<Tab>	If you press the Tab key midword, the CLI either spells the rest of this parameter at the command line or does nothing. If the CLI does nothing, it means that this string of characters represents more than one possible next parameter, so the CLI does not know which one to spell out.
command parm1 **?**	If a space is inserted before the question mark, the CLI lists all the next parameters and gives a brief explanation of each.

When you enter the **?**, the Cisco IOS CLI reacts immediately; that is, you don't need to press the Enter key or any other keys. The device running Cisco IOS also redisplays what you entered before the **?** to save you some keystrokes. If you press Enter immediately after the **?**, Cisco IOS tries to execute the command with only the parameters you have entered so far.

command represents any command, not the word *command*. Likewise, *parm* represents a command's parameter, not the word *parameter*.

The information supplied by using help depends on the CLI mode. For example, when **?** is entered in user mode, the commands allowed in user mode are displayed, but commands available only in enable mode (not in user mode) are not displayed. Also, help is available in configuration mode, which is the mode used to configure the switch. In fact, configuration mode has many different subconfiguration modes, as explained in the section "Configuration Submodes and Contexts." So, you can get help for the commands available in each configuration submode as well.

Cisco IOS stores the commands that you enter in a history buffer, storing ten commands by default. The CLI allows you to move backward and forward in the historical list of commands and then edit the command before reissuing it. These key sequences can help you use the CLI more quickly on the exams. Table 8-5 lists the commands used to manipulate previously entered commands.

Table 8-5 *Key Sequences for Command Edit and Recall*

Keyboard Command	What Happens
Up arrow or Ctrl-p	This displays the most recently used command. If you press it again, the next most recent command appears, until the history buffer is exhausted. (The p stands for previous.)
Down arrow or Ctrl-n	If you have gone too far back into the history buffer, these keys take you forward to the more recently entered commands. (The n stands for next.)
Left arrow or Ctrl-b	This moves the cursor backward in the currently displayed command without deleting characters. (The b stands for back.)
Right arrow or Ctrl-f	This moves the cursor forward in the currently displayed command without deleting characters. (The f stands for forward.)
Backspace	This moves the cursor backward in the currently displayed command, deleting characters.
Ctrl-a	This moves the cursor directly to the first character of the currently displayed command.
Ctrl-e	This moves the cursor directly to the end of the currently displayed command.
Ctrl-r	This redisplays the command line with all characters. It's useful when messages clutter the screen.
Ctrl-d	This deletes a single character.
Esc-b	This moves back one word.
Esc-f	This moves forward one word.

The debug and show Commands

By far, the single most popular Cisco IOS command is the **show** command. The **show** command has a large variety of options, and with those options, you can find the status of almost every feature of Cisco IOS. Essentially, the **show** command lists the currently known facts about the switch's operational status. The only work the switch does in reaction to **show** commands is to find the current status and list the information in messages sent to the user.

A less popular command is the **debug** command. Like the **show** command, **debug** has many options. However, instead of just listing messages about the current status, the **debug** command asks the switch to continue monitoring different processes in the switch. The switch then sends ongoing messages to the user when different events occur.

The effects of the **show** and **debug** commands can be compared to a photograph and a movie. Like a photo, a **show** command shows what's true at a single point in time, and it takes little effort. The **debug** command shows what's true over time, but it requires more effort. As a result, the **debug** command requires more CPU cycles, but it lets you watch what is happening in a switch while it is happening.

Cisco IOS handles the messages created with the **debug** command much differently than with the **show** command. When any user issues a **debug** command, the debug options in the command are enabled. The messages Cisco IOS creates in response to all **debug** commands, regardless of which user(s) issued the **debug** commands, are treated as a special type of message called a *log message*. Any remote user can view log messages by simply using the **terminal monitor** command. Additionally, these log messages also appear at the console automatically. So, whereas the **show** command lists a set of messages for that single user, the **debug** command lists messages for all interested users to see, requiring remote users to ask to view the **debug** and other log messages.

The options enabled by a single **debug** command are not disabled until the user takes action or until the switch is reloaded. A **reload** of the switch disables all currently enabled debug options. To disable a single debug option, repeat the same **debug** command with those options, prefaced by the word **no**. For example, if the **debug spanning-tree** command was been issued earlier, issue the **no debug spanning-tree** command to disable that same debug. Also, the **no debug all** and **undebug all** commands disable all currently enabled debugs.

Be aware that some **debug** options create so many messages that Cisco IOS cannot process them all, possibly resulting in a crash of Cisco IOS. You might want to check the current switch CPU utilization with the **show process** command before issuing any **debug** command. To be more careful, before enabling an unfamiliar **debug** command option, issue a **no debug all** command, and then issue the **debug** that you want to use. Then quickly retrieve the **no debug all** command using the up arrow or Ctrl-p key sequence twice. If the debug quickly degrades switch performance, the switch may be too busy to listen to what you are typing. The process described in this paragraph saves a bit of typing and may be the difference between preventing the switch from failing, or not.

Configuring Cisco IOS Software

You must understand how to configure a Cisco switch to succeed on the exam and in real networking jobs. This section covers the basic configuration processes, including the concept of a configuration file and the locations in which the configuration files can be stored. Although this section focuses on the configuration process, and not on the configuration commands themselves, you should know all the commands covered in this chapter for the exams, in addition to the configuration processes.

Configuration mode is another mode for the Cisco CLI, similar to user mode and privileged mode. User mode lets you issue nondisruptive commands and displays some information. Privileged mode supports a superset of commands compared to user mode, including commands that might harm the switch. However, none of the commands in user or privileged mode changes the switch's configuration. Configuration mode accepts *configuration commands*—commands that tell the switch the details of what to do, and how to do it. Figure 8-7 illustrates the relationships among configuration mode, user EXEC mode, and privileged EXEC mode.

Figure 8-7 *CLI Configuration Mode Versus Exec Modes*

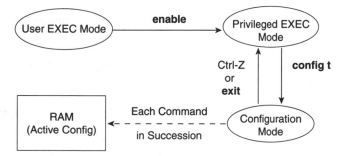

Commands entered in configuration mode update the active configuration file. *These changes to the configuration occur immediately each time you press the Enter key at the end of a command.* Be careful when you enter a configuration command!

Configuration Submodes and Contexts

Configuration mode itself contains a multitude of subcommand modes. *Context-setting commands* move you from one configuration subcommand mode, or context, to another. These context-setting commands tell the switch the topic about which you will enter the next few configuration commands. More importantly, the context tells the switch the topic you care about right now, so when you use the **?** to get help, the switch gives you help about that topic only.

> **NOTE** Context setting is not a Cisco term—it's just a term used here to help make sense of configuration mode.

The **interface** command is one of the most commonly used context-setting configuration commands. For example, the CLI user could enter interface configuration mode by entering the **interface FastEthernet 0/1** configuration command. Asking for help in interface configuration mode displays only commands that are useful when configuring Ethernet interfaces. Commands used in this context are called *subcommands*—or, in this specific case, *interface subcommands*. When you begin practicing with the CLI with real equipment, the navigation between modes can become natural. For now, consider Example 8-1, which shows the following:

■ Movement from enable mode to global configuration mode by using the **configure terminal** EXEC command

■ Using a **hostname Fred** global configuration command to configure the switch's name

■ Movement from global configuration mode to console line configuration mode (using the **line console 0** command)

■ Setting the console's simple password to **hope** (using the **password hope** line subcommand)

■ Movement from console configuration mode to interface configuration mode (using the **interface** command)

■ Setting the speed to 100 Mbps for interface Fa0/1 (using the **speed 100** interface subcommand)

■ Movement from console line configuration mode back to global configuration mode (using the **exit** command)

Example 8-1 *Navigating Between Different Configuration Modes*

```
Switch#configure terminal
Switch(config)#hostname Fred
Fred(config)#line console 0
Fred(config-line)#password hope
Fred(config-line)#interface FastEthernet 0/1
Fred(config-if)#speed 100
Fred(config-if)#exit
Fred(config)#
```

The text inside parentheses in the command prompt identifies the configuration mode. For example, the first command prompt after you enter configuration mode lists (config), meaning global configuration mode. After the **line console 0** command, the text expands to (config-line), meaning line configuration mode. Table 8-6 shows the most common command prompts in configuration mode, the names of those modes, and the context setting commands used to reach those modes.

Table 8-6 *Common Switch Configuration Modes*

Prompt	Name of Mode	Context-setting Command(s) to Reach This Mode
hostname(config)#	Global	None—first mode after **configure terminal**
hostname(config-line)#	Line	**line console 0** **line vty 0 15**
hostname(config-if)#	Interface	**interface** *type number*

No set rules exist for what commands are global commands or subcommands. Generally, however, when multiple instances of a parameter can be set in a single switch, the command used to set the parameter is likely a configuration subcommand. Items that are set once for the entire switch are likely global commands. For example, the **hostname** command is a global command because there is only one hostname per switch. Conversely, the **duplex** command is an interface subcommand to allow the switch to use a different setting on the different interfaces.

Both the Ctrl-z key sequence and the **end** command exit the user from any part of configuration mode and go back to privileged EXEC mode. Alternatively, the **exit** command backs you out of configuration mode one subconfiguration mode at a time.

Storing Switch Configuration Files

When you configure a switch, it needs to use the configuration. It also needs to be able to retain the configuration in case the switch loses power. Cisco switches contain Random Access Memory (RAM) to store data while Cisco IOS is using it, but RAM loses its contents when the switch loses power. To store information that must be retained when the switch loses power, Cisco switches use several types of more permanent memory, none of which has any moving parts. By avoiding components with moving parts (such as traditional disk drives), switches can maintain better uptime and availability.

The following list details the four main types of memory found in Cisco switches, as well as the most common use of each type.

- **RAM:** Sometimes called DRAM for Dynamic Random-Access Memory, RAM is used by the switch just as it is used by any other computer: for working storage. The running (active) configuration file is stored here.

- **ROM:** Read-Only Memory (ROM) stores a bootstrap (or boothelper) program that is loaded when the switch first powers on. This bootstrap program then finds the full Cisco IOS image and manages the process of loading Cisco IOS into RAM, at which point Cisco IOS takes over operation of the switch.

■ **Flash memory:** Either a chip inside the switch or a removable memory card, Flash memory stores fully functional Cisco IOS images and is the default location where the switch gets its Cisco IOS at boot time. Flash memory also can be used to store any other files, including backup copies of configuration files.

■ **NVRAM:** Nonvolatile RAM (NVRAM) stores the initial or startup configuration file that is used when the switch is first powered on and when the switch is reloaded.

Figure 8-8 summarizes this same information in a briefer and more convenient form for memorization and study.

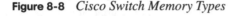

Figure 8-8 *Cisco Switch Memory Types*

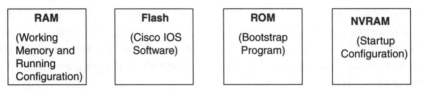

Cisco IOS stores the collection of configuration commands in a *configuration file*. In fact, switches use multiple configuration files—one file for the initial configuration used when powering on, and another configuration file for the active, currently used running configuration as stored in RAM. Table 8-7 lists the names of these two files, their purpose, and their storage location.

Table 8-7 *Names and Purposes of the Two Main Cisco IOS Configuration Files*

Configuration Filename	Purpose	Where It Is Stored
Startup-config	Stores the initial configuration used any time the switch reloads Cisco IOS.	NVRAM
Running-config	Stores the currently used configuration commands. This file changes dynamically when someone enters commands in configuration mode.	RAM

Essentially, when you use configuration mode, you change only the running-config file. This means that the configuration example earlier in this chapter (Example 8-1) updates only the running-config file. However, if the switch lost power right after that example, all that configuration would be lost. If you want to keep that configuration, you have to copy the running-config file into NVRAM, overwriting the old startup-config file.

Example 8-2 demonstrates that commands used in configuration mode change only the running configuration in RAM. The example shows the following concepts and steps:

Step 1   The original **hostname** command on the switch, with the startup-config file matching the running-config file.

Step 2   The **hostname** command changes the hostname, but only in the running-config file.

Step 3   The **show running-config** and **show startup-config** commands are shown, with only the hostname commands displayed for brevity, to make the point that the two configuration files are now different.

Example 8-2 *How Configuration Mode Commands Change the Running-config File, not the Startup-config File*

```
! Step 1 next (two commands)
!
hannah#show running-config
! (lines omitted)
hostname hannah
! (rest of lines omitted)

hannah#show startup-config
! (lines omitted)
hostname hannah
! (rest of lines omitted)
! Step 2 next. Notice that the command prompt changes immediately after
! the hostname command.
!hannah#configure terminal
hannah(config)#hostname jessie
jessie(config)#exit
! Step 3 next (two commands)
!
jessie#show running-config
! (lines omitted)
hostname jessie
! (rest of lines omitted - notice that the running configuration reflects the
!  changed hostname)
jessie# show startup-config
! (lines omitted)
hostname hannah
! (rest of lines omitted - notice that the changed configuration is not
! shown in the startup config)
```

> **NOTE** Cisco uses the term *reload* to refer to what most PC operating systems call rebooting or restarting. In each case, it is a reinitialization of the software. The **reload** exec command causes a switch to reload.

Copying and Erasing Configuration Files

If you reload the switch at the end of Example 8-2, the hostname reverts to Hannah, because the running-config file has not been copied into the startup-config file. However, if you want to keep the new hostname of jessie, you would use the command **copy running-config startup-config**, which overwrites the current startup-config file with what is currently in the running configuration file. The **copy** command can be used to copy files in a switch, most typically a configuration file or a new version of Cisco IOS Software. The most basic method for moving configuration files in and out of a switch is to use the **copy** command to copy files between RAM or NVRAM on a switch and a TFTP server. The files can be copied between any pair, as shown in Figure 8-9.

Figure 8-9 *Locations for Copying and Results from Copy Operations*

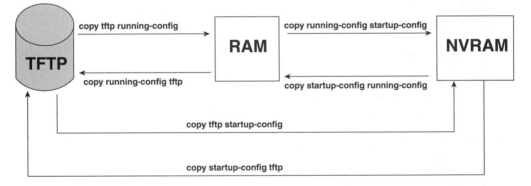

The commands for copying Cisco IOS configurations can be summarized as follows:

```
copy {tftp | running-config | startup-config} {tftp | running-config | startup-config}
```

The first set of parameters enclosed in braces ({ }) is the "from" location; the next set of parameters is the "to" location.

The **copy** command always replaces the existing file when the file is copied into NVRAM or into a TFTP server. In other words, it acts as if the destination file was erased and the new file completely replaced the old one. However, when the **copy** command copies a configuration file into the running-config file in RAM, the configuration file in RAM is not replaced, but is merged instead. Effectively, any **copy** into RAM works just as if you entered the commands in the "from" configuration file in the order listed in the config file.

Who cares? Well, we do. If you change the running config and then decide that you want to revert to what's in the startup-config file, the result of the **copy startup-config running-config** command may not cause the two files to actually match. The only way to guarantee that the two configuration files match is to issue the **reload** command, which reloads, or reboots, the switch, which erases RAM and then copies the startup-config into RAM as part of the reload process.

You can use three different commands to erase the contents of NVRAM. The **write erase** and **erase startup-config** commands are older, whereas the **erase nvram:** command is the more recent, and recommended, command. All three commands simply erase the contents of the NVRAM configuration file. Of course, if the switch is reloaded at this point, there is no initial configuration. Note that Cisco IOS does not have a command that erases the contents of the running-config file. To clear out the running-config file, simply erase the startup-config file, and then **reload** the switch.

> **NOTE** Making a copy of all current switch and router configurations should be part of any network's overall security strategy, mainly so that you can replace a device's configuration if an attack changes the configuration.

Although startup-config and running-config are the most common names for the two configuration files, Cisco IOS defines a few other more formalized names for these files. These more formalized filenames use a format defined by the *Cisco IOS File System* (IFS), which is the name of the file system created by Cisco IOS to manage files. For example, the **copy** command can refer to the startup-config file as nvram:startup-config. Table 8-8 lists the alternative names for these two configuration files.

Table 8-8 *IFS Filenames for the Startup and Running Config Files*

Config File Common Name	Alternative Names
startup-config	nvram: nvram:startup-config
running-config	system:running-config

Initial Configuration (Setup Mode)

Cisco IOS Software supports two primary methods of giving a switch an initial basic configuration—configuration mode, which has already been covered in this chapter, and setup mode. Setup mode leads a switch administrator to a basic switch configuration by using questions that prompt the administrator for basic configuration parameters. Because configuration mode is required for most configuration tasks, most networking personnel do not use setup at all. However, new users sometimes like to use setup mode, particularly until they become more familiar with the CLI configuration mode.

Figure 8-10 and Example 8-3 describe the process used by setup mode. Setup mode is used most frequently when the switch boots, and it has no configuration in NVRAM. You can also enter setup mode by using the **setup** command from privileged mode.

Figure 8-10 *Getting into Setup Mode*

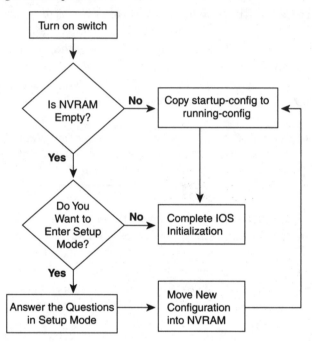

Example 8-3 *Initial Configuration Dialog Example*

```
--- System Configuration Dialog ---

Would you like to enter the initial configuration dialog? [yes/no]: yes

At any point you may enter a question mark '?' for help.
Use ctrl-c to abort configuration dialog at any prompt.
Default settings are in square brackets '[]'.


Basic management setup configures only enough connectivity
for management of the system, extended setup will ask you
```

Example 8-3 *Initial Configuration Dialog Example (Continued)*

```
to configure each interface on the system

Would you like to enter basic management setup? [yes/no]: yes
Configuring global parameters:

  Enter host name [Switch]: fred

  The enable secret is a password used to protect access to
  privileged EXEC and configuration modes. This password, after
  entered, becomes encrypted in the configuration.
  Enter enable secret: cisco

  The enable password is used when you do not specify an
  enable secret password, with some older software versions, and
  some boot images.
  Enter enable password: notcisco

  The virtual terminal password is used to protect
  access to the switch over a network interface.
  Enter virtual terminal password: wilma
  Configure SNMP Network Management? [no]:

Current interface summary

Any interface listed with OK? value "NO" does not have a valid configuration

Interface                IP-Address        OK? Method Status           Protocol
Vlan1                    unassigned        NO  unset  up               up
FastEthernet0/1          unassigned        YES unset  up               up
FastEthernet0/2          unassigned        YES unset  up               up
FastEthernet0/3          unassigned        YES unset  up               up
!
!Lines ommitted for brevity
!
GigabitEthernet0/1       unassigned        YES unset  down             down
GigabitEthernet0/2       unassigned        YES unset  down             down

The following configuration command script was created:

hostname fred
enable secret 5 $1$wNE7$4JSktD3uN1Af5FpctmPz11
enable password notcisco
line vty 0 15
password wilma
no snmp-server
```

continues

Example 8-3 *Initial Configuration Dialog Example (Continued)*

```
!
!
interface Vlan1
shutdown
no ip address
!
interface FastEthernet0/1
!
interface FastEthernet0/2
!
interface FastEthernet0/3
!
interface FastEthernet0/4
!
interface FastEthernet0/5
!
! Lines ommitted for brevity
!
interface GigabitEthernet0/1
!
interface GigabitEthernet0/2
!
end


[0] Go to the IOS command prompt without saving this config.
[1] Return back to the setup without saving this config.
[2] Save this configuration to nvram and exit.

Enter your selection [2]: 2
Building configuration...
[OK]

Use the enabled mode 'configure' command to modify this configuration.
Press RETURN to get started!
```

Setup behaves as shown in Example 8-3, regardless of whether Setup was reached by booting with an empty NVRAM or whether the **setup** privileged EXEC command was used. First, the switch asks whether you want to enter the initial configuration dialog. Answering **y** or **yes** puts you in setup mode. At that point, the switch keeps asking questions, and you keep answering, until you have answered all the setup questions.

When you are finished answering the configuration questions, the switch asks you to choose from one of three options:

0: Do not save any of this configuration, and go to the CLI command prompt.

1: Do not save any of this configuration, but start over in setup mode.

2: Save the configuration in both the startup-config and the running-config, and go to the CLI command prompt.

You can also abort the setup process before answering all the questions, and get to a CLI prompt, by pressing **Ctrl-C**. Note that answer **2** actually writes the configuration to both the startup-config and running-config file, whereas configuration mode changes only the running-config file.

Exam Preparation Tasks

Review All the Key Topics

Review the most important topics from this chapter, noted with the key topics icon. Table 8-9 lists these key topics and where each is discussed.

Table 8-9 *Key Topics for Chapter 8*

Key Topic Element	Description	Page Number
List	A Cisco switch's default console port settings	207
Table 8-6	A list of configuration mode prompts, the name of the configuration mode, and the command used to reach each mode	217
Figure 8-8	Types of memory in a switch	218
Table 8-7	The names and purposes of the two configuration files in a switch or router	218

Complete the Tables and Lists from Memory

Print a copy of Appendix H, "Memory Tables" (found on the CD), or at least the section for this chapter, and complete the tables and lists from memory. Appendix I, "Memory Tables Answer Key," also on the CD, includes completed tables and lists for you to check your work.

Definitions of Key Terms

Define the following key terms from this chapter and check your answers in the glossary:

command-line interface (CLI), Secure Shell (SSH), enable mode, user mode, configuration mode, startup-config file, running-config file, setup mode

Command References

Table 8-10 lists and briefly describes the configuration commands used in this chapter.

Table 8-10 *Chapter 8 Configuration Commands*

Command	Mode and Purpose
line console 0	Global command that changes the context to console configuration mode.
line vty *1st-vty 2nd-vty*	Global command that changes the context to vty configuration mode for the range of vty lines listed in the command.
login	Line (console and vty) configuration mode. Tells IOS to prompt for a password (no username).
password *pass-value*	Line (console and vty) configuration mode. Lists the password required if the **login** command (with no other parameters) is configured.
interface *type port-number*	Global command that changes the context to interface mode—for example, interface Fastethernet 0/1.
shutdown **no shutdown**	Interface subcommand that disables or enables the interface, respectively.
hostname *name*	Global command that sets this switch's hostname, which is also used as the first part of the switch's command prompt.
enable secret *pass-value*	Global command that sets the automatically encrypted enable secret password. The password is used for any user to reach enable mode.
enable password *pass-value*	Global command that sets the clear-text enable password, which is used only when the enable secret password is not configured.
exit	Moves back to the next higher mode in configuration mode.
end	Exits configuration mode and goes back to enable mode from any of the configuration submodes.
Ctrl-Z	This is not a command, but rather a two-key combination (the Ctrl key and the letter z) that together do the same thing as the **end** command.

Table 8-11 lists and briefly describes the EXEC commands used in this chapter.

Table 8-11   *Chapter 8 EXEC Command Reference*

Command	Purpose
no debug all **undebug all**	Enable mode EXEC command to disable all currently enabled debugs.
show process	EXEC command that lists statistics about CPU utilization.
terminal monitor	EXEC command that tells Cisco IOS to send a copy of all syslog messages, including debug messages, to the Telnet or SSH user who issues this command.
reload	Enable mode EXEC command that reboots the switch or router.
copy *from-location to-location*	Enable mode EXEC command that copies files from one file location to another. Locations include the startup-config and running-config files, files on TFTP and RPC servers, and flash memory.
copy running-config startup-config	Enable mode EXEC command that saves the active config, replacing the startup-config file used when the switch initializes.
copy startup-config running-config	Enable mode EXEC command that merges the startup config file with the currently active config file in RAM.
show running-config	Lists the contents of the running-config file.
write erase **erase startup-config** **erase nvram:**	All three enable mode EXEC commands erase the startup-config file.
setup	Enable mode EXEC command that places the user in setup mode, in which Cisco IOS asks the user for input on simple switch configurations.
quit	EXEC command that disconnects the user from the CLI session.
show system:running-config	Same as the **show running-config** command.
show startup-config	Lists the contents of the startup-config (initial config) file.

Table 8-11   *Chapter 8 EXEC Command Reference (Continued)*

Command	Purpose
show nvram:startup-config **show nvram:**	Same as the **show startup-config** command.
enable	Moves the user from user mode to enable (privileged) mode and prompts for an enable password if configured.
disable	Moves the user from enable mode to user mode.
configure terminal	Enable mode command that moves the user into configuration mode.

This chapter covers the following subjects:

Configuration Features in Common with Routers: This section explains how to configure a variety of switch features that happen to be configured exactly like the same feature on Cisco routers.

LAN Switch Configuration and Operation: This section explains how to configure a variety of switch features that happen to be unique to switches, and are not used on routers, or are configured differently than the configuration on Cisco routers.

CHAPTER 9

Ethernet Switch Configuration

Chapter 3, "Fundamentals of LANs," and Chapter 7, "Ethernet LAN Switching Concepts," have already explained the most common Ethernet LAN concepts. Those chapters explained how Ethernet cabling and switches work, including the concepts of how switches forward Ethernet frames based on the frames' destination MAC addresses.

Cisco LAN switches perform their core functions without any configuration. You can buy a Cisco switch, plug in the right cables to connect various devices to the switch, plug in the power cable, and the switch works. However, in most networks, the network engineer needs to configure and troubleshoot various switch features. This chapter explains how to configure various switch features, and Chapter 10, "Ethernet Switch Troubleshooting," explains how to troubleshoot problems on Cisco switches.

"Do I Know This Already?" Quiz

The "Do I Know This Already?" quiz allows you to assess whether you should read the entire chapter. If you miss no more than one of these eight self-assessment questions, you might want to move ahead to the "Exam Preparation Tasks" section. Table 9-1 lists the major headings in this chapter and the "Do I Know This Already?" quiz questions covering the material in those sections. This helps you assess your knowledge of these specific areas. The answers to the "Do I Know This Already?" quiz appear in Appendix A.

Table 9-1 *"Do I Know This Already?" Foundation Topics Section-to-Question Mapping*

Foundation Topics Section	Questions
Configuration of Features in Common with Routers	1–3
LAN Switch Configuration and Operation	4–8

1. Imagine that you have configured the **enable secret** command, followed by the **enable password** command, from the console. You log out of the switch and log back in at the console. Which command defines the password that you had to enter to access privileged mode?

    a. **enable password**

    b. **enable secret**

    c. Neither

    d. The **password** command, if it's configured

2. An engineer had formerly configured a Cisco 2960 switch to allow Telnet access so that the switch expected a password of **mypassword** from the Telnet user. The engineer then changed the configuration to support Secure Shell. Which of the following commands could have been part of the new configuration?

    a. A **username** *name* **password** *password* command in vty config mode

    b. A **username** *name* **password** *password* global configuration command

    c. A **transport input ssh** command in vty config mode

    d. A **transport input ssh** global configuration command

3. The following command was copied and pasted into configuration mode when a user was telnetted into a Cisco switch:

    ```
    banner login this is the login banner
    ```

    Which of the following are true about what occurs the next time a user logs in from the console?

    a. No banner text is displayed.

    b. The banner text "his is" is displayed.

    c. The banner text "this is the login banner" is displayed.

    d. The banner text "Login banner configured, no text defined" is displayed.

4. Which of the following is not required when configuring port security without sticky learning?

    a. Setting the maximum number of allowed MAC addresses on the interface with the **switchport port-security maximum** interface subcommand

    b. Enabling port security with the **switchport port-security** interface subcommand

c. Defining the allowed MAC addresses using the **switchport port-security mac-address** interface subcommand

d. All of the other answers list required commands

5. An engineer's desktop PC connects to a switch at the main site. A router at the main site connects to each branch office via a serial link, with one small router and switch at each branch. Which of the following commands must be configured, in the listed configuration mode, to allow the engineer to telnet to the branch office switches?

a. The **ip address** command in VLAN 1 configuration mode

b. The **ip address** command in global configuration mode

c. The **ip default-gateway** command in VLAN 1 configuration mode

d. The **ip default-gateway** command in global configuration mode

e. The **password** command in console line configuration mode

f. The **password** command in vty line configuration mode

6. Which of the following describes a way to disable IEEE standard autonegotiation on a 10/100 port on a Cisco switch?

a. Configure the **negotiate disable** interface subcommand

b. Configure the **no negotiate** interface subcommand

c. Configure the **speed 100** interface subcommand

d. Configure the **duplex half** interface subcommand

e. Configure the **duplex full** interface subcommand

f. Configure the **speed 100** and **duplex full** interface subcommands

7. In which of the following modes of the CLI could you configure the duplex setting for interface fastethernet 0/5?

a. User mode

b. Enable mode

c. Global configuration mode

d. Setup mode

e. Interface configuration mode

8. The **show vlan brief** command lists the following output:

    ```
    2    my-vlan                          active    Fa0/13, Fa0/15
    ```

    Which of the following commands could have been used as part of the configuration for this switch?

    a. The **vlan 2** global configuration command

    b. The **name MY-VLAN** vlan subcommand

    c. The **interface range Fa0/13 - 15** global configuration command

    d. The **switchport vlan 2** interface subcommand

Foundation Topics

Many Cisco Catalyst switches use the same Cisco IOS Software command-line interface (CLI) as Cisco routers. In addition to having the same look and feel, the switches and routers sometimes support the exact same configuration and **show** commands. Additionally, as mentioned in Chapter 8, some of the same commands and processes shown for Cisco switches work the same way for Cisco routers.

This chapter explains a wide variety of configurable items on Cisco switches. Some topics are relatively important, such as the configuration of usernames and passwords so that any remote access to a switch is secure. Some topics are relatively unimportant, but useful, such as the ability to assign a text description to an interface for documentation purposes. However, this chapter does contain the majority of the switch configuration topics for this book, with the exception of Cisco Discovery Protocol (CDP) configuration commands in Chapter 10.

Configuration of Features in Common with Routers

This first of the two major sections of this chapter examines the configuration of several features that are configured the exact same way on both switches and routers. In particular, this section examines how to secure access to the CLI, plus various settings for the console.

Securing the Switch CLI

To reach a switch's enable mode, a user must reach user mode either from the console or from a Telnet or SSH session, and then use the **enable** command. With default configuration settings, a user at the console does not need to supply a password to reach user mode or enable mode. The reason is that anyone with physical access to the switch or router console could reset the passwords in less than 5 minutes by using the password recovery procedures that Cisco publishes. So, routers and switches default to allow the console user access to enable mode.

> **NOTE** To see the password recovery/reset procedures, go to Cisco.com and search on the phrase "password recovery." The first listed item probably will be a web page with password recovery details for most every product made by Cisco.

To reach enable mode from a vty (Telnet or SSH), the switch must be configured with several items:

■ An IP address

■ Login security on the vty lines

■ An enable password

Most network engineers will want to be able to establish a Telnet or SSH connection to each switch, so it makes sense to configure the switches to allow secure access. Additionally, although someone with physical access to the switch can use the password recovery process to get access to the switch, it still makes sense to configure security even for access from the console.

This section examines most of the configuration details related to accessing enable mode on a switch or router. The one key topic not covered here is the IP address configuration, which is covered later in this chapter in the section "Configuring the Switch IP Address." In particular, this section covers the following topics:

■ Simple password security for the console and Telnet access

■ Secure Shell (SSH)

■ Password encryption

■ Enable mode passwords

Configuring Simple Password Security

An engineer can reach user mode in a Cisco switch or router from the console or via either Telnet or SSH. By default, switches and routers allow a console user to immediately access user mode after logging in, with no password required. With default settings, Telnet users are rejected when they try to access the switch, because a vty password has not yet been configured. Regardless of these defaults, it makes sense to password protect user mode for console, Telnet, and SSH users.

A user in user mode can gain access to enable mode by using the enable command, but with different defaults depending on whether the user is at the console or has logged in remotely using Telnet or SSH. By default, the **enable** command allows console users into enable mode without requiring a password, but Telnet users are rejected without even a chance to supply a password. Regardless of these defaults, it makes sense to password protect enable mode using the **enable secret** global configuration command.

> **NOTE** The later section "The Two Enable Mode Passwords" explains two options for configuring the password required by the **enable** command, as configured with the **enable secret** and **enable password** commands, and why the **enable secret** command is preferred.

Example 9-1 shows a sample configuration process that sets the console password, the vty (Telnet) password, the enable secret password, and a hostname for the switch. The example shows the entire process, including command prompts, which provide some reminders of the different configuration modes explained in Chapter 8, "Operating Cisco LAN Switches."

Example 9-1 *Configuring Basic Passwords and a Hostname*

```
Switch>enable
Switch#configure terminal
Switch(config)#enable secret cisco
Switch(config)#hostname Emma
Emma(config)#line console 0
Emma(config-line)#password faith
Emma(config-line)#login
Emma(config-line)#exit
Emma(config)#line vty 0 15
Emma(config-line)#password love
Emma(config-line)#login
Emma(config-line)#exit
Emma(config)#exit
Emma#
! The next command lists the switch's current configuration (running-config)
Emma#show running-config
!
Building configuration...

Current configuration : 1333 bytes
!
version 12.2
no service pad
service timestamps debug uptime
service timestamps log uptime
!
hostname Emma
!
enable secret 5 $1$YXRN$11zOe1Lb0Lv/nHyTquobd.
```

continues

Example 9-1   *Configuring Basic Passwords and a Hostname (Continued)*

```
!
spanning-tree mode pvst
spanning-tree extend system-id
!
interface FastEthernet0/1
!
interface FastEthernet0/2
!
! Several lines have been omitted here - in particular, lines for FastEthernet
! interfaces 0/3 through 0/23.
!
interface FastEthernet0/24
!
interface GigabitEthernet0/1
!
interface GigabitEthernet0/2
!
interface Vlan1
 no ip address
 no ip route-cache
!
ip http server
ip http secure-server
!
control-plane
!
!
line con 0
 password faith
 login
line vty 0 4
 password love
 login
line vty 5 15
 password love
 login
```

Example 9-1 begins by showing the user moving from enable mode to configuration mode by using the **configure terminal** EXEC command. As soon as the user is in global configuration mode, he enters two global configuration commands (**enable secret** and **hostname**) that add configuration that applies to the whole switch.

For instance, the **hostname** global configuration command simply sets the one and only name for this switch (in addition to changing the switch's command prompt). The **enable secret** command sets the only password used to reach enable mode, so it is also a global command. However, the **login** command (which tells the switch to ask for a text password, but no username) and the **password** command (which defines the required password) are shown in both console and vty line configuration submodes. So, these commands are subcommands in these two different configuration modes. These subcommands define different console and vty passwords based on the configuration submodes in which the commands were used, as shown in the example.

Pressing the Ctrl-z key sequence from any part of configuration mode takes you all the way back to enable mode. However, the example shows how to repeatedly use the **exit** command to move back from a configuration submode to global configuration mode, with another **exit** command to exit back to enable mode. The **end** configuration mode command performs the same action as the Ctrl-z key sequence, moving the user from any part of configuration mode back to privileged EXEC mode.

The second half of Example 9-1 lists the output of the **show running-config** command. This command shows the currently used configuration in the switch, which includes the changes made earlier in the example. The output highlights in gray the configuration commands added due to the earlier configuration commands.

> **NOTE**   The output of the **show running-config** command lists five vty lines (0 through 4) in a different location than the rest (5 through 15). In earlier IOS releases, Cisco IOS routers and switches had five vty lines, numbered 0 through 4, which allowed five concurrent Telnet connects to a switch or router. Later, Cisco added more vty lines (5 through 15), allowing 16 concurrent Telnet connections into each switch and router. That's why the command output lists the two vty line ranges separately.

Configuring Usernames and Secure Shell (SSH)

Telnet sends all data, including all passwords entered by the user, as clear text. The Secure Shell (SSH) application provides the same function as Telnet, displaying a terminal emulator window and allowing the user to remotely connect to another host's CLI. However, SSH encrypts the data sent between the SSH client and the SSH server, making SSH the preferred method for remote login to switches and routers today.

To add support for SSH login to a Cisco switch or router, the switch needs several configuration commands. For example, SSH requires that the user supply both a username and password instead of just a password. So, the switch must be reconfigured to use one of two user authentication methods that require both a username and password: one method with the usernames and passwords configured on the switch, and the other with the usernames and passwords configured on an external server called an Authentication, Authorization, and Accounting (AAA) server. (This book covers the configuration using locally configured usernames/passwords.) Figure 9-1 shows a diagram of the configuration and process required to support SSH.

Figure 9-1 *SSH Configuration Concepts*

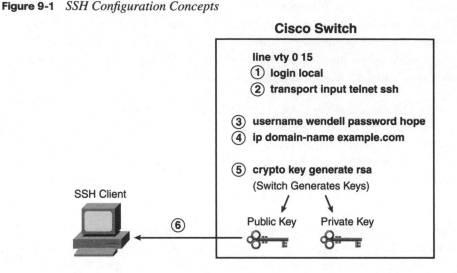

The steps in the figure, explained with the matching numbered list that follows, detail the required transactions before an SSH user can connect to the switch using SSH:

Step 1   Change the vty lines to use usernames, with either locally configured usernames or an AAA server. In this case, the **login local** subcommand defines the use of local usernames, replacing the **login** subcommand in vty configuration mode.

Step 2   Tell the switch to accept both Telnet and SSH with the **transport input telnet ssh** vty subcommand. (The default is **transport input telnet**, omitting the **ssh** parameter.)

Step 3   Add one or more **username** *name* **password** *pass-value* global configuration commands to configure username/password pairs.

Step 4   Configure a DNS domain name with the **ip domain-name** *name* global configuration command.

Step 5   Configure the switch to generate a matched public and private key pair, as well as a shared encryption key, using the **crypto key generate rsa** global configuration command.

Step 6   Although no switch commands are required, each SSH client needs a copy of the switch's public key before the client can connect.

> **NOTE**   This book contains several step lists that refer to specific configuration steps, such as the one shown here for SSH. You do not need to memorize the steps for the exams; however, the lists can be useful for study—in particular, to help you remember all the required steps to configure a certain feature.

Example 9-2 shows the same switch commands shown in Figure 9-1, entered in configuration mode.

Example 9-2 *SSH Configuration Process*

```
Emma#
Emma#configure terminal
Enter configuration commands, one per line.  End with CNTL/Z.
Emma(config)#line vty 0 15
! Step 1's command happens next
Emma(config-line)#login local
! Step 2's command happens next
Emma(config-line)#transport input telnet ssh
Emma(config-line)#exit
! Step 3's command happens next
Emma(config)#username wendell password hope
! Step 4's command happens next
Emma(config)#ip domain-name example.com
! Step 5's command happens next
Emma(config)#crypto key generate rsa
The name for the keys will be: Emma.example.com
Choose the size of the key modulus in the range of 360 to 2048 for your
  General Purpose Keys. Choosing a key modulus greater than 512 may take
  a few minutes.

How many bits in the modulus [512]: 1024
% Generating 1024 bit RSA keys ...[OK]

00:03:58: %SSH-5-ENABLED: SSH 1.99 has been enabled
Emma(config)#^Z
! Next, the contents of the public key are listed; the key will be needed by the SSH
  client.
Emma#show crypto key mypubkey rsa
% Key pair was generated at: 00:03:58 UTC Mar 1 1993
Key name: Emma.example.com
 Usage: General Purpose Key
 Key is not exportable.
 Key Data:
  30819F30 0D06092A 864886F7 0D010101 05000381 8D003081 89028181 00DB43DC
  49C258FA 8E0B8EB2 0A6C8888 A00D29CE EAEE615B 456B68FD 491A9B63 B39A4334
  86F64E02 1B320256 01941831 7B7304A2 720A57DA FBB3E75A 94517901 7764C332
  A3A482B1 DB4F154E A84773B5 5337CE8C B1F5E832 8213EE6B 73B77006 BA8782DE
  180966D9 9A6476D7 C9164ECE 1DC752BB 955F5BDE F82BFCB2 A273C58C 8B020301 0001
% Key pair was generated at: 00:04:01 UTC Mar 1 1993
Key name: Emma.example.com.server
 Usage: Encryption Key
 Key is not exportable.
```

continues

Example 9-2 *SSH Configuration Process (Continued)*

```
Key Data:
  307C300D 06092A86 4886F70D 01010105 00036B00 30680261 00AC339C D4916728
  6ACB627E A5EE26A5 00946AF9 E63FF322 A2DB4994 9E37BFDA AB1C503E AAF69FB3
  2A22A5F3 0AA94454 B8242D72 A8582E7B 0642CF2B C06E0710 B0A06048 D90CBE9E
  F0B88179 EC1C5EAC D551109D 69E39160 86C50122 9A37E954 85020301 0001
```

The example shows a gray highlighted comment just before the configuration commands at each step. Also, note the public key created by the switch, listed in the highlighted portion of the output of the **show crypto key mypubkey rsa** command. Each SSH client needs a copy of this key, either by adding this key to the SSH client's configuration beforehand, or by letting the switch send this public key to the client when the SSH client first connects to the switch.

For even tighter security, you might want to disable Telnet access completely, requiring all the engineers to use SSH to remotely log in to the switch. To prevent Telnet access, use the **transport input ssh** line subcommand in vty configuration mode. If the command is given only the SSH option, the switch will no longer accept Telnet connections.

Password Encryption

Several of the configuration commands used to configure passwords store the passwords in clear text in the running-config file, at least by default. In particular, the simple passwords configured on the console and vty lines, with the **password** command, plus the password in the **username** command, are all stored in clear text by default. (The **enable secret** command automatically hides the password value.)

To prevent password vulnerability in a printed version of the configuration file, or in a backup copy of the configuration file stored on a server, you can encrypt or encode the passwords using the **service password-encryption** global configuration command. The presence or absence of the **service password-encryption** global configuration command dictates whether the passwords are encrypted as follows:

- When the **service password-encryption** command is configured, all existing console, vty, and **username** command passwords are immediately encrypted.

- If the **service password-encryption** command has already been configured, any future changes to these passwords are encrypted.

- If the **no service password-encryption** command is used later, the passwords remain encrypted, until they are changed—at which point they show up in clear text.

Example 9-3 shows an example of these details.

> **NOTE** The **show running-config | begin line vty** command, as used in Example 9-3, lists the running configuration, beginning with the first line, which contains the text **line vty**. This is just a shorthand way to see a smaller part of the running configuration.

Example 9-3 *Encryption and the* **service password-encryption** *Command*

```
Switch3#show running-config | begin line vty
line vty 0 4
 password cisco
 login
Switch3#configure terminal
Enter configuration commands, one per line.  End with CNTL/Z.
Switch3(config)#service password-encryption
Switch3(config)#^Z
Switch3#show running-config | begin line vty
line vty 0 4
 password 7 070C285F4D06
 login
end
Switch3#configure terminal
Enter configuration commands, one per line.  End with CNTL/Z.
Switch3(config)#no service password-encryption
Switch3(config)#^Z
Switch3#show running-config | begin line vty
line vty 0 4
 password 7 070C285F4D06
 login
end
Switch3#configure terminal
Enter configuration commands, one per line.  End with CNTL/Z.
Switch3(config)#line vty 0 4
Switch3(config-line)#password cisco
Switch3(config-line)#^Z
Switch3#show running-config | begin line vty
line vty 0 4
 password cisco
 login
```

> **NOTE** The encryption type used by the **service password-encryption** command, as noted with the "7" in the **password** commands, refers to one of several underlying password encryption algorithms. Type 7, the only type used by the **service password-encryption** command, is a weak encryption algorithm, and the passwords can be easily decrypted.

The Two Enable Mode Passwords

The **enable** command moves you from user EXEC mode (with a prompt of hostname>) to privileged EXEC mode (with a prompt of hostname#). A router or switch can be configured to require a password to reach enable mode according to the following rules:

Key Topic

- If the global configuration command **enable password** *actual-password* is used, it defines the password required when using the **enable** EXEC command. This password is listed as *clear text* in the configuration file by default.

- If the global configuration command **enable secret** *actual-password* is used, it defines the password required when using the **enable** EXEC command. This password is listed as *a hidden MD5 hash value* in the configuration file.

- If *both commands* are used, the password set in the **enable secret** command defines which password is required.

When the **enable secret** command is configured, the router or switch automatically hides the password. While it is sometimes referenced as being encrypted, the enable secret password is not actually encrypted. Instead, IOS applies a mathematical function to the password, called a Message Digest 5 (MD5) hash, storing the results of the formula in the configuration file. IOS references this style of encoding the password as type 5 in the output in Example 9-4. Note that the MD5 encoding is much more secure than the encryption used for other passwords with the **service password-encryption** command. The example shows the creation of the **enable secret** command, its format, and its deletion.

Example 9-4 *Encryption and the* **enable secret** *Command*

```
Switch3(config)#enable secret ?
  0       Specifies an UNENCRYPTED password will follow
  5       Specifies an ENCRYPTED secret will follow
  LINE    The UNENCRYPTED (cleartext) 'enable' secret
  level   Set exec level password

Switch3(config)#enable secret fred
Switch3(config)#^Z
Switch3#show running-config
! all except the pertinent line has been omitted!
enable secret 5 $1$ZGMA$e8cmvkz4UjiJhVp7.maLE1

Switch3#configure terminal
Enter configuration commands, one per line.  End with CNTL/Z.
Switch3(config)#no enable secret
Switch3(config)#^Z
```

When you use the (recommended) **enable secret** command, rather than the **enable password** command, the password is automatically encrypted. Example 9-4 uses the **enable secret fred** command, setting the password text to **fred**. However, the syntax **enable**

secret 0 fred could have been used, with the **0** implying that the password that followed was clear text. IOS then takes the command, applies the encryption type used by the **enable secret** command (type 5 in this case, which uses an MD5 hash), and stores the encrypted or encoded value in the running configuration. The **show running-configuration** command shows the resulting configuration command, listing encryption type 5, with the gobbledygook long text string being the encrypted/encoded password.

Thankfully, to delete the enable secret password, you can simply use the **no enable secret** command, without even having to enter the password value. For instance, in Example 9-4, the command **no enable secret** deletes the enable secret password. Although you can delete the enable secret password, more typically, you will want to change it to a new value, which can be done with the **enable secret** *another-password* command, with *another-password* simply meaning that you put in a new text string for the new password.

Console and vty Settings

This section covers a few small configuration settings that affect the behavior of the CLI connection from the console and/or vty (Telnet and SSH).

Banners

Cisco routers and switches can display a variety of banners depending on what a router or switch administrator is doing. A banner is simply some text that appears on the screen for the user. You can configure a router or switch to display multiple banners, some before login and some after. Table 9-2 lists the three most popular banners and their typical use.

Table 9-2 *Banners and Their Use*

Banner	Typical Use
Message of the Day (MOTD)	Shown before the login prompt. For temporary messages that may change from time to time, such as "Router1 down for maintenance at midnight."
Login	Shown before the login prompt but after the MOTD banner. For permanent messages such as "Unauthorized Access Prohibited."
Exec	Shown after the login prompt. Used to supply information that should be hidden from unauthorized users.

The **banner** global configuration command can be used to configure all three types of these banners. In each case, the type of banner is listed as the first parameter, with MOTD being the default option. The first nonblank character after the banner type is called a beginning delimiter character. The banner text can span several lines, with the CLI user pressing Enter at the end of each line. The CLI knows that the banner has been configured as soon as the user enters the same delimiter character again.

Example 9-5 shows all three types of banners from Table 9-2, with a user login that shows the banners in use. The first banner in the example, the MOTD banner, omits the banner type in the **banner** command as a reminder that **motd** is the default banner type. The first two **banner** commands use a # as the delimiter character. The third **banner** command uses a Z as the delimiter, just to show that any character can be used. Also, the last **banner** command shows multiple lines of banner text.

Example 9-5 *Banner Configuration*

```
! Below, the three banners are created in configuration mode. Note that any
! delimiter can be used, as long as the character is not part of the message
! text.
SW1(config)#banner #
Enter TEXT message.  End with the character '#'.
Switch down for maintenance at 11PM Today #
SW1(config)#banner login #
Enter TEXT message.  End with the character '#'.
Unauthorized Access Prohibited!!!!
#
SW1(config)#banner exec Z
Enter TEXT message.  End with the character 'Z'.
Company picnic at the park on Saturday
 Don't tell outsiders!
Z
SW1(config)#^Z
! Below, the user of this router quits the console connection, and logs back in,
! seeing the motd and login banners, then the password prompt, and then the
! exec banner.
SW1#quit

SW1 con0 is now available

Press RETURN to get started.

Switch down for maintenance at 11PM Today
Unauthorized Access Prohibited!!!!

User Access Verification

Username: fred
Password:
Company picnic at the park on Saturday
don't tell outsiders!
 SW1>
```

History Buffer Commands

When you enter commands from the CLI, the last several commands are saved in the history buffer. As mentioned in Chapter 8, you can use the up-arrow key, or Ctrl-p, to move back in the history buffer stack to retrieve a command you entered a few commands ago. This feature makes it very easy and fast to use a set of commands repeatedly. Table 9-3 lists some of the key commands related to the history buffer.

Table 9-3   *Commands Related to the History Buffer*

Command	Description
show history	Lists the commands currently held in the history buffer.
history size *x*	From console or vty line configuration mode, sets the default number of commands saved in the history buffer for the user(s) of the console or vty lines, respectively.
terminal history size *x*	From EXEC mode, this command allows a single user to set, just for this one connection, the size of his or her history buffer.

The logging synchronous and exec-timeout Commands

The console automatically receives copies of all unsolicited syslog messages on a switch or router; that feature cannot be disabled. The idea is that if the switch or router needs to tell the network administrator some important and possibly urgent information, the administrator may be at the console and may notice the message. Normally a switch or router puts these syslog messages on the console's screen at any time—including right in the middle of a command you are entering, or in the middle of the output of a **show** command.

To make using the console a little easier, you can tell the switch to display syslog messages only at more convenient times, such as at the end of output from a **show** command or to prevent the interruption of a command text input. To do so, just configure the **logging synchronous** console line subcommand.

You can also make using the console or vty lines more convenient by setting a different inactivity timeout on the console or vty. By default, the switch or router automatically disconnects users after 5 minutes of inactivity, for both console users and users who connect to vty lines using Telnet or SSH. When you configure the **exec-timeout** *minutes seconds* line subcommand, the switch or router can be told a different inactivity timer. Also, if you set the timeout to 0 minutes and 0 seconds, the router never times out the console connection. Example 9-6 shows the syntax for these two commands.

Example 9-6   *Defining Console Inactivity Timeouts and When to Display Log Messages*

```
line console 0
 login
 password cisco
 exec-timeout 0 0
 logging synchronous
```

LAN Switch Configuration and Operation

One of the most convenient facts about LAN switch configuration is that Cisco switches work without any configuration. Cisco switches ship from the factory with all interfaces enabled (a default configuration of **no shutdown**) and with autonegotiation enabled for ports that run at multiple speeds and duplex settings (a default configuration of **duplex auto** and **speed auto**). All you have to do is connect the Ethernet cables and plug in the power cord to a power outlet, and the switch is ready to work—learning MAC addresses, making forwarding/filtering decisions, and even using STP by default.

The second half of this chapter continues the coverage of switch configuration, mainly covering features that apply only to switches and not routers. In particular, this section covers the following:

■   Switch IP configuration

■   Interface configuration (including speed and duplex)

■   Port security

■   VLAN configuration

■   Securing unused switch interfaces

Configuring the Switch IP Address

To allow Telnet or SSH access to the switch, to allow other IP-based management protocols such as Simple Network Management Protocol (SNMP) to function as intended, or to allow access to the switch using graphical tools such as Cisco Device Manager (CDM), the switch needs an IP address. Switches do not need an IP address to be able to forward Ethernet frames. The need for an IP address is simply to support overhead management traffic, such as logging into the switch.

A switch's IP configuration essentially works like a host with a single Ethernet interface. The switch needs one IP address and a matching subnet mask. The switch also needs to know its default gateway—in other words, the IP address of some nearby router. As with hosts, you can statically configure a switch with its IP address/mask/gateway, or the switch can dynamically learn this information using DHCP.

An IOS-based switch configures its IP address and mask on a special virtual interface called the *VLAN 1 interface*. This interface plays the same role as an Ethernet interface on a PC. In effect, a switch's VLAN 1 interface gives the switch an interface into the default VLAN used on all ports of the switch—namely, VLAN 1. The following steps list the commands used to configure IP on a switch:

Step 1 Enter VLAN 1 configuration mode using the **interface vlan 1** global configuration command (from any config mode).

Step 2 Assign an IP address and mask using the **ip address** *ip-address mask* interface subcommand.

Step 3 Enable the VLAN 1 interface using the **no shutdown** interface subcommand.

Step 4 Add the **ip default-gateway** *ip-address* global command to configure the default gateway.

Example 9-7 shows a sample configuration.

Example 9-7 *Switch Static IP Address Configuration*

```
Emma#configure terminal
Emma(config)#interface vlan 1
Emma(config-if)#ip address 192.168.1.200 255.255.255.0
Emma(config-if)#no shutdown
00:25:07: %LINK-3-UPDOWN: Interface Vlan1, changed state to up
00:25:08: %LINEPROTO-5-UPDOWN: Line protocol on Interface Vlan1, changed
  state to up
Emma(config-if)#exit
Emma(config)#ip default-gateway 192.168.1.1
```

Of particular note, this example shows how to enable any interface, VLAN interfaces included. To administratively enable an interface on a switch or router, you use the **no shutdown** interface subcommand. To administratively disable an interface, you would use the **shutdown** interface subcommand. The messages shown in Example 9-7, immediately following the **no shutdown** command, are syslog messages generated by the switch stating that the switch did indeed enable the interface.

To verify the configuration, you can again use the **show running-config** command to view the configuration commands and confirm that you entered the right address, mask, and default gateway.

For the switch to act as a DHCP client to discover its IP address, mask, and default gateway, you still need to configure it. You use the same steps as for static configuration, with the following differences in Steps 2 and 4:

Step 2: Use the **ip address dhcp** command, instead of the **ip address** *ip-address mask* command, on the VLAN 1 interface.

Step 4: Do not configure the **ip default-gateway** global command.

Example 9-8 shows an example of configuring a switch to use DHCP to acquire an IP address.

Example 9-8   *Switch Dynamic IP Address Configuration with DHCP*

```
Emma#configure terminal
Enter configuration commands, one per line.  End with CNTL/Z.
Emma(config)#interface vlan 1
Emma(config-if)#ip address dhcp
Emma(config-if)#no shutdown
Emma(config-if)#^Z
Emma#
00:38:20: %LINK-3-UPDOWN: Interface Vlan1, changed state to up
00:38:21: %LINEPROTO-5-UPDOWN: Line protocol on Interface Vlan1, changed state to up
Emma#
Interface Vlan1 assigned DHCP address 192.168.1.101, mask 255.255.255.0
Emma#show dhcp lease
Temp IP addr: 192.168.1.101  for peer on Interface: Vlan1
Temp   sub net mask: 255.255.255.0
   DHCP Lease server: 192.168.1.1, state: 3 Bound
   DHCP transaction id: 1966
   Lease: 86400 secs,  Renewal: 43200 secs,  Rebind: 75600 secs
Temp default-gateway addr: 192.168.1.1
   Next timer fires after: 11:59:45
   Retry count: 0    Client-ID: cisco-0019.e86a.6fc0-Vl1
   Hostname: Emma
Emma#show interface vlan 1
Vlan1 is up, line protocol is up
  Hardware is EtherSVI, address is 0019.e86a.6fc0 (bia 0019.e86a.6fc0)
  Internet address is 192.168.1.101/24
  MTU 1500 bytes, BW 1000000 Kbit, DLY 10 usec,
     reliability 255/255, txload 1/255, rxload 1/255
! lines omitted for brevity
```

When configuring a static interface IP address, you can use the **show running-config** command to see the IP address. However, when using the DHCP client, the IP address is not in the configuration, so you need to use the **show dhcp lease** command to see the (temporarily) leased IP address and other parameters.

> **NOTE**   Some older models of Cisco IOS switches might not support the DHCP client function on the VLAN 1 interface. Example 9-8 was taken from a 2960 switch running Cisco IOS Software Release 12.2.

Finally, the output of the **show interface vlan 1** command, shown at the end of Example 9-8, lists two very important details related to switch IP addressing. First, this **show** command lists the interface status of the VLAN 1 interface—in this case, "up and up." If the VLAN 1 interface is not up, the switch cannot use its IP address to send and receive traffic. Notably, if you forget to issue the **no shutdown** command, the VLAN 1 interface remains in its default shutdown state and is listed as "administratively down" in the **show** command output. Second, note that the output lists the interface's IP address on the third line of the output. If the switch fails to acquire an IP address with DHCP, the output would instead list the fact that the address will (hopefully) be acquired by DHCP. As soon as an address has been leased using DHCP, the output of the command looks like Example 9-8. However, nothing in the **show interface vlan 1** command output mentions that the address is either statically configured or DHCP-leased.

Configuring Switch Interfaces

IOS uses the term *interface* to refer to physical ports used to forward data to and from other devices. Each interface may be configured with several settings, each of which might differ from interface to interface.

IOS uses interface subcommands to configure these settings. For instance, interfaces can be configured to use the **duplex** and **speed** interface subcommands to configure those settings statically, or an interface can use autonegotiation (the default). Example 9-9 shows how to configure duplex and speed, as well as the **description** command, which is simply a text description of what an interface does.

Example 9-9 *Interface Configuration Basics*

```
Emma#configure terminal
Enter configuration commands, one per line.  End with CNTL/Z.
Emma(config)#interface FastEthernet 0/1
Emma(config-if)#duplex full
Emma(config-if)#speed 100
Emma(config-if)#description Server1 connects here
Emma(config-if)#exit
Emma(config)#interface range FastEthernet 0/11 - 20
Emma(config-if-range)#description end-users connect_here
Emma(config-if-range)#^Z
Emma#
Emma#show interfaces status


Port      Name               Status      Vlan     Duplex Speed Type
Fa0/1     Server1 connects h notconnect  1          full   100 10/100BaseTX
Fa0/2                        notconnect  1          auto  auto 10/100BaseTX
Fa0/3                        notconnect  1          auto  auto 10/100BaseTX
```
continues

Example 9-9 *Interface Configuration Basics (Continued)*

```
Fa0/4                              connected   1    a-full a-100 10/100BaseTX
Fa0/5                              notconnect  1       auto   auto 10/100BaseTX
Fa0/6                              connected   1    a-full a-100 10/100BaseTX
Fa0/7                              notconnect  1       auto   auto 10/100BaseTX
Fa0/8                              notconnect  1       auto   auto 10/100BaseTX
Fa0/9                              notconnect  1       auto   auto 10/100BaseTX
Fa0/10                             notconnect  1       auto   auto 10/100BaseTX
Fa0/11    end-users connect       notconnect  1       auto   auto 10/100BaseTX
Fa0/12    end-users connect       notconnect  1       auto   auto 10/100BaseTX
Fa0/13    end-users connect       notconnect  1       auto   auto 10/100BaseTX
Fa0/14    end-users connect       notconnect  1       auto   auto 10/100BaseTX
Fa0/15    end-users connect       notconnect  1       auto   auto 10/100BaseTX
Fa0/16    end-users connect       notconnect  1       auto   auto 10/100BaseTX
Fa0/17    end-users connect       notconnect  1       auto   auto 10/100BaseTX
Fa0/18    end-users connect       notconnect  1       auto   auto 10/100BaseTX
Fa0/19    end-users connect       notconnect  1       auto   auto 10/100BaseTX
Fa0/20    end-users connect       notconnect  1       auto   auto 10/100BaseTX
Fa0/21                             notconnect  1       auto   auto 10/100BaseTX
Fa0/22                             notconnect  1       auto   auto 10/100BaseTX
Fa0/23                             notconnect  1       auto   auto 10/100BaseTX
Fa0/24                             notconnect  1       auto   auto 10/100BaseTX
Gi0/1                              notconnect  1       auto   auto 10/100/1000BaseTX
Gi0/2                              notconnect  1       auto   auto 10/100/1000BaseTX
Emma#
```

You can see some of the details of interface configuration with both the **show running-config** command (not shown in the example) and the handy **show interfaces status** command. This command lists a single line for each interface, the first part of the interface description, and the speed and duplex settings. Note that interface FastEthernet 0/1 (abbreviated as Fa0/1 in the command output) lists a speed of 100, and duplex full, as configured earlier in the example. Compare those settings with Fa0/2, which does not have any cable connected yet, so the switch lists this interface with the default setting of auto, meaning autonegotiate. Also, compare these settings to interface Fa0/4, which is physically connected to a device and has completed the autonegotiation process. The command output lists the results of the autonegotiation, in this case using 100 Mbps and full duplex. The **a-** in **a-full** and **a-100** refers to the fact that these values were autonegotiated.

Also, note that for the sake of efficiency, you can configure a command on a range of interfaces at the same time using the **interface range** command. In the example, the **interface range FastEthernet 0/11 - 20** command tells IOS that the next subcommand(s) apply to interfaces Fa0/11 through Fa0/20.

Port Security

If the network engineer knows what devices should be cabled and connected to particular interfaces on a switch, the engineer can use *port security* to restrict that interface so that only the expected devices can use it. This reduces exposure to some types of attacks in which the attacker connects a laptop to the wall socket that connects to a switch port that has been configured to use port security. When that inappropriate device attempts to send frames to the switch interface, the switch can issue informational messages, discard frames from that device, or even discard frames from all devices by effectively shutting down the interface.

Port security configuration involves several steps. Basically, you need to make the port an access port, which means that the port is not doing any VLAN trunking. You then need to enable port security and then configure the actual MAC addresses of the devices allowed to use that port. The following list outlines the steps, including the configuration commands used:

Step 1   Make the switch interface an access interface using the **switchport mode access** interface subcommand.

Step 2   Enable port security using the **switchport port-security** interface subcommand.

Step 3   (Optional) Specify the maximum number of allowed MAC addresses associated with the interface using the **switchport port-security maximum** *number* interface subcommand. (Defaults to one MAC address.)

Step 4   (Optional) Define the action to take when a frame is received from a MAC address other than the defined addresses using the **switchport port-security violation** {**protect** | **restrict** | **shutdown**} interface subcommand. (The default action is to shut down the port.)

Step 5A   Specify the MAC address(es) allowed to send frames into this interface using the **switchport port-security mac-address** *mac-address* command. Use the command multiple times to define more than one MAC address.

Step 5B   Alternatively, instead of Step 5A, use the "sticky learning" process to dynamically learn and configure the MAC addresses of currently connected hosts by configuring the **switchport port-security mac-address sticky** interface subcommand.

For example, in Figure 9-2, Server 1 and Server 2 are the only devices that should ever be connected to interfaces FastEthernet 0/1 and 0/2, respectively. When you configure port security on those interfaces, the switch examines the source MAC address of all frames received on those ports, allowing only frames sourced from the configured MAC addresses. Example 9-10 shows a sample port security configuration matching Figure 9-2, with interface Fa0/1 being configured with a static MAC address, and with interface Fa0/2 using sticky learning.

Figure 9-2   *Port Security Configuration Example*

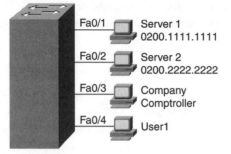

Fa0/1   Server 1
         0200.1111.1111

Fa0/2   Server 2
         0200.2222.2222

Fa0/3   Company
         Comptroller

Fa0/4   User1

Example 9-10   *Using Port Security to Define Correct MAC Addresses of Particular Interfaces*

```
fred#show running-config
(Lines omitted for brevity)


interface FastEthernet0/1
 switchport mode access
 switchport port-security
 switchport port-security mac-address 0200.1111.1111
!
interface FastEthernet0/2
 switchport mode access
 switchport port-security
 switchport port-security mac-address sticky


fred#show port-security interface fastEthernet 0/1
Port Security              : Enabled
Port Status                : Secure-shutdown
Violation Mode             : Shutdown
Aging Time                 : 0 mins
Aging Type                 : Absolute
SecureStatic Address Aging : Disabled
Maximum MAC Addresses      : 1
Total MAC Addresses        : 1
Configured MAC Addresses   : 1
Sticky MAC Addresses       : 0
Last Source Address:Vlan   : 0013.197b.5004:1
Security Violation Count   : 1
fred#show port-security interface fastEthernet 0/2
```

Example 9-10 *Using Port Security to Define Correct MAC Addresses of Particular
Interfaces (Continued)*

```
Port Security            : Enabled
Port Status              : Secure-up
Violation Mode           : Shutdown
Aging Time               : 0 mins
Aging Type               : Absolute
SecureStatic Address Aging : Disabled
Maximum MAC Addresses    : 1
Total MAC Addresses      : 1
Configured MAC Addresses : 1
Sticky MAC Addresses     : 1
Last Source Address:Vlan : 0200.2222.2222:1
Security Violation Count : 0
fred#show running-config
(Lines omitted for brevity)
interface FastEthernet0/2
 switchport mode access
 switchport port-security
 switchport port-security mac-address sticky
 switchport port-security mac-address sticky 0200.2222.2222
```

For FastEthernet 0/1, Server 1's MAC address is configured with the **switchport port-
security mac-address 0200.1111.1111** command. For port security to work, the 2960 must
think that the interface is an access interface, so the **switchport mode access** command is
required. Furthermore, the **switchport port-security** command is required to enable port
security on the interface. Together, these three interface subcommands enable port security,
and only MAC address 0200.1111.1111 is allowed to use the interface. This interface uses
defaults for the other settings, allowing only one MAC address on the interface, and causing
the switch to disable the interface if the switch receives a frame whose source MAC address
is not 0200.1111.111.

Interface FastEthernet 0/2 uses a feature called *sticky secure MAC addresses*. The
configuration still includes the **switchport mode access** and **switchport port-security**
commands for the same reasons as on FastEthernet 0/1. However, the **switchport port-
security mac-address sticky** command tells the switch to learn the MAC address from the
first frame sent to the switch and then add the MAC address as a secure MAC to the running
configuration. In other words, the first MAC address heard "sticks" to the configuration,
so the engineer does not have to know the MAC address of the device connected to the
interface ahead of time.

The **show running-config** output at the beginning of Example 9-10 shows the
configuration for Fa0/2, before any sticky learning occurred. The end of the example
shows the configuration after an address was sticky-learned, including the **switchport**

port-security mac-address sticky 0200.2222.2222 interface subcommand, which the switch added to the configuration. If you wanted to save the configuration so that only 0200.2222.2222 is used on that interface from now on, you would simply need to use the **copy running-config startup-config** command to save the configuration.

As it turns out, a security violation has occurred on FastEthernet 0/1 in Example 9-10, but no violations have occurred on FastEthernet 0/2. The **show port-security interface fastethernet 0/1** command shows that the interface is in a *secure-shutdown* state, which means that the interface has been disabled due to port security. The device connected to interface FastEthernet 0/1 did not use MAC address 0200.1111.1111, so the switch received a frame in Fa0/1 with a different source MAC, causing a violation.

The switch can be configured to use one of three actions when a violation occurs. All three configuration options cause the switch to discard the offending frame, but some of the configuration options include additional actions. The actions include the sending of syslog messages to the console and SNMP trap message to the network management station, as well as whether the switch should shut down (err-disable) the interface. The **shutdown** option actually puts the interface in an error disabled (err-disabled) state, making it unusable. An interface in err-disabled state requires that someone manually **shutdown** the interface and then use the **no shutdown** command to recover the interface. Table 9-4 lists the options on the **switchport port-security violation** command and which actions each option sets.

Table 9-4 *Actions When Port Security Violation Occurs*

Option on the switchport port-security violation Command	Protect	Restrict	Shutdown[*]
Discards offending traffic	Yes	Yes	Yes
Sends log and SNMP messages	No	Yes	Yes
Disables the interface, discarding all traffic	No	No	Yes

[*]**shutdown** is the default setting.

VLAN Configuration

Cisco switch interfaces are considered to be either access interfaces or trunk interfaces. By definition, access interfaces send and receive frames only in a single VLAN, called the access VLAN. Trunking interfaces send and receive traffic in multiple VLANs. The concept and configuration for VLAN trunking is beyond the scope of this book, but it is covered in detail in the *ICND2 Official Exam Certification Guide*, Chapters 1 and 3. This book focuses on VLAN configuration for access interfaces, which by definition must be assigned to a single VLAN.

For a Cisco switch to forward frames on access interfaces in a particular VLAN, the switch must be configured to believe that the VLAN exists. Additionally, the switch must have one or more access interfaces assigned to the VLAN. By default, Cisco switches already have VLAN 1 configured, and all interfaces default to be assigned to VLAN 1. However, to add another VLAN, and assign access interfaces to be in that VLAN, you can follow these steps:

Step 1 To configure a new VLAN:

> a. From configuration mode, use the **vlan** *vlan-id* global configuration command to create the VLAN and move the user into VLAN configuration mode.
>
> b. (Optional) Use the **name** *name* VLAN subcommand to list a name for the VLAN. If not configured, the VLAN name is VLANZZZZ, where ZZZZ is the four-digit decimal VLAN ID.

Step 2 To configure a VLAN for each access interface:

> a. Use the **interface** command to move into interface configuration mode for each desired interface.
>
> b. Use the **switchport access vlan** *id-number* interface subcommand to specify the VLAN number associated with that interface.
>
> c. (Optional) To disable trunking so that the switch will not dynamically decide to use trunking on the interface, and it will remain an access interface, use the **switchport mode access** interface subcommand.

Example 9-11 shows the configuration process to add a new VLAN and assign access interfaces to it. Figure 9-3 shows the network used in the example, with one LAN switch (SW1) and two hosts in each of two VLANs (1 and 2). Example 9-11 shows the details of the two-step configuration process for VLAN 2 and the two access interfaces assigned to VLAN 2.

Figure 9-3 *Network with One Switch and Two VLANs*

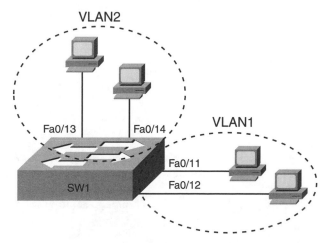

Example 9-11 *Configuring VLANs and Assigning Them to Interfaces*

```
! to begin, 5 VLANs exist, with all interfaces assigned to VLAN 1 (default setting)
SW1#show vlan brief
VLAN Name                             Status    Ports
---- -------------------------------- --------- -------------------------------
1    default                          active    Fa0/1, Fa0/2, Fa0/3, Fa0/4
                                                Fa0/5, Fa0/6, Fa0/7, Fa0/8
                                                Fa0/9, Fa0/10, Fa0/11, Fa0/12
                                                Fa0/13, Fa0/14, Fa0/15, Fa0/16
                                                Fa0/17, Fa0/18, Fa0/19, Fa0/20
                                                Fa0/21, Fa0/22, Fa0/23, Fa0/24
                                                Gi0/1, Gi0/2
1002 fddi-default                     act/unsup
1003 token-ring-default               act/unsup
1004 fddinet-default                  act/unsup
1005 trnet-default                    act/unsup
! Above, VLAN 2 did not yet exist. Below, VLAN 2 is added, with name Freds-vlan,
! with two interfaces assigned to VLAN 2.
SW1#configure terminal
Enter configuration commands, one per line.  End with CNTL/Z.
SW1(config)#vlan 2
SW1(config-vlan)#name Freds-vlan
SW1(config-vlan)#exit
SW1(config)#interface range fastethernet 0/13 - 14
SW1(config-if)#switchport access vlan 2
SW1(config-if)#exit
! Below, the show running-config command lists the interface subcommands on
! interfaces Fa0/13 and Fa0/14. The vlan 2 and name Freds-vlan commands do
! not show up in the running-config.
SW1#show running-config
! lines omitted for brevity
interface FastEthernet0/13
 switchport access vlan 2
 switchport mode access
!
interface FastEthernet0/14
 switchport access vlan 2
 switchport mode access
!
SW1#show vlan brief

VLAN Name                             Status    Ports
---- -------------------------------- --------- -------------------------------
1    default                          active    Fa0/1, Fa0/2, Fa0/3, Fa0/4
                                                Fa0/5, Fa0/6, Fa0/7, Fa0/8
                                                Fa0/9, Fa0/10, Fa0/11, Fa0/12
                                                Fa0/15, Fa0/16, Fa0/17, Fa0/18
```

Example 9-11 *Configuring VLANs and Assigning Them to Interfaces (Continued)*

```
                                          Fa0/19, Fa0/20, Fa0/21, Fa0/22
                                          Fa0/23, Fa0/24, Gi0/1, Gi0/2
2    Freds-vlan                 active    Fa0/13, Fa0/14
1002 fddi-default               act/unsup
1003 token-ring-default         act/unsup
1004 fddinet-default            act/unsup
1005 trnet-default              act/unsup
```

The example begins with the **show vlan brief** command confirming the default settings of five nondeletable VLANs (VLANs 1 and 1002–1005), with all interfaces assigned to VLAN 1. In particular, note that this 2960 switch has 24 Fast Ethernet ports (Fa0/1–Fa0/24) and two Gigabit Ethernet ports (Gi0/1 and Gi0/2), all of which are listed as being assigned to VLAN 1.

Following the first **show vlan brief** command, the example shows the entire configuration process. The configuration shows the creation of VLAN 2, named "Freds-vlan," and the assignment of interfaces Fa0/13 and Fa0/14 to VLAN 2. Note in particular that the example uses the **interface range** command, which causes the **switchport access vlan 2** interface subcommand to be applied to both interfaces in the range, as confirmed in the **show running-config** command output at the end of the example.

After the configuration has been added, to list the new VLAN, the example repeats the **show vlan brief** command. Note that this command lists VLAN 2, named "Freds-vlan," and the interfaces assigned to that VLAN (Fa0/13 and Fa0/14).

Securing Unused Switch Interfaces

Cisco originally chose the default interface configuration settings on Cisco switches so that the interfaces would work without any overt configuration. The interfaces automatically negotiate the speed and duplex, and each interface begins in an enabled (**no shutdown**) state, with all interfaces assigned to VLAN 1. Additionally, every interface defaults to negotiate to use VLAN features called VLAN trunking and VLAN Trunking Protocol (VTP), which are covered in more detail in Chapter 2 of the *CCNA ICND2 Official Exam Certification Guide*.

The good intentions of Cisco for "plug and play" operation have an unfortunate side effect in that the defaults expose switches to some security threats. So, for any currently unused switch interfaces, Cisco makes some general recommendations to override the default interface settings to make the unused ports more secure. The recommendations for unused interfaces are as follows:

■   Administratively disable the interface using the **shutdown** interface subcommand.

■   Prevent VLAN trunking and VTP by making the port a nontrunking interface using the **switchport mode access** interface subcommand.

■   Assign the port to an unused VLAN using the **switchport access vlan** *number* interface subcommand.

Frankly, if you just shut down the interface, the security exposure goes away, but the other two tasks prevent any immediate problems if someone else comes around and enables the interface by configuring a **no shutdown** command.

Exam Preparation Tasks

Review All the Key Topics

Review the most important topics from this chapter, noted with the key topics icon. Table 9-5 describes these key topics and where each is discussed.

Key
Topic

> **NOTE** There is no need to memorize any configuration step list referenced as a key topic; these lists are just study aids.

Table 9-5 *Key Topics for Chapter 9*

Key Topic Element	Description	Page Number
Example 9-1	Example showing basic password configuration	237-238
Figure 9-1	Five-step SSH configuration process example	240
List	Five-step list for SSH configuration	240
List	Key points about **enable secret** and **enable password**	244
Table 9-3	List of commands related to the command history buffer	247
List	Configuration checklist for a switch's IP address and default gateway configuration	249
List	Port security configuration checklist	253
Table 9-4	Port security actions and the results of each action	256
List	VLAN configuration checklist	257
List	Suggested security actions for unused switch ports	260
Table 9-7	**show** and **debug** command reference (at the end of the chapter). This chapter describes many small but important commands!	265

Complete the Tables and Lists from Memory

Print a copy of Appendix H, "Memory Tables" (found on the CD), or at least the section for this chapter, and complete the tables and lists from memory. Appendix I, "Memory Tables Answer Key," also on the CD, includes completed tables and lists for you to check your work.

Definitions of Key Terms

Define the following key terms from this chapter and check your answers in the glossary:

access interface, trunk interface

Command References

Table 9-6 lists and briefly describes the configuration commands used in this chapter.

Table 9-6 *Chapter 9 Configuration Command Reference*

Command	Mode/Purpose/Description
Basic Password Configuration **The following four commands are related to basic password configuration.**	
line console 0	Changes the context to console configuration mode.
line vty *1st-vty 2nd-vty*	Changes the context to vty configuration mode for the range of vty lines listed in the command.
login	Console and vty configuration mode. Tells IOS to prompt for a password.
password *pass-value*	Console and vty configuration mode. Lists the password required if the **login** command (with no other parameters) is configured.
Username/Password and SSH Configuration **The following four commands are related to username/password and SSH configuration.**	
login local	Console and vty configuration mode. Tells IOS to prompt for a username and password, to be checked against locally configured **username** global configuration commands on this switch or router.
username *name* **password** *pass-value*	Global command. Defines one of possibly multiple usernames and associated passwords, used for user authentication. Used when the **login local** line configuration command has been used.

Table 9-6 *Chapter 9 Configuration Command Reference (Continued)*

Command	Mode/Purpose/Description
crypto key generate rsa	Global command. Creates and stores (in a hidden location in flash memory) the keys required by SSH.
**transport input {telnet	ssh}**	vty line configuration mode. Defines whether Telnet and/or SSH access is allowed into this switch. Both values can be configured on one command to allow both Telnet and SSH access (the default).
IP Address Configuration **The following four commands are related to IP address configuration.**	
interface vlan *number*	Changes the context to VLAN interface mode. For VLAN 1, allows the configuration of the switch's IP address.
ip address *ip-address subnet-mask*	VLAN interface mode. Statically configures the switch's IP address and mask.
ip address dhcp	VLAN interface mode. Configures the switch as a DHCP client to discover its IP address, mask, and default gateway.
ip default-gateway *address*	Global command. Configures the switch's default gateway IP address. Not required if the switch uses DHCP.
Interface Configuration **The following six commands are related to interface configuration.**	
interface *type port-number*	Changes context to interface mode. The type is typically FastEthernet or gigabitEthernet. The possible port numbers vary depending on the model of switch—for example, Fa0/1, Fa0/2, and so on.
interface range *type port-range*	Changes the context to interface mode for a range of consecutively numbered interfaces. The subcommands that follow then apply to all interfaces in the range.
shutdown **no shutdown**	Interface mode. Disables or enables the interface, respectively.
**speed {10	100	1000	auto}**	Interface mode. Manually sets the speed to the listed speed or, with the **auto** setting, automatically negotiates the speed.

continues

Table 9-6 *Chapter 9 Configuration Command Reference (Continued)*

Command	Mode/Purpose/Description
duplex {**auto** | **full** | **half**}	Interface mode. Manually sets the duplex to half or full, or to autonegotiate the duplex setting.
description *text*	Interface mode. Lists any information text that the engineer wants to track for the interface, such as the expected device on the other end of the cable.
Miscellaneous **The remaining commands are related to miscellaneous configuration topics.**	
hostname *name*	Global command. Sets this switch's hostname, which is also used as the first part of the switch's command prompt.
enable secret *pass-value*	Global command. Sets this switch's password that is required for any user to reach enable mode.
history size *length*	Line config mode. Defines the number of commands held in the history buffer, for later recall, for users of those lines.
switchport port-security mac-address *mac-address*	Interface configuration mode command that statically adds a specific MAC address as an allowed MAC address on the interface.
switchport port-security mac-address sticky	Interface subcommand that tells the switch to learn MAC addresses on the interface and add them to the configuration for the interface as secure MAC addresses.
switchport port-security maximum *value*	Interface subcommand that sets the maximum number of static secure MAC addresses that can be assigned to a single interface.
switchport port-security violation {**protect** | **restrict** | **shutdown**}	Interface subcommand that tells the switch what to do if an inappropriate MAC address tries to access the network through a secure switch port.

Table 9-7 lists and briefly describes the EXEC commands used in this chapter.

Table 9-7   *Chapter 9 EXEC Command Reference*

Command	Purpose
show mac address-table dynamic	Lists the dynamically learned entries in the switch's address (forwarding) table.
show dhcp lease	Lists any information the switch acquires as a DHCP client. This includes IP address, subnet mask, and default gateway information.
show crypto key mypubkey rsa	Lists the public and shared key created for use with SSH using the **crypto key generate rsa** global configuration command.
show interfaces status	Lists one output line per interface, noting the description, operating state, and settings for duplex and speed on each interface.
show interfaces vlan 1	Lists the interface status, the switch's IP address and mask, and much more.
show port-security interface *type number*	Lists an interface's port security configuration settings and security operational status.

Key
Topic

This chapter covers the following subjects:

Perspectives on Network Verification and Troubleshooting: This is the first chapter dedicated to troubleshooting, and this section introduces the concept of troubleshooting computer networks.

Verifying the Network Topology with Cisco Discovery Protocol: This section focuses on CDP—specifically, how it can be used to verify network documentation.

Analyzing Layer 1 and 2 Interface Status: This section explains how to find and interpret interface status and how to find problems even when the interface appears to be working.

Analyzing the Layer 2 Forwarding Path with the MAC Address Table: This section examines how to link the concepts of how switches forward frames with the output of switch **show** commands.

CHAPTER 10

Ethernet Switch Troubleshooting

This chapter has two main goals. First, it covers the remaining Ethernet-oriented topics for this book—specifically, some of the commands and concepts related to verifying that a switched Ethernet LAN works. If the network doesn't work, this chapter suggests tools you can use to find out why. Additionally, this chapter suggests some troubleshooting methods and practices that might improve your troubleshooting skills. Although the troubleshooting processes explained in this book are not directly tested on the exams, they can help you prepare to correctly answer some of the more difficult exam questions.

"Do I Know This Already?" Quiz

The "Do I Know This Already?" quiz allows you to assess whether you should read the entire chapter. If you miss no more than one of these eight self-assessment questions, you might want to move ahead to the "Exam Preparation Tasks" section. Table 10-1 lists the major headings in this chapter and the "Do I Know This Already?" quiz questions covering the material in those sections. This helps you assess your knowledge of these specific areas. The answers to the "Do I Know This Already?" quiz appear in Appendix A.

Table 10-1 *"Do I Know This Already?" Foundation Topics Section-to-Question Mapping*

Foundation Topics Section	Questions
Perspectives on Network Verification and Troubleshooting	—
Verifying the Network Topology with Cisco Discovery Protocol	1, 2
Analyzing Layer 1 and 2 Interface Status	3–6
Analyzing the Layer 2 Forwarding Path with the MAC Address Table	7, 8

1. Imagine that a switch connects via an Ethernet cable to a router, and the router's hostname is Hannah. Which of the following commands could tell you information about the IOS version on Hannah without establishing a Telnet connection to Hannah?

   a. **show neighbor Hannah**

   b. **show cdp**

   c. **show cdp neighbor**

   d. **show cdp neighbor Hannah**

   e. **show cdp entry Hannah**

   f. **show cdp neighbor detail**

2. Which of the following CDP commands could identify a neighbor's model of hardware?

   a. **show neighbors**

   b. **show neighbors Hannah**

   c. **show cdp**

   d. **show cdp interface**

   e. **show cdp neighbors**

   f. **show cdp entry hannah**

3. The output of the **show interfaces status** command on a 2960 switch shows interface Fa0/1 in a "disabled" state. Which of the following is true about interface Fa0/1?

   a. The interface is configured with the **shutdown** command.

   b. The **show interfaces fa0/1** command will list the interface with two status codes of administratively down and down.

   c. The **show interfaces fa0/1** command will list the interface with two status codes of up and down.

   d. The interface cannot currently be used to forward frames.

   e. The interface can currently be used to forward frames.

4. Switch SW1 uses its gigabit 0/1 interface to connect to switch SW2's gigabit 0/2 interface. SW2's Gi0/2 interface is configured with the **speed 1000** and **duplex full** commands. SW1 uses all defaults for interface configuration commands on its Gi0/1 interface. Which of the following is true about the link after it comes up?

   a. The link works at 1000 Mbps (1 Gbps).

   b. SW1 attempts to run at 10 Mbps because SW2 has effectively disabled IEEE standard autonegotiation.

c. The link runs at 1 Gbps, but SW1 uses half duplex, and SW2 uses full duplex.

d. Both switches use full duplex.

5. The following line of output was taken from a **show interfaces fa0/1** command:

```
Full-duplex, 100Mbps, media type is 10/100BaseTX
```

Which of the following is/are true about the interface?

a. The speed was definitely configured with the **speed 100** interface subcommand.

b. The speed may have been configured with the **speed 100** interface subcommand.

c. The duplex was definitely configured with the **duplex full** interface subcommand.

d. The duplex may have been configured with the **duplex full** interface subcommand.

6. Switch SW1, a Cisco 2960 switch, has all default settings on interface Fa0/1, the **speed 100** command configured on Fa0/2, and both the **speed 100** and **duplex half** commands on Fa0/3. Each interface is cabled to a 10/100 port on different Cisco 2960 switches, with those switches using all default settings. Which of the following is true about the interfaces on the other 2960 switches?

a. The interface connected to SW1's Fa0/1 runs at 100 Mbps and full duplex.

b. The interface connected to SW1's Fa0/2 runs at 100 Mbps and full duplex.

c. The interface connected to SW1's Fa0/3 runs at 100 Mbps and full duplex.

d. The interface connected to SW1's Fa0/3 runs at 100 Mbps and half duplex.

e. The interface connected to SW1's Fa0/2 runs at 100 Mbps and half duplex.

7. A frame just arrived on interface Fa0/2, source MAC address 0200.2222.2222, destination MAC address 0200.2222.2222. (The frame was created as part of a security attack; it is not normal to see frames with the same source and destination MAC address.) Interface Fa0/2 is assigned to VLAN 2. Consider the following command output:

```
SW2#show mac address-table dynamic
          Mac Address Table
-------------------------------------------
Vlan    Mac Address       Type        Ports
----    -----------       --------    -----
   1    0200.1111.1111    DYNAMIC     Gi0/2
   1    0200.2222.2222    DYNAMIC     Fa0/13
Total Mac Addresses for this criterion: 2
```

Which of the following describes how the switch will forward the frame if the destination address is 0200.2222.2222?

a.   The frame will likely be flooded on all other interfaces in VLAN 2, unless the switch has a static entry for 0200.2222.2222, VLAN 2, in the MAC address table.

b.   The frame will be flooded out all other interfaces in VLAN 2.

c.   The switch will add an entry to its MAC address table for MAC address 0200.2222.2222, interface Fa0/2, and VLAN 2.

d.   The switch will replace the existing entry for 0200.2222.2222 with an entry for address 0200.2222.2222, interface Fa0/2, and VLAN 2.

8.   Which of the following commands list the MAC address table entries for MAC addresses configured by port security?

a.   **show mac address-table dynamic**

b.   **show mac address-table**

c.   **show mac address-table static**

d.   **show mac address-table port-security**

Foundation Topics

This chapter contains the first specific coverage of topics related to verification and troubleshooting. Verification refers to the process of examining a network to confirm that it is working as designed. Troubleshooting refers to examining the network to determine what is causing a particular problem so that it can be fixed.

As mentioned in the Introduction to this book, over the years, the CCNA exams have been asking more and more questions related to verification and troubleshooting. Each of these questions typically uses a unique topology. They typically require you to apply networking knowledge to unique problems, rather than just being ready to answer questions about lists of facts you've memorized. (For more information and perspectives on these types of exam questions, go back to the Introduction to this book, in the section titled "Format of the CCNA Exams.")

To help you prepare to answer questions that require troubleshooting skills, this book and the *CCNA ICND2 Official Exam Certification Guide* devote several chapters, plus sections of other chapters, to verification and troubleshooting. This chapter is the first such chapter in either book, so this chapter begins with some perspectives on troubleshooting networking problems. Following this coverage, the chapter examines three major topics related to troubleshooting networks built with LAN switches.

Perspectives on Network Verification and Troubleshooting

> **NOTE**   The information in this section is a means to help you learn troubleshooting skills. However, the specific processes and comments in this section, up to the next major heading ("Verifying the Network Topology with Cisco Discovery Protocol"), do not cover any specific exam objective for any of the CCNA exams.

You need several skills to be ready to answer the more challenging questions on today's CCNA exams. However, the required skills differ when comparing the different types of questions. This section starts with some perspectives on the various question types, followed by some general comments on troubleshooting.

Attacking Sim Questions

Sim questions provide a text description of a network, a network diagram, and software that simulates the network. Regardless of the details, sim questions can be reduced to the following: "The network is not working completely, so either complete the configuration, or find a problem with the existing configuration and fix it." In short, the solution to a sim question is by definition a configuration change.

One plan of attack for these problems is to use a more formalized troubleshooting process in which you examine each step in how data is forwarded from the sending host to the destination host. However, studies and experience show that when engineers think that the configuration might have a problem, the first troubleshooting step is to look at the various configuration files. To find and solve Sim questions on the exam, quickly comparing the router and/or switch configuration to what you remember about the normal configuration needed (based on the question text) might be all you require.

Sim questions do allow you to have more confidence about whether your answer is correct, at least for the technologies covered on the CCNA exams. The correct answer should solve the original problem. For example, if the sim question essentially states "Router R1 cannot ping router R2; fix it," you can use pings to test the network and confirm that your configuration changes solved the problem.

If you cannot find the problem by looking at the configuration, a more detailed process is required, mainly using **show** commands. The troubleshooting chapters and sections in this book and in the *CCNA ICND2 Official Exam Certification Guide* combine to provide the details of the more complex processes for examining different types of problems.

Simlet Questions

Simlet questions can force the exam taker to interpret the meaning of various **show** and **debug** commands. Simlet questions might not tell you the enable password, so you cannot even look at the configuration, removing the option to simply look at the configuration to find the root cause of a problem. In that case, the question text typically states the details of the scenario, requiring you to remember or find the right **show** commands, use them, and then interpret the output. Also, because simlet questions might not allow you to change the configuration, you do not get the positive feedback that your answer is correct.

For example, a simlet question may show a diagram of a switched LAN, stating that PC1 can ping PC2 but not PC3. You would need to remember the correct **show** commands to use (or take the time to find the commands using the **?** key) to find the root cause of the problem.

You can use several different approaches to attack these types of problems; no single way is necessarily better than another. The first step is to think about what should normally occur in the network, based on any network diagram and information in the question. Then, many people start by trying the **show** commands (that they remember) that are somehow related to the question. The question text probably gives some hints as to the problem area. For example, maybe the problem is related to port security. Many people then just try the commands they know that are related to that topic, such as **show port-security**, just to see if the answer jumps out at them—and that's a reasonable plan of attack. This plan uses common sense, and intuition to some degree, and it can work well and quickly.

If the answer does not become obvious when you look at the most obvious commands, a more organized approach may be useful. The troubleshooting chapters in this book, and large troubleshooting sections of other chapters, review technology and suggest a more organized approach to each topic—approaches that may be useful when the answer does not quickly become obvious.

Multiple-Choice Questions

Like simlets, multiple-choice questions can force the exam taker to interpret the meaning of various **show** and **debug** commands. Multiple-choice questions might simply list the output of some commands, along with a figure, and ask you to identify what would happen. For example, a multiple-choice question might show the **show mac address-table dynamic** command that lists a switch's dynamically learned MAC table entries. The question may then require you to predict how that switch would forward a frame sent by one device, destined for another device. This would require you to apply the concepts of LAN switching to the output shown in the command.

Multiple-choice questions that list **show** and **debug** command output require much of the same thinking as simlet questions. As with simlet questions, the first step for some multiple-choice questions is to think about what should normally occur in the network, based on any network diagram and information in the question. Next, compare the information in the question text, including the sample command output, to see if it confirms that the network is working normally, or if there is a problem. (The network might be working correctly, and the question is designed to confirm that you know why a particular command confirms that a particular part of the network is working well.) The big difference in this case, however, is that the multiple-choice questions do not require you to remember the commands to use. The command output is either supplied in the question, or it is not.

> **NOTE**   Refer to http://www.cisco.com/web/learning/wwtraining/certprog/training/ cert_exam_tutorial.html for a tutorial about the various types of CCNA exam questions.

Approaching Questions with an Organized Troubleshooting Process

If the answer to a sim, simlet, or multiple-choice question is not obvious after you use the more obvious and quicker options just discussed, you need to implement a more thorough and organized thought process. This more organized process may well be what a typical network engineer would do when faced with more complex real-world problems.

Unfortunately, the exams are timed, and thinking through the problem in more detail requires more time.

By thinking through the troubleshooting process as you prepare for the exam, you can be better prepared to attack problems on the exam. To that end, this book includes many suggested troubleshooting processes. The troubleshooting processes are not ends unto themselves, so you do not need to memorize them for the exams. They are a learning tool, with the ultimate goal being to help you correctly and quickly find the answers to the more challenging questions on the exams.

This section gives an overview of a general troubleshooting process. As you progress through this book, the process will be mentioned occasionally as it relates to other technology areas, such as IP routing. The three major steps in this book's organized troubleshooting process are as follows:

Step 1   **Analyzing/predicting normal operation:** Predict the details of what should happen if the network is working correctly, based on documentation, configuration, and **show** and **debug** command output.

Step 2   **Problem isolation:** Determine how far along the expected path the frame/packet goes before it cannot be forwarded any further, again based on documentation, configuration, and **show** and **debug** command output.

Step 3   **Root cause analysis:** Identify the underlying causes of the problems identified in the preceding step—specifically, the causes that have a specific action with which the problem can be fixed.

Following this process requires a wide variety of learned skills. You need to remember the theory of how networks should work, as well as how to interpret the **show** command output that confirms how the devices are currently behaving. This process requires the use of testing tools, such as **ping** and **traceroute**, to isolate the problem. Finally, this approach requires the ability to think broadly about everything that could affect a single component.

For example, imagine a simple LAN with two switches connected to each other, and two PCs (PC1 and PC2) each connected to one of the switches. Originally, PC1 could ping PC2 successfully, but the ping now fails. You could examine the documentation, as well as **show** command output, to confirm the network topology and predict its normal working behavior based on your knowledge of LAN switching. As a result, you could predict where a frame sent by PC1 to PC2 should flow. To isolate the problem, you could look in the switch MAC tables to confirm the interfaces out which the frame should be forwarded, possibly then finding that the interface connected to PC2 has failed. However, knowing that the interface has failed does not identify the root cause of the problem. So you would then need to broaden your thinking to any and all reasons why an interface might fail—from an unplugged cable, to electrical interference, to port security disabling the interface. **show** commands can either confirm that a specific root cause is the problem, or at least give some hints as to the root cause.

Isolating Problems at Layer 3, and Then at Layers 1 and 2

Before moving to the specific topics on Ethernet LAN troubleshooting, it is helpful to consider the larger picture. Most troubleshooting in real IP networks today begins with what the end user sees and experiences. From there, the analysis typically moves quickly to an examination of how well Layer 3 is working. For example, imagine that the user of PC1 in Figure 10-1 can usually connect to the web server on the right by entering www.example.com in PC1's web browser, but the connection to the web server currently fails. The user calls the help desk, and the problem is assigned to a network engineer to solve.

Figure 10-1 *Layer 3 Problem Isolation*

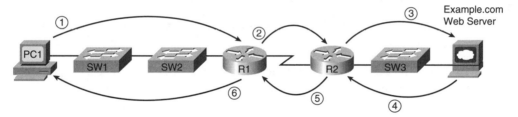

After knowing about the problem, the engineer can work to confirm that PC1 can resolve the hostname (www.example.com) into the correct IP address. At that point, the Layer 3 IP problem isolation process can proceed, to determine which of the six routing steps shown in the figure has failed. The routing steps shown in Figure 10-1 are as follows:

Step 1   PC1 sends the packet to its default gateway (R1) because the destination IP address is in a different subnet.

Step 2   R1 forwards the packet to R2 based on R1's routing table.

Step 3   R2 forwards the packet to the web server based on R2's routing table.

Step 4   The web server sends a packet back toward PC1 based on the web server's default gateway setting (R2).

Step 5   R2 forwards the packet destined for PC1 by forwarding the packet to R1 according to R2's routing table.

Step 6   R1 forwards the packet to PC1 based on R1's routing table.

Chapter 15, "Troubleshooting IP Routing," examines this process in much greater detail. For now, consider what happens if the Layer 3 problem isolation process discovers that Step 1, 3, 4, or 6 is the step that fails. Further isolating the problem would require more Layer 3 analysis. However, at some point, all the potential problems at Layer 3 might be ruled out, so the next problem isolation step would be to figure out why the Layer 1 and 2 details at that routing step do not work.

For example, imagine that the Layer 3 analysis determined that PC1 cannot even send a packet to its default gateway (R1), meaning that Step 1 in Figure 10-1 fails. To further isolate the problem and find the root causes, the engineer would need to determine the following:

■   The MAC address of PC1 and of R1's LAN interface

■   The switch interfaces used on SW1 and SW2

■   The interface status of each interface

■   The expected forwarding behavior of a frame sent by PC1 to R1 as the destination MAC address

By gathering and analyzing these facts, the engineer can most likely isolate the problem's root cause and fix it.

Troubleshooting as Covered in This Book

This book has three main troubleshooting chapters or sections, plus a few smaller troubleshooting sections interspersed in other chapters. The main coverage is as follows:

■   Chapter 10, "Ethernet Switch Troubleshooting"

■   Chapter 15, "Troubleshooting IP Routing"

■   Chapter 17, "WAN Configuration"

Essentially, Chapter 15 covers the analysis of problems related to Layer 3, as generally shown in Figure 10-1. This chapter covers some of the details of how to attack problems as soon as you know that the problem may be related to a LAN. Chapter 17 covers the troubleshooting steps in cases where the problem might be with a WAN link.

These three troubleshooting chapters spend some time on the more formalized troubleshooting process, but as a means to an end—focusing on predicting normal behavior, isolating problems, and determining the root cause. The end goal is to help you know the tools, concepts, configuration commands, and how to analyze a network based on **show** commands to solve a problem.

If you have both this book and the *CCNA ICND2 Official Exam Certification Guide*, the ICND2 book provides even more details about troubleshooting and how to use a more formalized troubleshooting process, if needed. The reason for putting more detail in the ICND2 book is that by the time you reach the troubleshooting topics in that book, you will have completed all the CCNA-level materials for a particular technology area. Because troubleshooting requires interpreting a broad range of concepts, configuration, and command output, the ICND2 book's troubleshooting chapters/sections occur at the end of each major topic, summarizing the important materials and helping show how the topics are interrelated.

The rest of this chapter examines three major topics, each of which has something to do with at least one of the three major components of the formalized troubleshooting process:

■ **Cisco Discovery Protocol (CDP):** Used to confirm the documentation, and learn about the network topology, to predict normal operation of the network.

■ **Examining interface status:** Interfaces must be in a working state before a switch will forward frames on the interface. You must determine if an interface is working, as well as determine the potential root causes for a failed switch interface.

■ **Analyzing where frames will be forwarded:** You must know how to analyze a switch's MAC address table and how to then predict how a switch will forward a particular frame.

Verifying the Network Topology with Cisco Discovery Protocol

The proprietary Cisco Discovery Protocol (CDP) discovers basic information about neighboring routers and switches without needing to know the passwords for the neighboring devices. To discover information, routers and switches send CDP messages out each of their interfaces. The messages essentially announce information about the device that sent the CDP message. Devices that support CDP learn information about others by listening for the advertisements sent by other devices.

From a troubleshooting perspective, CDP can be used to either confirm or fix the documentation shown in a network diagram, or even discover the devices and interfaces used in a network. Confirming that the network is actually cabled to match the network diagram is a good step to take before trying to predict the normal flow of data in a network.

On media that support multicasts at the data link layer, CDP uses multicast frames; on other media, CDP sends a copy of the CDP update to any known data-link addresses. So, any CDP-supporting device that shares a physical medium with another CDP-supporting device can learn about the other device.

CDP discovers several useful details from the neighboring Cisco devices:

- **Device identifier:** Typically the hostname

- **Address list:** Network and data-link addresses

- **Local interface:** The interface on the router or switch issuing the **show cdp** command with which the neighbor was discovered

- **Port identifier:** Text that identifies the port used by the neighboring device to send CDP messages to the local device

- **Capabilities list:** Information on what type of device it is (for instance, a router or a switch)

- **Platform:** The model and OS level running in the device

Table 10-2 lists the **show cdp** EXEC commands that include at least some of the details from the preceding list.

Table 10-2   show cdp *Commands That List Information About Neighbors*

Command	Description
show cdp neighbors [*type number*]	Lists one summary line of information about each neighbor, or just the neighbor found on a specific interface if an interface was listed.
show cdp neighbors detail	Lists one large set (approximately 15 lines) of information, one set for every neighbor.
show cdp entry *name*	Lists the same information as the **show cdp neighbors detail** command, but only for the named neighbor (case-sensitive).

Like many switch and router features that are enabled by default, CDP actually creates a security exposure when enabled. To avoid the possibility of allowing an attacker to learn details about each switch, CDP can be easily disabled. Cisco recommends that CDP be disabled on all interfaces that do not have a specific need for it. The most likely interfaces to need to use CDP are interfaces connected to other Cisco routers and switches and interfaces connected to Cisco IP Phones. Otherwise, CDP can be disabled per interface using the **no cdp enable** interface subcommand. (The **cdp enable** interface subcommand re-enables CDP.) Alternatively, the **no cdp run** global command disables CDP for the entire switch, with the **cdp run** global command re-enabling CDP globally.

Figure 10-2 shows a small network with two switches, one router, and a couple of PCs. Example 10-1 shows the **show** commands listed in Table 10-2, as well as several commands that list information about CDP itself, rather than about neighboring devices.

Figure 10-2 *Small Network Used in CDP Examples*

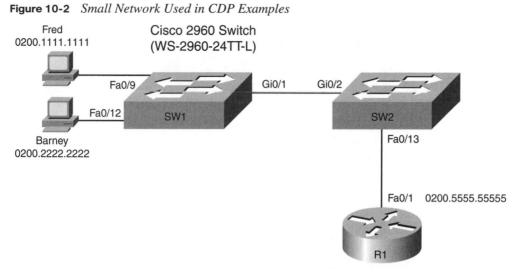

Example 10-1 **show cdp** *Command Examples: SW2*

```
SW2#show cdp ?
  entry      Information for specific neighbor entry
  interface  CDP interface status and configuration
  neighbors  CDP neighbor entries
  traffic    CDP statistics
  |          Output modifiers
  <cr>
! Next, the show cdp neighbors command lists SW2's local interface, and both R1's
! and SW1's interfaces  (in the "port" column), along with other details.
!
SW2#show cdp neighbors
Capability Codes: R - Router, T - Trans Bridge, B - Source Route Bridge
                  S - Switch, H - Host, I - IGMP, r - Repeater, P - Phone

Device ID          Local Intrfce      Holdtme   Capability   Platform   Port ID
SW1                Gig 0/2            173         S I        WS-C2960-2Gig 0/1
R1                 Fas 0/13           139        R S I        1841      Fas 0/1
SW2#show cdp neighbors detail
-------------------------
Device ID: SW1
Entry address(es):
Platform: cisco WS-C2960-24TT-L,  Capabilities: Switch IGMP
Interface: GigabitEthernet0/2,  Port ID (outgoing port): GigabitEthernet0/1
Holdtime : 167 sec
```

continues

Example 10-1   **show cdp** *Command Examples: SW2 (Continued)*

```
Version :
Cisco IOS Software, C2960 Software (C2960-LANBASEK9-M), Version 12.2(25)SEE2, RELEASE
  SOFTWARE (fc1)
Copyright (c) 1986-2006 by Cisco Systems, Inc.
Compiled Fri 28-Jul-06 11:57 by yenanh

advertisement version: 2
Protocol Hello:  OUI=0x00000C, Protocol ID=0x0112; payload len=27,
  value=00000000FFFFFFFF010221FF000
0000000000019E86A6F80FF0000
VTP Management Domain: 'fred'
Native VLAN: 1
Duplex: full
Management address(es):
! The info for router R1 follows.
-----------------------
Device ID: R1
Entry address(es):
  IP address: 10.1.1.1
Platform: Cisco 1841,  Capabilities: Router Switch IGMP
Interface: FastEthernet0/13,  Port ID (outgoing port): FastEthernet0/1
Holdtime : 131 sec

Version :
Cisco IOS Software, 1841 Software (C1841-ADVENTERPRISEK9-M), Version 12.4(9)T, RELEASE
  SOFTWARE (fc1)
Technical Support: http://www.cisco.com/techsupport
Copyright (c) 1986-2006 by Cisco Systems, Inc.
Compiled Fri 16-Jun-06 21:26 by prod_rel_team

advertisement version: 2
VTP Management Domain: ''
Duplex: full
Management address(es):
!
! Note that the show cdp entry R1 command repeats the same information shown in
! the show cdp neighbors detail command, but just for R1.
SW2#show cdp entry R1
-----------------------
Device ID: R1
Entry address(es):
  IP address: 10.1.1.1
Platform: Cisco 1841,  Capabilities: Router Switch IGMP
Interface: FastEthernet0/13,  Port ID (outgoing port): FastEthernet0/1
Holdtime : 176 sec
```

Example 10-1 **show cdp** *Command Examples: SW2 (Continued)*

```
Version :
Cisco IOS Software, 1841 Software (C1841-ADVENTERPRISEK9-M), Version 12.4(9)T, RELEASE
  SOFTWARE (fc1)
Technical Support: http://www.cisco.com/techsupport
Copyright (c) 1986-2006 by Cisco Systems, Inc.
Compiled Fri 16-Jun-06 21:26 by prod_rel_team


advertisement version: 2
VTP Management Domain: ''
Duplex: full
Management address(es):
SW2#show cdp
Global CDP information:
    Sending CDP packets every 60 seconds
    Sending a holdtime value of 180 seconds
    Sending CDPv2 advertisements is  enabled
SW2#show cdp interfaces
FastEthernet0/1 is administratively down, line protocol is down
  Encapsulation ARPA
  Sending CDP packets every 60 seconds
  Holdtime is 180 seconds
FastEthernet0/2 is administratively down, line protocol is down
  Encapsulation ARPA
  Sending CDP packets every 60 seconds
  Holdtime is 180 seconds
!
! Lines omitted for brevity
!
SW2#show cdp traffic
CDP counters :
    Total packets output: 54, Input: 49
    Hdr syntax: 0, Chksum error: 0, Encaps failed: 0
    No memory: 0, Invalid packet: 0, Fragmented: 0
    CDP version 1 advertisements output: 0, Input: 0
    CDP version 2 advertisements output: 54, Input: 49
```

A little more than the first half of the example shows a comparison of the output of the three commands listed in Table 10-2. The **show cdp neighbors** command lists one line per neighbor, but with lots of key details such as the local device's interface used to connect to the neighbor and the neighboring device's interface (under the Port heading). For example, SW2's **show cdp neighbors** command lists an entry for SW1, with SW2's local interface of Gi0/2, and SW1's interface of Gi0/1 (see Figure 10-2 for reference). The **show cdp neighbors** output also lists the platform, so if you know the Cisco product line to some degree, you know the specific model of the neighboring router or switch. So, even using this basic information, you could either construct a figure like Figure 10-2 or confirm that the details in the figure are correct.

Take a few moments to examine the output of the **show cdp neighbors detail** command and the **show cdp entry R1** commands in Example 10-1. Both commands supply the exact same messages, with the first supplying the information for all neighbors, rather than for one neighbor at a time. Note that the output of these two commands lists additional details, such as the full name of the model of switch (WS-2960-24TT-L) and the IP address configured on the 1841 router. (Had SW1's IP address been configured, it would also have been displayed.)

The bottom portion of Example 10-1 lists sample output from some of the **show cdp** commands that identify information about how CDP is operating. These commands do not list any information about neighbors. Table 10-3 lists these commands and their purpose for easy reference.

Table 10-3 *Commands Used to Verify CDP Operations*

Command	Description
show cdp	States whether CDP is enabled globally, and lists the default update and holdtime timers.
show cdp interface [*type number*]	States whether CDP is enabled on each interface, or a single interface if the interface is listed, and states update and holdtime timers on those interfaces.
show cdp traffic	Lists global statistics for the number of CDP advertisements sent and received.

Analyzing Layer 1 and 2 Interface Status

A Cisco switch interface must be in a working state before the switch will process frames received on the interface or send frames out the interface. Additionally, the interface might be in a working state, but intermittent problems might still be occurring. So, a somewhat obvious troubleshooting step is to examine the interface state, ensure that each interface is working, and also verify that no intermittent problems are occurring. This section examines the **show** commands you can use to determine the status of each interface, the reasons why an interface might not be working, and some issues that can occur even when the interfaces are in a working state.

Interface Status Codes and Reasons for Nonworking States

Cisco switches actually use two different sets of interface status codes—one set of two codes (words) that use the same conventions as do router interface status codes, and another set with a single code (word). Both sets of status codes can determine whether an interface is working.

The switch **show interfaces** and **show interfaces description** commands list the two-code status just like routers. The two codes are named the *line status* and *protocol status*. They generally refer to whether Layer 1 is working (line status) and whether Layer 2 is working (protocol status). LAN switch interfaces typically show an interface with both codes with the same value, either "up" or "down."

NOTE This book refers to these two status codes in shorthand by just listing the two codes with a slash between them, such as "up/up."

The **show interfaces status** command lists a different single interface status code. This single interface status code corresponds to different combinations of the traditional two-code interface status codes and can be easily correlated to those codes. For example, the **show interfaces status** command lists a "connect" state for working interfaces. It corresponds to the up/up state seen with the **show interfaces** and **show interfaces description** commands.

Any interface state other than connect or up/up means that the switch will not forward or receive frames on the interface. Each nonworking interface state has a small set of root causes. Also, note that the exams could easily ask a question that showed only one or the other type of status code, so be prepared to see both types of status codes on the exams, and know the meanings of both. Table 10-4 lists the code combinations and some root causes that could have caused a particular interface status.

Table 10-4 *LAN Switch Interface Status Codes*

Key Topic

Line Status	Protocol Status	Interface Status	Typical Root Cause
Administratively Down	Down	disabled	The interface is configured with the **shutdown** command.
Down	Down	notconnect	No cable; bad cable; wrong cable pinouts; the speeds are mismatched on the two connected devices; the device on the other end of the cable is powered off or the other interface is **shutdown**.
Up	Down	notconnect	An interface up/down state is not expected on LAN switch interfaces.
Down	down (err-disabled)	err-disabled	Port security has disabled the interface.
Up	Up	connect	The interface is working.

Most of the reasons for the notconnect state were covered earlier in this book. For example, to troubleshoot problems, you should remember the cabling pinout details explained in Chapter 3, "Fundamentals of LANs." However, one topic can be particularly difficult to troubleshoot—the possibility for both speed and duplex mismatches, as explained in the next section.

Interface Speed and Duplex Issues

Switch interfaces can find their speed and duplex settings in several ways. Many interfaces that use copper wiring are capable of multiple speeds, and duplex settings use the IEEE standard (IEEE 802.3X) autonegotiation process. These same network interface cards (NIC) and interfaces can also be configured to use a specific speed or duplex setting rather than using autonegotiation. On switches and routers, the **speed** {**10** | **100** | **1000**} interface subcommand and the **duplex** {**half** | **full**} interface subcommand set these values. Note that configuring both speed and duplex on a switch interface disables the IEEE-standard autonegotiation process on that interface.

The **show interfaces** and **show interfaces status** commands list both the speed and duplex settings on an interface, as demonstrated in Example 10-2.

Example 10-2   *Displaying Speed and Duplex Settings on Switch Interfaces*

```
SW1#show interfaces status

Port      Name            Status         Vlan       Duplex  Speed Type
Fa0/1                     notconnect     1            auto   auto 10/100BaseTX
Fa0/2                     notconnect     1            auto   auto 10/100BaseTX
Fa0/3                     notconnect     1            auto   auto 10/100BaseTX
Fa0/4                     connected      1          a-full  a-100 10/100BaseTX
Fa0/5                     connected      1          a-full  a-100 10/100BaseTX
Fa0/6                     notconnect     1            auto   auto 10/100BaseTX
Fa0/7                     notconnect     1            auto   auto 10/100BaseTX
Fa0/8                     notconnect     1            auto   auto 10/100BaseTX
Fa0/9                     notconnect     1            auto   auto 10/100BaseTX
Fa0/10                    notconnect     1            auto   auto 10/100BaseTX
Fa0/11                    connected      1          a-full     10 10/100BaseTX
Fa0/12                    connected      1            half    100 10/100BaseTX
Fa0/13                    connected      1          a-full  a-100 10/100BaseTX
Fa0/14                    disabled       1            auto   auto 10/100BaseTX
Fa0/15                    notconnect     3            auto   auto 10/100BaseTX
Fa0/16                    notconnect     3            auto   auto 10/100BaseTX
Fa0/17                    connected      1          a-full  a-100 10/100BaseTX
Fa0/18                    notconnect     1            auto   auto 10/100BaseTX
Fa0/19                    notconnect     1            auto   auto 10/100BaseTX
Fa0/20                    notconnect     1            auto   auto 10/100BaseTX
Fa0/21                    notconnect     1            auto   auto 10/100BaseTX
```

Example 10-2 *Displaying Speed and Duplex Settings on Switch Interfaces (Continued)*

```
Fa0/22                          notconnect    1          auto   auto 10/100BaseTX
Fa0/23                          notconnect    1          auto   auto 10/100BaseTX
Fa0/24                          notconnect    1          auto   auto 10/100BaseTX
Gi0/1                           connected     trunk      full   1000 10/100/1000BaseTX
Gi0/2                           notconnect    1          auto   auto 10/100/1000BaseTX
SW1#show interfaces fa0/13
FastEthernet0/13 is up, line protocol is up (connected)
  Hardware is Fast Ethernet, address is 0019.e86a.6f8d (bia 0019.e86a.6f8d)
  MTU 1500 bytes, BW 100000 Kbit, DLY 100 usec,
     reliability 255/255, txload 1/255, rxload 1/255
  Encapsulation ARPA, loopback not set
  Keepalive set (10 sec)
  Full-duplex, 100Mbps, media type is 10/100BaseTX
  input flow-control is off, output flow-control is unsupported
  ARP type: ARPA, ARP Timeout 04:00:00
  Last input 00:00:05, output 00:00:00, output hang never
  Last clearing of "show interface" counters never
  Input queue: 0/75/0/0 (size/max/drops/flushes); Total output drops: 0
  Queueing strategy: fifo
  Output queue: 0/40 (size/max)
  5 minute input rate 0 bits/sec, 0 packets/sec
  5 minute output rate 0 bits/sec, 0 packets/sec
     85022 packets input, 10008976 bytes, 0 no buffer
     Received 284 broadcasts (0 multicast)
     0 runts, 0 giants, 0 throttles
     0 input errors, 0 CRC, 0 frame, 0 overrun, 0 ignored
     0 watchdog, 281 multicast, 0 pause input
     0 input packets with dribble condition detected
     95226 packets output, 10849674 bytes, 0 underruns
     0 output errors, 0 collisions, 1 interface resets
     0 babbles, 0 late collision, 0 deferred
     0 lost carrier, 0 no carrier, 0 PAUSE output
     0 output buffer failures, 0 output buffers swapped out
```

Although both commands in the example can be useful, only the **show interfaces status** command implies how the switch determined the speed and duplex settings. The command output lists autonegotiated settings with a prefix of **a-**. For example, **a-full** means full duplex as autonegotiated, whereas **full** means full duplex but as manually configured. The example shades the command output that implies that the switch's Fa0/12 interface's speed and duplex were not found through autonegotiation, but Fa0/13 did use autonegotiation. Note that the **show interfaces fa0/13** command (without the **status** option) simply lists the speed and duplex for interface FastEthernet0/13, with nothing implying that the values were learned through autonegotiation.

When the IEEE autonegotiation process works on both devices, both devices agree to the fastest speed supported by both devices. Additionally, the devices use full duplex if it is supported by both devices, or half duplex if it is not. However, when one device has disabled autonegotiation, and the other device uses autonegotiation, the device using autonegotiation chooses the default duplex setting based on the current speed. The defaults are as follows:

Key Topic

■ If the speed is not known, use 10 Mbps, half duplex.

■ If the speed is somehow known to be 10 or 100 Mbps, default to use half duplex.

■ If the speed is somehow known to be 1000 Mbps, default to use full duplex.

> **NOTE** Ethernet interfaces using speeds faster than 1 Gbps always use full duplex.

Cisco switches can determine speed in a couple of ways even when IEEE standard autonegotiation fails. First, the switch knows the speed if the **speed** interface subcommand was manually configured. Additionally, even when IEEE autonegotiation fails, Cisco switches can automatically sense the speed used by the device on the other end of the cable, and can use that speed based on the electrical signals on the cable.

For example, in Figure 10-3, imagine that SW2's Gi0/2 interface was configured with the **speed 100** and **duplex full** commands (not recommended settings on a gigabit-capable interface, by the way). SW2 would use those settings and disable the IEEE-standard autonegotiation process, because both the **speed** and **duplex** commands have been configured. If SW1's Gi0/1 interface did not have a **speed** command configured, SW1 would still recognize the speed (100 Mbps)—even though SW2 would not use IEEE-standard negotiation—and SW1 would also use a speed of 100 Mbps. Example 10-3 shows the results of this specific case on SW1.

Figure 10-3 *Sample Network Showing Ethernet Autonegotiation Defaults*

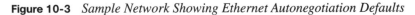

Example 10-3 *Displaying Speed and Duplex Settings on Switch Interfaces*

```
SW1#show interfaces gi0/1 status

Port      Name            Status      Vlan    Duplex  Speed Type
Gi0/1                     connected   trunk   a-half  a-100 10/100/1000BaseTX
```

The speed and duplex still show up with a prefix of **a-** in the output, implying autonegotiation. The reason is that in this case, the speed was found automatically, and the duplex setting was chosen because of the default values used by the IEEE autonegotiation process. SW1 sensed the speed without using IEEE standard autonegotiation, because SW2 disabled autonegotiation. SW1 then defaulted to use half duplex based on the IEEE default recommendation for links running at 100 Mbps.

This example shows one case of a duplex mismatch, because SW1 uses half duplex and SW2 uses full duplex. Finding a duplex mismatch can be much more difficult than finding a speed mismatch, because *if the duplex settings do not match on the ends of an Ethernet segment, the switch interface will still be in a connect (up/up) state*. In this case, the interface works, but it may work poorly, with poor performance, and with symptoms of intermittent problems. The reason is that the device using half duplex uses CSMA/CD logic, waiting to send when receiving a frame, believing collisions occur when they physically do not—and actually stopping sending a frame because the switch thinks a collision occurred. With enough traffic load, the interface could be in a connect state, but it's essentially useless for passing traffic.

To identify duplex mismatch problems, check the duplex setting on each end of the link, and watch for incrementing collision and late collision counters, as explained in the next section.

Common Layer 1 Problems on Working Interfaces

Some Layer 1 problems prevent a switch interface from ever reaching the connect (up/up) state. However, when the interface reaches the connect state, the switch tries to use the interface and keep various interface counters. These interface counters can help identify problems that can occur even though the interface is in a connect state. This section explains some of the related concepts and a few of the most common problems.

First, consider a couple of common reasons why Ethernet frames experience errors during transmission. When an Ethernet frame passes over a UTP cable, the electrical signal may encounter problems. The cable could be damaged, for example, if it lies under carpet. If the user's chair keeps squashing the cable, eventually the electrical signal can degrade. Additionally, many sources of electromagnetic interference (EMI) exist; for example, a nearby electrical power cable can cause EMI. EMI can change the electrical signal on the Ethernet cable.

Regardless of the root cause, whenever the electrical signal degrades, the receiving device may receive a frame whose bits have changed value. These frames do not pass the error detection logic as implemented in the FCS field in the Ethernet trailer, as covered in Chapter 3. The receiving device discards the frame and counts it as some kind of input error.

Cisco switches list this error as a CRC error (cyclic redundancy check [CRC] is an older term referring to the frame check sequence [FCS] concept), as highlighted in Example 10-4.

Example 10-4 *Interface Counters for Layer 1 Problems*

```
SW1#show interfaces fa0/13
! lines omitted for brevity
    Received 284 broadcasts (0 multicast)
    0 runts, 0 giants, 0 throttles
    0 input errors, 0 CRC, 0 frame, 0 overrun, 0 ignored
    0 watchdog, 281 multicast, 0 pause input
    0 input packets with dribble condition detected
    95226 packets output, 10849674 bytes, 0 underruns
    0 output errors, 0 collisions, 1 interface resets
    0 babbles, 0 late collision, 0 deferred
    0 lost carrier, 0 no carrier, 0 PAUSE output
    0 output buffer failures, 0 output buffers swapped out
```

Next, consider the concept of an Ethernet collision versus a late collision, both of which are tracked with interface counters by Cisco switches. Collisions occur as a normal part of the half-duplex logic imposed by CSMA/CD, so a switch interface with an increasing collisions counter may not even have a problem. However, if a LAN design follows cabling guidelines, all collisions should occur by the end of the 64th byte of any frame. When a switch has already sent 64 bytes of a frame, and the switch receives a frame on that same interface, the switch senses a collision. In this case, the collision is a late collision, and the switch increments the late collision counter in addition to the usual CSMA/CD actions to send a jam signal, wait a random time, and try again. (Note that the collision counters are actually listed in the output counters section of the command output.)

Three common LAN problems can be found using these counters: excessive interference on the cable, a duplex mismatch, and jabber. Excessive interference on the cable can cause the various input error counters to keep growing larger, especially the CRC counter. In particular, if the CRC errors grow, but the collisions counters do not, the problem may simply be interference on the cable. (The switch counts each collided frame as one form of input error as well.)

Both duplex mismatches and jabber can be partially identified by looking at the collisions and late collision counters. Jabber refers to cases in which the NIC ignores Ethernet rules and sends frame after frame without a break between the frames. With both problems, the collisions and late collision counters could keep growing. In particular, a significant problem exists if the collision counters show that more than .1% of all the output frames have collided. Duplex mismatch problems can be further isolated by using the **show interface** command options shown in the earlier section "Interface Speed and Duplex

Issues." Isolating jabber problems requires much more effort, typically using more specialized LAN cabling troubleshooting tools.

> **NOTE**   To find the percentage of collisions versus output frames, divide the collisions counter by the "packets output" counter, as highlighted in Example 10-4.

Finally, an incrementing late collisions counter typically means one of two things:

■ The interface is connected to a collision domain whose cabling exceeds Ethernet cable length standards.

■ The interface is using half duplex, and the device on the other end of the cable is using full duplex.

Table 10-5 summarizes the main points about these three general types of interface problems that occur even when the interface is in a connect (up/up) state.

Table 10-5   *Common LAN Layer 1 Problem Indicators*

Type of Problem	Counter Values Indicating This Problem	Common Root Causes
Excessive noise	Many input errors, few collisions	Wrong cable category (Cat 5, 5E, 6); damaged cables; EMI
Collisions	More than roughly .1% of all frames are collisions	Duplex mismatch (seen on the half-duplex side); jabber; DoS attack
Late collisions	Increasing late collisions	Collision domain or single cable too long; duplex mismatch

Analyzing the Layer 2 Forwarding Path with the MAC Address Table

As explained in Chapter 7, "Ethernet LAN Switching Concepts," switches learn MAC addresses and then use the entries in the MAC address table to make a forwarding/filtering decision for each frame. To know exactly how a particular switch will forward an Ethernet frame, you need to examine the MAC address table on a Cisco switch.

The **show mac address-table** EXEC command displays the contents of a switch's MAC address table. This command lists all MAC addresses currently known by the switch. The output includes some static overhead MAC addresses used by the switch and any statically configured MAC addresses, such as those configured with the port security feature. The command also lists all dynamically learned MAC addresses. If you want to see only the dynamically learned MAC address table entries, simply use the **show mac address-table dynamic** EXEC command.

The more formal troubleshooting process begins with a prediction of what should happen in a network, followed by an effort to isolate any problems that prevent the normal expected results. As an exercise, go back and review Figure 10-2, and try to create a MAC address table on paper for each switch. Include the MAC addresses for both PCs, as well as the Fa0/1 MAC address for R1. Then predict which interfaces would be used to forward a frame sent by Fred, Barney, and R1 to every other device. Even though the path the frames should take may be somewhat obvious in this exercise, it might be worthwhile, because it forces you to correlate what you'd expect to see in the MAC address table with how the switches forward frames. Example 10-5 shows the MAC address tables on both switches from Figure 10-2 so that you can check your answers.

The next step in the troubleshooting process is to isolate any problems with forwarding frames. Example 10-5 shows an example using the small network depicted in Figure 10-2, with no problems occurring. This example shows the MAC address table of both SW1 and SW2. Also, for this example, SW1 has been configured to use port security on its Fa0/9 interface, for MAC address 0200.1111.1111 (Fred's MAC address), just so the example can point out the differences between dynamically learned MAC addresses and statically configured MAC addresses.

Example 10-5   *Examining SW1's and SW2's MAC Address Tables*

```
SW1#show mac address-table
          Mac Address Table
-------------------------------------------

Vlan    Mac Address       Type        Ports
----    -----------       --------    -----
 All    0100.0ccc.cccc    STATIC      CPU
 All    0100.0ccc.cccd    STATIC      CPU
 All    0180.c200.0000    STATIC      CPU
 All    0180.c200.0001    STATIC      CPU
 All    0180.c200.0002    STATIC      CPU
 All    0180.c200.0003    STATIC      CPU
 All    0180.c200.0004    STATIC      CPU
 All    0180.c200.0005    STATIC      CPU
 All    0180.c200.0006    STATIC      CPU
 All    0180.c200.0007    STATIC      CPU
 All    0180.c200.0008    STATIC      CPU
 All    0180.c200.0009    STATIC      CPU
 All    0180.c200.000a    STATIC      CPU
 All    0180.c200.000b    STATIC      CPU
```

Example 10-5 *Examining SW1's and SW2's MAC Address Tables (Continued)*

```
All    0180.c200.000c    STATIC    CPU
All    0180.c200.000d    STATIC    CPU
All    0180.c200.000e    STATIC    CPU
All    0180.c200.000f    STATIC    CPU
All    0180.c200.0010    STATIC    CPU
All    ffff.ffff.ffff    STATIC    CPU
  1    0019.e859.539a    DYNAMIC   Gi0/1
! The next three entries are for Fred (statically-configured due to port security),
!  Barney (dynamically learned), and router R1 (dynamically learned)
!
  1    0200.1111.1111    STATIC    Fa0/9
  1    0200.2222.2222    DYNAMIC   Fa0/12
  1    0200.5555.5555    DYNAMIC   Gi0/1
Total Mac Addresses for this criterion: 24
!
! The next command just lists dynamically learned MAC addresses, so it does not list
  Fred's
! MAC address, because it is considered static due to the port security configuration.
!
SW1#show mac address-table dynamic
          Mac Address Table
-------------------------------------------


Vlan    Mac Address       Type       Ports
----    -----------       --------   -----
   1    0019.e859.539a    DYNAMIC    Gi0/1
   1    0200.2222.2222    DYNAMIC    Fa0/12
   1    0200.5555.5555    DYNAMIC    Gi0/1
Total Mac Addresses for this criterion: 3
! The same command on SW2 lists the same MAC addresses, but SW2's interfaces used
! to reach those addresses.
SW2#show mac address-table dynamic
          Mac Address Table
-------------------------------------------


Vlan    Mac Address       Type       Ports
----    -----------       --------   -----
   1    0019.e86a.6f99    DYNAMIC    Gi0/2
   1    0200.1111.1111    DYNAMIC    Gi0/2
   1    0200.2222.2222    DYNAMIC    Gi0/2
   1    0200.5555.5555    DYNAMIC    Fa0/13
Total Mac Addresses for this criterion: 4
! The highlighted line above for 0200.5555.5555 will be used in the explanations
! following this example.
```

When predicting the MAC address table entries, you need to imagine a frame sent by a device to another device on the other side of the LAN and then determine which switch ports the frame would enter as it passes through the LAN. For example, if Barney sends a frame to router R1, the frame would enter SW1's Fa0/12 interface, so SW1 has a MAC table entry that lists Barney's 0200.2222.2222 MAC address with Fa0/12. SW1 would forward Barney's frame to SW2, arriving on SW2's Gi0/2 interface, so SW2's MAC table lists Barney's MAC address (0200.2222.2222) with interface Gi0/2.

> **NOTE** The MAC table entries in Example 10-5 list several additional entries, entries that list a port of "CPU" and refer to MAC addresses used by the switch for overhead traffic such as CDP and STP. These entries tell the switch to send frames destined for these MAC addresses to the switch's CPU.

After you predict the expected contents of the MAC address tables, you can then examine what is actually happening on the switches, as described in the next section.

Analyzing the Forwarding Path

To analyze the actual path taken by a frame in this network, a few reminders are necessary. As mentioned earlier, this book's coverage of VLANs assumes that no trunks exist, so all interfaces are access interfaces—meaning that they are assigned to be in a single VLAN. So, although it isn't shown in Example 10-5, assume that the **show vlan brief** command lists all the interfaces on each switch as being assigned to default VLAN 1.

The switch forwarding logic can be summarized as follows:

Key
Topic

Step 1 Determine the VLAN in which the frame should be forwarded. On access interfaces this is based on the access VLAN associated with the incoming interface.

Step 2 Look for the frame's destination MAC address in the MAC address table, but only for entries in the VLAN identified in Step 1. If the destination MAC is...

    A. **Found (unicast)**, forward the frame out the only interface listed in the matched address table entry.

   B. **Not found (unicast)**, flood the frame out all other access ports (except the incoming port) in that same VLAN.

   C. **Broadcast or multicast**, flood the frame out all other access ports (except the incoming port) in that same VLAN.

> **NOTE**   Chapter 3 in the *ICND2 Official Exam Certification Guide* includes a more extensive summary of the forwarding process, including comments on the impact of VLAN trunking and STP on the forwarding process.

Using this process as a guide, consider a frame sent by Barney to its default gateway, R1 (0200.5555.5555). Using the same switch forwarding logic steps, the following occurs:

Step 1   SW1 receives the frame on its Fa0/12 interface and sees that it is assigned to access VLAN 1.

Step 2   SW1 looks for its MAC table entry for 0200.5555.5555, in the incoming interface's VLAN (VLAN 1), in its MAC address table.

   A. SW1 finds an entry, associated with VLAN 1, outgoing interface Gi0/1, so SW1 forwards the frame only out interface Gi0/1.

At this point, the frame with source 0200.2222.2222 (Barney) is on its way to SW2. You can then pick up SW2's logic, with the following explanation numbered to match the forwarding process summary:

Step 1   SW2 receives the frame on its Gi0/2 interface and sees that Gi0/2 is assigned to access VLAN 1.

Step 2   SW2 looks for its MAC table entry for 0200.5555.5555, in the incoming interface's VLAN (VLAN 1), in its MAC address table.

   A. SW2 finds an entry, associated with VLAN 1, outgoing interface Fa0/13, so SW2 forwards the frame only out interface Fa0/13.

At this point, the frame should be on its way, over the Ethernet cable between SW2 and R1.

Port Security and Filtering

Frankly, in real life, you will likely find any switching-related problems before you get to the point of having to think about every possible interface out which a switch forwards a frame. However, the exam can easily test you on the forwarding logic used in switches.

When it appears that all interfaces are up and working, and the switching table would allow a frame to be delivered, but the frame still does not arrive, the problem is likely to be related to some kind of filtering. LAN switches can be configured with access control lists (ACL), which filter frames. Additionally, routers can configure and use ACLs, so if a router is either the sender or receiver of a frame, the router's ACL might be filtering the frame. However, switch ACLs are not covered for the CCNA exams, although router ACLs are covered as part of the *CCNA ICND2 Exam Certification Guide*.

This book does cover one filtering tool that could make it appear that a frame can be delivered (according to the MAC address tables), but the switch discards the frame. With port security enabled with a violate action to shut down the interface, the switch may discard frames. Because of the shutdown violating action, the switch would disable the interface, making it easy to discover the reason why the frame was discarded by simply looking at the interface status. However, with either the **protect** or **restrict** violation action configured, the switch discards the offending traffic, but it leaves the port in a connect (up/ up) state. So, a simple **show interface** or **show interface status** command does not identify the reason for the problem.

For example, imagine that Barney (0200.2222.2222) is again sending a frame to router R1 (0200.5555.5555), but SW1 has been configured for port security in a way that disallows traffic from MAC address 0200.2222.2222 on port Fa0/12 of SW1, with a **protect** action. An analysis of the MAC address table on both SW1 and SW2 might well look exactly like it does in Example 10-5, with SW1's entry for 0200.5555.5555 referring out interface Gi0/ 1, and SW2's entry referring to Fa0/13. However, SW1 never even attempts to forward the frame because of the port security violation based on the source MAC address of Barney's frame as it enters SW1's Fa0/12 interface.

Exam Preparation Tasks

Review All the Key Topics

Review the most important topics from this chapter, noted with the key topics icon. Table 10-6 describes these key topics and where each is discussed.

Table 10-6 *Key Topics for Chapter 10*

Key Topic Element	Description	Page Number
List	Information gathered by CDP	278
Table 10-2	Three CDP **show** commands that list information about neighbors	278
Table 10-4	Two types of interface state terms and their meanings	283
List	Defaults for IEEE autonegotiation	286
Table 10-5	Common reasons for Layer 1 LAN problems even when the interface is up	289
List	Summary of switch forwarding steps	292

Complete the Tables and Lists from Memory

Print a copy of Appendix H, "Memory Tables" (found on the CD), or at least the section for this chapter, and complete the tables and lists from memory. Appendix I, "Memory Tables Answer Key," also on the CD, includes completed tables and lists for you to check your work.

Definitions of Key Terms

Define the following key terms from this chapter, and check your answers in the glossary:

CDP neighbor, up and up, error disabled, problem isolation, root cause

Command References

Tables 10-7 and 10-8 list only commands specifically mentioned in this chapter, but the command references at the end of Chapters 8 and 9 also cover some related commands. Table 10-7 lists and briefly describes the configuration commands used in this chapter.

Table 10-7   *Commands for Catalyst 2950 Switch Configuration*

Command	Description
shutdown **no shutdown**	Interface subcommands that administratively disable and enable an interface, respectively.
switchport port-security violation {**protect** | **restrict** | **shutdown**}	Interface subcommand that tells the switch what to do if an inappropriate MAC address tries to access the network through a secure switch port.
cdp run **no cdp run**	Global commands that enable and disable, respectively, CDP for the entire switch or router.
cdp enable **no cdp enable**	Interface subcommands that enable and disable, respectively, CDP for a particular interface.
speed {**10** | **100** | **1000**}	Interface subcommand that manually sets the interface speed.
duplex {**auto** | **full** | **half**}	Interface subcommand that manually sets the interface duplex.

Table 10-8 lists and briefly describes the EXEC commands used in this chapter.

Table 10-8   *Chapter 10 EXEC Command Reference*

Command	Description
show mac address-table [**dynamic** | **static**] [**address** *hw-addr*] [**interface** *interface-id*] [**vlan** *vlan-id*]	Displays the MAC address table. The security option displays information about the restricted or static settings.
show port-security [**interface** *interface-id*] [**address**]	Displays information about security options configured on an interface.
show cdp neighbors [*type number*]	Lists one summary line of information about each neighbor, or just the neighbor found on a specific interface if an interface was listed.
show cdp neighbors detail	Lists one large set of information (approximately 15 lines) for every neighbor.
show cdp entry *name*	Displays the same information as the **show cdp neighbors detail** command, but only for the named neighbor.
show cdp	States whether CDP is enabled globally, and lists the default update and holdtime timers.

Table 10-8   *Chapter 10 EXEC Command Reference (Continued)*

show cdp interface [*type number*]	States whether CDP is enabled on each interface, or a single interface if the interface is listed, and states update and holdtime timers on those interfaces.
show cdp traffic	Displays global statistics for the number of CDP advertisements sent and received.
show interfaces [*type number*]	Displays detailed information about interface status, settings, and counters.
show interfaces status [*type number*]	Displays summary information about interface status and settings, including actual speed and duplex, and whether the interface was autonegotiated.

This chapter covers the following subjects:

Wireless LAN Concepts: This section explains the basic theory behind transmitting data with radio waves using wireless LAN standards.

Deploying WLANs: This section lists a set of generic steps for installing small WLANs, with no product-specific details.

Wireless LAN Security: This section explains the various WLAN security options that have progressed through the years.

CHAPTER 11

Wireless LANs

So far, this book has dedicated a lot of attention to (wired) Ethernet LANs. Although they are vitally important, another style of LAN, wireless LANs (WLAN), fills a particularly important role in providing network access to end users. In particular, WLANs allow the user to communicate over the network without requiring any cables, enabling mobile devices while removing the expense and effort involved in running cables. This chapter examines the basic concepts, standards, installation, and security options for some of the most common WLAN technologies today.

As a reminder if you're following the optional reading plan listed in the Introduction to this book, you will be moving on to Chapter 1 of the *CCNA ICND2 Official Exam Certification Guide* following this chapter.

"Do I Know This Already?" Quiz

The "Do I Know This Already?" quiz allows you to assess whether you should read the entire chapter. If you miss no more than one of these nine self-assessment questions, you might want to move ahead to the "Exam Preparation Tasks" section. Table 11-1 lists the major headings in this chapter and the "Do I Know This Already?" quiz questions covering the material in those sections. This helps you assess your knowledge of these specific areas. The answers to the "Do I Know This Already?" quiz appear in Appendix A.

Table 11-1 *"Do I Know This Already?" Foundation Topics Section-to-Question Mapping*

Foundation Topics Section	Questions
Wireless LAN Concepts	1–4
Deploying WLANs	5–7
Wireless LAN Security	8, 9

1. Which of the following IEEE wireless LAN standards uses only the U-NII band of frequencies (around 5.4 GHz)?

    a. 802.11a

    b. 802.11b

    c. 802.11g

    d. 802.11i

2. Which of the following answers is the correct maximum speed at which two IEEE WLAN devices can send data with a particular standard?

    a. 802.11b, using OFDM, at 54 Mbps

    b. 802.11g, using OFDM, at 54 Mbps

    c. 802.11a, using DSSS, at 54 Mbps

    d. 802.11a, using DSSS, at 11 Mbps

3. Which of the following lists the nonoverlapping channels when using 802.1b DSSS in the U.S.?

    a. 1, 2, 3

    b. 1, 5, 9

    c. 1, 6, 11

    d. a, b, g

    e. 22, 33, 44

4. Which of the following terms refers to a WLAN mode that allows a laptop to roam between different access points?

    a. ESS

    b. BSS

    c. IBSS

    d. None of the other answers are correct.

5. When configuring a wireless access point, which of the following are typical configuration choices?

    a. SSID

    b. The speed to use

c. The wireless standard to use

d. The size of the desired coverage area

6. Which of the following is true about an ESS's connections to the wired Ethernet LAN?

a. The AP connects to the Ethernet switch using a crossover cable.

b. The various APs in the same WLAN need to be assigned to the same VLAN by the Ethernet switches.

c. The APs must have an IP address configured to forward traffic.

d. The APs using mixed 802.11g mode must connect via a Fast Ethernet or faster connection to an Ethernet switch.

7. Which of the following are not common reasons why a newly installed WLAN does not allow a client to connect through the WLAN into the wired infrastructure?

a. The AP is installed on top of a metal filing cabinet.

b. The client is near a fast-food restaurant's microwave oven.

c. The client is sitting on top of a big bundle of currently used Cat5 Ethernet cables.

d. The AP was configured to use DSSS channel 1 instead of the default channel 6, and no one configured the client to use channel 6.

8. Which of the following WLAN security standards refer to the IEEE standard?

a. WPA

b. WPA2

c. WEP

d. 802.11i

9. Which of the following security features were not in the original WEP security standard but are now in the WPA2 security standard?

a. Dynamic key exchange

b. Preshared Keys (PSK)

c. 802.1x authentication

d. AES encryption

Foundation Topics

This chapter examines the basics of WLANs. In particular, the first section introduces the concepts, protocols, and standards used by many of the most common WLAN installations today. The chapter then examines some basic installation steps. The last major section looks at WLAN security, which is particularly important because the WLAN signals are much more susceptible to being intercepted by an attacker than Ethernet LANs.

Wireless LAN Concepts

Many people use WLANs on a regular basis today. PC sales continue to trend toward more laptop sales versus desktop computers, in part to support a more mobile workforce. PC users need to connect to whatever network they are near, whether at work, at home, in a hotel, or at a coffee shop or bookstore. The migration toward a work model in which you find working moments wherever you are, with a need to be connected to the Internet at any time, continues to push the growth of wireless LANs.

For example, Figure 11-1 shows the design of a LAN at a retail bookstore. The bookstore provides free Internet access via WLANs while also supporting the bookstore's devices via a wired LAN.

The wireless-capable customer laptops communicate with a WLAN device called an access point (AP). The AP uses wireless communications to send and receive frames with the WLAN clients (the laptops). The AP also connects to the same Ethernet LAN as the bookstore's own devices, allowing both customers and employees to communicate with other sites.

This section begins the chapter by explaining the basics of WLANs, starting with a comparison of similarities between Ethernet LANs and WLANs. The rest of the section then explores some of the main differences.

Comparisons with Ethernet LANs

WLANs are similar to Ethernet LANs in many ways, the most important being that WLANs allow communications to occur between devices. The IEEE defines standards for both, using the IEEE 802.3 family for Ethernet LANs and the 802.11 family for WLANs. Both standards define a frame format with a header and trailer, with the header including a source and destination MAC address field, each 6 bytes in length. Both define rules about how the devices should determine when they should send frames and when they should not.

Figure 11-1 *Sample WLAN at a Bookstore*

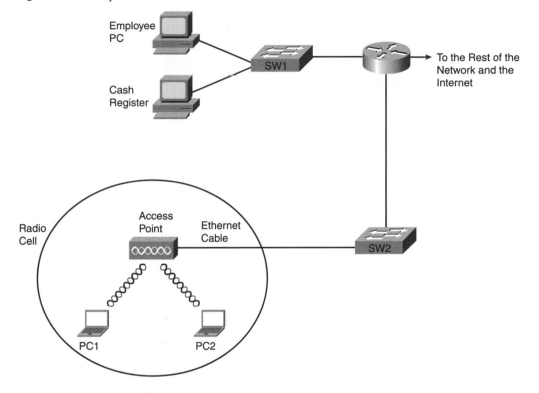

The biggest difference between the two lies in the fact that WLANs use radiated energy waves, generally called radio waves, to transmit data, whereas Ethernet uses electrical signals flowing over a cable (or light on optical cabling). Radio waves pass through space, so technically there is no need for any physical transmission medium. In fact, the presence of matter—in particular, walls, metal objects, and other obstructions—gets in the way of the wireless radio signals.

Several other differences exist as well, mainly as a side effect of the use of wireless instead of wires. For example, Chapter 7, "Ethernet LAN Switching Concepts," explains how Ethernet can support full-duplex (FDX) communication if a switch connects to a single device rather than a hub. This removes the need to control access to the link using carrier sense multiple access collision detect (CSMA/CD). With wireless, if more than one device at a time sends radio waves in the same space at the same frequency, neither signal is intelligible, so a half-duplex (HDX) mechanism must be used. To arbitrate the use of the frequency, WLANs use the carrier sense multiple access with collision avoidance (CSMA/CA) algorithm to enforce HDX logic and avoid as many collisions as possible.

Wireless LAN Standards

At the time this book was published, the IEEE had ratified four major WLAN standards: 802.11, 802.11a, 802.11b, and 802.11g. This section lists the basic details of each WLAN standard, along with information about a couple of other standards bodies. This section also briefly mentions the emerging 802.1n standard, which the IEEE had not yet ratified by the time this book was published.

Four organizations have a great deal of impact on the standards used for wireless LANs today. Table 11-2 lists these organizations and describes their roles.

Table 11-2   *Organizations That Set or Influence WLAN Standards*

Organization	Standardization Role
ITU-R	Worldwide standardization of communications that use radiated energy, particularly managing the assignment of frequencies
IEEE	Standardization of wireless LANs (802.11)
Wi-Fi Alliance	An industry consortium that encourages interoperability of products that implement WLAN standards through their Wi-Fi certified program
Federal Communications Commission (FCC)	The U.S. government agency with that regulates the usage of various communications frequencies in the U.S.

Of the organizations listed in this table, the IEEE develops the specific standards for the different types of WLANs used today. Those standards must take into account the frequency choices made by the different worldwide regulatory agencies, such as the FCC in the U.S. and the ITU-R, which is ultimately controlled by the United Nations (UN).

The IEEE introduced WLAN standards with the creation of the 1997 ratification of the 802.11 standard. This original standard did not have a suffix letter, whereas later WLAN standards do. This naming logic, with no suffix letter in the first standard, followed by other standards with a suffix letter, is like the original IEEE Ethernet standard. That standard was 802.3, with later, more-advanced standards having a suffix, such as 802.3u for Fast Ethernet.

The original 802.11 standard has been replaced by more-advanced standards. In order of ratification, the standards are 802.11b, 802.11a, and 802.11g. Of note, the 802.11n standard is likely to be ratified by the end of 2008, with prestandard products available in 2007. Table 11-3 lists some key points about the currently ratified standards.

Table 11-3 *WLAN Standards*

Feature	802.11a	802.11b	802.11g
Year ratified	1999	1999	2003
Maximum speed using DSSS	—	11 Mbps	11 Mbps
Maximum speed using OFDM	54 Mbps	—	54 Mbps
Frequency band	5 GHz	2.4 GHz	2.4 GHz
Channels (nonoverlapped)*	23 (12)	11 (3)	11 (3)
Speeds required by standard (Mbps)	6, 12, 24	1, 2, 5.5, 11	6, 12, 24

*These values assume a WLAN in the U.S.

This table lists a couple of features that have not yet been defined but that are described in this chapter.

Modes of 802.11 Wireless LANs

WLANs can use one of two modes—ad hoc mode or infrastructure mode. With ad hoc mode, a wireless device wants to communicate with only one or a few other devices directly, usually for a short period of time. In these cases, the devices send WLAN frames directly to each other, as shown in Figure 11-2.

Figure 11-2 *Ad Hoc WLAN*

PC1   PC2

In infrastructure mode, each device communicates with an AP, with the AP connecting via wired Ethernet to the rest of the network infrastructure. Infrastructure mode allows the WLAN devices to communicate with servers and the Internet in an existing wired network, as shown earlier in Figure 11-1.

> **NOTE** Devices in an infrastructure WLAN cannot send frames directly to each other; instead, they send frames to the AP, which can then in turn forward the frames to another WLAN device.

Infrastructure mode supports two sets of services, called *service sets*. The first, called a Basic Service Set (BSS), uses a single AP to create the wireless LAN, as shown in Figure 11-1. The other, called Extended Service Set (ESS), uses more than one AP, often with overlapping cells to allow roaming in a larger area, as shown in Figure 11-3.

Figure 11-3 *Infrastructure Mode BSS and ESS WLANs*

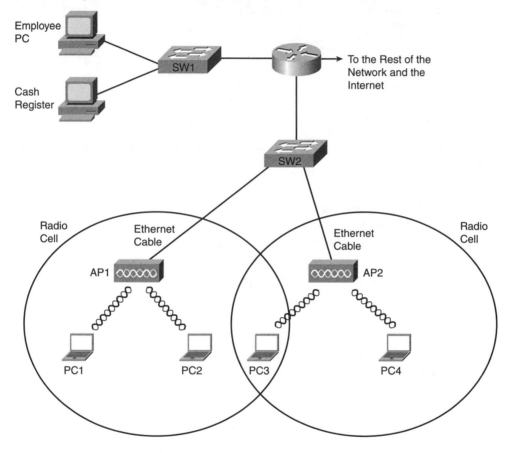

The ESS WLANs allow roaming, which means that users can move around inside the coverage area and stay connected to the same WLAN. As a result, the user does not need to change IP addresses. All the device has to do is sense when the radio signals from the current AP are getting weaker; find a new, better AP with a stronger or better signal; and start using the new AP.

Table 11-4 summarizes the WLAN modes for easy reference.

Table 11-4 *Different WLAN Modes and Names*

Mode	Service Set Name	Description
Ad hoc	Independent Basic Service Set (IBSS)	Allows two devices to communicate directly. No AP is needed.
Infrastructure (one AP)	Basic Service Set (BSS)	A single wireless LAN created with an AP and all devices that associate with that AP.
Infrastructure (more than one AP)	Extended Service Set (ESS)	Multiple APs create one wireless LAN, allowing roaming and a larger coverage area.

Wireless Transmissions (Layer 1)

WLANs transmit data at Layer 1 by sending and receiving radio waves. The WLAN network interface cards (NIC), APs, and other WLAN devices use a radio and its antenna to send and receive the radio waves, making small changes to the waves to encode data. Although the details differ significantly compared to Ethernet, the idea of encoding data by changing the energy signal that flows over a medium is the same idea as Ethernet encoding.

Similar to electricity on copper wires and light over optical cables, WLAN radio waves have a repeating signal that can be graphed over time, as shown in Figure 11-4. When graphed, the curve shows a repeating periodic waveform, with a frequency (the number of times the waveform repeats per second), amplitude (the height of the waveform, representing signal strength), and phase (the particular point in the repeating waveform). Of these items, frequency, measured in hertz (Hz), is the most important in discussions of WLANs.

Figure 11-4 *Graph of an 8-KHz Signal*

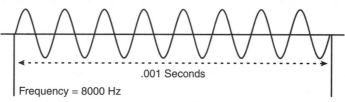

.001 Seconds

Frequency = 8000 Hz

Many electronic devices radiate energy at varying frequencies, some related to the device's purpose (for example, a wireless LAN or a cordless telephone). In other cases the radiated energy is a side effect. For example, televisions give off some radiated energy. To prevent the energy radiated by one device from interfering with other devices, national government agencies, regulate and oversee the frequency ranges that can be used inside that country. For example, the Federal Communications Commission (FCC) in the U.S. regulates the electromagnetic spectrum of frequencies.

The FCC or other national regulatory agencies specify some ranges of frequencies, called frequency bands. For example, in the U.S., FM and AM radio stations must register with the FCC to use a particular range (band) of frequencies. A radio station agrees to transmit its radio signal at or under a particular power level so that other radio stations in other cities can use the same frequency band. However, only that one radio station can use a particular frequency band in a particular location.

A frequency band is so named because it is actually a range of consecutive frequencies. An FM radio station needs about 200 kilohertz (KHz) of frequency in which to send a radio signal. When the station requests a frequency from the FCC, the FCC assigns a base frequency, with 100 KHz of bandwidth on either side of the base frequency. For example, an FM radio station that announces something like "The greatest hits are at 96.5 FM" means that the base signal is 96.5 megahertz (MHz), with the radio transmitter using the frequency band between 96.4 MHz and 96.6 MHz, for a total bandwidth of .2 MHz, or 200 KHz.

The wider the range of frequencies in a frequency band, the greater the amount of information that can be sent in that frequency band. For example, a radio signal needs about 200 KHz (.2 MHz) of bandwidth, whereas a broadcast TV signal, which contains a lot more information because of the video content, requires roughly 4.5 MHz.

> **NOTE** The use of the term bandwidth to refer to speeds of network interfaces is just a holdover from the idea that the width (range) of a frequency band is a measurement of how much data can be sent in a period of time.

The FCC, and equivalent agencies in other countries, license some frequency bands, leaving some frequency bands unlicensed. Licensed bands are used for many purposes; the most common are AM and FM radio, Ultra High Frequency (UHF) radio (for example, for police department communications), and mobile phones. Unlicensed frequencies can be used by all kinds of devices; however, the devices must still conform to the rules set up by the regulatory agency. In particular, a device using an unlicensed band must use power levels at or below a particular setting. Otherwise, the device might interfere too much with other devices sharing that unlicensed band. For example, microwave ovens happen to radiate energy in the 2.4 gigahertz (GHz) unlicensed band as a side effect of cooking food. That same unlicensed band is used by some WLAN standards and by many cordless telephones. In some cases, you cannot hear someone on the phone or surf the Internet using a WLAN when someone's heating up dinner.

The FCC defines three unlicensed frequency bands. The bands are referenced by a particular frequency in the band, although by definition, a frequency band is a range of frequencies. Table 11-5 lists the frequency bands that matter to some degree for WLAN communications.

Table 11-5 *FCC Unlicensed Frequency Bands of Interest*

Key
Topic

Frequency Range	Name	Sample Devices
900 MHz	Industrial, Scientific, Medical (ISM)	Older cordless telephones
2.4 GHz	ISM	Newer cordless phones and 802.11, 802.11b, 802.11g WLANs
5 GHz	Unlicensed National Information Infrastructure (U-NII)	Newer cordless phones and 802.11a, 802.11n WLANs

Wireless Encoding and Nonoverlapping DSSS Channels

When a WLAN NIC or AP sends data, it can modulate (change) the radio signal's frequency, amplitude, and phase to encode a binary 0 or 1. The details of that encoding are beyond the scope of this book. However, it is important to know the names of three general classes of encoding, in part because the type of encoding requires some planning and forethought for some WLANs.

Frequency Hopping Spread Spectrum (FHSS) uses all frequencies in the band, hopping to different ones. By using slightly different frequencies for consecutive transmissions, a device can hopefully avoid interference from other devices that use the same unlicensed band, succeeding at sending data at some frequencies. The original 802.11 WLAN standards used FHSS, but the current standards (802.11a, 802.11b, and 802.11g) do not.

Direct Sequence Spread Spectrum (DSSS) followed as the next general class of encoding type for WLANs. Designed for use in the 2.4 GHz unlicensed band, DSSS uses one of several separate channels or frequencies. This band has a bandwidth of 82 MHz, with a range from 2.402 GHz to 2.483 GHz. As regulated by the FCC, this band can have 11 different overlapping DSSS channels, as shown in Figure 11-5.

Although many of the channels shown in the figure overlap, three of the channels (the channels at the far left and far right, and the channel in the center) do not overlap enough to impact each other. These channels (channels 1, 6, and 11) can be used in the same space for WLAN communications, and they won't interfere with each other.

Figure 11-5   *Eleven Overlapping DSSS Channels at 2.4 GHz*

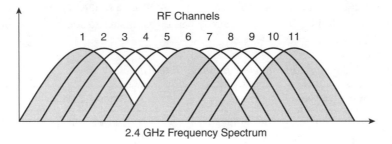

The significance of the nonoverlapping DSSS channels is that when you design an ESS WLAN (more than one AP), APs with overlapping coverage areas should be set to use different nonoverlapping channels. Figure 11-6 shows the idea.

Key Topic

Figure 11-6   *Using Nonoverlapping DSSS 2.4-GHz Channels in an ESS WLAN*

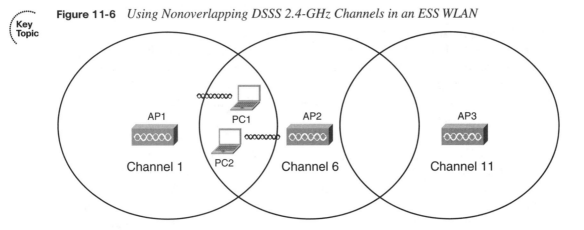

In this design, the devices in one BSS (devices communicating through one AP) can send at the same time as the other two BSSs and not interfere with each other, because each uses the slightly different frequencies of the nonoverlapping channels. For example, PC1 and PC2 could sit beside each other and communicate with two different APs using two different channels at the exact same time. This design is typical of 802.11b WLANs, with each cell running at a maximum data rate of 11 Mbps. With the nonoverlapping channels, each half-duplex BSS can run at 11 Mbps, for a cumulative bandwidth of 33 Mbps in this case. This cumulative bandwidth is called the WAN's *capacity*.

The last of the three categories of encoding for WLANs is called Orthogonal Frequency Division Multiplexing (OFDM). Like DSSS, WLANs that use OFDM can use multiple nonoverlapping channels. Table 11-6 summarizes the key points and names of the main three options for encoding.

Table 11-6 *Encoding Classes and IEEE Standard WLANs*

Name of Encoding Class	What It Is Used By
Frequency Hopping Spread Spectrum (FHSS)	802.11
Direct Sequence Spread Spectrum (DSSS)	802.11b
Orthogonal Frequency Division Multiplexing (OFDM)	802.11a, 802.11g

NOTE The emerging 802.11n standard uses OFDM as well as multiple antennas, a technology sometimes called multiple input multiple output (MIMO).

Wireless Interference

WLANs can suffer from interference from many sources. The radio waves travel through space, but they must pass through whatever matter exists inside the coverage area, including walls, floors, and ceilings. Passing through matter causes the signal to be partially absorbed, which reduces signal strength and the size of the coverage area. Matter can also reflect and scatter the waves, particularly if there is a lot of metal in the materials, which can cause dead spots (areas in which the WLAN simply does not work), and a smaller coverage area.

Additionally, wireless communication is impacted by other radio waves in the same frequency range. The effect is the same as trying to listen to a radio station when you're taking a long road trip. You might get a good clear signal for a while, but eventually you drive far enough from the radio station's antenna that the signal is weak, and it is hard to hear the station. Eventually, you get close enough to the next city's radio station that uses the same frequency range, and you cannot hear either station well because of the interference. With WLANs, the interference may simply mean that the data only occasionally makes it through the air, requiring lots of retransmissions, and resulting in poor efficiency.

One key measurement for interference is the Signal-to-Noise Ratio (SNR). This calculation measures the WLAN signal as compared to the other undesired signals (noise) in the same space. The higher the SNR, the better the WLAN devices can send data successfully.

Coverage Area, Speed, and Capacity

A WLAN coverage area is the space in which two WLAN devices can successfully send data. The coverage area created by a particular AP depends on many factors, several of which are explained in this section.

First, the transmit power by an AP or WLAN NIC cannot exceed a particular level based on the regulations from regulatory agencies such as the FCC. The FCC limits the transmit power to ensure fairness in the unlicensed bands. For example, if two neighbors bought Linksys APs and put them in their homes to create a WLAN, the products would conform to FCC regulations. However, if one person bought and installed high-gain antennas for her AP, and greatly exceeded the FCC regulations, she might get a much wider coverage area—maybe even across the whole neighborhood. However, it might prevent the other person's AP from working at all because of the interference from the overpowered AP.

NOTE The power of an AP is measured based on the Effective Isotropic Radiated Power (EIRP) calculation. This is the radio's power output, plus the increase in power caused by the antenna, minus any power lost in the cabling. In effect, it's the power of the signal as it leaves the antenna.

The materials and locations of the materials near the AP also impact an AP's coverage area. For example, putting the AP near a large metal filing cabinet increases reflections and scattering, which shrinks the coverage area. Certainly, concrete construction with steel rebar reduces the coverage area in a typical modern office building. In fact, when a building's design means that interference will occur in some areas, APs may use different types of antennas that change the shape of the coverage area from a circle to some other shape.

As it turns out, weaker wireless signals cannot pass data at higher speeds, but they can pass data at lower speeds. So, WLAN standards support the idea of multiple speeds. A device near the AP may have a strong signal, so it can transmit and receive data with the AP at higher rates. A device at the edge of the coverage area, where the signals are weak, may still be able to send and receive data—although at a slower speed. Figure 11-7 shows the idea of a coverage area, with varying speeds, for an IEEE 802.11b BSS.

The main ways to increase the size of the coverage area of one AP are to use specialized antennas and to increase the power of the transmitted signal. For example, you can increase the antenna gain, which is the power added to the radio signal by the antenna. To double the coverage area, the antenna gain must be increased to quadruple the original gain. Although this is useful, the power output (the EIRP) must still be within FCC rules (in the U.S.).

The actual size of the coverage area depends on a large number of factors that are beyond the scope of this book. Some of the factors include the frequency band used by the WLAN standard, the obstructions between and near the WLAN devices, the interference from other sources of RF energy, the antennas used on both the clients and APs, and the options used by DSSS and OFDM when encoding data over the air. Generally speaking, WLAN standards that use higher frequencies (U-NII band standards 802.11a and the future 802.11n) can send data faster, but with the price of smaller coverage areas. To cover all the required space, an ESS that uses higher frequencies would then require more APs, driving up the cost of the WLAN deployment.

Figure 11-7 *Coverage Area and Speed*

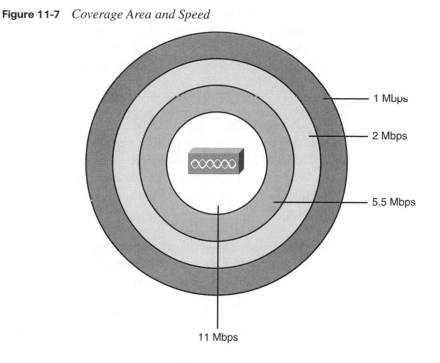

Table 11-7 lists the main IEEE WLAN standards that had been ratified at the time this book was published, the maximum speed, and the number of nonoverlapping channels.

Table 11-7 *WLAN Speed and Frequency Reference*

IEEE Standard	Maximum Speed (Mbps)	Other Speeds* (Mbps)	Frequency	Nonoverlapping Channels
802.11b	11 Mbps	1, 2, 5.5	2.4 GHz	3
802.11a	54 Mbps	**6**, 9, **12**, 18, **24**, 36, 48	5 GHz	12
802.11g	54 Mbps	Same as 802.11a	2.4 GHz	3

*The speeds listed in bold text are required speeds according to the standards. The other speeds are optional.

NOTE   The original 802.11 standard supported speeds of 1 and 2 Mbps.

Finally, note that the number of (mostly) nonoverlapping channels supported by a standard, as shown in Figures 11-5 and 11-6, affects the combined available bandwidth. For example, in a WLAN that exclusively uses 802.11g, the actual transmissions could occur at 54 Mbps. But three devices could sit beside each other and send at the same time, using three different channels, to three different APs. Theoretically, that WLAN could support a throughput of 3 * 54 Mbps, or 162 Mbps, for these devices in that part of the WLAN. Along the same line of reasoning, an 802.11a WLAN can transmit data at 54 Mbps, but with 12 nonoverlapping channels, for a theoretical maximum of 12 * 54 Mbps = 648 Mbps of bandwidth capacity.

Media Access (Layer 2)

Ethernet LANs began life using a shared medium (a coaxial cable), meaning that only one device could send data at a time. To control access to this half-duplex (HDX) medium, Ethernet defined the use of the CSMA/CD algorithm. As Ethernet progressed with continually improved standards, it started using switches, with one device cabled to each switch port, allowing the use of full duplex (FDX). With FDX, no collisions can occur, so the CSMA/CD algorithm is disabled.

With wireless communications, devices cannot be separated onto different cable segments to prevent collisions, so collisions can always occur, even with more-advanced WLAN standards. In short, if two or more WLAN devices send at the same time, using overlapping frequency ranges, a collision occurs, and none of the transmitted signals can be understood by those receiving the signal. To make matters worse, the device that is transmitting data cannot concurrently listen for received data. So, when two WLAN devices send at the same time, creating a collision, the sending devices do not have any direct way to know the collision occurred.

The solution to the media access problem with WLANs is to use the *carrier sense multiple access with collision avoidance (CSMA/CA)* algorithm. The collision avoidance part minimizes the statistical chance that collisions could occur. However, CSMA/CA does not prevent collisions, so the WLAN standards must have a process to deal with collisions when they do occur. Because the sending device cannot tell if its transmitted frame collided with another frame, the standards all require an acknowledgment of every frame. Each WLAN device listens for the acknowledgment, which should occur immediately after the frame is sent. If no acknowledgment is received, the sending device assumes that the frame was lost or collided, and it resends the frame.

The following list summarizes the key points about the CSMA/CA algorithm, omitting some of the details for the sake of clarity:

Step 1   Listen to ensure that the medium (space) is not busy (no radio waves currently are being received at the frequencies to be used).

Step 2   Set a random wait timer before sending a frame to statistically reduce the chance of devices all trying to send at the same time.

Step 3   When the random timer has passed, listen again to ensure that the medium is not busy. If it isn't, send the frame.

Step 4   After the entire frame has been sent, wait for an acknowledgment.

Step 5   If no acknowledgment is received, resend the frame, using CSMA/CA logic to wait for the appropriate time to send again.

This concludes the brief introduction to wireless LAN concepts. Next, this chapter covers the basics of what you should do when installing a new wireless LAN.

Deploying WLANs

WLAN security is one of the more important features of WLANs, and for good reason. The same security exposures exist on WLANs as for Ethernet LANs, plus WLANs are exposed to many more vulnerabilities than wired Ethernet LANs. For example, someone could park outside a building and pick up the WLAN signals from inside the building, reading the data. Therefore, all production WLAN deployments should include the currently best security options for that WLAN.

Although security is vitally important, the installation of a new WLAN should begin with just getting the WLAN working. As soon as a single wireless device is talking to an AP, security configuration can be added and tested. Following that same progression, this section examines the process of planning and implementing a WLAN, with no security enabled. The final major section of this chapter, "Wireless LAN Security," examines the concepts behind WLAN security.

Wireless LAN Implementation Checklist

The following basic checklist can help guide the installation of a new BSS WLAN:

Step 1   Verify that the existing wired network works, including DHCP services, VLANs, and Internet connectivity.

Step 2   Install the AP and configure/verify its connectivity to the wired network, including the AP's IP address, mask, and default gateway.

Step 3   Configure and verify the AP's wireless settings, including Service Set Identifier (SSID), but no security.

Step 4   Install and configure one wireless client (for example, a laptop), again with no security.

Step 5   Verify that the WLAN works from the laptop.

Step 6   Configure wireless security on the AP and client.

Step 7   Verify that the WLAN works again, in the presence of the security features.

This section examines the first five tasks. The last major section of this chapter discusses the concepts behind WLAN security but does not explain the large number of detailed options for configuring WLAN security.

Step 1: Verify the Existing Wired Network

Most of the other chapters in this book explain the details of how to understand, plan, design, and implement the switches and routers that create the rest of the network, so there is no need to repeat those details here. However, it can be helpful to consider a couple of items related to testing an existing wired network before connecting a new WLAN.

First, the Ethernet switch port to which the AP's Ethernet port connects typically is a switch access port, meaning that it is assigned to a particular VLAN. Also, in an ESS design with multiple APs, all the Ethernet switch ports to which the APs attach should be in the same VLAN. Figure 11-8 shows a typical ESS design for a WLAN, with the VLAN IDs listed.

Figure 11-8   *ESS WLAN with All APs in Ethernet VLAN 2*

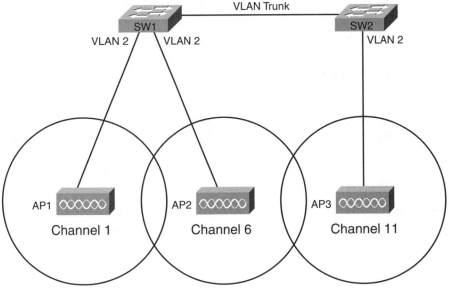

To test the existing network, you could simply connect a laptop Ethernet NIC to the same Ethernet cable that will be used for the AP. If the laptop can acquire an IP address, mask, and other information using DHCP, and communicate with other hosts, the existing wired network is ready to accept the AP.

Step 2: Install and Configure the AP's Wired and IP Details

Just like an Ethernet switch, wireless APs operate at Layer 2 and do not need an IP address to perform their main functions. However, just as an Ethernet switch in an Enterprise network should have an IP address so that it can be easily managed, APs deployed in an Enterprise network should also have an IP address.

The IP configuration details on an AP are the same items needed on an Ethernet switch, as covered in the section "Configuring the Switch IP Address" in Chapter 9, "Ethernet Switch Configuration." In particular, the AP needs an IP address, subnet mask, default gateway IP address, and possibly the IP address of a DNS server.

The AP uses a straight-through Ethernet cable to connect to the LAN switch. Although any speed Ethernet interface works, when using the faster WLAN speeds, using a Fast Ethernet interface on a switch helps improve overall performance.

Step 3: Configure the AP's WLAN Details

Most of the time, WLAN APs can be installed with no configuration, and they work. For example, many homes have consumer-grade wireless APs installed, connected to a high-speed Internet connection. Often, the AP, router, and cable connection terminate in the same device, such as the Linksys Dual-Band Wireless A+G Broadband Router. (Linksys is a division of Cisco Systems that manufactures and distributes consumer networking devices.) Many people just buy these devices, plug in the power and the appropriate cables for the wired part of the connection, and leave the default WLAN settings, and the AP works.

Both consumer-grade and Enterprise-grade APs can be configured with a variety of parameters. The following list highlights some of the features mentioned earlier in this chapter that may need to be configured:

■ IEEE standard (a, b, g, or multiple)

■ Wireless channel

■ Service Set Identifier (SSID, a 32-character text identifier for the WLAN)

■ Transmit power

This chapter has already explained most of the concepts behind these four items, but the SSID is new. Each WLAN needs a unique name to identify the WLAN. Because a simple WLAN with a single AP is called a Basic Service Set (BSS), and a WLAN with multiple APs is called an Extended Service Set (ESS), the term for the identifier of a WLAN is the Service Set Identifier (SSID). The SSID is a 32-character ASCII text value. When you configure an ESS WLAN, each of the APs should be configured with the same SSID, which allows for roaming between APs, but inside the same WLAN.

Also note that many APs today support multiple WLAN standards. In some cases, they can support multiple standards on the same AP at the same time. However, these mixed-mode implementations, particularly with 802.11b/g in this same AP, tend to slow down the WLAN. In practice, deploying some 802.11g-only APs and some mixed-mode b/g APs in the same coverage area may provide better performance than using only APs configured in b/g mixed mode.

Step 4: Install and Configure One Wireless Client

A wireless client is any wireless device that associates with an AP to use a WLAN. To be a WLAN client, the device simply needs a WLAN NIC that supports the same WLAN standard as the AP. The NIC includes a radio, which can tune to the frequencies used by the supported WLAN standard(s), and an antenna. For example, laptop computer manufacturers typically integrate a WLAN NIC into every laptop, and you can then use a laptop to associate with an AP and send frames.

The AP has several required configuration settings, but the client may not need anything configured. Typically, clients by default do not have any security enabled. When the client starts working, it tries to discover all APs by listening on all frequency channels for the WLAN standards it supports by default. For example, if a client were using the WLAN shown in Figure 11-6, with three APs, each using a different channel, the client might actually discover all three APs. The client would then use the AP from which the client receives the strongest signal. Also, the client learns the SSID from the AP, again removing the need for any client configuration.

WLAN clients may use wireless NICs from a large number of vendors. To help ensure that the clients can work with Cisco APs, Cisco started the *Cisco Compatible Extensions Program (CCX)*. This Cisco-sponsored program allows any WLAN manufacturer to send its products to a third-party testing lab, with the lab performing tests to see if the WLAN NIC works well with Cisco APs. Cisco estimates that 95 percent of the wireless NICs on the market have been certified through this program.

With Microsoft operating systems, the wireless NIC may not need to be configured because of the Microsoft *Zero Configuration Utility (ZCF)*. This utility, part of the OS, allows the PC to automatically discover the SSIDs of all WLANs whose APs are within range on the NIC. The user can choose the SSID to connect to. Or the ZCF utility can automatically pick the AP with the strongest signal, thereby automatically connecting to a wireless LAN without the user's needing to configure anything.

Note that most NIC manufacturers also provide software that can control the NIC instead of the operating system's built-in tools such as Microsoft ZCF.

Step 5: Verify That the WLAN Works from the Client

The first step to verify proper operation of the first WLAN client is to check whether the client can access the same hosts used for testing in Step 1 of this installation process. (The laptop's wired Ethernet connection should be disconnected so that the laptop uses only its WLAN connection.) At this point, if the laptop can get a response from another host, such as by pinging or browsing a web page on a web server, the WLAN at least works.

If this test does not work, a wide variety of tasks could be performed. Some of the tasks relate to work that is often done in the planning stages, generally called a *site survey*. During a wireless site survey, engineers tour the site for a new WLAN, looking for good AP locations, transmitting and testing signal strength throughout the site. In that same line of thinking, if the new client cannot communicate, you might check the following:

- Is the AP at the center of the area in which the clients reside?

- Is the AP or client right next to a lot of metal?

- Is the AP or client near a source of interference, such as a microwave oven or gaming system?

- Is the AP's coverage area wide enough to reach the client?

In particular, you could take a laptop with a wireless card and, using the NIC's tools, walk around while looking at signal quality measurement. Most WLAN NIC software shows signal strength and quality, so by walking around the site with the laptop, you can gauge whether any dead spots exist and where clients should have no problems hearing from the AP.

Besides the site survey types of work, the following list notes a few other common problems with a new installation:

- Check to make sure that the NIC and AP's radios are enabled. In particular, most laptops have a physical switch with which to enable or disable the radio, as well as a software setting to enable or disable the radio. This allows the laptop to save power (and extend the time before it must be plugged into a power outlet again). It also can cause users to fail to connect to an AP, just because the radio is turned off.

- Check the AP to ensure that it has the latest firmware. AP firmware is the OS that runs in the AP.

- Check the AP configuration—in particular, the channel configuration—to ensure that it does not use a channel that overlaps with other APs in the same location.

This completes the explanations of the first five steps of installing a simple wireless LAN. The final major section of this chapter examines WLAN security, which also completes the basic installation steps.

Wireless LAN Security

All networks today need good security, but WLANs have some unique security requirements. This section examines some of the security needs for WLANs and the progression and maturation of the WLAN security options. It also discusses how to configure the security features.

WLAN Security Issues

WLANs introduce a number of vulnerabilities that do not exist for wired Ethernet LANs. Some of these vulnerabilities give hackers an opportunity to cause harm by stealing information, accessing hosts in the wired part of the network, or preventing service through a denial-of-service (DoS) attack. Other vulnerabilities may be caused by a well-meaning but uninformed employee who installs an AP without the IT department's approval, with no security. This would allow anyone to gain access to the rest of the Enterprise's network.

The Cisco-authorized CCNA-related courses suggest several categories of threats:

■ **War drivers:** The attacker often just wants to gain Internet access for free. This person drives around, trying to find APs that have no security or weak security. The attacker can use easily downloaded tools and high-gain directional antennas (easily purchased and installed).

■ **Hackers:** The motivation for hackers is to either find information or deny services. Interestingly, the end goal may be to compromise the hosts inside the wired network, using the wireless network as a way to access the Enterprise network without having to go through Internet connections that have firewalls.

■ **Employees:** Employees can unwittingly help hackers gain access to the Enterprise network in several ways. An employee could go to an office supply store and buy an AP for less than $100, install the AP in his office, using default settings of no security, and create a small wireless LAN. This would allow a hacker to gain access to the rest of the Enterprise from the coffee shop across the street. Additionally, if the client does not use encryption, company data going between the legitimate employee client PC and the Enterprise network can be easily copied and understood by attackers outside the building.

■ **Rogue AP:** The attacker captures packets in the existing wireless LAN, finding the SSID and cracking security keys (if they are used). Then the attacker can set up her own AP, with the same settings, and get the Enterprise's clients to use it. In turn, this can cause the individuals to enter their usernames and passwords, aiding in the next phase of the attacker's plan.

To reduce the risk of such attacks, three main types of tools can be used on a WLAN:

- Mutual authentication

- Encryption

- Intrusion tools

Mutual authentication should be used between the client and AP. The authentication process uses a secret password, called a key, on both the client and the AP. By using some sophisticated mathematical algorithms, the AP can confirm that the client does indeed know the right key value. Likewise, the client can confirm that the AP also has the right key value. The process never sends the key through the air, so even if the attacker is using a network analysis tool to copy every frame inside the WLAN, the attacker cannot learn the key value. Also, note that by allowing mutual authentication, the client can confirm that the AP knows the right key, thereby preventing a connection to a rogue AP.

The second tool is encryption. Encryption uses a secret key and a mathematical formula to scramble the contents of the WLAN frame. The receiving device then uses another formula to decrypt the data. Again, without the secret encryption key, an attacker may be able to intercept the frame, but he or she cannot read the contents.

The third class of tools includes many options, but this class generally can be called intrusion tools. These tools include Intrusion Detection Systems (IDS) and Intrusion Prevention Systems (IPS), as well as WLAN-specific tools. Cisco defines the Structured Wireless-Aware Network (SWAN) architecture. It includes many tools, some of which specifically address the issue of detecting and identifying rogue APs, and whether they represent threats. Table 11-8 lists the key vulnerabilities, along with the general solution.

Table 11-8 *WLAN Vulnerabilities and Solutions*

Vulnerability	Solution
War drivers	Strong authentication
Hackers stealing information in a WLAN	Strong encryption
Hackers gaining access to the rest of the network	Strong authentication
Employee AP installation	Intrusion Detection Systems (IDS), including Cisco SWAN
Rogue AP	Strong authentication, IDS/SWAN

Key Topic

The Progression of WLAN Security Standards

WLAN standards have progressed over the years in response to a growing need for stronger security and because of some problems in the earliest WLAN security standard. This section examines four significant sets of WLAN security standards in chronological order, describing their problems and solutions.

> **NOTE**   WLAN standards address the details of how to implement the authentication and encryption parts of the security puzzle, and they are covered in this section. The intrusion-related tools (IDS and IPS) fall more into an Enterprise-wide security framework and are not covered in this chapter.

The initial security standard for WLANs, called *Wired Equivalent Privacy (WEP)*, had many problems. The other three standards covered here represent a progression of standards whose goal in part was to fix the problems created by WEP. In chronological order, Cisco first addressed the problem with some proprietary solutions. Then the Wi-Fi Alliance, an industry association, helped fix the problem by defining an industry-wide standard. Finally, the IEEE completed work on an official public standard, 802.11i. Table 11-9 lists these four major WLAN security standards.

Table 11-9   *WLAN Security Standards*

Name	Year	Who Defined It
Wired Equivalent Privacy (WEP)	1997	IEEE
The interim Cisco solution while awaiting 802.11i	2001	Cisco, IEEE 802.1x Extensible Authentication Protocol (EAP)
Wi-Fi Protected Access (WPA)	2003	Wi-Fi Alliance
802.11i (WPA2)	2005+	IEEE

The word *standard* is used quite loosely in this chapter when referring to WLAN security. Some of the standards are true open standards from a standards body—namely, the IEEE. Some of the standards flow from the Wi-Fi Alliance, making them de facto industry standards. Additionally, Cisco created several proprietary interim solutions for its products, making the use of the word more of a stretch. However, all of these standards helped improve the original WEP security, so the text will take a closer look at each standard.

Wired Equivalent Privacy (WEP)

WEP was the original 802.11 security standard, providing authentication and encryption services. As it turns out, WEP provided only weak authentication and encryption, to the point that its authentication and encryption can be cracked by a hacker today, using easily downloaded tools. The main problems were as follows:

■ **Static Preshared Keys (PSK):** The key value had to be configured on each client and each AP, with no dynamic way to exchange the keys without human intervention. As a result, many people did not bother to change the keys on a regular basis, especially in Enterprises with a large number of wireless clients.

■ **Easily cracked keys:** The key values were short (64 bits, of which only 40 were the actual unique key). This made it easier to predict the key's value based on the frames copied from the WLAN. Additionally, the fact that the key typically never changed meant that the hacker could gather lots of sample authentication attempts, making it easier to find the key.

Because of the problems with WEP, and the fact that the later standards include much better security features, WEP should not be used today.

SSID Cloaking and MAC Filtering

Because of WEP's problems, many vendors included a couple of security-related features that are not part of WEP. However, many people associated these features with WEP just because of the timing with which the features were announced. Neither feature provides much real security, and they are not part of any standard, but it is worth discussing the concepts in case you see them mentioned elsewhere.

The first feature, *SSID cloaking*, changes the process by which clients associate with an AP. Before a client can communicate with the AP, it must know something about the AP—in particular, the AP's SSID. Normally, the association process occurs like this:

Step 1 The AP sends a periodic Beacon frame (the default is every 100 ms) that lists the AP's SSID and other configuration information.

Step 2 The client listens for Beacons on all channels, learning about all APs in range.

Step 3 The client associates with the AP with the strongest signal (the default), or with the AP with the strongest signal for the currently preferred SSID.

Step 4 The authentication process occurs as soon as the client has associated with the AP.

Essentially, the client learns about each AP and its associated SSIDs via the Beacon process. This process aids in the roaming process, allowing the client to move around and reassociate with a new AP when the old AP's signal gets weaker. However, the Beacons allow an attacker to easily and quickly find out information about the APs to begin trying to associate and gain access to the network.

SSID cloaking is an AP feature that tells the AP to stop sending periodic Beacon frames. This seems to solve the problem with attackers easily and quickly finding all APs. However, clients still need to be able to find the APs. Therefore, if the client has been configured with a null SSID, the client sends a Probe message, which causes each AP to respond with its SSID. In short, it is simple to cause all the APs to announce their SSIDs, even with cloaking enabled on the APs, so attackers can still find all the APs.

> **NOTE**   Enterprises often use SSID cloaking to prevent curious people from trying to access the WLAN. Public wireless hotspots tend to let their APs send Beacon frames so that the customers can easily find their APs.

The second extra feature often implemented along with WEP is MAC address filtering. The AP can be configured with a list of allowed WLAN MAC addresses, filtering frames sent by WLAN clients whose MAC address is not in the list. As with SSID cloaking, MAC address filtering may prevent curious onlookers from accessing the WLAN, but it does not stop a real attack. The attacker can use a WLAN adapter that allows its MAC address to be changed, copy legitimate frames out of the air, set its own MAC address to one of the legitimate MAC addresses, and circumvent the MAC address filter.

The Cisco Interim Solution Between WEP and 802.11i

Because of the problems with WEP, vendors such as Cisco, and the Wi-Fi Alliance industry association, looked to solve the problem with their own standards, concurrent with the typically slower IEEE standardization process. The Cisco answer included some proprietary improvements for encryption, along with the IEEE 802.1x standard for end-user authentication. The main features of Cisco enhancements included the following:

- Dynamic key exchange (instead of static preshared keys)

- User authentication using 802.1x

- A new encryption key for each packet

The use of a dynamic key exchange process helps because the clients and AP can then change keys more often, without human intervention. As a result, if the key is discovered, the exposure can be short-lived. Also, when key information is exchanged dynamically, a new key can be delivered for each packet, allowing encryption to use a different key each time. That way, even if an attacker managed to discover a key used for a particular packet, he or she could decrypt only that one packet, minimizing the exposure.

Cisco created several features based on the then-to-date known progress on the IEEE 802.11i WLAN security standard. However, Cisco also added user authentication to its suite of security features. User authentication means that instead of authenticating the device by checking to see if the device knows a correct key, the user must supply a username and password. This extra authentication step adds another layer of security. That way, even if the keys are temporarily compromised, the attacker must also know a person's username and password to gain access to the WLAN.

Wi-Fi Protected Access (WPA)

The Cisco solution to the difficulties of WEP included proprietary protocols as well as IEEE standard 802.1x. After Cisco integrated its proprietary WLAN security standards into Cisco APs, the Wi-Fi Alliance created a multivendor WLAN security standard. At the same time, the IEEE was working on the future official IEEE WLAN security standard, 802.11i, but the WLAN industry needed a quicker solution than waiting on the IEEE standard. So, the Wi-Fi alliance took the current work-in-progress on the 802.11i committee, made some assumptions and predictions, and defined a de facto industry standard. The Wi-Fi Alliance then performed its normal task of certifying vendors' products as to whether they met this new industry standard, calling it *Wi-Fi Protected Access (WPA)*.

WPA essentially performed the same functions as the Cisco proprietary interim solution, but with different details. WPA includes the option to use dynamic key exchange, using the Temporal Key Integrity Protocol (TKIP). (Cisco used a proprietary version of TKIP.) WPA allows for the use of either IEEE 802.1X user authentication or simple device authentication using preshared keys. And the encryption algorithm uses the Message Integrity Check (MIC) algorithm, again similar to the process used in the Cisco-proprietary solution.

WPA had two great benefits. First, it improved security greatly compared to WEP. Second, the Wi-Fi Alliance's certification program had already enjoyed great success when WPA came out, so vendors had great incentive to support WPA and have their products become WPA-certified by the Wi-Fi Alliance. As a result, PC manufacturers could choose from many wireless NICs, and customers could buy APs from many different vendors, with confidence that WPA security would work well.

> **NOTE** The Cisco-proprietary solutions and the WPA industry standard are incompatible.

IEEE 802.11i and WPA-2

The IEEE ratified the 802.11i standard in 2005; additional related specifications arrived later. Like the Cisco-proprietary solution, and the Wi-Fi Alliance's WPA industry standard, 802.11i includes dynamic key exchange, much stronger encryption, and user authentication. However, the details differ enough so that 802.11i is not backward-compatible with either WPA or the Cisco-proprietary protocols.

One particularly important improvement over the interim Cisco and WPA standards is the inclusion of the *Advanced Encryption Standard (AES)* in 802.11i. AES provides even better encryption than the interim Cisco and WEP standards, with longer keys and much more secure encryption algorithms.

The Wi-Fi Alliance continues its product certification role for 802.11i, but with a twist on the names used for the standard. Because of the success of the WPA industry standard and the popularity of the term "WPA," the Wi-Fi Alliance calls 802.11i WPA2, meaning the second version of WPA. So, when buying and configuring products, you will more likely see references to WPA2 rather than 802.11i.

Table 11-10 summarizes the key features of the various WLAN security standards.

Table 11-10   *Comparisons of WLAN Security Features*

Standard	Key Distribution	Device Authentication	User Authentication	Encryption
WEP	Static	Yes (weak)	None	Yes (weak)
Cisco	Dynamic	Yes	Yes (802.1x)	Yes (TKIP)
WPA	Both	Yes	Yes (802.1x)	Yes (TKIP)
802.11i (WPA2)	Both	Yes	Yes (802.1x)	Yes (AES)

Exam Preparation Tasks

Review All the Key Topics

Review the most important topics from this chapter, noted with the key topics icon. Table 11-11 lists these key topics and where each is discussed.

Table 11-11 *Key Topics for Chapter 11*

Key Topic Element	Description	Page Number
Table 11-2	WLAN standards organizations and their roles	304
Table 11-3	Comparison of 802.11a, 802.11b, and 802.11g	305
Table 11-4	WLAN modes, their formal names, and descriptions	307
Table 11-5	Unlicensed bands, their general names, and the list of standards to use each band	309
Figure 11-6	DSSS frequencies, showing the three nonoverlapping channels	310
List	WLAN configuration checklist	315
List	Common WLAN installation problems related to the work done in the site survey	319
List	Other common WLAN installation problems	319
Table 11-8	Common WLAN security threats	321
Table 11-9	WLAN security standards	322
Table 11-10	Comparison of WLAN security standards	326

Complete the Tables and Lists from Memory

Print a copy of Appendix H, "Memory Tables" (found on the CD), or at least the section for this chapter, and complete the tables and lists from memory. Appendix I, "Memory Tables Answer Key," also on the CD, includes completed tables and lists for you to check your work.

Definitions of Key Terms

Define the following key terms from this chapter and check your answers in the glossary:

802.11a, 802.11b, 802.11g, 802.11i, 802.11n, access point, ad hoc mode, Basic Service Set (BSS), CSMA/CA, Direct Sequence Spread Spectrum, Extended Service Set (ESS), Frequency Hopping Spread Spectrum, infrastructure mode, Orthogonal Frequency Division Multiplexing, Service Set Identifier (SSID), Wi-Fi Alliance, Wi-Fi Protected Access (WPA), wired equivalent privacy (WEP), WLAN client, WPA2

Cisco Published ICND1 Exam Topics* Covered in This Part:

Describe the operation of data networks

- Use the OSI and TCP/IP models and their associated protocols to explain how data flows in a network
- Interpret network diagrams
- Determine the path between two hosts across a network
- Describe the components required for network and Internet communications
- Identify and correct common network problems at Layers 1, 2, 3, and 7 using a layered model approach
- Differentiate between LAN/WAN operation and features

Implement an IP addressing scheme and IP services to meet network requirements for a small branch office

- Describe the need and role of addressing in a network
- Create and apply an addressing scheme to a network
- Assign and verify valid IP addresses to hosts, servers, and networking devices in a LAN environment
- Describe and verify DNS operation
- Describe the operation and benefits of using private and public IP addressing
- Enable NAT for a small network with a single ISP and connection using SDM and verify operation using CLI and ping
- Configure, verify, and troubleshoot DHCP and DNS operation on a router (including: CLI/SDM)
- Implement static and dynamic addressing services for hosts in a LAN environment
- Identify and correct IP addressing issues

Implement a small routed network

- Describe basic routing concepts (including: packet forwarding, router lookup process)
- Describe the operation of Cisco routers (including: router bootup process, POST, router components)
- Select the appropriate media, cables, ports, and connectors to connect routers to other network devices and hosts
- Configure, verify, and troubleshoot RIPv2
- Access and utilize the router CLI to set basic parameters
- Connect, configure, and verify operation status of a device interface
- Verify device configuration and network connectivity using ping, traceroute, Telnet, SSH, or other utilities
- Perform and verify routing configuration tasks for a static or default route given specific routing requirements
- Manage IOS configuration files (including: save, edit, upgrade, restore)
- Manage Cisco IOS
- Implement password and physical security
- Verify network status and router operation using basic utilities (including: ping, traceroute, Telnet, SSH, ARP, ipconfig), show and debug commands

Identify security threats to a network and describe general methods to mitigate those threats

- Describe security recommended practices including initial steps to secure network devices

*Always recheck http://www.cisco.com for the latest posted exam topics.

Part III: IP Routing

This chapter covers the following subjects:

Exam Preparation Tools for Subnetting: This section lists the various tools that can help you practice your subnetting skills.

IP Addressing and Routing: This section moves beyond the basic concepts in Chapter 5, "Fundamentals of IP Addressing and Routing," introducing the purpose and meaning of the subnet mask.

Math Operations Used When Subnetting: This section explains how to convert between IP address and subnet mask formats.

Analyzing and Choosing Subnet Masks: This section explains the meaning behind subnet masks, how to choose a subnet mask to meet stated design goals, and how to interpret a mask chosen by someone else.

Analyzing Existing Subnets: This section shows how to determine an IP address's resident subnet, broadcast address, and range of addresses in the subnet.

Design: Choosing the Subnets of a Classful Network: This section explains how to find all subnets of a single classful network.

CHAPTER 12

IP Addressing and Subnetting

The concepts and application of IP addressing and subnetting may well be the most important topics to understand both for being a well-prepared network engineer and for being ready to do well on the ICND1, ICND2, and CCNA exams. To design a new network, engineers must be able to begin with some IP address range and break it into subdivisions called subnets, choosing the right size of each subnet to meet design requirements. Engineers need to understand subnet masks, and how to pick the right masks to implement the designs that were earlier drawn on paper. Even more often, engineers need to understand, operate, and troubleshoot pre-existing networks, tasks that require mastery of addressing and subnetting concepts and the ability to apply those concepts from a different perspective than when designing the network.

This chapter begins Part III of the book, which is focused on the role of routers in an internetwork. As introduced in Chapter 5, the network layer defines and uses addressing, routing, and routing protocols to achieve its main goals. After this chapter goes into depth on addressing, the rest of the chapters in Part III focus on how to implement IP addresses, routing, and routing protocols inside Cisco routers.

All the topics in this chapter have a common goal, which is to help you understand IP addressing and subnetting. To prepare you for both real jobs and the exams, this chapter goes far beyond the concepts as covered on the exam, preparing you to apply these concepts when designing a network and when you operate and troubleshoot a network. Additionally, this chapter creates a structure from which you can repeatedly practice the math processes used to get the answers to subnetting questions.

"Do I Know This Already?" Quiz

The "Do I Know This Already?" quiz allows you to assess if you should read the entire chapter. If you miss no more than one of these 14 self-assessment questions, you might want to move ahead to the "Exam Preparation Tasks" section. Table 12-1 lists the major headings in this chapter and the "Do I Know This Already?" quiz questions covering the material in those headings so you can assess your knowledge of these specific areas. The answers to the "Do I Know This Already?" quiz appear in Appendix A.

Table 12-1   *"Do I Know This Already?" Foundation Topics Section-to-Question Mapping*

Foundation Topics Section	Questions
Exam Preparation Tools for Subnetting	None
IP Addressing and Routing	1
Math Operations Used When Subnetting	2, 3
Analyzing and Choosing Subnet Masks	4–8
Analyzing Existing Subnets	9–12
Design: Choosing the Subnets of a Classful Network	13, 14

1. Which of the following are private IP networks?

    a. 172.31.0.0

    b. 172.32.0.0

    c. 192.168.255.0

    d. 192.1.168.0

    e. 11.0.0.0

2. Which of the following is the result of a Boolean AND between IP address 150.150.4.100 and mask 255.255.192.0?

    a. 1001 0110 1001 0110 0000 0100 0110 0100

    b. 1001 0110 1001 0110 0000 0000 0000 0000

    c. 1001 0110 1001 0110 0000 0100 0000 0000

    d. 1001 0110 0000 0000 0000 0000 0000 0000

3. Which of the following shows the equivalent of subnet mask 255.255.248.0, but in prefix notation?

    a. /248

    b. /24

    c. /28

    d. /21

    e. /20

    f. /23

4. If mask 255.255.255.128 were used with a Class B network, how many subnets could exist, with how many hosts per subnet, respectively?

    a. 256 and 256

    b. 254 and 254

    c. 62 and 1022

    d. 1022 and 62

    e. 512 and 126

    f. 126 and 510

5. A Class B network needs to be subnetted such that it supports 100 subnets and 100 hosts/subnet. For this design, if multiple masks meet those design requirements, the engineer should choose the mask that maximizes the number of hosts per subnet. Which of the following masks meets the design criteria?

    a. 255.255.255.0

    b. /23

    c. /26

    d. 255.255.252.0

6. If mask 255.255.255.240 were used with a Class C network, how many subnets could exist, with how many hosts per subnet, respectively?

    a. 16 and 16

    b. 14 and 14

    c. 16 and 14

    d. 8 and 32

    e. 32 and 8

    f. 6 and 30

7. Which of the following subnet masks lets a Class B network have up to 150 hosts per subnet, and supports 164 subnets?

    a. 255.0.0.0

    b. 255.255.0.0

    c. 255.255.255.0

    d. 255.255.192.0

    e. 255.255.240.0

    f. 255.255.252.0

8. Which of the following subnet masks let a Class A network have up to 150 hosts per subnet and supports 164 subnets?

   a. 255.0.0.0

   b. 255.255.0.0

   c. 255.255.255.0

   d. 255.255.192.0

   e. 255.255.252.0

   f. 255.255.255.192

9. Which of the following IP addresses are not in the same subnet as 190.4.80.80, mask 255.255.255.0?

   a. 190.4.80.1

   b. 190.4.80.50

   c. 190.4.80.100

   d. 190.4.80.200

   e. 190.4.90.1

   f. 10.1.1.1

10. Which of the following IP addresses is not in the same subnet as 190.4.80.80, mask 255.255.240.0?

    a. 190.4.80.1

    b. 190.4.80.50

    c. 190.4.80.100

    d. 190.4.80.200

    e. 190.4.90.1

    f. 10.1.1.1

11. Which of the following IP addresses are not in the same subnet as 190.4.80.80/25?

    a. 190.4.80.1

    b. 190.4.80.50

    c. 190.4.80.100

    d. 190.4.80.200

    e. 190.4.90.1

    f. 10.1.1.1

12. Each of the following answers lists a dotted decimal number and a subnet mask. The dotted decimal number might be a valid IP address that can be used by a host or it might be a subnet number or broadcast address. Which of the answers show an address that can be used by a host?

    a. 10.0.0.0, 255.0.0.0

    b. 192.168.5.160, 255.255.255.192

    c. 172.27.27.27, 255.255.255.252

    d. 172.20.49.0, 255.255.254.0

13. Which of the following are valid subnet numbers in network 180.1.0.0 when using mask 255.255.248.0?

    a. 180.1.2.0

    b. 180.1.4.0

    c. 180.1.8.0

    d. 180.1.16.0

    e. 180.1.32.0

    f. 180.1.40.0

14. Which of the following are not valid subnet numbers in network 180.1.0.0 when using mask 255.255.255.0?

    a. 180.2.2.0

    b. 180.1.4.0

    c. 180.1.8.0

    d. 180.1.16.0

    e. 180.1.32.0

    f. 180.1.40.0

Foundation Topics

This chapter is fundamentally different from the other chapters in this book. Like the other chapters, this chapter explains a related set of concepts—in this case, the concepts, thought processes, and math used to attack IP addressing and subnetting questions on the CCNA exams. However, more so than for any other chapter in this book, you must practice the concepts and math in this chapter before you take the exam(s). It is very much like math classes in school—if you do not do the homework, you probably will not do as well on the test.

This chapter begins with a few comments about how to prepare for subnetting questions on the exam. Then the chapter spends a few pages reviewing what has been covered already in regard to IP addressing and routing, two topics that are tightly linked. The rest of the major sections of the chapter tackle a particular type of subnetting question in depth, with each section ending with a list of suggested steps to take to practice your subnetting skills.

Exam Preparation Tools for Subnetting

To help you prepare for the exam, this chapter explains the subnetting concepts and shows multiple examples. Each section also lists the specific steps required to solve a particular type of problem. Often, two sets of steps are provided, one that uses binary math, and another that uses only decimal math.

More so than for any other single chapter in this book, you should also practice and review the topics in this chapter until you have mastered the concepts. To that end, this book includes several tools, some of which are located on the CD-ROM that comes with this book, in addition to this chapter:

- **Appendix D, "Subnetting Practice":** This large appendix lists numerous practice problems, with solutions that show how to use the processes explained in this chapter.

- **Appendix E, "Subnetting Reference Pages":** This short appendix includes a few handy references, including a 1-page summary of each of the subnetting processes listed in this chapter.

- **Subnetting videos (DVD):** Several of the most important subnetting processes described in this chapter are explained in videos on the DVD in the back of this book. The goal of these videos is to ensure that you understand these key processes completely, and hopefully move you quickly to the point of mastering the process.

- **Cisco Binary Game at the Cisco CCNA Prep Center:** If you want to use the processes that use binary math, you can use the Cisco Binary Game to practice your binary-to-decimal and decimal-to-binary conversion accuracy and speed. The CCNA Prep Center is at http://www.cisco.com/go/prepcenter. The binary game is also included on the CD in the back of the book.

■ **Subnetting Game at the Cisco CCNA Prep Center:** As of the time of writing this chapter, the CCNA Prep Center had a Beta version of the Subnetting Game available. The game requires that you choose a mask, pick subnets, calculate the subnet number and broadcast address of the subnets, and assign IP addresses in the subnets.

■ **Subnetting calculators:** You can make up your own practice problems, and use a subnetting calculator to find the answers to check your work. This allows you to have unlimited amounts of practice to get better and get faster. The CCNA Prep Center also has the Cisco Subnet Calculator for free download.

■ **Glossary:** The topics of IP addressing and subnetting use a wide variety of terminology. The glossary in the back of this book includes the subnetting terms used in this book.

Suggested Subnetting Preparation Plan

Over the years, some readers have asked for a suggested subnetting study plan. At the same time, the CCNA exam questions have been getting more difficult. To help you better prepare, the following list outlines a suggested study plan:

Step 1   If you have not done so already, load the CD-ROM and get familiar with its user interface, install the exam engine software, and verify that you can find the tools listed in the preceding list. You may want to go ahead and print Appendix E, and if you expect you will want to use a printed version of Appendix D, print that as well (be warned, Appendix D is almost 100 pages in length).

Step 2   Keep reading this chapter through the end of the second major section, "IP Addressing and Routing."

Step 3   For each subsequent major section, read the section and then follow the instructions in the subsection "Practice Suggestions." This short part of each major section points you to the items that would be of the most help to stop and practice at that point. These suggestions include the use of the tools listed earlier. The following major sections include a "Practice Suggestions" subsection:

   • Math Operations Used When Subnetting

   • Analyzing and Choosing Subnet Masks

   • Analyzing Existing Subnets

   • Design: Choosing the Subnets of a Classful Network

Step 4 When finished with the chapter, if you feel the need for more practice, make up your own practice problems, and check your answers using a subnet calculator (more information is provided after this list). I recommend the Cisco Subnet Calculator because its user interface displays the information in a convenient format for doing extra questions.

Step 5 At any point in your study, feel free to visit the CCNA Prep Center (http://www.cisco.com/go/prepcenter) to use both the Cisco Binary Game and the Subnetting Game. Both help you build skills for doing subnetting problems. (The CCNA Prep Center requires you to log in with a Cisco.com User ID; if you do not have one, the preceding URL has a link to Cisco.com registration.) Once in the CCNA Prep Center, you can find the games under the Additional Information tab.

You can certainly deviate from this plan to suit your personal preferences, but at the end of this process, you should be able to confidently answer straightforward subnetting questions, such as those in Appendix D. In fact, you should be able to answer in 10–12 seconds a straightforward question such as, "In what subnet does IP address 10.143.254.17, with mask 255.255.224.0, reside?" That is a subjective time period, based on my experience teaching classes, but the point is that you need to understand it all, and practice to the point of being pretty fast.

However, perfecting your subnetting math skills is not enough. The exams ask questions that require you to prove you have the skills to attack real-life problems, problems such as how to design an IP network by subnetting a classful network, how to determine all the subnets of a classful network, and how to pick subnets to use in an internetwork design. The wording of the exam problems, in some cases, is similar to that of the math word problems back in school—many people have trouble translating the written words into a math problem that can be worked. Likewise, the exam questions may well present a scenario, and then leave it to you to figure out what subnetting math is required to find the answer.

To prepare for these skills-based questions, Chapter 15, "Troubleshooting IP Routing," covers a wide variety of topics that help you analyze a network to solve subnetting-related problems. These extra tips help you sift through the wording in problems, and tell you how to approach the problems, so that you can then find the answers. So, in addition to this chapter, read through Chapter 15 as well, which includes coverage of tips for troubleshooting IP addressing problems.

More Practice Using a Subnet Calculator

If you want even more practice, you can essentially get unlimited practice using a subnet calculator. For the purpose of CCNA study, I particularly like the Cisco Subnet Calculator, which can be downloaded from the Cisco CCNA Prep Center. You can then make up your own problems like those found in this chapter, work the problem, and then check your work using the calculator.

For example, you could pick an IP network and mask. Then, you could find all subnets of that network, using that single mask. To check your work, you could type in the network number and mask in the Cisco Subnet Calculator, and click the **Subnets/hosts** tab, which then displays all the subnet numbers, from which you can check your answers. As another example, you could pick an IP address and mask, try to find the subnet number, broadcast address, and range of addresses, and then check your work with the calculator using the **Subnet** tab. After you have typed the IP address and mask, this tab displays the subnet number, broadcast address, and range of usable addresses. And yet another example: You can even choose an IP address and mask, and try to find the number of network, subnet, and host bits—and again check your work with the calculator. In this case, the calculator even uses the same format as this chapter to represent the mask, with N, S, and H for the network, subnet, and host parts of the address.

Now that you have a study plan, the next section briefly reviews the core IP addressing and routing concepts covered previously in Chapter 5. Following that, four major sections describe the various details of IP addressing and subnetting.

IP Addressing and Routing

This section primarily reviews the addressing and routing concepts found in earlier chapters of this book, particularly in Chapter 5. It also briefly introduces IP Version 6 (IPv6) addressing and the concept of private IP networks.

IP Addressing Review

The vast majority of IP networks today use a version of the IP protocol called IP Version 4 (IPv4). Rather than refer to it as IPv4, most texts, this one included, simply refer to it as IP. This section reviews IPv4 addressing concepts as introduced in Chapter 5.

Many different Class A, B, and C networks exist. Table 12-2 summarizes the possible network numbers, the total number of each type, and the number of hosts in each Class A, B, and C network.

NOTE   In Table 12-2, the "Valid Network Numbers" row shows actual network numbers. There are several reserved cases. For example, network 0.0.0.0 (originally defined for use as a broadcast address) and network 127.0.0.0 (still available for use as the loopback address) are reserved.

Table 12-2 *List of All Possible Valid Network Numbers*

	Class A	Class B	Class C
First Octet Range	1 to 126	128 to 191	192 to 223
Valid Network Numbers	1.0.0.0 to 126.0.0.0	128.0.0.0 to 191.255.0.0	192.0.0.0 to 223.255.255.0
Number of Networks in This Class	$2^7 - 2$	2^{14}	2^{21}
Number of Hosts Per Network	$2^{24} - 2$	$2^{16} - 2$	$2^8 - 2$
Size of Network Part of Address (Bytes)	1	2	3
Size of Host Part of Address (Bytes)	3	2	1

> **NOTE** This chapter uses the term *network* to refer to a *classful network*—in other words, a Class A, B, or C network. This chapter also uses the term *subnet* to refer to smaller parts of a classful network. However, note that many people use these terms more loosely, interchanging the words network and subnet, which is fine for general conversation, but can be problematic when trying to be exact.

Figure 12-1 shows the structure of three IP addresses, each from a different network, when no subnetting is used. One address is in a Class A network, one is in a Class B network, and one is in a Class C network.

Figure 12-1 *Class A, B, and C IP Addresses and Their Formats*

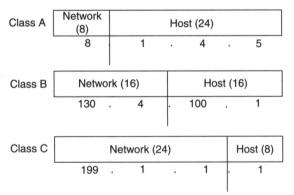

By definition, an IP address that begins with 8 in the first octet is in a Class A network, so the network part of the address is the first byte, or first octet. An address that begins with 130 is in a Class B network. By definition, Class B addresses have a 2-byte network part, as shown. Finally, any address that begins with 199 is in a Class C network, which has a 3-byte network part. Also by definition, a Class A address has a 3-byte host part, Class B has a 2-byte host part, and Class C has a 1-byte host part.

Humans can simply remember the numbers in Table 12-2 and the concepts in Figure 12-1 and then quickly determine the network and host parts of an IP address. Computers, however, use a mask to define the size of the network and the host parts of an address. The logic behind the mask results in the same conventions of Class A, B, and C networks that you already know, but the computer can deal with it better as a binary math problem.

The mask is a 32-bit binary number, usually written in dotted decimal format. The purpose of the mask is to define the structure of an IP address. In short, the mask defines the size of the host part of an IP address, representing the host part of the IP address with binary 0s in the mask. The first part of the mask contains binary 1s, which represents the network part of the addresses (if no subnetting is used), or both the network and subnet parts of the addresses (if subnetting is used).

When subnetting is not used, each class of IP address uses the default mask for that class. For example, the default Class A mask ends with 24 bits of binary 0s, which means that the last three octets of the mask are 0s, representing the 3-byte host part of Class A addresses. Table 12-3 summarizes the default masks and reflects the sizes of the two parts of an IP address.

Table 12-3   *Class A, B, and C Networks: Network and Host Parts and Default Masks*

Key Topic

Class of Address	Size of Network Part of Address in Bits	Size of Host Part of Address in Bits	Default Mask for Each Class of Network
A	8	24	255.0.0.0
B	16	16	255.255.0.0
C	24	8	255.255.255.0

Public and Private Addressing

The ICANN (formerly IANA) and its member organizations manage the process of assigning IP network numbers, or even smaller ranges of IP addresses, to companies that want to connect to the Internet. After a company is assigned a range of IP addresses, only that company can use that range. Additionally, the routers in the Internet can then learn routes to reach these networks, so that everyone in the entire Internet can forward packets to that IP network. Because these IP addresses can be reached by packets in the public Internet, these networks are often called public networks, and the addresses in these networks are called *public addresses*.

Some computers will never be connected to the Internet. So, engineers building a network consisting of only such computers could use IP addresses that are duplicates of registered public IP addresses in the Internet. So, when designing the IP addressing convention for such a network, an organization could pick and use any network number(s) that it wanted, and all would be well. For instance, you can buy a few routers, connect them together in your office, and configure IP addresses in network 1.0.0.0 and make it work, even though some company also uses Class A network 1 as its registered public IP network. The IP addresses that you use might be duplicates of real IP addresses in the Internet, but if all you want to do is learn on the lab in your office, all is well.

However, using the same IP addresses used by another company is unnecessary in this situation, because TCP/IP RFC 1918 defines a set of *private networks* that can be used for internetworks that do not connect to the Internet. More importantly, this set of private networks will never be assigned by ICANN to any organization for use as registered public network numbers. So, when building a private network, like one in a lab, you can use numbers in a range that is not used by anyone in the public Internet. Table 12-4 shows the private address space defined by RFC 1918.

Key Topic

Table 12-4 *RFC 1918 Private Address Space*

Private IP Networks	Class of Networks	Number of Networks
10.0.0.0	A	1
172.16.0.0 through 172.31.0.0	B	16
192.168.0.0 through 192.168.255.0	C	256

In other words, any organization can use these network numbers. However, no organization is allowed to advertise these networks using a routing protocol on the Internet.

Many of you might be wondering, "Why bother reserving special private network numbers when it does not matter whether the addresses are duplicates?" Well, as it turns out, private networks can be used inside a company and that company can still connect to the Internet today, using a function called Network Address Translation (NAT). Chapter 16, "WAN Concepts," and Chapter 17, "WAN Configuration," expand on the concepts of NAT and private addressing, and how the two work together.

IP Version 6 Addressing

IPv6 defines many improvements over IPv4. However, the primary goal of IPv6 is to significantly increase the number of available IP addresses. To that end, IPv6 uses a 128-bit IP address, rather than the 32 bits defined by IPv4. To appreciate the size of the address structure, a 128-bit address structure provides well over 10^{38} possible IP addresses. If you consider the fact that the Earth currently has less than 10^{10} people, you can see that you could have literally billions, trillions, or gazillions of IP addresses per person and still not run out.

> **NOTE** In case you are wondering, IP Version 5 was defined for experimental reasons but was never deployed. To avoid confusion, the next attempt to update the IP protocol was named IPv6.

IPv6 has been defined since the mid-1990s, but the migration from IPv4 to IPv6 has been rather slow. IPv6 was created to solve an overcrowding problem in the IPv4 address space. Some other short-term solutions in IPv4 (notably, NAT, as covered in Chapter 16) helped relieve the IPv4 overcrowding. However, in 2007, IPv6 deployment has started to quicken. Many large service providers have migrated to IPv6 to support the large number of mobile devices that can connect to the Internet, and the U.S. government has mandated migration to IPv6 for its member agencies.

The 128-bit IPv6 address is written in hexadecimal notation, with colons between each quartet of symbols. Even in hexadecimal, the addresses can be long. However, IPv6 also allows for abbreviations, as is shown in Table 12-5. The table also summarizes some of the pertinent information comparing IPv4 addresses with IPv6.

Table 12-5 *IPv4 Versus IPv6*

Feature	IPv4	IPv6
Size of address (bits or bytes per octets)	32 bits, 4 octets	128 bits, 16 octets
Example address	10.1.1.1	0000:0000:0000:0000:FFFF:FFFF:0A01:0101
Same address, abbreviated	—	::FFFF:FFFF:0A01:0101
Number of possible addresses, ignoring reserved values	2^{32}, (roughly 4 billion)	2^{128}, or roughly 3.4×10^{38}

IP Subnetting Review

IP subnetting creates larger numbers of smaller groups of IP addresses compared with simply using Class A, B, and C conventions. You can still think about the Class A, B, and C rules, but now a single Class A, B, or C network can be subdivided into many smaller groups. Subnetting treats a subdivision of a single Class A, B, or C network as if it were a network itself. By doing so, a single Class A, B, or C network can be subdivided into many nonoverlapping subnets.

Figure 12-2 shows a reminder of the basics of how to subnet a classful network, using the same internetwork shown in Figure 5-6 in Chapter 5. This figure shows Class B network 150.150.0.0, with a need for six subnets.

Figure 12-2 *Same Network Topology Using One IP Network with Six Subnets*

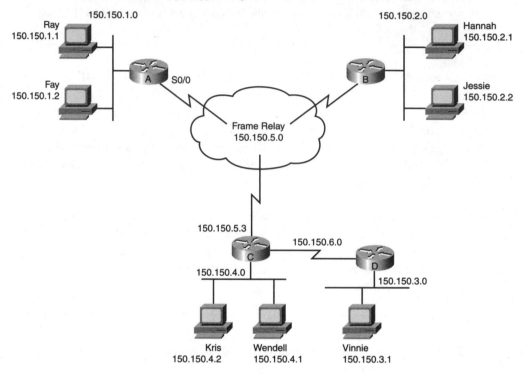

> **NOTE** The term *network* might be used to refer to a Class A, B, or C IP network, or might be used to simply refer to a collection of switches, routers, cables, and end-user devices. To avoid confusion, this chapter uses the term internetwork to refer to the collection of networking devices (internetwork meaning "interconnected networks"), and the term network specifically for a Class A, B, or C IP network.

This design subnets Class B network 150.150.0.0. The IP network designer has chosen a mask of 255.255.255.0, the last octet of which implies 8 host bits. Because it is a Class B network, there are 16 network bits. Therefore, there are 8 subnet bits, which happen to be bits 17 through 24—in other words, the third octet.

> **NOTE** Note that the next major section explains the use and purpose of subnet masks, so do not be concerned at this point if the analysis in this paragraph does not yet make sense.

The network parts (the first two octets in this example) all begin with 150.150, meaning that each of the six subnets is a subnet of Class B network 150.150.0.0.

With subnetting, the third part of an IP address—namely, the subnet part—appears in the middle of the address. This field is created by "stealing" or "borrowing" bits from the host part of the address. The size of the network part of the address never shrinks. In other words, Class A, B, and C rules still apply when you define the size of the network part of an address. However, the host part of the address shrinks to make room for the subnet part of the address. Figure 12-3 shows the format of addresses when subnetting is used.

Figure 12-3 *Address Formats When Subnetting Is Used*

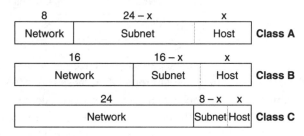

IP Routing Review

IP routing and IP addressing were designed with each other in mind. IP routing presumes the structure of IP subnetting, in which ranges of consecutive IP addresses reside in a single subnet. IP addressing RFCs define subnetting so that consecutively numbered IP addresses can be represented as a subnet number (subnet address) and a subnet mask. This allows routers to succinctly list subnets in their routing tables.

Routers need a good way to list the subnet number in their routing tables. This information must somehow imply the IP addresses in the subnet. For example, the subnet at the bottom of figure 12-2, which contains host Kris, can be described as follows:

> All IP addresses that begin with 150.150.4; more specifically, the numbers 150.150.4.0 through 150.150.4.255.

Although true, the preceding statement is not very succinct. Instead, a router's routing table would list the subnet number and subnet mask as follows:

> 150.150.4.0, 255.255.255.0

The subnet number and mask together means the same thing as the earlier long text statement, but just using numbers. This chapter explains how to examine a subnet number and mask and figure out the range of consecutive IP addresses that comprises the subnet.

One reason you need to be able to figure out the range of addresses in a subnet is to understand, analyze, and troubleshoot routing problems. To see why, again consider router A's route for subnet 150.150.4.0, 255.255.255.0 in Figure 12-2. Each route in a router's routing table lists the destination (a subnet number and mask), plus instructions on how the router should forward packets to that subnet. The forwarding instructions typically include the IP address of the next router to which the packet should be forwarded, and the local router's interface to use when forwarding the packet. For example, router A's route to that subnet would look like the information in Table 12-6.

Table 12-6   *Routing Table Entry in Router A*

Subnet and Mask	Next-hop Router	Outgoing Interface
150.150.4.0, 255.255.255.0	150.150.5.3	S0/0

Now, to see how this information is related to subnetting, consider a packet sent by Ray to Kris (150.150.4.2). Ray sends the packet to router A because Ray knows that 150.150.4.2 is in a different subnet, and Ray knows that router A is Ray's default gateway. Once router A has the packet, it compares the destination IP address (150.150.4.2) to A's routing table. Router A typically will not find the address 150.150.4.2 in the routing table—instead, the router has a list of subnets (subnet numbers and corresponding subnet masks), like the route listed in Table 12-6. So, the router must ask itself the following:

> Of the subnets in my routing table, which subnet's range of IP addresses includes the destination IP address of this packet?

In other words, the router must match the packet's destination address to the correct subnet. In this case, the subnet listed in Table 12-6 includes all addresses that begin with 150.150.4, so the packet destined to Kris (150.150.4.2) matches the route. In this case, router A forwards the packet to router C (150.150.5.3), with router A using its S0/0 interface to forward the packet.

> **NOTE**   The exams might expect you to apply this knowledge to solve a routing problem. For example, you might be asked to determine why PC1 cannot ping PC2, and the problem is that the second of three routers between PC1 and PC2 does not have a route that matches the destination IP address of PC2.

This chapter explains many features of IP addressing and subnetting, as an end to itself. The next section focuses on some basic math tools. The section following that, "Analyzing and Choosing Subnet Masks," examines the meaning of the subnet mask and how it represents the structure of an IP address—both from a design perspective and the perspective of analyzing an existing internetwork. Following that, the next section, "Analyzing Existing

Subnets," explains the processes by which you can analyze an existing IP internetwork, and find the subnet numbers, broadcast addresses, and range of IP addresses in each subnet. Finally, the last section, "Design: Choosing the Subnets of a Classful Network," explains how to go about designing a subnetting scheme for a Class A, B, or C network, including how to find all possible subnets.

Math Operations Used When Subnetting

Computers, especially routers, think about IP addresses in terms of 32-bit binary numbers. This is fine, because technically that is what IP addresses are. Also, computers use a subnet mask to define the structure of these binary IP addresses. Acquiring a full understanding of what this means is not too difficult with a little reading and practice. However, getting accustomed to doing the binary math in your head can be challenging, particularly if you do not do it every day.

In this section, you will read about three key math operations that will be used throughout the discussion of answering CCNA addressing and subnetting questions:

■   Converting IP addresses and masks from binary to decimal, and decimal to binary

■   Performing a binary math operation called a Boolean AND

■   Converting between two formats for subnet masks: dotted decimal and prefix notation

> **NOTE**   This chapter includes many summarized processes of how to do some work with IP addresses and subnets. There is no need to memorize the processes. Most people find that after practicing the processes sufficiently to get good and fast enough to do well on the exams, they internalize and memorize the important steps as a side effect of the practice.

Converting IP Addresses and Masks from Decimal to Binary and Back Again

If you already know how binary works, how binary-to-decimal and decimal-to-binary conversion work, and how to convert IP addresses and masks from decimal to binary and back, skip to the next section, "Performing a Boolean AND Operation."

IP addresses are 32-bit binary numbers written as a series of decimal numbers separated by periods (called *dotted decimal* format). To examine an address in its true form, binary, you need to convert from decimal to binary. To put a 32-bit binary number in the decimal form that is needed when configuring a router, you need to convert the 32-bit number back to decimal 8 bits at a time.

One key to the conversion process for IP addresses is remembering these facts:

Key Topic

When you convert from one format to the other, each decimal number represents 8 bits.

When you convert from decimal to binary, each decimal number converts to an 8-bit number.

When you convert from binary to decimal, each set of 8 consecutive bits converts to one decimal number.

Consider the conversion of IP address 150.150.2.1 to binary. The number 150, when converted to its 8-bit binary equivalent, is 10010110. (You can refer to the conversion chart in Appendix B, "Decimal to Binary Conversion Table," to easily convert the numbers.) The next byte, another decimal 150, is converted to 10010110. The third byte, decimal 2, is converted to 00000010. Finally, the fourth byte, decimal 1, is converted to 00000001. The combined series of 8-bit numbers is the 32-bit IP address—in this case, 10010110 10010110 00000010 00000001.

If you start with the binary version of the IP address, you first separate it into four sets of eight digits. Then you convert each set of eight binary digits to its decimal equivalent. For example, writing an IP address as follows is correct, but not very useful:

10010110100101100000000100000001

To convert this number to a more-convenient decimal form, first separate it into four sets of eight digits:

10010110 10010110 00000010 00000001

Then look in the conversion chart in Appendix B. You see that the first 8-bit number converts to 150, and so does the second. The third set of 8 bits converts to 2, and the fourth converts to 1, giving you 150.150.2.1.

Using the chart in Appendix B makes this much easier, but you will not have the chart at the exam, of course! So, you have two main options. First, you can learn and practice how to do the conversion. This may not be as hard as it might seem at first, particularly if you are willing to practice. The Cisco CCNA Prep Center has a Binary Game that helps you practice the conversions, and its very effective. The second option is to use the decimal-math-only processes listed in this chapter, which removes the need to be good at doing the conversions. However, you do not need to decide right now whether to get really good at doing the conversions—keep reading, understand both methods, and then pick which way works best for you.

Keep in mind that with subnetting, the subnet and host parts of the address might span only part of a byte of the IP address. But when you convert from binary to decimal and decimal to binary, the rule of always converting an 8-bit binary number to a decimal number is always true. However, when thinking about subnetting, you need to ignore byte boundaries and think of IP addresses as 32-bit numbers without specific byte boundaries. This is explained more in the section "Finding the Subnet Number: Binary."

Here are some websites that might help you if you want more information:

- For a description of the conversion process, try http://doit.ort.org/course/inforep/135.htm.

- For another, try http://www.wikihow.com/Convert-from-Binary-to-Decimal and http://www.wikihow.com/Convert-from-Decimal-to-Binary.

- To practice the conversions, use the Cisco Binary Game at the CCNA Prep Center (http://www.cisco.com/go/prepcenter).

Performing a Boolean AND Operation

George Boole, a mathematician who lived in the 1800s, created a branch of mathematics that came to be called Boolean math after its creator. Boolean math has many applications in computing theory. In fact, you can find subnet numbers given an IP address and subnet mask using a Boolean AND.

A *Boolean AND* is a math operation performed on a pair of one-digit binary numbers. The result is another one-digit binary number. The actual math is even simpler than those first two sentences! The following list shows the four possible inputs to a Boolean AND, and the result:

- 0 AND 0 yields a 0

- 0 AND 1 yields a 0

- 1 AND 0 yields a 0

- 1 AND 1 yields a 1

In other words, the input to the equation consists of two one-digit binary numbers, and the output of the equation is one single-digit binary number. The only time the result is a binary 1 is when both input numbers are also binary 1; otherwise, the result of a Boolean AND operation is a 0.

You can perform a Boolean AND operation on longer binary numbers, but you are really just performing an AND operation on each pair of numbers. For instance, if you wanted to

AND together two four-digit numbers, 0110 and 0011, you would perform an AND on the first digit of each number and write down the answer. Then you would perform an AND operation on the second digit of each number, and so on, through the four digits. Table 12-7 shows the general idea.

Table 12-7 *Bitwise Boolean AND Between Two Four-Digit Numbers*

	Four-Digit Binary	First Digit	Second Digit	Third Digit	Fourth Digit
First Number	0110	0	1	1	0
Second Number	0011	0	0	1	1
Boolean AND Result	0010	0	0	1	0

This table separates the four digits of each original number to make the point more obvious. Look at the "First Digit" column. The first digit of the first number is 0, and the first digit of the second number is also 0. 0 AND 0 yields a binary 0, which is listed as the Boolean AND operation result in that same column. Similarly, the second digits of the two original numbers are 1 and 0, respectively, so the Boolean AND operation result in the "Second Digit" column shows a 0. For the third digit, the two original numbers' third digits are 1 and 1, so the AND result this time shows a binary 1. Finally, the fourth digits of the two original numbers are 0 and 1, so the Boolean AND result is 0 for that column.

When you Boolean AND together two longer binary numbers, you perform what is called a *bitwise Boolean AND*. This term simply means that you do what the previous example shows: you AND together the first digits from each of the two original numbers, and then the second digits, and then the third, and so on, until each pair of single-digit binary numbers has been ANDed.

IP subnetting math frequently uses a Boolean AND operation between two 32-bit binary numbers. The actual operation works just like the example in Table 12-7, except it is 32 bits long.

To discover the subnet number in which a particular IP address resides, you perform a bitwise AND operation between the IP address and the subnet mask. Although humans can sometimes look at an IP address and mask in decimal and derive the subnet number, routers and other computers use a bitwise Boolean AND operation between the IP address and the subnet mask to find the subnet number, so you need to understand this process. In this chapter, you will also read about a process by which you can find the subnet number without using binary conversion or Boolean ANDs. Table 12-8 shows an example of the derivation of a subnet number.

Table 12-8 *Bitwise Boolean AND Example*

	Decimal	Binary
Address	150.150.2.1	1001 0110 1001 0110 0000 0010 **0000 0001**
Mask	255.255.255.0	1111 1111 1111 1111 1111 1111 **0000 0000**
Result of AND	150.150.2.0	1001 0110 1001 0110 0000 0010 **0000 0000**

First, focus only on the third column of the table. The binary version of the IP address 150.150.2.1 is listed first. The next row shows the 32-bit binary version of the subnet mask (255.255.255.0). The last row shows the results of a bitwise AND of the two numbers. In other words, the first bit in each number is ANDed, and then the second bit in each number, and then the third, and so on, until all 32 bits in the first number have been ANDed with the bit in the same position in the second number.

The resulting 32-bit number is the subnet number in which 150.150.2.1 resides. All you have to do is convert the 32-bit number back to decimal 8 bits at a time. The subnet number in this case is 150.150.2.0.

While this process may seem long, and make you want to avoid converting all these numbers, do not worry. By the end of this chapter you will see how that, even using binary, you can use a small shortcut so that you only have to convert one octet to binary and back in order to find the subnet. For now, just be aware of the conversion table in Appendix B, and remember the Boolean AND process.

Prefix Notation/CIDR Notation

Subnet masks are actually 32-bit numbers, but for convenience, they are typically written as dotted decimal numbers—for example, 255.255.0.0. However, another way to represent a mask, called *prefix notation*, and sometimes referred to as *CIDR notation*, provides an even more succinct way to write, type, or speak the value of a subnet mask. To understand prefix notation, it is important to know that all subnet masks have some number of consecutive binary 1s, followed by binary 0s. In other words, a subnet mask cannot have 1s and 0s interspersed throughout the mask. The mask always has some number of binary 1s, followed only by binary 0s.

For the purpose of writing or typing the subnet mask, prefix notation simply denotes the number of binary 1s in a mask, preceded by a /. For example, for subnet mask 255.255.255.0, whose binary equivalent is 11111111 11111111 11111111 00000000, the equivalent prefix notation is /24, because there are 24 consecutive binary 1s in the mask.

When talking about subnets, you can say things like "That subnet uses a *slash 24 prefix*" or "That subnet has a 24-bit prefix" instead of saying something like "That subnet uses a mask of two-fifty-five dot two-fifty-five dot two-fifty-five dot two-fifty-five." As you can tell, the prefix notation alternative—simply saying something like "slash twenty-four"—is much easier.

Binary Process to Convert Between Dotted Decimal and Prefix Notation

To be prepared for both real networking jobs and the exams, you should be able to convert masks between dotted decimal and prefix notation. Routers display masks in both formats, depending on the **show** command, and configuration commands typically require dotted decimal notation. Also, you might see written documentation with different mask formats. Practically speaking, network engineers simply need to be able to convert between the two often.

This section describes the relatively straightforward process of converting between the two formats, using binary math, with the following section explaining how to convert using only decimal math. To convert from dotted decimal to prefix notation, you can follow this simple binary process:

Step 1 Convert the dotted decimal mask to binary.

Step 2 Count the number of binary 1s in the 32-bit binary mask; this is the value of the prefix notation mask.

For example, the dotted decimal mask of 255.255.240.0 converts to 11111111 11111111 11110000 00000000 in binary. The mask has 20 binary 1s, so the prefix notation of the same mask is /20.

To convert from prefix notation to a dotted decimal number, you can follow what is essentially the reverse process, as follows:

Step 1 Write down *x* binary 1s, where *x* is the value listed in the prefix version of the mask.

Step 2 Write down binary 0s after the binary 1s until you have written down a 32-bit number.

Step 3 Convert this binary number, *8 bits at a time*, to decimal, to create a dotted decimal number; this value is the dotted decimal version of the subnet mask.

For example, with a /20 prefix, you would first write:

11111111 11111111 1111

Then, you would write binary 0s, to complete the 32-bit number, as follows:

11111111 11111111 111**10000 00000000**

At the third step, you would convert this number, 8 bits at a time, back to decimal, resulting in a dotted decimal mask of 255.255.240.0.

Decimal Process to Convert Between Dotted Decimal and Prefix Notation

The binary process for converting masks between dotted decimal format and prefix format is relatively easy, particularly once you can do the binary/decimal conversions quickly. However, due to the time pressure on the exam, practice that process until you can do it quickly. Some people might be able to work more quickly using a decimal shortcut, so this section describes a shortcut. In either case, you should practice using either binary or the decimal process listed here until you can find the answer quickly, and with confidence.

The decimal processes assume you have access to the information in Table 12-9. This table lists the nine possible decimal numbers that can be used in a subnet mask, along with the binary equivalent. And just to make it obvious, the table also lists the number of binary 0s and binary 1s in the binary version of these decimal numbers.

Table 12-9 *Nine Possible Decimal Numbers in a Subnet Mask*

Key Topic

Subnet Mask's Decimal Octet	Binary Equivalent	Number of Binary 1s	Number of Binary 0s
0	**00000000**	0	8
128	1**0000000**	1	7
192	11**000000**	2	6
224	111**00000**	3	5
240	1111**0000**	4	4
248	11111**000**	5	3
252	111111**00**	6	2
254	1111111**0**	7	1
255	11111111	8	0

For the exams, you will want to memorize the table. As it turns out, if you practice subnetting problems enough to get really good and fast, then you will probably end up memorizing the table as a side effect of all the practice. So, don't just sit and memorize— wait until you have practiced subnetting, and then decide if you really need to work on memorizing the table or not.

To convert a mask from dotted decimal to prefix format, use the following process:

Step 1 Start with a prefix value of 0.

Step 2 For each dotted decimal octet, add the number of binary 1s listed for that decimal value in Table 12-9.

Step 3 The prefix length is /x, where x is the sum calculated at Step 2.

For example, with a mask of 255.255.240.0 again, for Step 1, you start with a value of 0. At Step 2, you add the following:

Because of the first octet value of 255, add 8.

Because of the second octet value of 255, add 8.

Because of the third octet value of 240, add 4.

Because of the fourth octet value of 0, add 0.

The end result, 20, is the prefix length, written as /20.

Converting from prefix format to dotted decimal may be somewhat intuitive, but the written process is a bit more laborious than the previous process. The process refers to the prefix value as x; the process is as follows:

Step 1 Divide x by 8 (x/8), noting the number of times 8 fully goes into x (the dividend, represented as a d), and the number left over (the remainder, represented as an r).

Step 2 Write down d octets of value 255. (This in effect begins the mask with 8, 16, or 24 binary 1s.)

Step 3 For the next octet, find the decimal number that begins with r binary 1s, followed by all binary 0s. (Table 12-9 will be useful for this step.)

Step 4 For any remaining octets, write down a decimal 0.

The steps may not be so obvious as written, so an example can help. If the prefix length is 20, then at Step 1, 20/8 should be interpreted as "a dividend of 2, with a remainder of 4." At Step 2, you would write down two octets of decimal 255, as follows:

255.255

Then, for Step 3, you will find from Table 12-9 that decimal 240's binary equivalent begins with four binary 1s, so you would write down an octet of value 240:

255.255.**240**

For Step 4, you would complete the subnet mask, 255.255.240.0.

No matter whether you use the binary or decimal shortcut to make these conversions, you should practice until you can make the conversions quickly, confidently, and correctly. To that end, CD-only Appendix D lists some sample questions, with answers.

Practice Suggestions

Before moving on to the next major section, consider taking the time now to practice a few items from this section. First, pick at least one of the processes (binary or decimal) for converting between mask formats, and practice until you can quickly and easily find the right answer. To that end, you can use this chapter, the practice questions in (CD-ROM) Appendix D. Also, if you begin to think that you will want to use the binary process, use the Binary Game at the CCNA Prep Center to refine your skills.

> **NOTE**   For those of you using or intending to use Appendix E, the processes covered in this section are summarized in reference pages RP-1A and RP-1B in that appendix.

Now that the basic tools have been covered, the next section explains how to use these tools to understand and choose subnet masks.

Analyzing and Choosing Subnet Masks

The process of subnetting subdivides a *classful network*—a Class A, B, or C network—into smaller groups of addresses, called subnets. When an engineer designs an internetwork, the engineer often chooses to use a single subnet mask in a particular classful network. The choice of subnet mask revolves around some key design requirements—namely, the need for some number of subnets, and some number of hosts per subnet. The choice of subnet mask then defines how many subnets of that classful network can exist, and how many host addresses exist in each subnet, as well as the specific subnets.

The first part of this section examines how to analyze the meaning of subnet masks once some other network engineer has already chosen the classful network and mask used in an internetwork. The second part of this section describes how an engineer could go about choosing which subnet mask to use when designing a new internetwork. Note that in real life, the first task, analyzing the meaning of the mask someone else chose, is the more common task.

> **NOTE**   This section assumes a single mask in each classful network, a convention sometimes called *static length subnet masking (SLSM)*. The *ICND2 Official Exam Certification Guide* covers the details of an alternative, using different masks in a single classful network, called *variable-length subnet masking (VLSM)*.

Analyzing the Subnet Mask in an Existing Subnet Design

The engineer's choice of using a particular classful network, with a particular single subnet mask, determines the number of possible subnets and number of hosts per subnet. Based on the network number and subnet mask, you should be able to figure out how many network, subnet, and host bits are used with that subnetting scheme. From those facts, you can easily figure out how many hosts exist in the subnet and how many subnets you can create in that network using that subnet mask.

This section begins with a general discussion of how to analyze an IP subnetting design, particularly how to determine the number of network, subnet, and host bits used in the design. Then, the text describes two different formal processes to find these facts, one using binary math, and the other using decimal math. As usual, you should read about both, but you should practice one of these processes until it becomes second nature. Finally, this section ends with the description of how to find the number of possible subnets, and number of possible hosts per subnet.

The Three Parts: Network, Subnet, and Host

You have already learned that Class A, B, and C networks have 8, 16, or 24 bits in their network fields, respectively. Those rules do not change. You have also read that, without subnetting, Class A, B, and C addresses have 24, 16, or 8 bits in their host fields, respectively. With subnetting, the network part of the address does not shrink or change, but the host field shrinks to make room for the subnet field. So the key to answering these types of questions is to figure out how many host bits remain after the engineer has implemented subnetting by choosing a particular subnet mask. Then you can tell the size of the subnet field, with the rest of the answers following from those two facts.

The following facts tell you how to find the sizes of the network, subnet, and host parts of an IP address:

- The network part of the address is always defined by class rules.

- The host part of the address is always defined by the subnet mask. The number of binary 0s in the mask (always found at the end of the mask) defines the number of host bits in the host part of the address.

- The subnet part of the address is what is left over in the 32-bit address.

> **NOTE**   The preceding list assumes a classful approach to IP addressing, which can be useful for learning subnetting. However, a classless view of addressing, which combines the network and subnet fields into one field, can be used as well. For consistency, this chapter uses a classful view of addressing.

Table 12-10 shows an example, with the last three rows showing the analysis of the three parts of the IP address based on the three rules just listed. (If you have forgotten the ranges of values in the first octet for addresses in Class A, B, and C networks, refer to Table 12-2.)

Table 12-10 *First Example, with Rules for Learning the Network, Subnet, and Host Part Sizes*

Step	Example	Rules to Remember
Address	8.1.4.5	
Mask	255.255.0.0	
Number of Network Bits	8	Always defined by Class A, B, C
Number of Host Bits	16	Always defined as the number of binary 0s in the mask
Number of Subnet Bits	8	32 – (network size + host size)

This example has 8 network bits because the address is in a Class A network, 8.0.0.0. There are 16 host bits because 255.255.0.0 in binary has 16 binary 0s—the last 16 bits in the mask. (Feel free to convert this mask to binary as a related exercise.) The size of the subnet part of the address is what is left over, or 8 bits.

Two other examples with easy-to-convert masks might help your understanding. Consider address 130.4.102.1 with mask 255.255.255.0. First, 130.4.102.1 is in a Class B network, so there are 16 network bits. A subnet mask of 255.255.255.0 has only eight binary 0s, implying 8 host bits, which leaves 8 subnet bits in this case.

As another example, consider 199.1.1.100 with mask 255.255.255.0. This example does not even use subnetting! 199.1.1.100 is in a Class C network, which means that there are 24 network bits. The mask has eight binary 0s, yielding 8 host bits, with no bits remaining for the subnet part of the address. In fact, if you remembered that the default mask for Class C networks is 255.255.255.0, you might have already realized that no subnetting was being used in this example.

Binary Process: Finding the Number of Network, Subnet, and Host Bits

You probably can calculate the number of host bits easily if the mask uses only decimal 255s and 0s, because it is easy to remember that decimal 255 represents eight binary 1s and decimal 0 represents eight binary 0s. So, for every decimal 0 in the mask, there are 8 host bits. However, when the mask uses decimal values besides 0 and 255, deciphering the number of host bits is more difficult.

Examining the subnet masks in binary helps overcome the challenge because the binary mask directly defines the number of network and subnet bits combined, and the number of host bits, as follows:

- The mask's binary 1s define the combined network and subnet parts of the addresses.

- The mask's binary 0s define the host part of the addresses.

- The class rules define the size of the network part.

Applying these three facts to a binary mask allows you to easily find the size of the network, subnet, and host parts of addresses in a particular subnetting scheme. For example, consider the addresses and masks, including the binary versions of the masks, shown in Table 12-11.

Table 12-11 *Two Examples Using More-Challenging Masks*

Mask in Decimal	Mask in Binary
130.4.102.1, mask 255.255.252.0	1111 1111 1111 1111 1111 1100 0000 0000
199.1.1.100, mask 255.255.255.224	1111 1111 1111 1111 1111 1111 1110 0000

The number of host bits implied by a mask becomes more apparent after you convert the mask to binary. The first mask, 255.255.252.0, has ten binary 0s, implying a 10-bit host field. Because that mask is used with a Class B address (130.4.102.1), implying 16 network bits, there are 6 remaining subnet bits. In the second example, the mask has only five binary 0s, for 5 host bits. Because the mask is used with a Class C address, there are 24 network bits, leaving only 3 subnet bits.

The following list formalizes the steps you can take, in binary, to find the sizes of the network, subnet, and host parts of an address:

Step 1 Compare the first octet of the address to the table of Class A, B, C addresses; write down the number of network bits depending on the address class.

Step 2 Find the number of hosts bits by:

a. Converting the subnet mask to binary.

b. Counting the number of binary 0s in the mask.

Step 3 Calculate the number of subnet bits by subtracting the number of combined network and host bits from 32.

Decimal Process: Finding the Number of Network, Subnet, and Host Bits

It is very reasonable to use the binary process to find the number of network, subnet, and host bits in any IP address. With a little practice, and mastery of the binary/decimal conversion process, the process should be quick and painless. However, some people prefer processes that use more decimal math, and less binary math. To that end, this section briefly outlines an alternative decimal process, as follows:

Step 1 (Same as Step 1 in the binary process.) Compare the first octet of the address to the table of Class A, B, C addresses; write down the number of network bits depending on the address class.

Step 2 If the mask is in dotted decimal format, convert the mask to prefix format.

Step 3 To find the number of host bits, subtract the prefix length value from 32.

Step 4 (Same as Step 4 in the binary process.) Calculate the number of subnet bits by subtracting the number of combined network and host bits from 32.

The key to this process is that the mask in prefix format lists the number of binary 1s in the mask, so it is easy to figure out how many binary 0s are in the mask. For example, a mask of 255.255.224.0, converted to prefix format, is /19. Knowing that the mask has 32 bits in it, and knowing that /19 means "19 binary 1s," you can easily calculate the number of binary 0s as 32 − 19 = 13 host bits. The rest of the process follows the same logic used in the binary process, but these steps do not require any binary math.

Determining the Number of Subnets and Number of Hosts Per Subnet

Both in real networking jobs and for the exams, you should be able to answer questions such as the following:

Given an address (or classful network number), and a single subnet mask that is used throughout the classful network, how many subnets could exist in that classful network? And how many hosts are there in each subnet?

Two simple formulas provide the answers. If you consider the number of subnet bits to be s, and the number of host bits to be h, the following formulas provide the answers:

Number of subnets = 2^s

Number of hosts per subnet = $2^h - 2$

Both formulas are based on the fact that to calculate the number of things that can be numbered using a binary number, you take 2 to the power of the number of bits used. For example, with 3 bits, you can create $2^3 = 8$ unique binary numbers: 000, 001, 010, 011, 100, 101, 110, and 111.

IP addressing conventions reserve two IP addresses per subnet: the first/smallest number (which has all binary 0s in the host field) and the last/largest number (which has all binary 1s in the host field). The smallest number is used as the subnet number, and the largest number is used as the subnet broadcast address. Because these numbers cannot be assigned to a host to use as an IP address, the formula to calculate the number of hosts per subnet includes the "minus 2."

Number of Subnets: Subtract 2, or Not?

Before seeing more of the math, this chapter needs to explain a bit of related information about which math to use when calculating the number of possible subnets. In some cases, two of the subnets in a single classful IP network are reserved, and should not be used. In other cases, these two subnets are not reserved, and can be used. This section describes these two subnets, and explains when they can be used, and when they cannot be used.

The first of the two possibly reserved subnets in a network is called the *zero subnet*, or *subnet zero*. Of all the subnets of the classful network, it has the smallest numeric value. The subnet number of the zero subnet also happens to always be the exact same number as the classful network number itself. For example, for Class B network 150.150.0.0, the zero subnet number would be 150.150.0.0—which creates a bit of ambiguity at first glance. This ambiguity is one of the reasons that the zero subnet was first reserved.

The other of the two possibly reserved subnets is called the *broadcast subnet*. It is the largest numeric subnet number in a network. The reason why this subnet was not used at one point in time relates to the fact that this subnet's broadcast address—used to send one packet to all hosts in the subnet—happens to be the same number as the network-wide broadcast address. For example, a packet sent to address 150.150.255.255 might mean "send this packet to all hosts in Class B network 150.150.0.0," but in other cases mean that the packet should be delivered to just all the hosts in a single subnet. This ambiguity in the meaning of a broadcast address is the reason why such subnets were avoided.

To succeed in real networking jobs and on the exams, you need to be able to determine when a zero subnet and broadcast subnet can be used. If allowed, the formula for the number of subnets is 2^s, where s is the number of subnet bits; if not allowed, the formula for the number of subnets is $2^s - 2$, which essentially does not count these two special subnets. Also, the exams might ask you to pick subnets to use, and part of that question might require you to figure out which subnets are zero subnets and broadcast subnets, and to know if these should be used.

For the exams, three main factors dictate when you can use these two subnets, and when you cannot. First, if the routing protocol is classless, use these two subnets, but if the routing protocol is classful, do not use these two subnets. (Chapter 14, "Routing Protocol Concepts and Configuration," explains the terms classless routing protocol and classful routing protocol; the details are not important for now.) Additionally, if the question uses VLSM—the practice of using different masks in the same classful network—then the two special subnets are allowed.

The third factor that defines whether the two special subnets should be used is based on a global configuration command: **ip subnet zero**. If configured, this command tells the router that an IP address in a zero subnet can be configured on an interface. If the opposite is configured—the **no ip subnet zero** command—then an IP address in a zero subnet cannot be configured. Note that the **ip subnet zero** command is a default setting in Cisco IOS, meaning that IOS allows the zero subnet by default. So, if the **ip subnet zero** command is configured, or not listed, then the zero subnet and the other special subnet, the broadcast subnet, are both allowed.

For the exams, any time that the zero subnet or broadcast subnet may impact the answer to the question, use the information in Table 12-12 to help you decide whether to allow these two special subnets.

Table 12-12 *When to Use Which Formula for the Number of Subnets*

Use the $2^s - 2$ formula, and avoid the zero and broadcast subnet, if...	Use the 2^s formula, and use the zero and broadcast subnet, if...
Classful routing protocol	Classless routing protocol
RIP Version 1 or IGRP as the routing protocol	RIP Version 2, EIGRP, or OSPF as the routing protocol
The **no ip subnet zero** command is configured	The **ip subnet zero** command is configured or omitted (default)
	VLSM is used
	No other clues provided

Of particular importance, for the CCNA exams, if a question simply does not give any clues as to whether to allow these two special subnets or not, assume you can use these subnets, and use the 2^s formula.

Now, back to the core purpose of this chapter. The remainder of the chapter will assume that these two special subnets can be used, but it will also point out how to identify these two special subnets to prepare you for the exam.

Practice Examples for Analyzing Subnet Masks

This chapter will use five different IP addresses and masks as examples for various parts of the subnetting analysis. For practice right now, go ahead and determine the number of network, subnet, and host bits, and the number of subnets and the number of hosts per subnet, for each of the following five example problems:

- 8.1.4.5/16

- 130.4.102.1/24

- 199.1.1.100/24

- 130.4.102.1/22

- 199.1.1.100/27

Table 12-13 lists the answers for reference.

Table 12-13   *Five Examples of Addresses/Masks, with the Number of Network, Subnet, and Host Bits*

Address	8.1.4.5/16	130.4.102.1/24	199.1.1.100/24	130.4.102.1/22	199.1.1.100/27
Mask	255.255.0.0	255.255.255.0	255.255.255.0	255.255.252.0	255.255.255.224
Number of Network Bits	8	16	24	16	24
Number of Host Bits	16	8	8	10	5
Number of Subnet Bits	8	8	0	6	3
Number of Hosts Per Subnet	$2^{16} - 2$, or 65,534	$2^8 - 2$, or 254	$2^8 - 2$, or 254	$2^{10} - 2$, or 1022	$2^5 - 2$, or 30
Number of Subnets	2^8, or 256	2^8, or 256	0	2^6, or 64	2^3, or 8

Choosing a Subnet Mask that Meets Design Requirements

This chapter's previous discussions about subnet masks assumed that an engineer had already chosen the subnet mask. However, someone has to choose which mask to use. This section describes the concepts related to choosing an appropriate subnet mask, based on a set of design requirements.

When a network engineer designs a new internetwork, the engineer must choose a subnet mask to use, based on the requirements for the new internetwork. The mask needs to define enough host and subnet bits so that the design allows for enough hosts in each subnet (based on the $2^h - 2$ formula) and enough different subnets (based on the 2^s or the $2^s - 2$ formula, depending on whether the zero and broadcast subnets can be used). The exams might test this same skill, asking questions like this:

> You are using Class B network X, and you need 200 subnets, with at most 200 hosts per subnet. Which of the following subnet masks can you use? (This is followed by some subnet masks from which you choose the answer.)

> **NOTE**   The questions may not be that straightforward, but still ask that you do the same reasoning to find the answers.

To find the correct answers to these types of questions, you first need to decide how many subnet bits and host bits you need to meet the requirements. Basically, the number of hosts per subnet is $2^h - 2$, where h is the number of host bits as defined by the subnet mask. Likewise, the number of subnets in a network, assuming that the same subnet mask is used all over the network, is 2^s, but with s being the number of subnet bits. Alternately, if the question implies that the two special subnets (zero subnet and broadcast subnet) should not be used, you would use the $2^s - 2$ formula. As soon as you know how many subnet bits and host bits are required, you can figure out what mask or masks meet the stated design goals in the question.

In some cases, the design requirements only allow for a single possible subnet mask, whereas in other cases, several masks may meet the design requirements. The next section shows an example for which only one possible mask could be used, followed by a section that uses an example where multiple masks meet the design requirements.

Finding the Only Possible Mask

Next, consider the following question, which happens to lead you to only one possible subnet mask that meets the requirements:

> Your network can use Class B network 130.1.0.0. What subnet masks meet the requirement that you plan to allow at most 200 subnets, with at most 200 hosts per subnet?

First you need to figure out how many subnet bits allow for 200 subnets. You can use the formula 2^s and plug in values for s until one of the numbers is at least 200. In this case, s turns out to be 8, because $2^7 = 128$, which is not enough subnets, but $2^8 = 256$, which provides enough subnets. In other words, you need at least 8 subnet bits to allow for 200 subnets.

Similarly, to find the number of required host bits, plug in values for h in the formula $2^h - 2$ until you find the smallest value of h that results in a value of 200 or more. In this case, $h = 8$.

If you do not want to keep plugging values into the formulas based on 2^x, you can instead memorize Table 12-14.

Table 12-14 *Maximum Number of Subnets/Hosts*

Number of Bits in the Host or Subnet Field	Maximum Number of Hosts ($2^h - 2$)	Maximum Number of Subnets (2^s)
1	0	2
2	2	4
3	6	8
4	14	16
5	30	32
6	62	64
7	126	128
8	254	256
9	510	512
10	1022	1024
11	2046	2048
12	4094	4096
13	8190	8192
14	16,382	16,384

As you can see, if you already have the powers of 2 memorized, you really do not need to memorize the table—just remember the formulas.

Continuing this same example with Class B network 130.1.0.0, you need to decide what mask(s) to use, knowing that you must have at least 8 subnet bits and 8 host bits to meet the design requirements. In this case, because the network is a Class B network, you know you will have 16 network bits. Using the letter *N* to represent network bits, the letter *S* to represent subnet bits, and the letter *H* to represent host bits, the following shows the sizes of the various fields in the subnet mask:

NNNNNNNN NNNNNNNN SSSSSSSS HHHHHHHH

In this example, because there are 16 network bits, 8 subnet bits, and 8 host bits already defined, you have already allocated all 32 bits of the address structure. Therefore, only one possible subnet mask works. To figure out the mask, you need to write down the 32-bit subnet mask, applying the following fact and subnet masks:

> The network and subnet bits in a subnet mask are, by definition, all binary 1s. Similarly, the host bits in a subnet mask are, by definition, all binary 0s.

So, the only valid subnet mask, in binary, is

11111111 11111111 11111111 00000000

When converted to decimal, this is 255.255.255.0, or /24 in prefix format.

Finding Multiple Possible Masks

In some cases, more than one mask may meet the design requirements. This section shows an example, with some ideas about how to find all the possible subnet masks. This section also uses an example question, in this case with multiple subnet masks meeting the criteria, as follows:

> Your internetwork design calls for 50 subnets, with the largest subnet having 200 hosts. The internetwork uses a class B network, and will not get any larger. What subnet masks meet these requirements?

For this design, you need 16 network bits, because the design uses a Class B network. You need at least 8 host bits, because $2^7 - 2 = 126$ (not enough), but $2^8 - 2 = 254$, which does provide enough hosts per subnet. Similarly, you now need only 6 subnet bits, because 6 subnet bits allows for 2^6, or 64, subnets, whereas 5 subnet bits only allows for 32 subnets.

If you follow the same process of noting network, subnet, and host bits with the letters N, S, and H, you get the following format:

NNNNNNNN NNNNNNNN SSSSSS_ _ HHHHHHHH

This format represents the minimum number of network (16), subnet (6), and host (8) bits. However, it leaves 2 bit positions empty, namely, the last 2 bits in the third octet. For these bit positions, write an **X** for "wildcard" bits—bits that can be either subnet or host bits. In this example:

NNNNNNNN NNNNNNNN SSSSSS**XX** HHHHHHHH

The wildcard bits, shown as **X** in the structure, can be either subnet or host bits, while still meeting the design requirements. In this case, there are 2 bits, so you might think that four possible answers exist; however, only three valid answers exist, because of a very important fact about subnet masks:

> All masks must start with one unbroken consecutive string of binary 1s, followed by one unbroken consecutive string of binary 0s.

This statement makes more sense by applying the concept to a particular example. Continuing the same example, the following list includes the three correct answers, all of which show consecutive 1s and 0s. The list also includes one invalid combination of wildcard bits—an answer which shows nonconsecutive binary 1s and 0s. Note that the wildcard bits (the bits that could either be subnet bits or host bits) are shown in bold.

11111111 11111111 11111111 00000000 (8 subnet, 8 host)

11111111 11111111 11111110 00000000 (7 subnet, 9 host)

11111111 11111111 11111100 00000000 (6 subnet, 10 host)

11111111 11111111 11111101 00000000 illegal (nonconsecutive 1s)

The first three lines maintain the requirement of an unbroken string of binary 1s followed by one unbroken string of binary 0s. However, the last line in the list shows 22 binary 1s, then a binary 0, followed by another binary 1, which makes this value illegal for use as a subnet mask.

The final answer to this problem is to list the three valid subnet masks in decimal or prefix format, as follows:

255.255.255.0   /24   8 subnet bits, 8 host bits

255.255.254.0   /23   7 subnet bits, 9 host bits

255.255.252.0   /22   6 subnet bits, 10 host bits

Choosing the Mask that Maximizes the Number of Subnets or Hosts

Finally, on the exams, a question might ask you to find the subnet mask that meets the stated requirements, but either maximizes or minimizes the number of subnets. Alternately, the question might ask that you pick the mask that either maximizes or minimizes the number of hosts per subnet. To pick among the various subnet masks, simply keep the following in mind when comparing the multiple masks that meet the stated design requirements:

- **The mask with the most subnet bits:** The mask for which the wildcard bits were set to binary 1, thereby making the subnet part of the addresses larger, maximizes the number of subnets and minimizes the number of hosts per subnet.

- **The mask with the most host bits:** The mask for which the wildcard bits were set to binary 0, thereby making the host part of the addresses larger, maximizes the number of hosts per subnet and minimizes the number of subnets.

Completing this same example, with three possible masks, mask 255.255.255.0 (/24)—with 8 subnet bits and 8 host bits—both maximizes the number of subnets and minimizes the number of hosts per subnet (while still meeting the design requirements). Conversely, the mask of 255.255.252.0 (/22)—with 6 subnet bits and 10 host bits—maximizes the number of hosts per subnet and minimizes the number of subnets, again while still meeting the design requirements.

For reference, the following list summarizes the steps to choose a new subnet mask, based on a set of requirements, assuming that the zero and broadcast subnet can be used.

Step 1 Find the number of network bits (N) based on Class A, B, C rules.

Step 2 Find the number of subnet bits (S) based on the formula 2^s, such that 2^s => the required number of subnets.

Step 3 Find the number of host bits (H) based on the formula $2^h - 2$, such that $2^h - 2$ => the required number of hosts per subnet.

Step 4 Write down, starting on the left, N + S binary 1s.

Step 5 Write down, starting on the right, H binary 0s.

Step 6 If the number of binary 1s and 0s together adds up to less than 32:

   a. Fill in the remaining "wildcard" bit positions—between the binary 1s and 0s—with the letter X.

   b. Find all combinations of bits for the wildcard bit positions that meet the requirements for only having one consecutive string of binary 1s in the binary mask.

Step 7 Convert the mask(s) to decimal or prefix format as appropriate.

Step 8 To find the mask that maximizes the number of subnets, pick the mask that has the most binary 1s in it. To find the mask that maximizes the number of hosts per subnet, pick the mask that has the largest number of binary 0s in it.

Practice Suggestions

Before moving on to the next major section, take a few moments and practice the processes covered in this section. In particular:

- Refer to Appendix E, specifically the following processes, which summarize the processes covered in this section:

  — RP-2: Analyzing Unsubnetted IP Addresses

  — RP-3A: Analyzing an Existing Subnet Mask: Binary Version

  — RP-3B: Analyzing an Existing Subnet Mask: Decimal Version

  — RP-4: Choosing a Subnet Mask

- Do the following problem sets from Appendix D:

  — Problem Set 2, which covers how to analyze an unsubnetted IP address

  — Problem Set 3, which covers how to analyze the meaning of an existing subnet mask

  — Problem Set 4, which covers how to choose a new subnet mask to use

You should practice these problems until you can look at a given IP network and mask and determine the number of hosts per subnet, and the number of subnets, in around 15 seconds. You should also practice the design-oriented process of choosing a new subnet mask, given an IP network and a set of requirements for the number of hosts and subnets, within about 30 seconds. (These timings are admittedly subjective and are meant to give you a goal to help reduce the time pressure you may feel on exam day.)

Analyzing Existing Subnets

One of the most common subnetting-related tasks—both in real networking jobs and for the exams—is to analyze and understand some key facts about existing subnets. You might be given an IP address and subnet mask, and you need to then answer questions about the subnet in which the address resides—sometimes referred to as the *resident subnet*. The question might be straightforward, like "What is the subnet number in which the address resides?" or it might be more subtle, like "Which of the following IP addresses are in the same subnet as the stated address?" In either case, if you can dissect an IP address as described in this chapter, you can answer any variation on this type of question.

This section describes how to find three key facts about any subnet, once you know an IP address and subnet mask for a host in that subnet:

- The subnet number (subnet address)

- The subnet broadcast address for that subnet

- The range of usable IP addresses in that subnet

This section begins by showing how to use binary-based processes to find all three of these facts about a subnet. Following that, the text describes a decimal-based process that helps you find the same answers, but with a little practice, the decimal-based process will help you find these answers much more quickly.

Finding the Subnet Number: Binary

A *subnet number*, or *subnet address*, is a dotted decimal number that represents a subnet. You most often see subnet numbers in written documentation and in routers' routing tables. Each subnet might contain hundreds of consecutively numbered IP addresses, but a router typically represents that range of IP addresses as a subnet number and mask in its IP routing table. Listing the subnet number and mask in the routing table allows a router to concisely refer to the subnet—a consecutive range of IP addresses—without requiring a routing table entry for every individual host address.

Earlier in this chapter, you learned that computers perform a Boolean AND of an IP address and mask to find the resident subnet number. Humans can certainly use the same process, formalized as follows:

Step 1 Convert the IP address from decimal to binary.

Step 2 Convert the subnet mask to binary, writing this number down below the IP address from Step 1.

Step 3 Perform a bitwise Boolean AND of the two numbers. To do so:

a. AND the first bit of the address with the first bit of the subnet mask, recording the result below those numbers.

b. AND the second bit of each number, recording the result below those numbers.

c. Repeat for each pair of bits, resulting in a 32-bit binary number.

Step 4 Convert the resulting binary number, *8 bits at a time*, back to decimal. This value is the subnet number.

Key
Topic

Tables 12-15 through 12-19 show the results of all four steps, for five different examples. The tables include the binary version of the address and mask and the results of the Boolean AND.

Table 12-15 *Boolean AND Calculation for the Subnet with Address 8.1.4.5, Mask 255.255.0.0*

Address	8.1.4.5	00001000 00000001 00000100 00000101
Mask	255.255.0.0	11111111 11111111 **00000000 00000000**
AND Result	8.1.0.0	00001000 00000001 00000000 00000000

Table 12-16 *Boolean AND Calculation for the Subnet with Address 130.4.102.1, Mask 255.255.255.0*

Address	130.4.102.1	10000010 00000100 01100110 00000001
Mask	255.255.255.0	11111111 11111111 11111111 **00000000**
AND Result	130.4.102.0	10000010 00000100 01100110 00000000

Table 12-17 *Boolean AND Calculation for the Subnet with Address 199.1.1.100, Mask 255.255.255.0*

Address	199.1.1.100	11000111 00000001 00000001 01100100
Mask	255.255.255.0	11111111 11111111 11111111 **00000000**
AND Result	199.1.1.0	11000111 00000001 00000001 00000000

Table 12-18 *Boolean AND Calculation for the Subnet with Address 130.4.102.1, Mask 255.255.252.0*

Address	130.4.102.1	10000010 00000100 01100110 00000001
Mask	255.255.252.0	11111111 11111111 111111**00 00000000**
AND Result	130.4.100.0	10000010 00000100 01100100 00000000

Table 12-19 *Boolean AND Calculation for the Subnet with Address 199.1.1.100, Mask 255.255.255.224*

Address	199.1.1.100	11000111 00000001 00000001 01100100
Mask	255.255.255.224	11111111 11111111 11111111 111**00000**
AND Result	199.1.1.96	11000111 00000001 00000001 01100000

The last step in the formalized process—converting the binary number back to decimal—causes problems for many people new to subnetting. The confusion typically arises when the boundary between the subnet and host part of the address is in the middle of a byte, which occurs when the subnet mask has a value besides 0 or 255 decimal. For example, with 130.4.102.1, mask 255.255.252.0 (Table 12-18), the first 6 bits of the third octet comprise the subnet field, and the last 2 bits of the third octet, plus the entire fourth octet, comprise the host field. Because of these facts, some people convert the 6-bit subnet part from binary to decimal, and then they convert the 10-bit host part to decimal. However, when converting binary to decimal, to find the dotted decimal IP address, you always convert the entire octet—even if part of the octet is in the subnet part of the address and part is in the host part of the address.

So, in the example shown in Table 12-18, the subnet number (130.4.100.0) in binary is 1000 0010 0000 0100 **0110 0100** 0000 0000. The entire third octet is shown in bold, which converts to 100 in decimal. When you convert the whole number, each set of 8 bits is converted to decimal, giving you 130.4.100.0.

Finding the Subnet Number: Binary Shortcut

Even if you tend to prefer the binary processes for subnetting, you might still find it a bit laborious to convert two dotted decimal numbers to binary, do the Boolean AND for 32 bits, and then convert the result back into dotted decimal. However, as you practice this process, you should start to notice some important trends, which can help you optimize and simplify the binary process. This section specifically notes these trends and shows how you can reduce the Boolean AND process down to a single octet's worth of effort.

First, think about each octet separately. Any single octet of any IP address, when ANDed with a string of eight binary 1s from the mask, yields the same number you started with in the address. Of course, when the mask has an octet of value decimal 255, that number represents eight binary 1s. As a result, for any octet in which the mask shows a decimal value of 255, the result of the Boolean AND leaves the IP address's corresponding octet unchanged.

For example, the first octet of the example in Table 12-19 (199.1.1.100, mask 255.255.255.224) has an IP address value of 199, with a mask value of 255. After converting the IP address value of decimal 199 to binary 11000111, and the mask value of decimal 255 to binary 11111111, and ANDing the two numbers, you still end up with 11000111—or decimal 199. So, although you can convert the whole IP address and mask to binary, for any mask octets of value 255, you can almost ignore that octet, knowing that the subnet number matches the original IP address for this octet.

Similarly, as you consider each octet separately again, you will notice that any IP address octet, ANDed with eight binary 0s, yields an octet of eight binary 0s. Of course, a mask octet of value decimal 0 represents eight binary 0s. As a result, for any octet in which the mask shows a value of decimal 0, the result of the Boolean AND is a decimal 0.

For example, in Table 12-15 (8.1.4.5, mask 255.255.0.0), the last octet has an IP address value of decimal 5, or 00000101 in binary. The fourth octet of the mask has a value of decimal 0, or binary 00000000. The Boolean AND for that octet yields a value of all binary 0s, or decimal 0.

These two facts may help you start developing a few shortcuts of your own. Summarizing, if you want to find the resident subnet by using an AND on the IP address and mask, you could follow this shortcut:

Step 1 Record the decimal mask in the first row of a table and the decimal IP address in the second row.

Step 2 For any mask octets of value decimal 255, copy the IP address's octet value for the same octet of the decimal subnet number.

Step 3 Similarly, for any mask octets of value decimal 0, write down a decimal 0 for the same octet of the subnet number.

Step 4 If the subnet number still has one remaining octet to be filled in, do the following for that one octet:

   a. Convert that one remaining octet of the IP address to binary.

   b. Convert that one remaining octet of the mask to binary.

   c. AND the two 8-bit numbers together.

   d. Convert the 8-bit number to decimal, and place that value in the one remaining octet of the subnet number.

Using this logic, when the mask only has 255s and 0s in it, you can find the subnet number without any binary math. In other cases, you can find three of the four octets easily, and then just Boolean AND the address and mask values for the remaining octet, to complete the subnet number.

Finding the Subnet Broadcast Address: Binary

The subnet broadcast address, sometimes called the *directed broadcast address*, can be used to send a packet to every device in a single subnet. For example, subnet 8.1.4.0/24 has a subnet broadcast address of 8.1.4.255. A packet sent to a destination address of 8.1.4.255 will be forwarded across the internetwork, until it reaches a router connected to that subnet. That final router, when forwarding the packet onto the subnet, encapsulates the packet in a data-link broadcast frame. For instance, if this subnet existed on an Ethernet LAN, the packet would be forwarded inside an Ethernet frame with a destination Ethernet address of FFFF.FFFF.FFFF.

Although interesting as an end to itself, a more interesting use for the subnet broadcast address today is that it helps you more easily calculate the largest valid IP address in the subnet, which is an important part of answering subnetting questions. The next section, "Finding the Range of Valid IP Addresses in a Subnet," explains the details. By definition, a subnet's broadcast address has the same value as the subnet number in the network and subnet parts of the address, but all binary 1s in the host part of the broadcast address.

(The subnet number, by definition, happens to have all binary 0s in the host part.) In other words, the subnet number is the lower end of the range of addresses, and the subnet broadcast address is the high end of the range.

There is a binary math operation to calculate the subnet broadcast address based on the subnet number, but there is a much easier process for humans, especially if you already have the subnet number in binary:

> To calculate the subnet broadcast address, if you already know the binary version of the subnet number, change all the host bit values in the subnet number to binary 1s.

You already know how to identify the host bits, based on the mask's bits of value binary 0. You can examine the simple math behind calculating the subnet broadcast address in Tables 12-20 through 12-24. The host parts of the addresses, masks, subnet numbers, and broadcast addresses are in bold.

Table 12-20 *Calculating the Broadcast Address: Address 8.1.4.5, Mask 255.255.0.0*

Address	8.1.4.5	00001000 00000001 **00000100 00000101**
Mask	255.255.0.0	11111111 11111111 **00000000 00000000**
AND Result	8.1.0.0	00001000 00000001 **00000000 00000000**
Broadcast	8.1.255.255	00001000 00000001 **11111111 11111111**

Table 12-21 *Calculating the Broadcast Address: Address 130.4.102.1, Mask 255.255.255.0*

Address	130.4.102.1	10000010 00000100 01100110 **00000001**
Mask	255.255.255.0	11111111 11111111 11111111 **00000000**
AND Result	130.4.102.0	10000010 00000100 01100110 **00000000**
Broadcast	130.4.102.255	10000010 00000100 01100110 **11111111**

Table 12-22 *Calculating the Broadcast Address: Address 199.1.1.100, Mask 255.255.255.0*

Address	199.1.1.100	11000111 00000001 00000001 **01100100**
Mask	255.255.255.0	11111111 11111111 11111111 **00000000**
AND Result	199.1.1.0	11000111 00000001 00000001 **00000000**
Broadcast	199.1.1.255	11000111 00000001 00000001 **11111111**

Table 12-23 *Calculating the Broadcast Address: Address 130.4.102.1, Mask 255.255.252.0*

Address	130.4.102.1	10000010 00000100 01100110 00000001
Mask	255.255.252.0	11111111 11111111 11111100 00000000
AND Result	130.4.100.0	10000010 00000100 01100100 00000000
Broadcast	130.4.103.255	10000010 00000100 01100111 11111111

Table 12-24 *Calculating the Broadcast Address: Address 199.1.1.100, Mask 255.255.255.224*

Address	199.1.1.100	11000111 00000001 00000001 01100100
Mask	255.255.255.224	11111111 11111111 11111111 11100000
AND Result	199.1.1.96	11000111 00000001 00000001 01100000
Broadcast	199.1.1.127	11000111 00000001 00000001 01111111

By examining the subnet broadcast addresses in binary, you can see that they are identical to the subnet numbers, except that all host bits have a value of binary 1 instead of binary 0. (Look for the bold digits in the examples.)

> **NOTE**   In case you want to know the Boolean math, to derive the broadcast address, start with the subnet number and mask in binary. Invert the mask (change all the 1s to 0s and all the 0s to 1s), and then do a bitwise Boolean OR between the two 32-bit numbers. (An OR yields a 0 when both bits are 0 and yields a 1 in any other case.) The result is the subnet broadcast address.

For reference, the following process summarizes the concepts described in this section for how to find the subnet broadcast address:

Step 1   Write down the subnet number (or IP address), and subnet mask, in binary form. Make sure that the binary digits line up directly on top of the other.

Step 2   Separate the host part of these numbers from the network/subnet part by drawing a vertical line. Place this line between the rightmost binary 1 in the mask and the leftmost binary 0. Extend this line up and down an inch or two.

Step 3   To find the subnet broadcast address, in binary:

   a. Copy the bits of the subnet number (or IP address) that are to the left of the vertical line.

b. Write down binary 1s for the bits to the right of the vertical line.

Step 4 Convert the 32-bit binary subnet broadcast address to decimal, 8 bits at a time, ignoring the vertical line.

Finding the Range of Valid IP Addresses in a Subnet

You also need to be able to figure out which IP addresses are in a particular subnet and which are not. You already know how to do the hard part of finding that answer. In every subnet, two numbers are reserved and cannot be used as IP addresses by hosts: the subnet number itself and the subnet broadcast address. The subnet number is the numerically smallest number in the subnet, and the broadcast address is the numerically largest number. So, the range of valid IP addresses starts with the IP address that is 1 more than the subnet number, and ends with the IP address that is 1 less than the broadcast address. It is that simple.

Here is a formal definition of the "algorithm" to find the first and last IP addresses in a subnet when you know the subnet number and broadcast addresses:

Step 1 To find the first IP address, copy the subnet number, but add 1 to the *fourth octet*.

Key
Topic

Step 2 To find the last IP address, copy the subnet broadcast address, but subtract 1 from the *fourth octet*.

The math for this process is pretty obvious; however, take care to add 1 (Step 1) and subtract 1 (Step 2) only in the fourth octet—no matter what the class of network and no matter what subnet mask is used. Tables 12-25 through 12-29 summarize the answers for the five examples used throughout this chapter.

Table 12-25 *Subnet Chart: 8.1.4.5/255.255.0.0*

Octet	1	2	3	4
Address	8	1	4	5
Mask	255	255	0	0
Subnet Number	8	1	0	0
First Address	8	1	0	1
Broadcast	8	1	255	255
Last Address	8	1	255	254

Table 12-26   *Subnet Chart: 130.4.102.1/255.255.255.0*

Octet	1	2	3	4
Address	130	4	102	1
Mask	255	255	255	0
Subnet Number	130	4	102	0
First Address	130	4	102	1
Broadcast	130	4	102	255
Last Address	130	4	102	254

Table 12-27   *Subnet Chart: 199.1.1.100/255.255.255.0*

Octet	1	2	3	4
Address	199	1	1	100
Mask	255	255	255	0
Subnet Number	199	1	1	0
First Address	199	1	1	1
Broadcast	199	1	1	255
Last Address	199	1	1	254

Table 12-28   *Subnet Chart: 130. 4.102.1/255.255.252.0*

Octet	1	2	3	4
Address	130	4	102	1
Mask	255	255	252	0
Subnet Number	130	4	100	0
First Address	130	4	100	1
Broadcast	130	4	103	255
Last Address	130	4	103	254

Table 12-29   *Subnet Chart: 199.1.1.100/255.255.255.224*

Octet	1	2	3	4
Address	199	1	1	100
Mask	255	255	255	224
Subnet Number	199	1	1	96
First Address	199	1	1	97
Broadcast	199	1	1	127
Last Address	199	1	1	126

Finding the Subnet, Broadcast Address, and Range of Addresses: Decimal Process

Using the binary math required to find the subnet number and broadcast address forces you to think about subnetting, which really does help you understand subnetting better. However, many people feel too much time pressure on the exam when they have to do a lot of binary math. This section describes some decimal processes for finding the subnet number and subnet broadcast address. From there, you can easily find the range of assignable addresses in the subnet, as described in the previous section.

Decimal Process with Easy Masks

Of all the possible subnet masks, only three masks—255.0.0.0, 255.255.0.0, and 255.255.255.0—use only 255s and 0s. I call these masks "easy masks" because you can find the subnet number and broadcast address easily, without any real math tricks. In fact, many people intuitively see how to find the answers with easy masks, so feel free to skip to the next section, "Decimal Process with Difficult Masks," if you already see how to find the subnet number and broadcast address.

Of these three easy masks, 255.0.0.0 does not cause any subnetting. Therefore, this section describes only how to use the two easy masks that can be used for subnetting—255.255.0.0 and 255.255.255.0.

The process is simple. To find the subnet number when given an IP address and a mask of 255.255.0.0 or 255.255.255.0, do the following:

Step 1   For each *subnet mask octet* of value 255, copy the *IP address* octet value.

Step 2   For the remaining octets, write down a 0.

Yes, it is that easy. Finding the subnet broadcast address is just as easy:

> Perform the same Step 1 as when finding the subnet number, but at Step 2, write down 255s instead of 0s.

As soon as you know the subnet number and broadcast address, you can easily find the first and last IP addresses in the subnet using the same simple logic covered earlier:

■ To find the first valid IP address in the subnet, copy the subnet number, but add 1 to the fourth octet.

■ To find the last valid IP address in the subnet, copy the broadcast address, but subtract 1 from the fourth octet.

Decimal Process with Difficult Masks

When the subnet mask is not 255.0.0.0, 255.255.0.0, or 255.255.255.0, I consider the mask to be difficult. Why is it difficult? Well, it is difficult only in that most people cannot easily derive the subnet number and broadcast address without using binary math.

You can always use the binary processes covered earlier in this chapter, all the time, whether the mask is easy or difficult—and consistently find the right answers. However, most people can find the correct answer much more quickly by spending some time practicing the decimal process described in this section.

The decimal process uses a table to help organize the problem, an example of which is found in Table 12-30. The text refers to this table as a *subnet chart*.

Table 12-30 *Generic Subnet Chart*

Octet	1	2	3	4
Mask				
Address				
Subnet Number				
First Address				
Last Address				
Broadcast Address				

The following steps list the formal process for finding the subnet number, using a decimal process, assuming a difficult mask is used.

Step 1 Write down the subnet mask in the first empty row of the subnet chart and the IP address in the second empty row.

Step 2   Find the octet for which the *subnet mask's value* is not 255 or 0. This octet is called the *interesting octet*. Draw a dark rectangle around the interesting octet's column of the table, top to bottom.

Step 3   Record the subnet number's value for the uninteresting octets, as follows:

    a. For each octet to the left of the rectangle drawn in Step 2: Copy the *IP address's* value in that same octet.

    b. For each octet to the right of the rectangle: Write down a decimal 0.

Step 4   At this point, the subnet number row of the subnet chart has three octets filled in, with only the interesting octet remaining. To find the subnet number's value for this interesting octet:

    a. Calculate the magic number by subtracting the *subnet mask's interesting octet value* from 256.

    b. Calculate the multiples of the magic number, starting at 0, up through 256.

    c. Find the subnet number's interesting octet's value, as follows: find the multiple of the magic number that is *closest to, but not greater than*, the IP address's interesting octet value.

As you can see, the process itself seems a bit detailed, but do not let the detail deter you from trying this process. The majority of the first three steps—other than drawing a rectangle around the interesting octet—use the same logic used with easy masks. The fourth step is detailed, but it can be learned, mastered, and forgotten once you see the decimal patterns behind subnetting. Also, note that you do not need to memorize the process as an end to itself. If you practice this process long enough to get good and fast at finding the right answer, then you will likely internalize the process to the point that you make the process your own, and then you can ignore the specific steps listed here.

The best way to understand this process is to see it in action. The DVD that comes with this book includes three video examples of how to use the process described here. This would be an excellent place to pause and at least watch subnetting video 1. Video 1 describes a full treatment of the process. You can also watch subnetting videos 2 and 3, which provide additional examples.

You can also learn the process just by reading the examples in this book. For example, consider 130.4.102.1, with mask 255.255.252.0. Because the third octet of the mask is not a 0 or 255, the third octet is where the interesting part of this decimal process takes place. For Step 1, you create a subnet chart and fill in the mask and address in the first two rows. For Step 2, just draw a rectangle around the third octet's column in the subnet chart. For Step 3, fill in the first two octets of the subnet number by copying the IP address's first two octets and writing a zero in the fourth octet. Table 12-31 shows the results of these steps.

Table 12-31 *Subnet Chart: 130.4.102.1/255.255.252.0, Through Step 3A*

Octet	1	2	3	4
Mask	255	255	252	0
Address	130	4	102	1
Subnet Number	130	4		0
First Address				
Last Address				
Broadcast Address				

The last (fourth) step is the only step that may seem a little odd, but at least it lets you use decimal math, and no binary, to find the subnet number. First you find what I call the "magic number": 256 minus the *mask's interesting octet*. In this case, the magic number is 256 – 252, or 4. Then you find the multiple of the magic number that is closest to the *address's interesting octet*, but less than or equal to it. In this example, 100 is a multiple of the magic number (4×25), and this multiple is less than or equal to 102. The next-higher multiple of the magic number, 104, is, of course, more than 102, so that is not the right number. So, to complete this example, simply plug in 100 for the third octet of the subnet number in Table 12-30.

As soon as you know the subnet number, you can easily find the first valid IP address in the subnet:

To find the first valid IP address in the subnet, copy the subnet number, but add 1 to the fourth octet.

That is all. Table 12-32 continues the same example, but with the subnet number and first valid IP address.

Table 12-32 *Subnet Chart: 130.4.102.1/255.255.252.0 with Subnet and First IP Address*

Octet	1	2	3	4	Comments
Mask	255	255	252	1	
Address	130	4	102	1	
Subnet Number	130	4	**100**	0	Magic number = 256 – 252 = 4; 100 is the multiple of 4 closest to, but not higher than, 102.
First Address	130	4	**100**	1	Add 1 to the subnet's last octet.
Last Address					
Broadcast Address					

Finding the Broadcast Address: Decimal

If you used the decimal process to find the subnet number, finding the subnet broadcast address using only decimal math is easy. Once you find the broadcast address, you already know how to find the last usable IP address in the subnet: You simply subtract 1 from the fourth octet of the broadcast address. To find the subnet broadcast address after finding the subnet number, assuming a difficult mask, use the following process:

Step 1   Fill in the subnet broadcast address octets to the left of the rectangle by copying the subnet number's same octets.

Step 2   Fill in the subnet broadcast address octets to the right of the rectangle with decimal 255s.

Step 3   Find the value for the interesting octet by adding the *subnet number's* value in the interesting octet to the *magic number, and subtract 1.*

The only possibly tricky part of the process again relates to the interesting octet. To fill in the interesting octet of the broadcast address, you again use the magic number. The magic number is 256 minus the mask's interesting octet. In this example, the magic number is 4 (256 – 252). Then you add the magic number to the interesting octet value of the subnet number and subtract 1. The result is the broadcast address's value in the interesting octet. In this case, the value is

100 (subnet number's third octet) + 4 (magic number) – 1 = 103.

Table 12-33 shows the completed answers, with annotations.

Table 12-33   *Subnet Chart: 130.4.102.1/255.255.252.0 Completed*

Octet	1	2	3	4	Comments
Mask	255	255	252	0	
Address	130	4	102	1	
Subnet Number	130	4	100	0	Magic number = 256 – 252 = 4. 4 × 25 = 100, the closest multiple <= 102.
First Address	130	4	100	1	Add 1 to the subnet's last octet.
Last Address	130	4	103	254	Subtract 1 from the broadcast address's fourth octet.
Broadcast	130	4	103	255	Subnet's interesting octet, plus the magic number, minus 1 (100 + 4 – 1).

> **NOTE**   Subnetting videos 4, 5, and 6 continue the examples shown in videos 1, 2, and 3, respectively, focusing on finding the broadcast address and range of valid addresses. If this process is not clear, take the time now to stop and watch the videos.

Summary of Decimal Processes to Find the Subnet, Broadcast, and Range

The entire process of dissecting IP addresses that use difficult masks is now complete. The following list summarizes the tasks in each step:

Key Topic

Step 1   Write down the subnet mask in the first empty row of the subnet chart and the IP address in the second empty row.

Step 2   Find the octet for which the *subnet mask's value* is not 255 or 0. This octet is called the *interesting octet*. Draw a dark rectangle around the interesting octet's column of the table, top to bottom.

Step 3   Record the subnet number's value for the uninteresting octets, as follows:

   a. For each octet to the left of the rectangle drawn in Step 2: Copy the *IP address's* value in that same octet.

   b. For each octet to the right of the rectangle: Write down a decimal 0.

Step 4   To find the subnet number's value for this interesting octet:

   a. Calculate the magic number by subtracting the *subnet mask's interesting octet value* from 256.

   b. Calculate the multiples of the magic number, starting at 0, up through 256.

   c. Write down the interesting octet's value, calculated as follows: Find the multiple of the magic number that is *closest to, but not greater than*, the IP address's interesting octet value.

Step 5   Find the subnet broadcast address, as follows:

   a. For each *subnet mask octet* to the left of the rectangle: Copy the *IP address* octet value.

   b. For each *subnet mask octet* to the right of the rectangle: Write down 255.

   c. Find the value for the interesting octet by adding the *subnet number's* value in the interesting octet to the *magic number, and subtract 1*.

Step 6   To find the first IP address, copy the decimal subnet number, but add 1 to the fourth octet.

Step 7   To find the last IP address, copy the decimal subnet broadcast address, but subtract 1 from the fourth octet.

> **NOTE**   For those of you using the subnetting reference pages in Appendix E, note that instead of the preceding seven-step process, RP-5C and RP-6C separate the process into two parts—one to find the subnet number (Steps 1–4 from the preceding list), and one to find the rest of the information (Steps 5–7 from the preceding list).

Practice Suggestions

Becoming proficient at both the binary and decimal processes to find the subnet number, broadcast address, and range of valid addresses takes some practice. The binary process is relatively straightforward, but requires conversions between binary and decimal. The decimal process has much easier math, but requires repetition to internalize the details of the many steps.

If you are using the decimal process, please practice it until you no longer think about the process as stated in this book. You should practice it until the concept is obvious, and second nature. It is the same idea as how you learn and master multiplication. For example, as an adult, multiplying 22 times 51 is simple enough that it would take you much longer to explain how to do it than to actually do it. Through practice, you should become equally familiar with the decimal process to find the subnet number.

Appendix D contains practice problems that ask you to find the subnet number, broadcast address, and range of addresses for a given IP address and mask. Regardless of whether you use binary or decimal processes, you should strive to be able to answer each problem within about 10–15 seconds after you have finished reading the problem.

The following list outlines the specific tools that may be useful for practicing the processes covered in this section:

■   Refer to Appendix E, specifically the following processes:

— RP-5A and RP-5A-shortcut, which focus on the binary process to find the subnet number

— RP-5B and RP-5C, which focus on the decimal process to find the subnet number

— RP-6A, which focuses on the binary process to find the broadcast address and range of addresses in a subnet

— RP-6B and RP-6C, which focus on the decimal process to find the broadcast address and range of addresses in a subnet

- Do Appendix D Problem Set 5, which includes 25 problems that require that you find the subnet number, broadcast address, and range of usable addresses in each subnet.

- For more practice, make up problems and check your answers using a subnet calculator.

The final major section of this chapter examines the processes by which a network engineer might choose a single subnet mask for a particular classful IP network and determine the subnets that can be used based on that design.

Design: Choosing the Subnets of a Classful Network

The final general type of IP addressing and subnetting question covered in this chapter asks you to list all the subnets of a particular classful network. You could use a long process that requires you to count in binary and convert many numbers from binary to decimal. However, because most people either learn the decimal shortcut or use a subnet calculator in their jobs, I decided to just show you the shortcut method for this particular type of question.

First, the question needs a better definition—or at least a more complete one. The question might be better stated like this:

> If the same subnet mask is used for all subnets of one Class A, B, or C network, what are the valid subnets?

This general type of question assumes that the internetwork uses static-length subnet masking (SLSM), although variable-length subnet masking (VLSM) may also be used. This chapter shows you how to approach questions using SLSM. Chapter 5, "VLSM and Route Summarization," in the *CCNA ICND2 Official Exam Certification Guide* examines this problem in light of VLSM.

The decimal process to find all subnets can be a bit wordy. To make learning a little easier, the text first shows the process with an additional constraint—the process as first explained here only works when there are fewer than 8 subnet bits. This assumption allows the wording in the formal process and upcoming examples to be a bit briefer. Then, once you know the process, the text will describe the more general cases.

Finding All Subnets with Fewer Than 8 Subnet Bits

The following easy decimal process lists all the valid subnets, assuming both that SLSM is used and that fewer than 8 subnet bits are used. First, the process uses another table or chart, called a list-all-subnets chart in this book. Like the subnet chart used earlier in this chapter, the chart is simply a tool to help you organize the information found by a particular process.

Table 12-34 presents a generic version of the list-all-subnets chart.

Table 12-34   *Generic List-All-Subnets Chart*

Octet	1	2	3	4
Mask				
Magic Number				
Network Number/Zero Subnet				
Next Subnet				
Next Subnet				
Last Subnet				
Broadcast Subnet				
Out of Range (Used by Process)				

The process starts with the assumption that you already know the classful network number and subnet mask (dotted decimal format). If the question gives you an IP address and mask instead of the network number and mask, just write down the network number of which that IP address is a member. If the mask is in prefix format, go ahead and convert it to dotted decimal.

The key to this decimal process is the following:

The various subnet numbers' interesting octet values are multiples of the magic number.

Key Topic

For example, as you read in the previous section, with Class B network 130.4.0.0, mask 255.255.252.0, the magic number is 256 – 252 = 4. So, the subnets of 130.4.0.0/ 255.255.252.0, in the third octet, are multiples of 4—namely, 130.4.0.0 (zero subnet), 130.4.4.0, 130.4.8.0, 130.4.12.0, 130.4.16.0, and so on, up through 130.4.252.0 (broadcast subnet).

If that intuitively makes sense to you, great, you are ahead of the game. If not, the rest of this section details the steps of the process, from which you can practice until you master the process. For reference, the process for finding all subnets of a classful network, assuming SLSM with 8 or fewer subnet bits, is as follows:

Step 1   Write down the subnet mask, in decimal, in the first empty row of the table.

Step 2   Identify the interesting octet, which is the one octet of the mask with a value other than 255 or 0. Draw a rectangle around the column of the interesting octet.

Step 3   Calculate the magic number by subtracting the *subnet mask's interesting octet* from 256. (Record this number in the list-all-subnets chart, inside the rectangle, for easy reference.)

Step 4   Write down the classful network number, which is the same number as the zero subnet, in the next empty row of the list-all-subnets chart.

Step 5   To find each successive subnet number:

a. For the three uninteresting octets, copy the previous subnet number's values.

b. For the interesting octet, add the magic number to the previous subnet number's interesting octet.

Step 6   Once the sum calculated in Step 5b reaches 256, stop the process. The number with the 256 in it is out of range, and the previous subnet number is the broadcast subnet.

Again, the written process is long, but with practice, most people can find the answers much more quickly than by using binary math.

> **NOTE**   Subnetting video 7 describes an example of using this process to list all subnets. This would be an excellent time to pause to view that video.

Before you see a few examples, you should know that in every case, the classful network number is the exact same number as the zero subnet number. *Subnet zero*, or the *zero subnet*, is numerically the first subnet, and it is one of the two possibly reserved subnet numbers, as mentioned earlier in this chapter. Interestingly, a network's zero subnet always has the exact same numeric value as the network itself—which is the main reason why the zero subnet was originally avoided.

Now on to some examples. Table 12-35 shows the results of the process for finding all subnets, through Step 4. In particular, at Steps 1 and 2, the subnet mask is recorded, with a box being drawn around the third octet because of the mask's value of 252 in the third octet. At Step 3, the magic number—256 minus the mask's interesting octet value of 252, or 4—is written on the next row. At Step 4, the classful network number, which is also the same number as the zero subnet, is recorded.

Table 12-35   *List-All-Subnets Chart: 130.4.0.0/22—After Finding the Zero Subnet*

Octet	1	2	3	4
Mask	255	255	252	0
Magic Number			4	
Classful Network/Subnet Zero	130	4	0	0

Next, Step 5 continues the process, finding a new subnet number each time Step 5 is repeated. Per Step 5A, octets 1, 2, and 4 are copied from the subnet zero row. For Step 5B, the magic number (4) is added to the zero subnet's interesting octet value of 0, completing the subnet number of 130.4.4.0. By repeating this process, you end up with 130.4.8.0 next, 130.4.12.0 after that, and so on. Table 12-36 lists all the values, including the last few values from which you can determine when to stop the process.

Table 12-36   *List-All-Subnets Chart: 130.4.0.0/22—After Finding Where to Stop the Process*

Octet	1	2	3	4
Mask	255	255	252	0
Magic Number			4	
Classful Network/Subnet Zero	130	4	0	0
First Nonzero Subnet	130	4	4	0
Next Subnet	130	4	8	0
Next Subnet	130	4	12	0
Next Subnet	130	4	16	0
Next Subnet	130	4	20	0
Next Subnet	130	4	24	0
(Skipping many subnets—shorthand)	130	4	X	0
Largest Numbered Nonbroadcast Subnet	130	4	248	0
Broadcast Subnet	130	4	252	0
Invalid—Used by Process	130	4	256	0

The six-step process directs you to create a new subnet by repeating Step 5 continually, but you need to know when to stop. Basically, you keep going until the interesting octet is 256. The number written in that row is invalid, and the number before it is the broadcast subnet.

> **NOTE** Depending on the exam question, you may or may not be able to use the zero subnet and broadcast subnet. If you do not recall the details, refer to the section "Number of Subnets: Subtract 2, or Not?" earlier in this chapter.

Finding All Subnets with Exactly 8 Subnet Bits

When exactly 8 subnet bits exist, the process of finding all subnets can be somewhat intuitive. In fact, consider Class B network 130.4.0.0, mask 255.255.255.0 for a moment. If you think about what subnets should exist in this network and then check your answers against upcoming Table 12-37, you may realize that you intuitively know how to get the answer. If so, great—move on to the next section in this chapter. However, if not, consider a few brief words that will hopefully unlock the process.

With exactly 8 subnet bits, the mask will be either a 255.255.0.0 mask used with a Class A network or a 255.255.255.0 mask used with a Class B network. In each case, the subnet part of the address is one entire octet. Inside that octet, the subnet numbers begin with a number identical to the classful network number (the zero subnet), and increment by 1 in that one subnet octet. For example, for 130.4.0.0, mask 255.255.255.0, the entire third octet is the subnet field. The zero subnet is 130.4.0.0, the next subnet is 130.4.1.0 (adding 1 in the third octet), the next subnet is 130.4.2.0, and so on.

You can think about the problem in the same terms as the process used when fewer than 8 subnet bits exist. One change is required, however, when exactly 8 subnet bits exist, because the interesting octet is not easily identified. So, with exactly 8 subnet bits, to find the interesting octet:

> The interesting octet is the octet in which all 8 subnet bits reside.

For example, consider network 130.4.0.0/255.255.255.0 again. As stated earlier, the entire third octet is the subnet part of the addresses, making the third octet the interesting octet. From that point, just use the same basic process used when fewer than 8 subnet bits exist. For example, the magic number is 1, because 256 minus 255 (the mask's third octet value) is 1. The zero subnet is equal to the Class B network number (130.4.0.0), with each successive subnet being 1 larger in the third octet, because the magic number is 1. Table 12-37 lists the work in progress for this example, with all steps completed.

Table 12-37   *List-All-Subnets Chart: 130.4.0.0/24*

Octet	1	2	3	4
Mask	255	255	255	0
Magic Number			1	
Classful Network/Subnet Zero	130	4	0	0
First Nonzero Subnet	130	4	1	0
Next Subnet	130	4	2	0
Next Subnet	130	4	3	0
(Skipping many subnets—shorthand)	130	4	X	0
Largest Numbered Nonbroadcast Subnet	130	4	254	0
Broadcast Subnet	130	4	255	0
Invalid—Used by Process	130	4	256	0

Practice Suggestions

The process to find all subnets of a network, assuming SLSM is used and assuming more than 8 subnet bits exist, requires some imagination on your part. So, before tackling that problem, it is helpful to master the process to find all subnets when the process is more concise. To that end, take the time now to do Appendix D Problem Set 6, which includes problems about finding all subnets of a network, using a mask that implies fewer than 8 subnet bits. You can refer to Appendix E reference page RP-7A as well, which summarizes the process in this chapter.

Also, if you have not yet done so, feel free to watch subnetting video 7, which explains this same process.

Finding All Subnets with More Than 8 Subnet Bits

When reading this section, particularly for the first time, consider the fact that when more than 8 subnet bits exist, there will be a lot of subnets. Also, note that the subnet part of the addresses exists in at least two different octets, possibly three octets. So, the process will need to work in multiple octets.

The explanation works better by starting with an example. (At your option, you may choose to go ahead and watch subnetting video 8, which also explains the process shown here.) The first example in this written chapter is using Class B network 130.4.0.0 again, now with 10 subnet bits, meaning a mask of 255.255.255.192. The following list notes the first 13 subnets:

■ 130.4.0.0 (zero subnet)

■ 130.4.0.64

■ 130.4.0.128

■ 130.4.0.192

■ 130.4.1.0

■ 130.4.1.64

■ 130.4.1.128

■ 130.4.1.192

■ 130.4.2.0

■ 130.4.2.64

■ 130.4.2.128

■ 130.4.2.192

■ 130.4.3.0

You can see some obvious patterns in the subnet numbers. For example, each successive subnet number is larger than the previous subnet number. The last octet's values repeat over time (0, 64, 128, and 192 in this case), whereas the third octet seems to be growing steadily by 1 for each set of four subnets.

Now, consider the following version of the full process for finding all subnets. The process follows the same first five steps of the process used when there are fewer than 8 subnet bits. However, instead of the old Step 6, do the following:

Key Topic

Step 6 When any step's addition results in a sum of 256:

   a. For the octet whose sum would have been 256, write down a 0.

   b. For the octet to the left, add 1 to the previous subnet's value in that octet.

   c. For any other octets copy the values of the same octets in the previous
      subnet number.

   d. Start again with RP-7A Step 5.

Step 7   Each time the process results in a sum of 256, repeat step 6 of this RP-7B
             process.

Step 8   Repeat until the addition in Step 6b would actually change the value of
             the network portion of the subnet number.

For example, consider this revised process, now applied to 130.4.0.0/255.255.255.192.
In this case, the fourth octet is the interesting octet. Table 12-38 shows the work in
progress, up through the point at which a 256 is recorded, triggering the new and
revised Step 6.

Table 12-38   *Incorrect Entry in the List-All-Subnets Chart: First Addition to 256*

Octet	1	2	3	4
Mask	255	255	255	192
Magic Number (256 – 192 = 64)				64
Classful Network/Subnet Zero	130	4	0	0
First Nonzero Subnet	130	4	0	64
Next Subnet	130	4	0	128
Next Subnet	130	4	0	192
A 256 in the Fourth Octet...	130	4	0	256

According to Step 6 of the process listed just before the table, you should not have written
down the contents in the last row of Table 12-38. Instead, you should have

   Written a 0 in the fourth octet.

   Added 1 to the value in the octet to the left (third octet in this case), for a total of 1.

Table 12-39 shows the revised entry, and the next three subnets (found by continuing Step 5,
which adds the magic number *in the interesting octet*). The table lists the subnets up to the
point that the next step would again generate a sum of 256.

Table 12-39 *Correct Entry in the List-All-Subnets Chart: First Addition to 256*

Octet	1	2	3	4
Mask	255	255	255	192
Magic Number				64
Classful Network/Subnet Zero	130	4	0	0
First Nonzero Subnet	130	4	0	64
Next Subnet	130	4	0	128
Next Subnet	130	4	0	192
Correct Next Subnet (found by writing 0 in the fourth octet, and adding 1 to the third octet)	130	4	1	0
Next Subnet	130	4	1	64
Next Subnet	130	4	1	128
Next Subnet	130	4	1	192

If you continued the process using the last row in the table, and added the magic number (64) to the interesting (fourth) octet yet again, the sum would total 256 again. With the revised Step 6, that means you would again instead write a 0 for the interesting octet, and add 1 to the octet to the left—in this case resulting in 130.4.2.0.

If you continue with this process, you will find all subnet numbers. However, as usual, it helps to know when to stop. In this case, you would eventually get to subnet 130.4.255.192. Then, when adding the magic number (64) to the interesting (fourth) octet, you would get 256—so instead, you would write down a 0 in the interesting octet, and add 1 to the octet to the left. However, the third octet would then be a value of 256. If you look at the literal wording in the process, any time you try to add, and the result is 256, you should instead write down a 0, and add 1 to the octet to the left. In this case, the next result would then be

130.5.0.0

As you can see, this value is in a totally different Class B network, because one of the two Class B network octets has been changed. So, when the network octets are changed by the process, you should stop. The previous subnet—in this case 130.4.255.192—is the broadcast subnet.

More Practice Suggestions

Now that you have seen the even more involved process when the length of the subnet field is more than 8 bits, you can do a few more practice problems. To practice this process a few times, take the time now to do Appendix D Problem Set 7, which includes problems about finding all subnets of a network, using a mask that implies at least 8 subnet bits. You can refer to Appendix E reference page RP-7B as well, which summarizes the process in this chapter.

Also, if you have not yet done so, feel free to watch subnetting video 8, which explains this same process.

Exam Preparation Tasks

Review All the Key Topics

Review the most important topics from inside the chapter, noted with the key topics icon in the outer margin of the page. Table 12-40 lists a reference of these key topics and the page numbers on which each is found.

This chapter contains a lot of lists that summarize the process used to find a particular answer. These processes do not need to be memorized. Instead, practice your chosen method to find each set of facts about IP addressing, whether it is one of the binary or decimal processes found in this chapter, or elsewhere. The processes are listed here as key topics for easier study and reference. Note that the topics that could be helpful to memorize or study as an end to themselves are shaded in the table.

Table 12-40   *Key Topics for Chapter 12*

Key Topic Element	Description	Page Number
Table 12-2	Reference table for the number of networks, size of the network part, and size of the host part, for Class A, B, and C IP networks	340
Table 12-3	Class A, B, and C networks with their default masks	341
Table 12-4	Reference table of the private (RFC 1918) IP networks	342
List	Tips for doing binary-to-decimal and decimal-to-binary conversion for IP addresses	348
Process list	Binary process for converting a mask from dotted decimal to prefix notation	352
Process list	Binary process for converting a mask from prefix to dotted decimal notation	352
Table 12-9	Nine decimal values allowed in subnet masks, with the binary equivalent values	353
Process list	Decimal process for converting a mask from dotted decimal to prefix notation	354
Process list	Decimal process for converting a mask from prefix to dotted decimal notation	354

Table 12-40 *Key Topics for Chapter 12 (Continued)*

Key Topic Element	Description	Page Number
List	Facts about how to analyze and find the size of the network, subnet, and host parts of an IP address	356
List	Facts about how the subnet mask identifies part of the structure of an IP address	358
Process list	Binary process to find the structure (network, subnet, and host parts) of an IP address	358
Process list	Decimal process to find the structure (network, subnet, and host parts) of an IP address	359
List	Key facts about how to calculate the number of subnets and number of hosts per subnet	359
Table 12-12	How to determine which formula to use to calculate the number of available subnets	361
Paragraph	Important fact about the binary values in subnet masks	365
List	Tips for understanding how to find the mask that provides the most subnets or most hosts per subnet	366
Process list	Summarizes how to choose a subnet mask based on a set of requirements	367
Process list	Binary process, with no binary shortcuts, to find an address's resident subnet by using a Boolean AND	369
Process list	Binary process to find a subnet broadcast address	372
Process list	Decimal process to find the range of addresses in a subnet, after having found the subnet number and subnet broadcast address	374
Process list	Fnding the range of valid IP addresses in a subnet	375
Process list	Decimal process to find the subnet number, broadcast address, and range of addresses in a subnet	382
Paragraph	A note that the subnet numbers of a classful network are multiples of the magic number	385
Process list	Decimal process to find all subnets of a classful network, with one mask and fewer than 8 subnet bits	386
Process list	Decimal process to find all subnets of a classful network, with one mask and more than 8 subnet bits	390

Complete the Tables and Lists from Memory

Print a copy of Appendix H, "Memory Tables" (found on the CD-ROM), or at least the section for this chapter, and complete the tables and lists from memory. Appendix I, "Memory Tables Answer Key," also on the CD-ROM, includes completed tables and lists to check your work.

Definitions of Key Terms

Define the following key terms from this chapter and check your answers in the glossary.

bitwise Boolean AND, Boolean AND, broadcast subnet, classful network, default mask, prefix notation/CIDR notation, private IP address, public IP address, subnet, subnet mask, subnet number/subnet address, zero subnet

Read Appendix F Scenario 1, Part A

Appendix F, "Additional Scenarios," contains two detailed scenarios that give you a chance to analyze different designs, problems, and command output, as well as show you how concepts from several different chapters interrelate. Reviewing Appendix F Scenario 1, Part A, would be useful at this time because it provides an opportunity to practice IP address planning.

Subnetting Questions and Processes

This chapter contains a large number of explanations on how to find a particular piece of information about a subnet, along with formalized processes. These formalized processes provide a clear method for practicing the process to get the correct answer.

The specific processes themselves are not the focus of the chapter. Instead, through practice, you should understand the various tasks, and use the processes to find the right answer, until it begins to become natural. At that point, you probably will not think about the specific steps listed in this chapter—the process will be integrated into how you think about IP addressing and subnetting. By the time you have finished this chapter, and the associated suggested practice throughout the chapter, you should be able to answer the following types of questions. Read over the following questions, and if the process by which you would find the answer is not clear, please refer back to the corresponding section of this chapter, listed with each question, for additional review and practice.

1.   For IP address a.b.c.d, what is the classful IP network in which it reside? ("IP Addressing Review")

2.   For mask e.f.g.h, what is the same value in prefix notation? ("Prefix Notation/CIDR Notation")

3. For prefix /x, what is the same value in dotted decimal notation? ("Prefix Notation/ CIDR Notation")

4. For IP address a.b.c.d, mask e.f.g.h, how many network bits exist? Subnet bits? Host bits? ("Analyzing the Subnet Mask in an Existing Subnet Design")

5. For a particular classful network, with mask e.f.g.h, how many subnets are supported? How many hosts per subnet? ("Analyzing the Subnet Mask in an Existing Subnet Design")

6. For a given classful network, with a need for X subnets, and Y hosts per subnet, assuming the same mask is used throughout the network, what masks meet the requirements? ("Choosing a Subnet Mask that Meets Design Requirements")

7. For a given classful network, with a need for X subnets, and Y hosts per subnet, of the masks that meet these requirements, which mask maximizes the number of hosts per subnet? Which mask maximizes the number of subnets? ("Choosing a Subnet Mask that Meets Design Requirements")

8. Given IP address a.b.c.d, mask e.f.g.h, what is the resident subnet? Broadcast address? Range of addresses in the subnet? ("Analyzing Existing Subnets")

9. Which of the following subnets are subnets of a given classful network, using mask e.f.g.h for all subnets? ("Design: Choosing the Subnets of a Classful Network")

This chapter covers the following subjects:

Installing Cisco Routers: This section gives some perspectives on the purpose of enterprise-class routers and consumer-grade routers, and how the routers connect users to a network.

Cisco Router IOS CLI: This section examines the similarities between the Cisco IOS router CLI and the Cisco IOS switch CLI (introduced in Chapter 8, "Operating Cisco LAN Switches") and also covers some of the features that are unique to routers.

Upgrading Cisco IOS Software and the Cisco IOS Software Boot Process: This section examines how a router boots, including how a router chooses which Cisco IOS software image to load.

CHAPTER 13

Operating Cisco Routers

Routers differ from switches in terms of their core purposes. Switches forward Ethernet frames by comparing the frame's destination MAC address to the switch's MAC address table, whereas routers forward packets by comparing the destination IP address to the router's IP routing table. Ethernet switches today typically have only one or more types of Ethernet interfaces, whereas routers have Ethernet interfaces, serial WAN interfaces, and other interfaces with which to connect via cable and digital subscriber line (DSL) to the Internet. Routers understand how to forward data to devices connected to these different types of interfaces, whereas Ethernet switches focus solely on forwarding Ethernet frames to Ethernet devices. So, while both switches and routers forward data, the details of what can be forwarded, and to what devices, differ significantly.

Even though their core purposes differ, Cisco routers and switches use the same CLI. This chapter covers the CLI features on routers that differ from the features on switches, particularly features that differ from the switch CLI features as covered in Chapter 8. This chapter also explains more details about the physical installation of Cisco routers, along with some details about how routers choose and load IOS.

"Do I Know This Already?" Quiz

The "Do I Know This Already?" quiz allows you to assess if you should read the entire chapter. If you miss no more than one of these nine self-assessment questions, you might want to move ahead to the "Exam Preparation Tasks" section. Table 13-1 lists the major headings in this chapter and the "Do I Know This Already?" quiz questions covering the material in those headings so you can assess your knowledge of these specific areas. The answers to the "Do I Know This Already?" quiz appear in Appendix A.

Table 13-1   *"Do I Know This Already?" Foundation Topics Section-to-Question Mapping*

Foundation Topics Section	Questions
Installing Cisco Routers	1, 2
Cisco Router IOS CLI	3–7
Upgrading Cisco IOS Software and the Cisco IOS Software Boot Process	8, 9

1. Which of the following installation steps are typically required on a Cisco router, but not typically required on a Cisco switch?

    a. Connect Ethernet cables

    b. Connect serial cables

    c. Connect to the console port

    d. Connect the power cable

    e. Turn the on/off switch to "on"

2. Which of the following roles does a SOHO router typically play in regards to IP address assignment?

    a. DHCP server on the interface connected to the ISP

    b. DHCP server on the interface connected to the PCs at the home/office

    c. DHCP client on the interface connected to the ISP

    d. DHCP client on the interface connected to the PCs at the home/office

3. Which of the following features would you typically expect to be associated with the router CLI, but not with the switch CLI?

    a. The **clock rate** command

    b. The **ip address** *address mask* command

    c. The **ip address dhcp** command

    d. The **interface vlan 1** command

4. You just bought two Cisco routers for use in a lab, connecting each router to a different LAN switch with their Fa0/0 interfaces. You also connected the two routers' serial interfaces using a back-to-back cable. Which of the following steps is not required to be able to forward IP on both routers' interfaces?

    a. Configuring an IP address on each router's FastEthernet and serial interfaces

    b. Configuring the **bandwidth** command on one router's serial interface

    c. Configuring the **clock rate** command on one router's serial interface

    d. Setting the interface **description** on both the FastEthernet and serial interface of each router

5. The output of the **show ip interface brief** command on R1 lists interface status codes of "down" and "down" for interface Serial 0/0. Which of the following could be true?

   a. The **shutdown** command is currently configured for that interface.

   b. R1's serial interface has been configured to use Frame Relay, but the router on the other end of the serial link has been configured to use PPP.

   c. R1's serial interface does not have a serial cable installed.

   d. Both routers have been cabled to a working serial link (CSU/DSUs included), but only one router has been configured with an IP address.

6. Which of the following commands does not list the IP address and mask of at least one interface?

   a. **show running-config**

   b. **show protocols** *type number*

   c. **show ip interface brief**

   d. **show interfaces**

   e. **show version**

7. Which of the following is different on the Cisco switch CLI as compared with the Cisco router CLI?

   a. The commands used to configure simple password checking for the console

   b. The number of IP addresses configured

   c. The types of questions asked in setup mode

   d. The configuration of the device's host name

   e. The configuration of an interface description

8. Which of the following could cause a router to change the IOS that is loaded when the router boots?

   a. **reload** EXEC command

   b. **boot** EXEC command

   c. **reboot** EXEC command

   d. **boot system** configuration command

   e. **reboot system** configuration command

   f. configuration register

9. Which of the following hexadecimal values in the last nibble of the configuration register would cause a router to not look in Flash memory for an IOS?

   a. 0

   b. 2

   c. 4

   d. 5

   e. 6

Foundation Topics

Installing Cisco Routers

Routers collectively provide the main feature of the network layer—the capability to forward packets end-to-end through a network. As introduced in Chapter 5, "Fundamentals of IP Addressing and Routing," routers forward packets by connecting to various physical network links, like Ethernet, serial links, and Frame Relay, and then using Layer 3 routing logic to choose where to forward each packet. As a reminder, Chapter 3, "Fundamentals of LANs," covered the details of making those physical connections to Ethernet networks, while Chapter 4, "Fundamentals of WANs," covered the basics of cabling with WAN links.

This section examines some of the details of router installation and cabling, first from the enterprise perspective, and then from the perspective of connecting a typical small office/home office (SOHO) to an ISP using high-speed Internet.

Installing Enterprise Routers

A typical enterprise network has a few centralized sites as well as lots of smaller remote sites. To support devices at each site (the computers, IP phones, printers, and other devices), the network includes at least one LAN switch at each site. Additionally, each site has a router, which connects to the LAN switch and to some WAN link. The WAN link provides connectivity from each remote site, back to the central site, and to other sites via the connection to the central site.

Figure 13-1 shows one way to draw part of an enterprise network. The figure shows a typical branch office on the left, with a router, some end-user PCs, and a nondescript generic drawing of an Ethernet. The central site, on the right, has basically the same components, with a point-to-point serial link connecting the two routers. The central site includes a server farm with two servers, with one of the main purposes of this internetwork being to provide remote offices with access to the data stored on these servers.

Figure 13-1 purposefully omits several details to show the basic concepts. Figure 13-2 shows the same network, but now with more detail about the cabling used at each site.

Figure 13-1   *Generic Enterprise Network Diagram*

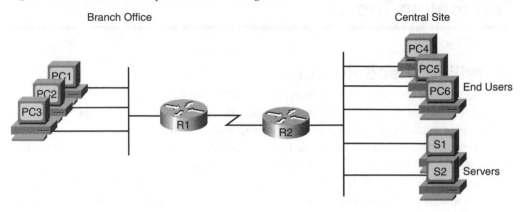

Figure 13-2   *More Detailed Cabling Diagram for the Same Enterprise Network*

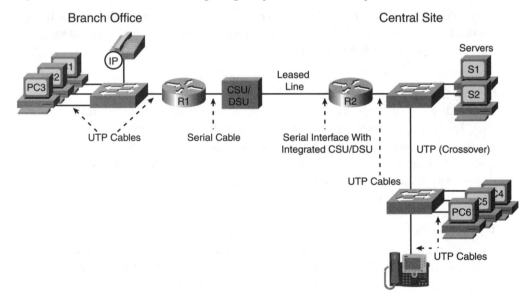

Figure 13-2 shows the types of LAN cables (UTP), with a couple of different WAN cables. The LAN connections all use UTP straight-through cabling pinouts, except for the UTP cable between the two switches, which is a crossover cable.

The serial link in the figure shows the two main options for where the channel service unit/ digital service unit (CSU/DSU) hardware resides: either outside the router (as shown at the branch office in this case) or integrated into the router's serial interface (as shown at the central site). Most new installations today include the CSU/DSU in the router's serial interface. The WAN cable installed by the telco typically has an RJ-48 connector, which is the same size and shape as an RJ-45 connector. The telco cable with the RJ-48 connector inserts into the CSU/DSU, meaning it connects directly into the central site router in this case, but into the external CSU/DSU at the branch office router. At the branch, the external CSU/DSU would then be cabled, using a serial cable, to the branch router's serial port. (See Figure 4-4 in Chapter 4 for a reminder of WAN serial cables.)

Cisco Integrated Services Routers

Product vendors, including Cisco, typically provide several different types of router hardware, including some routers that just do routing, with other routers that serve other functions in addition to routing. A typical enterprise branch office needs a router for WAN/LAN connectivity, and a LAN switch to provide a high-performance local network and connectivity into the router and WAN. Many branches also need Voice over IP (VoIP) services, and several security services as well. (One popular security service, virtual private networking (VPN), is covered in Chapter 6, "Fundamentals of TCP/IP Transport, Applications, and Security.") Rather than require multiple separate devices at one site, as shown in Figure 13-2, Cisco offers single devices that act as both router and switch, and provide other functions as well.

Following that concept further, Cisco offers several router model series in which the routers support many other functions. In fact, Cisco has several router product series called Integrated Services Routers (ISR), with the name emphasizing the fact that many functions are integrated into a single device. If you have not seen Cisco routers before, you can go to http://www.cisco.com/go/isr and click any of the 3D Product Demonstration links to see interactive views of a variety of Cisco ISR routers. However, for the sake of learning and understanding the different functions, the CCNA exams focus on using a separate switch and separate router, which provides a much cleaner path for learning the basics.

Figure 13-3 shows a couple of pictures taken from the interactive demo of the Cisco 1841 ISR, with some of the more important features highlighted. The top part of the figure shows a full view of the back of the router. It also shows a magnified view of the back of the router, with a clearer view of the two FastEthernet interfaces, the console and auxiliary ports, and a serial card with an internal CSU/DSU. (You can find the interactive demo from which these photos were taken at the same ISR web page mentioned in the previous paragraph.)

Figure 13-3 *Photos of a Model 1841 Cisco Integrated Services Router (ISR)*

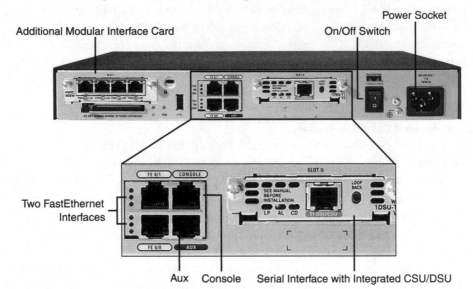

Physical Installation

Armed with the planning information shown in Figure 13-2, and the perspectives shown in Figure 13-3, you can physically install a router. To install a router, follow these steps:

Step 1   Connect any LAN cables to the LAN ports.

Step 2   If using an external CSU/DSU, connect the router's serial interface to the CSU/DSU, and the CSU/DSU to the line from the telco.

Step 3   If using an internal CSU/DSU, connect the router's serial interface to the line from the telco.

Step 4   Connect the router's console port to a PC (using a rollover cable), as needed, to configure the router.

Step 5   Connect a power cable from a power outlet to the power port on the router.

Step 6   Turn on the router.

Note that the steps generally follow the same steps used for installation of LAN switches—install the cables for the interfaces, connect the console (as needed), and connect the power. However, note that most of the Cisco Catalyst switches do not have a power on/off switch—once the switch is connected to power, the switch is on. However, Cisco routers do have on/off switches.

Installing Internet Access Routers

Routers play a key role in SOHO networks, connecting the LAN-attached end-user devices to a high-speed Internet access service. Once connected to the Internet, SOHO users can send packets to and from their enterprise network at their company or school.

As in the enterprise networking market, product vendors tend to sell integrated networking devices that perform many functions. However, in keeping with the CCNA strategy of understanding each function separately, this section first examines the various networking functions needed at a typical SOHO network, using a separate device for each function. Following that, a more realistic example is shown, with the functions combined into a single device.

A SOHO Installation with a Separate Switch, Router, and Cable Modem

Figure 13-4 shows an example of the devices and cables used in a SOHO network to connect to the Internet using cable TV (CATV) as the high-speed Internet service. For now, keep in mind that the figure shows one alternative for the devices and cables, whereas many variations are possible.

Figure 13-4 *Devices in a SOHO Network with High-Speed CATV Internet*

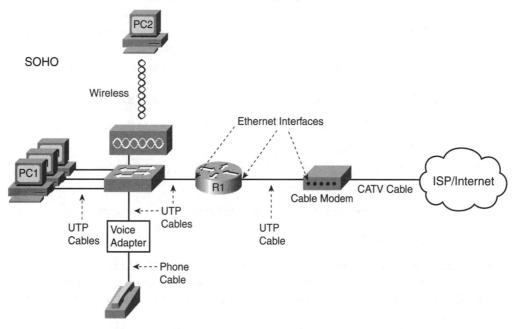

This figure has many similarities to Figure 13-2, which shows a typical enterprise branch office. The end-user PCs still connect to a switch, and the switch still connects to a router's Ethernet interface. The router still provides routing services, forwarding IP packets. The voice details differ slightly between Figure 13-2 and Figure 13-4, mainly because

Figure 13-4 shows a typical home-based Internet phone service, which uses a normal analog phone and a voice adapter to convert from analog voice to IP.

The main differences between the SOHO connection in Figure 13-4 and the enterprise branch in Figure 13-2 relate to the connection into the Internet. An Internet connection that uses CATV or DSL needs a device that converts between the Layer 1 and 2 standards used on the CATV cable or DSL line, and the Ethernet used by the router. These devices, commonly called *cable modems* and *DSL modems*, respectively, convert electrical signals between an Ethernet cable and either CATV or DSL.

In fact, while the details differ greatly, the purpose of the cable modem and DSL modem is similar to a CSU/DSU on a serial link. A CSU/DSU converts between the Layer 1 standards used on a telco's WAN circuit and a serial cable's Layer 1 standards—and routers can use serial cables. Similarly, a cable modem converts between CATV signals and a Layer 1 (and Layer 2) standard usable by a router—namely, Ethernet. Similarly, DSL modems convert between the DSL signals over a home telephone line and Ethernet.

To physically install a SOHO network with the devices shown in Figure 13-4, you basically need the correct UTP cables for the Ethernet connections, and either the CATV cable (for cable Internet services) or a phone line (for DSL services). Note that the router used in Figure 13-4 simply needs to have two Ethernet interfaces—one to connect to the LAN switch, and one to connect to the cable modem. Thinking specifically just about the router installation, you would need to use the following steps to install this SOHO router:

Step 1 Connect a UTP straight-through cable from the router to the switch.

Step 2 Connect a UTP straight-through cable from the router to the cable modem.

Step 3 Connect the router's console port to a PC (using a rollover cable), as needed, to configure the router.

Step 4 Connect a power cable from a power outlet to the power port on the router.

Step 5 Turn on the router.

A SOHO Installation with an Integrated Switch, Router, and DSL Modem

Today, most new SOHO installations use an integrated device rather than the separate devices shown in Figure 13-4. In fact, you can buy SOHO devices today that include all of these functions:

■ Router

■ Switch

■ Cable or DSL modem

- Voice Adapter

- Wireless AP

- Hardware-enabled encryption

The CCNA exams do indeed focus on separate devices to aid the learning process. However, a newly installed high-speed SOHO Internet connection today probably looks more like Figure 13-5, with an integrated device.

Figure 13-5 *SOHO Network, Using Cable Internet and an Integrated Device*

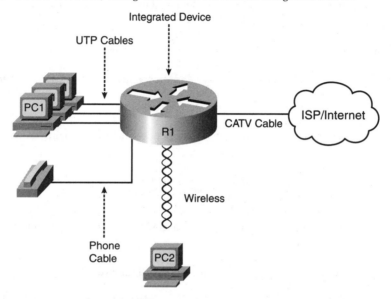

Regarding the SOHO Devices Used in This Book

Cisco sells products to both enterprise customers and consumers. Cisco sells its consumer products using the Linksys brand. These products are easily found online and in office supply stores. Cisco mainly sells enterprise products either directly to its customers or through Cisco Channel Partners (resellers). However, note that the CCNA exams do not use Linksys products or their web-based user interface, instead focusing on the IOS CLI used by Cisco enterprise routing products.

Cisco Router IOS CLI

Cisco routers use the same switch IOS CLI as described in Chapter 8. However, because routers and switches perform different functions, the actual commands differ in some cases. This section begins by listing some of the key features that work exactly the same on both switches and routers, and then lists and describes in detail some of the key features that differ between switches and routers.

Comparisons Between the Switch CLI and Router CLI

The following list details the many items covered in Chapter 8 for which the router CLI behaves the same. If these details are not fresh in your memory, it might be worthwhile to spend a few minutes briefly reviewing Chapter 8.

The configuration commands used for the following features are the same on both routers and switches:

Key Topic

- User and Enable (privileged) mode

- Entering and exiting configuration mode, using the **configure terminal**, **end**, and **exit** commands, and the Ctrl-Z key sequence

- Configuration of console, Telnet, and enable secret passwords

- Configuration of SSH encryption keys and username/password login credentials

- Configuration of the host name and interface description

- Configuration of Ethernet interfaces that can negotiate speed, using the **speed** and **duplex** commands

- Configuring an interface to be administratively disabled (**shutdown**) and administratively enabled (**no shutdown**)

- Navigation through different configuration mode contexts using commands like **line console 0** and **interface**

- CLI help, command editing, and command recall features

- The meaning and use of the startup-config (in NVRAM), running-config (in RAM), and external servers (like TFTP), along with how to use the **copy** command to copy the configuration files and IOS images

- The process of reaching setup mode either by reloading the router with an empty startup-config or by using the **setup** command

At first glance, this list seems to cover most everything covered in Chapter 8—and it does cover most of the details. However, a couple of topics covered in Chapter 8 do work differently with the router CLI as compared to the switch CLI, namely:

Key Topic

- The configuration of IP addresses differs in some ways.

- The questions asked in setup mode differ.

- Routers have an auxiliary (Aux) port, intended to be connected to an external modem and phone line, to allow remote users to dial into the router, and access the CLI, by making a phone call.

Beyond these three items from Chapter 8, the router CLI does differ from a switch CLI just because switches and routers do different things. For instance, Example 10-5 in Chapter 10, "Ethernet Switch Troubleshooting," shows the output of the **show mac address-table dynamic** command, which lists the most important table that a switch uses for forwarding frames. The router IOS does not support this command—instead, routers support the **show ip route** command, which lists the IP routes known to the router, which of course is the most important table that a router uses for forwarding packets. As you might imagine, the Cisco Layer 2 switches covered on the CCNA exams do not support the **show ip route** command because they do not do any IP routing.

The rest of this section explains a few of the differences between the router IOS CLI and the switch IOS CLI. Chapter 14, "Routing Protocol Concepts and Configuration," goes on to show even more items that differ, in particular how to configure router interface IP addresses and IP routing protocols. For now, this chapter examines the following items:

- Router interfaces

- Router IP address configuration

- Router setup mode

Router Interfaces

The CCNA exams refer to two general types of physical interfaces on routers: Ethernet interfaces and serial interfaces. The term *Ethernet interface* refers to any type of Ethernet interface. However, on Cisco routers, the name referenced by the CLI refers to the fastest speed possible on the interface. For example, some Cisco routers have an Ethernet interface capable of only 10 Mbps, so to configure that type of interface, you would use the **interface ethernet** *number* configuration command. However, other routers have interfaces capable of 100 Mbps, or even of auto-negotiating to use 10 Mbps or 100 Mbps, so routers refer to these interfaces by the fastest speed, with the **interface fastethernet** *number* command. Similarly, interfaces capable of Gigabit Ethernet speeds are referenced with the **interface gigabitethernet** *number* command.

Serial interfaces are the second major type of physical interface on routers. As you may recall from Chapter 4, point-to-point leased lines and Frame Relay access links both use the same underlying Layer 1 standards. To support those same standards, Cisco routers use serial interfaces. The network engineer then chooses which data link layer protocol to use, such as High-Level Data Link Control (HDLC) or Point-to-Point Protocol (PPP) for leased lines or Frame Relay for Frame Relay connections, and configures the router to use the correct data link layer protocol. (Serial interfaces default to use HDLC as the data link layer protocol.)

Routers use numbers to distinguish between the different interfaces of the same type. On routers, the interface numbers might be a single number, or two numbers separated by a slash, or three numbers separated by slashes. For example, all three of the following configuration commands are correct on at least one model of Cisco router:

```
interface ethernet 0
interface fastEthernet 0/1
interface serial 1/0/1
```

You can view information about interfaces by using several commands. To see a brief list of interfaces, use the **show ip interface brief** command. To see brief details about a particular interface, use the **show protocols** *type number* command. (Note that the **show protocols** command is not available in all versions of Cisco IOS Software.) You can also see a lot of detail about each interface, including statistics about the packets flowing in and out of the interface, by using the **show interfaces** command. Optionally, you can include the interface type and number on many commands, for example, **show interfaces** *type number*, to see details for just that interface. Example 13-1 shows sample output from these three commands.

Example 13-1 *Listing the Interfaces in a Router*

```
Albuquerque#show ip interface brief
Interface              IP-Address      OK? Method Status                 Protocol
FastEthernet0/0        unassigned      YES unset  up                     up
FastEthernet0/1        unassigned      YES unset  administratively down  down
Serial0/0/0            unassigned      YES unset  administratively down  down
Serial0/0/1            unassigned      YES unset  up                     up
Serial0/1/0            unassigned      YES unset  up                     up
Serial0/1/1            unassigned      YES unset  administratively down  down
Albuquerque#show protocols fa0/0
FastEthernet0/0 is up, line protocol is up
Albuquerque#show interfaces s0/1/0
Serial0/1/0 is up, line protocol is up
  Hardware is GT96K Serial
  MTU 1500 bytes, BW 1544 Kbit, DLY 20000 usec,
     reliability 255/255, txload 1/255, rxload 1/255
  Encapsulation HDLC, loopback not set
  Keepalive set (10 sec)
  CRC checking enabled
  Last input 00:00:03, output 00:00:01, output hang never
  Last clearing of "show interface" counters never
  Input queue: 0/75/0/0 (size/max/drops/flushes); Total output drops: 0
  Queueing strategy: weighted fair
  Output queue: 0/1000/64/0 (size/max total/threshold/drops)
     Conversations  0/1/256 (active/max active/max total)
     Reserved Conversations 0/0 (allocated/max allocated)
     Available Bandwidth 1158 kilobits/sec
```

Example 13-1 *Listing the Interfaces in a Router (Continued)*

```
5 minute input rate 0 bits/sec, 0 packets/sec
5 minute output rate 0 bits/sec, 0 packets/sec
   70 packets input, 6979 bytes, 0 no buffer
   Received 70 broadcasts, 0 runts, 0 giants, 0 throttles
   0 input errors, 0 CRC, 0 frame, 0 overrun, 0 ignored, 0 abort
   36 packets output, 4557 bytes, 0 underruns
   0 output errors, 0 collisions, 8 interface resets
   0 output buffer failures, 0 output buffers swapped out
   13 carrier transitions
   DCD=up  DSR=up  DTR=up  RTS=up  CTS=up
```

> **NOTE** Commands that refer to router interfaces can be significantly shortened by truncating the words. For example, **sh int fa0/0** can be used instead of **show interfaces fastethernet 0/0**. In fact, many network engineers, when looking over someone's shoulder, would say something like "just do a show int F-A-oh-oh command" in this case, rather than speaking the long version of the command.

Interface Status Codes

Each of the commands in Example 13-1 lists two *interface status codes*. For a router to use an interface, the two interface status codes on the interface must be in an "up" state. The first status code refers essentially to whether Layer 1 is working, and the second status code mainly (but not always) refers to whether the data link layer protocol is working. Table 13-2 summarizes these two status codes.

Table 13-2 *Interface Status Codes and Their Meanings*

Name	Location	General Meaning
Line status	First status code	Refers to the Layer 1 status—for example, is the cable installed, is it the right/wrong cable, is the device on the other end powered on?
Protocol status	Second status code	Refers generally to the Layer 2 status. It is always down if the line status is down. If the line status is up, a protocol status of down usually is caused by mismatched data link layer configuration.

Key Topic

Four combinations of settings exist for the status codes when troubleshooting a network. Table 13-3 lists the four combinations, along with an explanation of the typical reasons why an interface would be in that state. As you review the list, note that if the line status (the first status code) is not "up," the second will always be "down," because the data link layer functions cannot work if the physical layer has a problem.

Table 13-3 *Typical Combinations of Interface Status Codes*

Line and Protocol Status	Typical Reasons
Administratively down, down	The interface has a **shutdown** command configured on it.
down, down	The interface has a **no shutdown** command configured, but the physical layer has a problem. For example, no cable has been attached to the interface, or with Ethernet, the switch interface on the other end of the cable is shut down, or the switch is powered off.
up, down	Almost always refers to data link layer problems, most often configuration problems. For example, serial links have this combination when one router was configured to use PPP, and the other defaults to use HDLC.
up, up	All is well, interface is functioning.

Router Interface IP Addresses

As has been mentioned many times throughout this book, routers need an IP address on each interface. If no IP address is configured, even if the interface is in an up/up state, the router will not attempt to send and receive IP packets on the interface. For proper operation, for every interface a router should use for forwarding IP packets, the router needs an IP address.

The configuration of an IP address on an interface is relatively simple. To configure the address and mask, simply use the **ip address** *address mask* interface subcommand. Example 13-2 shows an example configuration of IP addresses on two router interfaces, and the resulting differences in the **show ip interface brief** and **show interfaces** commands from Example 13-1. (No IP addresses were configured when the output in Example 13-1 was gathered.)

Example 13-2 *Configuring IP Addresses on Cisco Routers*

```
Albuquerque#configure terminal
Enter configuration commands, one per line.  End with CNTL/Z.
Albuquerque (config)#interface Fa0/0
Albuquerque (config-if)#ip address 10.1.1.1 255.255.255.0
Albuquerque (config-if)#interface S0/0/1
Albuquerque (config-if)#ip address 10.1.2.1 255.255.255.0
Albuquerque (config-if)#^Z
Albuquerque#show ip interface brief
Interface               IP-Address      OK? Method Status                Protocol
FastEthernet0/0         10.1.1.1        YES manual up                    up
FastEthernet0/1         unassigned      YES NVRAM  administratively down down
Serial0/0/0             unassigned      YES NVRAM  administratively down down
Serial0/0/1             10.1.2.1        YES manual up                    up
Serial0/1/0             unassigned      YES NVRAM  up                    up
Serial0/1/1             unassigned      YES NVRAM  administratively down down
```

Example 13-2 *Configuring IP Addresses on Cisco Routers (Continued)*

```
Albuquerque#show interfaces fa0/0
FastEthernet0/0 is up, line protocol is up
  Hardware is Gt96k FE, address is 0013.197b.5004 (bia 0013.197b.5004)
  Internet address is 10.1.1.1/24
! lines omitted for brevity
```

Bandwidth and Clock Rate on Serial Interfaces

Ethernet interfaces use either a single speed or one of a few speeds that can be auto-negotiated. However, as mentioned in Chapter 4, WAN links can run at a wide variety of speeds. To deal with the wide range of speeds, routers physically slave themselves to the speed as dictated by the CSU/DSU through a process called *clocking*. As a result, routers can use serial links without the need for additional configuration or autonegotiation to sense the serial link's speed. The CSU/DSU knows the speed, the CSU/DSU sends clock pulses over the cable to the router, and the router reacts to the clocking signal. In effect, the CSU/DSU tells the router when to send the next bit over the cable, and when to receive the next bit, with the router just blindly reacting to the CSU/DSU for that timing.

The physical details of how clocking works prevent routers from sensing and measuring the speed used on a link with CSU/DSUs. So, routers use two different interface configuration commands that specify the speed of the WAN link connected to a serial interface, namely the **clock rate** and **bandwidth** interface subcommands.

The **clock rate** command dictates the actual speed used to transmit bits on a serial link, but only when the physical serial link is actually created with cabling in a lab. The lab networks used to build the examples in this book, and probably in any labs engineers use to do proof-of-concept testing, or even labs you use in CCNA classes, use *back-to-back serial cables* (see the Chapter 4 section "Building a WAN Link in a Lab" for a reminder). Back-to-back WAN connections do not use a CSU/DSU, so one router must supply the clocking, which defines the speed at which bits are transmitted. The other router works as usual when CSU/DSUs are used, slaving itself to the clocking signals received from the other router. Example 13-3 shows an example configuration for a router named Albuquerque, with a couple of important commands related to WAN links.

NOTE Example 13-3 omits some of the output of the **show running-config** command, specifically the parts that do not matter to the information covered here.

Example 13-3 *Albuquerque Router Configuration with* **clock rate** *Command*

```
Albuquerque#show running-config
! lines omitted for brevity
interface Serial0/0/1
 clock rate 128000
```

continues

Example 13-3 *Albuquerque Router Configuration with* **clock rate** *Command (Continued)*

```
!
interface Serial0/1/0
 clock rate 128000
 bandwidth 128
!
interface FastEthernet0/0
! lines omitted for brevity
Albuquerque#show controllers serial 0/0/1
Interface Serial0
Hardware is PowerQUICC MPC860
DCE V.35, clock rate 128000
idb at 0x8169BB20, driver data structure at 0x816A35E4
! Lines omitted for brevity
```

The **clock rate** *speed* interface subcommand sets the rate in bits per second on the router that has the DCE cable plugged into it. If you do not know which router has the DCE cable in it, you can find out by using the **show controllers** command, which lists whether the attached cable is DCE (as shown in Example 13-3) or DTE. Interestingly, IOS accepts the **clock rate** command on an interface only if the interface already has a DCE cable installed, or if no cable is installed. If a DTE cable has been plugged in, IOS silently rejects the command, meaning that IOS does not give you an error message, but IOS ignores the command.

The second interface subcommand that relates to the speed of the serial link is the **bandwidth** *speed* command, as shown on interface serial 0/1/0 in Example 13-3. The **bandwidth** command tells IOS the speed of the link, in kilobits per second, regardless of whether the router is supplying clocking. However, the **bandwidth** setting does not change the speed at which bits are sent and received on the link. Instead, the router uses it for documentation purposes, in calculations related to the utilization rates of the link, and for many other purposes. In particular, the EIGRP and OSPF routing protocols use the interface **bandwidth** settings to set their default metrics, with the metrics impacting a router's choice of the best IP route to reach each subnet. (The *CCNA ICND2 Official Exam Certification Guide* covers these two routing protocols, including how the **bandwidth** command impacts the routing protocol metrics.)

Every router interface has a default setting of the **bandwidth** command that is used when there is no **bandwidth** command configured on the interface. For serial links, the default bandwidth is 1544, meaning 1544 kbps, or 1.544 Mbps—in other words, the speed of a T1 line. Router Ethernet interfaces default to a bandwidth setting that reflects the current speed of the interface. For example, if a router's FastEthernet interface is running at 100 Mbps, the bandwidth is 100,000 (kbps); if the interface is currently running at 10 Mbps, the router automatically changes the bandwidth to 10,000 kbps. Note that the configuration of the **bandwidth** command on an interface overrides these defaults.

> **NOTE** The **clock rate** command uses a unit of bps, whereas the **bandwidth** command uses a unit of kbps. In other words, a **show** command that lists bandwidth as 10,000 means 10,000 kbps, or 10 Mbps.

Router Auxiliary (Aux) Port

Routers have an auxiliary (Aux) port that allows access to the CLI by using a terminal emulator. Normally, the Aux port is connected via a cable (RJ-45, 4 pair, with straight-through pinouts) to an external analog modem. The modem connects to a phone line. Then, the engineer uses a PC, terminal emulator, and modem to call the remote router. Once connected, the engineer can use the terminal emulator to access the router CLI, starting in user mode as usual.

Aux ports can be configured beginning with the **line aux 0** command to reach aux line configuration mode. From there, all the commands for the console line, covered mostly in Chapter 8, can be used. For example, the **login** and **password** *passvalue* commands could be used to set up simple password checking when a user dials in.

Cisco switches do not have an Aux port.

Initial Configuration (Setup Mode)

The processes related to setup mode in routers follow the same rules as for switches. You can refer to the Chapter 8 section "Initial Configuration Using Setup Mode" for more details, but the following statements summarize some of the key points, all of which are true on both switches and routers:

- Setup mode is intended to allow basic configuration by prompting the CLI user via a series of questions.

- You can reach setup mode either by booting a router after erasing the startup-config file or by using the **setup** enable-mode EXEC command.

- At the end of the process, you get three choices (0, 1, or 2), to either ignore the answers and go back to the CLI (0); ignore the answers but begin again in setup mode (1); or to use the resulting configuration (2).

- If you tire of the process, the Ctrl-C key combination will eject the user out of setup mode and back to the previous CLI mode.

- If you select to use the resulting configuration, the router writes the configuration to the startup-config file, as well as the running-config file.

The main difference between the setup mode on switches and routers relates to the information requested while in setup mode. For example, routers need to know the IP address and mask for each interface on which you want to configure IP, whereas switches have only one IP address. To be complete, Example 13-4 demonstrates the use of setup mode. If you do not have a router with which to practice setup mode, take the time to review the example, and see the kinds of information requested in the various questions.

> **NOTE**   The questions asked, and the default answers, differ on some routers in part due to the IOS revision, feature set, and router model.

Example 13-4   *Router Setup Configuration Mode*

```
--- System Configuration Dialog ---

Would you like to enter the initial configuration dialog? [yes/no]: yes
At any point you may enter a question mark '?' for help.
Use ctrl-c to abort configuration dialog at any prompt.
Default settings are in square brackets '[]'.Basic management setup configures
only enough connectivity
for management of the system, extended setup will ask you
to configure each interface on the system

Would you like to enter basic management setup? [yes/no]: no
First, would you like to see the current interface summary? [yes]:
Any interface listed with OK? value "NO" does not have a valid configuration

Interface               IP-Address      OK? Method Status              Protocol
Ethernet0               unassigned      NO  unset  up                  down
Serial0                 unassigned      NO  unset  down                down
Serial1                 unassigned      NO  unset  down                down

Configuring global parameters:

  Enter host name [Router]: R1
      The enable secret is a password used to protect access to
      privileged EXEC and configuration modes. This password, after
      entered, becomes encrypted in the configuration.
      Enter enable secret: cisco
    The enable password is used when you do not specify an
      enable secret password, with some older software versions, and
      some boot images.
      Enter enable password: fred
    The virtual terminal password is used to protect
      access to the router over a network interface.
      Enter virtual terminal password: barney
  Configure SNMP Network Management? [yes]: no
  Configure bridging? [no]:
  Configure DECnet? [no]:
  Configure AppleTalk? [no]:
  Configure IPX? [no]:
```

Example 13-4 *Router Setup Configuration Mode (Continued)*

```
     Configure IP? [yes]:
     Configure RIP routing? [yes]:
Configure CLNS? [no]:
  Configure bridging? [no]:

Configuring interface parameters:
     Do you want to configure Ethernet0  interface? [yes]:
     Configure IP on this interface? [yes]:
     IP address for this interface: 172.16.1.1
     Subnet mask for this interface [255.255.0.0] : 255.255.255.0
     Class B network is 172.16.0.0, 24 subnet bits; mask is /24
     Do you want to configure Serial0  interface? [yes]:
       Configure IP on this interface? [yes]:
     Configure IP unnumbered on this interface? [no]:
     IP address for this interface: 172.16.12.1
     Subnet mask for this interface [255.255.0.0] : 255.255.255.0
     Class B network is 172.16.0.0, 24 subnet bits; mask is /24
     Do you want to configure Serial1  interface? [yes]:
     Configure IP on this interface? [yes]:
     Configure IP unnumbered on this interface? [no]:
     IP address for this interface: 172.16.13.1
     Subnet mask for this interface [255.255.0.0] : 255.255.255.0
     Class B network is 172.16.0.0, 24 subnet bits; mask is /24

     The following configuration command script was created:

     hostname R1
     enable secret 5 $1$VOLh$pkIe0Xjx2sgjgZ/Y6Gt1s.
     enable password fred
     line vty 0 4
     password barney
     no snmp-server
     !
     ip routing
      !
     interface Ethernet0
     ip address 172.16.1.1 255.255.255.0
     !
     interface Serial0
     ip address 172.16.12.1 255.255.255.0
     !
     interface Serial1
     ip address 172.16.13.1 255.255.255.0
     !
     router rip
     network 172.16.0.0
     !
```

continues

Example 13-4   *Router Setup Configuration Mode (Continued)*

```
end

[0] Go to the IOS command prompt without saving this config.
[1] Return back to the setup without saving this config.
[2] Save this configuration to nvram and exit.

Enter your selection [2]: 2
Building configuration...
[OK]Use the enabled mode 'configure' command to modify this configuration.
Press RETURN to get started!
```

NOTE   Although not shown in this example, routers that use an IOS feature set that includes additional security features will also ask the user if they want to configure *Cisco Auto Secure*. This feature automatically configures many router security best practice settings, for example, disabling CDP.

Upgrading Cisco IOS Software and the Cisco IOS Software Boot Process

Engineers need to know how to upgrade IOS to move to a later release or version of IOS. Typically, a router has one IOS image in Flash memory, and that is the IOS image that is used. (The term *IOS image* simply refers to a file containing IOS.) The upgrade process might include steps such as copying a newer IOS image into Flash memory, configuring the router to tell it which IOS image to use, and deleting the old one when you are confident that the new release works well. Alternately, you could copy a new image to a TFTP server, with some additional configuration on the router to tell it to get the new IOS from the TFTP server the next time the router is reloaded.

This section shows how to upgrade IOS by copying a new IOS file into Flash memory and telling the router to use the new IOS. Because the router decides which IOS to use when the router boots, this is also a good place to review the process by which routers boot (initialize). Switches follow the same basic process as described here, with some minor differences, as specifically noted.

Upgrading a Cisco IOS Software Image into Flash Memory

Routers and switches typically store IOS images in Flash memory. Flash memory is rewriteable, permanent storage, which is ideal for storing files that need to be retained when the router loses power. Cisco purposefully uses Flash memory instead of disk drives in its products because there are no moving parts in Flash memory, so there is a smaller chance of failure as compared with disk drives. Additionally, the IOS image can be placed on an external TFTP server, but using an external server typically is done for testing; in production, practically every Cisco router loads an IOS image stored in the only type of large, permanent memory in a Cisco router—Flash memory.

Figure 13-6 illustrates the process to upgrade an IOS image into Flash memory:

Step 1 Obtain the IOS image from Cisco, typically by downloading the IOS image from Cisco.com using HTTP or FTP.

Step 2 Place the IOS image into the default directory of a TFTP server that is accessible from the router.

Step 3 Issue the **copy** command from the router, copying the file into Flash memory.

You also can use an FTP or remote copy (rcp) server, but the TFTP feature has been around a long time and is a more likely topic for the exams.

Figure 13-6 *Complete Cisco IOS Software Upgrade Process*

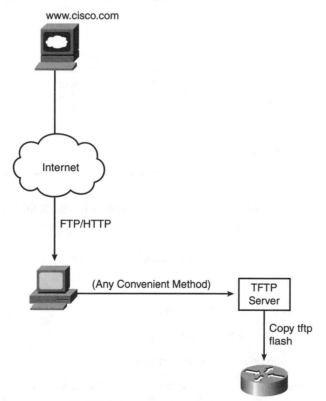

Example 13-5 provides an example of the final step, copying the IOS image into Flash memory. Note that the **copy tftp flash** command shown here works much like the **copy tftp startup-config** command that can be used to restore a backup copy of the configuration file into NVRAM.

Example 13-5   **copy tftp flash** *Command Copies the IOS Image to Flash Memory*

```
R1#copy tftp flash

System flash directory:
File  Length    Name/status
  1   7530760   c4500-d-mz.120-2.bin
[7530824 bytes used, 857784 available, 8388608 total]
Address or name of remote host [255.255.255.255]? 134.141.3.33
Source file name? c4500-d-mz.120-5.bin
Destination file name [c4500-d-mz.120-5.bin]?
Accessing file c4500-d-mz.120-5.bin ' on 134.141.3.33...
Loading c4500-d-mz.120-5.bin from 134.141.3.33 (via Ethernet0): ! [OK]

Erase flash device before writing? [confirm]
Flash contains files. Are you sure you want to erase? [confirm]

Copy 'c4500-d-mz.120-5.bin ' from server
  as 'c4500-d-mz.120-5.bin ' into Flash WITH erase? [yes/no]y
Erasing device... eeeeeeeeeeeeeeeeeeeeeeeeeeeeeeeee ...erased
Loading c4500-d-mz.120-5.bin  from 134.141.3.33 (via Ethernet0):
  !!!!!!!!!!!!!!!!!!!!!!!!!!!!!!!!!!!!!!!!!!!!!!!!!!!!!!!!!!!!!!!!!!!!!!!!!!!!!!!
  !!!!!!!!!!!!!!!!!!!!!!!!!!!!!!!!!!!!!!!!!!!!! (leaving out lots of exclamation points)
[OK  7530760/8388608 bytes]

Verifying checksum...  OK (0xA93E)
Flash copy took 0:04:26 [hh:mm:ss]
```

During this process of copying the IOS image into Flash memory, the router needs to discover several important facts:

1. What is the IP address or host name of the TFTP server?

2. What is the name of the file?

3. Is space available for this file in Flash memory?

4. Does the server actually have a file by that name?

5. Do you want the router to erase the old files?

The router will prompt you for answers, as necessary. For each question, you should either type an answer or press Enter if the default answer (shown in square brackets at the end of the question) is acceptable. Afterward, the router erases Flash memory if directed, copies the file, and then verifies that the checksum for the file shows that no errors occurred in transmission. You can then use the **show flash** command to verify the contents of Flash memory, as demonstrated in Example 13-6. (The **show flash** output can vary among router families. Example 13-6 is output from a 2500 series router.)

Example 13-6 *Verifying Flash Memory Contents with the* **show flash** *Command*

```
fred#show flash
System flash directory:
File  Length    Name/status
  1   13305352  c2500-ds-1.122-1.bin
[13305416 bytes used, 3471800 available, 16777216 total]
16384K bytes of processor board System flash (Read ONLY)
```

The shaded line in Example 13-6 lists the amount of Flash memory, the amount used, and the amount of free space. When copying a new IOS image into Flash, the **copy** command will ask you if you want to erase Flash, with a default answer of [yes]. If you reply with an answer of **no**, and IOS realizes that not enough available Flash memory exists, the copy will fail. Additionally, even if you answer **yes**, and erase all of Flash memory, the new Flash IOS image must be of a size that fits into flash memory; if not, the **copy** command will fail.

Once the new IOS has been copied into Flash, the router must be reloaded to use the new IOS image. The next section, which covers the IOS boot sequence, explains the details of how to configure a router so that it loads the right IOS image.

The Cisco IOS Software Boot Sequence

Cisco routers perform the same types of tasks that a typical computer performs when you power it on or reboot (reload) it. Most computers have a single operating system (OS) installed, and that OS boots by default. However, a router can have multiple IOS images available both in Flash memory and on external TFTP servers, so the router needs to know which IOS image to load. This section examines the entire boot process, with extra emphasis on the options that impact a router's choice of what IOS image to load.

NOTE The boot sequence details in this section, particularly those regarding the configuration register and the ROMMON OS, differ from Cisco LAN switches, but they do apply to most every model of Cisco router. This book does not cover the equivalent options in Cisco switches.

When a router first powers on, it follows these four steps:

1. The router performs a power-on self-test (POST) to discover the hardware components and verify that all components work properly.

2. The router copies a bootstrap program from ROM into RAM, and runs the bootstrap program.

3. The bootstrap program decides which IOS image (or other OS) to load into RAM, and loads that OS. After loading the IOS image, the bootstrap program hands over control of the router hardware to the newly loaded OS.

4. If the bootstrap program loaded IOS, IOS finds the configuration file (typically the startup-config file in NVRAM) and loads it into RAM as the running-config.

All routers attempt all four steps each time that the router is powered on or reloaded. The first two steps do not have any options to choose; these steps either work or the router initialization fails and you typically need to call the Cisco Technical Assistance Center (TAC) for support. However, Steps 3 and 4 have several configurable options that tell the router what to do next. Figure 13-7 depicts those options, referencing Steps 2 through 4 shown in the earlier boot process.

Figure 13-7 *Loading the Cisco IOS*

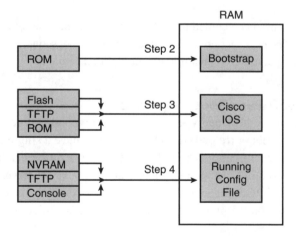

As you can see, the router can get the IOS image from three locations and can get the initial configuration from three locations as well. Frankly, routers almost always load the configuration from NVRAM (the startup-config file), when it exists. There is no real advantage to storing the initial configuration anywhere else except NVRAM. So, this chapter will not look further into the options of Step 4. However, there are good reasons for putting multiple IOS images in Flash, and keeping images on external servers, so the rest of this section examines Step 3 in more detail. In particular, the next few pages explain a few facts about some alternate router operating systems besides IOS, and a router feature called the *configuration register*, before showing how a router chooses which IOS image to load.

> **NOTE**   The IOS image is typically a compressed file so that it consumes less space in Flash memory. The router decompresses the IOS image as is it loaded into RAM.

The Three Router Operating Systems

A router typically loads and uses a Cisco IOS image that allows the router to perform its normal function of routing packets. However, Cisco routers can use a different OS to perform some troubleshooting, to recover router passwords, and to copy new IOS files into Flash when Flash has been inadvertently erased or corrupted. In the more recent additions to the Cisco router product line (for example, 1800 and 2800 series routers), Cisco routers use only one other OS, whereas older Cisco routers (for example, 2500 series routers) actually had two different operating systems to perform different subsets of these same functions. Table 13-4 lists the other two router operating systems, and a few details about each.

Table 13-4   *Comparing ROMMON and RxBoot Operating Systems*

Operating Environment	Common Name	Stored In	Used in...
ROM Monitor	ROMMON	ROM	Old and new routers
Boot ROM	RxBoot, boot helper	ROM	Only in older routers

Key Topic

Because the RxBoot OS is only available in older routers and is no longer needed in the newer routers, this chapter will mainly refer to the OS that continues to be available for these special functions, the ROMMON OS.

The Configuration Register

The configuration register is a special 16-bit number that can be set on any Cisco router. The configuration register's bits control different settings for some low-level operating characteristics of the router. For example, the console runs at a speed of 9600 bps by default, but that console speed is based on the default settings of a couple of bits in the configuration register.

You can set the *configuration register* value with the **config-register** global configuration command. Engineers set the configuration register to different values for many reasons, but the most common are to help tell the router what IOS image to load, as explained in the next few pages, and in the password recovery process. For example, the command **config-register 0x2100** sets the value to hexadecimal 2100, which causes the router to load the ROMMON OS instead of IOS—a common practice when recovering lost passwords. Interestingly, this value is automatically saved when you press Enter at the end of the **config-register** command—you do not need to save the running-config file into the startup-config file after changing the configuration register. However, the configuration register's new value is not used until the next time the router is reloaded.

> **TIP**   The **show version** command, shown near the end of this chapter in Example 13-7, shows the configuration register's current value and, if different, the value that will be used once the router is reloaded.

> **NOTE**   On most Cisco routers, the default configuration register setting is hexadecimal 2102.

How a Router Chooses Which OS to Load

A router chooses the OS to load based on the low-order 4 bits in the configuration register and the details configured in any **boot system** global configuration commands found in the startup-config file. The low-order 4 bits (the 4th hex digit) in the configuration register are called the *boot field*, with the value of these bits being the first value a router examines when choosing which OS to try and load. The boot field's value when the router is powered on or reloaded tells the router how to proceed with choosing which OS to load.

> **NOTE**   Cisco represents hexadecimal values by preceding the hex digit(s) with 0x—for example, 0xA would mean a single hex digit A.

The process to choose which OS to load, on more modern routers that do not have an RxBoot OS, happens as follows (note that "boot" refers to the boot field in the configuration register):

Key Topic

Step 1   If boot field = 0, use the ROMMON OS.

Step 2   If boot field = 1, load the first IOS file found in Flash memory.

Step 3   If boot field = 2-F:

   a. Try each **boot system** command in the startup-config file, in order, until one works.

   b. If none of the **boot system** commands work, load the first IOS file found in Flash memory.

> **NOTE**   The actual step numbers are not important—the list is just numbered for easier reference.

The first two steps are pretty straightforward, but Step 3 then tells the router to look to the second major method to tell the router which IOS to load: the **boot system** global configuration command. This command can be configured multiple times on one router, with details about files in Flash memory, and filenames and IP addresses of servers, telling the router where to look for an IOS image to load. The router tries to load the IOS images, in the order of the configured **boot system** commands. Once the router succeeds in loading one of the referenced IOS images, the process is complete, and the router can ignore the remaining **boot system** commands. If the router fails to load an IOS based on the **boot system** commands, the router then tries what Step 1 suggests, which is to load the first IOS file found in Flash memory.

Both Step 2 and Step 3b refer to a concept of the "first" IOS file, a concept which needs a little more explanation. Routers number the files stored in Flash memory, with each new file typically getting a higher and higher number. When a router tries Step 2 or Step 3b from the preceding list, the router will look in Flash memory, starting with file number 1, and then file number 2, and so on, until it finds the lowest numbered file that happens to be an IOS image. The router will then load that file.

Interestingly, most routers end up using Step 3b to find their IOS image. From the factory, Cisco routers do not have any **boot system** commands configured; in fact, they do not have any configuration in the startup-config file at all. Cisco loads Flash memory with a single IOS when it builds and tests the router, and the configuration register value is set to 0x2102, meaning a boot field of 0x2. With all these settings, the process tries Step 3 (because boot = 2), finds no **boot system** commands (because the startup-config is empty), and then looks for the first file in Flash memory at Step 3b.

Figure 13-8 shows a diagram that summarizes the key concepts behind how a router chooses the OS to load.

Key
Topic

Figure 13-8   *Choices for Choosing the OS at Boot Time: Modern Cisco Router*

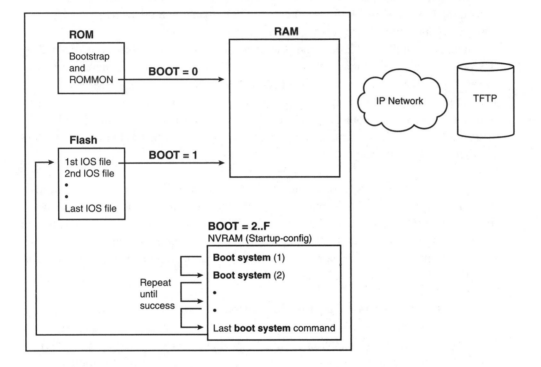

The **boot system** commands need to refer to the exact file that the router should load.
Table 13-5 shows several examples of the commands.

Table 13-5   *Sample* **boot system** *Commands*

Boot System Command	Result
boot system flash	The first file from Flash memory is loaded.
boot system flash *filename*	IOS with the name *filename* is loaded from Flash memory.
boot system tftp *filename* **10.1.1.1**	IOS with the name *filename* is loaded from the TFTP server.

In some cases, a router fails to load on OS based on the three-step process listed earlier in
this section. For example, someone might accidentally erase all the contents of Flash,
including the IOS image. So, routers need more options to help recover from these
unexpected but possible scenarios. If no OS is found by the end of Step 3, the router will
send broadcasts looking for a TFTP server, guess at a filename for the IOS image, and load

an IOS image (assuming that a TFTP server is found). In practice it is highly unlikely to work. The final step is to simply load ROMMON, which is designed in part to provide tools to recover from these unexpected types of problems. For example, an IOS image can be copied into Flash from a TFTP server while using ROMMON.

For older models of Cisco router that have an RxBoot (boot helper) OS in ROM, the process to choose which OS to load works generally the same, with two differences. When the boot field is 0x1, the router loads the RxBoot OS stored in ROM. Also, in the final efforts to find an OS as described in the previous paragraph, if the effort to find an image from a TFTP server fails, and the router has an RxBoot image, the router first tries to load RxBoot before trying to load the ROM Monitor OS.

The show version Command and Seeing the Configuration Register's Value

The **show version** command supplies a wide variety of information about a router, including both the current value of the configuration register and the expected value at the next reload of the router. The following list summarizes some of the other very interesting information in this command:

1. The IOS version

2. The uptime (the length of time that has passed since the last reload)

3. The reason for the last reload of IOS (**reload** command, power off/on, software failure)

4. The time of the last loading of IOS (if the router's clock has been set)

5. The source from which the router loaded the current IOS

6. The amount of RAM memory

7. The number and types of interfaces

8. The amount of NVRAM memory

9. The amount of Flash memory

10. The configuration register's current and future setting (if different)

Example 13-7 demonstrates output from the **show version** command, highlighting the key pieces of information. Note that the preceding list is in the same order in which the highlighted information appears in the example.

Example 13-7 **show version** *Command Output*

```
Albuquerque#show version
Cisco IOS Software, 1841 Software (C1841-ADVENTERPRISEK9-M), Version 12.4(9)T, RELEASE
  SOFTWARE (fc1)
Technical Support: http://www.cisco.com/techsupport
Copyright (c) 1986-2006 by Cisco Systems, Inc.
```
continues

Example 13-7   show version *Command Output (Continued)*

```
Compiled Fri 16-Jun-06 21:26 by prod_rel_team

ROM: System Bootstrap, Version 12.3(8r)T8, RELEASE SOFTWARE (fc1)

Albuquerque uptime is 5 hours, 20 minutes
System returned to ROM by reload at 13:12:26 UTC Wed Jan 17 2007
System restarted at 13:13:38 UTC Wed Jan 17 2007
System image file is "flash:c1841-adventerprisek9-mz.124-9.T.bin"


This product contains cryptographic features and is subject to United
States and local country laws governing import, export, transfer and
use. Delivery of Cisco cryptographic products does not imply
third-party authority to import, export, distribute or use encryption.
Importers, exporters, distributors and users are responsible for
compliance with U.S. and local country laws. By using this product you
agree to comply with applicable laws and regulations. If you are unable
to comply with U.S. and local laws, return this product immediately.

A summary of U.S. laws governing Cisco cryptographic products may be found at:
http://www.cisco.com/wwl/export/crypto/tool/stqrg.html

If you require further assistance please contact us by sending email to
export@cisco.com.

Cisco 1841 (revision 4.1) with 354304K/38912K bytes of memory.
Processor board ID FTX0906Y03T
2 FastEthernet interfaces
4 Serial(sync/async) interfaces
1 Virtual Private Network (VPN) Module
DRAM configuration is 64 bits wide with parity disabled.
191K bytes of NVRAM.
125440K bytes of ATA CompactFlash (Read/Write)

Configuration register is 0x2102 (will be 0x2101 at next reload)
```

Most of the information highlighted in the example can be easily found in comparison to the list preceding Example 13-7. However, note that the amount of RAM, listed as 354304K/38912K, shows the RAM in two parts. The sum of these two parts is the total amount of available RAM, about 384 MB in this case.

Exam Preparation Tasks

Review All the Key Topics

Review the most important topics from inside the chapter, noted with the key topics icon in the outer margin of the page. Table 13-6 lists a reference of these key topics and the page numbers on which each is found.

Key
Topic

Table 13-6 *Key Topics for Chapter 13*

Key Topic	Description	Page Number
List	Steps required to install a router	406
List	Similarities between router CLI and switch CLI	410
List	Items covered for switches in Chapter 8 that differ in some way on routers	410
Table 13-2	Router interface status codes and their meanings	413
Table 13-3	Combinations of the two interface status codes and the likely reasons for each combination	414
List	Summary of important facts about the initial configuration dialog (setup mode)	417
List	The four steps a router performs when booting	424
Table 13-4	Comparison of ROMMON and RxBoot operating systems	425
List	Steps a router uses to choose which IOS image to load	426
Figure 13-8	Diagram of how a router chooses which IOS image to load	428
List	A list of the many important facts that can be seen in the output from the **show version** command	429

Complete the Tables and Lists from Memory

Print a copy of Appendix H, "Memory Tables" (found on the CD-ROM), or at least the section for this chapter, and complete the tables and lists from memory. Appendix I, "Memory Tables Answer Key," also on the CD-ROM, includes completed tables and lists to check your work.

Definitions of Key Terms

Define the following key terms from this chapter and check your answers in the glossary.

bandwidth, boot field, clock rate, configuration register, IOS image, power-on self-test (POST), ROMMON, RxBoot

Read Appendix F Scenario 2

Appendix F, "Additional Scenarios," contains two detailed scenarios that give you a chance to analyze different designs, problems, and command output, as well as show you how concepts from several different chapters interrelate. At this point in your reading, Appendix F scenario 2, which shows how to use Cisco Discovery Protocol (CDP), would be particularly useful to read.

Command References

Although you should not necessarily memorize the information in the tables in this section, this section does include a reference for the configuration commands (Table 13-7) and EXEC commands (Table 13-8) covered in this chapter. Practically speaking, you should memorize the commands as a complement to reading the chapter and doing all the activities in this exam preparation section. To check to see how well you have memorized the commands, cover the left side of the table with a piece of paper, read the descriptions in the right side, and see if you remember the command.

Table 13-7 *Chapter 13 Configuration Command Reference*

Command	Description
bandwidth *kbps*	Interface command that sets the router's perception of bandwidth of the interface, in a unit of kbps.
clock rate *rate*	Interface command that sets the speed at which the router supplies a clocking signal, applicable only when the router has a DCE cable installed. The unit is bits/second.
config-register *value*	Global command that sets the hexadecimal value of the configuration register.
boot system {*file-url*	*filename*}	Global command that identifies an externally located IOS image using a URL.
boot system flash [*flash-fs:*] [*filename*]	Global command that identifies the location of an IOS image in Flash memory.

Table 13-7 *Chapter 13 Configuration Command Reference (Continued)*

Command	Description
boot system rom	Global command that tells the router to load the RxBoot OS found in ROM, if one exists.
boot system {rcp | tftp | ftp} *filename* [*ip-address*]	Global command that identifies an external server, protocol, and filename to use to load an IOS from an external server.

Table 13-8 *Chapter 13 EXEC Command Reference*

Command	Purpose
show interfaces *[type number]*	Lists a large set of informational messages about each interface, or about the one specifically listed interface.
show ip interface brief	Lists a single line of information about each interface, including the IP address, line and protocol status, and the method with which the address was configured (manual or DHCP).
show protocols *type number*	Lists a single line of information about the listed interface, including the IP address, mask, and line/protocol status.
show controllers *[type number]*	Lists many lines of information per interface, or for one interface, for the hardware controller of the interface. On serial interfaces, this command identifies the cable as either a DCE or DTE cable.
show version	Lists the IOS version, as well as a large set of other useful information (see Example 13-7).
setup	Starts the setup (initial configuration) dialog in which the router prompts the user for basic configuration settings.
copy *source-url destination-url*	Copies a file from the first listed URL to the destination URL.
show flash	Lists the names and size of the files in Flash memory, as well as noting the amount of Flash memory consumed and available.
reload	Enable mode command that reinitializes (reboots) the router.

This chapter covers the following subjects:

Connected and Static Routes: This section covers the basics of how routers learn routes to connected subnets and how to configure static routes.

Routing Protocol Overview: This section explains the terminology and theory related to routing protocols in general and Routing Information Protocol (RIP) in particular.

Configuring and Verifying RIP-2: This section explains how to configure RIP Version 2 (RIP-2) and how to confirm that RIP-2 is working correctly.

CHAPTER 14

Routing Protocol Concepts and Configuration

The United States Postal Service routes a huge number of letters and packages each day. To do so, the postal sorting machines run fast, sorting lots of letters. Then the letters are placed in the correct container and onto the correct truck or plane to reach the final destination. However, if no one programs the letter-sorting machines to know where letters to each ZIP code should be sent, the sorter cannot do its job. Similarly, Cisco routers can route many packets, but if the router does not know any routes—routes that tell the router where to send the packets—the router cannot do its job.

This chapter introduces the basic concepts of how routers fill their routing tables with routes. Routers learn routes by being directly connected to local subnets, by being statically configured with information about routes, and by using dynamic routing protocols.

As you might guess by now, to fully appreciate the nuances of how routing protocols work, you need a thorough understanding of routing—the process of forwarding packets—as well as subnetting. So, this chapter includes a few additional comments on routing and subnetting, to link the ideas from Chapter 5, "Fundamentals of IP Addressing and Routing," Chapter 12, "IP Addressing and Subnetting," and Chapter 13, "Operating Cisco Routers," together so you can better understand dynamic routing protocols.

"Do I Know This Already?" Quiz

The "Do I Know This Already?" quiz allows you to assess if you should read the entire chapter. If you miss no more than one of these ten self-assessment questions, you might want to move ahead to the "Exam Preparation Tasks" section. Table 14-1 lists the major headings in this chapter and the "Do I Know This Already?" quiz questions covering the material in those headings so you can assess your knowledge of these specific areas. The answers to the "Do I Know This Already?" quiz appear in Appendix A.

Table 14-1 *"Do I Know This Already?" Foundation Topics Section-to-Question Mapping*

Foundation Topics Section	Questions
Connected and Static Routes	1, 2
Routing Protocol Overview	3–6
Configuring and Verifying RIP-2	7–10

1. Which of the following must be true for a static route to be installed in a router's IP routing table?

    a. The outgoing interface associated with the route must be in an "up and up" state.

    b. The router must receive a routing update from a neighboring router.

    c. The **ip route** command must be added to the configuration.

    d. The outgoing interface's **ip address** command must use the **special** keyword.

2. Which of the following commands correctly configures a static route?

    a. **ip route 10.1.3.0 255.255.255.0 10.1.130.253**

    b. **ip route 10.1.3.0 serial 0**

    c. **ip route 10.1.3.0 /24 10.1.130.253**

    d. **ip route 10.1.3.0 /24 serial 0**

3. Which of the following routing protocols are considered to use distance vector logic?

    a. RIP

    b. IGRP

    c. EIGRP

    d. OSPF

4. Which of the following routing protocols are considered to use link-state logic?

    a. RIP

    b. RIP-2

    c. IGRP

    d. EIGRP

    e. OSPF

    f. Integrated IS-IS

5. Which of the following routing protocols support VLSM?

    a. RIP

    b. RIP-2

    c. IGRP

    d. EIGRP

    e. OSPF

    f. Integrated IS-IS

6. Which of the following routing protocols are considered to be capable of converging quickly?

   a. RIP

   b. RIP-2

   c. IGRP

   d. EIGRP

   e. OSPF

   f. Integrated IS-IS

7. Router1 has interfaces with addresses 9.1.1.1 and 10.1.1.1. Router2, connected to Router1 over a serial link, has interfaces with addresses 10.1.1.2 and 11.1.1.2. Which of the following commands would be part of a complete RIP Version 2 configuration on Router2, with which Router2 advertises out all interfaces, and about all routes?

   a. **router rip**

   b. **router rip 3**

   c. **network 9.0.0.0**

   d. **version 2**

   e. **network 10.0.0.0**

   f. **network 10.1.1.1**

   g. **network 10.1.1.2**

   h. **network 11.0.0.0**

   i. **network 11.1.1.2**

8. Which of the following **network** commands, following a **router rip** command, would cause RIP to send updates out two interfaces whose IP addresses are 10.1.2.1 and 10.1.1.1, mask 255.255.255.0?

   a. **network 10.0.0.0**

   b. **network 10.1.1.0 10.1.2.0**

   c. **network 10.1.1.1. 10.1.2.1**

   d. **network 10.1.0.0 255.255.0.0**

   e. **network 10**

   f. You cannot do this with only one **network** command.

9. What command(s) list(s) information identifying the neighboring routers that are sending routing information to a particular router?

    a. **show ip**

    b. **show ip protocol**

    c. **show ip routing-protocols**

    d. **show ip route**

    e. **show ip route neighbor**

    f. **show ip route received**

10. Review the snippet from a **show ip route** command on a router:

    ```
    R       10.1.2.0 [120/1] via 10.1.128.252, 00:00:13, Serial0/0/1
    ```

    Which of the following statements are true regarding this output?

    a. The administrative distance is 1.

    b. The administrative distance is 120.

    c. The metric is 1.

    d. The metric is not listed.

    e. The router added this route to the routing table 13 seconds ago.

    f. The router must wait 13 seconds before advertising this route again.

Foundation Topics

Connected and Static Routes

Routers need to have routes in their IP routing tables for the packet forwarding process (routing) to work. Two of the most basic means by which a router adds routes to its routing table are by learning about the subnets connected to its interfaces, and by configuring a route by using a global configuration command (called a static route). This section explains both, with the remainder of the chapter focusing on the third method of learning routes— dynamic routing protocols.

Connected Routes

A router adds routes to its routing table for the subnets connected to each of the router's interfaces. For this to occur, the router must have an IP address and mask configured on the interface (statically with the **ip address** command or dynamically using Dynamic Host Configuration Protocol [DHCP]) and both interface status codes must be "up." The concept is simple: if a router has an interface in a subnet, the router has a way to forward packets into that subnet, so the router needs a route in its routing table.

Figure 14-1 illustrates a sample internetwork that will be used in Example 14-1 to show some connected routes and some related **show** commands. Figure 14-1 shows an internetwork with six subnets, with each of the three routers having three interfaces in use. Each of the LANs in this figure could consist of one switch, one hub, or lots of switches and/or hubs together—but for the purposes of this chapter, the size of the LAN does not matter. Once the interfaces have been configured as shown in the figure, and once each interface is up and working, each of the routers should have three connected routes in their routing tables.

Example 14-1 shows the connected routes on Albuquerque after its interfaces have been configured with the addresses shown in Figure 14-1. The example includes several comments, with more detailed comments following the example.

Figure 14-1   *Sample Internetwork Used Throughout Chapter 14*

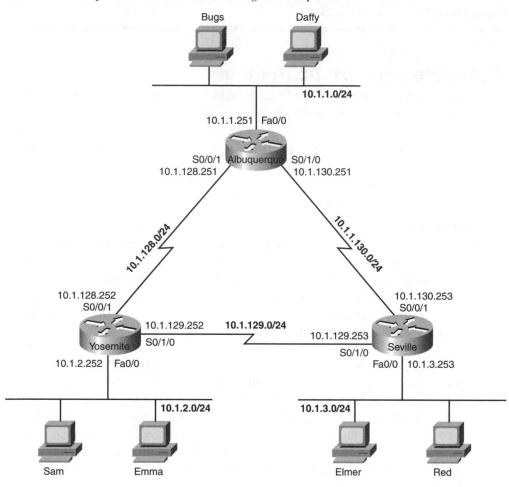

Example 14-1   *Albuquerque Connected Routes*

```
! The following command just lists the IP address configuration on Albuquerque.
! The output has been edited to show only the three interfaces used in Figure
! 14-1.
!
Albuquerque#show running-config
interface FastEthernet0/0
 ip address 10.1.1.251 255.255.255.0
!
interface Serial 0/0/1
 ip address 10.1.128.251 255.255.255.0
!
interface Serial 0/1/0
 ip address 10.1.130.251 255.255.255.0
```

Example 14-1 *Albuquerque Connected Routes (Continued)*

```
! Lines omitted for brevity
! The next command lists the interfaces, and confirms that Albuquerque's three
! interfaces shown in Figure 14-1 are in an "up and up" status.
!
Albuquerque#show ip interface brief
Interface               IP-Address      OK? Method Status             Protocol
FastEthernet0/0         10.1.1.251      YES manual up                    up
FastEthernet0/1         unassigned      YES manual administratively down down
Serial0/0/0             unassigned      YES NVRAM  administratively down down
Serial0/0/1             10.1.128.251    YES NVRAM  up                    up
Serial0/1/0             10.1.130.251    YES NVRAM  up                    up
Serial0/1/1             unassigned      YES NVRAM  administratively down down
!
! The next command lists the routes known by Albuquerque - all connected routes
!
Albuquerque#show ip route
Codes: C - connected, S - static, I - IGRP, R - RIP, M - mobile, B - BGP
       D - EIGRP, EX - EIGRP external, O - OSPF, IA - OSPF inter area
       N1 - OSPF NSSA external type 1, N2 - OSPF NSSA external type 2
       E1 - OSPF external type 1, E2 - OSPF external type 2, E - EGP
       i - IS-IS, L1 - IS-IS level-1, L2 - IS-IS level-2, ia - IS-IS inter area
       * - candidate default, U - per-user static route, o - ODR
       P - periodic downloaded static route
Gateway of last resort is not set


     10.0.0.0/24 is subnetted, 3 subnets
C       10.1.1.0 is directly connected, FastEthernet0/0
C       10.1.130.0 is directly connected, Serial0/1/0
C       10.1.128.0 is directly connected, Serial0/0/1
!
! The next command changes the mask format used by the show ip route command
!
Albuquerque#terminal ip netmask-format decimal
Albuquerque#show ip route
Codes: C - connected, S - static, I - IGRP, R - RIP, M - mobile, B - BGP
       D - EIGRP, EX - EIGRP external, O - OSPF, IA - OSPF inter area
       N1 - OSPF NSSA external type 1, N2 - OSPF NSSA external type 2
       E1 - OSPF external type 1, E2 - OSPF external type 2, E - EGP
       i - IS-IS, L1 - IS-IS level-1, L2 - IS-IS level-2, ia - IS-IS inter area
       * - candidate default, U - per-user static route, o - ODR
       P - periodic downloaded static route

Gateway of last resort is not set


     10.0.0.0 255.255.255.0 is subnetted, 3 subnets
C       10.1.1.0 is directly connected, FastEthernet0/0
C       10.1.130.0 is directly connected, Serial0/1/0
C       10.1.128.0 is directly connected, Serial0/0/1
```

To begin, the **show ip interface brief** command in Example 14-1 confirms that Albuquerque's three interfaces meet the requirements to have their connected subnets added to the routing table. Note that all three interfaces are in an "up and up" state and have an IP address configured.

The output of the **show ip route** command confirms that Albuquerque indeed added a route to all three subnets to its routing table. The output begins with a single-letter code legend, with "C" meaning "connected." The individual routes begin with a code letter on the far left—in this case, all three routes have the letter C. Also, note that the output lists the mask in prefix notation by default. Additionally, in cases when one mask is used throughout a single classful network—in other words, static-length subnet masking (SLSM) is used— the **show ip route** command output lists the mask on a heading line above the subnets of that classful network. For example, the lines with 10.1.1.0, 10.1.128.0, and 10.1.130.0 do not show the mask, but the line just above those three lines does list classful network 10.0.0.0 and the mask, as highlighted in the example.

Finally, you can change the format of the display of the subnet mask in **show** commands, for the duration of your login session to the router, using the **terminal ip netmask-format decimal** EXEC command, as shown at the end of Example 14-1.

> **NOTE** To be well prepared for the exams, you should look at all items in the output of the **show ip interface brief** and **show ip route** commands in each example in this chapter. Example 14-6, later in this chapter, provides more detailed comments about the **show ip route** command's output.

Static Routes

Although the connected routes on each router are important, routers typically need other routes to forward packets to all subnets in an internetwork. For example, Albuquerque can successfully ping the IP addresses on the other end of each serial link, or IP addresses on its local connected LAN subnet (10.1.1.0/24). However, a ping of an IP address in a subnet besides the three connected subnets will fail, as demonstrated in Example 14-2. Note that this example assumes that Albuquerque still only knows the three connected routes shown in Example 14-1.

Example 14-2 *Albuquerque Pings—Works to Connected Subnets Only*

```
! This first ping is a ping of Yosemite's S0/0/1 interface
Albuquerque#ping 10.1.128.252
Type escape sequence to abort.
Sending 5, 100-byte ICMP Echos to 10.1.128.252, timeout is 2 seconds:
!!!!!
Success rate is 100 percent (5/5), round-trip min/avg/max = 4/4/8 ms
```

Example 14-2 *Albuquerque Pings—Works to Connected Subnets Only (Continued)*

```
! This next ping is a ping of Yosemite's Fa0/0 interface
Albuquerque#ping 10.1.2.252
Type escape sequence to abort.
Sending 5, 100-byte ICMP Echos to 10.1.2.252, timeout is 2 seconds:
.....
Success rate is 0 percent (0/5)
```

The **ping** command sends an ICMP echo request packet to the stated destination address. The TCP/IP software at the destination then replies to the ping echo request packet with a similar packet, called an *ICMP echo reply*. The **ping** command sends the first packet and waits on the response. If a response is received, the command displays a "!". If no response is received within the default timeout of 2 seconds, the **ping** command displays a ".". The Cisco IOS software **ping** command sends five of these packets by default.

In Example 14-2, the **ping 10.1.128.252** command works (showing all !'s), because Albuquerque's route to 10.1.128.0/24 matches the destination address of 10.1.128.252. However, the **ping** to 10.1.2.252 does not work, because Albuquerque does not have a route for the subnet in which 10.1.2.252 resides, subnet 10.1.2.0/24. As a result, Albuquerque cannot even send the five ping packets, so the output lists five periods.

The simple and typical solution to this problem is to configure a routing protocol on all three routers. However, you can configure static routes instead. Example 14-3 shows two **ip route** global configuration commands on Albuquerque, which add static routes for the two LAN subnets connected to Yosemite and Seville. The addition of the first of the two **ip route** commands makes the failed ping from Example 14-2 work.

Example 14-3 *Static Routes Added to Albuquerque*

```
Albuquerque#configure terminal
Albuquerque(config)#ip route  10.1.2.0 255.255.255.0  10.1.128.252
Albuquerque(config)#ip route  10.1.3.0 255.255.255.0  10.1.130.253
Albuquerque#show ip route static
     10.0.0.0/24 is subnetted, 5 subnets
S       10.1.3.0 [1/0] via 10.1.130.253
S       10.1.2.0 [1/0] via 10.1.128.252
```

Key
Topic

The **ip route** global configuration command supplies the subnet number, mask, and the next-hop IP address. One **ip route** command defines a route to 10.1.2.0 (mask 255.255.255.0), which is located off Yosemite, so the next-hop IP address as configured on Albuquerque is 10.1.128.252, which is Yosemite's Serial0/0/1 IP address. Similarly, Albuquerque's route to 10.1.3.0/24, the subnet off Seville, points to Seville's Serial0/0/1 IP address, 10.1.130.253. Note that the next-hop IP address should be an IP address in a directly connected subnet. Now Albuquerque knows how to forward routes to both subnets.

Whereas you can see all routes using the **show ip route** command, the **show ip route static** command lists only statically configured IP routes. The "S" in the first column means that these two routes were statically configured. Also, to actually be added to the IP routing table, the **ip route** command must be configured, and the outgoing interface implied by the next-hop router IP address must be in an "up and up" state. For example, the next-hop address on the first **ip route** command is 10.1.128.252, which is in the subnet connected to Albuquerque's S0/0/1 interface. If Albuquerque's S0/0/1 interface is not currently in an "up and up" state, this static route would not be listed in the IP routing table.

The **ip route** command allows a slightly different syntax on point-to-point serial links. For such links, you can configure the outgoing interface instead of the next-hop IP address. For instance, you could have configured **ip route 10.1.2.0 255.255.255.0 serial0/0/1** for the first route in Example 14-3.

Unfortunately, adding these two static routes to Albuquerque does not solve all the network's routing problems—you would also need to configure static routes on the other two routers as well. Currently, the static routes help Albuquerque deliver packets to these two remote LAN subnets, but the other two routers do not have enough routing information to forward packets back toward Albuquerque's LAN subnet (10.1.1.0/24). For instance, PC Bugs cannot ping PC Sam in this network yet. The problem is that although Albuquerque has a route to subnet 10.1.2.0, where Sam resides, Yosemite does not have a route to 10.1.1.0, where Bugs resides. The ping request packet goes from Bugs to Sam correctly, but Sam's ping response packet cannot be routed by the Yosemite router back through Albuquerque to Bugs, so the ping fails.

Extended ping Command

In real life, you might not be able to find a user, like Bugs, to ask to test your network by pinging, and it might be impractical to physically travel to some other site just to type a few **ping** commands on some end-user PCs. A better alternative might be to telnet to a router connected to that user's subnet, and use the IOS **ping** command to try similar tests. However, to make the **ping** command on the router more closely resemble a **ping** issued by the end user requires the extended **ping** command.

The extended IOS **ping** command, available from privileged EXEC mode, allows the CLI user to change many options for what the **ping** command does, including the source IP address used for the ICMP echo requests sent by the command. To see the significance of this option, Example 14-4 shows Albuquerque with the working standard **ping 10.1.2.252** command, but with an extended **ping** command that works similarly to a **ping** from Bugs to Sam—a **ping** that fails in this case, because router Yosemite cannot send the ICMP echo reply back to Albuquerque.

Example 14-4 *Albuquerque: Working Ping After Adding Default Routes, Plus Failing Extended ping*

```
Albuquerque#show ip route static
     10.0.0.0/24 is subnetted, 5 subnets
S       10.1.3.0 [1/0] via 10.1.130.253
S       10.1.2.0 [1/0] via 10.1.128.252
Albuquerque#ping 10.1.2.252

Type escape sequence to abort.
Sending 5, 100-byte ICMP Echos to 10.1.2.252, timeout is 2 seconds:
!!!!!
Success rate is 100 percent (5/5), round-trip min/avg/max = 4/4/8 ms

Albuquerque#ping
Protocol [ip]:
Target IP address: 10.1.2.252
Repeat count [5]:
Datagram size [100]:
Timeout in seconds [2]:
Extended commands [n]: y
Source address or interface: 10.1.1.251
Type of service [0]:
Set DF bit in IP header? [no]:
Validate reply data? [no]:
Data pattern [0xABCD]:
Loose, Strict, Record, Timestamp, Verbose[none]:
Sweep range of sizes [n]:
Type escape sequence to abort.
Sending 5, 100-byte ICMP Echos to 10.1.2.252, timeout is 2 seconds:
. . . . .
Success rate is 0 percent (0/5)
```

The simple (standard) **ping 10.1.2.252** command works for one obvious reason and one not-so-obvious reason. First, Albuquerque can forward a packet to subnet 10.1.2.0 because of the static route. The return packet, sent by Yosemite, is sent to address 10.1.128.251—Albuquerque's Serial0/0/1 IP address. Why? Well, the following points are true about the **ping** command on a Cisco router:

- The Cisco **ping** command uses, by default, the output interface's IP address as the packet's source address, unless otherwise specified in an extended **ping**. The first ping in Example 14-4 uses a source of 10.1.128.251, because Albuquerque's route used to send the packet to 10.1.2.252 refers to interface Serial0/0/1 as the outgoing interface—and Albuquerque's S0/0/1 interface IP address is 10.1.128.251.

■ Ping response packets reverse the IP addresses used in the original ping request. So, in this example, Albuquerque used 10.1.128.251 as the source IP address of the original packet, so Yosemite uses 10.1.128.251 as the destination of the ping response packet—and Yosemite has a connected route to reach subnet 10.1.128.0/24, which includes address 10.1.128.251.

When you troubleshoot this internetwork, you can use the extended **ping** command to act like you issued a **ping** from a computer on that subnet, without having to call a user and ask to enter a **ping** command for you on the PC. The extended version of the **ping** command can be used to refine the problem's underlying cause by changing several details of what the **ping** command sends in its request. In real networks, when a **ping** from a router works, but a **ping** from a host does not, the extended ping could help you re-create the problem without needing to work with the end user on the phone.

For example, in Example 14-4, the extended **ping** command on Albuquerque uses a source IP address of 10.1.1.251 (Albuquerque's Fa0/0 interface IP address), destined to 10.1.2.252 (Yosemite's Fa0/0 IP address). According to the command output, no ping response was received by Albuquerque. Normally, Albuquerque's **ping** would be sourced from the IP address of the outgoing interface. With the use of the extended ping source address option, the source IP address of the echo packet is set to Albuquerque's Fa0/0 IP address, 10.1.1.251. Because the ICMP echo generated by the extended ping is sourced from an address in subnet 10.1.1.0, the packet looks more like a packet from an end user in that subnet. Yosemite builds a reply, with destination 10.1.1.251—but Yosemite does not have a route to subnet 10.1.1.0/24. So, Yosemite cannot send the ping reply packet back to Albuquerque, causing the ping to fail.

The solution in this case is pretty simple: either add a static route on Yosemite for subnet 10.1.1.0/24, or enable a routing protocol on all three routers.

Default Routes

As part of the routing (forwarding) process, a router compares each packet's destination IP address to the router's routing table. If the router does not match any routes, the router discards the packet, and makes no attempt to recover from the loss.

A *default route* is a route that is considered to match all destination IP addresses. With a default route, when a packet's destination IP address does not match any other routes, the router uses the default route for forwarding the packet.

Default routes work best when only one path exists to a part of the network. For example, in Figure 14-2, R1 is a branch office router with a single serial link connecting it to the rest of the enterprise network. There may be hundreds of subnets located outside R1's branch office. The engineer has three main options for helping R1 know routes to reach all the rest of the subnets:

■ Configure hundreds of static routes on R1—but all of those routes would use S0/1 as R1's outgoing interface, with next-hop IP address 172.16.3.2 (R2).

■ Enable a routing protocol on the routers to learn the routes.

■ Add a default route to R1 with outgoing interface S0/1.

Figure 14-2 *Sample Network in Which a Default Route Is Useful*

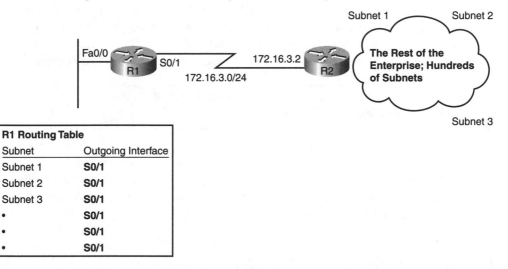

By coding a special static route called a default route, R1 can have a single route that forwards all packets out its S0/1 interface toward R2. The **ip route** command lists a special subnet and mask value, each 0.0.0.0, which means "match all packets." Example 14-5 shows the default static route on R1, pointing to R2 (172.16.3.2) as the next-hop router.

Example 14-5 *R1 Static Default Route Configuration and Routing Table*

```
R1(config)#ip route  0.0.0.0  0.0.0.0  172.16.3.2
R1#show ip route
Codes: C - connected, S - static, I - IGRP, R - RIP, M - mobile, B - BGP
       D - EIGRP, EX - EIGRP external, O - OSPF, IA - OSPF inter area
       N1 - OSPF NSSA external type 1, N2 - OSPF NSSA external type 2
       E1 - OSPF external type 1, E2 - OSPF external type 2, E - EGP
       i - IS-IS, L1 - IS-IS level-1, L2 - IS-IS level-2, ia - IS-IS inter area
       * - candidate default, U - per-user static route, o - ODR
       P - periodic downloaded static route

                                                                    continues
```

Example 14-5   *R1 Static Default Route Configuration and Routing Table (Continued)*

```
Gateway of last resort is 172.16.3.2 to network 0.0.0.0

     172.16.0.0/24 is subnetted, 3 subnets
C        172.16.1.0 is directly connected, FastEthernet0/0
C        172.16.3.0 is directly connected, Serial0/1
S*       0.0.0.0/0 [1/0] via 172.16.3.2
```

The **show ip route** command shows a couple of interesting facts about this special default route. The output lists a code of "S" just like other static routes, but with an * as well. The * means that the route might be used as the default route, meaning it will be used for packets that do not match any other routes in the routing table. Without a default route, a router discards packets that do not match the routing table. With a default route, the router forwards packets that do not match any other routes, as in the case in this example.

> **NOTE**   Chapter 4, "IP Routing," in the *CCNA ICND2 Official Exam Certification Guide*, explains default routes in more detail.

You could use static routes, including static default routes, on all routers in an internetwork. However, most enterprises use a dynamic routing protocol to learn all the routes. The next section covers some additional concepts and terminology for routing protocols, with the remainder of the chapter focusing on how to configure RIP-2.

Routing Protocol Overview

IP routing protocols have one primary goal: to fill the IP routing table with the current best routes it can find. The goal is simple, but the process and options can be complicated.

Routing protocols help routers learn routes by having each router advertise the routes it knows. Each router begins by knowing only connected routes. Then, each router sends messages, defined by the routing protocol, that list the routes. When a router hears a routing update message from another router, the router hearing the update learns about the subnets and adds routes to its routing table. If all the routers participate, all the routers can learn about all subnets in an internetwork.

When learning routes, routing protocols must also prevent loops from occurring. A loop occurs when a packet keeps coming back to the same router due to errors in the routes in the collective routers' routing tables. These loops can occur with routing protocols, unless the routing protocol makes an effort to avoid the loops.

This section starts by explaining how RIP-2 works in a little more detail than was covered in Chapter 5. Following that, the various IP routing protocols are compared.

RIP-2 Basic Concepts

Routers using RIP-2 advertise a small amount of simple information about each subnet to their neighbors. Their neighbors in turn advertise the information to their neighbors, and so on, until all routers have learned the information. In fact, it works a lot like how rumors spread in a neighborhood, school, or company. You might be out in the yard, stop to talk to your next-door neighbor, and tell your neighbor the latest gossip. Then, that neighbor sees his other next-door neighbor, and tells them the same bit of gossip—and so on, until everyone in the neighborhood knows the latest gossip. Distance vector protocols work the same way, but hopefully, unlike rumors in a real neighborhood, the rumor has not changed by the time everyone has heard about it.

For example, consider what occurs in Figure 14-3. The figure shows RIP-2 advertising a subnet number, mask (shown in prefix notation), and metric to its neighbors.

Figure 14-3 *Example of How RIP-2 Advertises Routes*

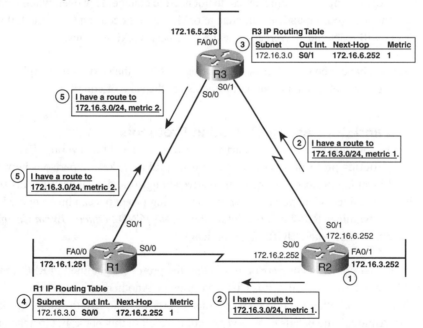

For the sake of keeping the figure less cluttered, Figure 14-3 only shows how the routers advertise and learn routes for subnet 172.16.3.0/24, even though the routers do advertise about other routes as well. Following the steps in the figure:

1. Router R2 learns a connected route for subnet 172.16.3.0/24.

2. R2 sends a *routing update* to its neighbors, listing a subnet (172.16.3.0), mask (/24), and a distance, or metric (1 in this case).

3. R3 hears the routing update, and adds a route to its routing table for subnet 172.16.3.0/24, referring to R2 as the next-hop router.

4. Around the same time, R1 also hears the routing update sent directly to R1 by R2. R1 then adds a route to its routing table for subnet 172.16.3.0/24, referring to R2 as the next-hop router.

5. R1 and R3 then send a routing update to each other, for subnet 172.16.3.0/24, metric 2.

By the end of this process, both R1 and R3 have heard of two possible routes to reach subnet 172.16.3.0/24—one with metric 1, and one with metric 2. Each router uses its respective lower-metric (metric 1) routes to reach 172.16.3.0.

Interestingly, distance vector protocols such as RIP-2 repeat this process continually on a periodic basis. For example, RIP routers send periodic routing updates about every 30 seconds by default. As long as the routers continue to hear the same routes, with the same metrics, the routers' routing tables do not need to change. However, when something changes, the next routing update will change or simply not occur due to some failure, so the routers will react and converge to use the then-best working routes.

Now that you have seen the basics of one routing protocol, the next section explains a wide variety of features of different routing protocols for the sake of comparison.

Comparing and Contrasting IP Routing Protocols

IP's long history and continued popularity has driven the need for several different competing routing protocols over time. So, it is helpful to make comparisons between the different IP routing protocols to see their relative strengths and weaknesses. This section describes several technical points on which the routing protocols can be compared. Then, this chapter examines RIP-2 in more detail; the *CCNA ICND2 Official Exam Certification Guide* explains OSPF and EIGRP in more detail.

One of the first points of comparison is whether the protocol is defined in RFCs, making it a public standard, or whether it is Cisco proprietary. Another very important consideration is whether the routing protocol supports variable-length subnet masking (VLSM). Although the details of VLSM are not covered in this book, but instead are covered in the *CCNA ICND2 Official Exam Certification Guide*, VLSM support is an important consideration today. This section introduces several different terms and concepts used to compare the various IP routing protocols, with Table 14-4 at the end of this section summarizing the comparison points for many of the IP routing protocols.

Interior and Exterior Routing Protocols

IP routing protocols fall into one of two major categories:

- **Interior Gateway Protocol (IGP):** A routing protocol that was designed and intended for use inside a single autonomous system

- **Exterior Gateway Protocol (EGP):** A routing protocol that was designed and intended for use between different autonomous systems

> **NOTE** The terms IGP and EGP include the word *gateway* because routers used to be called gateways.

These definitions use another new term: *autonomous system.* An autonomous system is an internetwork under the administrative control of a single organization. For instance, an internetwork created and paid for by a single company is probably a single autonomous system, and an internetwork created by a single school system is probably a single autonomous system. Other examples include large divisions of a state or national government, where different government agencies may be able to build their own separate internetworks.

Some routing protocols work best inside a single autonomous system, by design, so these routing protocols are called IGPs. Conversely, only one routing protocol, *Border Gateway Protocol (BGP)*, is used today to exchange routes between routers in different autonomous systems, so it is called an EGP.

Each autonomous system can be assigned a number, called (unsurprisingly) an *autonomous system number (ASN)*. Like public IP addresses, the Internet Corporation for Assigned Network Numbers (ICANN) controls the worldwide rights to assign ASNs, delegating that authority to other organizations around the planet, typically to the same organizations that assign public IP addresses. By assigning each autonomous organization an ASN, BGP can ensure that packets do not loop around the global Internet by making sure that packets do not pass through the same autonomous system twice.

Figure 14-4 shows a small view into the worldwide Internet. Two companies and three ISPs use IGPs (OSPF and EIGRP) inside their own networks, with BGP being used between the ASNs.

Figure 14-4 *Comparing Locations for Using IGPs and EGPs*

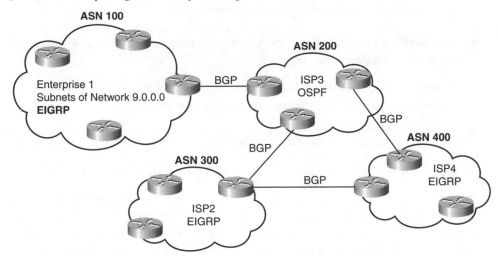

Routing Protocol Types/Algorithms

Each IGP can be classified as using a particular class, or type, of underlying logic. Table 14-2 lists the three options, noting which IGPs use which class of algorithm.

Table 14-2 *Routing Protocol Classes/Algorithms and Protocols that Use Them*

Class/Algorithm	IGPs
Distance vector	RIP-1, RIP-2, IGRP
Link-state	OSPF, Integrated IS-IS
Balanced hybrid (also called advanced distance vector)	EIGRP

The *CCNA ICND2 Official Exam Certification Guide* covers the theory behind each of these classes of routing protocols. However, because the only IGP this book covers to any level of detail is RIP-2, most of the conceptual materials in this chapter actually show how distance vector protocols work.

Metrics

Routing protocols must have some way to decide which route is best when a router learns of more than one route to reach a subnet. To that end, each routing protocol defines a *metric* that gives an objective numeric value to the "goodness" of each route. The lower the metric, the better the route. For example, earlier, in Figure 14-3, R1 learned a metric 1 route for subnet 172.16.3.0/24 from R2, and a metric 2 route for that same subnet from R3, so R1 chose the lower-metric (1) route through R2.

Some metrics work better than others. To see why, consider Figure 14-5. The figure shows two analyses of the same basic internetwork, focusing on router B's choice of a route to reach subnet 10.1.1.0, which is on the LAN on the left side of router A. In this case, the link between A and B is only a 64-kbps link, whereas the other two links are T1s, running at 1.544 Mbps each. The top part of the figure shows router B's choice of route when using RIP (Version 1 or Version 2), whereas the bottom part of the figure shows router B's choice when the internetwork uses EIGRP.

Figure 14-5 *Comparing the Effect of the RIP and EIGRP Metrics*

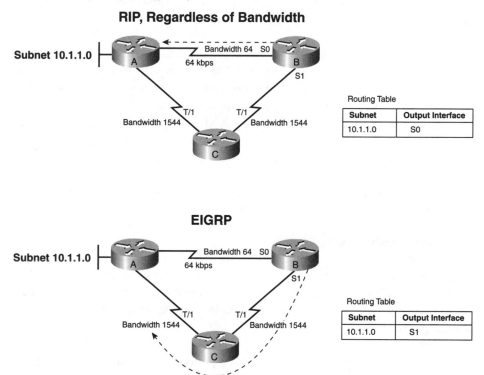

RIP uses a metric called hop count, which measures the number of routers (hops) between a router and a subnet. With RIP, router B would learn two routes to reach subnet 10.1.1.0: a one-hop route through router A, and a two-hop route first through router C and then to router A. So, router B, using RIP, would add a route for subnet 10.1.1.0 pointing to router A as the next-hop IP address (represented as the dashed line in Figure 14-5).

EIGRP, on the other hand, uses a metric that (by default) considers both the interface bandwidth and interface delay settings as input into a mathematical formula to calculate the metric. If routers A, B, and C were configured with correct **bandwidth** interface subcommands, as listed in Figure 14-5, EIGRP would add a route for subnet 10.1.1.0 to its routing table, but with router C as the next-hop router, again shown with a dashed line.

> **NOTE**   For a review of the **bandwidth** command, refer to the section "Bandwidth and Clock Rate on Serial Interfaces" in Chapter 13, "Operating Cisco Routers."

Autosummarization and Manual Summarization

Routers generally perform routing (forwarding) more quickly with smaller routing tables, and less quickly with larger routing tables. Route summarization helps shorten the routing table while retaining all the needed routes in the network.

Two general types of route summarization can be done, with varying support for these two types depending on the routing protocol. The two types, both of which are introduced in this section, are called *autosummarization* and *manual summarization*. Manual summarization gives the network engineer a great deal of control and flexibility, allowing the engineer to choose what summary routes to advertise, instead of just being able to summarize with a classful network. As a result, support for manual summarization is the more useful feature as compared to autosummarization.

Chapter 5 in the *CCNA ICND2 Official Exam Certification Guide* explains both autosummarization and manual summarization in great detail.

Classless and Classful Routing Protocols

Some routing protocols must consider the Class A, B, or C network number that a subnet resides in when performing some of its tasks. Other routing protocols can ignore Class A, B, and C rules altogether. Routing protocols that must consider class rules are called *classful routing protocols*; those that do not need to consider class rules are called *classless routing protocols*.

Classless routing protocols and classful routing protocols are identified by the same three criteria, as summarized in Table 14-3.

Table 14-3   *Comparing Classless and Classful Routing Protocols*

Feature	Classless	Classful
Supports VLSM	Yes	No
Sends subnet mask in routing updates	Yes	No
Supports manual route summarization	Yes	No

Convergence

The term *convergence* refers to the overall process that occurs with routing protocols when something changes in a network topology. When a link comes up or fails, or when a router fails or is first turned on, the possible routes in the internetwork change. The processes used by routing protocols to recognize the changes, to figure out the now-best routes to each subnet, and to change all the routers' routing tables, is called convergence.

Some routing protocols converge more quickly than others. As you might imagine, the capability to converge quickly is important, because in some cases, until convergence completes, users might not be able to send their packets to particular subnets. (Table 14-4 in the next section summarizes the relative convergence speed of various IP routing protocols, along with other information.)

Miscellaneous Comparison Points

Two other minor comparison points between the various IGPs are interesting as well. First, the original routing protocol standards defined that routing updates should be sent to the IP all-local-hosts broadcast address of 255.255.255.255. After those original routing protocols were defined, IP multicast emerged, which allowed newer routing protocols to send routing updates only to other interested routers by using various IP multicast IP addresses.

The earlier IGPs did not include any authentication features. As time went on, it became obvious that attackers could form a denial-of-service (DoS) attack by causing problems with routing protocols. For example, an attacker could connect a router to a network and advertise lots of lower-metric routes for many subnets, causing the packets to be routed to the wrong place—and possibly copied by the attacker. The later-defined IGPs typically support some type of authentication, hoping to mitigate the exposure to these types of DoS attacks.

Summary of Interior Routing Protocols

For convenient comparison and study, Table 14-4 summarizes the most important features of interior routing protocols. Note that the most important routing protocol for the ICND1 exam is RIP, specifically RIP-2. The ICND2 and CCNA exams include more detailed coverage of RIP-2 theory, as well as the theory, configuration, and troubleshooting of OSPF and EIGRP.

Table 14-4 *Interior IP Routing Protocols Compared*

Feature	RIP-1	RIP-2	EIGRP	OSPF	IS-IS
Classless	No	Yes	Yes	Yes	Yes
Supports VLSM	No	Yes	Yes	Yes	Yes
Sends mask in update	No	Yes	Yes	Yes	Yes
Distance vector	Yes	Yes	No[1]	No	No
Link-state	No	No	No[1]	Yes	Yes
Supports autosummarization	Yes	Yes	Yes	No	No
Supports manual summarization	No	Yes	Yes	Yes	Yes
Proprietary	No	No	Yes	No	No
Routing updates sent to a multicast IP address	No	Yes	Yes	Yes	N/A
Supports authentication	No	Yes	Yes	Yes	Yes
Convergence	Slow	Slow	Very fast	Fast	Fast

1. EIGRP is often described as a balanced hybrid routing protocol, instead of link-state or distance vector. Some documents refer to EIGRP as an advanced distance vector protocol.

> **NOTE**   For reference, IGRP has the same characteristics as RIP-1 in Table 14-4, with the exception that IGRP is proprietary and RIP-1 is not.

Configuring and Verifying RIP-2

RIP-2 configuration is actually somewhat simple as compared to the concepts related to routing protocols. The configuration process uses three required commands, with only one command, the **network** command, requiring any real thought. You should also know the more-popular **show** commands for helping you analyze and troubleshoot routing protocols.

RIP-2 Configuration

The RIP-2 configuration process takes only the following three required steps, with the possibility that the third step might need to be repeated:

Step 1   Use the **router rip** configuration command to move into RIP configuration mode.

Step 2   Use the **version 2** RIP subcommand to tell the router to use RIP Version 2 exclusively.

Step 3 Use one or more **network** *net-number* RIP subcommands to enable RIP
on the correct interfaces.

Step 4 (Optional) As needed, disable RIP on an interface using the **passive-interface** *type number* RIP subcommand.

Of the required first three steps, only the third step—the RIP **network** command—requires much thought. Each RIP **network** command enables RIP on a set of interfaces.
The RIP **network** command only uses a classful network number as its one parameter.
For any of the router's interface IP addresses in that entire classful network, the router
does the following three things:

- The router multicasts routing updates to a reserved IP multicast IP address, 224.0.0.9.

Key
Topic

- The router listens for incoming updates on that same interface.

- The router advertises about the subnet connected to the interface.

Sample RIP Configuration

Keeping these facts in mind, now consider how to configure RIP on a single router.
Examine Figure 14-6 for a moment and try to apply the first three configuration steps to this
router and anticipate the configuration required on the router to enable RIP on all interfaces.

Figure 14-6 *RIP-2 Configuration: Sample Router with Four Interfaces*

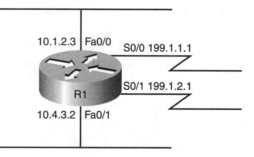

The first two configuration commands are easy, **router rip**, followed by **version 2**, with no
parameters to choose. Then you need to pick which **network** commands need to be
configured at Step 3. To match interface S0/0, you have to figure out that address 199.1.1.1
is in Class C IP network 199.1.1.0, meaning you need a **network 199.1.1.0** RIP
subcommand. Similarly, to match interface S0/1, you need a **network 199.1.2.0** command,
because IP address 199.1.2.1 is in Class C network 199.1.2.0. Finally, both of the LAN
interfaces have an IP address in Class A network 10.0.0.0, so a single **network 10.0.0.0**
command matches both interfaces. Example 14-6 shows the entire configuration process,
with all five configuration commands.

Example 14-6 *Sample Router Configuration with RIP Enabled*

```
R1#configure terminal
R1(config)#router rip
R1(config-router)#version 2
R1(config-router)#network 199.1.1.0
R1(config-router)#network 199.1.2.0
R1(config-router)#network 10.0.0.0
```

With this configuration, R1 starts using RIP—sending RIP updates, listening for incoming RIP updates, and advertising about the connected subnet—on each of its four interfaces. However, imagine that for some reason you wanted to enable RIP on R1's Fa0/0 interface, but did not want to enable RIP on Fa0/1's interface. Both interfaces are in network 10.0.0.0, so both are matched by the **network 10.0.0.0** command.

RIP configuration does not provide a way to enable RIP on only some of the interfaces in a single Class A, B, or C network. So, if you needed to enable RIP only on R1's Fa0/0 interface, and not on the Fa0/1 interface, you would actually need to use the **network 10.0.0.0** command to enable RIP on both interfaces, and then disable the sending of RIP updates on Fa0/1 using the **passive-interface** *type number* RIP subcommand. For example, to enable RIP on all interfaces of router R1 in Figure 14-6, except for Fa0/1, you could use the same configuration in Example 14-6, but then also add the **passive-interface fa0/1** subcommand while in RIP configuration mode. This command tells R1 to stop sending RIP updates out its Fa0/1 interface, disabling one of the main functions of RIP.

> **NOTE** The **passive-interface** command only stops the sending of RIP updates on the interface. Other features outside the scope of this book could be used to disable the processing of received updates and the advertisement of the connected subnet.

One final note on the **network** command: IOS will actually accept a parameter besides a classful network number on the command, and IOS does not supply an error message, either. However, IOS, knowing that the parameter must be a classful network number, changes the command. For example, if you typed **network 10.1.2.3** in RIP configuration mode, IOS would accept the command, with no error messages. However, when you look at the configuration, you would see a **network 10.0.0.0** command, and the **network 10.1.2.3** command that you had typed would not be there. The **network 10.0.0.0** command would indeed match all interfaces in network 10.0.0.0.

RIP-2 Verification

IOS includes three primary **show** commands that are helpful to confirm how well RIP-2 is working. Table 14-5 lists the commands and their main purpose.

Table 14-5 *RIP Operational Commands*

Command	Purpose
show ip interface brief	Lists one line per router interface, including the IP address and interface status; an interface must have an IP address, and be in an "up and up" status, before RIP begins to work on the interface.
show ip route [rip]	Lists the routing table, including RIP-learned routes, and optionally just RIP-learned routes.
show ip protocols	Lists information about the RIP configuration, plus the IP addresses of neighboring RIP routers from which the local router has learned routes.

To better understand these commands, this section uses the internetwork shown in Figure 14-1. First, consider the RIP-2 configuration required on each of the three routers. All three interfaces on all three routers are in classful network 10.0.0.0. So each router needs only one **network** command, **network 10.0.0.0**, to match all three of its interfaces. The configuration needs to be the same on all three routers, as follows:

```
router rip
 version 2
 network 10.0.0.0
```

Now, to focus on the **show** commands, Example 14-7 lists a couple of variations of the **show ip route** command, with some explanations in the example, and some following the example. Following that, Example 14-8 focuses on the **show ip protocols** command. Note that Example 14-1, earlier in this chapter, shows the output from the **show ip interfaces brief** command on the Albuquerque router, so it is not repeated here.

Example 14-7 *The **show ip route** Command*

```
Albuquerque#show ip route
Codes: C - connected, S - static, R - RIP, M - mobile, B - BGP
       D - EIGRP, EX - EIGRP external, O - OSPF, IA - OSPF inter area
       N1 - OSPF NSSA external type 1, N2 - OSPF NSSA external type 2
       E1 - OSPF external type 1, E2 - OSPF external type 2
       i - IS-IS, su - IS-IS summary, L1 - IS-IS level-1, L2 - IS-IS level-2
       ia - IS-IS inter area, * - candidate default, U - per-user static route
       o - ODR, P - periodic downloaded static route
Gateway of last resort is not set

     10.0.0.0/24 is subnetted, 6 subnets
R       10.1.3.0 [120/1] via 10.1.130.253, 00:00:16, Serial0/1/0
R       10.1.2.0 [120/1] via 10.1.128.252, 00:00:09, Serial0/0/1
C       10.1.1.0 is directly connected, FastEthernet0/0
```

continues

Example 14-7   *The* **show ip route** *Command (Continued)*

```
C        10.1.130.0 is directly connected, Serial0/1/0

R        10.1.129.0 [120/1] via 10.1.130.253, 00:00:16, Serial0/1/0
                    [120/1] via 10.1.128.252, 00:00:09, Serial0/0/1
C        10.1.128.0 is directly connected, Serial0/0/1
!
! The next command lists just the RIP routes, so no code legend is listed
!
Albuquerque#show ip route rip
     10.0.0.0/24 is subnetted, 6 subnets
R        10.1.3.0 [120/1] via 10.1.130.253, 00:00:20, Serial0/1/0
R        10.1.2.0 [120/1] via 10.1.128.252, 00:00:13, Serial0/0/1
R        10.1.129.0 [120/1] via 10.1.130.253, 00:00:20, Serial0/1/0
                    [120/1] via 10.1.128.252, 00:00:13, Serial0/0/1
!
! The next command lists the route matched by this router for packets going to the
! listed IP address 10.1.2.1.
!
Albuquerque#show ip route 10.1.2.1
Routing entry for 10.1.2.0/24
  Known via "rip", distance 120, metric 1
  Redistributing via rip
  Last update from 10.1.128.252 on Serial0/0/1, 00:00:18 ago
  Routing Descriptor Blocks:
  * 10.1.128.252, from 10.1.128.252, 00:00:18 ago, via Serial0/0/1
      Route metric is 1, traffic share count is 1
!
! The same command again, but for an address that does not have a matching route in
! the routing table.
Albuquerque#show ip route 10.1.7.1
% Subnet not in table
Albuquerque#
```

Interpreting the Output of the show ip route Command

Example 14-7 shows the **show ip route** command, which lists all IP routes, the **show ip route rip** command, which lists only RIP-learned routes, and the **show ip route** *address* command, which lists details about the route matched for packets sent to the listed IP address. Focusing on the **show ip route** command, note that the legend lists "R," which means that a route has been learned by RIP, and that three of the routes list an R beside them. Next, examine the details in the route for subnet 10.1.3.0/24, highlighted in the example. The important details are as follows:

- The subnet number is listed, with the mask in the heading line above.

- The next-hop router's IP address, 10.1.130.253, which is Seville's S0/0/1 IP address.

- Albuquerque's S0/1/0 interface is the outgoing interface.

- The length of time since Albuquerque last heard about this route in a periodic RIP update, 16 seconds ago in this case.

- The RIP metric for this route (1 in this case), listed as the second number in the square brackets. For example, between Albuquerque and subnet 10.1.3.0/24, one other router (Seville) exists.

- The administrative distance of the route (120 in this case; the first number in brackets).

Take the time now to review the other two RIP routes, noting the values for these various items in those routes. As you can see, the **show ip route rip** command output lists the routes in the exact same format, the difference being that only RIP-learned routes are shown, and the legend is not displayed at the top of the command output. The **show ip route** *address* command lists more detailed output about the route that matches the destination IP address listed in the command, with the command output supplying more detailed information about the route.

Administrative Distance

When an internetwork has redundant links, and uses a single routing protocol, each router may learn multiple routes to reach a particular subnet. As stated earlier in this chapter, the routing protocol then uses a metric to choose the best route, and the router adds that route to its routing table.

In some cases, internetworks use multiple IP routing protocols. In such cases, a router might learn of multiple routes to a particular subnet using different routing protocols. In these cases, the metric does not help the router choose which route is best, because each routing protocol uses a metric unique to that routing protocol. For example, RIP uses the hop count as the metric, but EIGRP uses a math formula with bandwidth and delay as inputs. A route with RIP metric 1 might need to be compared to an EIGRP route, to the same subnet, but with metric 4,132,768. (Yes, EIGRP metrics tend to be large numbers.) Because the numbers have different meanings, there is no real value in comparing the metrics.

The router still needs to choose the best route, so IOS solves this problem by assigning a numeric value to each routing protocol. IOS then chooses the route whose routing protocol has the lower number. This number is called the *administrative distance (AD)*. For example, EIGRP defaults to use an AD of 90, and RIP defaults to use the value of 120, as seen in the routes in Example 14-7. So, an EIGRP route to a subnet would be chosen instead of a competing RIP route. Table 14-6 lists the AD values for the most common sources of routing information.

Table 14-6 *IOS Defaults for Administrative Distance*

Route Source	Administrative Distance
Connected routes	0
Static routes	1
EIGRP	90
IGRP	100
OSPF	110
IS-IS	115
RIP (V1 and V2)	120
Unknown or unbelievable	255

While this may be a brief tangent away from RIP and routing protocols, now that this chapter has explained administrative distance, the concept behind a particular type of static route, called a *backup static route*, can be explained. Static routes have a default AD that is better than all routing protocols, so if a router has a static route defined for a subnet, and the routing protocol learns a route to the same subnet, the static route will be added to the routing table. However, in some cases, the static route is intended to be used only if the routing protocol fails to learn a route. In these cases, an individual static route can be configured with an AD higher than the routing protocol, making the routing protocol more believable.

For example, the **ip route 10.1.1.0 255.255.255.0 10.2.2.2 150** command sets this static route's AD to 150, which is higher than all the default AD settings in Table 14-6. If RIP-2 learned a route to 10.1.1.0/24 on this same router, the router would place the RIP-learned route into the routing table, assuming a default AD of 120, which is better than the static route's AD in this case.

The show ip protocols Command

The final command for examining RIP operations is the **show ip protocols** command. This command identifies some of the details of RIP operation. Example 14-8 lists the output of this command, again on Albuquerque. Due to the variety of information in the command output, the example includes many comments inside the example.

Example 14-8 *The* **show ip protocols** *Command*

```
Albuquerque#show ip protocols
Routing Protocol is "rip"
  Outgoing update filter list for all interfaces is not set
  Incoming update filter list for all interfaces is not set
!
! The next line identifies the time interval for periodic routing updates, and when this
! router will send its next update.
  Sending updates every 30 seconds, next due in 22 seconds
  Invalid after 180 seconds, hold down 180, flushed after 240
  Redistributing: rip
!
! The next few lines result from the version 2 command being configured
  Default version control: send version 2, receive version 2
    Interface            Send  Recv  Triggered RIP  Key-chain
    FastEthernet0/0      2     2
    Serial0/0/1          2     2
    Serial0/1/0          2     2
  Automatic network summarization is in effect
  Maximum path: 4
!
! The next two lines reflect the fact that this router has a single network command,
! namely network 10.0.0.0. If other network commands were configured, these networks
! would also be listed.
  Routing for Networks:
    10.0.0.0
!
! The next section lists the IP addresses of neighboring routers from which Albuquerque
! has received routing updates, and the time since this router last heard from the
! neighbors. Note 10.1.130.253 is Seville, and 10.1.128.252 is Yosemite.
  Routing Information Sources:
    Gateway         Distance      Last Update
    10.1.130.253         120      00:00:25
    10.1.128.252         120      00:00:20
  Distance: (default is 120)
```

Key
Topic

Of particular importance for real-life troubleshooting and for the exam, focus on both the version information and the routing information sources. If you forget to configure the **version 2** command on one router, that router will send only RIP-1 updates by default, and the column labeled "Send" would list a 1 instead of a 2. The other routers, only listening for Version 2 updates, could not learn routes from this router.

Also, a quick way to find out if the local router is hearing RIP updates from the correct routers is to look at the list of routing information sources listed at the end of the **show ip protocols** command. For example, given the internetwork in Figure 14-1, you should expect Albuquerque to receive updates from two other routers (Yosemite and Seville). The end of Example 14-8 shows exactly that, with Albuquerque having heard from both routers in the last 30 seconds. If only one router was listed in this command's output, you could figure out which one Albuquerque was hearing from, and then investigate the problem with the missing router.

Examining RIP Messages with debug

The best way to understand whether RIP is doing its job is to use the **debug ip rip** command. This command enables a debug option that tells the router to generate log messages each time the router sends and receives a RIP update. These messages include information about every subnet listed in those advertisements as well, and the meaning of the messages is relatively straightforward.

Example 14-9 shows the output generated by the **debug ip rip** command on the Albuquerque router, based on Figure 14-1. Note that to see these messages, the user needs to be connected to the console of the router, or use the **terminal monitor** privileged mode EXEC command if using Telnet or SSH to connect to the router. The notes inside the example describe some of the meaning of the messages, in five different groups. The first three groups of messages describe Albuquerque's updates sent on each of its three RIP-enabled interfaces; the fourth group includes messages generated when Albuquerque receives an update from Seville; and the last group describes the update received from Yosemite.

Example 14-9 *Example RIP Debug Output*

```
Albuquerque#debug ip rip
RIP protocol debugging is on
Albuquerque#

! Update sent by Albuquerque out Fa0/0:
! The next two messages tell you that the local router is sending a version 2 update
! on Fa0/0, to the 224.0.0.9 multicast IP address. Following that, 5 lines list the
! 5 subnets listed in the advertisement.
*Jun  9 14:35:08.855: RIP: sending v2 update to 224.0.0.9 via FastEthernet0/0 (10.1.1.251)
*Jun  9 14:35:08.855: RIP: build update entries
*Jun  9 14:35:08.855:    10.1.2.0/24 via 0.0.0.0, metric 2, tag 0
*Jun  9 14:35:08.855:    10.1.3.0/24 via 0.0.0.0, metric 2, tag 0
*Jun  9 14:35:08.855:    10.1.128.0/24 via 0.0.0.0, metric 1, tag 0
*Jun  9 14:35:08.855:    10.1.129.0/24 via 0.0.0.0, metric 2, tag 0
*Jun  9 14:35:08.855:    10.1.130.0/24 via 0.0.0.0, metric 1, tag 0
```

Example 14-9 *Example RIP Debug Output (Continued)*

```
! The next 5 debug messages state that this local router is sending an update on its
! S0/1/0 interface, listing 3 subnets/masks
*Jun  9 14:35:10.351: RIP: sending v2 update to 224.0.0.9 via Serial0/1/0 (10.1.130.251)
*Jun  9 14:35:10.351: RIP: build update entries
*Jun  9 14:35:10.351:    10.1.1.0/24 via 0.0.0.0, metric 1, tag 0
*Jun  9 14:35:10.351:    10.1.2.0/24 via 0.0.0.0, metric 2, tag 0
*Jun  9 14:35:10.351:    10.1.128.0/24 via 0.0.0.0, metric 1, tag 0

! The next 5 debug messages state that this local router is sending an update on its
! S0/0/1 interface, listing 3 subnets/masks
*Jun  9 14:35:12.443: RIP: sending v2 update to 224.0.0.9 via Serial0/0/1 (10.1.128.251)
*Jun  9 14:35:12.443: RIP: build update entries
*Jun  9 14:35:12.443:    10.1.1.0/24 via 0.0.0.0, metric 1, tag 0
*Jun  9 14:35:12.443:    10.1.3.0/24 via 0.0.0.0, metric 2, tag 0
*Jun  9 14:35:12.443:    10.1.130.0/24 via 0.0.0.0, metric 1, tag 0

! The next 4 messages are about a RIP version 2 (v2) update received by Albuquerque
! from Seville (S0/1/0), listing three subnets. Note the mask is listed as /24.
*Jun  9 14:35:13.819: RIP: received v2 update from 10.1.130.253 on Serial0/1/0
*Jun  9 14:35:13.819:      10.1.2.0/24 via 0.0.0.0 in 2 hops
*Jun  9 14:35:13.819:      10.1.3.0/24 via 0.0.0.0 in 1 hops
*Jun  9 14:35:13.819:      10.1.129.0/24 via 0.0.0.0 in 1 hops

! The next 4 messages are about a RIP version 2 (v2) update received by Albuquerque
! from Yosemite (S0/0/1), listing three subnets. Note the mask is listed as /24.
*Jun  9 14:35:16.911: RIP: received v2 update from 10.1.128.252 on Serial0/0/1
*Jun  9 14:35:16.915:      10.1.2.0/24 via 0.0.0.0 in 1 hops
*Jun  9 14:35:16.915:      10.1.3.0/24 via 0.0.0.0 in 2 hops
*Jun  9 14:35:16.915:      10.1.129.0/24 via 0.0.0.0 in 1 hops

Albuquerque#undebug all
All possible debugging has been turned off
Albuquerque#show process
CPU utilization for five seconds: 0%/0%; one minute: 0%; five minutes: 0%
 PID QTy       PC Runtime (ms)    Invoked   uSecs    Stacks TTY Process
   1 Cwe 601B2AE8              0          1       0 5608/6000   0 Chunk Manager
```

First, if you take a broader look at the five sets of messages, it helps reinforce the expected updates that Albuquerque should both send and receive. The messages state that Albuquerque is sending updates on Fa0/0, S0/0/1, and S0/1/0, on which RIP should be enabled. Additionally, other messages state that the router received updates on interface S0/1/0, which is the link connected to Seville, and S0/0/1, which is the link connected to Yosemite.

Most of the details in the messages can be easily guessed. Some messages mention "v2," for RIP Version 2, and the fact that the messages are being sent to multicast IP address 224.0.0.9. (RIP-1 sends updates to the 255.255.255.255 broadcast address.) The majority of the messages in the example describe the routing information listed in each update, specifically the subnet and prefix length (mask), and the metric.

A close examination of the number of subnets in each routing update shows that the routers do not advertise all routes in the updates. In Figure 14-1, six subnets exist. However, the updates in the example have either three or five subnets listed. The reason has to do with the theory behind RIP, specifically a feature called split horizon. This loop-avoidance feature, which is described in Chapter 8 of the ICND2 book, limits which subnets are advertised in each update to help avoid some forwarding loops.

> **NOTE**   Chapter 8, "Routing Protocol Theory," in the *CCNA ICND2 Official Exam Certification Guide* covers split horizon in greater detail.

Finally, a few comments about the **debug** command itself can be helpful. First, before using the **debug** command, it is helpful to look at the router's CPU utilization with the **show process** command, as shown at the end of Example 14-9. This command lists the router's CPU utilization as a rolling average over three short time periods. On routers with a higher CPU utilization, generally above 30 to 40 percent, be very cautious when enabling debug options, as this may drive the CPU to the point of impacting packet forwarding. Also, you might have noticed the time stamps on the debug messages; to make the router generate time stamps, you need to configure the **service timestamps** global configuration command.

Exam Preparation Tasks

Review All the Key Topics

Review the most important topics in the chapter, noted with the key topics icon in the outer margin of the page. Table 14-7 lists a reference of these key topics and the page numbers on which each is found.

Key Topic

Table 14-7 *Key Topics for Chapter 14*

Key Topic Element	Description	Page Number
Example 14-3	Shows how to configure static routes	443
Definitions	IGP and EGP	451
Table 14-2	List of IGP algorithms and the IGPs that use them	452
Table 14-3	Comparison points for classless and classful routing protocols	454
Table 14-4	Summary of comparison points for IGPs	456
List	RIP-2 configuration checklist	456-457
List	The three things that occur on an interface matched by a RIP network command	457
Table 14-6	List of routing protocols and other routing sources and their default administrative distance settings	462
Example 14-8	Lists the **show ip protocol** command and how it can be used to troubleshoot RIP problems	463

Complete the Tables and Lists from Memory

Print a copy of Appendix H, "Memory Tables" (found on the CD-ROM), or at least the section for this chapter, and complete the tables and lists from memory. Appendix I, "Memory Tables Answer Key," also on the CD-ROM, includes completed tables and lists to check your work.

Definitions of Key Terms

Define the following key terms from this chapter and check your answers in the glossary.

administrative distance, autonomous system, backup static route, balanced hybrid, classful routing protocol, classless routing protocol, convergence, default route, distance vector, Exterior Gateway Protocol (EGP), Interior Gateway Protocol (IGP), link state, metric, routing update, variable-length subnet masking (VLSM)

Command References

Although you should not necessarily memorize the information in the tables in this section, this section does include a reference for the configuration commands (Table 14-8) and EXEC commands (Table 14-9) covered in this chapter. Practically speaking, you should memorize the commands as a side effect of reading the chapter and doing all the activities in this exam preparation section. To check to see how well you have memorized the commands, cover the left side of the table with a piece of paper, read the descriptions in the right side, and see if you remember the command.

Table 14-8 *Chapter 14 Configuration Command Reference*

Command	Description
router rip	Global command that moves the user into RIP configuration mode.
network *network-number*	RIP subcommand that lists a classful network number, enabling RIP on all of that router's interfaces in that classful network.
version {1	2}	RIP subcommand that sets the RIP version.
passive-interface [default] {*interface-type interface-number*}	RIP subcommand that tells RIP to no longer advertise RIP updates on the listed interface.
ip address *ip-address mask*	Interface subcommand that sets the router's interface IP address and mask.
ip route *prefix mask* {*ip-address*	*interface-type interface-number*}	Global command that defines a static route.
service timestamps	Global command that tells the router to put a timestamp on log messages, including debug messages.

Table 14-9 *Chapter 14 EXEC Command Reference*

Command	Purpose
show ip interface brief	Lists one line per router interface, including the IP address and interface status; an interface must have an IP address, and be in an "up and up" status, before RIP begins to work on the interface.
show ip route [rip | static | connected]	Lists the routing table, including RIP-learned routes, and optionally just RIP-learned routes.
show ip route *ip-address*	Lists details about the route the router would match for a packet sent to the listed IP address.
show ip protocols	Lists information about the RIP configuration, plus the IP addresses of neighboring RIP routers from which the local router has learned routes.
show process	Lists information about the various processes running in IOS, and most importantly, overall CPU utilization statistics.
terminal ip netmask-format decimal	For the length of the user's session, causes IOS to display mask information in dotted-decimal format instead of prefix format.
debug ip rip	Tells the router to generate detailed messages for each sent and received RIP update.

This chapter covers the following subjects:

IP Troubleshooting Tips and Tools: This section suggests some tips for how to approach host routing issues, routing related to routers, and IP addressing problems, including how to use several additional tools not covered elsewhere in this book.

A Troubleshooting Scenario: This section shows a three-part scenario, with tasks for each part that can be performed before seeing the answers.

CHAPTER 15

Troubleshooting IP Routing

This chapter has two main goals. First, this chapter covers some topics that are not covered elsewhere in this book, namely some troubleshooting commands on both hosts and routers. Second, this chapter reviews the core concepts of addressing and routing, but with a focus on how to approach new problems to analyze and understand how to troubleshoot any problems. Additionally, this chapter includes a troubleshooting scenario that shows how to use some of the tools and concepts from earlier in this chapter, with an opportunity for you to try and discover the problems before the text explains the answers.

For those of you following the reading plan using both this book and the *CCNA ICND2 Official Exam Certification Guide*, note that after this chapter, you should proceed to the ICND2 book and read the chapters in Parts II and III.

"Do I Know This Already?" Quiz

The "Do I Know This Already?" quiz allows you to assess if you should read the entire chapter. If you miss no more than one of these nine self-assessment questions, you might want to move ahead to the "Exam Preparation Tasks" section. Table 15-1 lists the major headings in this chapter and the "Do I Know This Already?" quiz questions covering the material in those headings so you can assess your knowledge of these specific areas. The answers to the "Do I Know This Already?" quiz appear in Appendix A.

Table 15-1 *"Do I Know This Already?" Foundation Topics Section-to-Question Mapping*

Foundation Topics Section	Questions
IP Troubleshooting Tips and Tools	1–6
A Routing Troubleshooting Scenario	7–9

1. An internetwork diagram shows a router, R1, with the **ip subnet-zero** command configured. The engineer has typed several configuration commands into a word processor for later pasting into the router's configuration. Which of the following IP addresses could not be assigned to the router's Fa0/0 interface?

    a. 172.16.0.200 255.255.255.128

    b. 172.16.0.200 255.255.255.0

    c. 225.1.1.1 255.255.255.0

    d. 10.43.53.63 255.255.255.192

2. Which of the following is a useful command on some Microsoft OSs for discovering a host's current IP address and mask?

    a. **tracert**

    b. **ipconfig /all**

    c. **arp –a**

    d. **ipconfig /displaydns**

3. Examine the following command output. If the user typed the **resume** command, what would happen?

    ```
    R1#show sessions
    Conn Host               Address        Byte  Idle Conn Name
       1 Fred                10.1.1.1         0     0  Fred
    *  2 Barney              10.1.2.1         0     0  Barney
    ```

    a. The command would be rejected, and the R1 CLI command prompt would be displayed again.

    b. The CLI user would be connected to a suspended Telnet connection to the router with IP address 10.1.1.1.

    c. The CLI user would be connected to a suspended Telnet connection to the router with IP address 10.1.2.1.

    d. The result cannot be accurately predicted from the information shown.

    Refer to the following figure for questions 4–9:

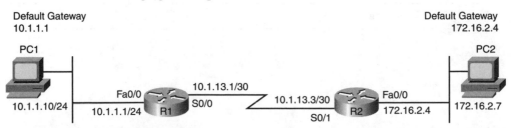

4. If PC3 were added to the LAN on the left, with IP address 10.1.1.130/25, default gateway 10.1.1.1, which of the following would be true?

    a. If PC1 issued a **ping 10.1.1.130** command, PC1 would use ARP to learn PC3's MAC address.

    b. If PC3 issued a **ping 10.1.1.10** command, PC3 would ARP trying to learn PC1's MAC address.

    c. If PC1 issued a **ping 10.1.13.1** command, PC1 would ARP trying to learn the MAC address of 10.1.13.1.

    d. If R1 issued a **ping 10.1.1.130** command, R1 would ARP trying to learn the MAC address of 10.1.1.130.

5. A new network engineer is trying to troubleshoot a problem for the user of PC1. Which of the following tasks and results would most likely point to a Layer 1 or 2 Ethernet problem on the LAN on the left side of the figure?

    a. A **ping 10.1.1.1** command on PC1 did not succeed.

    b. A **ping 10.1.13.3** command from PC1 succeeded, but a **ping 172.16.2.4** did not.

    c. A **ping 10.1.1.1** command from PC1 succeeded, but a **ping 10.1.13.1** did not.

    d. A **ping 10.1.1.10** command from PC1 succeeded.

6. The PC2 user issues the **tracert 10.1.1.10** command. Which of the following IP addresses could be shown in the command output?

    a. 10.1.1.10

    b. 10.1.1.1

    c. 10.1.13.1

    d. 10.1.13.3

    e. 172.16.2.4

7. All the devices in the figure just booted, and none of the devices has yet sent any data frames. Both PCs use statically configured IP addresses. Then PC1 successfully pings PC2. Which of the following ARP table entries would you expect to see?

    a. An entry on PC1's ARP cache for IP address 172.16.2.7

    b. An entry on PC1's ARP cache for IP address 10.1.1.1

    c. An entry on R1's ARP cache for IP address 10.1.1.10

    d. An entry on R1's ARP cache for IP address 172.16.2.7

8. All the devices in the figure just booted, and none of the devices has yet sent any data frames. Both PCs use statically configured IP addresses. Then PC1 successfully pings PC2. Which of the following ARP requests would you expect to occur?

   a. PC1 would send an ARP broadcast looking for R1's MAC address of the interface with IP address 10.1.1.1.

   b. PC2 would send an ARP broadcast looking for R2's MAC address of the interface with IP address 172.16.2.4.

   c. R1 would send an ARP broadcast looking for PC1's MAC address.

   d. R2 would send an ARP broadcast looking for PC2's MAC address.

   e. PC1 would send an ARP broadcast looking for PC2's MAC address.

9. PC1 is successfully pinging PC2 in the figure. Which of the following is true about the packets?

   a. The frame going left-to-right, as it crosses the left-side LAN, has a destination MAC address of R1's MAC address.

   b. The frame going left-to-right, as it crosses the right-side LAN, has a destination MAC address of R2's MAC address.

   c. The frame going left-to-right, as it crosses the serial link, has a destination IP address of PC2's IP address.

   d. The frame going right-to-left, as it crosses the left-side LAN, has a source MAC address of PC2's MAC address.

   e. The frame going right-to-left, as it crosses the right-side LAN, has a source MAC address of PC2's MAC address.

   f. The frame going right-to-left, as it crosses the serial link, has a source MAC address of R2's MAC address.

Foundation Topics

IP Troubleshooting Tips and Tools

The primary goal of this chapter is to better prepare you for the more challenging exam problems that involve potential Layer 3 problems. These problems often require the same thought processes and tools that you would use to troubleshoot networking problems in a real job. The first half of this chapter reviews the main types of problems that can occur, mainly related to addressing, host routing, and a router's routing logic. The second half of the chapter shows a scenario that explains one internetwork that has several problems, giving you a chance to first analyze the problems, and then showing how to solve the problems.

IP Addressing

This section includes some reminders relating to some of the basic features of IP addressing. More importantly, the text includes some tips on how to apply this basic knowledge to a given exam question, helping you know how to attack a particular type of problem.

Avoiding Reserved IP Addresses

One of the first things to check in an exam question that includes a larger scenario is whether the IP addresses are reserved and should not be used as unicast IP addresses. These reserved addresses can be categorized into one of three groups:

- Addresses that are always reserved

- Two addresses that are reserved in each subnet

- Addresses in two special subnets of each classful network, namely the zero subnet and broadcast subnet.

The first category of reserved addresses includes two Class A networks that are always reserved, plus all Class D (multicast) and Class E (experimental) IP addresses. You can easily recognize these IP addresses based on the value of their first octet, as follows:

- 0 (because network 0.0.0.0 is always reserved)

- 127 (because network 127.0.0.0 is always reserved)

- 224–239 (all Class D multicast IP addresses)

- 240–255 (all Class E experimental IP addresses)

Key Topic

The second category of reserved IP addresses includes the two reserved addresses inside each subnet. When subnetting, each subnet reserves two numbers—the smallest and largest numbers in the subnet—otherwise known as

- The subnet number

- The subnet's broadcast address

So the ability to quickly and confidently determine the subnet number and subnet broadcast address has yet another application, when attempting to confirm that the addresses shown in a question can be legally used.

The third category of reserved IP addresses may or may not apply to a particular internetwork or question. For a given classful network, depending on several factors, the following two subnets may not be allowed to be used:

- The zero subnet

- The broadcast subnet

If an exam question includes an address in the zero subnet or broadcast subnet, you must then consider whether the question allows neither subnet to be used, or both. Table 15-2 summarizes the clues to look for in exam questions to determine whether a question allows the use of both subnets or not.

Table 15-2   *Determining Whether a Question Allows the Use of the Zero and Broadcast Subnets*

Clues in the Question	Subnets Reserved?
Says nothing about it (default for the exam)	No
Lists the **ip subnet-zero** configuration command	No
Uses a classless routing protocol (RIP-2, EIGRP, OSPF)	No
Lists the **no ip subnet-zero** configuration command	Yes
Uses a classful routing protocol (RIP-1)	Yes

One Subnet, One Mask, for Each LAN

The hosts on a single LAN or VLAN (a single broadcast domain) should all be in the same subnet. As a result, each host, each router interface attached to the LAN, and each switch management address in that LAN should also use the same mask.

For the exam, you should check all the details documented in the question to determine the mask used by the various devices on the same LAN. Oftentimes, a question that is intended to test your knowledge will not just list all the information in a nice organized figure. Instead, you might have to look at the configuration and diagrams and use **show** commands to gather the information, and then apply the subnetting math explained in Chapter 12, "IP Addressing and Subnetting."

Figure 15-1 shows an example of a LAN that could be part of a test question. For convenience, the figure lists several details about IP addresses and masks, but for a given question, you might have to gather some of the facts from a figure, a simulator, and from an exhibit that lists command output.

Figure 15-1   *One LAN with Three Different Opinions About the Subnet*

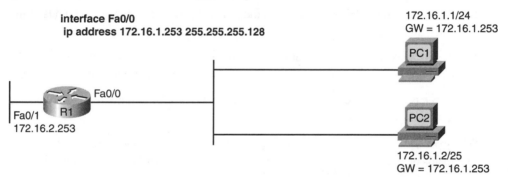

From the information in Figure 15-1, you can quickly tell that the two PCs use different masks (listed in prefix notation). In this case, you would need to know to look in the configuration for the subnet mask in the **ip address** interface subcommand, and then convert that mask to prefix notation to compare it with the other masks in this example. Table 15-3 lists the three differing opinions about the subnet.

Table 15-3   *Different Opinions About the Subnet in Figure 15-1*

	R1 Fa0/0	PC1	PC2
Mask	255.255.255.128	255.255.255.0	255.255.255.128
Subnet number	172.16.1.128	172.16.1.0	172.16.1.0
Broadcast address	172.16.1.255	172.16.1.255	172.16.1.127

In this case, several problem symptoms occur. For example, PC1 thinks 172.16.1.253 (R1) is in the same subnet, and PC1 thinks that it can forward packets to R1 over the LAN. However, R1 does not think that PC1 (172.16.1.1) is in the same subnet, so R1's connected route on the LAN interface (172.16.1.128/25) will not provide a route that R1 can use to forward packets back to PC1. For the exam, recognizing the fact that the hosts on the same LAN do not have the same opinion about the subnet should be enough to either answer the question, or to know what to fix in a Sim question. Table 15-4, found a little later in this chapter, summarizes the router commands that can be used to find the information required to analyze such problems.

Summary of IP Addressing Tips

Generally speaking, keep the following tips and facts in mind when you approach the exam questions that include details about IP addresses:

1.   Check the mask used on each device in the same LAN; if different, then the devices cannot have the same view of the range of addresses in the subnet.

2.   On point-to-point WAN links, check the IP addresses and masks on both ends of the link, and confirm that the two IP addresses are in the same subnet.

3.   When checking to confirm that hosts are in the same subnet, do not just examine the subnet number. Also check the subnet mask, and the implied range of IP addresses.

4.   Be ready to use the commands summarized in Table 15-4 to quickly find the IP addresses, masks, and subnet numbers.

The next section, in addition to reviewing a host's routing logic, introduces some commands on Microsoft operating systems that list the host's IP address and mask.

Host Networking Commands

Chapter 5, "Fundamentals of IP Addressing and Routing," explained the simple two-step logic a host uses when forwarding packets, in addition to how a host typically uses DHCP, DNS, ARP, and ICMP. These details can be summarized as follows:

Routing: If the packet's destination is on the same subnet, send the packet directly; if not, send the packet to the default gateway.

Address assignment: Before sending any packets, the host may use DHCP client services to learn its IP address, mask, default gateway, and DNS IP addresses. The host could also be statically configured with these same details.

Name resolution: When the user directly or indirectly references a host name, the host typically uses DNS name resolution requests to ask a DNS to identify that host's IP address unless the host already has that information in its name cache.

IP-to-MAC resolution: The host uses ARP requests to find the other host's MAC address, or the default gateway's IP address, unless the information is already in the host's ARP cache.

Of these four items, note that only the routing (forwarding) process happens for each packet. The address assignment function usually happens once, soon after booting. Name resolution and ARPs occur as needed, typically in reaction to something done by the user.

To analyze how well a host has accomplished these tasks, to troubleshoot problems, and to do the equivalent for exam questions, it is helpful to know a few networking commands on a host. Table 15-4 lists several of the commands on Microsoft Windows XP, but other similar commands exist for other operating systems. Example 15-1 following the table shows the output from some of these commands.

Table 15-4 *Microsoft Windows XP Network Command Reference*

Command	Function
ipconfig /all	Displays detailed IP configuration information for all interfaces, including IP address, mask, default gateway, and DNS IP addresses
ipconfig /release	Releases any DHCP-leased IP addresses
ipconfig /renew	Acquires an IP address and related information using DHCP
nslookup *name*	Sends a DNS request for the listed name
arp –a	Lists the host's ARP cache
ipconfig /displaydns	Lists the host's name cache
ipconfig /flushdns	Removes all DNS-found name cache entries
arp -d	Flushes (empties) the host's ARP cache
netstat -rn	Displays a host's routing table

Example 15-1 shows an example of the **ping www.cisco.com** command on a host running Windows XP, just after the ARP cache and hostname cache have been deleted (flushed). The example first shows the DHCP-learned addressing and DNS details, and then shows the flushing of the two caches. At that point, the example shows the **ping www.cisco.com** command, which forces the host to use DNS to learn the IP address of the Cisco web server, and then ARP to learn the MAC address of the default gateway, before sending an ICMP echo request to the Cisco web server.

NOTE   The **ping** fails in this example, probably due to ACLs on routers or firewalls in the Internet. However, the **ping** command still drives the DNS and ARP processes as shown in the example. Also, the text is from a DOS window in Windows XP.

Example 15-1 *Example Use of Host Networking Commands*

```
C:\>ipconfig /all
! Some lines omitted for brevity
Ethernet adapter Local Area Connection:

        Connection-specific DNS Suffix  . : cinci.rr.com
        Description . . . . . . . . . . . : Broadcom NetXtreme 57xx Gigabit Cont
roller
        Physical Address. . . . . . . . . : 00-11-11-96-B5-13
        Dhcp Enabled. . . . . . . . . . . : Yes
        Autoconfiguration Enabled . . . . : Yes
        IP Address. . . . . . . . . . . . : 192.168.1.102
        Subnet Mask . . . . . . . . . . . : 255.255.255.0
        Default Gateway . . . . . . . . . : 192.168.1.1
        DHCP Server . . . . . . . . . . . : 192.168.1.1
        DNS Servers . . . . . . . . . . . : 65.24.7.3
                                            65.24.7.6
        Lease Obtained. . . . . . . . . . : Thursday, March 29, 2007 6:32:59 AM
        Lease Expires . . . . . . . . . . : Friday, March 30, 2007 6:32:59 AM
! Next, the ARP and name cache are flushed.
C:\>arp -d
C:\>ipconfig /flushdns
Windows IP Configuration

Successfully flushed the DNS Resolver Cache.

! The ping command lists the IP address (198.133.219.25), meaning that the DNS request
  worked.
! However, the ping does not complete, probably due to ACLs filtering ICMP traffic.
C:\>ping www.cisco.com

Pinging www.cisco.com [198.133.219.25] with 32 bytes of data:
Request timed out.
Request timed out.
Request timed out.
Request timed out.

Ping statistics for 192.133.219.25:
    Packets: Sent = 4, Received = 0, Lost = 4 (100% loss),

! Next, the ARP cache lists an entry for the default gateway.
C:\>arp -a

Interface: 192.168.1.102 --- 0x2
  Internet Address      Physical Address      Type
  192.168.1.1           00-13-10-d4-de-08     dynamic
! Next, the local name cache lists the name used in the ping command and the IP address
```
continues

Example 15-1   *Example Use of Host Networking Commands (Continued)*

```
! learned from the DNS server.
C:\>ipconfig /displaydns

Windows IP Configuration

        www.cisco.com
        ----------------------------------------
        Record Name . . . . . : www.cisco.com
        Record Type . . . . . : 1
        Time To Live  . . . . : 26190
        Data Length . . . . . : 4
        Section . . . . . . . : Answer
        A (Host) Record . . . : 198.133.219.25
! Lines omitted for brevity
```

> **NOTE**   At press time, the simulator used on the Cisco exams did not include host networking commands; however, the exam can still require you to interpret the output of host commands, and the simulator could include these commands in the future.

In addition to these commands, Figure 15-2 shows an example of the windows used to statically configure a host's IP address, mask, default gateway, and DNS server IP addresses. These details can be configured with commands as well, but most people prefer the easier graphical interface.

Figure 15-2   *Configuring Static IP Addresses on Windows XP*

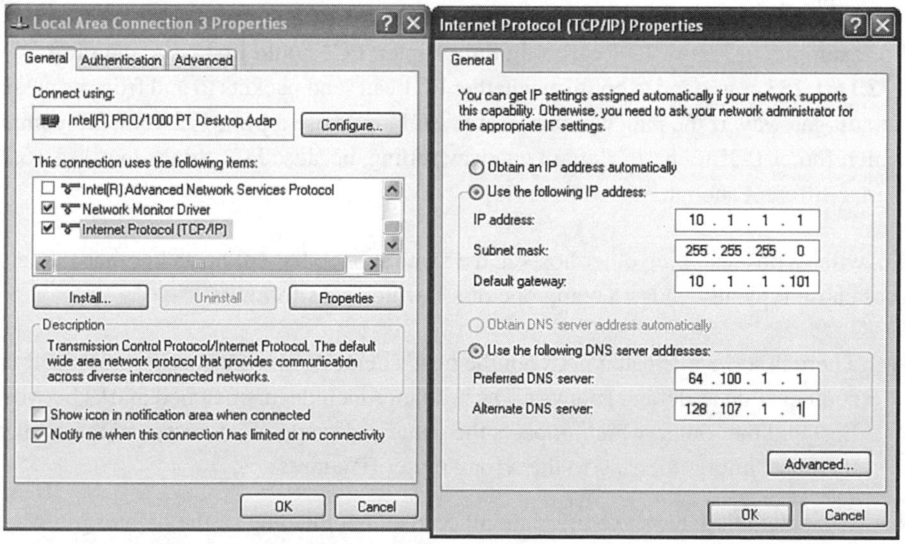

Troubleshooting Host Routing Problems

Troubleshooting host routing problems should begin with the same two-step routing logic used by a host. The first question to ask is whether the host can ping other hosts inside the same subnet. If a ping of a same-subnet host fails, the root cause typically falls into one of two categories:

Key Topic

- The two hosts have incorrect IP address and mask configurations, typically so that at least one of the two hosts thinks it is in a different subnet.

- The two hosts have correct IP address and mask configurations, but the underlying Ethernet has a problem.

For the exam, start by looking at the host's addresses and masks, and determine the subnet number and range of addresses for each. If the subnets are the same, then move on to Layer 1 and 2 Ethernet troubleshooting as covered in Chapter 10, "Ethernet Switch Troubleshooting," and in the *CCNA ICND2 Exam Certification Guide*, Chapter 3, "Troubleshooting LAN Switching."

If the host can ping other hosts in the same subnet, the next step is to confirm if the host can ping IP addresses in other subnets, thereby testing the second branch of a host's routing logic. Two different pings can be helpful at this step:

- Ping the default gateway IP address to confirm that the host can send packets over the LAN to and from the default gateway.

- Ping a different IP address on the default gateway/router, but not the IP address on the same LAN.

For example, in Figure 15-1 earlier in this chapter, PC1 could first issue the **ping 172.16.1.253** command to confirm whether PC1 can send packets to and from its presumed default gateway. If the ping was successful, PC1 could use a **ping 172.16.2.253** command, which forces PC1 to use its default gateway setting, because PC1 thinks that 172.16.2.253 is in a different subnet.

So, when a host can ping other hosts in the same subnet, but not hosts in other subnets, the root cause typically ends up being one of a few items, as follows:

Key Topic

- There is some mismatch between the host's default gateway configuration and the router acting as default gateway. The problems include mismatched masks between the host and the router, which impacts the perceived range of addresses in the subnet, or the host simply referring to the wrong router IP address.

- If the default gateway settings are all correct, but the ping of the default gateway IP address fails, there is probably some Layer 1 or 2 problem on the LAN.

■ If the default gateway settings are all correct and the ping of the default gateway works, but the ping of one of the other router interface IP addresses fails (like the **ping 172.16.2.253** command based on Figure 15-1), then the router's other interface may have failed.

While all the details in this section can be helpful when troubleshooting problems on hosts, keep in mind that many of the problems stem from incorrect IP address and mask combinations. For the exam, be ready to find the IP address and masks, and apply the math from Chapter 12 to quickly determine where these types of problems exist.

Finding the Matching Route on a Router

Chapter 5 summarized the process by which a router forwards a packet. A key part of that process is how a router compares the destination IP address of each packet with the existing contents of that router's IP routing table. The route that matches the packet's destination tells the router out which interface to forward the packet and, in some cases, the IP address of the next-hop router.

In some cases, a particular router's routing table might have more than one route that matches an individual destination IP address. Some legitimate and normal reasons for the overlapping routes in a routing table include auto-summary, route summarization, and the configuration of static routes.

The exams can test your understanding of IP routing by asking questions about which route would be matched for a packet sent to particular IP addresses. To answer such questions, you should keep the following important facts in mind:

■ When a particular destination IP address matches more than one route in a router's routing table, the router uses the most specific route—in other words, the route with the longest prefix length.

■ Although the router uses binary math to compare the destination IP address to the routing table entries, you can simply compare the destination IP address to each subnet in the routing table. If a subnet's implied address range includes the packet's destination address, the route matches the packet's destination.

■ If the question includes a simulator, you can easily find the matched route by using the **show ip route** *address* command, which lists the route matched for the IP address listed in the command.

Example 15-2 shows a sample IP routing table for a router, with many overlapping routes. Read the example, and before reading the explanations after the example, predict which route this router would match for packets destined to the following IP addresses: 172.16.1.1, 172.16.1.2, 172.16.2.2, and 172.16.4.3.

Example 15-2 **show ip route** *Command with Overlapping Routes*

```
R1#show ip route rip
Codes: C - connected, S - static, R - RIP, M - mobile, B - BGP
       D - EIGRP, EX - EIGRP external, O - OSPF, IA - OSPF inter area
       N1 - OSPF NSSA external type 1, N2 - OSPF NSSA external type 2
       E1 - OSPF external type 1, E2 - OSPF external type 2
       i - IS-IS, su - IS-IS summary, L1 - IS-IS level-1, L2 - IS-IS level-2
       ia - IS-IS inter area, * - candidate default, U - per-user static route
       o - ODR, P - periodic downloaded static route

Gateway of last resort is not set

     172.16.0.0/16 is variably subnetted, 5 subnets, 4 masks
R       172.16.1.1/32 [120/1] via 172.16.25.2, 00:00:04, Serial0/1/1
R       172.16.1.0/24 [120/2] via 172.16.25.129, 00:00:09, Serial0/1/0
R       172.16.0.0/22 [120/1] via 172.16.25.2, 00:00:04, Serial0/1/1
R       172.16.0.0/16 [120/2] via 172.16.25.129, 00:00:09, Serial0/1/0
R       0.0.0.0/0 [120/3] via 172.16.25.129, 00:00:09, Serial0/1/0
R1#show ip route 172.16.4.3
Routing entry for 172.16.0.0/16
  Known via "rip", distance 120, metric 2
  Redistributing via rip
  Last update from 172.16.25.129 on Serial0/1/0, 00:00:19 ago
  Routing Descriptor Blocks:
  * 172.16.25.129, from 172.16.25.129, 00:00:19 ago, via Serial0/1/0
      Route metric is 2, traffic share count is 1
```

For the exam, to find the matching route, all you need to know is the destination IP address of the packet and the router's IP routing table. By examining each subnet and mask in the routing table, you can determine the range of IP addresses in each subnet. Then, you can compare the packet's destination to the ranges of addresses, and find all matching routes. In cases where a particular destination IP address falls within the IP address range for multiple routes, then you pick the route with the longest prefix length. In this case:

■ Destination address 172.16.1.1 matches all five routes, but the host route for specific IP address 172.16.1.1, prefix length /32, has the longest prefix length.

■ Destination address 172.16.1.2 matches four of the routes (all except the host route for 172.16.1.1), but the route to 172.16.1.0/24 has the longest prefix.

■ Destination address 172.16.2.2 matches the last three routes listed in R1's routing table in the example, with the route for 172.16.0.0/22 having the longest prefix length.

■ Destination address 172.16.4.3 matches the last two routes listed in R1's routing table in the example, with the route for 172.16.0.0/16 having the longest prefix length.

Finally, note the output of the **show ip route 172.16.4.3** command at the end of Example 15-2. This command shows which route the router would match to reach IP address 172.16.4.3—a very handy command for both real life and for Sim questions on the exams. In this case, a packet sent to IP address 172.16.4.3 would match the route for the entire Class B network 172.16.0.0/16, as highlighted near the end of the example.

Troubleshooting Commands

The most popular troubleshooting command on a router or switch is the **ping** command. Chapter 14, "Routing Protocol Concepts and Configuration," already introduced this command, in both its standard form and the extended form. Basically, the **ping** command sends a packet to another host, and the receiving host sends back a packet to the original host, testing to see if packets can be routed between the two hosts.

This section introduces three additional Cisco IOS commands that can be useful when troubleshooting routing problems, namely the **show ip arp**, **traceroute**, and **telnet** commands.

The show ip arp Command

The **show ip arp** command lists the contents of a router's ARP cache. Example 15-3 lists sample output from this command, taken from router R1 in Figure 15-1, after the router and hosts were changed to all use a /24 mask.

Example 15-3 *Sample* **show ip arp** *Command Output*

```
R1#show ip arp
Protocol  Address         Age (min)  Hardware Addr   Type   Interface
Internet  172.16.1.1              8  0013.197b.2f58  ARPA   FastEthernet0/0
Internet  172.16.1.253           -  0013.197b.5004  ARPA   FastEthernet0/0
Internet  172.16.2.253           -  0013.197b.5005  ARPA   FastEthernet0/1
```

The most important parts of each entry are the IP address, MAC address, and interface. When a router needs to send a packet out a particular interface, the router will only use entries associated with that interface. For example, for R1 to send a packet to host PC1 in Figure 15-1 (address 172.16.1.1), R1 needs to forward the packet out its Fa0/0 interface, so R1 will only use ARP cache entries associated with Fa0/0.

Additionally, the Age heading includes a few interesting facts. If it lists a number, the Age value represents the number of minutes since the router last received a packet from the host. For example, it had been 8 minutes since R1 had received a packet from host PC1, source IP address 172.16.1.1, source MAC address 0013.197b.2f58. The Age does not mean how long it has been since the ARP request/reply; the timer is reset to 0 each time a matching packet is received. If the Age is listed as a dash, the ARP entry actually represents an IP address assigned to the router—for example, R1's Fa0/0 interface in Figure 15-1 is shown as 172.16.1.253, which is the second entry in Example 15-3.

The traceroute Command

The Cisco IOS **traceroute** command, like the Cisco IOS **ping** command, tests the route between a router and another host or router. However, the **traceroute** command also identifies the IP addresses of the routers in the route. For example, consider Figure 15-3 and Example 15-4. The figure shows an internetwork with three routers, with the **traceroute 172.16.2.7** command being used on router R1. The arrowed lines show the three IP addresses identified by the command output, which is shown in Example 15-4.

Figure 15-3 *Internetwork Used in* **traceroute** *Example*

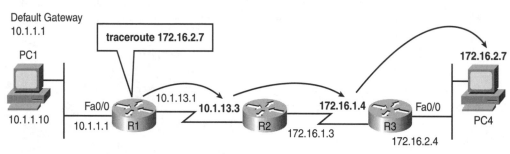

Example 15-4 *Sample* **traceroute** *Command Output*

```
R1#traceroute 172.16.2.7

Type escape sequence to abort.
Tracing the route to 172.16.2.7

  1 10.1.13.3   8 msec 4 msec 4 msec
  2 172.16.1.4   24 msec 25 msec 26 msec
  3 172.16.2.7   26 msec 26 msec 28 msec
```

The example shows a working **traceroute** command. However, if a routing problem exists, the command will not complete. For example, imagine that R1 had a route that matched 172.16.2.7, so R1 could forward packets to R2. However, R2 does not have a route that matches destination 172.16.2.7. In that case, the **traceroute** command would list the first line that refers to a router (highlighted in Example 15-4). However, no other routers would be listed, and the user would have to stop the command, typically by pressing the Ctrl-Shift-6 key sequence a few times. However, 10.1.13.3 is an IP address on the router that has a routing problem (R2), so the next step would be to telnet to R2 and find out why it does not have a route matching destination 172.16.2.7.

It is important to note that the **traceroute** command lists the IP addresses considered to be the next-hop device. For example, in Example 15-4, the first IP address (R2, 10.1.13.3) is the next-hop IP address in the route R1 uses to route the packet. Similarly, the next IP address (R3, 172.16.1.4) is the next-hop router in the route used by R2. (Chapter 7, "Troubleshooting IP Routing," in the *CCNA ICND2 Official Exam Certification Guide* explains how the **traceroute** command finds these IP addresses.)

> **NOTE**   Many operating systems have a similar command, including the Microsoft OS **tracert** command, which achieves the same goal.

Telnet and Suspend

Many engineers troubleshoot network problems sitting at their desks. To get access to a router or switch, the engineer just needs to use Telnet or SSH on their desktop PC to connect to each router or switch, oftentimes opening multiple Telnet or SSH windows to connect to multiple devices. As an alternative, the engineer could connect to one router or switch using a Telnet or SSH client on their desktop computer, and then use the **telnet** or **ssh** Cisco IOS EXEC commands to connect to other routers and switches. These commands acts as a Telnet or SSH client, respectively, so that you can easily connect to other devices when troubleshooting. When finished, the user could just use the **exit** command to disconnect the Telnet or SSH session.

Frankly, many people who rarely troubleshoot just use multiple windows on their desktop and ignore the Cisco IOS **telnet** and **ssh** commands. However, those who do a lot more troubleshooting tend to use these commands because, with practice, they enable you to move between routers and switches more quickly.

One of the most important advantages of using the Cisco IOS **telnet** and **ssh** commands is the suspend feature. The suspend feature allows a Telnet or SSH connection to remain active while creating another Telnet or SSH connection, so that you can make many concurrent connections, and then easily switch between the connections. Figure 15-4 shows a sample internetwork with which the text will demonstrate the suspend feature and its power.

The router administrator is using the PC named Bench to telnet into the Cincy router. When connected to the Cincy CLI, the user telnets to router Milwaukee. When in Milwaukee, the user suspends the Telnet session by pressing Ctrl-Shift-6, followed by pressing the letter x. The user then telnets to New York and again suspends the connection. At the end of the example, the user is concurrently telnetted into all three routers, with the ability to switch between the connections with just a few keystrokes. Example 15-5 shows example output, with annotations to the side.

Figure 15-4 *Telnet Suspension*

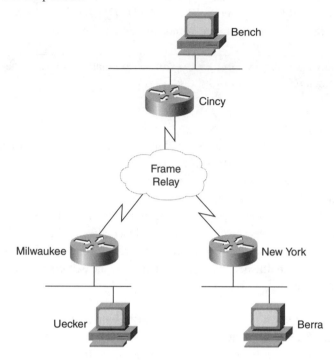

Example 15-5 *Telnet Suspensions*

```
Cincy#telnet milwaukee                  (User issues command to Telnet to Milwaukee)
Trying Milwaukee (10.1.4.252)... Open


User Access Verification

Password:                  (User plugs in password, can type commands at Milwaukee)
Milwaukee>
Milwaukee>
Milwaukee>
                          (Note: User pressed Ctrl-Shift-6 and then x)
Cincy#telnet NewYork              (User back at Cincy because Telnet was suspended)
Trying NewYork (10.1.6.253)... Open
                    (User is getting into New York now, based on telnet NewYork command)


User Access Verification

                                                               continues
```

Example 15-5 *Telnet Suspensions (Continued)*

```
Password:
NewYork>                         (User can now type commands on New York)
NewYork>
NewYork>
NewYork>
                    (Note: User pressed Ctrl-Shift-6 and then x)


Cincy#show sessions             (This command lists suspended Telnet sessions)
Conn Host               Address          Byte  Idle Conn Name
   1 Milwaukee          10.1.4.252          0     0 Milwaukee
*  2 NewYork            10.1.6.253          0     0 NewYork

Cincy#where                     (where does the same thing as show sessions)
Conn Host               Address          Byte  Idle Conn Name
   1 Milwaukee          10.1.4.252          0     0 Milwaukee
*  2 NewYork            10.1.6.253          0     0 NewYork


Cincy#resume 1       (Resume connection 1 (see show session) to Milwaukee)
[Resuming connection 1 to milwaukee ... ]


Milwaukee>                         (User can type commands on Milwaukee)
Milwaukee>
Milwaukee>
! (Note: User pressed Ctrl-Shift-6 and then x, because the user wants to
! go back to Cincy)
Cincy#        (WOW! User just pressed Enter and resumes the last Telnet)
 [Resuming connection 1 to milwaukee ... ]


Milwaukee>
Milwaukee>
Milwaukee>
                    (Note: User pressed Ctrl-Shift-6 and then x)
Cincy#disconnect 1             (No more need to use Milwaukee  Telnet terminated!)
Closing connection to milwaukee [confirm]        (User presses Enter to confirm)
Cincy#
[Resuming connection 2 to NewYork ... ]
                 (Pressing Enter resumes most recently suspended active Telnet)


NewYork>
NewYork>
NewYork>
                    (Note: User pressed Ctrl-Shift-6 and then x)
Cincy#disconnect 2                        (Done with New York, terminate Telnet)
Closing connection to NewYork [confirm]           (Just press Enter to confirm)
Cincy#
```

The play-by-play notes in the example explain most of the details. Example 15-5 begins with the Cincy command prompt that would be seen in the Telnet window from host Bench. After telnetting to Milwaukee, the Telnet connection was suspended because the user pressed Ctrl-Shift-6, let go, and then pressed x and let go. Then, after establishing a Telnet connection to New York, that connection was suspended with the same key sequence.

The two connections can be suspended or resumed easily. The **resume** command can be used to resume any suspended connection. To reconnect to a particular session, the **resume** command can list a connection ID, which is shown in the **show sessions** command. (The **where** command provides the same output.) If the **resume** command is used without a connection ID, the command reconnects the user to the most recently suspended connection. Also, instead of using the **resume** command, you can just use the session number as a command. For instance, just typing the command **2** does the same thing as typing the command **resume 2**.

The interesting and potentially dangerous nuance here is that if a Telnet session is suspended and you simply press Enter, Cisco IOS Software resumes the connection to the most recently suspended Telnet connection. That is fine, until you realize that you tend to press the Enter key occasionally to clear some of the clutter from the screen. With a suspended Telnet connection, pressing Enter a few times to unclutter the screen might reconnect to another router. This is particularly dangerous when you are changing the configuration or using potentially damaging EXEC commands, so be careful about what router you are actually using when you have suspended Telnet connections.

If you want to know which session has been suspended most recently, look for the session listed in the **show sessions** command that has an asterisk (*) to the left of the entry. The asterisk marks the most recently suspended session.

In addition to the commands in Example 15-5 that show how to suspend and resume Telnet and SSH connections, two other commands can list useful information about sessions for users logged into a router. The **show users** command lists all users logged into the router on which the command is used. This command lists all sessions, including users at the console, and those connecting using both Telnet and SSH. The **show ssh** command lists the same kind of information, but only for users that connected using SSH. Note that these commands differ from the **show sessions** command, which lists suspended Telnet/SSH sessions from the local router to other devices.

This concludes the first half of the chapter. The remainder of the chapter focuses on how to apply many of the troubleshooting tips covered earlier in this chapter by analyzing an internetwork that has a few problems.

A Routing Troubleshooting Scenario

This section describes a three-part scenario. Each part (A, B, and C) uses figures, examples, and text to explain part of what is happening in an internetwork and asks you to complete some tasks and answer some questions. For each part, the text shows sample answers for the tasks and questions.

The goal of this scenario is to demonstrate how to use some of the troubleshooting tips covered earlier in this chapter. The scenario is not designed to match any particular type of question you might see on the CCNA exams. Instead, it is just one more tool to help you learn how to apply your knowledge to new unique scenarios, which is exactly what the exam will require you to do.

Note that Appendix F, "Additional Scenarios," has two additional scenarios about other topics in this book. Appendix F, "Additional Scenarios," in the *ICND2 Official Exam Certification Guide* has five additional scenarios, again with the goal of providing more practice with troubleshooting and analysis skills for new scenarios.

Scenario Part A: Tasks and Questions

The scenario begins with an internetwork that has just been installed, but the documentation is incomplete. Your job is to examine the existing documentation (in the form of an internetwork diagram), along with the output of several **show** commands. From that information, you should

- Determine the IP address and subnet mask/prefix length of each router interface.

- Calculate the subnet number for each subnet in the diagram.

- Complete the internetwork diagram, listing router IP addresses and prefix lengths, as well as the subnet numbers.

- Identify any existing problems with the IP addresses or subnets shown in the existing figure.

- Suggest solutions to any problems you find.

Examples 15-6 through 15-8 list command output from routers R1, R2, and R3 in Figure 15-5. Example 15-9 lists commands as typed into a text editor, which were later pasted into R4's configuration mode.

Figure 15-5   *Scenario 3: Incomplete Network Diagram*

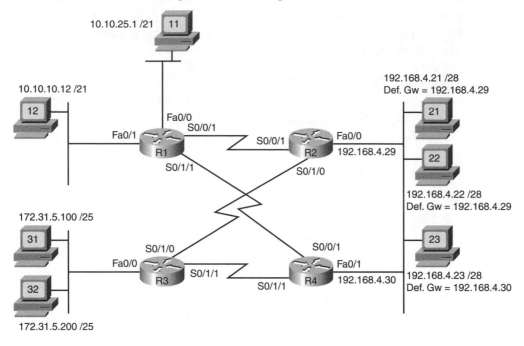

Example 15-6   *Scenario Output: Router R1*

```
R1#show ip interface brief
Interface                  IP-Address      OK? Method Status                 Protocol
FastEthernet0/0            10.10.24.1      YES NVRAM  up                     up
FastEthernet0/1            10.10.15.1      YES NVRAM  up                     up
Serial0/0/0                unassigned      YES NVRAM  administratively down  down
Serial0/0/1                192.168.1.1     YES NVRAM  up                     up
Serial0/1/0                unassigned      YES NVRAM  administratively down  down
Serial0/1/1                192.168.1.13    YES NVRAM  up                     up
R1#show protocols
Global values:
  Internet Protocol routing is enabled
FastEthernet0/0 is up, line protocol is up
  Internet address is 10.10.24.1/21
FastEthernet0/1 is up, line protocol is up
  Internet address is 10.10.15.1/21
Serial0/0/0 is administratively down, line protocol is down
Serial0/0/1 is up, line protocol is up
  Internet address is 192.168.1.1/30
Serial0/1/0 is administratively down, line protocol is down
Serial0/1/1 is up, line protocol is up
  Internet address is 192.168.1.13/30
```

Example 15-7 *Scenario Output: Router R2*

```
R2#show protocols
Global values:
  Internet Protocol routing is enabled
FastEthernet0/0 is up, line protocol is up
  Internet address is 192.168.4.29/28
FastEthernet0/1 is administratively down, line protocol is down
Serial0/0/0 is administratively down, line protocol is down
Serial0/0/1 is up, line protocol is up
  Internet address is 192.168.1.2/30
Serial0/1/0 is up, line protocol is up
  Internet address is 192.168.1.6/30
Serial0/1/1 is administratively down, line protocol is down
```

Example 15-8 *Scenario Output: Router R3*

```
R3#show ip interface brief
Interface              IP-Address      OK? Method Status                Protocol
FastEthernet0/0        172.31.5.1      YES NVRAM  up                    up
FastEthernet0/1        unassigned      YES NVRAM  administratively down down
Serial0/0/0            unassigned      YES NVRAM  administratively down down
Serial0/0/1            unassigned      YES NVRAM  administratively down down
Serial0/1/0            192.168.1.5     YES NVRAM  up                    up
Serial0/1/1            192.168.1.18    YES NVRAM  up                    up
R3#show ip route connected
      172.31.0.0/25 is subnetted, 1 subnets
C        172.31.5.0 is directly connected, FastEthernet0/0
      192.168.1.0/24 is variably subnetted, 5 subnets, 2 masks
C        192.168.1.4/30 is directly connected, Serial0/1/0
C        192.168.1.16/30 is directly connected, Serial0/1/1
```

Example 15-9 *Scenario Output: Router R4*

```
! The following commands are in a text editor, and will be pasted into
! configuration mode on R4.
interface fa0/1
 ip address 192.168.4.30 255.255.255.240
!
interface serial 0/0/1
 ip address 192.168.1.14 255.255.255.252
!
interface serial 0/1/1
 ip address 192.168.1.19 255.255.255.252
!
! The following three lines correctly configure RIP Version 2
router rip
 version 2
 network 192.168.1.0
 network 192.168.4.0
```

Scenario Part A: Answers

Examples 15-6, 15-7, and 15-8 list the IP addresses of each interface on routers R1, R2, and R3, respectively. However, some of the commands used in the examples do not provide mask information. In particular, the **show ip interface brief** command—a great command for getting a quick look at interfaces, their IP addresses, and the status—does not list the mask. The **show protocols** command lists that same information, as well as the subnet mask.

Example 15-8 (R3) does list the mask information directly, but it may take a little work to find it. You can see the interfaces and their configured IP addresses in the **show ip interfaces brief** command output, and then compare that information to the output of the **show ip route connected** command. This command does list the mask information, and the subnet number connected to an interface. A router determines the subnet number and mask for each connected route based on the configured **ip address** interface subcommand on each interface. From these facts, you can determine the mask used on each of R3's interfaces.

Finally, Example 15-9 lists configuration commands that will be pasted into router R4. These commands explicitly list the IP addresses and subnet masks in the various **ip address** configuration commands.

Figure 15-6 shows the answers to the first three tasks in Part A, listing the IP addresses and masks of each interface, as well as the subnet numbers.

Figure 15-6 *Scenario Part A: Subnet Numbers*

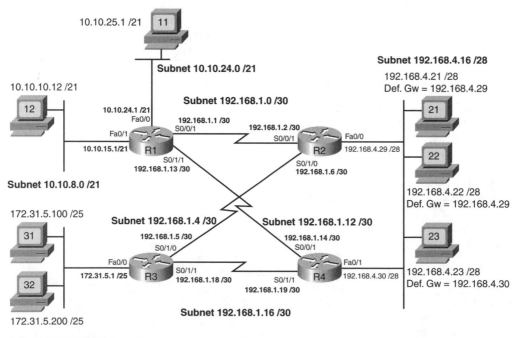

With all the information listed in one internetwork diagram, you can use the suggestions and tips from earlier in this chapter to analyze the IP addresses and subnets. In this case, you should have found two different addressing problems. The first of the two IP addressing problems is the disagreement between PC31 and PC32 regarding the subnet numbers and range of addresses on the lower-left LAN in Figure 15-6. In this case, PC32, with IP address 172.31.5.200 and a prefix length of /25, thinks it is in subnet 172.31.5.128/25, with a range of addresses from 172.31.5.129 to 172.31.5.254. PC31 and R3, attached to the same LAN, think they are attached to subnet 172.31.5.0/25, with the range of addresses being 172.31.5.1–172.31.5.126.

This particular problem results in R3 not being able to forward packets to PC32, because R3's connected route for that interface will refer to subnet 172.31.5.0/25. As a result, packets sent to PC32's IP address would not match that connected route. Additionally, PC32's setting for its default gateway IP address (172.31.5.1) is invalid, because the default gateway IP address should be in the same subnet as the host.

The second addressing problem in this scenario is that on the serial link between routers R3 and R4, R4's IP address and mask (192.168.1.19/30) is actually a broadcast address in subnet 192.168.1.16/30. Subnet 192.168.1.16/30 has an address range of 192.168.1.17–192.168.1.18, with a subnet broadcast address of 192.168.1.19. Note that the scenario suggested that the commands in Example 15-9 would be pasted into R4's configuration mode; R4 would actually reject the **ip address 192.168.1.19 255.255.255.252** command because it is a subnet broadcast address.

Several possible working solutions exist for both problems, but the simple solution in each case is to assign a valid but unused IP address from the correct subnets. In PC32's case, any IP address between 172.31.5.1 and 172.31.5.126, not already used by PC31 or R3, would work fine. For R4, IP address 192.168.1.17 would be the only available IP address, because R3 has already been assigned 192.168.1.18.

Scenario Part B: Analyze Packet/Frame Flow

Part B of this scenario continues with the network shown in Figure 15-6—including the IP addressing errors from Part A. However, no other problems exist. In this case, all physical connections and links are working, and RIP-2 has been correctly configured, and is functional.

With those assumptions in mind, answer the following questions. Note that to answer some questions, you need to refer to MAC addresses that are not otherwise specified. In these cases, a pseudo MAC address is listed—for example, R1-Fa0/1-MAC for R1's Fa0/1 interface's MAC address.

1. PC12 successfully pings PC21, with the packet flowing over the R1-R2 link. What ARP table entries are created to support the forwarding of the ICMP Echo Request packet?

2. Assume when PC12 pings PC23 that the ICMP echo request goes over the R1-R4 path. What ARP table entries are required on PC12? R1? R4?

3. Assume when PC12 pings PC23 that the ICMP echo request goes over the R1-R2 path. What ARP table entries are required in support of the ICMP echo reply from PC23, on PC23? R2? R4? R1?

4. PC31 sends a packet to PC22. When the packet passes over the Ethernet on the right side of the figure, what is the source MAC address? Destination MAC address? Source IP address? Destination IP address?

5. PC31 sends a packet to PC22. When the packet passes over the serial link between R3 and R2, what is the source MAC address? Destination MAC address? Source IP address? Destination IP address?

6. PC21 sends a packet to PC12, with the packet passing over the R2-R1 path. When the packet passes over the Ethernet on the right side of the figure, what is the source MAC address? Destination MAC address? Source IP address? Destination IP address?

7. PC21 sends a packet to PC12, with the packet passing over the R2-R1 path. When the packet passes over the Ethernet on the left side of the figure, what is the source MAC address? Destination MAC address? Source IP address? Destination IP address?

Scenario Part B: Answers

Scenario Part B requires that you think about the theory behind the IP forwarding process. That process includes many details covered in Chapter 5. In particular, to answer the questions in Part B correctly, you need to remember the following key facts:

Key Topic

■ The IP packet flows from the sending host to the receiving host.

■ The data link header and trailer, which encapsulate the packet, do not flow over the complete end-to-end route—instead, each individual data link helps move the packet from a host to a router, between two routers, or from a router to the destination host.

■ For the process to work, the data link frame's destination address lists the next device's data link address.

- The IP header lists the IP address of the sending host and receiving host.

- Routers discard the data link header and trailer for received frames and build a new data link header and trailer—appropriate for the outgoing interface—before forwarding the frame.

- On LANs, hosts and routers use ARP to discover the Ethernet MAC address used by other devices on the same LAN.

- On point-to-point WAN links, ARP is not needed, and the data link addressing is uninteresting and can be ignored.

If your reading of this list caused you to doubt some of your answers, feel free to go back and reevaluate your answers before looking at the actual answers.

Scenario Part B: Question 1

This question focuses on the packet flow from PC12 to PC21, assuming the packet passes over the R1-R2 link. The fact that the packet is created due to a **ping** command, and contains an ICMP echo request, does not impact the answer at all. The question specifically asks about which ARP table entries must be used by each device.

To answer the question, you need to remember how a host or router will choose to which device it sends the frame. PC12 sends the frame to R1 because the destination IP address is in a different subnet than PC12. R1 then sends a new frame to R2. Finally, R2 sends yet another new frame (with new data link header and trailer) to PC21. Figure 15-7 shows the frames, with just the destination MAC address and destination IP address shown.

To analyze the frame sent by PC12, remember that PC12's logic is basically "the destination IP address is on another subnet, so send this packet to my default gateway." To do so, PC12 needs to encapsulate the IP packet in an Ethernet frame so that the frame arrives at R1, PC12's default gateway. So, PC12 must find the MAC address of its default gateway (10.10.15.1) in PC12's ARP table. If the ARP table entry exists, PC12 can immediately build the frame shown in Figure 15-7 at step 1. If not, PC12 must first send an ARP broadcast, and receive a reply, to build the correct entry in its ARP table.

Also, note that PC12 does not need to know PC21's MAC address, because PC12 is not trying to send the packet directly to PC21. Instead, PC12 is trying to send the packet to its default gateway, so PC12 needs to know its default gateway's MAC address.

Figure 15-7 *Scenario Part B: Answer to Question 1*

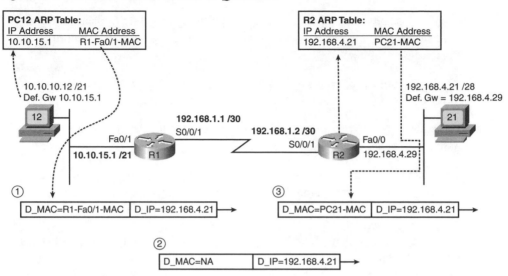

Step 2, as marked in Figure 15-7, shows the frame after R1 has stripped off the incoming frame's Ethernet header and trailer, R1 has decided to forward the packet out R1's S0/0/1 interface to R2 next, and R1 has added a (default) HDLC header and trailer to encapsulate the IP packet. The packet's destination IP address (192.168.4.21) is unchanged. HDLC, used only on point-to-point links, does not use MAC addresses, so it does not need ARP at all. So, no ARP table entries are needed on R1 for forwarding this packet.

Finally, step 3 again shows the frame after the router (R2) has stripped off the incoming HDLC frame's header and trailer and built the new Ethernet header and trailer. R2 needs to forward the packet out R2's Fa0/0 interface, directly to PC21, so R2 builds a header with PC21's MAC address as the destination. To make that happen, R2 needs an ARP table entry listing PC21's IP address (192.168.4.21) and its corresponding MAC address. Again, if R2 does not have an ARP table entry for IP address 192.168.4.21, R2 will send an ARP request (broadcast), and wait for a reply, before R2 would forward the packet.

Scenario Part B: Question 2

The answer to question 2 uses the same logic and reasoning as the answer to question 1. In this case, PC12, R1, and R4 will forward the packet in three successive steps, as follows:

1. PC12 decides to send the packet to its default gateway, because the destination (192.16.4.23) is on a different subnet than PC12. So, PC12 needs an ARP table entry listing the MAC address of its default gateway (10.10.15.1, or R1).

2. R1 receives the frame, strips off the data link header and trailer, and decides to forward the packet over the serial link to R4. The link uses HDLC, so R1 does not need ARP at all.

3. R4 receives the frame and strips off the incoming frame's HDLC header and trailer. R4 then decides to forward the packet directly to PC23, out R4's Fa0/1 interface, so R4 needs an ARP table entry listing the MAC address of host 192.168.4.23 (PC23).

Figure 15-8 shows the ARP table entries required for the flow of a packet from PC12 to PC23. Note that the figure also shows the correlation between the next-hop IP address and the MAC address, with the MAC address then being added to a new Ethernet data link header.

Figure 15-8 *Required ARP Table Entries: Question 2*

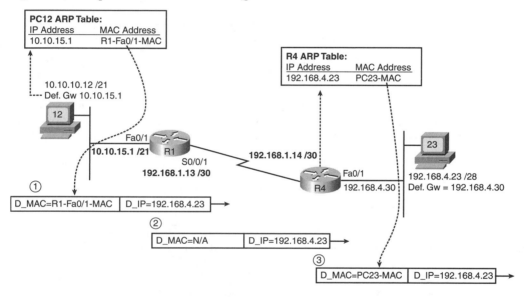

Scenario Part B: Question 3

The tricky part of this particular question relates to the fact that two routers connect to the subnet on the right of Figure 15-6, so PC23 appears to have two possible routers to use as its default gateway. The question suggests that an ICMP echo request packet goes from PC12, through R1, then R2, and over the LAN to PC23. PC23 then needs to send the ICMP echo reply to PC12, so to answer the question fully, you need to understand where the packet flows, and then determine the required ARP table entries on each device.

PC23 still uses the same familiar host logic when sending a packet—if the destination is on a different subnet, PC23 will send the packet to its default gateway. In this case, PC23 needs to send the ICMP echo reply to PC12, which is in another subnet, so PC23 will send the packet to 192.168.4.30 (R4)—PC23's configured default gateway. Presumably, R4 would then forward the packet to R1, and then R1 would forward the packet directly to PC12.

The ARP entries required for sending packets from PC23, to R4, to R1, and then to PC12 are as follows:

1. PC23 decides to send the packet to its default gateway, R4. So, PC23 needs an ARP table entry listing the MAC address of its default gateway (192.168.4.30).

2. R4 receives the frame, strips off the data link header and trailer, and decides to forward the packet over the serial link to R1. This links uses HDLC, so R4 does not need ARP at all.

3. R1 receives the frame from R4 and strips off the incoming frame's HDLC header and trailer. R1 then decides to forward the packet directly to PC12, out R1's Fa0/1 interface, so R1 needs an ARP table entry listing the MAC address of host 10.10.10.12 (PC12).

Figure 15-9 shows the ARP table entries required for the flow of a packet from PC23 to PC12. Note that the figure also shows the correlation between the next-hop IP address and the MAC address, with the MAC address then being added to a new Ethernet data link header.

Figure 15-9 *Required ARP Table Entries: Question 3*

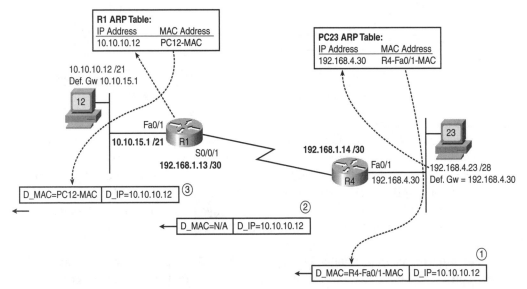

Scenario Part B: Question 4

This question uses a packet sent from PC31 to PC22, but with the question focusing on the packet as it crosses the LAN on the right side of Figure 15-6. To answer this question fully, you need to recall that while the source and destination IP addresses of the packet remain unchanged from sending host to receiving host, the data link source and destination addresses change each time a router builds a new data link header when forwarding a packet. Additionally, you need to realize that the R3→R4 serial link has been misconfigured (R4's proposed IP address of 192.168.1.19 was invalid), so no IP packets can be forwarded over the link between R1 and R4. As a result, the packet will go over this path: PC31→R3→R2→PC22.

The packet in question here (from PC31 to PC22) passes over the LAN on the right side of the figure when R2 forwards the packet over the LAN to PC22. In this case, R2 will build a new Ethernet header, with a source MAC address of R2's Fa0/0 interface MAC address. The destination MAC address will be PC22's MAC address. The source and destination IP addresses of 172.31.5.100 (PC31) and 192.168.4.22 (PC22), respectively, remain unchanged.

Figure 15-10 shows both data link addresses and both network layer addresses in each frame sent from PC31 to PC22. Note that the figure shows the addresses in the data link and network layer headers for each stage of its passage from PC31 to PC22.

Scenario Part B: Question 5

This question uses the same packet flow as question 4, but it focuses on the frame that passes the serial link between R3 and R2. The question can be easily answered as long as you remember that the router discards the data link headers of received frames, and then encapsulates the packet in a new data link header and trailer before forwarding the packet. This new data link header and trailer must be appropriate for the outgoing interface.

In this case, the routers use HDLC, which is the default point-to-point serial data link protocol on Cisco routers. HDLC headers do not include MAC addresses at all—in fact, HDLC addressing is completely uninteresting, because any frame sent by R3 on that link must be destined for R2, because R2 is the only other device on the other end of the link. As a result, there are no MAC addresses, but the source and destination IP addresses of 172.31.5.100 (PC31) and 192.168.4.22 (PC22), respectively, remain unchanged. Figure 15-9, found in the previous answer, shows a representation of the HDLC frame, mainly pointing out that it does not contain MAC addresses.

Figure 15-10 *Required ARP Table Entries: Question 4*

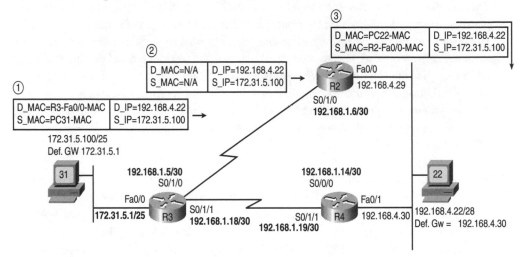

Scenario Part B: Question 6

This question focuses on a packet sent from PC21 to PC12, as the packet crosses the LAN on the right side of Figure 15-6. Also, the question tells you that the packet goes from PC21 to R2, then to R1, then to PC12.

In this case, PC21 forwards the packet, encapsulated in an Ethernet frame, to R2. To do so, the Ethernet header lists PC21 as the source MAC address, and R2's Fa0/0 interface MAC address as the destination MAC address. The IP addresses—a source of 192.168.4.21 (PC21) and a destination of 10.10.10.12 (PC12)—remain the same for the entire journey from PC21 to PC12. Figure 15-11 summarizes the frame contents for both this question and the next.

Figure 15-11 *Required ARP Table Entries: Questions 6 and 7*

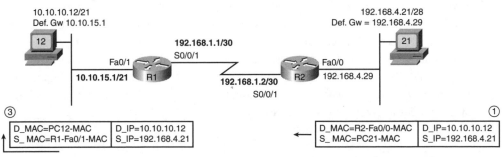

Scenario Part B: Question 7

Question 7 continues question 6 by examining the same packet, sent from PC21 to PC12, as the packet crosses the LAN on the upper-left part of Figure 15-6. The route taken by this packet is from PC21 to R2, then to R1, then to PC12.

To begin, PC21 sends the IP packet, with a source of 192.168.4.21 (PC21) and a destination of 10.10.10.12 (PC12). To send this packet, PC21 encapsulates the packet in an Ethernet frame to deliver the packet to its default gateway (R2). R2 strips off the Ethernet header of the received frame, and before forwarding the packet to R1, R2 encapsulates the packet in an HDLC frame. When R1 receives the HDLC frame, R1 removes the HDLC header and trailer, deciding to forward the packet out R1's Fa0/1 interface to PC12. As usual, the packet's source and destination address do not change at all during this process.

Before R1 forwards the packet out its Fa0/1 interface, R1 adds an Ethernet header and trailer. The source MAC address is R1's Fa0/1 interface MAC address, and the destination, found in R1's ARP table, is PC12's MAC address. Note that Figure 15-11, shown in the previous section, shows this frame on the left side of the figure.

Scenario Part C: Analyze Connected Routes

For Part C of this scenario, predict the output that would be displayed of the **show ip route connected** command on R4 and R1. You may continue to assume that any IP addressing problems found in Part A still have *not* been corrected. You may refer back to Example 15-5 through Example 15-9, as well as the completed IP address reference of Figure 15-6, for reference.

Scenario Part C: Answers

Routers add connected IP routes to their IP routing tables, referencing the subnet that is connected to an interface, assuming the following are true:

■   The interface's two status codes are "up" and "up."

■   The interface has an IP address correctly configured.

Key
Topic

For each interface meeting these two requirements, the router calculates the subnet number based on the IP address and subnet mask listed in the **ip address** interface subcommand. Based on details included in Parts A and B of this scenario, all router interfaces shown in Figure 15-5 have an IP address and are up/up, with the exception of R4's S0/1/1 interface. This one serial interface was to be assigned an IP address that was really a subnet broadcast address, so the router would have rejected the **ip address** command. Table 15-5 lists the location and connected routes added to R1 and R4.

Table 15-5 *Connected Routes Added to R1 and R4*

Location	IP Address	Subnet	Outgoing Interface
R1 Fa0/0	10.10.24.1/21	10.10.24.0/21	Fa0/0
R1 Fa0/1	10.10.15.1/21	10.10.8.0/21	Fa0/1
R1 S0/0/1	192.168.1.1/30	192.168.1.0/30	S0/0/1
R1 S0/1/1	192.168.1.13/30	192.168.1.12/30	S0/1/1
R4 S0/0/1	192.168.1.14/30	192.168.1.12/30	S0/0/1
R4 Fa0/1	192.168.4.30/28	192.168.4.16/28	Fa0/1

To see the connected routes in a concise command, you can use the **show ip route connected** EXEC command. This command simply lists a subset of the routes in the routing table—those that are connected routes. Example 15-10 and Example 15-11 show the contents of the **show ip route connected** command on both R1 and R4, respectively.

Example 15-10 **show ip route connected** *Command Output for R1*

```
R1#show ip route connected
     10.0.0.0/21 is subnetted, 2 subnets
C       10.10.8.0 is directly connected, FastEthernet0/0
C       10.10.24.0 is directly connected, FastEthernet0/1
     192.168.1.0/24 is variably subnetted, 5 subnets, 2 masks
C       192.168.1.12/30 is directly connected, Serial0/1/1
C       192.168.1.0/30 is directly connected, Serial0/0/1
```

Example 15-11 **show ip route connected** *Command on R4*

```
R4#show ip route connected
     192.168.4.0/28 is subnetted, 1 subnets
C       192.168.4.16 is directly connected, FastEthernet0/1
     192.168.1.0/24 is variably subnetted, 5 subnets, 2 masks
C       192.168.1.12/30 is directly connected, Serial0/0/1
```

If you compare the highlighted portions of Example 15-11 with Example 15-9's **ip address 192.168.4.30 255.255.255.240** command, a subcommand under R4's Fa0/1 interface, you can correlate the information. The mask from the **ip address** command can be used to determine the prefix notation version of the same mask—/28. The address and mask together can be used to determine the subnet number of 192.168.4.16. These same pieces of information are highlighted in the output of the **show ip route connected** command in Example 15-11.

Exam Preparation Tasks

Review All the Key Topics

Review the most important topics from inside the chapter, noted with the key topics icon in the outer margin of the page. Table 15-6 lists a reference of these key topics and the page numbers on which each is found.

Table 15-6 *Key Topics for Chapter 15*

Key Topic Element	Description	Page Number
List	First octet values of addresses that are always reserved and cannot be assigned to hosts	475
Table 15-2	Summary of reasons why an exam question should or should not allow the use of the zero and broadcast subnets	476
List	Summary of four tips when approaching IP addressing related questions on the exams	478
List	Summary of how a host thinks about routing, address assignment, name resolution, and ARP	478
List	Two typical reasons why a host cannot ping other hosts in the same subnet	482
List	Three typical reasons why a host can ping other hosts in the same subnet, but not hosts in other subnets	482-483
List	Tips regarding how a router matches a packet's destination IP address as part of the routing process	483
Figure 15-3	Shows the IP addresses discovered by the Cisco IOS **traceroute** command	486
List	Reminders that are helpful when thinking about the source and destination MAC and IP addresses used at various points in an internetwork	496
List	Two key requirements for a router to add a connected route	503

Complete the Tables and Lists from Memory

Print a copy of Appendix H, "Memory Tables" (found on the CD-ROM), or at least the section for this chapter, and complete the tables and lists from memory. Appendix I, "Memory Tables Answer Key," also on the CD-ROM, includes completed tables and lists to check your work.

Command Reference

Table 15-7 lists the EXEC commands used in this chapter and a brief description of their use. Additionally, you might want to review the host commands listed earlier in the chapter in Table 15-4. (This chapter did not introduce any new configuration commands.)

Table 15-7   *Chapter 15* **show** *and* **debug** *Command Reference*

Command	Purpose
show sessions	Lists the suspended Telnet and SSH session on the router from which the Telnet and SSH sessions were created
where	Does the same thing as the **show sessions** command
telnet {*hostname* | *ip_address*}	Connects the CLI to another host using Telnet
ssh –l *username* {*hostname* | *ip_address*}	Connects the CLI to another host using SSH
disconnect [*connection_number*]	Disconnects a currently suspended Telnet or SSH connection, based on the connection number as seen with the **show sessions** command
resume [*connection_number*]	Connects the CLI to a currently suspended Telnet or SSH connection, based on the connection number as seen with the **show sessions** command
traceroute {*hostname* | *ip_address*}	Discovers if a path from the router to a destination IP address is working, listing each next-hop router in the route
Ctrl-Shift-6, **x**	The key sequence required to suspend a Telnet or SSH connection
show ip arp	Lists the contents of the router's ARP cache
show arp	Lists the contents of the router's ARP cache
show ssh	Lists information about the users logged in to the router using SSH
show users	Lists information about users logged in to the router, including Telnet, SSH, and console users

Cisco Published ICND1 Exam Topics* Covered in This Part:

Describe the operation of data networks

- Interpret network diagrams

- Determine the path between two hosts across a network

- Describe the components required for network and Internet communications

- Identify and correct common network problems at Layers 1, 2, 3, and 7 using a layered model approach

- Differentiate between LAN/WAN operation and features

Implement an IP addressing scheme and IP services to meet network requirements for a small branch office

- Explain the basic uses and operation of NAT in a small network connecting to one ISP

- Describe the operation and benefits of using private and public IP addressing

- Enable NAT for a small network with a single ISP and connection using SDM and verify operation using CLI and ping

Implement and verify WAN links

- Describe different methods for connecting to a WAN

- Configure and verify a basic WAN serial connection

*Always recheck http://www.cisco.com for the latest posted exam topics.

Part IV: Wide-Area Networks

This chapter covers the following subjects:

WAN Technologies: This section examines several additional WAN technologies that were not covered in Chapter 4, namely modems, DSL, cable, and ATM.

IP Services for Internet Access: This section examines how an Internet access router uses DHCP client and server functions, as well as NAT.

CHAPTER 16

WAN Concepts

Chapter 4, "Fundamentals of WANs," introduced two important WAN technologies common in enterprise networks today:

- Leased lines, which use either High-Level Data Link Control (HDLC) or Point-to-Point Protocol (PPP)

- Frame Relay

Part IV of this book covers the remainder of the WAN-specific topics in this book. In particular, this chapter examines a broader range of WAN technologies, including commonly used Internet access technologies. Chapter 17, "WAN Configuration," focuses on how to implement several features related to WAN connections, including several Layer 3 services required for a typical Internet connection from a small office or home (SOHO) today.

"Do I Know This Already?" Quiz

The "Do I Know This Already?" quiz allows you to assess if you should read the entire chapter. If you miss no more than one of these eight self-assessment questions, you might want to move ahead to the "Exam Preparation Tasks" section. Table 16-1 lists the major headings in this chapter and the "Do I Know This Already?" quiz questions covering the material in those headings so you can assess your knowledge of these specific areas. The answers to the "Do I Know This Already?" quiz appear in Appendix A.

Table 16-1 *"Do I Know This Already?" Foundation Topics Section-to-Question Mapping*

Foundation Topics Section	Questions
WAN Technologies	1–5
IP Services for Internet Access	6–8

1. Which of the following best describes the function of demodulation by a modem?

   a. Encoding an incoming analog signal from the PC as a digital signal for transmission into the PSTN

   b. Decoding an incoming digital signal from the PSTN into an analog signal

   c. Encoding a set of binary digits as an analog electrical signal

   d. Decoding an incoming analog electrical signal from thc PSTN into a digital signal

   e. Encoding a set of binary digits as a digital electrical signal

2. Which of the following standards has a limit of 18,000 feet for the length of the local loop?

   a. ADSL

   b. Analog modems

   c. ISDN

   d. Cable Internet service

3. Which of the following is true regarding the location and purpose of a DSLAM?

   a. Typically used at a home or small office to connect the phone line to a DSL router

   b. Typically used at a home or small office instead of a DSL router

   c. Typically used inside the telco's CO to prevent any voice traffic from reaching the ISP's router

   d. Typically used inside the telco's CO to separate the voice traffic from the data traffic

4. Which of the following remote-access technologies support specifications that allow both symmetric speeds and asymmetric speeds?

   a. Analog modems

   b. WWW

   c. DSL

   d. Cable modems

5. Which of the following remote-access technologies, when used to connect to an ISP, is considered to be an "always on" Internet service?

   a. Analog modems

   b. DSL

   c. Cable modems

   d. All of these answers are correct.

6. For a typical Internet access router, using either cable or DSL, which of the following does the router typically do on the router interface connected to the LAN with the PCs in the small or home office?

   a. Acts as a DHCP server

   b. Acts as a DHCP client

   c. Performs NAT/PAT for the source address of packets that exit the interface

   d. Acts as DNS server

7. For a typical Internet access router, using either cable or DSL, which of the following does the router typically do on the router interface connected toward the Internet?

   a. Acts as a DHCP server

   b. Acts as a DHCP client

   c. Performs NAT/PAT for the source address of packets that exit the interface

   d. Acts as DNS server

8. This question examines a home-based network with a PC, a DSL router, and a DSL line. The DSL router uses typical default settings and functions. The PC connected to the router has IP address 10.1.1.1. This PC opens a browser and connects to the www.cisco.com web server. Which of the following are true in this case?

   a. The web server can tell it is communicating with a host at IP address 10.1.1.1.

   b. The PC learns the IP address of the www.cisco.com web server as a public IP address.

   c. The 10.1.1.1 address would be considered an inside local IP address.

   d. The 10.1.1.1 address would be considered an inside global IP address.

Foundation Topics

WANs differ from LANs in several ways. Most significantly, WAN links typically go much longer distances, with the WAN cabling being installed underground in many cases to prevent accidental damage by people walking on them or cars driving over them. Governments typically do not let the average person dig around other people's property, so WAN connections use cabling installed by a service provider, with the service provider having permission from the appropriate government agencies to install and maintain the cabling. The service provider then sells the WAN services to various enterprises. This difference between WANs and LANs can be summed up with the old adage "You own LANs, but you lease WANs."

This chapter has two major sections. The first section examines a broad range of WAN connectivity options, including switched circuits, DSL, cable, and ATM. The second half then explains how Internet connections from a home or small office often need several Layer 3 services before the WAN connection can be useful. The second section goes on to explain why DHCP and NAT are needed for routers connecting to the Internet, with particular attention to the NAT function.

WAN Technologies

This section introduces four different types of WAN technologies in addition to the leased-line and Frame Relay WANs introduced in Chapter 4. The first of these technologies, analog modems, can be used to communicate between most any two devices, and can be used to connect to the Internet through an ISP. The next two technologies, DSL and cable Internet, are almost exclusively used for Internet access. The last of these, ATM, is a packet-switching service used like Frame Relay to connect enterprise routers, as well as for other purposes not discussed in this book.

Before introducing each of these types of WANs, this section starts by explaining a few details about the telco's network, particularly because modems and DSL use the phone line installed by the telco.

Perspectives on the PSTN

The term Public Switched Telephone Network (PSTN) refers to the equipment and devices that telcos use to create basic telephone service between any two phones in the world. This term refers to the combined networks of all telephone companies. The "public" part of PSTN refers to the fact that it is available for public use (for a fee), and the "switched" part refers to the fact that you can change or switch between phone calls with different people at will. Although the PSTN was originally built to support voice traffic, two of the three Internet access technologies covered in this chapter happen to use the PSTN to send data, so a basic understanding of the PSTN can help you appreciate how modems and DSL work.

Sound waves travel through the air by vibrating the air. The human ear hears the sound because the ear vibrates as a result of the air inside the ear moving, which, in turn, causes the brain to process the sounds that were heard by the ear.

The PSTN, however, cannot forward sound waves. Instead, a telephone includes a microphone, which simply converts the sound waves into an analog electrical signal. (The electrical signal is called analog because it is analogous to the sound waves.) The PSTN can send the analog electrical signal between one phone and another using an electrical circuit. On the receiving side, the phone converts the analog electrical signal back to sound waves using a speaker that is inside the part of the phone that you put next to your ear.

The original PSTN predated the invention of the digital computer by quite a while, with the first telephone exchanges being created in the 1870s, soon after the invention of the telephone by Alexander Graham Bell. In its original form, a telephone call required an electrical circuit between the two phones. With the advent of digital computers, however, in the mid-1950s telcos began updating the core of the PSTN to use digital electrical signals, which gave the PSTN many advantages in speed, quality, manageability, and capability to scale to a much larger size.

Next, consider what the telco has to do to make your home phone work. Between your home and some nearby telco central office (CO), the telco typically installs a cable with a pair of wires, called the *local loop*. (In the United States, if you have ever seen a two- to three-foot-high light-green post in your neighborhood, that is the collection point for the local loop cables that connect to the houses on that street.) One end of the cable enters your house and connects to the phone outlets in your house. The other end (possibly miles away) connects to a computer in the CO, generically called a voice switch. Figure 16-1 shows the concept, along with some other details.

The local loop supports analog electrical signals to create a voice call. The figure shows two local loops, one connected to Andy's phone, and the other connected to Barney's. Andy and Barney happen to live far enough apart that their local loops connect to different COs.

Figure 16-1 *Analog Voice Calls Through a Digital PSTN*

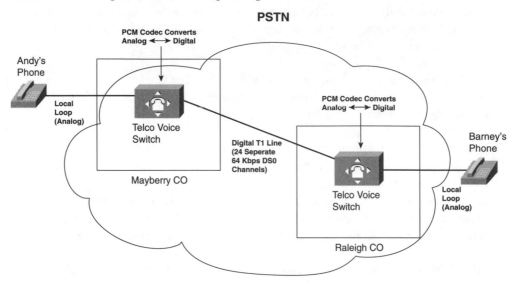

When Andy calls Barney, the phone call works, but the process is more complicated than just setting up an electrical circuit between the two phones. In particular, note that

■   The phones use analog electrical signals only.

■   The voice switches use a digital circuit to forward the voice (a T1 in this case).

■   The voice switch must convert between analog electricity and digital electricity in both directions.

To make it all work, the phone company switch in the Mayberry CO performs analog-to-digital (A/D) conversion of Andy's incoming analog voice. When the switch in Raleigh gets the digital signal from the Mayberry switch, before sending it out the analog line to Barney's house, the Raleigh switch reverses the A/D process, converting the digital signal back to analog. The analog signal going over the local line to Barney's house is roughly the same analog signal that Andy's phone sent over his local line; in other words, it is the same sounds.

The original standard for converting analog voice to a digital signal is called *pulse-code modulation (PCM)*. PCM defines that an incoming analog voice signal should be sampled 8000 times per second by the A/D converter, using an 8-bit code for each sample. As a result, a single voice call requires 64,000 bits per second—which amazingly fits perfectly into 1 of the 24 available 64-kbps DS0 channels in a T1. (As you may recall from Chapter 4, a T1 holds 24 separate DS0 channels, 64 kbps each, plus 8 kbps of management overhead, for a total of 1.544 Mbps.)

The details and complexity of the PSTN as it exists today go far beyond this brief introduction. However, these few pages do introduce a few key points that will give you some perspectives on how other WAN technologies work. In summary:

■ The telco voice switch in the CO expects to send and receive analog voice over the physical line to a typical home (the *local loop*).

■ The telco voice switch converts the received analog voice to the digital equivalent using a codec.

■ The telco converts the digital voice back to the analog equivalent for transmission over the local loop at the destination.

■ The voice call, with the PCM codec in use, consumes 64 kbps through the digital part of the PSTN (when using links like T1s and T3s inside the telco).

Analog Modems

Analog modems allow two computers to send and receive a serial stream of bits over the same voice circuit normally used between two phones. The modems can connect to a normal local phone line (local loop), with no physical changes required on the local loop cabling and no changes required on the voice switch at the telco's CO. Because the switch in the CO expects to send and receive analog voice signals over the local loop, modems simply send an analog signal to the PSTN and expect to receive an analog signal from the PSTN. However, that analog signal represents some bits that the computer needs to send to another computer, instead of voice created by a human speaker. Similar in concept to a phone converting sound waves into an analog electrical signal, a modem converts a string of binary digits on a computer into a representative analog electrical signal.

To achieve a particular bit rate, the sending modem could modulate (change) the analog signal at that rate. For instance, to send 9600 bps, the sending modem would change the signal (as necessary) every 1/9600th of a second. Similarly, the receiving modem would sample the incoming analog signal every 1/9600th of a second, interpreting the signal as a binary 1 or 0. (The process of the receiving end is called *demodulation*. The term *modem* is a shortened version of the combination of the two words *modulation* and *demodulation*.)

Because modems represent data as an analog electrical signal, modems can connect to a PSTN local loop, make the equivalent of a phone call to another site that has a modem connected to its phone line, and send data. As a result, modems can be used at most any location that has a phone line installed.

The PSTN refers to a communications path between the two modems as a circuit. Because the modems can switch to a different destination just by hanging up and dialing another phone number, this type of WAN service is called a *switched circuit*. Figure 16-2 shows an example, now with Andy and Barney connecting their PCs to their home phone lines using a modem.

Figure 16-2   *Basic Operation of Modems over PSTN*

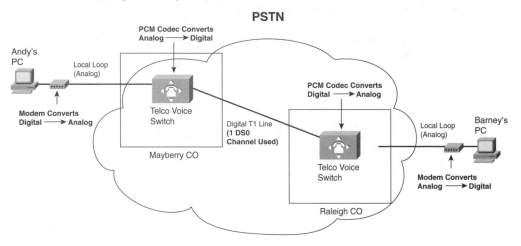

Once the circuit has been established, the two computers have a Layer 1 service, meaning that they can pass bits between each other. The computers also need to use some data link layer protocol on the circuit, with PPP being a popular option today. The telco has no need to try and interpret what the bits sent by the modem mean—in fact, the telco does not even care to know if the signal represents voice or data.

To be used as an Internet access WAN technology, the home-based user connects via a modem to a router owned by an ISP. The home user typically has a modem in their computer (internal modem) or outside the computer (external modem). The ISP typically has a large bank of modems. The ISP then publishes a phone number for the phone lines installed into the ISP router's modem bank, and the home user dials that number to connect to the ISP's router.

The circuit between two modems works and acts like a leased line in some regards; however, the link differs in regards to clocking and synchronization. The CSU/DSUs on the ends of a leased line create what is called a synchronous circuit, because not only do the CSU/DSUs try to run at the same speed, they adjust their speeds to match or synchronize with the other CSU/DSU. Modems create an asynchronous circuit, which means that the two modems try to use the same speed, but they do not adjust their clock rates to match the other modem.

Modems have the great advantage of being the most pervasively available remote-access technology, usable most anywhere that a local phone line is available. The cost is relatively low, particularly if the phone line is already needed for basic voice service; however, modems run at a relatively slow speed. Even with modern compression technologies, the bit rate for modems is only a little faster than 100 kbps. Additionally, you cannot concurrently talk on the phone and send data with a modem on the same phone line.

Digital Subscriber Line

By the time *digital subscriber line (DSL)* came around in the mid- to late 1990s, the main goal for remote-access WAN technology had changed. The need to connect to any other computer anywhere had waned, but the need to connect to the Internet was growing quickly. In years past, modems were used to dial a large variety of different computers, which was useful. Today you can think of the Internet as a utility, just like you think of the electric company, the gas company, and so on. The Internet utility provides IP connectivity to the rest of the world, so if you can just get connected to the Internet, you can communicate with anyone else in the world.

Because most people today just want access to the utility—in other words, the Internet— DSL was defined a little differently than modems. In fact, DSL was designed to provide high-speed access between a home or business and the local CO. By limiting the scope of where DSL needed to work, design engineers were able to define DSL to support much faster speeds than modems.

DSL's basic services have some similarities, as well as differences, to analog modems. Some of the key features are as follows:

■ DSL allows analog voice signals and digital data signals to be sent over the same local loop wiring at the same time.

■ The local loop must be connected to something besides a traditional voice switch at the local CO, in this case a device called a *DSL access multiplexer (DSLAM)*.

■ DSL allows for a concurrent voice call to be up at the same time as the data connection.

■ Unlike modems, DSL's data component is always on; in other words, you do not have to signal or dial a phone number to set up a data circuit.

DSL really does provide some great benefits—you can use the same old phones that you already have, you can keep the same phone number, and, once DSL is installed, you can just sit down and start using your "always on" Internet service without having to dial a number. Figure 16-3 shows some of the details of a typical DSL connection.

Figure 16-3   *DSL Connection from the Home to an ISP*

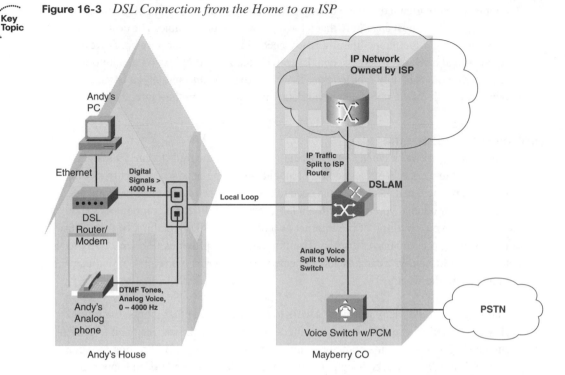

The figure shows a generic-looking device labeled "DSL Router/Modem" which connects via a standard telephone cable to the same phone jack on the wall. Many options exist for the DSL hardware at the home: There could be a separate router and DSL modem, the two could be combined as shown in the figure, or the two could be combined along with a LAN switch and a wireless AP. (Figure 13-4 and Figure 13-5 in Chapter 13, "Operating Cisco Routers," show a couple of the cabling options for the equivalent design when using cable Internet, which has the same basic hardware options.)

In the home, a DSL modem or DSL-capable router is connected to the phone line (the local loop) using a typical telephone cable, as shown on the left side of Figure 16-3. The same old analog telephones can be connected to any other available phone jacks, at the same time. The cable from the phone or DSL modem to the telephone wall jack uses RJ-11 connectors, as is typical for a cable for an analog phone or a modem.

DSL supports concurrent voice and data, so you can make a phone call without disrupting the always-on DSL Internet connection. The phone generates an analog signal at frequency ranges between 0 and 4000 Hz; the DSL modem uses frequencies higher than 4000 Hz so that the phone and DSL signals do not interfere with each other very much. You typically need to put a filter, a small device about the size of a small packet of chewing gum, between each phone and the wall socket (not shown) to prevent interference from the higher-frequency DSL signals.

The DSLAM at the local CO plays a vitally important role in allowing the digital data and analog voice to be processed correctly. When migrating a customer from just using voice to instead support voice and DSL, the phone company has to disconnect the local loop cable from the old voice switch and move it to a DSLAM. The local loop wiring itself does not have to change. The DSLAM directs (multiplexes) the analog voice signal—the frequency range between 0 Hz and 4000 Hz—to a voice switch, and the voice switch treats that signal just like any other analog voice line. The DSLAM multiplexes the data traffic to a router owned by the ISP providing the service in Figure 16-3.

The design with a local loop, DSLAM, and ISP router enables a business model in which you buy Internet services from an ISP that is not the local phone company. The local telco owns the local loop. However, many ISPs that are not a local telco sell DSL Internet access. The way it works is that you pay the ISP a monthly fee for DSL service, and the ISP works with the telco to get your local loop connected to the telco's DSLAM. The telco then configures the DSLAM to send data traffic from your local loop to that ISP's router. You pay the ISP for high-speed DSL Internet service, and the ISP keeps part of the money and gives part of the money to the local telco.

DSL Types, Speeds, and Distances

DSL technology includes many options at many speeds, with some variations getting more attention in the marketplace. So, it is helpful to consider at least a few of the options.

One key difference in the types of DSL is whether the DSL service is symmetric or asymmetric. *Symmetric* DSL means that the link speed in each direction is the same, whereas *asymmetric* means that the speeds are different. As it turns out, SOHO users tend to need to receive much more data than they need to send. For example, a home user might type in a URL in a browser window, sending a few hundred bytes of data to the ISP. The web page returned from the Internet may be many megabytes large. Asymmetric DSL allows for much faster downstream (Internet toward home) speeds, but with lower upstream (home toward Internet) speeds, as compared with symmetric DSL. For example, an ADSL connection might use a 1.5-Mbps speed downstream (toward the end user), and a 384-Kbps speed upstream toward the Internet. Table 16-2 lists some of the more popular types of DSL, and whether each is asymmetric or symmetric.

Table 16-2   *DSL Types*

Acronym	Spelled Out	Type
ADSL	Asymmetric DSL	Asymmetric
CDSL (G.lite)	Consumer DSL	Asymmetric
VDSL	Very-high-data-rate DSL	Asymmetric

continues

Table 16-2   *DSL Types (Continued)*

Acronym	Spelled Out	Type
SDSL	Symmetric DSL	Symmetric
HDSL	High-data-rate DSL	Symmetric
IDSL	ISDN DSL	Symmetric

Typically, most consumer DSL installations in the United States use ADSL.

The speed of a DSL line is a difficult number to pin down. DSL standards list maximum speeds, but in practice the speed can vary widely, based on many factors, including:

Key Topic

- The distance between the CO and the consumer (the longer the distance, the slower the speed)

- The quality of the local loop cabling (the worse the wiring, the slower the speed)

- The type of DSL (each standard has different maximum theoretical speeds)

- The DSLAM used in the CO (older equipment may not have recent improvements that allow for faster speeds on lower-grade local loops)

For example, ADSL has theoretical downstream speeds of close to 10 Mbps, with the Cisco ICND1 course currently making a minor reference to a maximum of 8.192 Mbps. However, most ISPs, if they quote any numbers at all, state that the lines will run at about 1.5 Mbps downstream, and 384 kbps upstream—numbers much more realistic compared to the actual speeds experienced by their customers. Regardless of the actual speeds, these speeds are significantly faster than modem speeds, making DSL very popular in the marketplace for high-speed Internet access.

Besides the factors that limit the speed, DSL lines typically do not work at all if the local loop exceeds that particular DSL standard's maximum cabling length. For example, ADSL has become popular in part because it supports local loops that are up to 18,000 feet (a little over 3 miles/5 kilometers). However, if you live in the country, far away from the CO, chances are DSL is not an option.

DSL Summary

DSL brings high-speed remote-access capabilities to the home. It supports concurrent voice and data, using the same old analog phones and same old local loop cabling. The Internet data service is always on—no dialing required. Furthermore, the speed of the DSL service itself does not degrade when more users are added to the network.

DSL has some obvious drawbacks. DSL simply will not be available to some people, particularly those in rural areas, based on the distance from the home to the CO. The local telco must have DSL equipment in the CO before it, or any ISP, can offer DSL services. Even when the home is close enough to the CO, sites farther from the CO might run slower than sites closer to the CO.

Cable Internet

Of all the Internet access technologies covered in this chapter, cable modem technology is the only one that does not use a phone line from the local telco for physical connectivity. Many homes also have a cable TV service supplied by a coaxial cable—in other words, over the cable TV (CATV) cabling. Cable modems provide an always-on Internet access service, while allowing you to surf the Internet over the cable and make all the phone calls you want over your telephone line—and you can watch TV at the same time!

> **NOTE**   Cable companies today also offer digital voice services, competing with the local telcos. The voice traffic also passes over the same CATV cable.

Cable modems (and cable routers with integrated cable modems, similar in concept to DSL) use some of the capacity in the CATV cable that otherwise might have been allocated for new TV channels, using those frequency bands for transferring data. It is a little like having an "Internet" channel to go along with CNN, TBS, ESPN, The Cartoon Network, and all your other favorite cable channels.

To appreciate how cable modems work, you need a little perspective on some cable TV terminology. Cable TV traditionally has been a one-way service—the cable provider sends electrical signals down the cable for all the channels. All you have to do, after the physical installation is complete, is choose the channel you want to watch. While you are watching The Cartoon Network, the electrical signals for CNN still are coming into your house over the cable—your TV is just ignoring that part of the signal. If you have two TVs in your house, you can watch two different channels because the signals for all the channels are being sent down the cable.

Cable TV technology has its own set of terminology, just like most of the other access technologies covered in this chapter. Figure 16-4 outlines some of the key terms.

The cable modem or cable router connects to the CATV cable, shown as a dotted line in the figure. In a typical house or apartment, there are several cable wall plates installed, so the cable modem/router just connects to one of those wall jacks. And like DSL modems/routers, the cable modem/router connects to the PCs in the home using an Ethernet connection.

Figure 16-4 *Cable TV Terminology*

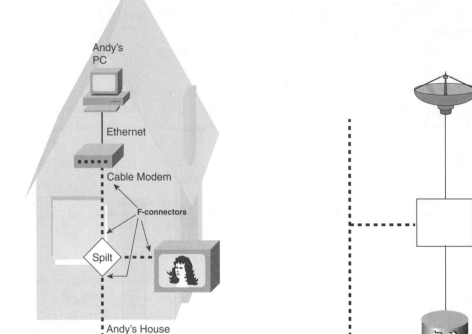

The other end of the cable connects to equipment in the cable company's facilities, generally called the head-end. Equipment on the head-end can split the channels used for Internet over to an ISP router, much like a DSLAM splits data off the telco local loop over to an ISP's router. That same equipment collects TV signals (typically from a satellite array) and feeds those over other channels on the cable to provide TV service.

Cable Internet service has many similarities to DSL services. It is intended to be used to access some ISP's router, with that service being always on and available. It is asymmetric, with much faster downstream speeds. The SOHO user needs a cable modem and router, which may be in a single device or in separate devices.

There are some key differences, as you might imagine. Cable Internet service runs faster than DSL, with practical speeds from two to five times faster than the typically quoted 1.5 Mbps for DSL. Cable speeds do not degrade due to the length of the cable (distance from the cable company's facilities). However, the effective speed of cable Internet does degrade as more and more traffic is sent over the cable by other users, because the cable is shared among users in certain parts of the CATV cable plant, whereas DSL does not suffer from this problem. To be fair, the cable companies can engineer around these contention problems and improve the effective speed for those customers.

> **NOTE**   Pinning down exact answers to the questions "how fast is cable?" and "how fast is DSL?" is difficult because the speeds vary depending on many factors. However, you can test the actual amount of data transferred using one of many speed-testing websites. I tend to use CNET's website, which can be found by searching the web for "Internet speed test CNET" or at http://reviews.cnet.com/7004-7254_7-0.html.

Comparison of Remote-Access Technologies

This chapter scratches the surface of how modems, cable, and DSL work. Consumers choose between these options for Internet access all the time, and network engineers choose between these options for supporting their work-at-home users as well. So, Table 16-3 lists some of the key comparison points for these options.

Table 16-3   *Comparison of Modems, DSL, and Cable*

Key Topic

	Analog Modems	DSL	Cable Modems
Transport	Telco local loop	Telco local loop	CATV cable
Supports symmetric speeds	Yes	Yes	No
Supports asymmetric speeds	Yes	Yes	Yes
Typical practical speeds (may vary)	Up to 100 kbps	1.5 Mbps downstream	3 to 6 Mbps downstream
Allows concurrent voice and data	No	Yes	Yes
Always-on Internet service	No	Yes	Yes
Local loop distance issues	No	Yes	No
Throughput degrades under higher loads	No	No	Yes

ATM

The other WAN technologies introduced in this book can all be used for Internet access from the home or a small office. Asynchronous Transfer Mode (ATM) is most often used today either as a packet-switching service, similar in purpose to Frame Relay, or as a switching technology used inside the core network built by telcos. This section introduces ATM as a packet-switching service.

To use ATM, routers connect to an ATM service via an access link to an ATM switch inside the service provider's network—basically the same topology as Frame Relay. For multiple sites, each router would need a single access link to the ATM network, with a virtual circuit (VC) between sites as needed. ATM can use permanent VCs (PVC) like Frame Relay.

Of course, there are differences between Frame Relay and ATM; otherwise, you would not need both! First, ATM typically supports much higher-speed physical links, especially those using a specification called Synchronous Optical Network (SONET). The other big difference is that ATM does not forward frames—it forwards *cells*. A cell, just like a packet or frame, is a string of bits sent over some network. The difference is that while packets and frames can vary in size, ATM cells are always a fixed 53 bytes in length.

ATM cells contain 48 bytes of payload (data) and a 5-byte header. The header contains two fields that together act like the data-link connection identifier (DLCI) for Frame Relay by identifying each VC. The two fields are named *Virtual Path Identifier (VPI)* and *Virtual Channel Identifier (VCI)*. Just like Frame Relay switches forward frames based on the DLCI, devices called ATM switches, resident in the service provider network, forward cells based on the VPI/VCI pair.

The end users of a network typically connect using Ethernet, and Ethernet devices do not create cells. So, how do you get traffic off an Ethernet and onto an ATM network? A router connects both to the LAN and to the ATM WAN service via an access link. When a router receives a packet from the LAN and decides to forward the packet over the ATM network, the router creates the cells by breaking the packet into smaller pieces. This cell-creation process involves breaking up a data link layer frame into 48-byte-long segments. Each segment is placed in a cell along with the 5-byte header. Figure 16-5 shows the general idea, as performed on R2.

Figure 16-5 *ATM Segmentation and Reassembly*

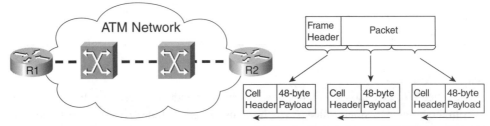

R1 actually reverses the segmentation process after receiving all the cells—a process called *reassembly.* The entire concept of segmenting a frame into cells, and reassembling them, is called *segmentation and reassembly (SAR).* Cisco routers use specialized ATM interfaces to support ATM. The ATM cards include special hardware to perform the SAR function quickly. They also often include special hardware to support SONET.

Because of its similar function to Frame Relay, ATM also is considered to be a type of packet-switching service. However, because it uses fixed-length cells, it more often is called a *cell-switching* service.

Packet Switching Versus Circuit Switching

Many WAN technologies can be categorized as either a circuit-switching service or a packet-switching service. In traditional telco terminology, a circuit provides the physical ability to send voice or data between two endpoints. The origins of the term circuit relate to how the original phone systems actually created an electrical circuit between two telephones in order to carry the voice signal. The leased lines explained in Chapter 4 are circuits, providing the physical ability to transfer bits between two endpoints.

Packet switching means that the devices in the WAN do more than pass the bits or electrical signal from one device to another. With packet switching, the provider's networking devices interpret the bits sent by the customers by reading some type of address field in the header. The service makes choices, switching one packet to go in one direction, and the next packet to go in another direction to another device. Table 16-4 summarizes a few of the key comparison points between these two types of WANs.

Table 16-4 *Comparing Circuits and Packet Switching*

Feature	Circuits	Packet Switching
Service implemented as OSI layer . . .	1	2
Point-to-point (two devices) or more	Point-to-point	Multipoint (more than two)

Ethernet as a WAN Service

Before moving on to a discussion of some Internet access issues, it is useful to note a major development in WAN services: Ethernet as a WAN service, or Metropolitan Ethernet (Metro E). To supply a Metro E service, the service provider provides an Ethernet cable, oftentimes optical to meet the longer distance requirements, into the customer site. The customer can then connect the cable to a LAN switch or router.

Additionally, the service provider can offer both Fast Ethernet and Gigabit Ethernet speeds, but, like Frame Relay, offer a lower committed information rate (CIR). For example, a customer might need 20 Mbps of bandwidth between routers located at large data centers on either side of a city. The provider installs a Fast Ethernet link between the sites, contracting with the customer for 20 Mbps. The customer then configures the routers so that they will purposefully send only 20 Mbps, on average, using a feature called shaping. The end result is that the customer gets the bandwidth, typically at a better price than other options (like using a T3).

Metro E offers many design options as well, including simply connecting one customer site to an ISP, or connecting all of a customer's sites to each other using various VLANs over a single Ethernet access link. Although the details are certainly beyond the CCNA exams, it is an interesting development to watch as it becomes more popular in the marketplace.

Next, this chapter changes focus completely, examining several features that are required for a typical Internet connection using DSL and cable.

IP Services for Internet Access

DSL and cable Internet access have many similar features. In particular, both use a router, with that router being responsible for forwarding packets from the computers in the home or office to a router on the other side of the cable/DSL line, and vice versa. This second major section of this chapter examines several IP-related functions that must be performed by the DSL/cable router, in particular a couple of ways to use DHCP, as well as a feature called Network Address Translation (NAT).

The equipment used at a SOHO to connect to the Internet using DSL or cable may be a single integrated device, or several separate devices, as introduced in Figures 13-4 and 13-5 in Chapter 13. For the sake of explaining the details in this chapter, the figures will show separate devices, as in Figure 16-6.

Figure 16-6 *Internet Access Equipment, Separate Devices*

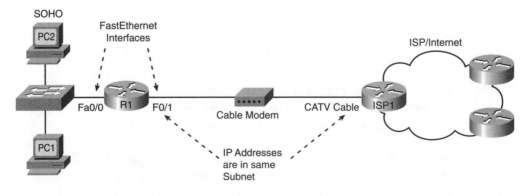

Thinking about the flow of data left-to-right in the figure, a PC sends data to its default gateway, which is the local access router. The LAN switch just forwards frames to the access router. The router makes a routing decision to forward the packet to the ISP router as the next-hop router. Then, the cable modem converts the Ethernet frame received from the router to meet cable specifications, the details of which are beyond the scope of this book. Finally, the ISP router has a routing table for all routes in the Internet, so it can forward the packet to wherever the packet needs to go.

Of the three devices at the small office, this section examines the router in detail. Besides basic routing, the access router needs to perform three additional important functions, as will be explained in this section: assign addresses, learn routes, and translate addresses (NAT).

Address Assignment on the Internet Access Router

The Internet access router in Figure 16-6 has two LAN interfaces—one facing the Internet and one facing the devices at that site. As was mentioned in Part III of this book on many occasions, to be able to route packets on those two interfaces, the router needs an IP address on each interface. However, instead of choosing and statically configuring the IP addresses with the **ip address** interface subcommand, the IP addresses are chosen per the following rules:

- The Internet-facing interface needs one public IP address so that the routers in the Internet know how to route packets to the access router.

- The ISP typically assigns that public (and globally routable) IP address dynamically, using DHCP.

- The local PCs typically need to dynamically learn IP addresses with DHCP, so the access router will act as a DHCP server for the local hosts.

- The router needs a statically configured IP address on the local subnet, using a private network number.

- The local LAN subnet will use addresses in a private network number.

> **NOTE** The section "Public and Private Addressing" in Chapter 12, "IP Addressing and Subnetting," introduces the concept of private networks and lists the ranges of addresses in private networks.

Figure 16-7 shows the net results of the DHCP exchanges between the various devices, ignoring some of the cabling details.

Figure 16-7 *DHCP Server and Client Functions on an Internet Access Router*

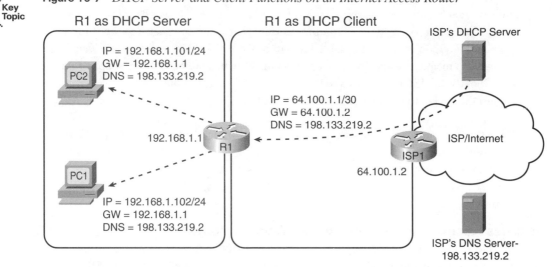

For the process in Figure 16-7 to work, the access router (R1) needs a statically configured IP address on the local interface, a DHCP server function enabled on that interface, and a DHCP client function enabled on the Internet interface. R1 learns its Internet interface IP address from the ISP, in this case 64.100.1.1. After being configured with IP address 192.168.1.1/24 on the local interface, R1 starts answering DHCP requests, assigning IP addresses in that same subnet to PC1 and PC2. Note that R1's DHCP messages list the DNS IP address (198.133.219.2) learned from the ISP's DHCP server.

Routing for the Internet Access Router

Besides the IP address details, router R1 needs to be able to route packets to and from the Internet. R1 has two connected routes, as normal. However, instead of learning all the routes in the global Internet using a routing protocol, R1 can use a default route. In fact, the topology is a classic case for using a default route—the access router has one possible physical route to use to reach the rest of the Internet, namely the route connecting the access router to the ISP's router.

Instead of requiring a static route configuration, the access router can add a default route based on the default gateway learned by the DHCP client function. For example, in Figure 16-7, R1 learned a default gateway IP address of 64.100.1.2, which is router ISP1's interface connected to the DSL or cable service. The access router creates a default route with that default gateway IP address as the next-hop router. Figure 16-8 shows this default route, along with a few other important routes, as solid lines with arrows.

Figure 16-8 *Routing in an Internet Access Router*

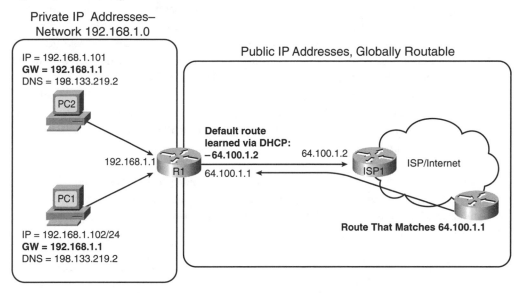

The default gateway settings on the local PCs, along with the default route on the access router (R1), allow the PCs to send packets that reach the Internet. At that point, the Internet routers should be able to forward the packets anywhere in the Internet. However, the routes pointing in the reverse direction, from the Internet back to the small office, seem incomplete at this point. Because R1's Internet-facing IP address (64.100.1.1 in Figure 16-8) is from the public registered IP address range, all the routers in the Internet should have a matching route, enabling them to forward packets to that address. However, Internet routers should never have any routes for private IP addresses, like those in private networks, such as private network 192.168.1.0/24 as used in Figure 16-8.

The solution to this problem is not related to routing; instead, the solution is to make the local hosts on the LAN look as if they are using R1's publicly registered IP address by using NAT and PAT. Hosts in the Internet will send the packets to the access router's public IP address (64.100.1.1 in Figure 16-8), and the access router will translate the address to match the correct IP address on the hosts on the local LAN.

NAT and PAT

Before getting to the details of how NAT and Port Address Translation (PAT) solve this last part of the puzzle, a few other related perspectives can help you to understand NAT and PAT—one related to IP address conservation, and one related to how TCP and UDP use ports.

First, the Internet Corporation for Assigned Names and Numbers (ICANN) manages the process of assigning public IP addresses in the global IPv4 address space—and we are slowly running out of addresses. So, when an ISP adds a new DSL or cable customer, the ISP wants to assign as few public IP addresses to that customer as possible. Additionally, the ISP prefers to assign the address dynamically, so if a customer decides to move to another ISP, the ISP can quickly reclaim and reuse the IP address for another customer. So, for a typical DSL or cable connection to the Internet, the ISP assigns a single publicly routable IP address, using DHCP, as was shown earlier in Figure 16-7. In particular, the ISP does not want to assign multiple public IP addresses to each PC (like PC1 and PC2 in Figure 16-7), again to conserve the public IPv4 address space.

The second thing to think about is that, from a server's perspective, there is no important difference between some number of TCP connections from different hosts, versus the same number of TCP connections from the same host. Figure 16-9 details an example that helps make the logic behind PAT more obvious.

Figure 16-9 *Three TCP Connections: From Three Different Hosts, and from One Host*

Three Connections from Three PCs

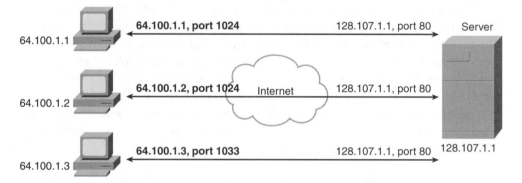

Three Connections from One PC

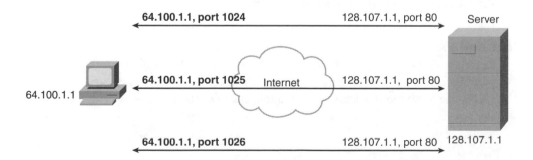

The top part of the figure shows a network with three different hosts connecting to a web server using TCP. The bottom half of the figure shows the same network later in the day, with three TCP connections from one client. All six connections connect to the server IP address (128.107.1.1) and port (80, the well-known port for web services). In each case, the server is able to differentiate between the various connections because each has a unique combination of IP address and port number.

Keeping the address conservation and port number concepts in mind, next examine how PAT allows the local hosts to use private IP addresses while the access router uses a single public IP address. PAT takes advantage of the fact that a server really does not care if it has one connection each to three different hosts or three connections to a single host IP address. So, to support lots of local hosts at the small office, using a single publicly routable IP address on the router, PAT translates the local hosts' private IP addresses to the one registered public IP address. To tell which packets need to be sent back to which local host, the router keeps track of both the IP address and TCP or UDP port number. Figure 16-10 shows an example, using the same IP addresses and routers shown previously in Figure 16-7.

Figure 16-10 *PAT Function on an Internet Access Router*

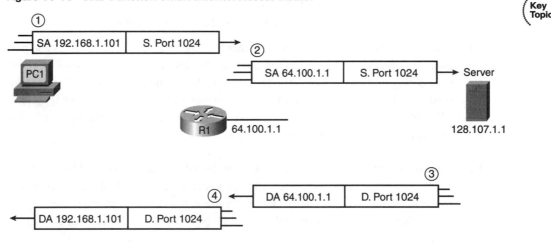

Key
Topic

NAT Translation Table

Inside Local	Inside Global
192.168.1.101:1024	64.100.1.1: 1024
192.168.1.102:1024	64.100.1.1: 1025

The figure shows a packet sent by PC1 to the server in the Internet on the right. The top part of the figure (steps 1 and 2) shows the packet's source IP address and source port both before and after R1 performs PAT. The lower part of the figure (steps 3 and 4) shows the return packet from the server, which shows the destination IP address and destination port, again both before and after R1 performs the PAT function. (The server, when replying to a packet with a particular source IP address and port, uses those same values in the response packet.) The numbered steps in the figure follow this logic:

1. PC1 sends a packet to server 128.107.1.1 and, per PC1's default gateway setting, sends the packet to access router R1.

2. R1 performs PAT, based on the details in the router's NAT translation table, changing the local host's IP from the private IP address used on the local LAN to the one globally routable public IP address available to R1, namely 64.100.1.1 in this case. R1 forwards the packet based on its default route.

3. When the server replies to the packet sent from PC1, the server sends the packet to destination address 64.100.1.1, destination port 1024, because those were the values in the source fields of the packet at step 2. The Internet routers know how to forward this packet back to R1, because the destination is a globally routable public IP address.

4. R1 changes the destination IP address and port per the NAT table, switching from destination address/port 64.100.1.1/1024 to 192.168.1.101/1024. R1 knows a route to reach 192.168.1.101, because this address is in a subnet connected to R1.

More generally, the PAT feature causes the router to translate the source IP address and port for packets leaving the local LAN, and to translate the destination IP address and port on packets returning to the local LAN. The end result is that, as far as hosts in the Internet are concerned, all the packets coming from this one customer are from one host (64.100.1.1 in Figure 16-10), for which all the routers in the Internet should have a matching route. This allows the ISP to conserve public IPv4 addresses.

The terms *inside local* and *inside global*, as listed in the NAT translation table in Figure 16-10, have some very specific and important meanings in the world of NAT. When speaking of NAT, the terms have the perspective of the enterprise network engineer, rather than someone working at the ISP. Keeping that in mind, NAT uses the following terms (and many others):

Key Topic

Inside host: Refers to a host in the enterprise network, like PC1 and PC2 in the last few figures.

Inside local: Refers to an IP address in an IP header, with that address representing a local host as the packet passes over the local enterprise network (not the Internet). In this case, 192.168.1.101 and .102 are inside local IP addresses, and the packets at steps 1 and 4 in Figure 16-10 show inside local IP addresses.

Inside global: Refers to an IP address in an IP header, with that address representing a local host as the packet passes over the global Internet (not the enterprise). In this case, 64.100.1.1 is the one inside global IP address, and the packets at steps 2 and 3 in Figure 16-10 show the inside global IP address.

Inside interface: The router interface connected to the same LAN as the inside hosts.

Outside interface: The router interface connected to the Internet.

Now that you have seen an example of how PAT works, a more exact definition of the terms NAT and PAT can be described. So, when using the terms in a very specific, formal manner, NAT refers to the translation of network layer (IP) addresses, with no translation of ports, whereas PAT refers to the translation of IP addresses as well as transport layer (TCP and UDP) port numbers. However, with a broader definition of the term NAT, PAT is simply one of several ways to configure and use NAT. In real life, in fact, most people refer to this broader definition of NAT. So, an engineer might say "we use NAT with our Internet connection to conserve our public IP addresses"; technically the function is PAT, but most everyone simply calls it NAT.

In closing, some of you who have installed a cable router or DSL router in your home may have found that it was easy to get that router to work—much easier than trying to understand the details explained in this chapter. If you buy a consumer-grade cable router or DSL router, it comes preconfigured to use a DHCP client, DHCP server, and PAT as described in this section. (In fact, your product may have one RJ-45 port labeled "Internet" or "Uplink"—that is the port that by default acts as a DHCP client, and it would be the Internet-facing interface in the figures presented toward the end of this chapter.) So, these functions happen, but they happen with no effort required on your part. However, to do the same functions with an enterprise-class Cisco router, the router needs to be configured, because the Cisco enterprise routers ship from the factory with no initial configuration. Chapter 17 will show how to configure the features described in this section on Cisco routers.

Exam Preparation Tasks

Review All the Key Topics

Key Topic

Review the most important topics from inside the chapter, noted with the key topics icon in the outer margin of the page. Table 16-5 lists a reference of these key topics and the page numbers on which each is found.

Table 16-5 *Key Topics for Chapter 16*

Key Topic Element	Description	Page Number
List	Comparison points between DSL and modems	519
Figure 16-3	Typical topology and devices used for DSL	520
List	Factors that affect the speed of a DSL line	522
Figure 16-4	Typical topology and devices used for cable	524
Table 16-3	Comparison points for Internet access technologies	525
Table 16-4	Comparison of circuit switching and packet switching	527
List	Factors that impact the IP addresses used by Internet access routers	529
Figure 16-7	Depicts DHCP client and server functions in an Internet access router	530
Figure 16-10	Shows how PAT translates IP addresses in Internet access routers	533
List	Definitions of several key NAT terms	534

Complete the Tables and Lists from Memory

Print a copy of Appendix H, "Memory Tables" (found on the CD-ROM), or at least the section for this chapter, and complete the tables and lists from memory. Appendix I, "Memory Tables Answer Key," also on the CD-ROM, includes completed tables and lists to check your work.

Definitions of Key Terms

Define the following key terms from this chapter and check your answers in the glossary.

ADSL, asymmetric, ATM, DSL, inside global, inside local, modem, NAT, PAT, PSTN, symmetric, telco

This chapter covers the following subjects:

Configuring Point-to-Point WANs: This section examines how to configure leased lines between two routers using HDLC and PPP.

Configuring and Troubleshooting Internet Access Routers: This section shows how to configure DHCP client, DHCP server, and PAT functions on an Internet access router using SDM.

CHAPTER 17

WAN Configuration

This chapter examines the configuration details for how to configure a few of the types of wide-area networks (WANs) covered in Chapter 4, "Fundamentals of WANs," and Chapter 16, "WAN Concepts." The first section of this chapter examines leased-line configuration using both High-Level Data Link Control (HDLC) and Point-to-Point Protocol (PPP). The second section of the chapter shows how to configure the Layer 3 features required for an Internet access router to connect to the Internet, specifically Dynamic Host Configuration Protocol (DHCP) and Network Address Translation/Port Address Translation (NAT/PAT). However, the configuration in the second half of the chapter does not use the command-line interface (CLI), but instead focuses on using the web-based router Security Device Manager (SDM) interface.

For those of you preparing specifically for the CCNA 640-802 exam by using the reading plan in the introduction to this book, note that you should move on to Part IV of the *CCNA ICND2 Official Exam Certification Guide* after completing this chapter.

"Do I Know This Already?" Quiz

The "Do I Know This Already?" quiz allows you to assess if you should read the entire chapter. If you miss no more than one of these seven self-assessment questions, you might want to move ahead to the "Exam Preparation Tasks" section. Table 17-1 lists the major headings in this chapter and the "Do I Know This Already?" quiz questions covering the material in those headings so you can assess your knowledge of these specific areas. The answers to the "Do I Know This Already?" quiz appear in Appendix A.

Table 17-1 *"Do I Know This Already?" Foundation Topics Section-to-Question Mapping*

Foundation Topics Section	Questions
Configuring and Troubleshooting Point-to-Point WANs	1–3
Configuring and Troubleshooting Internet Access Routers	4–7

1. Routers R1 and R2 connect using a leased line, with both routers using their respective Serial 0/0 interfaces. The routers can currently route packets over the link, which uses HDLC. Which of the following commands would be required to migrate the configuration to use PPP?

    a. **encapsulation ppp**

    b. **no encapsulation hdlc**

    c. **clock rate 128000**

    d. **bandwidth 128000**

2. Routers R1 and R2 have just been installed in a new lab. The routers will connect using a back-to-back serial link, using interface serial 0/0 on each router. Which of the following is true about how to install and configure this connection?

    a. If the DCE cable is installed in R1, the **clock rate** command must be configured on R2's serial interface.

    b. If the DTE cable is installed in R1, the **clock rate** command must be configured on R2's serial interface.

    c. If the **clock rate 128000** command is configured on R1, the **bandwidth 128** command must be configured on R2.

    d. None of the answers are correct.

3. Two brand new Cisco routers have been ordered and installed in two different sites, 100 miles apart. A 768-kbps leased line has been installed between the two routers. Which of the following commands is required on at least one of the routers in order to forward packets over the leased line, using PPP as the data link protocol?

    a. **no encapsulation hdlc**

    b. **encapsulation ppp**

    c. **clock rate 768000**

    d. **bandwidth 768**

    e. **description this is the link**

4. When configuring a DHCP server on an Internet access router using SDM, which of the following settings is typically configured on the Internet access router?

    a. The MAC addresses of the PCs on the local LAN

    b. The IP address of the ISP's router on the common cable or DSL link

   c. The range of IP addresses to be leased to hosts on the local LAN

   d. The DNS server IP address(es) learned via DHCP from the ISP

5. When configuring an access router with SDM, to use DHCP client services to learn an IP address from an ISP, and configure PAT at the same time, which of the following is true?

   a. The SDM configuration wizard requires PAT to be configured if the DHCP client function has been chosen to be configured.

   b. The SDM configuration wizard considers any interfaces that already have IP addresses configured as candidates to become inside interfaces for PAT.

   c. The SDM configuration wizard assumes the interface on which DHCP client services have been enabled should be an inside interface.

   d. None of the answers are correct.

6. Which of the following is true about the configuration process using SDM?

   a. SDM uses an SSH connection via the console or an IP network to configure a router.

   b. SDM uses a web interface from the IP network or from the console.

   c. SDM loads configuration commands into a router at the end of each wizard (after the user clicks the Finish button), saving the configuration in the running-config and startup-config files.

   d. None of these answers are correct.

7. Which of the following are common problems when configuring a new Internet access router's Layer 3 features?

   a. Omitting commonly used but optional information from the DHCP server features—for example, the IP address(es) of the DNS server(s)

   b. Setting the wrong interfaces as the NAT inside and outside interfaces

   c. Forgetting to configure the same routing protocol that the ISP uses

   d. Forgetting to enable CDP on the Internet-facing interface

Foundation Topics

Configuring Point-to-Point WANs

This brief section explains how to configure leased lines between two routers, using both HDLC and PPP. The required configuration is painfully simply—for HDLC, do nothing, and for PPP, add one interface subcommand on each router's serial interface (**encapsulation ppp**). However, several optional configuration steps can be useful, so this section explains those optional steps and their impact on the links.

> **NOTE**   This chapter assumes all serial links use an external channel service unit/data service unit (CSU/DSU). The configuration details of the external CSU/DSU, or an internal CSU/DSU, are beyond the scope of the book.

Configuring HDLC

Considering the lowest three layers of the OSI reference model on router Ethernet interfaces for a moment, there are no required configuration commands related to Layers 1 and 2 for the interface to be up and working, forwarding IP traffic. The Layer 1 details occur by default once the cabling has been installed correctly. Router IOS defaults to use Ethernet as the data link protocol on all types of Ethernet interfaces, so no Layer 2 commands are required. To make the interface operational for forwarding IP packets, the router needs one command to configure an IP address on the interface, and possibly a **no shutdown** command if the interface is in an "administratively down" state.

Similarly, serial interfaces on Cisco routers that use HDLC typically need no specific Layer 1 or 2 configuration commands. The cabling needs to be completed as described in Chapters 4 and 16, but there are no required configuration commands related to Layer 1. IOS defaults to use HDLC as the data link protocol, so there are no required commands that relate to Layer 2. As on Ethernet interfaces, the only required command to get IP working on the interface is the **ip address** command and possibly the **no shutdown** command.

However, many optional commands exist for serial links. The following list outlines some configuration steps, listing the conditions for which some commands are needed, plus commands that are purely optional:

Step 1   Configure the interface IP address using the **ip address** interface subcommand.

Step 2   The following tasks are required only when the specifically listed conditions are true:

  a.   If an **encapsulation** *protocol* interface subcommand that lists a protocol besides HDLC already exists on the interface, use the **encapsulation hdlc** interface subcommand to enable HDLC.

b. If the interface line status is administratively down, enable the interface using the **no shutdown** interface subcommand.

c. If the serial link is a back-to-back serial link in a lab (or a simulator), configure the clocking rate using the **clock rate** *speed* interface subcommand, but only on the one router with the DCE cable (per the **show controllers serial** *number* command).

Step 3 The following steps are always optional, and have no impact on whether the link works and passes IP traffic:

a. Configure the link's speed using the **bandwidth** *speed-in-kbps* interface subcommand.

b. For documentation purposes, configure a description of the purpose of the interface using the **description** *text* interface subcommand.

In practice, when you configure a Cisco router with no pre-existing interface configuration, and install a normal production serial link with CSU/DSUs, the **ip address** command is likely the one configuration command you would need. Figure 17-1 shows a sample internetwork, and Example 17-1 shows the configuration. In this case, the serial link was created with a back-to-back serial link in a lab, requiring Steps 1 (**ip address**) and 2c (**clock rate**) from the preceding list, plus optional Step 3b (**description**).

Figure 17-1 *Typical Serial Link Between Two Routers*

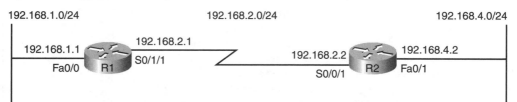

192.168.1.0/24   192.168.2.0/24   192.168.4.0/24

192.168.1.1   192.168.2.1
                                       192.168.2.2   192.168.4.2
Fa0/0   R1   S0/1/1
                          S0/0/1   R2   Fa0/1

Example 17-1 *HDLC Configuration*

```
R1#show running-config
! Note - only the related lines are shown
interface FastEthernet0/0
 ip address 192.168.1.1 255.255.255.0
!
interface Serial0/1/1
 ip address 192.168.2.1 255.255.255.0
 description link to R2
 clockrate 1536000
```

continues

Example 17-1 *HDLC Configuration (Continued)*

```
!
router rip
 version 2
 network 192.168.1.0
 network 192.168.2.0
!
R1#show controllers serial 0/1/1
Interface Serial0/1/1
Hardware is GT96K
DCE V.35, clock rate 1536000
! lines omitted for brevity
R1#show interfaces s0/1/1
Serial0/1/1 is up, line protocol is up
  Hardware is GT96K Serial
  Description: link to R2
  Internet address is 192.168.2.1/24
  MTU 1500 bytes, BW 1544 Kbit, DLY 20000 usec,
     reliability 255/255, txload 1/255, rxload 1/255
  Encapsulation HDLC, loopback not set
  Keepalive set (10 sec)
  Last input 00:00:06, output 00:00:03, output hang never
  Last clearing of "show interface" counters never
  Input queue: 0/75/0/0 (size/max/drops/flushes); Total output drops: 0
  Queueing strategy: weighted fair
  Output queue: 0/1000/64/0 (size/max total/threshold/drops)
     Conversations  0/1/256 (active/max active/max total)
     Reserved Conversations 0/0 (allocated/max allocated)
     Available Bandwidth 1158 kilobits/sec
  5 minute input rate 0 bits/sec, 0 packets/sec
  5 minute output rate 0 bits/sec, 0 packets/sec
     70 packets input, 4446 bytes, 0 no buffer
     Received 50 broadcasts, 0 runts, 0 giants, 0 throttles
     0 input errors, 0 CRC, 0 frame, 0 overrun, 0 ignored, 0 abort
     73 packets output, 5280 bytes, 0 underruns
     0 output errors, 0 collisions, 5 interface resets
     0 output buffer failures, 0 output buffers swapped out
     0 carrier transitions
     DCD=up  DSR=up  DTR=up  RTS=up  CTS=up
R1#show ip interface brief
Interface              IP-Address       OK? Method Status                 Protocol
FastEthernet0/0        192.168.1.1      YES manual up                     up
FastEthernet0/1        unassigned       YES NVRAM  administratively down  down
Serial0/0/0            unassigned       YES NVRAM  administratively down  down
Serial0/0/1            unassigned       YES manual administratively down  down
Serial0/1/0            unassigned       YES manual administratively down  down
Serial0/1/1            192.168.2.1      YES manual up                     up
```

Example 17-1 *HDLC Configuration (Continued)*

```
R1#show interfaces description
Interface                 Status         Protocol Description
Fa0/0                     up             up
Fa0/1                     admin down     down
Se0/0/0                   admin down     down
Se0/0/1                   admin down     down
Se0/1/0                   admin down     down
Se0/1/1                   up             up         link to R2
```

The configuration on R1 is relatively simple. The matching configuration on R2's S0/0/1 interface simply needs an **ip address** command, plus the default settings of **encapsulation hdlc** and **no shutdown**. The **clock rate** command would not be needed on R2, as R1 has the DCE cable, so R2 must be connected to a DTE cable.

The rest of the example lists the output of a few **show** commands. First, the output from the **show controllers** command for S0/1/1 confirms that R1 indeed has a DCE cable installed. The **show interfaces S0/1/1** command lists the various configuration settings near the top, including the default encapsulation value (HDLC) and default bandwidth setting on a serial interface (1544, meaning 1544 kbps or 1.544 Mbps). At the end of the example, the **show ip interface brief** and **show interfaces description** commands display a short status of the interfaces, with both listing the line status and protocol status codes.

Configuring PPP

Configuring the basics of PPP is just as simple as for HDLC, except that whereas HDLC is the default serial data-link protocol and requires no additional configuration, you must configure the **encapsulation ppp** command for PPP. Other than that, the list of possible and optional configuration steps is exactly the same as for HDLC. So, to migrate from a working HDLC link to a working PPP link, the only command needed is an **encapsulation ppp** command on each of the two routers' serial interfaces. Example 17-2 shows the serial interface configuration on both R1 and R2 from Figure 17-1, this time using PPP.

Example 17-2 *PPP Configuration*

```
R1#show running-config interface s0/1/1
Building configuration...

Current configuration : 129 bytes
!
interface Serial0/1/1
 description link to R2
 ip address 192.168.2.1 255.255.255.0
 encapsulation ppp
```

continues

Example 17-2 *PPP Configuration (Continued)*

```
 clockrate 1536000
end
```

```
! R2's configuration next
R2#show run interface s0/0/1
Building configuration...

Current configuration : 86 bytes
!
interface Serial0/0/1
 ip address 192.168.2.2 255.255.255.0
 encapsulation ppp
end
```

The example lists a new variation on the **show running-config** command as well as the PPP-related configuration. The **show running-config interface S0/1/1** command on R1 lists the interface configuration for interface S0/1/1, and none of the rest of the running-config. Note that on both routers, the **encapsulation ppp** command has been added; it is important that both routers use the same data link protocol, or the link will not work.

Configuring and Troubleshooting Internet Access Routers

As covered in Chapter 16, Internet access routers often connect to the Internet using one LAN interface, and to the local LAN using another interface. Routers that are built specifically for consumers as Internet access routers ship from the factory with DHCP client services enabled on the Internet-facing interface, DHCP server functions enabled on the local interface, and PAT functions enabled. Enterprise routers, which have many features and may not necessarily be used as Internet access routers, ship from the factory without these features enabled by default. This section shows how to configure these functions on a Cisco enterprise-class router.

Cisco routers support another configuration method besides using the CLI. In keeping with the exam topics published by Cisco for the ICND1 exam, this chapter shows how to configure the rest of the features in this chapter using this alternative tool, called *Cisco Router and Security Device Manager (SDM)*. Instead of using Telnet or SSH, the user connects to the router using a web browser. (To support the web browser, the router must first be configured from the CLI with at least one IP address, typically on the local LAN, so that the engineer's computer can connect to the router.) From there, SDM allows the engineer to configure a wide variety of router features, including the DHCP client, DHCP server, and PAT.

> **NOTE** Cisco switches also allow web access for configuration, using a tool called *Cisco Device Manager (CDM)*. The general concept of CDM matches the concepts of SDM.

Note that the features configured through SDM in the remainder of this chapter can also be done with the CLI.

Internet Access Router: Configuration Steps

You can configure the DHCP client, DHCP server, and PAT functions with SDM using the following five major steps:

Step 1 **Establish IP connectivity.** Plan and configure (from the CLI) IP addresses on the local LAN so that a PC on the LAN can ping the router's LAN interface.

Step 2 **Install and access SDM.** Install SDM on the router and access the router SDM interface using a PC that can ping the router's IP address (as implemented at Step 1).

Step 3 **Configure DHCP and PAT.** Use SDM to configure both DHCP client services and the PAT service on the router.

Step 4 **Plan for DHCP services.** Plan the IP addresses to be assigned by the router to the hosts on the local LAN, along with the DNS IP addresses, domain name, and default gateway settings that the router will advertise.

Step 5 **Configure the DHCP server.** Use SDM to configure the DHCP server features on the router.

The sections that follow examine each step in order in greater detail. The configuration will use the same internetwork topology that was used in the Chapter 16 discussion of Internet access routers, repeated here as Figure 17-2.

Step 1: Establish IP Connectivity

The Internet access router needs to use a private IP network on the local LAN, as mentioned in Chapter 16. For this step, you should choose the following details:

Step a Choose any private IP network number.

Step b Choose a mask that allows for enough hosts (typically the default mask is fine).

Step c Choose a router IP address from that network.

Figure 17-2   *Internet Access Router: Sample Network*

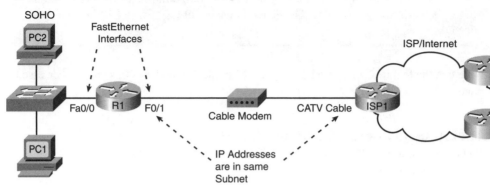

It does not really matter which private network you use, as long as it is a private network. Many consumer access routers use Class C network 192.168.1.0, as will be used in this chapter, and the default mask. If you work at a small company with a few sites, all connecting to the Internet, you can use the same private network at each site, because NAT/ PAT will translate the addresses anyway.

Step 2: Install and Access SDM

To be able to install the SDM software on the router (if it is not already installed on the router), and to allow the engineer's host to access the router using a web browser, the engineer needs to use a host with IP connectivity to reach the router. Typically, the engineer would use a host on the local LAN, configure the router's local LAN interface with the IP address planned at Step 1, and configure the host with another IP address in that same network. Note that SDM does not use Telnet or SSH, and the PC must be connected via an IP network—the console can only be used to access the CLI.

The network engineer must configure several additional commands on the router before a user can access and use it, the details of which are beyond the scope of this book. If you are curious, you can look for more details by searching www.cisco.com for "SDM installation." This configuration step was listed just in case you try using SDM with your own lab gear, to make you aware that there is more work to do. By the end of the process, a web browser should be able to connect to the router and see the SDM Home page for that router, like the example shown in Figure 17-3.

Figure 17-3 *SDM Home Page*

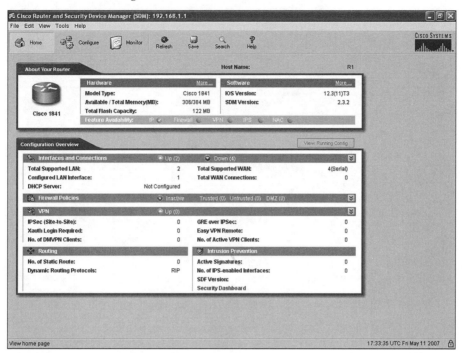

Step 3: Configure DHCP and PAT

The SDM user interface has a wide variety of configuration wizards that guide you through a series of web pages, asking for input. At the end of the process, SDM loads the corresponding configuration commands into the router.

One such wizard allows you to configure the DHCP client feature on the Internet-facing interface and, optionally, configure the PAT feature. This section shows sample windows for the configuration of router R1 in Figure 17-2.

From the SDM Home page shown in Figure 17-3:

1.   Click **Configure** near the top of the window.

2.   Click **Interfaces and Connections** at the top of the Tasks pane on the left side of the window.

Figure 17-4 shows the resulting Interfaces and Connections window, with the Create Connection tab displayed. (Note that the heavy arrowed lines are overlaid on the image of the page to point out the items referenced in the text.)

Figure 17-4 *SDM Configure Interfaces and Connections Window*

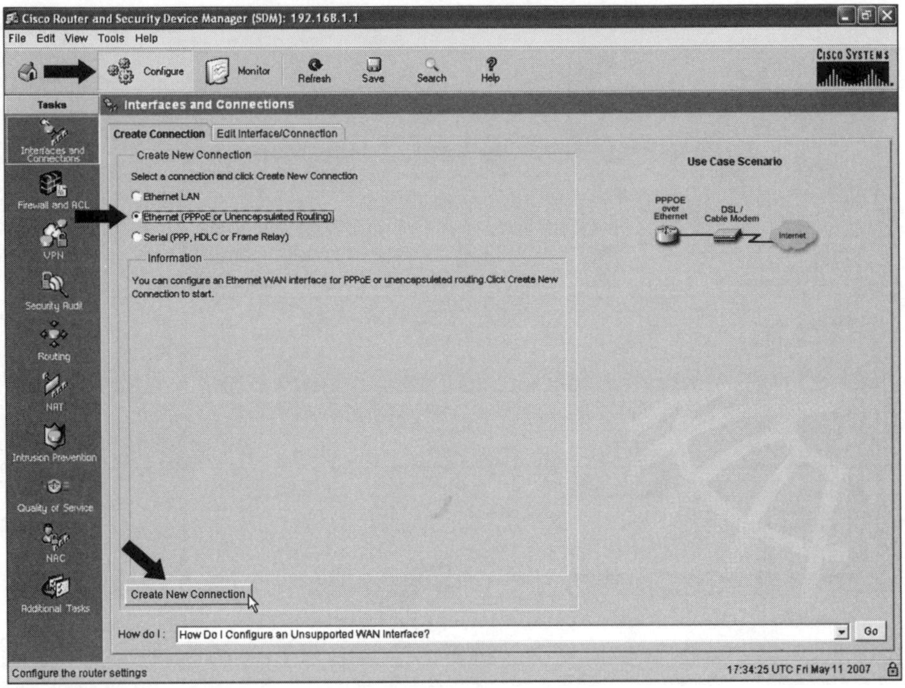

The network topology on the right side of this tab should look familiar, as it basically matches Figure 17-2, with a router connected to a cable or DSL modem. On the Create Connection tab, do the following:

1. Choose the **Ethernet (PPPoE or Unencapsulated Routing)** radio button.

2. Click the **Create New Connection** button near the bottom of the tab.

These actions open the SDM Ethernet Wizard, shown in Figure 17-5. The page in Figure 17-5 has no options to choose, so just click **Next** to keep going.

The next page of the wizard, shown in Figure 17-6, has only one option, a check box that, if checked, enables the protocol PPP over Ethernet (PPPoE). If the ISP asks that you use PPPoE, then check this box. Ordinarily, you simply leave this box unchecked, which implies unencapsulated routing. (Unencapsulated routing means that the router forwards Ethernet frames onto the interface, with an IP packet inside the Ethernet frame, as was covered in several places in Part III of this book.)

Figure 17-5 *SDM Ethernet Wizard Welcome Page*

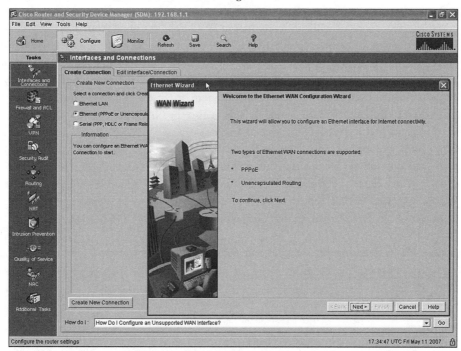

Figure 17-6 *SDM Ethernet Wizard: Choice to Use Encapsulation with PPPoE*

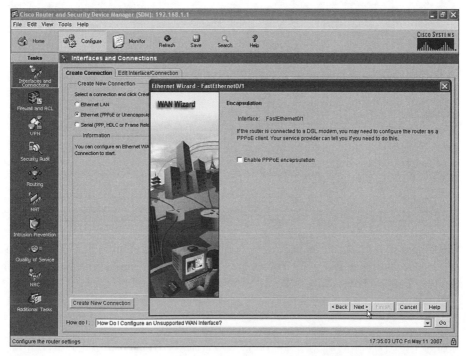

As you can see near the top of Figure 17-6, the wizard picked a Fast Ethernet interface, Fa0/1 in this case, as the interface to configure. The router used in this example has two LAN interfaces, one of which already has an IP address assigned from Step 1 (Fa0/0). Because this wizard will be configuring DHCP client services on this router, the wizard picked the only LAN interface that did not already have an IP address, namely Fa0/1, as the interface on which it will enable the DHCP client function. This choice is particularly important when troubleshooting a new installation, because this must be the LAN interface connected to the cable or DSL modem. This is also the NAT/PAT outside interface.

Click **Next**. Figure 17-7 shows the next page of the wizard, the IP Address page. This page gives you the option of statically configuring this interface's IP address. However, as explained in Chapter 16, the goal is to use a dynamically assigned IP address from the ISP—an address that happens to come from the globally routable IP address space. So, you want to use the default radio button option of **Dynamic (DHCP Client)**.

Figure 17-7   *SDM Ethernet Wizard: Static or DHCP Address Assignment*

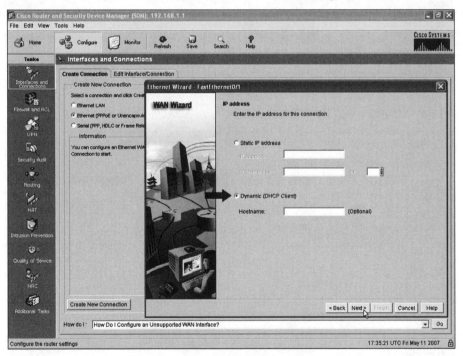

Click **Next** to move to the Advanced Options page, shown in Figure 17-8. This page asks if you want to enable PAT, which of course is also desired on an Internet access router. Simply click the **Port Address Translation** check box. If you do not want to enable PAT for some reason, do not check this box.

Figure 17-8 *SDM Ethernet Wizard: Enable PAT and Choose Inside Interface*

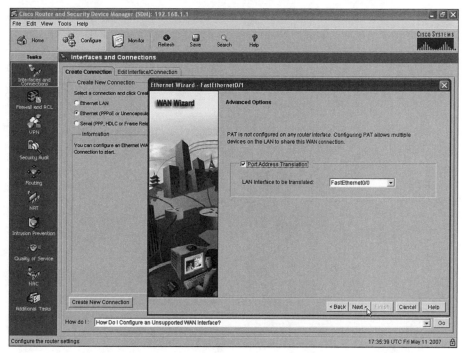

It is particularly important to note the LAN Interface to Be Translated drop-down box near the middle of the page. In NAT terminology, this box lists the inside interface, which means that the listed interface is connected to the local LAN. This example shows FastEthernet0/0 as the inside interface, as intended. Almost as important in this case is that the interface being configured for the DHCP client by this wizard, in this case FastEthernet0/1, is assumed to be the outside interface by the NAT feature, again exactly as intended.

Click **Next** to move to the Summary page shown in Figure 17-9, which summarizes the choices you made when using this wizard. The text on the screen is particularly useful, as it reminds you that:

■   The interface being configured is FastEthernet0/1.

■   FastEthernet0/1 will use DHCP client services to find its IP address.

■   PPPoE encapsulation is disabled, which means that unencapsulated routing is used.

■   PAT is enabled, with FastEthernet0/0 as the inside interface, and FastEthernet0/1 as the outside interface.

Figure 17-9 *SDM Ethernet Wizard: Request that the Configuration Changes Be Made*

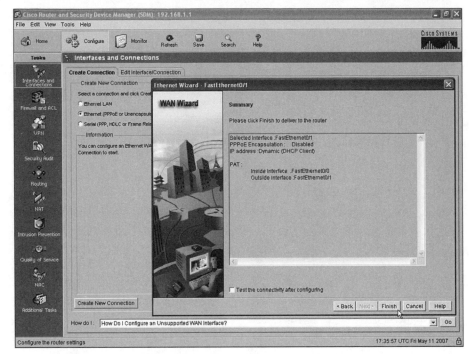

Click **Finish**. SDM builds the configuration and loads it into the router's running-config file. If you want to save the configuration, click the save button near the top of the SDM home page to make the router do a **copy running-config startup-config** command to save the configuration. However, without this extra action, the configuration will only be added to the running-config file.

At this point, the DHCP client and PAT functions have been configured. The remaining tasks are to plan the details of what to configure for the DHCP server function on the router for the local LAN, and to use SDM to configure that feature.

Step 4: Plan for DHCP Services

Before configuring the DHCP server function on the router, to support the local LAN, you need to plan a few of the values to be configured in the server. In particular, you need to choose the subset of the private IP network on the local LAN that you intend to allow to be assigned using DHCP. For the example in this chapter, part of the work at Step 1 was to choose a private IP network for the local LAN, in this case 192.168.1.0, and default mask 255.255.255.0. It makes sense to allow only a subset of the IP addresses in this network to be assigned with DHCP, leaving some IP addresses for static assignment. For example, router R1's Fa0/0 interface, connected to the local LAN, has already been configured with IP address 192.168.1.1, so that address should not be included in the range of addresses allowed to be assigned by the DHCP server.

The following list outlines the key items that you need to gather before you configure the router as a DHCP server. The first two items in the list relate to planning on the local LAN, and the last two items are just values learned from the ISP that need to be passed on to the hosts on the local LAN.

1. Recall the private IP network and mask used on the local LAN and then choose a subset of that network that can be assigned to hosts using DHCP.

2. Make a note of the router's IP address in that network; this address will be the local hosts' default gateway.

3. Find the DNS server IP addresses learned by the router using DHCP client services, using the **show dhcp server** EXEC command; the routers will then be able to inform the DHCP clients on the local LAN about the DNS server IP address(es).

4. Find the domain name, again with the **show dhcp server** EXEC command.

> **NOTE** Cisco uses the term *DHCP pool* for the IP addresses that can be assigned using DHCP.

For the example in this chapter, the first two items, IP network 192.168.1.0 with mask /24, have already been chosen back in Step 1 of the overall configuration process. The range 192.168.1.101–192.168.1.254 has been reserved for DHCP clients, leaving range 192.168.1.1–192.168.1.100 for static IP addresses. The router's 192.168.1.1 IP address, which was configured back at Step 1 so that the engineer could connect to the router using SDM, will be assigned as the local hosts' default gateway.

For the last two items in the planning list, the DNS server IP addresses and the domain name, Example 17-3 shows how to find those values using the **show dhcp server** command. This command lists information on a router acting as a DHCP client, information learned from each DHCP server from which the router has learned an IP address. The pieces of information needed for the DHCP server SDM configuration are highlighted in the example.

Example 17-3 *Finding the DNS Server IP Addresses and Domain Name*

```
R1#show dhcp server
  DHCP server: ANY (255.255.255.255)
    Leases:    8
    Offers:    8       Requests: 8     Acks: 8      Naks: 0
    Declines: 0        Releases: 21     Bad:  0
    DNS0:   198.133.219.2,   DNS1:   0.0.0.0
    Subnet: 255.255.255.252    DNS Domain: example.com
```

Step 5: Configure the DHCP Server

To configure the DHCP server with SDM, click **Configure** near the top of the SDM window and then click **Additional Tasks** at the bottom of the Tasks pane to open the Additional Tasks window, shown in Figure 17-10.

Figure 17-10 *SDM Additional Tasks Configuration Window*

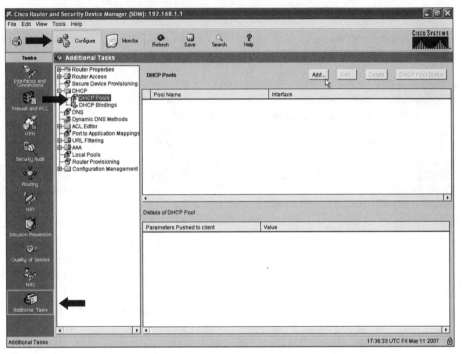

Select the **DHCP Pools** option on the left (as noted with one of the heavy arrows) and then click the **Add** button to open the Add DHCP Pool dialog box, shown in Figure 17-11. This dialog box has a place to type all the information gathered in the previous step, along with other settings. Figure 17-11 shows the screen used to configure router R1 in the ongoing example in this chapter.

The four planning items discussed in the previous overall configuration step (Step 4) are typed in obvious places in this dialog box:

- Range of addresses to be assigned with DHCP

- DNS server IP addresses

- Domain name

- Default router settings

Figure 17-11 *SDM DHCP Pool Dialog Box*

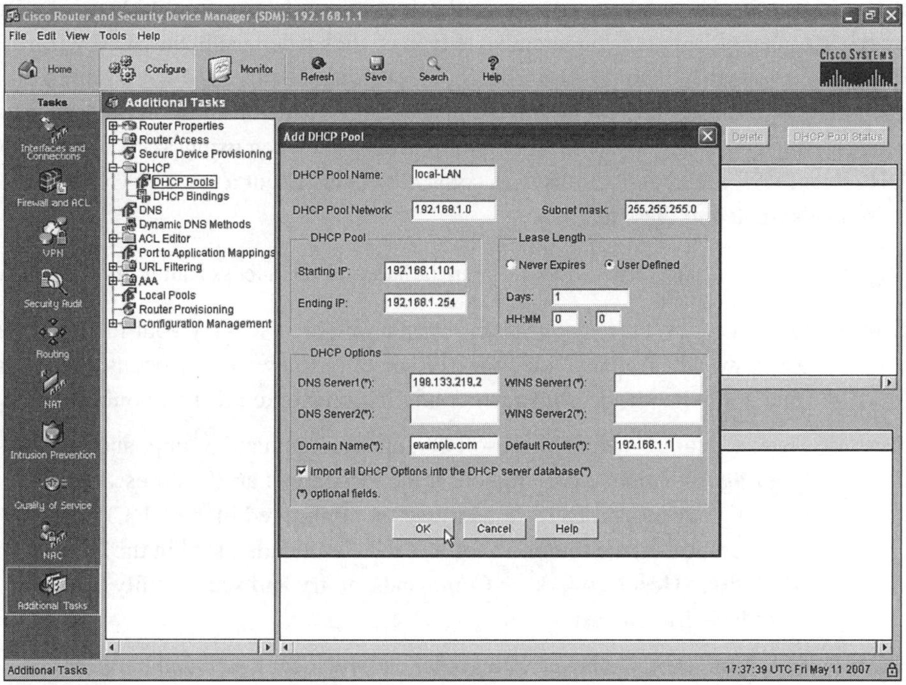

Additionally, the dialog box wants to know the subnet number and mask used on the subnet in which the addresses will be assigned. Also, you need to make up a name for this pool of DHCP addresses—the name can be most anything, but choose a meaningful name for that installation.

Whew! Configuring an Internet access router with SDM might seem to require a lot of steps and navigating through a lot of windows; however, it is certainly less detailed than configuring the same features from the CLI. The next section examines a few small verification and troubleshooting tasks.

Internet Access Router Verification

The choice to cover SDM configuration for DHCP and NAT/PAT, instead of the CLI configuration commands, has both some positives and negatives. The positives include the fact that the ICND1 exam, meant for entry-level network engineers, can cover a common set of features seen on Internet access routers, which are commonly used by smaller companies. Also, because the underlying configuration can be large (the configuration added by SDM for the examples in this chapter required about 20 configuration commands), the use of SDM avoided the time and effort to go over a lot of configuration options, keeping the topic a little more focused.

One negative of using SDM is that troubleshooting becomes a little more difficult because the configuration has not been covered in detail. As a result, true troubleshooting requires a review of the information you intended to type or click when using the SDM wizards, and double-checking that configuration from SDM. Showing all the SDM screens used to check each item would itself be a bit laborious. Instead of showing all those SDM screens, this section points out a few of the most common oversights when using SDM to configure DHCP and PAT, and then it closes with some comments about a few key CLI EXEC commands related to these features.

To perform some basic verification of the installation of the access router, try the following:

Key Topic

Step 1   Go to a PC on the local LAN and open a web browser. Try your favorite Internet-based website (for example, www.cisco.com). If a web page opens, that is a good indication that the access router configuration worked. If not, go to Step 2.

Step 2   From a local PC with a Microsoft OS, open a command prompt and use the **ipconfig /all** command to find out if the PC learned an IP address, mask, default gateway, and DNS IP addresses as configured in the DHCP server configuration on the router. If not, use the commands listed in the Chapter 15 section "Host Networking Commands" to try and successfully lease an IP address from a host.

Step 3   Check the cabling between the router and the local LAN, and between the router and the cable or DSL modem, noting which router interface connects to which part of the network. Then check the SDM configuration to ensure that the inside interface per the PAT configuration is the interface connected to the local LAN, and the outside interface per the PAT configuration is connected to the DSL/cable modem.

Step 4   Test the PAT function by generating traffic from a local PC to a host in the Internet. (More details on this item are given in the next few pages.)

The last item in the list provides a good opportunity to examine a few EXEC commands from the CLI. Example 17-4 lists the output of several CLI commands related to the access router configuration in this chapter, with some comments following the example.

Example 17-4   *Interesting EXEC Commands on the Access Router*

```
R1#show ip dhcp binding
Bindings from all pools not associated with VRF:
IP address       Client-ID/Hardware address/User name   Lease expiration      Type
192.168.1.101    0063.6973.636f.2d                       May 12 2007 08:24 PM  Automatic
192.168.1.111    0100.1517.1973.2c                       May 12 2007 08:26 PM  Automatic
R1#show ip nat translations
Pro Inside global      Inside local          Outside local        Outside global
tcp 64.100.1.1:36486   192.168.1.101:36486   192.168.7.1:80       192.168.7.1:80
udp 64.100.1.1:1027    192.168.1.111:1027    198.133.219.2:53     198.133.219.2:53
```

Example 17-4 *Interesting EXEC Commands on the Access Router (Continued)*

```
R1#clear ip nat translation *
R1#show ip nat translations

R1#
```

The **show ip dhcp binding** command output lists information about the IP addresses assigned to hosts on the local LAN by the DHCP server function in the access router. This command output can be compared to the results when trying to get hosts on the local LAN to acquire an IP address from the router's DHCP server function.

The **show ip nat translations** command output provides a few insights that confirm the normal operation of NAT and PAT. The output shown in Example 17-4 lists one heading line plus two actual NAT translation table entries. The two highlighted parts of the heading line refer to the inside global address and the inside local address. The inside local address should always be the IP address of a host on the local LAN, in this case 192.168.1.101. The router translates that IP address to the one globally routable public address known to the router—the 64.100.1.1 IP address learned via DHCP from the ISP.

The last command in the example, **clear ip nat translation ***, can be useful when the problem symptom is that some users' connections that need to use NAT work fine, and other users' connection that need to use NAT do not work at all. NAT table entries might need to be removed before a host can start sending data again, although this is probably a rare occurrence today. However, this command clears out all the entries in the table, and then the router creates new entries as the ensuing packets arrive. Note that this **clear** command could impact some applications.

Exam Preparation Tasks

Review All the Key Topics

Review the most important topics from inside the chapter, noted with the key topics icon in the outer margin of the page. Table 17-2 lists a reference of these key topics and the page numbers on which each is found.

Table 17-2 *Key Topics for Chapter 17*

Key Topic Element	Description	Page Number
List	Optional and required configuration steps for a serial link between two routers	542
List	IP addressing details planned and configured on the local LAN for an Internet access router	547
List	Planning items before configuring the DHCP server	555
List	Common items to check when troubleshooting access router installation	558

Complete the Tables and Lists from Memory

Print a copy of Appendix H, "Memory Tables" (found on the CD-ROM), or at least the section for this chapter, and complete the tables and lists from memory. Appendix I, "Memory Tables Answer Key," also on the CD-ROM, includes completed tables and lists to check your work.

Definitions of Key Terms

Define the following key terms from this chapter, and check your answers in the glossary.

Cisco Router and Security Device Manager

Command References

Although you should not necessarily memorize the information in the tables in this section, this section does include a reference for the configuration commands (Table 17-3) and EXEC commands (Table 17-4) covered in this chapter. Practically speaking, you should memorize the commands as a side effect of reading the chapter and doing all the activities in this exam preparation section. To check to see how well you have memorized the commands as a side effect of your other studies, cover the left side of the table with a piece of paper, read the descriptions in the right side, and see if you remember the command.

Table 17-3 *Chapter 17 Configuration Command Reference*

Command	Description
encapsulation {hdlc | ppp | frame-relay}	Serial interface subcommand that defines the data-link protocol to use on the link
clock rate *speed*	Serial interface subcommand that, when used on an interface with a DCE cable, sets the clock speed in bps
bandwidth *speed-kbps*	Interface subcommand that sets the router's opinion of the link speed, in kbps, but has no effect on the actual speed
description *text*	Interface subcommand that can set a text description of the interface

Table 17-4 *Chapter 17 EXEC Command Reference*

Command	Description
show ip nat translations	Lists the NAT/PAT translation table entries
show dhcp server	Lists information learned from a DHCP server, by a router acting as a DHCP client
clear ip nat translation *	Clears (removes) all dynamic entries in the NAT table
show interfaces	Lists several important settings on serial links, including encapsulation, bandwidth, keepalives, the two status codes, description, and IP address/ mask
show controllers serial *number*	Lists whether a cable is connected to the interface, and if so, whether it is a DTE or DCE cable
show interfaces [*type number*] **description**	Lists a single line per interface (or if the interface is included, just one line of output total) that lists the interface status and description
show ip interface brief	Lists a single line per interface, listing the IP address and interface status

Part V: Final Preparation

CHAPTER 18

Final Preparation

The first 17 chapters of this book cover the technologies, protocols, commands, and features you need to understand to pass the ICND2 exam. Although these chapters supply the detailed information, most people need more preparation than simply reading the first 17 chapters. This chapter details a set of tools and a study plan to help you complete your preparation for the exams.

If you're preparing for the CCNA exam by reading both this book and the *CCNA ICND2 Official Exam Certification Guide*, you know that both books have a final preparation chapter. However, you can refer to just this chapter to read about the suggested study plan, because this chapter refers to the tools in both this book and the ICND2 book. Just look for the text highlighted in gray, like this sentence, for suggestions that apply to CCNA (640-802) exam preparation, but not to ICND1 (640-816) exam preparation.

This short chapter has two main sections. The first section lists the exam preparation tools that can be useful at this point in your study process. The second section lists a suggested study plan now that you have completed all the earlier chapters.

> **NOTE** This chapter refers to many of the book's chapters and appendixes, as well as tools available on the CD. Some of the appendixes, beginning with Appendix D, are included only on the CD that comes with this book. To access those, just insert the CD and make the appropriate selection from the opening interface.

Tools for Final Preparation

This section lists some information about the available tools and how to access them.

Exam Engine and Questions on the CD

The CD includes an exam engine—software that displays and then grades a set of exam-realistic questions. These include simulation (sim) questions, drag-and-drop, and many scenario-based questions that require the same level of analysis as the questions on the ICND1 and CCNA exams. Using the exam engine, you can either practice with the questions in Study Mode or take a simulated (timed) ICND1 or CCNA exam.

The installation process has two major steps. The CD includes a recent copy of the exam engine software, supplied by Boson Software (http://www.boson.com). The practice exam—the database of ICND1 exam questions—is not on the CD. Instead, the practice exam resides on the http://www.boson.com web server, so the second major step is to activate and download the practice exam.

> **NOTE**   The cardboard CD case in the back of this book includes the CD and a piece of paper. The paper lists the activation key for the practice exam associated with this book. *Do not lose the activation key.*

Install the Software from the CD

The software installation process is pretty routine as compared with other software installation processes. The following steps outline the process:

Step 1   Insert the CD into your PC.

Step 2   The software that automatically runs is the Cisco Press software to access and use all CD-based features, including the exam engine, viewing a PDF file of this book, and viewing the CD-only appendixes. From the main menu, click the option to **Install the Exam Engine**.

Step 3   Respond to prompt windows, as you would with any typical software installation process.

The installation process might give you the option to register the software. This process requires that you establish a login at the http://www.boson.com website. You will need this login to activate the exam, so feel free to register when prompted. If you already have a login at the http://www.boson.com site, you don't need to register again. Just use your existing login.

Activate and Download the Practice Exam

After the exam engine is installed, you should activate the exam associated with this book:

Step 1   Start the Boson Exam Environment (BEE) software from the Start menu. It should be installed in a Cisco Press folder on your computer.

Step 2   The first time you start the software, it should ask you to either log in or register an account. If you do not already have an account with Boson, select the option to register a new account. (You must register to download and use the exam.)

Step 3   After you are registered, the software might prompt you to download the latest version of the software, which you should do. Note that this process updates the exam engine software (formally called the Boson Exam Environment). It doesn't activate the practice exam.

Step 4 To activate and download the exam associated with this book, from the exam engine main window, click the **Exam Wizard** button.

Step 5 From the Exam Wizard pop-up window, select **Activate a purchased exam** and click the **Next** button. (Although you did not purchase the exam directly, you purchased it indirectly when you purchased this book.)

Step 6 On the next screen, enter the Activation Key from the paper inside the cardboard CD holder, and click the **Next** button.

Step 7 The activation process downloads the practice exam. When this is done, the main exam engine menu should list a new exam, with a name such as "ExSim for Cisco Press ICND1 ECG." If you do not see the exam, be sure you have selected the **My Exams** tab on the menu. You may need to click the plus sign icon (+) to expand the menu and see the exam.

At this point, the software and practice exam are ready to use.

Activating Other Exams

You need to go through the exam software installation process and the registration process only once. After that, for each new exam, only a few steps are required. For instance, if you bought both this book and the *CCNA ICND2 Official Exam Certification Guide*, you could follow the steps just listed to install the software and activate the exam associated with this book. Then, for the practice exam associated with the ICND2 book, which has about 150 exam-realistic ICND2 questions, you need to follow only a few more steps. All you have to do is start the Boson exam environment (if it is not still up and running) and follow Steps 4 through 6 in the preceding list. In fact, if you purchase other Cisco Press books, or purchase a practice exam from Boson, you just need to activate each new exam as described in Steps 4 through 6.

You can also purchase additional practice exams from Boson directly from its website. When you purchase an exam, you receive an activation key, and then you can activate and download the exam—again without requiring any additional software installation.

The Cisco CCNA Prep Center

Cisco provides a wide variety of CCNA preparation tools at a Cisco Systems website called the CCNA Prep Center. The CCNA Prep Center includes demonstrations of the exam's user interface, sample questions, informational videos, discussion forums, and other tools.

To use the CCNA Prep Center, you need a registered login at http://www.cisco.com. To register, simply go to http://www.cisco.com, click **Register** at the top of the page, and supply some information. (You do not need to work for Cisco or one of its partners to get a login.)

After you have registered, proceed to http://www.cisco.com/go/prepcenter, and look for the link to the CCNA Prep Center. There you can log in and explore the many features.

Subnetting Videos, Reference Pages, and Practice Problems

Being able to analyze the IP addressing and subnetting used in any IPv4 network may be the single most important skill for all the CCNA exams. This book's Chapter 12, "IP Addressing and Subnetting," covers most of those details. The ICND2 book's Chapter 5, "VLSM and Route Summarization," adds to the puzzle by explaining VLSM.

This book includes several tools to help you practice and refine your subnetting skills:

■ **Subnetting reference pages:** CD-only Appendix E, "Subnetting Reference Pages," summarizes the binary and decimal shortcut processes explained in Chapter 12. Each reference page lists a single process related to subnetting, along with reference information useful for that process. These summarized processes may be a more convenient tool when you're practicing subnetting, as compared to flipping pages in the subnetting chapters, looking for the correct process.

■ **Subnetting videos:** The DVD included with this book has a series of subnetting videos. These videos show you how to use the shortcut processes to find the answers to popular subnetting questions. You can select and play the videos from a simple menu that starts when you insert the DVD into a DVD drive.

■ **Subnetting practice:** CD-only Appendix D, "Subnetting Practice," contains a variety of subnetting practice problems, including 25 problems for which you need to find the subnet number, subnet broadcast address, and range of valid IP addresses. This appendix shows you how to use both binary and shortcut processes to find the answers.

Scenarios

As mentioned in the Introduction to this book, some of the exam questions require you to use the same skills commonly used to troubleshoot problems in real networks. The troubleshooting sections and chapters of both the ICND1 and ICND2 books help prepare you for those kinds of questions.

Another way to prepare for troubleshooting questions on the exams is to think through many different network scenarios, predicting what should occur, and investigating whether the network is performing as it should. Appendix F, "Additional Scenarios," in both books includes some tasks that you should attempt before reading the suggested solutions listed later in the appendix. By reading these scenarios and doing the exercises, you can practice some of the skills required when analyzing and troubleshooting networks.

Study Plan

You could simply study using all the available tools, as mentioned earlier in this chapter. However, this section suggests a particular study plan, with a sequence of tasks that may work better than just using the tools randomly. However, feel free to use the tools in any way and at any time that helps you fully prepare for the exam.

If you are preparing for only the ICND1 exam, you can ignore the gray highlighted portions of this study plan. If you are studying for the CCNA exam by using the ICND2 book as well, include the tasks highlighted in gray.

The suggested study plan separates the tasks into four categories:

- **Recall the facts.** Activities that help you remember all the details from the first 17 chapters of this book.

- **Practice subnetting.** You must master subnetting to succeed on the ICND1, ICND2, and CCNA exams. This category lists the items you can use to practice subnetting skills.

- **Build troubleshooting skills using scenarios.** To answer some exam questions that present a scenario, you may need to recall facts, do subnetting math quickly and accurately, and use a hands-on simulator—all to answer a single question. This plan section suggests activities that help you pull together these different skills.

- **Use the exam engine to practice realistic questions.** You can use the exam engine on the CD to study using a bank of unique exam-realistic questions available only with this book.

Recall the Facts

As with most exams, you must recall many facts, concepts, and definitions to do well on the test. This section suggests a couple of tasks that should help you remember all the details:

Step 1 **Review and repeat, as needed, the activities in the "Exam Preparation Tasks" section at the end of each chapter.** Most of these activities help you refine your knowledge of a topic while also helping you memorize the facts. For CCNA exam preparation, do this for Chapters 2 through 17 in this book as well as Chapters 1 through 17 in the ICND2 book.

Step 2 **Review all the "Do I Know This Already?" quiz questions at the beginning of the chapters.** Although the questions may be familiar, reading through them again will help improve your recall of the topics covered in the questions. Also, the DIKTA questions tend to cover the most important topics from the chapter, and it never hurts to drill on those topics.

Practice Subnetting

Without question, absolutely the most important skill you need to succeed in passing the ICND1, ICND2, and CCNA exams is to be able to accurately, confidently, and quickly answer subnetting questions. The CCNA exams all have some element of time pressure; the most stressful questions are the sim, simlet, and subnetting questions. So, you should practice subnetting math and processes until you can consistently find the correct answer in a reasonable amount of time.

Before I suggest how you should prepare for subnetting questions, please note that there are many alternative methods for finding the answers to subnetting questions. For example, you can use binary math for all 32 bits of the addresses and subnet numbers. Alternatively, you could recognize that 3 of the 4 octets in most subnetting problems are easily predicted without binary math, and then use binary math in the final interesting octet. Another option would be to use decimal shortcuts. (This topic is covered in this book's Chapter 12, which is included in the ICND2 book's Appendix H.) Shortcuts require no binary math but do require you to practice a process until you've memorized it. You can even use variations on these processes as taught in other books or classes.

Whichever process you prefer, you should practice it until you can use it accurately, confidently, and quickly.

The following list of suggested activities includes practice activities that you can use regardless of the process you choose. In some cases, this list includes items that help you learn the shortcuts included with this book:

Step 1   **View or Print Appendix E, "Subnetting Reference Pages."** This short CD-only appendix includes a series of single-page summaries of the subnetting processes found in Chapter 12. Appendix E includes reference pages that summarize both the binary and decimal shortcut subnetting processes.

Step 2   **Watch the subnetting videos found on the CCNA video DVD found in the back of this book.** These videos show examples of how to use some of the more detailed shortcut processes to help ensure that you know how to use the processes. CCNA exam candidates: The subnetting videos are on DVDs included with both books. They are identical, so you can watch the videos from either DVD.

Step 3   **View or print Appendix D, "Subnetting Practice."** This CD-only appendix includes enough subnetting practice problems so that, through repetition, you can significantly improve your speed and internalize the shortcut processes. Plan on working on these problems until you can consistently get the right answer, quickly, and you no longer have to sit back and think about the process for finding the answer. The goal is to make the process of finding the answers to such problems automatic. CCNA exam candidates: The ICND2 Appendix D contains all the problems from ICND1's Appendix D, plus a few others, so use ICND2's Appendix D.

Step 4 **Practice subnetting with Cisco's subnetting game.** Cisco has a subnetting game, available at the Cisco CCNA Prep Center. It prompts you with various subnetting scenarios and makes practicing subnetting fun. Just go to the CCNA Prep Center (http://www.cisco.com/go/prepcenter), log in with your Cisco.com User ID, select the **Additional Information** tab, and look for the link to download the game. (If you do not have a login, you can establish one from this web page.)

Step 5 **Develop your own practice problems using a subnet calculator.** You can download many free subnet calculators from the Internet, including one available from Cisco as part of the CCNA Prep Center. You can make up your own subnetting problems like those in Appendix D, do the problems, and then test your answers by using the subnet calculator.

Build Troubleshooting Skills Using Scenarios

Just as a real problem in a real network may be caused by a variety of issues—a routing protocol, a bad cable, spanning tree, an incorrect ACL, or even errors in your documentation about the internetwork—the exam makes you apply a wide range of knowledge to answer individual questions. The one activity for this section is as follows:

■ **Review the scenarios included in Appendix F of this book.** These scenarios make you think about issues covered in multiple chapters of the book. They also require more abstract thought to solve the problem. CCNA exam candidates should review the scenarios in Appendix F of both books.

Use the Exam Engine

The exam engine includes two basic modes:

■ **Study mode** is most useful when you want to use the questions to learn and practice. In study mode, you can select options such as whether you want to randomize the order of the questions, randomize the order of the answers, automatically see the answers, refer to specific sections of the text that reside on the CD, and many other options.

■ **Simulation mode** presents questions in a timed environment, providing you with a more exam-realistic experience. However, it restricts your ability to see your score as you progress through the exam, view the answers as you are taking the exam, and refer to sections of the text. These timed exams not only allow you to study for the actual ICND1 and CCNA exams, they also help you simulate the time pressure of the actual exam.

Choosing Study or Simulation Mode

Both study mode and simulation mode are useful for preparing for the exams. It's easy to choose one of the modes from the exam engine's user interface. The following steps show you how to move to the screen where you select study or simulation mode:

Step 1   Click the **Choose Exam** button. The exam should be listed under the title **ExSim for Cisco Press ICND1 ECG**.

Step 2   Click the exam's name to highlight it.

Step 3   Click the **Load Exam** button.

The engine should display a window. Here you can choose **Study Mode** or **Simulation Mode** using the radio buttons.

Choosing the Right Exam Option

The exam engine has many options. You need to choose from one of the three listed exams on the left side of the window, and select either simulation or study mode. Additionally, depending on these two choices, you can potentially modify many other small settings. Although this is a useful tool, it can be difficult to figure out which options to choose to perform the following four primary tasks:

■   Study for the ICND1 exam

■   Study for the CCNA exam

■   Simulate the ICND1 exam

■   Simulate the CCNA exam

To support the ability to study for and simulate both the ICND1 and CCNA exams, the practice test includes two separate question banks. The first bank includes about 150 unique questions written specifically for the ICND1 exam. The second bank includes a subset of the ICND2 question bank written for the *CCNA ICND2 Official Exam Certification Guide*.

When studying for or simulating the CCNA exam, you have to choose an option that includes both the ICND2 and ICND1 questions. To study for or simulate the ICND1 exam, you need to choose an exam option that includes only ICND1 questions. The following list outlines the three options on the menu and the questions served by the exam engine for each choice:

■   **Cisco ICND1 Exam:** ICND1 questions only

■   **Custom Exam:** ICND1 questions only

■   **Full CCNA Exam:** Both ICND1 and ICND2 questions

You might want to experiment with some of the options. After you have chosen to either study using these questions or simulate an exam, Table 18-1 lists the four main options, along with how to pick the right options from the user interface.

Table 18-1   *Directions for What to Choose from the Menu to Study or Simulate the Exam*

If you want to:	. . . choose this exam:	. . . and this mode:	. . . and modify these additional settings:
Study for ICND1	Cisco ICND1 CD Exam	Study	No specific settings are required.
Simulate ICND1	Custom Exam	—	Select the timed exam option, 55 questions, 75 minutes. Deselect **Show current score during exam**, and select **Never** under **Show answers and explanations**.
Study for CCNA	Full CCNA Exam	Study	No specific settings are required.
Simulate CCNA	Full CCNA Exam	Simulation	No specific settings are required.

In addition to these main four study options, the custom exam option has a particularly useful feature for exam study. With this option, by clicking the **Modify Settings** button, you can select the questions to study by chapter. So, if you want to use the question bank for study, and you are studying by chapter or groups of chapters, you can select the questions associated with those chapters.

Summary

The tools and suggestions listed in this chapter were designed with one goal in mind: to help you develop the skills required to pass the ICND1 and CCNA exams. This book, and its companion ICND2 book, were developed not just to tell you the facts, but to help you learn how to apply the facts. No matter what your experience level when you take the exams, it is our hope that the broad range of preparation tools, and even the structure of the books and the focus on troubleshooting, will help you pass the exams with ease. I wish you well on the exams.

Part VI: Appendixes

Answers to the "Do I Know This Already?" Quizzes

Chapter 2

"Do I Know This Already?"

1. D and F

2. A and G

3. B. Adjacent-layer interaction occurs on one computer, with two adjacent layers in the model. The higher layer requests services from the next lower layer, and the lower layer provides the services to the next higher layer.

4. B. Same-layer interaction occurs on multiple computers. The functions defined by that layer typically need to be accomplished by multiple computers—for example, the sender setting a sequence number for a segment, and the receiver acknowledging receipt of that segment. A single layer defines that process, but the implementation of that layer on multiple devices is required to accomplish the function.

5. A. Encapsulation is defined as the process of adding a header in front of data supplied by a higher layer (and possibly adding a trailer as well).

6. D

7. C

8. A

9. F

10. C and E. OSI includes the transport layer (not transmission layer) and the network layer (not Internet layer).

Chapter 3

"Do I Know This Already?"

1. D

2. A

3. B

4. B, D, and E. Routers, wireless access point Ethernet ports, and PC NICs all send using pins 1 and 2, whereas hubs and switches send using pins 3 and 6. Straight-through cables are used when connecting devices that use the opposite pairs of pins to transmit data.

5. B

6. A

7. A and C

8. C and D

9. A

10. B, C, and E

11. C

Chapter 4

"Do I Know This Already?"

1. B

2. B

3. B

4. A

5. E

6. E. Although HDLC has an Address field, its value is immaterial on a point-to-point link, as there is only one intended recipient, the device on the other end of the circuit.

7. A

8. B. One of the main advantages of Frame Relay is that a router can use a single access link to support multiple VCs, with each VC allowing the router to send data to a different remote router. To identify each VC, the router must use a different DLCI, because the DLCI identifies the VC.

Chapter 5

"Do I Know This Already?"

1. A and C. The network layer defines logical addressing, in contrast to physical addressing. The logical address structure allows for easy grouping of addresses, which makes routing more efficient. Path selection refers to the process of choosing the best routes to use in the network. Physical addressing and arbitration typically are data link layer functions, and error recovery typically is a transport layer function.

2. C and E

3. A

4. B. 224.1.1.1 is a class D address. 223.223.223.255 is the network broadcast address for class C network 223.223.223.0, so it cannot be assigned to a host.

5. D

6. D and F. Without any subnetting in use, all addresses in the same network as 10.1.1.1—all addresses in Class A network 10.0.0.0—must be on the same LAN. Addresses separated from that network by some router cannot be in network 10.0.0.0. So, the two correct answers are the only two answers that list a valid unicast IP address that is not in network 10.0.0.0.

7. D

8. F

9. C

10. B and C

11. A and C

12. C

13. D

Chapter 6

"Do I Know This Already?"

1. D. PC1 interprets the absence of an acknowledgement to mean that PC1 cannot tell if PC2 got any of the segments. As a result, PC1 resends all segments.

2. D

3. D and E

4. D and E

5. C. TCP, not UDP, performs windowing, error recovery, and ordered data transfer. Neither performs routing or encryption.

6. C and F. The terms packet and L3PDU refer to the data encapsulated by Layer 3. Frame and L2PDU refer to the data encapsulated by Layer 2.

7. B. Note that the hostname is all the text between the // and the /. The text before the // identifies the application layer protocol, and the text after the / represents the name of the web page.

8. A and D. VoIP flows need better delay, jitter, and loss, with better meaning less delay, jitter, and loss, as compared with all data applications. VoIP typically requires less bandwidth than data applications.

9. C. Intrusion Detection Systems (IDS) monitor packets, comparing the contents of single packets, or multiple packets, to known combinations (signatures) that typically imply that a network attack is occurring.

10. A. A virtual private network (VPN) is a security feature in which two endpoints encrypt data before forwarding it through a public network such as the Internet, providing privacy of the data inside the packets.

Chapter 7

"Do I Know This Already?"

1. A. A switch compares the destination address to the MAC address table. If a matching entry is found, the switch knows out which interface to forward the frame. If no matching entry is found, the switch floods the frame.

2. C. A switch floods broadcast frames, multicast frames (if no multicast optimizations are enabled), and unknown unicast destination frames (frames whose destination MAC address is not in the MAC address table).

3. A. A switch floods broadcast frames, multicast frames (if no multicast optimizations are enabled), and unknown unicast destination frames (frames whose destination MAC address is not in the MAC address table).

4. B. Switches learn MAC table entries by noting the source MAC address of each received frame and the interface in which the frame was received, adding an entry that contains both pieces of information (MAC address and interface).

5. A and B. When the frame sent by PC3 arrives at the switch, the switch has learned a MAC address table entry for only 1111.1111.1111, PC1's MAC address. PC3's

frame, addressed to 2222.2222.2222, is flooded, which means it is forwarded out all interfaces except for the interface on which the frame arrived.

6. **A.** A collision domain contains all devices whose frames could collide with frames sent by all the other devices in the domain. Bridges, switches, and routers separate or segment a LAN into multiple collision domains, whereas hubs and repeaters do not.

7. **A, B, and C.** A broadcast domain contains all devices whose sent broadcast frames should be delivered to all the other devices in the domain. Hubs, repeaters, bridges, and switches do not separate or segment a LAN into multiple broadcast domains, whereas routers do.

8. **B and D**

Chapter 8

"Do I Know This Already?"

1. A and B

2. B

3. B

4. A

5. F

6. D

7. B and C

Chapter 9

"Do I Know This Already?"

1. **B.** If both commands are configured, IOS accepts only the password as configured in the **enable secret** command.

2. **B and C**

3. **B.** The first nonblank character after the **banner login** phrase is interpreted as the beginning delimiter character. In this case, it's the letter "t." So, the second letter "t"—the first letter in "the"—is interpreted as the ending delimiter. The resulting login banner is the text between these two "t"s—namely, "his is."

4. **A.** The setting for the maximum number of MAC addresses has a default of 1, so the **switchport port-security maximum** command does not have to be configured.

5. A, D, and F. To allow access via Telnet, the switch must have password security enabled, at a minimum using the **password** vty line configuration subcommand. Additionally, the switch needs an IP address (configured under the VLAN 1 interface) and a default gateway when the switch needs to communicate with hosts in a different subnet.

6. F

7. E

8. A. VLAN names are case-sensitive, so the **name MY-VLAN** command, while using the correct syntax, would set a different VLAN name than the name shown in the question. The **interface range** command in one of the answers includes interfaces Fa0/13, Fa0/14, and Fa0/15. Because Fa0/14 is not assigned to VLAN 2, this command would not have allowed the right VLAN assignment. To assign a port to a VLAN, the **switchport access vlan 2** command would have been required (not the **switchport vlan 2** command, which is syntactically incorrect).

Chapter 10

"Do I Know This Already?"

1. E and F. CDP discovers information about neighbors. **show cdp** gives you several options that display more or less information, depending on the parameters used.

2. E and F

3. A, B, and D. The disabled state in the **show interfaces status** command is the same as an "administratively down and down" state shown in the **show interfaces** command. The interface must be in a connect state (per the **show interfaces status** command) before the switch can send frames out the interface.

4. A and D. SW2 has effectively disabled IEEE standard autonegotiation by configuring both speed and duplex. However, Cisco switches can detect the speed used by the other device, even with autonegotiation turned off. Also, at 1 Gbps, the IEEE autonegotiation standard says to use full duplex if the duplex setting cannot be negotiated, so both ends use 1 Gbps, full duplex.

5. B and D. The **show interfaces** command lists the actual speed and duplex setting, but it does not imply anything about how the settings were configured or negotiated. The **show interfaces status** command lists a prefix of **a-** in front of the speed and duplex setting to imply that the setting was autonegotiated, leaving off this prefix if the setting was configured.

6. A, B, and D. For Fa0/1, autonegotiation should work normally, with both switches choosing the faster speed (100) and better duplex setting (full). Autonegotiation also works on SW1's Fa0/2, with both switches choosing the 100 Mbps and FDX setting.

Fa0/3 disables autonegotiation as a result of having both the speed and duplex configured. The other switch still automatically senses the speed (100 Mbps), but the autonegotiation failure results in the other switch using half duplex.

7. A and C. Switch forwarding logic and MAC table entries are separated per VLAN. Because the frame came in an interface in VLAN 2, it will only be forwarded based on VLAN 2's MAC table entries, and it will only cause the addition of MAC table entries in VLAN 2. The output from the **show mac address-table dynamic** command lists only dynamic MAC table entries, so you cannot definitively state how the frame will be forwarded, because the static entries are not listed.

8. B and C. IOS adds MAC addresses configured by the port security feature as static MAC addresses, so they do not show up in the output of the **show mac address-table dynamic** command. **show mac address-table port-security** is not a valid command.

Chapter 11

"Do I Know This Already?"

1. A. 802.11a uses the U-NNI band of frequencies (around 5.4 GHz). 802.11b and 802.11g use the ISM band (around 2.4 GHz). 802.11i is a security standard.

2. B. 802.11a uses only OFDM, and 802.11b uses only DSSS. 802.11g runs at a maximum of 54 Mbps using OFDM encoding.

3. C

4. A. The Extended Service Set (ESS) mode uses multiple access points, which then allows roaming between the APs. BSS uses a single AP, and IBSS (ad hoc mode) does not use an AP, so roaming between different APs cannot be done with BSS and IBSS.

5. A and C. APs need to know the SSID for the WLAN the AP is supporting and, if an AP is capable of multiple standards, the wireless standard to use. The AP uses the best speed to each device based on the signal quality between the AP and that device; the speed can vary from device to device. The size of the coverage area is not configured; instead, it is impacted by antenna choice, antenna gain, interference, and the wireless standard used.

6. B. The AP connects to a LAN switch using a straight-through cable, just like an end-user device. All APs in the same ESS should connect to the same VLAN, because all clients connected to the same WLAN should be in the same subnet. Like LAN switches, APs do not need IP configuration to forward traffic, although it is useful for managing and accessing the AP. The standard or speed used on the WLAN does not require any particular Ethernet speed on the wired side of the AP, although overall performance is better when using faster WLAN speeds by using at least 100-Mbps Ethernet.

7.   C and D. Ethernet cabling does not typically give off any radio frequency interference, so the cabling should not affect the WLAN communications. Clients discover APs by listening on all channels, so a configuration setting to a particular channel on an AP does not prevent the client from discovering the AP.

8.   B and D. The standard is IEEE 802.11i. The Wi-Fi alliance defined the term WPA2 to refer to that same standard.

9.   A, C, and D

Chapter 12

"Do I Know This Already?"

1.   A and C

2.   B

3.   D

4.   E. Class B networks imply 16 network bits; the mask implies 7 host bits (7 binary 0s in the mask), leaving 9 subnet bits. 2^9 yields 512 subnets, and $2^7 - 2$ yields 126 hosts per subnet.

5.   B. The design requirements mean that at least 7 subnet bits are needed, because $2^6 = 64$ and $2^7 = 128$. Similarly, 7 host bits are also needed, because $2^6 - 2 = 62$ (not enough) and $2^7 - 2 = 126$ (enough). Masks of /23, /24, and /25 (255.255.254.0, 255.255.255.0, and 255.255.255.128, respectively), when used with a Class B network, have at least 7 subnet bits and 7 host bits. The /23 mask maximizes the number of host bits (9 host bits in this case).

6.   C. Class C networks imply 24 network bits; the mask implies 4 host bits (4 binary 0s in the mask), leaving 4 subnet bits. 2^4 yields 16 subnets, and $2^4 - 2$ yields 14 hosts per subnet.

7.   C. You need 8 bits to number up to 150 hosts because $2^7 - 2$ is less than 150, but $2^8 - 2$ is greater than 150. Similarly, you need 8 subnet bits, because 2^7 is less than 164, but 2^8 is greater than 164. The only valid Class B subnet mask with 8 host and 8 subnet bits is 255.255.255.0.

8.   B, C, D, and E. To meet these requirements, the mask needs at least 8 subnet bits, because $2^8 = 256$, but $2^7 = 128$, which is not enough subnets. The mask also needs at least 8 host bits, because $2^8 - 2 = 254$, but $2^7 - 2 = 126$, which is not enough hosts per subnet. Because a Class A network is in use, the mask needs 8 network bits. As a result, the first 16 bits in the mask must be binary 1s, and the last 8 bits binary 0s, with any valid combination in the third octet.

9. E and F. IP address 190.4.80.80, with mask 255.255.255.0, is in subnet number 190.4.80.0, with broadcast address 190.4.80.255, and a range of valid addresses of 190.4.80.1 through 190.4.80.254.

10. F. 190.4.80.80, mask 255.255.240.0, is in subnet 190.4.80.0, broadcast address 190.4.95.255, with a range of valid addresses of 190.4.80.1 through 190.4.95.254.

11. D, E, F. 190.4.80.80, mask 255.255.255.128 (/25), is in subnet 190.4.80.0, broadcast address 190.4.80.127, with a range of valid addresses of 190.4.80.1 through 190.4.80.126.

12. B and D. To find the answer, you should use the presumed address and mask and try to find the subnet number and subnet broadcast address of that subnet. If the subnet number or broadcast address happens to be the same number you started with, as listed in the answer, then you have identified the fact that the number is a subnet number or broadcast address. For this question, note that 10.0.0.0 is a Class A network number, which is the same value as the zero subnet, no matter what mask is used—so it is definitely reserved. For 172.27.27.27, mask 255.255.255.252, you will find subnet 172.27.27.24, valid address range 172.27.27.25–26, and a subnet broadcast address of 172.27.27.27.

13. C, D, E, and F. In this case, the subnet numbers begin with 180.1.0.0 (subnet zero), and then 180.1.8.0, 180.1.16.0, 180.1.24.0, and so on, increasing by 8 in the third octet, up to 180.1.248.0 (broadcast subnet).

14. A. In this case, the subnet numbers begin with 180.1.0.0 (subnet zero), and then 180.1.1.0, 180.1.2.0, 180.1.3.0, and so on, increasing by 1 in the third octet, up to 180.1.255.0 (broadcast subnet).

Chapter 13

"Do I Know This Already?"

1. B and E. Cisco routers have an on/off switch, but Cisco switches generally do not.

2. B and C. SOHO routers oftentimes expect to connect users to the Internet, so they use DHCP client services to learn a publicly routable IP address from an ISP, and then use DHCP server functions to lease IP addresses to the hosts in the small office.

3. A. Both switches and routers configure IP addresses, so the **ip address** *address mask* and **ip address dhcp** commands could be used on both routers and switches. The **interface vlan 1** command applies only to switches.

4. B and D. To route packets, a router interface must have an IP address assigned and be in an "up and up" interface state. For a serial link created in a lab, without using

CSU/DSUs, one router must be configured with a **clock rate** command to the speed of the link. The **bandwidth** and **description** commands are not required to make a link operational.

5. C. If the first of the two status codes is "down," it typically means that a Layer 1 problem exists (for example, the physical cable is not connected to the interface).

6. C and E

7. B and C. A router has one IP address for each interface in use, whereas a LAN switch has a single IP address that is just used for accessing the switch. Setup mode prompts for some different details in routers and switches; in particular, routers ask for IP addresses and masks for each interface.

8. D and F. The router boot process considers the low-order 4 bits of the configuration register, called the boot field, as well as any configured **boot system** global configuration commands. This process allows an engineer to specify which IOS is loaded when the router is initialized.

9. A

Chapter 14

"Do I Know This Already?"

1. A and C. A router will add a static route to the routing table as long as the outgoing interface or next-hop information is currently valid.

2. A

3. A and B

4. E and F

5. B, D, E, and F

6. D, E, and F

7. A, D, E, and H. The configuration consists of the **router rip** command, the **version 2** command, and the **network 10.0.0.0** and **network 11.0.0.0** commands. The **network** command uses classful network numbers as the parameter, and the **version 2** command is required to make the router use only RIP Version 2. Router2 does not need a **network 9.0.0.0** command, because a router needs only **network** commands that match directly connected subnets.

8. A. The **network** command uses classful network numbers as the parameter, matching all of that router's interfaces whose addresses are in the classful network. The parameter must list the full network number, not just the network octets.

9. B

10. B and C. The bracketed numbers include first the administrative distance, and then the metric. The time counter (value 00:00:13) is an increasing counter that lists the time since this route was last included in a received RIP update. The counter resets to 00:00:00 upon receipt of each periodic routing update.

Chapter 15

1. C and D. Addresses that begin with 225 are Class D multicast IP addresses, so they cannot be assigned to interfaces to be used as unicast IP addresses. 10.43.53.63 255.255.255.192 is actually a subnet broadcast address for subnet 10.43.53.0 255.255.255.192.

2. B

3. C. The asterisk beside connection 2 identifies the connection number to which the **resume** command will connect the user if the **resume** command does not have any parameters.

4. A and D. LAN-based hosts ARP to find the MAC addresses of other hosts they perceive to be in the same subnet. PC1 thinks that 10.1.1.130 is in the same subnet, so PC1 will ARP looking for that host's MAC address. PC3 would not ARP for 10.1.1.10, because PC3's subnet, per its address and mask, is 10.1.1.128/25, range 10.1.1.129–10.1.1.254. R1 would have a connected route for subnet 10.1.1.0/24, range 10.1.1.1–10.1.1.254, so R1 would ARP looking for 10.1.1.130's MAC address.

5. A. A ping of a host's own IP address does not test whether the LAN is working or not, because the packet does not have to traverse the LAN. A ping that requires the packet to go from PC1 to the default gateway (R1) proves the LAN works, at least between PC1 and R1. The only answer that lists a command that causes a packet to need to cross the LAN from PC1 to R1 (although that process fails) is the **ping 10.1.1.1** command.

6. A, C, and E. The **tracert** (Microsoft operating systems) and **traceroute** (Cisco IOS Software) commands list the IP address of the intermediate routers and end host. The commands list the router's IP address closest to the host that issued the command.

7. B and C. A host only ARPs to find MAC addresses of other hosts in the same subnet. PC1 would need its default gateway's MAC address, and likewise, R1 would need PC1's MAC address in its ARP cache to send the return packet.

8. A and D. A host only ARPs to find MAC addresses of other hosts in the same subnet. However, a host learns the IP address to MAC address mapping information from a received ARP request. PC1 would send an ARP broadcast for R1's 10.1.1.1 IP address, which would cause PC1 to learn about R1's MAC address, and R1 to learn PC1's MAC address. Similarly, because the first packet is going from PC1 to PC2, R2 will need

to send an ARP broadcast looking for PC2's MAC address, through which PC2 will learn R2's MAC address, meaning that PC2 does not need to send an ARP broadcast looking for R2's MAC address.

9. A, C, and E. The IP header has a source IP address of 10.1.1.10 and a destination of 172.16.2.7 for the packets going left-to-right, with those addresses reversed for the ping reply packets that go right-to-left. The MAC addresses always represent the addresses of the devices on that local LAN. Note that HDLC, on the serial link, does not use MAC addresses.

Chapter 16

"Do I Know This Already?"

1. D. Modems demodulate an analog signal sent by the phone company into a digital signal. The goal is to re-create the original bits sent by the other modem, so the demodulation function converts the analog signal into the bits that it was intended to represent.

2. A. Of the Internet access options covered in this book, only DSL has distance limitations based on the length of the local telco loop.

3. D. The DSLAM separates, or multiplexes, the voice traffic from the data, splitting the voice traffic off to a voice switch, and the data traffic to a router.

4. A and C. Cable Internet supports only asymmetric speeds.

5. B and C

6. A. The router acts as a DHCP server on the local LAN segment, with a static IP address on the interface. It performs NAT/PAT, changing the source IP address of packets entering the interface. It does not act as a DNS server; although as DHCP server, it does tell the PCs on the local LAN the IP address(es) of any known DNS servers.

7. B and C. The router acts as a DHCP server on the local LAN segment, and as a DHCP client on the Internet-facing interface. It performs NAT/PAT, changing the source IP address of packets entering the local LAN interface and exiting the Internet-facing interface. It does not act as a DNS server; although as DHCP server, it does tell the PCs on the local LAN the IP address(es) of any known DNS servers.

8. B and C. In a typical installation, the router translates (with NAT/PAT) the local hosts' IP addresses, so the server would receive packets from a public IP address (known to the access router) instead of from private IP address 10.1.1.1. The PC user will use normal DNS services to learn the IP address of www.cisco.com, which would be a public IP address in the Internet. In NAT terminology, the inside local IP address is the private IP address for a local host in the enterprise network, whereas the inside global IP address is the public Internet IP address to which the inside local IP address is translated by NAT/PAT.

Chapter 17

1.   A. The **encapsulation** command resets the encapsulation (data-link), so only the **encapsulation ppp** command is required. The **clock rate** command only matters if a back-to-back serial link is used, and if that link already works, that means the clock rate command has already been configured. The **bandwidth** command is never required to make the link work.

2.   B. For a back-to-back serial link, the **clock rate** command is required on the router with the DCE cable installed. If R1 connects to a DTE cable, R2 must use a DCE cable, requiring the **clock rate** command on R2. The **bandwidth** command is never needed to make any interface work; it is merely a reference for other functions, such as for defaults for choosing routing protocol metrics for EIGRP and OSPF.

3.   B. The **clock rate** command is needed only when a back-to-back serial link is created in a lab, and this link uses a real leased line installed by a telco. Although the **bandwidth** command may be recommended, it is not required to make the link work. Because the routers are brand new, having not been configured before, the serial interfaces still have their default encapsulation of HDLC, so the **encapsulation ppp** command is required, on both routers, to make PPP operational.

4.   C and D. Other settings include the DHCP clients' default gateway, which is the access router's local LAN interface IP address, the subnet number, and subnet mask.

5.   B. The SDM configuration wizard allows DHCP client services to be configured, with an option to add PAT configuration or not. The PAT configuration option assumes all interfaces that already have IP addresses are candidates to be inside interfaces, with DHCP-client interfaces assumed to be outside interfaces.

6.   D. SDM uses a web browser on a PC and a web server function on the router, requiring the user to connect through an IP network rather than from the console. SDM does not use SSH at all. SDM loads the configuration into the router only after the user clicks the Finish button on any of the configuration wizards, but the configuration is added only to the running-config file.

7.   A and B. To enable a local host user to type names instead of IP addresses to access the Internet, the access router DHCP server needs to be configured with several details, including the IP addresses of the DNS servers advertised by the ISPs. Also, mixing up which interface should be the inside interface and which should be the outside interface is common. The other two answers have nothing to do with the required configuration on an Internet access router.

Decimal to Binary Conversion Table

This appendix provides a handy reference for converting between decimal and binary formats for the decimal numbers 0 through 255. Feel free to refer to this table when practicing any of the subnetting problems found in this book and on the CD-ROM.

Although this appendix is useful as a reference tool, note that if you plan to convert values between decimal and binary when doing the various types of subnetting problems on the exams, instead of using the shortcut processes that mostly avoid binary math, you will likely want to practice converting between the two formats before the exam. For practice, just pick any decimal value between 0 and 255, convert it to 8-bit binary, and then use this table to find out if you got the right answer. Also, pick any 8-bit binary number, convert it to decimal, and again use this table to check your work.

Decimal Value	Binary Value	Decimal Value	Binary Value	Decimal Value	Binary Value	Decimal Value	Binary Value
0	00000000	32	00100000	64	01000000	96	01100000
1	00000001	33	00100001	65	01000001	97	01100001
2	00000010	34	00100010	66	01000010	98	01100010
3	00000011	35	00100011	67	01000011	99	01100011
4	00000100	36	00100100	68	01000100	100	01100100
5	00000101	37	00100101	69	01000101	101	01100101
6	00000110	38	00100110	70	01000110	102	01100110
7	00000111	39	00100111	71	01000111	103	01100111
8	00001000	40	00101000	72	01001000	104	01101000
9	00001001	41	00101001	73	01001001	105	01101001
10	00001010	42	00101010	74	01001010	106	01101010
11	00001011	43	00101011	75	01001011	107	01101011
12	00001100	44	00101100	76	01001100	108	01101100
13	00001101	45	00101101	77	01001101	109	01101101
14	00001110	46	00101110	78	01001110	110	01101110
15	00001111	47	00101111	79	01001111	111	01101111
16	00010000	48	00110000	80	01010000	112	01110000
17	00010001	49	00110001	81	01010001	113	01110001
18	00010010	50	00110010	82	01010010	114	01110010
19	00010011	51	00110011	83	01010011	115	01110011
20	00010100	52	00110100	84	01010100	116	01110100
21	00010101	53	00110101	85	01010101	117	01110101
22	00010110	54	00110110	86	01010110	118	01110110
23	00010111	55	00110111	87	01010111	119	01110111
24	00011000	56	00111000	88	01011000	120	01111000
25	00011001	57	00111001	89	01011001	121	01111001
26	00011010	58	00111010	90	01011010	122	01111010
27	00011011	59	00111011	91	01011011	123	01111011
28	00011100	60	00111100	92	01011100	124	01111100
29	00011101	61	00111101	93	01011101	125	01111101
30	00011110	62	00111110	94	01011110	126	01111110
31	00011111	63	00111111	95	01011111	127	01111111

Decimal Value	Binary Value	Decimal Value	Binary Value	Decimal Value	Binary Value	Decimal Value	Binary Value
128	10000000	160	10100000	192	11000000	224	11100000
129	10000001	161	10100001	193	11000001	225	11100001
130	10000010	162	10100010	194	11000010	226	11100010
131	10000011	163	10100011	195	11000011	227	11100011
132	10000100	164	10100100	196	11000100	228	11100100
133	10000101	165	10100101	197	11000101	229	11100101
134	10000110	166	10100110	198	11000110	230	11100110
135	10000111	167	10100111	199	11000111	231	11100111
136	10001000	168	10101000	200	11001000	232	11101000
137	10001001	169	10101001	201	11001001	233	11101001
138	10001010	170	10101010	202	11001010	234	11101010
139	10001011	171	10101011	203	11001011	235	11101011
140	10001100	172	10101100	204	11001100	236	11101100
141	10001101	173	10101101	205	11001101	237	11101101
142	10001110	174	10101110	206	11001110	238	11101110
143	10001111	175	10101111	207	11001111	239	11101111
144	10010000	176	10110000	208	11010000	240	11110000
145	10010001	177	10110001	209	11010001	241	11110001
146	10010010	178	10110010	210	11010010	242	11110010
147	10010011	179	10110011	211	11010011	243	11110011
148	10010100	180	10110100	212	11010100	244	11110100
149	10010101	181	10110101	213	11010101	245	11110101
150	10010110	182	10110110	214	11010110	246	11110110
151	10010111	183	10110111	215	11010111	247	11110111
152	10011000	184	10111000	216	11011000	248	11111000
153	10011001	185	10111001	217	11011001	249	11111001
154	10011010	186	10111010	218	11011010	250	11111010
155	10011011	187	10111011	219	11011011	251	11111011
156	10011100	188	10111100	220	11011100	252	11111100
157	10011101	189	10111101	221	11011101	253	11111101
158	10011110	190	10111110	222	11011110	254	11111110
159	10011111	191	10111111	223	11011111	255	11111111

ICND1 Exam Updates: Version 1.0

Over time, reader feedback allows Cisco Press to gauge which topics give our readers the most problems when taking the exams. Additionally, Cisco may make small changes in the breadth of exam topics or in emphasis of certain topics. To assist readers with those topics, the author creates new materials clarifying and expanding upon those troublesome exam topics. As mentioned in the introduction, the additional content about the exam is contained in a PDF document on this book's companion website at http://www.ciscopress.com/title/1587201828. The document you are viewing is Version 1.0 of this appendix.

This appendix presents all the latest update information available at the time of this book's printing. To make sure you have the latest version of this document, you should be sure to visit the companion website to see if any more recent versions have been posted since this book went to press.

This appendix attempts to fill the void that occurs with any print book. In particular, this appendix does the following:

1. Mentions technical items that might not have been mentioned elsewhere in the book

2. Covers new topics when Cisco adds topics to the ICND1 or CCNA exam blueprints

3. Provides a way to get up-to-the-minute current information about content for the exam

Always Get the Latest at the Companion Website

You are reading the version of this appendix that was available when your book was printed. However, given that the main purpose of this appendix is to be a living, changing document, it is very important that you look for the latest version online at the book's companion website. To do so:

1. Browse to http://www.ciscopress.com/title/1587201828.

2. Select the **Downloads** option under the **More Information** box.

3. Download the latest "ICND1 Appendix C" document.

> **NOTE**   Note that the downloaded document has a version number. If the version of the PDF on the website is the same version as this appendix in your book, your book has the latest version, and there is no need to download or use the online version.

Technical Content

The current version of this appendix does not contain any additional technical coverage. This appendix is here simply to provide the instructions to check online for a later version of this appendix.

10BASE-T The 10-Mbps baseband Ethernet specification using two pairs of twisted-pair cabling (Categories 3, 4, or 5): One pair transmits data and the other receives data. 10BASE-T, which is part of the IEEE 802.3 specification, has a distance limit of approximately 100 m (328 feet) per segment.

100BASE-TX A name for the IEEE Fast Ethernet standard that uses two-pair copper cabling, a speed of 100 Mbps, and a maximum cable length of 100 meters.

1000BASE-T A name for the IEEE Gigabit Ethernet standard that uses four-pair copper cabling, a speed of 1000 Mbps (1 Gbps), and a maximum cable length of 100 meters.

802.1Q The IEEE standardized protocol for VLAN trunking.

802.11a The IEEE standard for wireless LANs using the U-NII spectrum, OFDM encoding, at speeds of up to 54 Mbps.

802.11b The IEEE standard for wireless LANs using the ISM spectrum, DSSS encoding, and speeds of up to 11 Mbps.

802.11g The IEEE standard for wireless LANs using the ISM spectrum, OFDM or DSSS encoding, and speeds of up to 54 Mbps.

802.11i The IEEE standard for wireless LAN security, including authentication and encryption.

A

AAA Authentication, Authorization, and Accounting. Authentication confirms the identity of the user or device. Authorization determines what the user or device is allowed to do. Accounting records information about access attempts, including inappropriate requests.

access interface   A LAN network design term that refers to a switch interface connected to end-user devices.

access link   In Frame Relay, the physical serial link that connects a Frame Relay DTE device, usually a router, to a Frame Relay switch. The access link uses the same physical layer standards as do point-to-point leased lines.

access point   A wireless LAN device that provides a means for wireless clients to send data to each other and to the rest of a wired network, with the AP connecting to both the wireless LAN and the wired Ethernet LAN.

accounting   In security, the recording of access attempts. *See* AAA.

ad hoc mode   In wireless LANs, a method or mode of operation in which clients send data directly to each other without the use of a wireless access point (AP).

adjacent-layer interaction   The general topic of how on one computer, two adjacent layers in a networking architectural model work together, with the lower layer providing services to the higher layer.

administrative distance   In Cisco routers, a means for one router to choose between multiple routes to reach the same subnet when those routes were learned by different routing protocols. The lower the administrative distance, the better the source of the routing information.

ADSL   Asymmetric digital subscriber line. One of many DSL technologies, ADSL is designed to deliver more bandwidth downstream (from the central office to the customer site) than upstream.

Anti-X   The term used by Cisco to refer to a variety of security tools that help prevent various attacks, including antivirus, anti-phishing, and anti-spam.

ARP   Address Resolution Protocol. An Internet protocol used to map an IP address to a MAC address. Defined in RFC 826.

asymmetric   A feature of many Internet access technologies, including DSL, cable, and modems, in which the downstream transmission rate is higher than the upstream transmission rate.

asynchronous   The lack of an imposed time ordering on a bit stream. Practically, both sides agree to the same speed, but there is no check or adjustment of the rates if they are slightly different. However, because only 1 byte per transfer is sent, slight differences in clock speed are not an issue.

ATM   Asynchronous Transfer Mode. The international standard for cell relay in which multiple service types (such as voice, video, and data) are conveyed in fixed-length (53-byte) cells. Fixed-length cells allow cell processing to occur in hardware, thereby reducing transit delays.

authentication   In security, the verification of the identity of a person or a process. *See* AAA.

authorization   In security, the determination of the rights allowed for a particular user or device. *See* AAA.

autonomous system   An internetwork in the administrative control of one organization, company, or governmental agency, inside which that organization typically runs an Interior Gateway Protocol (IGP).

auxiliary port   A physical connector on a router that is designed to be used to allow a remote terminal, or PC with a terminal emulator, to access a router using an analog modem.

B

back-to-back link   A serial link between two routers, created without CSU/DSUs, by connecting a DTE cable to one router and a DCE cable to the other. Typically used in labs to build serial links without the expense of an actual leased line from the telco.

balanced hybrid   A term that refers to a general type of routing protocol algorithm, the other two being distance vector and link state. The Enhanced Interior Gateway Routing Protocol (EIGRP) is the only routing protocol that Cisco classifies as using a balanced hybrid algorithm.

bandwidth   A reference to the speed of a networking link. Its origins come from earlier communications technology in which the range, or width, of the frequency band dictated how fast communications could occur.

basic service set (BSS)   In wireless LANs, a WLAN with a single access point.

bitwise Boolean AND   A Boolean AND between two numbers of the same length in which the first bit in each number is ANDed, and then the second bit in each number, and then the third, and so on.

Boolean AND   A math operation performed on a pair of one-digit binary numbers. The result is another one-digit binary number. 1 AND 1 yields 1; all other combinations yield a 0.

boot field   The low-order 4 bits of the configuration register in a Cisco router. The value in the boot field in part tells the router where to look for a Cisco IOS image to load.

BRI   Basic Rate Interface. An ISDN interface composed of two 64-kbps bearer (B) channels and one 16-kbps data (D) channel for circuit-switched communication of voice, video, and data.

broadcast address   *See* subnet broadcast address.

broadcast domain   A set of all devices that receive broadcast frames originating from any device within the set. Devices in the same VLAN are in the same broadcast domain.

broadcast frame   An Ethernet frame sent to destination address FFFF.FFFF.FFFF, meaning that the frame should be delivered to all hosts on that LAN.

broadcast subnet   When subnetting a Class A, B, or C network, the one subnet in each classful network for which all subnet bits have a value of binary 1. The subnet broadcast address in this subnet has the same numeric value as the classful network's network-wide broadcast address.

bus   A common physical signal path composed of wires or other media across which signals can be sent from one part of a computer to another.

C

CDP   Cisco Discovery Protocol. A media- and protocol-independent device-discovery protocol that runs on most Cisco-manufactured equipment, including routers, access servers, and switches. Using CDP, a device can advertise its existence to other devices and receive information about other devices on the same LAN or on the remote side of a WAN.

CDP neighbor   A device on the other end of some communications cable that is advertising CDP updates.

CIDR notation   *See* prefix notation.

circuit switching   A generic reference to network services, typically WAN services, in which the provider sets up a (layer 1) circuit between two devices, and the provider makes no attempt to interpret the meaning of the bits. *See also* packet switching.

classful network   An IPv4 Class A, B, or C network; called a classful network because these networks are defined by the class rules for IPv4 addressing.

classful routing protocol   Does not transmit the mask information along with the subnet number, and therefore must consider Class A, B, and C network boundaries and perform autosummarization at those boundaries. Does not support VLSM.

classless routing protocol   An inherent characteristic of a routing protocol, specifically that the routing protocol does send subnet masks in its routing updates, thereby removing any need to make assumptions about the addresses in a particular subnet or network, making it able to support VLSM and manual route summarization.

CLI   Command-line interface. An interface that enables the user to interact with the operating system by entering commands and optional arguments.

clock rate   The speed at which a serial link encodes bits on the transmission medium.

clock source   The device to which the other devices on the link adjust their speed when using synchronous links.

clocking   The process of supplying a signal over a cable, either on a separate pin on a serial cable or as part of the signal transitions in the transmitted signal, so that the receiving device can keep synchronization with the sending device.

codec   Coder-decoder. An integrated circuit device that transforms analog voice signals into a digital bit stream and then transforms digital signals back into analog voice signals.

collision domain   A set of network interface cards (NICs) for which a frame sent by one NIC could result in a collision with a frame sent by any other NIC in the same collision domain.

command-line interface   *See* CLI.

configuration mode   A part of the Cisco IOS Software CLI in which the user can type configuration commands that are then added to the device's currently used configuration file (running-config).

configuration register   In Cisco routers, a 16-bit, user-configurable value that determines how the router functions during initialization. In software, the bit position is set by specifying a hexadecimal value using configuration commands.

connection establishment   The process by which a connection-oriented protocol creates a connection. With TCP, a connection is established by a three-way transmission of TCP segments.

console port   A physical socket on a router or switch to which a cable can be connected between a computer and the router/switch, for the purpose of allowing the computer to use a terminal emulator and use the CLI to configure, verify, and troubleshoot the router/switch.

convergence   The time required for routing protocols to react to changes in the network, removing bad routes and adding new, better routes so that the current best routes are in all the routers' routing tables.

CPE   Customer premises equipment. Any equipment related to communications that is located at the customer site, as opposed to inside the telephone company's network.

crossover cable   An Ethernet cable that swaps the pair used for transmission on one device to a pair used for receiving on the device on the opposite end of the cable. In 10BASE-T and 100BASE-TX networks, this cable swaps the pair at pins 1,2 to pins 3,6 on the other end of the cable, and the pair at pins 3,6 to pins 1,2 as well.

CSMA/CA   Carrier sense multiple access with collision avoidance. A media-access mechanism that defines how devices decide when they can send, with a goal of avoiding collisions as much as possible. IEEE WLANs use CSMA/CA.

CSMA/CD   Carrier sense multiple access collision detect. A media-access mechanism in which devices ready to transmit data first check the channel for a carrier. If no carrier is sensed for a specific period of time, a device can transmit. If two devices transmit at once, a collision occurs and is detected by all colliding devices. This collision subsequently delays retransmissions from those devices for some random length of time.

CSU/DSU   Channel service unit/digital service unit. A device that understands the Layer 1 details of serial links installed by a telco and how to use a serial cable to communicate with networking equipment such as routers.

cut-through switching   One of three options for internal processing on some models of Cisco LAN switches in which the frame is forwarded as soon as possible, including forwarding the first bits of the frame before the whole frame is received.

D

DCE   Data communications equipment. From a physical layer perspective, the device providing the clocking on a WAN link, typically a CSU/DSU, is the DCE. From a packet-switching perspective, the service provider's switch, to which a router might connect, is considered the DCE.

decapsulation   On a computer that receives data over a network, the process in which the device interprets the lower-layer headers and, when finished with each header, removes the header, revealing the next-higher-layer PDU.

default gateway/default router   On an IP host, the IP address of some router to which the host sends packets when the packet's destination address is on a subnet other than the local subnet.

default mask   The mask used in a Class A, B, or C network that does not create any subnets; specifically, mask 255.0.0.0 for Class A networks, 255.255.0.0 for Class B networks, and 255.255.255.0 for Class C networks.

default route   On a router, the route that is considered to match all packets that are not otherwise matched by some more specific route.

demarc   The legal term for the demarcation or separation point between the telco's equipment and the customer's equipment.

denial of service (DoS)   A type of attack whose goal is to cause problems by preventing legitimate users from being able to access services, thereby preventing the normal operation of computers and networks.

DHCP   Dynamic Host Configuration Protocol. A protocol used by hosts to dynamically discover and lease an IP address, and learn the correct subnet mask, default gateway, and DNS server IP addresses.

Direct Sequence Spread Spectrum (DSSS)   A method of encoding data for transmission over a wireless LAN in which the device uses 1 of 11 (in the USA) nearby frequencies in the 2.4-GHz range.

directed broadcast address   *See* subnet broadcast address.

distance vector   The logic behind the behavior of some interior routing protocols, such as RIP. Distance vector routing algorithms call for each router to send its entire routing table in each update, but only to its neighbors. Distance vector routing algorithms can be prone to routing loops but are computationally simpler than link-state routing algorithms.

DNS   Domain Name System. An application layer protocol used throughout the Internet for translating hostnames into their associated IP addresses.

DS0   Digital signal level 0. A 64-kbps line or channel of a faster line inside a telco whose origins are to support a single voice call using the original voice (PCM) codecs.

DS1   Digital signal level 1. A 1.544-Mbps line from the telco, with 24 DS0 channels of 64 kbps each, plus an 8-kbps management and framing channel. Also called a T1.

DSL   Digital subscriber line. Public network technology that delivers high bandwidth over conventional telco local-loop copper wiring at limited distances. Typically used as an Internet access technology, connecting a user to an ISP.

DTE   Data terminal equipment. From a Layer 1 perspective, the DTE synchronizes its clock based on the clock sent by the DCE. From a packet-switching perspective, the DTE is the device outside the service provider's network, typically a router.

E

E1   Similar to a T1, but used in Europe. It uses a rate of 2.048 Mbps and 32 64-kbps channels, with one channel reserved for framing and other overhead.

enable mode   A part of the Cisco IOS CLI in which the user can use the most powerful and potentially disruptive commands on a router or switch, including the ability to then reach configuration mode and reconfigure the router.

encapsulation   The placement of data from a higher-layer protocol behind the header (and in some cases, between a header and trailer) of the next-lower-layer protocol. For example, an IP packet could be encapsulated in an Ethernet header and trailer before being sent over an Ethernet.

encryption   Applying a specific algorithm to data to alter the appearance of the data, making it incomprehensible to those who are not authorized to see the information.

error detection   The process of discovering whether or not a data-link level frame was changed during transmission. This process typically uses a Frame Check Sequence (FCS) field in the data-link trailer.

error disabled   An interface state on LAN switches that is the result of one of many security violations.

error recovery   The process of noticing when some transmitted data was not successfully received and resending the data until it is successfully received.

Ethernet   A series of LAN standards defined by the IEEE, originally invented by Xerox Corporation and developed jointly by Xerox, Intel, and Digital Equipment Corporation.

Extended Service Set (ESS)   In wireless LANs, a WLAN with multiple access points to create one WLAN, allowing roaming between the APs.

Exterior Gateway Protocol (EGP)   A routing protocol that was designed to exchange routing information between different autonomous systems.

F

filter   Generally, a process or a device that screens network traffic for certain characteristics, such as source address, destination address, or protocol, and determines whether to forward or discard that traffic based on the established criteria.

firewall   A device that forwards packets between the less secure and more secure parts of the network, applying rules that determine which packets are allowed to pass, and which are not.

Flash   A type of read/write permanent memory that retains its contents even with no power applied to the memory, and uses no moving parts, making the memory less likely to fail over time.

flooding   The result of the LAN switch forwarding process for broadcasts and unknown unicast frames. Switches forward these frames out all interfaces, except the interface in which the frame arrived. Switches also forward multicasts by default, although this behavior can be changed.

flow control   The process of regulating the amount of data sent by a sending computer toward a receiving computer. Several flow control mechanisms exist, including TCP flow control, which uses windowing.

forward   To send a frame received in one interface out another interface, toward its ultimate destination.

forward acknowledgment   A process used by protocols that do error recovery in which the number that acknowledges data lists the next data that should be sent, not the last data that was successfully received.

four-wire circuit   A line from the telco with four wires, composed of two twisted-pair wires. Each pair is used to send in one direction, so a four-wire circuit allows full-duplex communication.

fragment-free switching   One of three internal processing options on some Cisco LAN switches in which the first bits of the frame may be forwarded before the entire frame is received, but not until the first 64 bytes of the frame are received, in which case, in a well-designed LAN, collision fragments should not occur as a result of this forwarding logic.

frame   A term referring to a data-link header and trailer, plus the data encapsulated between the header and trailer.

Frame Relay   An international standard data-link protocol that defines the capabilities to create a frame-switched (packet-switched) service, allowing DTE devices (typically routers) to send data to many other devices using a single physical connection to the Frame Relay service.

Frequency Hopping Spread Spectrum   A method of encoding data on a wireless LAN in which consecutive transmissions occur on different nearby frequency bands as compared with the prior transmission. Not used in modern WLAN standards.

full duplex   Generically, any communication in which two communicating devices can concurrently send and receive data. In Ethernet LANs, the allowance for both devices to send and receive at the same time, allowed when both devices disable their CSMA/CD logic.

full mesh   A network topology in which more than two devices can physically communicate and, by choice, all pairs of devices are allowed to communicate directly.

H

half duplex   Generically, any communication in which only one device at a time can send data. In Ethernet LANs, the normal result of the CSMA/CD algorithm that enforces the rule that only one device should send at any point in time.

HDLC   High-Level Data Link Control. A bit-oriented synchronous data link layer protocol developed by the International Organization for Standardization (ISO).

head end   The upstream, transmit end of a cable TV (CATV) installation.

host   Any device that uses an IP address.

host address   The IP address assigned to a network card on a computer.

host part   A term used to describe a part of an IPv4 address that is used to uniquely identify a host inside a subnet. The host part is identified by the bits of value 0 in the subnet mask.

host route   A route with a /32 mask, which by virtue of this mask represents a route to a single host IP address.

HTML   Hypertext Markup Language. A simple document-formatting language that uses tags to indicate how a given part of a document should be interpreted by a viewing application, such as a web browser.

HTTP   Hypertext Transfer Protocol. The protocol used by web browsers and web servers to transfer files, such as text and graphic files.

hub   A LAN device that provides a centralized connection point for LAN cabling, repeating any received electrical signal out all other ports, thereby creating a logical bus. Hubs do not interpret the electrical signals as a frame of bits, so hubs are considered to be Layer 1 devices.

I

ICMP   Internet Control Message Protocol. A TCP/IP network layer protocol that reports errors and provides other information relevant to IP packet processing.

IEEE   Institute of Electrical and Electronics Engineers. A professional organization that develops communications and network standards, among other activities.

IEEE 802.2   An IEEE LAN protocol that specifies an implementation of the LLC sublayer of the data link layer.

IEEE 802.3   A set of IEEE LAN protocols that specifies the many variations of what is known today as an Ethernet LAN.

inactivity timer   For switch MAC address tables, a timer associated with each entry, which counts time upwards from 0 and is reset to 0 each time a switch receives a frame with the same MAC address. The entries with the largest timers can be removed to make space for additional MAC address table entries.

infrastructure mode   A mode of wireless LAN (WLAN) operation in which WLAN clients send and receive data with an access point (AP), which allows the clients to communicate with the wired infrastructure through the AP. Clients do not send data to each other directly; the AP must receive the data from one client, and then send the data to the other WLAN client.

inside global   For packets sent to and from a host that resides inside the trusted part of a network that uses NAT, a term referring to the IP address used in the headers of those packets when those packets traverse the global (public) Internet.

inside local   For packets sent to and from a host that resides inside the trusted part of a network that uses NAT, a term referring to the IP address used in the headers of those packets when those packets traverse the Enterprise (private) part of the network.

Interior Gateway Protocol (IGP)   *See* interior routing protocol.

interior routing protocol   A routing protocol designed for use within a single organization.

intrusion detection system (IDS)   A security function that examines more complex traffic patterns against a list of both known attack signatures and general characteristics of how attacks may be carried out, rating each perceived threat and reporting the threats.

intrusion prevention system (IPS)   A security function that examines more complex traffic patterns against a list of both known attack signatures and general characteristics of how attacks may be carried out, rating each perceived threat and reacting to prevent the more significant threats.

IOS   Cisco operating system software that provides the majority of a router's or switch's features, with the hardware providing the remaining features.

IOS Image   A file that contains the IOS.

IP   Internet Protocol. The network layer protocol in the TCP/IP stack, providing routing and logical addressing standards and services.

IP address   In IP Version 4 (IPv4), a 32-bit address assigned to hosts using TCP/IP. Each address consists of a network number, an optional subnetwork number, and a host number. The network and subnetwork numbers together are used for routing, and the host number is used to address an individual host within the network or subnetwork.

ISDN   Integrated Services Digital Network. A service offered by telephone companies that permits telephone networks to carry data, voice, and other traffic. Often used as an Internet access technology, as well as dial backup when routers lose their normal WAN communications links.

ISL   Inter-Switch Link. A Cisco-proprietary protocol that maintains VLAN information as traffic flows between switches and routers.

ISO   International Organization for Standardization. An international organization that is responsible for a wide range of standards, including many standards relevant to networking. The ISO developed the OSI reference model, a popular networking reference model.

K

keepalive   A proprietary feature of Cisco routers in which the router sends messages on a periodic basis as a means of letting the neighboring router know that the first router is still alive and well.

L

L4PDU   The data compiled by a Layer 4 protocol, including Layer 4 headers and encapsulated high-layer data, but not including lower-layer headers and trailers.

Layer 3 protocol   A protocol that has characteristics like OSI Layer 3, which defines logical addressing and routing. IP, IPX, and AppleTalk DDP are all Layer 3 protocols.

learning   The process used by switches for discovering MAC addresses, and their relative location, by looking at the source MAC address of all frames received by a bridge or switch.

leased line   A serial communications circuit between two points, provided by some service provider, typically a telephone company (telco). Because the telco does not sell a physical cable between the two endpoints, instead charging a monthly fee for the ability to send bits between the two sites, the service is considered to be a leased service.

link state   A classification of the underlying algorithm used in some routing protocols. Link-state protocols build a detailed database that lists links (subnets) and their state (up, down), from which the best routes can then be calculated.

LLC   Logical Link Control. The higher of the two data link layer sublayers defined by the IEEE. Synonymous with IEEE 802.2.

local loop   A line from the premises of a telephone subscriber to the telephone company CO.

logical address   A generic reference to addresses as defined by Layer 3 protocols, which do not have to be concerned with the physical details of the underlying physical media. Used mainly to contrast these addresses with data-link addresses, which are generically considered to be physical addresses because they differ based on the type of physical medium.

M

MAC   Media Access Control. The lower of the two sublayers of the data link layer defined by the IEEE. Synonymous with IEEE 802.3 for Ethernet LANs.

MAC address   A standardized data link layer address that is required for every device that connects to a LAN. Ethernet MAC addresses are 6 bytes long and are controlled by the IEEE. Also known as a *hardware address*, a *MAC layer address*, and a *physical address*.

metric   A unit of measure used by routing protocol algorithms to determine the best route for traffic to use to reach a particular destination.

microsegmentation   The process in LAN design by which every switch port connects to a single device, with no hubs connected to the switch ports, creating a separate collision domain per interface. The term's origin relates to the fact that one definition for the word "segment" is "collision domain," with a switch separating each switch port into a separate collision domain or segment.

modem   Modulator-demodulator. A device that converts between digital and analog signals so that a computer may send data to another computer using analog telephone lines. At the source, a modem converts digital signals to a form suitable for transmission over analog communication facilities. At the destination, the analog signals are returned to their digital form.

multimode   A type of fiber-optic cabling with a larger core than single-mode cabling, allowing light to enter at multiple angles. Such cabling has lower bandwidth than single-mode fiber but requires a typically cheaper light source, such as an LED rather than a laser.

N

name server   A server connected to a network that resolves network names into network addresses.

NAT   Network Address Translation. A mechanism for reducing the need for globally unique IP addresses. NAT allows an organization with addresses that are not globally unique to connect to the Internet by translating those addresses into public addresses in the globally routable address space.

network   A collection of computers, printers, routers, switches, and other devices that can communicate with each other over some transmission medium.

network address   *See* network number.

network broadcast address   In IPv4, a special address in each classful network that can be used to broadcast a packet to all hosts in that same classful network. Numerically, the address has the same value as the network number in the network part of the address, and all 255s in the host octets—for example, 10.255.255.255 is the network broadcast address for classful network 10.0.0.0.

network number   A number that uses dotted decimal notation like IP addresses, but the number itself represents all hosts in a single Class A, B, or C IP network.

network part   The portion of an IPv4 address that is either 1, 2, or 3 octets/bytes long, based on whether the address is in a Class A, B, or C network.

networking model   A generic term referring to any set of protocols and standards collected into a comprehensive grouping that, when followed by the devices in a network, allows all the devices to communicate. Examples include TCP/IP and OSI.

NVRAM   Nonvolatile RAM. A type of random-access memory (RAM) that retains its contents when a unit is powered off.

O

ordered data transfer   A networking function, included in TCP, in which the protocol defines how the sending host should number the data transmitted, defines how the receiving device should attempt to reorder the data if it arrives out of order, and specifies to discard the data if it cannot be delivered in order.

Orthogonal Frequency Division Multiplexing   A method of encoding data in wireless LANs that allows for generally higher data rates than the earlier FHSS and DSSS encoding methods.

OSI   Open System Interconnection reference model. A network architectural model developed by the ISO. The model consists of seven layers, each of which specifies particular network functions, such as addressing, flow control, error control, encapsulation, and reliable message transfer.

P

packet   A logical grouping of information that includes the network layer header and encapsulated data, but specifically does not include any headers and trailers below the network layer.

packet switching   A generic reference to network services, typically WAN services, in which the service examines the contents of the transmitted data to make some type of forwarding decision. This term is mainly used to contrast with the WAN term *circuit switching*, in which the provider sets up a (Layer 1) circuit between two devices, and the provider makes no attempt to interpret the meaning of the bits.

partial mesh   A network topology in which more than two devices could physically communicate but, by choice, only a subset of the pairs of devices connected to the network is allowed to communicate directly.

PCM   Pulse code modulation. A technique of encoding analog voice into a 64-kbps data stream by sampling with 8-bit resolution at a rate of 8000 times per second.

PDU   Protocol data unit. An OSI term to refer generically to a grouping of information by a particular layer of the OSI model. More specifically, an L*x*PDU would imply the data and headers as defined by Layer *x*.

ping   Packet Internet groper. An Internet Control Message Protocol (ICMP) echo message and its reply; ping often is used in IP networks to test the reachability of a network device.

pinout   The documentation and implementation of which wires inside a cable connect to each pin position in any connector.

port   In TCP and UDP, a number that is used to uniquely identify the application process that either sent (source port) or should receive (destination port) data. In LAN switching, another term for switch interface.

Port Address Translation (PAT)   A NAT feature in which one inside global IP address supports over 65,000 concurrent TCP and UDP connections.

port number   A field in a TCP or UDP header that identifies the application that either sent (source port) or should receive (destination port) the data inside the data segment.

positive acknowledgment and retransmission (PAR)   A generic reference to how the error recovery feature works in many protocols, including TCP, in which the receiver must send an acknowledgment that either implies that the data was (positively) received, or send an acknowledgement that implies that some data was lost, so the sender can then resend the lost data.

Power-on Self Test (POST)   The process on any computer, including routers and switches, in which the computer hardware first runs diagnostics on the required hardware before even trying to load a bootstrap program.

PPP   Point-to-Point Protocol. A protocol that provides router-to-router and host-to-network connections over synchronous point-to-point and asynchronous point-to-point circuits.

prefix notation   A shorter way to write a subnet mask in which the number of binary 1s in the mask is simply written in decimal. For instance, /24 denotes the subnet mask with 24 binary 1 bits in the subnet mask. The number of bits of value binary 1 in the mask is considered to be the prefix length.

PRI   Primary Rate Interface. An Integrated Services Digital Network (ISDN) interface to primary rate access. Primary rate access consists of a single 64-kbps D channel plus 23 (T1) or 30 (E1) B channels for voice or data.

private addresses   IP addresses in several Class A, B, and C networks that are set aside for use inside private organizations. These addresses, as defined in RFC 1918, are not routable through the Internet.

problem isolation   The part of the troubleshooting process in which the engineer attempts to rule out possible causes of the problem until the root cause of the problem can be identified.

protocol data unit (PDU)   A generic term referring to the header defined by some layer of a networking model, and the data encapsulated by the header (and possibly trailer) of that layer, but specifically not including any lower-layer headers and trailers.

Protocol Type field   A field in a LAN header that identifies the type of header that follows the LAN header. Includes the DIX Ethernet Type field, the IEEE 802.2 DSAP field, and the SNAP protocol Type field.

PSTN   Public Switched Telephone Network. A general term referring to the variety of telephone networks and services in place worldwide. Sometimes called *POTS*, or Plain Old Telephone Service.

PTT   Post, telephone, and telegraph. A government agency that provides telephone services. PTTs exist in most areas outside of North America and provide both local and long-distance telephone services.

public IP address   An IP address that is part of a registered network number, as assigned by an Internet Assigned Numbers Authority (IANA) member agency, so that only the organization to which the address is registered is allowed to use the address. Routers in the Internet should have routes allowing them to forward packets to all the publicly registered IP addresses.

R

RAM   Random-access memory. A type of volatile memory that can be read and written by a microprocessor.

RFC   Request For Comments. A document used as the primary means for communicating information about the TCP/IP protocols. Some RFCs are designated by the Internet Architecture Board (IAB) as Internet standards, and others are informational. RFCs are available online from numerous sources, including http://www.rfc-editor.org/.

RIP   Routing Information Protocol. An Interior Gateway Protocol (IGP) that uses distance vector logic and router hop count as the metric. RIP Version 1 (RIP-1) has become unpopular, with RIP Version 2 (RIP-2) providing more features, including support for VLSM.

RJ-45   A popular type of cabling connector used for Ethernet cabling. It is similar to the RJ-11 connector used for telephone wiring in homes in the United States. RJ-45 allows the connection of eight wires.

ROM   Read-only memory. A type of nonvolatile memory that can be read but not written by the microprocessor.

ROMMON   A shorter name for ROM Monitor, which is a low-level operating system that can be loaded into Cisco routers for several seldom needed maintenance tasks, including password recovery and loading a new IOS when Flash memory has been corrupted.

root cause   A troubleshooting term that refers to the reason why a problem exists, specifically a reason for which, if changed, the problem would either be solved or changed to a different problem.

routed protocol   A protocol which defines packets that can be routed by a router. Examples of routed protocols include AppleTalk, DECnet, and IP.

Router Security Device Manager   The administrative web-based interface on a router that allows for configuration and monitoring of the router, including the configuration of DHCP and NAT/PAT.

routing protocol   A set of messages and processes with which routers can exchange information about routes to reach subnets in a particular network. Examples of routing protocols include the Enhanced Interior Gateway Routing Protocol (EIGRP), the Open Shortest Path First (OSPF) protocol, and the Routing Information Protocol (RIP).

routing table   A list of routes in a router, with each route listing the destination subnet and mask, the router interface out which to forward packets destined to that subnet, and, as needed, the next-hop router's IP address.

routing update   A generic reference to any routing protocol's messages in which it sends routing information to a neighbor.

running-config file   In Cisco IOS switches and routers, the name of the file that resides in RAM memory, holding the device's currently used configuration.

RxBoot   A limited-function version of IOS stored in ROM in some older models of Cisco routers, for the purpose of performing some seldom needed low-level functions, including loading a new IOS into Flash memory when Flash has been deleted or corrupted.

S

same-layer interaction   The communication between two networking devices for the purposes of the functions defined at a particular layer of a networking model, with that communication happening by using a header defined by that layer of the model. The two devices set values in the header, send the header and encapsulated data, with the receiving device(s) interpreting the header to decide what action to take.

Secure Shell (SSH)   A TCP/IP application layer protocol that supports terminal emulation between a client and server, using dynamic key exchange and encryption to keep the communications private.

segment   In TCP, a term used to describe a TCP header and its encapsulated data (also called an *L4PDU*). Also in TCP, the process of accepting a large chunk of data from the application layer and breaking it into smaller pieces that fit into TCP segments. In Ethernet, a segment is either a single Ethernet cable or a single collision domain (no matter how many cables are used).

segmentation   The process of breaking a large piece of data from an application into pieces appropriate in size to be sent through the network.

serial cable   A type of cable with many different styles of connectors used to connect a router to an external CSU/DSU on a leased-line installation.

Service Set Identifier (SSID)   A text value used in wireless LANs to uniquely identify a single WLAN.

setup mode   An option on Cisco IOS switches and routers that prompts the user for basic configuration information, resulting in new running-config and startup-config files.

shared Ethernet   An Ethernet that uses a hub, or even the original coaxial cabling, which results in the devices having to take turns sending data, sharing the available bandwidth.

single-mode   A type of fiber-optic cabling with a narrow core that allows light to enter only at a single angle. Such cabling has a higher bandwidth than multimode fiber but requires a light source with a narrow spectral width (such as a laser).

sliding windows   For protocols such as TCP that allow the receiving device to dictate the amount of data the sender can send before receiving an acknowledgment—a concept called a window—a reference to the fact that the mechanism to grant future windows is typically just a number that grows upwards slowly after each acknowledgment, sliding upward.

SONET   Synchronous Optical Network. A standard format for transporting a wide range of digital telecommunications services over optical fiber.

Spanning Tree Protocol   A bridge protocol that uses the Spanning Tree algorithm, allowing a switch to dynamically work around loops in a network topology by creating a spanning tree. Switches exchange bridge protocol data unit (BPDU) messages with other bridges to detect loops and then remove the loops by shutting down selected bridge interfaces.

star   A network topology in which endpoints on a network are connected to a common central device by point-to-point links.

startup-config file   In Cisco IOS switches and routers, the name of the file that resides in NVRAM memory, holding the device's configuration that will be loaded into RAM as the running-config file when the device is next reloaded or powered on.

store-and-forward switching   One of three internal processing options on some Cisco LAN switches in which the Ethernet frame must be completely received before the switch can begin forwarding the first bit of the frame.

STP   Shielded twisted pair. Shielded twisted-pair cabling has a layer of shielded insulation to reduce electromagnetic interference (EMI).

straight-through cable   In Ethernet, a cable that connects the wire on pin 1 on one end of the cable to pin 1 on the other end of the cable, pin 2 on one end to pin 2 on the other end, and so on.

subnet   Subdivisions of a Class A, B, or C network, as configured by a network administrator. Subnets allow a single Class A, B, or C network to be used instead of multiple networks, and still allow for a large number of groups of IP addresses, as is required for efficient IP routing.

subnet address   *See* subnet number.

subnet broadcast address   A special address in each subnet, specifically the largest numeric address in the subnet, designed so that packets sent to this address should be delivered to all hosts in that subnet.

subnet mask   A 32-bit number that numerically describes the format of an IP address by representing the combined network and subnet bits in the address with mask bit values of 1, and representing the host bits in the address with mask bit values of 0.

subnet number   In IP v4, a dotted decimal number that represents all addresses in a single subnet. Numerically, the smallest value in the range of numbers in a subnet, reserved so that it cannot be used as a unicast IP address by a host.

subnet part   In a subnetted IPv4 address, interpreted with classful addressing rules, one of three parts of the structure of an IP address, with the subnet part uniquely identifying different subnets of a classful IP network.

subnetting   The process of subdividing a Class A, B, or C network into smaller groups called subnets.

switch   A network device that filters, forwards, and floods Ethernet frames based on the destination address of each frame.

switched Ethernet   An Ethernet that uses a switch, and particularly not a hub, so that the devices connected to one switch port do not have to contend to use the bandwidth available on another port. This term contrasts with *shared Ethernet*, in which the devices must share bandwidth, whereas switched Ethernet provides much more capacity, as the devices do not have to share the available bandwidth.

symmetric   A feature of many Internet access technologies in which the downstream transmission rate is the same as the upstream transmission rate.

synchronous   The imposition of time ordering on a bit stream. Practically, a device will try to use the same speed as another device on the other end of a serial link. However, by examining transitions between voltage states on the link, the device can notice slight variations in the speed on each end and can adjust its speed accordingly.

T

T1   A line from the telco that allows transmission of data at 1.544 Mbps, with the ability to treat the line as 24 different 64-kbps DS0 channels (plus 8 kbps of overhead).

TCP   Transmission Control Protocol. A connection-oriented transport layer TCP/IP protocol that provides reliable data transmission.

TCP/IP   Transmission Control Protocol/Internet Protocol. A common name for the suite of protocols developed by the U.S. Department of Defense in the 1970s to support the construction of worldwide internetworks. TCP and IP are the two best-known protocols in the suite.

telco   A common abbreviation for telephone company.

Telnet   The standard terminal-emulation application layer protocol in the TCP/IP protocol stack. Telnet is used for remote terminal connection, enabling users to log in to remote systems and use resources as if they were connected to a local system. Telnet is defined in RFC 854.

trace   Short for traceroute. A program available on many systems that traces the path that a packet takes to a destination. It is used mostly to debug routing problems between hosts.

transparent bridge   The name of a networking device that was a precursor to modern LAN switches. Bridges forward frames between LAN segments based on the destination MAC address. Transparent bridging is so named because the presence of bridges is transparent to network end nodes.

trunk interface   On a LAN switch, an interface that is currently using either 802.1Q or ISL trunking.

trunking   Also called *VLAN trunking*. A method (using either the Cisco ISL protocol or the IEEE 802.1q protocol) to support multiple VLANs that have members on more than one switch.

twisted pair   Transmission medium consisting of two insulated wires, with the wires twisted around each other in a spiral. An electrical circuit flows over the wire pair, with the current in opposite directions on each wire, which significantly reduces the interference between the two wires.

U

UDP   User Datagram Protocol. Connectionless transport layer protocol in the TCP/IP protocol stack. UDP is a simple protocol that exchanges datagrams without acknowledgments or guaranteed delivery.

unknown unicast frame   An Ethernet frame whose destination MAC address is not listed in a switch's MAC address table, so the switch must flood the frame.

up and up   Jargon referring to the two interface states on a Cisco IOS router or switch (line status and protocol status), with the first "up" referring to the line status, and the second "up" referring to the protocol status. An interface in this state should be able to pass data-link frames.

update timer   A timer used by a router to indicate when to send the next routing update.

URL   Universal Resource Locator. A standard for how to refer to any piece of information retrievable via a TCP/IP network, most notably used to identify web pages. For example, http://www.cisco.com/univercd is a URL that identifies the protocol (HTTP), hostname (www.cisco.com), and web page (/univercd).

user mode   A mode of the user interface to a router or switch in which the user can type only nondisruptive EXEC commands, generally just to look at the current status, but not to change any operational settings.

UTP   Unshielded twisted pair. A type of cabling, standardized by the Electronics Industry Alliance (EIA) and Telecommunications Industry Association (TIA), that holds twisted pairs of copper wires (typically four pair), and does not contain any shielding from outside interference.

V

variable-length subnet masks (VLSM)   The capability to specify a different subnet mask for the same Class A, B, or C network number on different subnets. VLSM can help optimize available address space.

virtual circuit   In packet-switched services like Frame Relay, VC refers to the ability of two DTE devices (typically routers) to send and receive data directly to each other, which supplies the same function as a physical leased line (leased circuit), but doing so without a physical circuit. This term is meant as a contrast with a leased line or leased circuit.

virtual LAN (VLAN)   A group of devices, connected to one or more switches, with the devices grouped into a single broadcast domain through switch configuration. VLANs allow switch administrators to separate the devices connected to the switches into separate VLANs without requiring separate physical switches, gaining design advantages of separating the traffic without the expense of buying additional hardware.

virtual private network (VPN)   The process of securing communication between two devices whose packets pass over some public and unsecured network, typically the Internet. VPNs encrypt packets so that the communication is private and authenticate the identity of the endpoints.

VoIP   Voice over IP. The transport of voice traffic inside IP packets over an IP network.

W

web server   Software, running on some computer, that stores web pages and sends those web pages to web clients (web browsers) that request the web pages.

well-known port   A TCP or UDP port number reserved for use by a particular application. The use of well-known ports allows a client to send a TCP or UDP segment to a server, to the correct destination port for that application.

Wi-Fi Alliance   An organization formed by many companies in the wireless industry (an industry association) for the purpose of getting multivendor certified-compatible wireless products to market in a more timely fashion than would be possible by simply relying on standardization processes.

Wi-Fi Protected Access (WPA)   A trademarked name of the Wi-Fi Alliance that represents a set of security specifications that predated the standardization of the IEEE 802.11i security standard.

window   The term window represents the number of bytes that can be sent without receiving an acknowledgment.

wired equivalent privacy (WEP)   An early WLAN security specification that used relatively weak security mechanisms, using only preshared keys and either no encryption or weak encryption.

WLAN client   A wireless device that wants to gain access to a wireless access point for the purpose of communicating with other wireless devices or other devices connected to the wired internetwork.

WPA2   The Wi-Fi Alliance trademarked name for the same set of security specifications defined in the IEEE 802.11i security standard.

Z

zero subnet   For every classful IPv4 network that is subnetted, the one subnet whose subnet number has all binary 0s in the subnet part of the number. In decimal, the zero subnet can be easily identified because it is the same number as the classful network number.

Index

O

objects, 152
octets, 106
    interesting octet, 379
OFDM (Orthogonal Frequency Division Multiplexing), 310
operating systems on Cisco routers, 425
operators
    AND operations, 349–350
    bitwise Boolean ANDing, 350–351
ordered data transfer, 144–145
OSI networking model, 21
OSI reference model, 32
    comparing to TCP/IP architectural model, 32–33
    layers, 34–35
        benefits of, 35–36
        encapsulation, 36–37
        mnemonics, 35
    network layer, 98–99
        addressing, 103–104
        interaction with data link layer, 101
        routing, 99–100
        routing protocols, 104
        utilities, 121–125
OUI (organizationally unique identifier), 64
output of show ip route command, interpreting, 460
outside interfaces, 535

P

packets, 28, 527
    acknowledgments, 25
    Frame Relay, 87
        access links, 87
        LAPF, 88
        VCs, 89–90
    scaling benefits, 86–87
    services, 86
PAR (Positive Acknowledgment and Retransmission), 142
passwords
    configuring on Catalyst switches, 244–245
    encryption, configuring on Cisco Catalyst switches, 242–243
    password-protecting switch console access, 208–210

    recovery, configuring on Cisco Catalyst switches, 236–238
PAT (Port Address Translation), 531, 535
    configuring on Internet access router, 552
path selection, 98
PCM (pulse code modulation), 82, 516
PDUs (protocol data units), 36–37
phishing attacks, 158
physical connectivity of point-to-point WANs, 78
pin positions, 53
ping command, 125, 442–444, 479
pinouts, 55–58
point-to-point WANs
    cabling
        RJ-48 connectors, 79
        serial cabling, 78, 80
    demarc, 78
    devices, legal ownership of, 78
    HDLC, configuring, 542–545
    Layer 1 operation, 74
    Layer 2
        HDLC, 83–84
        PPP, 85
    link speeds, 82
    physical connectivity, 78
    PPP, configuring, 545–546
port LED, 204
port numbers, 137
port security, 293
    configuring on Cisco Catalyst switches, 253–256
PPP (Point-to-Point Protocol), 85
    configuring, 545–546
practice exams
    accessing, 566
    downloading, 566–567
practice labs, 81
practicing
    with subnet calculator, 338–339
    subnetting, 383–384, 570–571
    practice examples, 361
prefix notation, 351–352
    binary process, 352–353
    decimal process, 353–355
preparing for exams
    ICND1 exam
        Cisco CCNA Prep Center, 567
        recommended study plan, 569–573

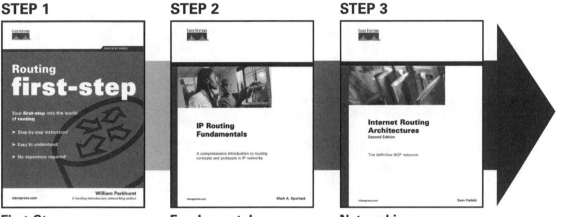

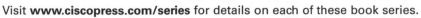

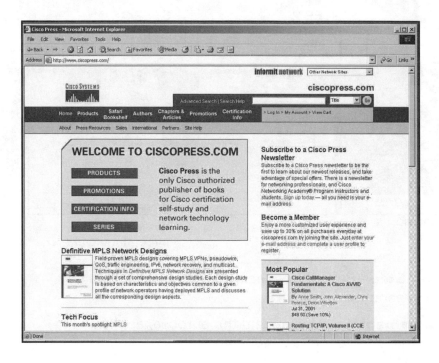

THIS BOOK IS SAFARI ENABLED

INCLUDES FREE 45-DAY ACCESS TO THE ONLINE EDITION

The Safari® Enabled icon on the cover of your favorite technology book means the book is available through Safari Bookshelf. When you buy this book, you get free access to the online edition for 45 days.

Safari Bookshelf is an electronic reference library that lets you easily search thousands of technical books, find code samples, download chapters, and access technical information whenever and wherever you need it.

TO GAIN 45-DAY SAFARI ENABLED ACCESS TO THIS BOOK:

● Go to **http://www.ciscopress.com/safarienabled**

● Complete the brief registration form

● Enter the coupon code found in the front of this book before the "Contents at a Glance" page

If you have difficulty registering on Safari Bookshelf or accessing the online edition, please e-mail customer-service@safaribooksonline.com.

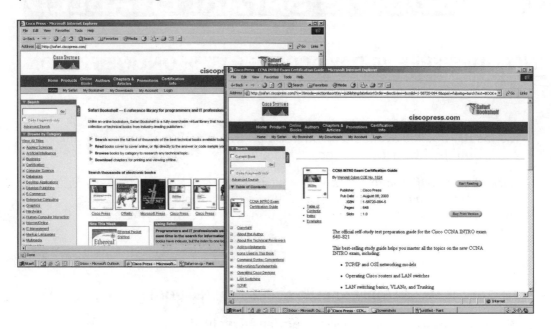